THE STORY OF CHRISTIANITY

THE STORY OF
CHRISTIANITY

Complete in One Volume
The Early Church to the Present Day

JUSTO L. GONZÁLEZ

PRINCE
PRESS

Prince Press, an imprint of Hendrickson Publishers
P.O. Box 3473
Peabody, Massachusetts 01961-3473

Printed in the United States of America

Prince Press edition

ISBN 1-56563-522-1

Sixth printing – September 2006

VOLUME ONE
The Early Church to the Dawn of the Reformation

To Catherine

Contents

PART III: MEDIEVAL CHRISTIANITY

Maps

Preface

The reader will probably be surprised to learn that I regard this book as in large measure autobiographical. It is so, first of all, because as Ortega y Gasset said, each generation stands on the shoulders of its predecessors like acrobats in a vast human pyramid. Thus, to tell the story of those whose heirs we are is to write a long preface to our own life stories.

But this book is also autobiographical in a second sense, for it deals with friends and companions with whom I have spent the last three decades. Since I first met Irenaeus, Athanasius, and the rest, and as I have read their writings and pondered their thoughts and deeds, they have accompanied me through the many turns and twists of life. Like contemporary friends, they have often been a joy, at other times a puzzlement, and even sometimes an aggravation. But still, they have become part of me, and as I write of them I am also aware that I am writing of my life with them.

It is customary in a preface to acknowledge those who have contributed to the writing of a book. This I find impossible, for I would have to name a long list of scholars, both living and dead—Origen, Eusebius, the Inca Garcilaso, Harnack, and the host of unknown monks who copied and recopied manuscripts.

Among my own contemporaries, however, there are two that I must mention. The first is my wife, Catherine Gunsalus González, Professor of Church History at Columbia Theological Seminary, Decatur, Georgia, who has shared with me the last decade of my journey with the ancients, and whose reading and criticism of my manuscript have proven invaluable. The naming of the second is a sign of our times, for this is my live-in, full-time secretary of six years: the word-processor on which I have prepared this manuscript. Many of the adjectives usually applied to typists in prefaces do apply to my word-processor: patient, careful, uncomplaining, always ready to serve. Indeed, this secretary has typed and retyped my manuscript with no more protest than an occasional beep. However, as I write these very last words of my manuscript, an electric storm has forced me to take pen in hand once again, thus reminding me that we are not as far removed as we sometimes think from the time of Origen and Eusebius!

As I send this book out into the world, it is my hope that others will enjoy the reading of it as much as I have enjoyed the writing of it.

¹/Introduction

In those days a decree went out from
Caesar Augustus that all the world should
be enrolled.
LUKE 2:1

From its very beginning, the Christian message was grafted onto human history. The Good News Christians have proclaimed through the ages is that in Jesus Christ, and for our salvation, God has entered human history in a unique way. History is crucial for understanding not only the life of Jesus, but also the entire biblical message. A good deal of the Old Testament is historical narrative. The Bible tells the story of God's revelation in the life and history of the people of God. Without that story, it is impossible to know that revelation.

The New Testament writers are quite clear about this. The Gospel of Luke tells us that the birth of Jesus took place during the reign of Augustus Caesar, "when Quirinius was governor of Syria" (2:2). Shortly before, the same Gospel places the narrative within the context of Palestinian history, recording that it took place "in the days of Herod, king of Judaea" (1:5). The Gospel of Matthew opens with a genealogy that places Jesus within the framework of the history and hopes of Israel, and then goes on to date the birth of Jesus "in the days of Herod the king" (2:1). Mark gives less chronological detail, but still does affirm that Jesus began his ministry "in those days"—that is, the days of John the Baptist (1:9). The Fourth Gospel wishes to make clear that the significance of these events is not transitory, and therefore begins by stating that the Word who was made flesh in human history (1:14) is the same Word who "was in the beginning with God" (1:2). Finally, a similar note is sounded in the First Epistle of John, whose opening lines declare "that which was from the beginning" is also that "which we have heard, which we have seen with our eyes, which we have looked upon and touched with our hands" (1:1).

After completing his Gospel, Luke continued the story of the Christian church in the book of Acts. He did not do this out of mere antiquarian curiosity, but rather out of some important theological considerations. According to Luke and to the entire New Testament, the presence of God among us did not end with the ascension of Jesus. On the contrary, Jesus himself promised his followers that he would not leave them alone, but would send another Counselor (John 14:16–26). At the beginning of Acts, immediately before the ascension, Jesus tells his disciples that they will receive the power of the Holy Spirit, by which they will be his witnesses "to the end of the earth" (1:8). Then follow the events of Pentecost, which mark the beginning of the witnessing life of the church. Thus, the theme of the book that is usually called "Acts of the Apostles" is not so much the deeds of the apostles as the deeds of the Holy Spirit through the apostles (and others). Luke has left us two books, the first on the deeds of Jesus, and the second on the deeds of the Spirit.

But Luke's second book does not seem to have a conclusion. At the end, Paul is still preaching in Rome, and the book does not tell us what became of him or of the rest of the church. Luke had a theological reason for this, for the story he was telling shall not come to an end before the end of all history.

What this means for those who share in Luke's faith is that the history of the church, while showing all the characteristics of human history, is much more than the history of an institution or of a movement. It is a history of the deeds of the Spirit in and through the men and women who have gone before in the faith.

There are episodes in the course of that history where it is difficult to see the action of the Holy Spirit. As our narrative unfolds, we shall find those who have used the faith of the church for their financial gain, or to increase their personal power. There will be others who will forget or twist the commandment of love, and will persecute their enemies with a vindictiveness unworthy of the name of Jesus. At other times it will appear to many of us that the church has forsaken the biblical faith, and some will even doubt that such a church can be truly called "Christian." At such points in our narrative, it may be well to remember two things.

The first of these is that, while this narrative is the history of the deeds of the Spirit, it is the history of those deeds through sinners such as us. This is clear as early as New Testament times, where Peter, Paul, and the rest are depicted both as people of faith and as sinners. And, if that example is not sufficiently stark, it should suffice to take another look at the "saints" to whom Paul addresses his first Epistle to the Corinthians!

The second is that it has been through those sinners and that church— and only through them—that the biblical message has come to us. Even in the darkest times of the life of the church, there were those Christians who loved, studied, kept, and copied the Scriptures, and thus bequeathed them to us.

What those earlier Christians have bequeathed to us, however, is more than the text of Scripture. They have also left the illuminating record of their striving to be faithful witnesses in the most diverse circumstances. In times of persecution, some witnessed with their blood, others with their writings, and still others with their loving acceptance of those who had weakened, and later repented. In times when the church was powerful, some sought to witness by employing that power, while others questioned the use of it. In times of invasions, chaos, and famine, there were those who witnessed to their Lord by seeking to restore order, so that the homeless might find shelter, and the hungry might have food. When vast lands until then unknown were opened to European Christians, there were those who rushed to those lands, there to preach the message of their faith. Throughout the centuries, some sought to witness by the word spoken and written, others by prayer and renunciation, and still others by the force of arms and the threat of inquisitorial fires.

Like it or not, we are heirs of this host of diverse and even contradictory witnesses. Some of their actions we may find revolting, and others inspiring. But all of them form part of our history. All of them, those whom we admire as well as those whom we despise, brought us to where we are now.

Without understanding that past, we are unable to understand ourselves, for in a sense the past still lives in us and influences who we are and how we understand the Christian message. When we read, for instance, that "the just shall live by faith," Martin Luther is whispering at our ear how we are to interpret those words—and this is true even for those of us who have never even heard of Martin Luther. When we hear that "Christ died for our sins," Anselm of Canterbury sits in the pew with us, even though we may not have the slightest idea who Anselm was. When we stand, sit, or kneel in church, when we sing a hymn, recite a creed, or refuse to recite one, when we build a church or preach a sermon, a past of which we may not be aware is one of the factors involved in our actions. The notion that we read the New Testament exactly as the early Christians did, without any weight of tradition coloring our interpretation, is an illusion. It is also a dangerous illusion, for it tends to absolutize our interpretation, confusing it with the Word of God.

One way in which we can avoid this danger is to know the past that colors our vision. A person wearing tinted glasses can avoid the conclusion that the entire world is tinted only by being conscious of the glasses themselves. Likewise, if we are to break free from an undue weight of tradition, we must begin by understanding what that tradition is, how we came to be where we are, and how particular elements in our past color our view of the present. It is then that we are free to choose which elements in the past—and in the present—we wish to reject, and which we will affirm.

It is at this point that the *doing* of history converges with the *making* of it. When we study the life and work of past generations, and when we interpret it, we are *doing* history. But we must remember that future generations will read about our times as past history. In that sense, like it or not, both by our action and by our inaction, we are *making* history. This is both an exhilarating opportunity and an awesome responsibility, and it demands that we *do* history in order to be able to *make* it more faithfully. Every renewal of the church, every great age in its history, has been grounded on a renewed reading of history. The same will be true as we prepare to move into the twenty-first century. Part of that preparation will be the *doing* of history to which this book invites its readers.

PART I

THE EARLY CHURCH

Chronology

Emperors	Bishops of Rome*	Authors and Documents**	Events
Augustus (27 B.C.– 14 A.D.)		(Philo)	Jesus
Tiberius (14–37)			
Caligula (37–41)			
Claudius (41–54)		Paul's Epistles (Flavius Josephus)	Jews expelled from Rome
Nero (54–68)	Linus (?)	Mark	Persecution Jerusalem Christians flee to Pella (66)
Galba (68–69)			
Otho (69)			
Vitellius (69)			
Vespasian (69–79)		Matthew (?)	Fall of Jerusalem (70)
	Anacletus (?)	Luke—Acts (?)	
Titus (79–81)			
Domitian (81–96)		John (?)	
	Clement	Revelation	Persecution
Nerva (96–98)			
Trajan (98–117)			
	Evaristus Alexander Sixtus	Ignatius	Persecution
Hadrian (117–138)		Quadratus Aristides	Persecution
	Telesphorus	Papias (Epictetus) Didache (?) Gospel of the Hebrews	Surge of Gnosticism Marcion in Rome

*Bishops whom the Roman Church does not recognize are in italics.
**Non-Christian authors are in parentheses.

Emperors	Bishops of Rome*	Authors and Documents**	Events
	Hyginius	Pseudo-Barnabas (?)	
Antoninus Pius (138–161)	Pius	Basilides	Persecution
		Aristo of Pella (130)	
		Hermas (c. 150)	
		Martyrdom of Polycarp	
		Roman Symbol	
		Valentinus	
		Gospel of Peter	
	Anicetus	Muratorian Fragment (160)	
		Fronto of Cirta	
		Epitaph of Pectorius (?)	Montanism
		Ascension of Isaiah (?)	
		Odes of Solomon (?)	
Marcus Aurelius (161–180)			Persecution
		Justin (165)	
Lucius Verus co-emperor (161–169)	Soter	Hegesippus (154–166)	
		Lucian of Samosata	
		Tatian	
		II Enoch (?)	
	Eleuterus (?–189)	Athenagoras	Martyrs of Gaul (177)
Commodus (180–192)		Theophilus of Antioch (Celsus)	

Emperors	Bishops of Rome*	Authors and Documents**	Events
		Irenaeus (c. 180)	
		Pantenus	Scillitan martyrs
	Victor (189–199)	Melito of Sardis (189)	Debate over date of
Pertinax (193)		Tertullian (195–220)	Easter
Didius Julian (193)			
Septimius Severus (193–211)		Minucius Felix (?)	
	Zephyrinus (199–217)	Epitaph of Abercius	Persecution Syncretistic
		Perpetua and Felicitas	policy
		Clement of Alexandria (200–215)	Tertullian Montanist
Caracalla (211–217)		Origen (215–253)	(207)
Macrinus (217–218)	Calixtus (217–222)	(Plotinus)	
Elagabalus (218–222)			
Alexander Severus (222–235)	Urban (222–230)	Pseudo-Clementine (?)	
	Hippolytus (222–235)		Two bishops in Rome
	Pontian (230–235)		Origen in Palestine
Maximin (235–238)	Anterus (235–236)		
	Fabian (236–250)		
Gordian I (238)			
Gordian II (238)			
Pupienus (238)		Sextus Julius Africanus	
Balbinus (238)			
Gordian III (238–244)		Gospel of Thomas (?)	
		Methodius	Manicheism founded
Philip the Arabian (244–249)		Heraclas	

Emperors	Bishops of Rome*	Authors and Documents**	Events
Decius (249–251)		Cyprian	Persecution
Hostilian (251)			
Gallus (251–253)	Cornelius (251–253)		Two bishops in Rome
	Novatian (251–258?)		
Aemilian (253)	Lucius (253–254)	Didascalia (?)	
Valerian (253–259)	Stephen (254–257)		
	Sixtus II (257–258)		
Gallienus (259–268)			
	Dionysius (260–268)	Dionysius of Alexandria	Paul of Samosata bishop of Antioch
		Lucian of Antioch	
		Gregory the Wonderworker	
	Felix (269–274)	Firmilian of Caesarea	
Claudius II (268–270)		Theognost	
Quintillus (270)		Gnostic papyri (?)	
Aurelian (270–275)		Gospel of Bartholomew	
Tacitus (275–276)	Eutychian (275–283)		
Florian (276)			
Probus (276–282)			
Carus (282–283)	Caius (283–296)		
Numerian (283–284)		Arnobius	
Carinus (283–285)			
Diocletian (284–305)			
Maximian (285–305)	Marcellinus (296–304)		
Constantius Chlorus (292–306)		Pierius	Great Persecution

Emperors	Bishops of Rome*	Authors and Documents**	Events
Galerius (292–311)			Edict of Toleration (311)
Maximinus Daia (305–313)	Marcellus (308–309)		
Constantine (306–337)	Eusebius (309–310)		
Severus (306–307)			
Maxentius (306–312)	Miltiades (311–314)		Battle of Milvian Bridge
Licinius (307–323)			Edict of Milan (313)
	Sylvester (314–335)		

2/The Fullness of Time

But when the time had fully come, God
sent forth his Son, born of woman, born
under the law.
GALATIANS 4:4

The early Christians did not believe that the time and place of the birth of Jesus had been left to chance. On the contrary, they saw the hand of God preparing the advent of Jesus in all events prior to the birth, and in all the historical circumstances around it. The same could be said about the birth of the church, which resulted from the work of Jesus. God had prepared the way so that the disciples, after receiving the power of the Holy Spirit, could be witnesses "in Jerusalem and in all Judea and Samaria and to the end of the earth" (Acts 1:8).

Therefore, the church was never disconnected from the world around it. The first Christians were first-century Jews, and it was as such that they heard and received the message. Then the faith spread, first among other Jews, and eventually among Gentiles both within and beyond the borders of the Roman Empire. In order to understand the history of Christianity in its early centuries, we must begin by looking at the world in which it evolved.

Judaism in Palestine

Palestine, the land in which Christianity first appeared, has long been a land of strife and suffering. In ancient times, this was due mostly to its geographical position, at the crossroads of the great trades routes that joined Egypt with Mesopotamia, and Asia Minor with Arabia. As we read the Old Testament, we see that, as empires came and went, they cast a covetous eye on that narrow strip of land; for this reason, its inhabitants repeatedly suffered invasion, bondage, and exile. In the fourth century B.C., with Alexander and his Macedonian armies, a new contender entered the arena. Upon defeating the Persians, Alexander became master of Palestine. But his death followed shortly thereafter, and his vast empire was dismembered. For a long time two

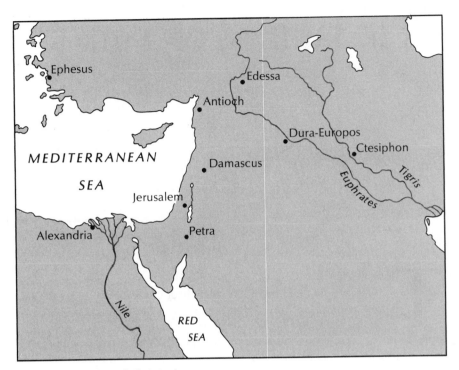

Palestine: Birthplace of Christianity

of the resulting dynasties, one in Egypt and one in Syria, fought for the possession of Palestine. The result was another period of unrest and political instability.

The conquests of Alexander had an ideological basis. He did not wish simply to conquer the world, but to unite it by spreading the insights of Greek civilization. The result, in which some elements of Greek origin combined, in various forms and degrees, with other elements taken from conquered civilizations, is known as *Hellenism*. Although the precise nature of Hellenism varied from place to place, it did provide the eastern Mediterranean basin with a unity that opened the way first to Roman conquest, and later to the preaching of the gospel.

But there were many Jews who did not regard Hellenism as a blessing. Since part of the Hellenistic ideology consisted in equating and mixing the gods of different nations, they saw in it a threat to Israel's faith in the One God. In a way, the history of Palestine from the time of Alexander's conquest to the destruction of Jerusalem in A.D. 70 may be seen as the constant struggle between Hellenizing pressures on the one hand and Jewish faithfulness to their God and their traditions on the other.

The high point of that struggle was the Jewish rebellion led by the family known as the Maccabees, in the second century B.C. For a while the Maccabees were able to gain a measure of religious and political independence. But

Palestine was coveted both because it was relatively fertile and because it was a crossroads for ancient trade.

eventually their successors gave way to the Hellenizing pressures of the Seleucids, who had succeeded Alexander in the rule of Syria. When some of the stricter Jews protested, they were persecuted. Eventually, partially as a result of all this, Rome intervened. In 63 B.C., Pompey conquered the land and deposed the last of the Maccabees, Aristobulus II.

In general, Roman policies towards the religion and customs of conquered people were rather tolerant. Shortly after the conquest, the Roman government gave the descendents of the Maccabees a measure of authority, and used them in governing the land, giving them the titles of High Priest and Ethnarch. Herod the Great, appointed King of Judea by the Romans in 40 B.C., had a distant Maccabean claim, for he had married a woman of that lineage.

But Roman tolerance could not understand the seeming obstinacy of the Jews, who insisted on worshiping only their God, and who threatened rebellion at the least challenge to their faith. Herod made an effort to Hellenize the country, and had temples built in Samaria and Caesarea in honor of Roma and Augustus. But when he dared place a Roman eagle at the entrance of the Temple there was an uprising, which he suppressed by force. His successors followed a similar policy, building new cities and encouraging the immigration of Gentiles.

This led to almost continuous rebellion. When Jesus was a child there was an uprising against Archelaus, Herod's son, who had to call in the Roman army. The Romans then destroyed a city in Galilee near Nazareth, and crucified two thousand Jews. It is to this rebellion that Gamaliel refers in Acts 5:37, as an example of useless revolt. The radical or Zealot party, tenaciously opposed to Roman rule, continued unabated in spite of such atrocities, and played an important role in the great rebellion that broke out in A.D. 66. Once again the Roman legions were called in, and in A.D. 70 they took Jerusalem and destroyed the Temple. Several years later the last stronghold of Jewish resistance, the rock fortress of Massada, was conquered after a heroic defense.

In the midst of such suffering and so many vicissitudes, Jewish religion took different shapes, and several parties appeared. The best known, both because the Gospels refer to it repeatedly and because later Judaism evolved from it, is the party of the Pharisees. They were the party of the populace, who did not enjoy the material benefits of Roman rule and Hellenistic civilization. To them, it was important to be faithful to the Law, and for that reason they studied and debated how the Law was to be applied in every conceivable situation. This has led to the charge that they were legalistic. That may be true to a degree. But, on the other hand, one must remember that they sought to make the faith of Israel relevant to everyday situations, and to new circumstances under Roman rule and Hellenizing threats. Besides this, they held some doctrines, such as the final resurrection and the existence of angels, which the more conservative Jews declared to be mere innovations.

Those more conservative Jews were the Sadducees. By and large, they belonged to the Jewish aristocracy, and they were conservative in both politics and religion. In matters of religion, their interest centered on the Temple, which they held with the support of the Romans, who in turn found their political conservatism much to their liking. They also rejected many of the doctrines of the Pharisees as unwarranted innovations.

This means that one must take care not to exaggerate the opposition of Jesus and the early Christians to the Pharisees. A great deal of the friction between Christians and Pharisees was due to the similarity of their views, rather than to their difference. Moving among the common people, Jesus and his followers had more opportunities to rub shoulders with the Pharisees than with the Sadducees.

There were many other sects and groups within first-century Judaism. The Zealots have already been mentioned. Another important group was that of the Essenes, an ascetic sect to which many attribute the Dead Sea Scrolls. This group, and probably others like it, sought to obey the Law by withdrawing from the rest of society, and often had a very intense expectation that the end was near.

On the other hand, this diversity of tendencies, sects, and parties should not obscure two fundamental tenets of all Jews: ethical monotheism and eschatological hope. Ethical monotheism means that there is only one God, and that this God requires, just as much as proper worship, proper relationships among human beings. The various parties might disagree as to the exact shape of such relationships, but they all agreed on the need to honor the only God with the whole of life.

Under the leadership of Judas Maccabeus, the Jews enjoyed a period of political freedom. Here he is seen as depicted by the fifteenth-century Italian painter Taddeo di Bartolo.

Eschatological hope was another common tenet in the faith of Israel. All, from the Sadducees to the Pharisees, kept the Messianic hope, and firmly believed that the day would come when God would intervene in order to restore Israel and fulfill the promise of a Kingdom of peace and justice. Some thought that they were to speed its coming by the force of arms. Others were convinced that such matters should be left entirely in the hands of God. But all looked to a future when God's promises would be fulfilled.

Of all these groups, the best-equipped to survive after the destruction of the Temple was that of the Pharisees. Their roots went back to the time of the Exile, when it was not possible to worship in Jerusalem, and religious life perforce centered on the Law. The same was true in the first century of the millions of Jews who lived in distant lands. When the Temple was destroyed in A.D. 70, the Sadducees received a mortal blow, while the theological tradition of the Pharisees continued to bloom into modern Judaism.

Diaspora Judaism

For centuries before the birth of Jesus, the number of Jews living away from Palestine had been increasing. From Old Testament times there were numerous Jews in Persia and Mesopotamia. In Egypt, they even built a temple in the seventh century B.C., and another five centuries later. By the time of Jesus, there were sizable Jewish communities in every major city in the Roman Empire. These Jews, scattered far and wide, but with strong emotional and religious connections with the land of their ancestors, are called the "Diaspora" or "Dispersion."

Diaspora Judaism is of crucial importance for the history of Christianity, for it was one of the main avenues through which the new faith expanded throughout the Roman Empire. Furthermore, Diaspora Judaism unwittingly provided the church with one of the most useful tools of its missionary expansion, the Greek translation of the Old Testament.

One of the common traits of Diaspora Judaism was that many of its members had forgotten the language of their ancestors. For this reason, it was necessary to translate the Hebrew Scriptures into languages that they understood—Aramaic in the eastern wing of the Diaspora, and Greek in its western wing, within the borders of the Roman Empire. After Alexander's conquests, Greek had become the common language of a great part of the Mediterranean. Egyptians, Jews, Cypriots, and even Romans used Greek to communicate with each other. Therefore, it was natural that when the Jews of the Diaspora began losing their Hebrew they would translate the Scriptures to Greek.

This translation, which originated in Alexandria—the main city in Egypt—is called the Septuagint, or the version of the Seventy (usually abbreviated as LXX). This was because of an ancient legend that a number of Jewish scholars were commissioned to translate the Scriptures and, after working independently, they found that their translations agreed exactly. The obvious purpose of the legend was to legitimize the translation as divinely inspired.

In any case, the Septuagint was of enormous importance for the early church. It is the text of Scripture quoted by most New Testament authors, and it profoundly influenced the formation of early Christian vocabulary—including the very name of "Christ," which was the Septuagint word for "Anointed One" or "Messiah." When the early Christians began their missionary spread, they used the Septuagint as a ready-made means of communicating their message to the Gentiles. For this and other reasons, the Jewish community produced other versions that were not as readily suitable for Christian use, and in effect left the church in sole possession of the Septuagint.

In the Diaspora, Judaism was forced to come to terms with Hellenism

This mosaic from Tunisia, depicting the Menorah, is one of many remains of the Diaspora.

in a manner that could be avoided in Palestine itself. Particularly in Alexandria, there was a movement within Judaism that sought to show the compatibility between the ancient faith and the best of Hellenistic culture. As early as the third century B.C., attempts were made to retell the history of Israel following the accepted patterns of Hellenistic historical writing. But the high point of this entire tradition was the work of Philo of Alexandria, a contemporary of Jesus who sought to show that the best of pagan philosophy agreed with the Hebrew Scriptures. He claimed that, since the Hebrew prophets antedated the Greek philosophers, the latter must have drawn from the wisdom of the former. According to Philo, such points of agreement are many, for ultimately the teachings of the philosophers coincide with those of Scripture. The difference is that Scripture speaks figuratively. This in turn means that it is to be understood by means of allegorical interpretation. Through such interpretation, Philo tried to prove that the God of Scripture is the same as the One of the philosophers, and that the moral teachings of the Hebrews are basically the same as those of the best among the Greek philosophers. As will be readily seen, this sort of argument provided ample ammunition for the early Christians in their efforts to show to the pagan world that their faith was credible.

The Greco-Roman World

The Roman Empire had brought to the Mediterranean basin an unprecedented political unity. Although each region kept some of its ancient laws and customs, the general policy of the Empire was to encourage as much uniform-

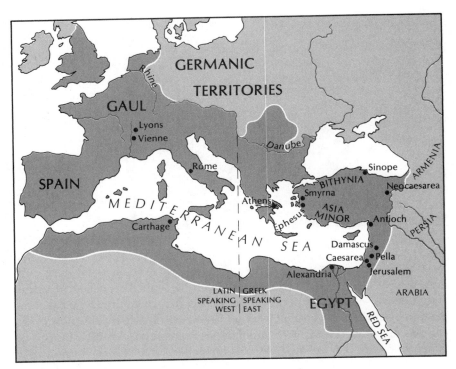

The Roman Empire

ity as possible without doing unnecessary violence to the uses of each area. In this they followed the example of Alexander. Both Alexander and the Roman Empire succeeded to a remarkable degree, and therefore Roman law and Hellenistic culture were the context in which the early church took shape.

The political unity wrought by the Roman Empire allowed the early Christians to travel without having to fear bandits or local wars. When reading about Paul's journeys, we see that the great threat to shipping at that time was bad weather. A few decades earlier, an encounter with pirates was much more to be feared than any storm. In the first century, well-paved and well-guarded roads ran to the most distant provinces. Since trade flourished, travel was constant; thus Christianity often reached a new region, not through the work of missionaries or preachers, but rather through traveling traders, slaves, and others. In that sense, the political circumstances favored the spread of Christianity.

But other aspects of those circumstances were a threat and a challenge to the early Christians. In order to achieve greater unity, imperial policy sought religious uniformity by following two routes: religious syncretism—the indiscriminate mixing of elements from various religions—and emperor worship.

Rome had a vested interest in having her subjects from different lands

The Appian Way was one of many well-paved and well-guarded roads that made trade and travel relatively safe.

believe that, although their gods had different names, they were ultimately the same gods. To the Roman Pantheon (temple of "all gods") were added numerous gods from different lands. The same roads and sea lanes that served Christian missionary expansion were traveled by people of all sorts of traditions and beliefs. These mingled in the plazas and markets of the cities, to the point that their original form was barely recognizable. Syncretism was the fashion of the time. In that atmosphere, Jews and Christians were seen as unbending fanatics who insisted on the sole worship of their One God —an alien cyst that must be removed for the good of society.

The syncretism of the times could also been seen in what historians now call "mystery religions." These were not centered on the ancient Olympian deities, but on others which seemed to be much more personal. In earlier times, people generally had followed the religion of their birthplace. But now, after the conquests of Alexander and Rome, which gods one was to serve became a matter of personal choice. Therefore, one did not belong to a mystery religion by birth, but rather by initiation. Most of these religions were based on myths regarding the origin of the world, the sustenance of life, and the life of the deity. From Egypt came the myth of Isis and Osiris, which explained the fertility of the Nile and all other fertility. Greece contributed rites that from time immemorial had been celebrated near Athens. The cult of Mithra, a god of Indo-Iranian origin, was very popular in the army. Others worshiped the Great Mother, of Semitic origin. Given the syncretism of all these religions, soon they were so intermingled that today it is exceedingly difficult for historians to determine which doctrine or practice arose in which context. Since the deities of the mysteries were not exclusivistic, like the God of Jews and Christians, many people who were initiated into various of these cults took elements from one to the other.

But it was another element in Roman religion that eventually became the reason for persecution. This was the worship of the ruling emperor. Roman authorities saw this as a means of unity and a test of loyalty. To refuse to burn incense before the emperor's image was a sign of treason or at least of disloyalty. When Christians refused to burn incense before the emperor's image, they did so as a witness to their faith; but the authorities condemned them as disloyal and seditious people.

To communicate their faith in the midst of Hellenistic culture, Christians found two philosophical traditions particularly attractive and helpful: Platonism and Stoicism.

Plato's teacher, Socrates, had been condemned to death as an incredulous corruptor of youth. Plato wrote several dialogues in his defense, and by the first century Socrates was considered one of the greatest sages of antiquity. Socrates, Plato, and many other philosophers had criticized the ancient gods, and had taught about a supreme being, perfect and immutable. Furthermore, both Socrates and Plato believed in the immortality of the soul. And Plato affirmed that, far above this world of fleeting things, there was a higher world of abiding truth. All this many early Christians found attractive and useful in their attempts to respond to the charges that they were ignorant and

The Great Mother of the Gods, commonly known as Cybele, came to Greece and Rome from Asia Minor.

unbelieving. Although at first these philosophical traditions were used for interpreting the faith to outsiders, eventually they began influencing the manner in which Christians understood their own faith.

Something similar happened with Stoicism. This philosophical school, slightly younger than Platonism, held very high moral standards. The early Stoics—in the third century B.C.—were materialists who believed that all things were made out of fire, and determinists who were convinced that all they could do was to train themselves to assent to the inexorable laws that rule events. By the time Christianity appeared on the scene, however, Stoicism had evolved to the point where it had religious overtones, and some of its philosophers spoke of using their wisdom to guide the course of events. In any case, all Stoics believed that the purpose of philosophy was to understand the law of nature, and to obey and adjust to it. The wise person is not one who knows a great deal, but rather one whose mind is so attuned to the universal law that reason prevails. When this happens, passions subside, and the philosopher approaches the ideal of *apatheia*—life without passions. The virtues one must cultivate are four: moral insight, courage, self-control, and justice. These, however, are different facets of the life of wisdom, and therefore a failure in one of them is a failure in all. Stoics were also critical of the religion of their time, which many saw as a way to have the gods satisfy their desires rather than as a call to virtue. They also rejected the traditional parochialism of earlier Greek culture, insisting on the universality of the law of reason and calling themselves citizens of the world.

Again, all this was very attractive to Christians, whose criticism of the religion and morals of the time was rarely well received. The church, which many Christians called a "new race" because it drew its members from all races, was living proof of the universal unity of humankind. The Stoic notion of natural law as the .guide to wisdom was soon taken up by Christian apologists and moralists who argued that the Christian life was life according to that law. In response to prejudice, ridicule and even martyrdom, the Stoic ideal of *apatheia* called believers to steadfastness. And many of the arguments that Stoic philosophers had used against the gods were now taken up by Christians.

This was the world into which Christianity was born. The Roman Empire and Hellenistic civilization provided avenues for the proclamation of the new faith; but they also provided obstacles and even dangers. In the next chapters, we shall see how the early Christians followed those avenues, attempted to overcome those obstacles, and responded to those dangers.

3/ The Church in Jerusalem

*And with great power the apostles gave
their testimony to the resurrection of the
Lord Jesus, and great grace was upon
them all.*

ACTS 4:33

The book of Acts affirms that from the very beginning there was
a strong church in Jerusalem. But then that very book moves on
to other matters, and tells us very little about the later history of
that Christian community. The rest of the New Testament offers
a few other bits of information. But it too deals mostly with the life of the
church in other parts of the Empire. Yet, by piecing together what the New
Testament tells us with information gathered from other authors, one can
come to a general idea as to the life of that earliest Christian community, and
its later history.

Unity and Diversity

The earliest Christian community is often idealized. Peter's firmness and
eloquence at Pentecost tend to eclipse his waverings as to what ought to be
done with the Gentiles who wished to join the church. The possession of all
things in common, commendable as it may be, did not abolish all tensions
between various groups, for "the Hellenists murmured against the Hebrews
because their widows were neglected in the daily distribution" (Acts 6:1).

These last words do not refer to a conflict between Jews and Gentiles,
for Acts makes clear that at that time there were still no Gentiles in the
church. It was rather a conflict between two groups of Jews, those who kept
the customs and language of their ancestors, and those who showed more
openness to Hellenistic influences. In Acts, the first are called "Hebrews,"
and the others the "Hellenists." In response to this crisis, the twelve

called an assembly that appointed seven men "to serve tables." Exactly what this meant is not altogether clear, although there is no doubt that the idea was that the seven would have administrative tasks, and that the twelve would continue preaching and teaching. In any case, it would seem that all seven were "Hellenists," for they had Greek names. Thus, the naming of the seven would appear as an attempt to give greater voice in the affairs of the church to the Hellenistic party, while the twelve, all "Hebrews," would continue being the main teachers and preachers.

The seventh chapter of Acts tells the story of Stephen, one of the seven. There is a hint (Acts 7:47–48) that his attitude towards the Temple was not entirely positive. In any case, the Jewish council, composed mostly of anti-Hellenistic Jews, refuses to listen to him and condemns him to death. This contrasts with the treatment given by the same council to Peter and John, who were released after being beaten and told to stop preaching (Acts 5:40). Furthermore, when persecution finally broke out and Christians had to flee Jerusalem, the apostles were able to remain. When Saul left for Damascus to seek out Christians who had taken refuge there, the apostles were still in Jerusalem, and Saul seemed to ignore them. All of this would seem to indicate that the earliest persecution was aimed mostly at the "Hellenistic" Christians, and that the "Hebrews" had much less difficulty. It is later, in chapter 12, that we are told of Herod (not the council) ordering the death of James, and arresting Peter.

Immediately after the death of Stephen, Acts turns to another of the

In Jerusalem, shortly after Pentecost, Christians already had to deal with the diversity in their midst.

seven, Philip, who founded a church in Samaria. Peter and John are then sent to supervise the life of that new community. Thus, a church is being born beyond the confines of Judea, and that church, although not founded by the apostles, still acknowledges their authority. This is a pattern that would often be repeated as the church extended to new areas.

By its ninth chapter, Acts becomes increasingly interested in Paul, and we hear less and less of the church in Jerusalem. What was happening was that the "Hellenistic" Jewish Christians were serving as a bridge to the Gentile world, and that Gentiles were joining the church in such numbers that they soon overshadowed the earlier Jewish Christian community. For this reason most of our story will deal with Gentile Christianity. And yet, we should not forget that earliest of churches, of which we have only fragmentary glimpses.

Religious Life

The earliest Christians did not consider themselves followers of a new religion. All their lives they had been Jews, and they still were. This was true of Peter and the twelve, of the seven, and of Paul. Their faith was not a denial of Judaism, but was rather the conviction that the Messianic age had finally arrived. Paul would say that he was persecuted "because of the hope of Israel" (Acts 28:20). The earliest Christians did not reject Judaism, but were convinced that their faith was the fullfilment of the age-long expectation of a Messiah.

This was why Christians in Jerusalem continued keeping the Sabbath and attending worship at the Temple. To this they added the observance of the first day of the week, in which they gathered in celebration of the resurrection of Jesus. Those early communion services did not center on the Lord's passion, but rather on his victory by which a new age had dawned. It was much later—centuries later—that the focus of Christian worship shifted towards the death of Jesus. In the earliest Christian community, the breaking of the bread took place "with glad and generous hearts" (Acts 2:46).

There were indeed times set aside for sorrow for one's sins. These were especially the two weekly days of fasting, which the church took from Jewish practice. At an early date, however, Christians began fasting, not on Mondays and Thursdays, like the Jews, but rather on Wednesdays and Fridays. It may be that this shift took place in commemoration of the betrayal and the crucifixion.

In that early church, authority was vested primarily on the twelve (although some scholars suggest that this emphasis on the authority of the apostles is slightly later, and appeared as part of an effort to tighten up the system of authority within the church). Of the apostles, Peter and John seem

*An Egyptian manuscript of Acts, circa A.D. 400. The loop on the
cross is shaped after an ancient hieroglyph meaning "life."*

to have been foremost, for Acts gives several indications of this, and they are
two of the "pillars" to whom Paul refers in Galatians 2:9.

The third such "pillar," however, was not one of the twelve. He was
James, the brother of the Lord. According to Paul (1 Cor. 15:7), the risen
Jesus had appeared to James. Whether because of his blood ties with Jesus,
or for some other reason, James soon became the leader of the church in
Jerusalem. Later, when church leaders were uniformly given the title of
"bishop," it was said that James was the first "bishop" of Jerusalem. Although
the title is clearly erroneous, it is probably true that he was the leader of the
church in Jerusalem.

The Waning of the Jewish Church

Soon persecution grew fiercer and more general. Herod Agrippa, the grandson of Herod the Great, ordered the death of James the brother of John—
not to be confused with James the brother of Jesus and head of the community. When this move was well received by his subjects, Herod had Peter
arrested, but he escaped. In A.D. 62 the other James, the brother of Jesus,
was killed by orders of the high priest, even against the desire and advice of
some of the Pharisees.

Soon thereafter, the leaders of the Christian community in Jerusalem
decided to move to Pella, a city beyond the Jordan whose population was

mostly Gentile. This move seems to have been prompted, not only by persecution at the hands of the Jews, but also by Roman suspicion as to the exact nature of the new religious sect. At that time Jewish nationalism had reached the boiling point, and in A.D. 66 a rebellion broke out that would lead, four years later, to the destruction of Jerusalem by the Roman armies. Christians were followers of one who they said was of the line of David, and who had been crucified by Roman authorities for claiming that he was King of the Jews. They were led first by James, the brother of the crucified, and then, after the death of James, by Simeon, another relative of Jesus. To allay the suspicions that all this created, the church decided to remove to Pella. But in spite of this such suspicions continued, and Simeon was eventually killed by the Romans, although it is not clear whether this was due to his Christian faith or to his claim to Davidic lineage. In any case, the result of all this was that the ancient Jewish church, rejected by both Jews and Gentiles, found itself in increasing isolation. Although by A.D. 135 a number of Jewish Christians returned to Jerusalem, their relationship with the rest of Christianity had been almost entirely severed, and leadership had passed to Gentile Christians.

In the desolate regions beyond the Jordan, Jewish Christianity made contact with various groups who had also abandoned orthodox Judaism. Lacking in contact with the rest of the church, that Jewish Christian community followed its own course, and was often influenced by the many sects among which it lived. When, in later centuries, Gentile Christians deigned to write a few words about that forgotten community, they would speak of its heretics and its strange customs, but they would have little of positive value to say about that church, which faded out of history in the fifth century.

A silver shekel from the first year of the Jewish War.

4/Mission to the Gentiles

I am not ashamed of the gospel: it is the power of God for salvation to every one who has faith, to the Jew first and also to the Greek.

ROMANS 1:16

Those Christians whom Acts called "Hellenists," while being Jewish, showed a degree of openness to Hellenistic culture. Since they were the first to be persecuted in Jerusalem, they were the first to be scattered throughout the neighboring towns, and thus they were also the first to take the Christian message to those areas.

The Scope of the Mission

According to Acts 8:1, these Christians "were all scattered throughout Judea and Samaria." Acts 9:32–42 speaks of visits by Peter to the Christian communities in Lydda, Sharon, and Joppa, all in Judea. Acts 8 tells of the work of Philip in Samaria, the conversion of Simon Magus, and the visit of Peter and John.

But, as early as Acts 9, we are also told that some of the fleeing Christians were scattered as far as Damascus, well beyond the borders of Judea. And Acts 11:19 adds further that "those who were scattered because of the persecution that arose over Stephen traveled as far as Phoenicia and Cyprus and Antioch." This does not mean that the mission was extended to the Gentiles, for Acts explains that they went to all these areas "speaking the word to none except Jews."

The mission of Philip in Samaria, and the conversion of the Ethiopian eunuch, are possibly the first indications of the church's willingness to receive non-Jews. But the issue is finally faced in Acts 10, in the episode of Peter and Cornelius, which eventually leads the church of Jerusalem to the surprised conclusion: "Then to the Gentiles also God has granted repentance unto life"

(Acts 11:18). Immediately thereafter we are told that something similar happened in Antioch, with the result that Barnabas was sent by the church in Jerusalem to investigate the matter, and "when he came and saw the grace of God, he was glad" (Acts 11:23). These various events show that, while the earliest Christian expansion was mostly the result of the witness of those Jewish Christians of Hellenistic tendencies who had to flee Jerusalem, the mother church approved of their work, both among Hellenistic Jews and among Gentiles.

A medieval illuminated manuscript depicting Pentecost, with the Spirit coming to the apostles in tongues of fire.

Naturally, this did not solve all problems, for there was always the question of whether Gentile converts to Christianity had to obey the Law of Israel. After some hesitation, the church in Jerusalem accepted them, declaring that "it has seemed good to the Holy Spirit and to us to lay upon you no other burden than these necessary things: that you abstain from what has been sacrificed to idols and from blood and from what is strangled and from unchastity" (Acts 15:28–29). This, however, did not end the matter, for Paul's epistles are full of evidence that there were for a time those who insisted on greater strictures.

Paul's Work

It is not necessary to retell here all of Paul's travels, to which the book of Acts devotes several chapters. It should suffice to say that, for some unknown reason, Barnabas went to Tarsus to look for Paul, and that together they spent a year in Antioch, where the followers of Jesus were first called "Christians." Then in a number of missionary voyages, first with Barnabas and then with others, Paul took the Gospel to the island of Cyprus, to several cities of Asia Minor, to Greece, to Rome, and perhaps—according to a tradition that cannot be confirmed—to Spain.

But to say that Paul took the Gospel to those areas is not to imply that he was the first to do so. The Epistle to the Romans shows that there was a church in the imperial capital before Paul's arrival. Furthermore, the spread of Christianity in Italy was such that when Paul arrived at the small seaport of Puteoli there were Christians there.

Therefore, Paul's significance for the early spread of Christianity ought not to be exaggerated. Although the New Testament speaks a great deal of Paul and his journeys, there were many others preaching in various regions. Barnabas and Mark went to Cyprus. The Alexandrine Jew Apollos preached in Ephesus and Corinth. And Paul himself, after complaining that "some preach Christ from envy and rivalry," rejoices that by all these Christ is proclaimed (Philippians 1:18).

Paul's greatest and unique contribution to the shaping of early Christianity was not so much in the actual founding of churches. Rather, it was in the epistles that he wrote in connection with that activity, since those epistles eventually became part of Christian Scripture, and thus have had a decisive and continuing impact in the life and thought of the Christian church.

The missionary task itself was undertaken, not only by Paul and others whose names are known—Barnabas, Mark, et al.—but also by countless and nameless Christians who went from place to place taking with them their faith and their witness. Some of these, like Paul, traveled as missionaries, impelled by their faith. But mostly these nameless Christians were merchants, slaves,

Paul is often shown holding a book of his epistles.

and others who traveled for various reasons, but whose travel provided the opportunity for the expansion of the Christian message.

Finally, while speaking of Paul's work, it is important to point out that, while he felt called to preach to the Gentiles, his usual procedure upon arriving at a new town was to go to the synagogue and the Jewish community. Again, he did not believe that he was preaching a new religion, but rather the fulfillment of the promises made to Israel. His message was not that Israel had been abandoned by God, but rather that now, through the resurrection of Jesus, the age of the Messiah had dawned, and that therefore the way was open for Gentiles to join the people of God.

The Apostles: Facts and Legends

The New Testament gives no indication as to the career of most of the apostles. Acts tells of the death of James, the brother of John. But that very book, after following Paul's career for a number of years, abruptly leaves him while preaching in Rome, awaiting trial. What became of Paul, Peter, and the other apostles? From an early date, traditions began to appear claiming that one or another of them had preached in a particular region, or had suffered martyrdom in one way or another. Most of these traditions are no more that the result of the desire of a church in a particular city to claim an apostolic origin. Others are more worthy of credit.

Of all these traditions, the most trustworthy is the one that affirms that Peter was in Rome, and that he suffered martyrdom in that city during the Neronian persecution. On these points, several writers of the first and second centuries agree. We are also told that he was crucified—according to one version, upside-down—and this seems to agree with the otherwise obscure words in John 21:18–19.

The case of Paul is somewhat more complex. The book of Acts leaves him while preaching in Rome. Ancient writers agree that he died in Rome —probably beheaded, as befitted a Roman citizen—at the time of Nero. But others say that he undertook some journeys that are not mentioned in Acts, including a trip to Spain. Some have tried to join these two traditions by supposing that Paul went to Spain between the end of Acts and the Neronian persecution. But this explanation encounters chronological difficulties. At best, all that can be said is that nothing is known for certain between the end of the book of Acts and Paul's death during the reign of Nero.

The task of reconstructing John's later career is complicated by the frequency with which the name of John appears in early records. There is an ancient tradition that claims that John was killed in a pot of boiling oil. But the book of Revelation places John, at about the same time, in exile on the island of Patmos. Another very trustworthy tradition speaks of John as a

In later Christian art, Peter was seen as a powerful pope.

teacher at Ephesus, where he died around A.D. 100. All this indicates that there were at least two people with the same name, and that later tradition confused them. A second-century Christian writer—Papias of Hierapolis—affirms that there were indeed two persons by the name of John in the early church: one the apostle, and another an elder at Ephesus, who received the visions of Patmos. In any case, there was indeed towards the end of the first century, in the city of Ephesus, a Christian teacher named John, whose authority was great in all the churches of Asia Minor.

Late in the second century, a development took place that greatly hinders the task of the historian who seeks to discern the later career of the apostles. What happened was that the churches in every important city began claiming apostolic origins. In her rivalry with Rome and Antioch, the church in Alexandria felt constrained to have an apostolic founder, and thus the tradition appeared according to which Saint Mark had founded the church there. Likewise, when Constantinople became a capital city in the Empire, its church too needed apostolic roots, and thus it was claimed that Philip had preached in Byzantium, the ancient site where Constantinople was later built.

There are other traditions regarding apostolic activities that are worthy of note, if not for their truthfulness, at least for their popularity and their significance for later history. This is particularly true of the traditions regarding the origins of Christianity in Spain and India.

Christians in Spain have claimed that their land was missionized, not only by Paul, but also by seven envoys of Saint Peter and by Saint James. The legend regarding Peter's missionaries to Spain appeared in the fifth century, but it was not as influential as that of James' visit to the country, which originated three centuries later. According to this tradition, James proclaimed the Gospel, without much success, in Galicia and Saragossa. On his way back, the Virgin appeared to him standing on a pillar, and gave him words of encouragement—this is the origin of the "Virgen del Pilar," still venerated by many in the Spanish tradition. Back in Jerusalem, James was beheaded by Herod, and then his disciples took his remains back to Compostela in Spain, where they are supposedly buried to this day.

This legend has been of great significance for the later history of Spain, for St. James (in Spanish, Santiago) became the patron saint of the nation. During the wars against the Moors, the name of "Santiago" was often the battle cry to which various small kingdoms rallied. At the same time, pilgrimages to the shrine of St. James in Compostela played an important role both in European religiosity and in the unification of northern Spain. The Order of Saint James was also a significant factor in Spanish history. Thus, although it is highly unlikely that James ever gave any thought to Spain, the legends regarding his visit were very influential in the later history of that country.

The tradition that claims Thomas visited India leaves historians somewhat baffled. It appears for the first time in the *Acts of Thomas,* which may have been written as early as the end of the second century. But already it is embellished with legendary tales, which make the entire account suspicious. We are told that an Indian king, Gondophares, was seeking an architect to build a palace, and that Thomas, who was no architect, offered himself for the job. When the king found that Thomas was giving to the poor the money allotted for the construction of the palace, he had the apostle put in prison. But then Gondophares' brother, Gad, died and came back from the dead. Upon his return he told his brother of the magnificent heavenly palace that he had seen, which was being built through Thomas' gifts to the poor. The king and his brother were then converted and baptized, and Thomas moved on to other parts of India, until he died as a martyr.

Obviously, much in this legend is of questionable authenticity, and historians have often discarded the whole of it as fictitious, for history had no record of Gondophares nor of any of the other details of the story. More recently, however, coins have been found that prove that there was indeed a ruler by that name, and that he had a brother named Gad. This, coupled with the undeniable antiquity of Christianity in India, and with the fact that at the time there was significant trade between India and the Near East, makes it more difficult to reject categorically the possibility that Thomas may have visited that land, and that later the story may have been embellished with all kinds of legendary accounts. In any case, it is significant that from a relatively early date there was a church in India, and that this church has repeatedly claimed Thomas as its founder.

In conclusion, it is certain that some of the apostles—particularly Peter, John, and Paul—did travel proclaiming the Gospel and supervising the churches that had been founded, either by them or by others. Perhaps other apostles, such as Thomas, did likewise. But most of the traditions regarding apostolic travels date from a later period, when it was believed that the apostles divided the world among themselves, and when the church in each country or city sought to claim apostolic origins. In truth, most of the missionary work was not carried out by the apostles, but rather by the countless and nameless Christians who for different reasons—persecution, business, or missionary calling—traveled from place to place taking the news of the Gospel with them.

5/First Conflicts with the State

From its very beginnings, Christianity was no easy matter. The Lord whom Christians served had died on the cross, condemned as a criminal. Soon thereafter Stephen was stoned to death following his witness before the council of the Jews. Then James was killed at Herod Agrippa's order. Ever since then, and up to our own days, there have been those who have had to seal their witness with their blood.

Yet, the reasons for persecution, and the manner in which it has been carried out, have varied. Already in the early decades of the life of the church there was a certain development in these matters.

A New Jewish Sect

The early Christians did not believe that they were following a new religion. They were Jews, and their main difference with the rest of Judaism was that they were convinced that the Messiah had come, whereas other Jews continued awaiting his advent. Therefore, the Christian message to Jews was not that they should abandon their Jewishness. On the contrary, now that the messianic age had begun, they were to be better Jews. Likewise, their early proclamation to the Gentiles was not an invitation to accept a newly born religion, but rather to become participants of the promises made to Abraham and his descendents. Gentiles were invited to become children of Abraham by faith, since they could not be so by flesh. This invitation was made possible because, since the time of the prophets, Judaism had believed that through the advent of the Messiah all nations would be brought to Zion. For those early Christians, Judaism was not a rival religion to Christianity, but the same faith, even though those who followed it did not see or believe that the prophecies had been fulfilled.

From the point of view of those Jews who rejected Christianity, the situation was understood in a similar manner. Christianity was not a new religion, but a heretical sect within Judaism. As we have seen, first-century Judaism was not a monolithic entity, but included various divergent sects and opinions. Therefore, when Christianity entered the scene, Jews saw it as simply another sect.

The attitude of those Jews toward Christianity is best understood by placing ourselves in their situation, and seeing Christianity from their perspective, as a new heresy going from town to town tempting good Jews to become heretics. Furthermore, many Jews believed, with some biblical foundation, that the reason why they had lost their independence and been made subjects of the Empire was that the people had not been sufficiently faithful to the traditions of their ancestors. Nationalistic and patriotic sentiment was aroused by the fear that these new heretics could once more bring the wrath of God upon Israel.

For these reasons, in most of the New Testament it is Jews who persecute Christians, who in turn seek refuge under the wing of Roman authorities. This happens, for instance, when some Jews in Corinth accuse Paul before Proconsul Gallio, saying that "this man is persuading men to worship God contrary to the law," to which Gallio answers, "If it were a matter of wrongdoing or vicious crime, I should have reason to hear you, O Jews; but since it is a matter of questions about words and names and your own law, see to it yourselves; I refuse to be a judge of these things" (Acts 18:14-15). Later, when there is a riot because some claim that Paul has brought a Gentile to the Temple, and some Jews try to kill the apostle, it is the Romans that save his life.

Thus, Romans, Jews, and Christians agreed that what was taking place was a conflict among Jews. As long as things were relatively orderly, Romans preferred to stay out of such matters. But when there was a riot or any disorderly conduct, they intervened to restore order, and sometimes to punish the disorderly.

A good illustration of this policy was the expulsion of Jews from Rome by Emperor Claudius, around A.D. 51. Acts 18:2 mentions that expulsion, but does not explain the reason for it. Suetonius, a Roman historian, says that Jews were expelled from the capital city for their disorderly conduct "because of Chrestus." Most historians agree that "Chrestus" is none other than "Christus," and that what actually took place in Rome was that Christian proclamation caused so many riots among Jews that the emperor decided to expel the lot. At that time, Romans still saw the conflict between Christians and Jews as an internal matter within Judaism.

But the distinction between Christians and Jews became clearer as the Church gained more converts from the Gentile population, and the ratio of Jews in its ranks diminished. There are also indications that, as Jewish nationalism increased and eventually led to rebellion against Rome, Christians—particularly the Gentiles among them—sought to put as much distance as possible between themselves and that movement. The result was that Roman authorities began to take cognizance of Christianity as a religion quite different from Judaism. This new consciousness was at the root of two-and-a-half centuries of persecution by the Roman Empire, from the time of Nero to the conversion of Constantine.

The story of Jewish-Christian relations in the first years of Christianity has had fateful consequences. While Christianity appeared as a heretical sect within Judaism, the latter tried to suppress it, as can be seen in various books of the New Testament. Since that time, however, Jews have not been in a position where they could persecute Christians—in fact, the opposite has often been the case. When Christianity became the official religion of the majority, there were those who, on the basis of what the New Testament says about the opposition of Judaism to Christianity, and without any regard for the different historical circumstances, declared the Jews to be a rejected race, persecuted them, and even massacred them. Such an attitude would have been abhorrent to Paul, who claimed that he was being persecuted "for the hope of Israel."

Persecution under Nero

Thanks to his mother's intrigues, Nero reached the Roman throne in October of 54. At first he was a reasonable ruler, not entirely unpopular, whose laws in favor of the dispossessed were well received by the Roman populace. But he became increasingly infatuated by his dreams of grandeur and lust for pleasure, and surrounded himself with a court where all vied to satisfy his every whim. Ten years after his accession to the throne, he was despised by the people as well as by the poets and artists, who were offended by the emperor's claim that he was one of them. Soon the rumor began circulating that he was mad.

Such was the state of things when, on the night of June 18, A.D. 64, a great fire broke out in Rome. It appears that Nero was several miles away, in his palace at Antium, and that as soon as he heard the news he hurried to Rome, where he tried to organize the fight against the fire. He opened to the homeless the gardens of his palace, as well as other public buildings. In spite of this, there were those who suspected the emperor, whom many believed mad, of having ordered that certain sections of the city be put to the torch. The fire lasted six days and seven nights, and then flared up

At first a reasonable ruler, Nero became increasingly unpopular; eventually, rumors circulated that he was mad.

sporadically for three more days. Ten of the fourteen sections of the city were destroyed. In the midst of their sufferings, the people clamored for justice. Soon the rumor arose—and persists to this day in many history books—that Nero had ordered the city destroyed so he could rebuild it according to his fancy. The Roman historian Tacitus, who may well have been present at the time, records several of the rumors that circulated, but seems inclined to believe that the fire began accidentally in an oil warehouse.

More and more, the people suspected the emperor. It began to be rumored that he had spent most of the time during the fire atop a tower on the Palatine, dressed as an actor, playing his lyre and singing about the destruction of Troy. Then the story was that, in his presumptuousness as a poet, he had ordered the city destroyed so that the fire would inspire in him a great epic poem. Nero tried to allay such suspicions, but it soon became clear that he would not succeed in this as long as there was no one else to blame. Two of the areas that had not burned had a very high proportion of Jewish and Christian population. Therefore, the Emperor decided to blame the Christians.

Tacitus tells the story:

In spite of every human effort, of the emperor's largesse, and of the sacrifices made to the gods, nothing sufficed to allay suspicion nor to destroy the opinion that the fire had been ordered. Therefore, in order to destroy this rumor, Nero blamed the Christians, who are hated for their abominations, and punished them with refined cruelty. Christ, from whom they take their name, was executed by Pontius Pilate during the reign of Tiberius. Stopped for a moment, this evil superstition reappeared, not only in Judea, where was the root of the evil, but also in Rome, where all things sordid and abominable from every corner of the world come together. Thus, first those who confessed [that they were Christians] were arrested, and on the basis of their testimony a great number were condemned, although not so much for the fire itself as for their hatred of humankind.*

These words from Tacitus are of great value, for they are one of the most ancient extant indications of how pagans viewed Christians. Reading these lines, it is clear that Tacitus does not believe that the fire in Rome was set by Christians. Furthermore, he does not approve of Nero's "refined cruelty." But, all the same, this good and cultured Roman believes a great deal of what is being said about the "abominations" of Christians and their "hatred of humankind." Tacitus and other contemporary authors do not tell us what these supposed "abominations" were. Second-century authors will be more explicit. But, in any case, Tacitus believes the rumors, and thinks that Christians hate humankind. This last charge makes sense if one remembers that all social activities—the theatre, the army, letters, sports—were so entwined with pagan worship that Christians often felt the need to abstain from them. Therefore, to the eyes of a Roman such as Tacitus, who loved his culture and society, Christians appeared as haters of humankind.

But Tacitus goes on:

Before killing the Christians, Nero used them to amuse the people. Some were dressed in furs, to be killed by dogs. Others were crucified. Still others were set on fire early in the night, so that they might illumine it. Nero opened his own gardens for these shows, and in the circus he himself became a spectacle, for he mingled with the people dressed as a charioteer, or he rode around in his chariot. All of this aroused the mercy of the people, even against these culprits who deserved an exemplary punishment, for it was clear that they were not being destroyed for the common good, but rather to satisfy the cruelty of one person.**

Once again the pagan historian, while showing no love for Christians, indicates that the reason for this persecution was not justice, but the whim of the emperor. These lines are also one of the few surviving pagan testimonies of the cruel tortures to which those early martyrs were subjected.

It is difficult to know the extent of the Neronian persecution. Christian writers from the latter part of the first century, and early in the second, recall the horrors of those days. It is also very likely that both Peter and Paul were among the Neronian martyrs. On the other hand, there is no mention of any persecution outside the city of Rome, and therefore it is quite likely that this persecution, although exceedingly cruel, was limited to the capital of the Empire.

Although at first Christians were charged with arson, soon they were persecuted for the mere fact of being Christians—and for all the supposed

---

*Annals 15.44.
**Ibid.

abominations connected with that name. Ancient writers tell us that Nero issued an edict against Christians. But such an edict, if it ever existed, is no longer extant.

In A.D. 68, Nero was deposed by a rebellion that gained the support of the Roman senate, and then killed himself. The persecution ceased, although nothing was done to rescind whatever laws Nero had passed against Christians. A period of political turmoil followed, to the point that A.D. 69 is known as "the year of four emperors." Eventually, Vespasian gained control of the government, and during his reign and that of his son Titus Christians were generally ignored by the authorities.

Persecution under Domitian

Domitian, who became emperor after Titus, at first paid no particular attention to Christians. Why he eventually turned against them is not clear. It is a fact that he loved and respected Roman traditions, and that he sought to restore them. Christians, in their rejection of Roman gods and of many Roman traditions, stood in the way of Domitian's dreams, and this may have been one of the causes of persecution.

Jews also found themselves in difficulty with the emperor. Since the Temple had been destroyed in A.D. 70, Domitian decided that all Jews should remit to the imperial coffers the annual offering they would otherwise have sent to Jerusalem. Some Jews refused to obey, while others sent the money but made clear that Rome had not taken the place of Jerusalem. In response, Domitian enacted strict laws against Judaism, and insisted on the offering in even harsher terms.

Since at that time the distinction between Jews and Christians was not clear in the minds of Roman authorities, imperial functionaries began persecuting any who followed "Jewish practices." Thus began a new persecution, which seems to have been directed against both Jews and Christians.

As in the case of Nero, it does not appear that this persecution was uniformly severe throughout the Empire. In fact, it is only from Rome and Asia Minor that there are trustworthy reports of persecution at this time.

In Rome, Flavius Clemens and his wife Flavia Domitilla, who may have been related to the emperor, were executed. They were accused of "atheism" and of "Jewish practices." Since Christians worshiped an invisible God, pagans often declared them to be atheists. Therefore, is is likely that Flavius Clemens and Domitilla died because they were Christians. If so, these are the only two Roman martyrs of this persecution whose names are known. But several ancient writers affirm that there were many martyrs, and a letter that the church in Rome addressed to the Corinthians speaks of "the continuous and unexpected evils which have come upon us."

*Christians abstained from pagan spectacles
such as those that took place in the Coliseum.*

In Asia Minor, this persecution resulted in the writing of the book of
Revelation, whose author was exiled on the island of Patmos. There are
indications that many were killed, and for generations the Church in Asia
Minor remembered the reign of Domitian as a time of trial.

In the midst of persecution, Revelation displays a much more negative
attitude towards Rome than the rest of the New Testament. Paul had instructed Christians in Rome to obey the authorities, whom he said had been
ordained by God. But now the seer of Patmos speaks of Rome as "the great
harlot . . . drunk with the blood of the saints and the blood of the martyrs
of Jesus" (Rev. 17:1, 6).

Fortunately, when persecution broke out Domitian's reign was coming
to an end. Like Nero, Domitian was increasingly seen as a tyrant. His enemies conspired against him, and he was murdered in his own palace. The

Roman senate then decreed that his name should be erased from every inscription, so that there would be no memory of him. As for Christians, no one seems to have taken notice of them, and therefore they were granted a few years of relative peace.

6/Persecution in the Second Century

Now I begin to be a disciple. . . . Let fire and cross, flocks of beasts, broken bones, dismemberment, . . . come upon me, so long as I attain to Jesus Christ.

IGNATIUS OF ANTIOCH

Although the Roman Empire began persecuting Christians from the time of Nero, throughout the first century the details of such persecutions are scarce. By the second century, however, records begin to afford a clearer view of the issues involved in the persecutions, and of the attitudes of Christians towards martyrdom. Of these, the most dramatic are the "acts of the martyrs," which retell the arrest, trial, and death of various martyrs. Some of these include so many trustworthy details about the trial that they seem to have been taken, in part at least, from official court records. Sometimes we are told that the writer was present at the trial and death of the martyr, and historians are inclined to believe that it was indeed so. On the other hand, a number of these supposed "acts of the martyrs" clearly come from a much later date, and deserve little credit. But, in any case, the genuine "acts" are among the most precious and inspiring documents of early Christianity. Secondly, we learn of the attitude of Christians towards martyrdom through other Christian writings. Of these, the most valuable is probably the set of seven letters that the aged Bishop Ignatius of Antioch wrote on his way to martyrdom. Finally, the second century offers further glimpses into the attitude of Roman authorities vis-a-vis the new faith. In this context, the correspondence between Pliny and Trajan is most illuminating.

The Correspondence between Pliny and Trajan

In A.D. 111, Pliny the Younger was appointed governor of Bithynia, on the northern shore of what today is Turkey. From various sources, it would appear that Pliny was a just man with a profound respect for Roman law and traditions. But in Bithynia he had to deal with an unexpected problem. There were many Christians in the region—so many, in fact, that Pliny declared that the pagan temples were almost deserted, and that the sellers of sacrificial victims found few buyers. When somebody sent the new governor a list of Christians, Pliny began inquiries, for he knew that this religion was illegal.

The governor had the accused brought before him, and thus began learning of the beliefs and practices of Christians. Many declared that they were not Christians, and others said that, although they had followed the new faith for a time, they had abandoned it. Of these Pliny required only that they pray to the gods, burn incense before the image of the emperor, and curse Christ, something that he had heard true Christians would never do. Once they performed these rites, he simply let them go.

Those who persisted in their faith posed a different problem. Pliny's practice was to offer them three opportunities to recant, while threatening them with death. If they refused, he had them executed, not so much for being Christians, as for their obstinacy. If they were Roman citizens, he had them sent to Rome, as the law required.

But Pliny considered himself a just man, and therefore felt obliged to find out what crimes, besides sheer obstinacy, Christians committed. All he could learn was that Christians gathered before dawn to sing to Christ "as to a god," and to join in an oath not to commit theft, adultery, or any such sins. They also used to gather for a common meal, but had discontinued this practice when the authorities had outlawed secret meetings. Not quite convinced that this was the whole truth, Pliny put two female Christian ministers to torture. But they simply confirmed what he already knew.

The question then was, should Christians be punished for concrete crimes, or should the very name "Christian" be considered a crime? Not knowing what course to follow, Pliny suspended the proceedings and wrote Emperor Trajan for further instructions.

The emperor's response was brief. When it comes to the punishment of Christians, there is no general rule that is equally valid in all circumstances. On the one hand, the nature of their crime is such that the state should not waste time seeking them out. On the other hand, if they are accused and refuse to recant they should be punished. Those who are willing to worship the gods should be pardoned without further inquiries. Finally, anonymous accusations should be disregarded, for they are a bad legal precedent and are unworthy of this age.

Almost a hundred years later the legal mind of Tertullian, a Christian in North Africa, rebelled against the injustice of such an edict, which was still in force:

What a necessarily confused sentence! It refuses to seek them out, as if they were innocent, and orders that they be punished as if they were guilty. It pardons, and yet is cruel. It ignores, and yet punishes. Why do you circumvent your own censure? If you condemn, why do you not inquire? And, if you do not inquire, why do you not also absolve?*

Yet, although Trajan's decision seemed to lack logic, it did not lack political sense. He understood what Pliny was saying: that Christians, by the mere fact of being such, were not committing any crime against society or against the state. Therefore, the resources of the state should not be wasted in seeking them out. But, once accused and brought before the authorities, Christians had to be forced to worship the gods of the Empire, or face punishment. Otherwise, imperial courts would lose their authority. In other words, Christians were not punished for crimes committed before being brought to trial, but for their seeming contempt of Roman courts. Those who openly refused to worship the gods and the emperor had to be punished, first, because the dignity of the courts required it; and, secondly, because in refusing to worship the emperor they seemed to be denying his right to rule.

For these reasons, the policies which Trajan outlined in his response to Pliny were followed far beyond the borders of Bithynia, and long after Trajan's death. Throughout the second century, and part of the third, it was imperial policy not to seek out Christians, but still to punish them when they were brought before the authorities. That this was true even before the correspondence between Pliny and Trajan may be seen in the circumstances surrounding Ignatius' seven letters.

Ignatius of Antioch, the Bearer of God

About A.D. 107, the elderly bishop of Antioch, Ignatius, was condemned to death by the imperial authorities. Since great festivities were being planned in Rome in celebration of a military victory, Ignatius was sent to the capital so that his death would help amuse the people. On his way to martyrdom, he wrote seven letters that are among the most valuable documents for our knowledge of early Christianity.

Ignatius was probably born around A.D. 30 or 35, and was well over seventy when his life ended in martyrdom. In his letters, he repeatedly calls himself "the bearer of God," as if this were a title by which he was known

---

*Apology 1.2.

—and this is an indication of the high respect in which he was held among Christians. Much later, by making a slight change in the Greek text of his letters, people began speaking of Ignatius as "he who was borne by God," and thus arose the legend according to which he was the little child whom Jesus picked up and placed in the midst of his disciples. In any case, by the beginning of the second century Ignatius had great prestige in the entire Christian community, because he was bishop (the second after the apostles) of one of the most ancient churches, that of Antioch.

Nothing is known about the arrest and trial of Ignatius, nor of who it was that brought in an accusation against him. From his letters, it is clear that there were several factions in Antioch, and that the elderly bishop had tenaciously opposed those doctrines he found heretical. It is not clear whether he was accused before the authorities by a pagan, or by a dissident Christian who sought to undo him. In any case, for one reason or another, Ignatius was arrested, tried, and condemned to die in Rome.

On their way to Rome, Ignatius and the soldiers guarding him passed through Asia Minor. A number of Christians from that area went to see him. Ignatius was able to see them and converse with them. He even had a Christian amanuensis who wrote the letters he dictated. It is clear from this that there was no general persecution of Christians throughout the Empire at this time, but that only those brought before the courts were condemned. This was why Ignatius could receive visitors who were obviously guilty of the same "crime" of which he stood convicted.

Ignatius' seven letters are the outcome of these visits. He had received the bishop, two elders, and a deacon from the church in Magnesia. From Tralles, Bishop Polybius had come. Ephesus had sent a delegation headed by Bishop Onesimus, who may well have been the same person about whom Paul wrote to Philemon. To each of these churches, Ignatius addressed a letter from Smyrna. Later, from Troas, he wrote three other letters: one to the church of Smyrna, another to its bishop Polycarp, and a third to the church in Philadelphia. But the most significant letter to help us understand the nature of persecution and martyrdom in the second century is the one that Ignatius wrote from Smyrna to the church in Rome.

Somehow, Ignatius had heard that Christians in Rome were considering

A sixth-century mosaic depicting scenes in Antioch.

the possibility of freeing him from death. He did not look upon this with favor. He was ready to seal his witness with his blood, and any move on the part of the Christians in Rome to save him would be an obstacle to his goal. He therefore wrote to them:

I fear your kindness, which may harm me. You may be able to achieve what you plan. But if you pay no heed to my request it will be very difficult for me to attain unto God.

As Ignatius goes on to say, his purpose is to be an imitator of the passion of his God, that is, Jesus Christ. As he faces the ultimate sacrifice, Ignatius believes that he begins to be a disciple; and therefore all that he wants from Christians in Rome is that they pray, not that he be freed, but that he may have the strength to face every trial, "so that I may not only be called a Christian, but also behave as such. . . . My love is crucified. . . . I no longer savor corruptible food . . . but wish to taste the bread of God, which is the flesh of Jesus Christ . . . and his blood I wish to drink, which is an immortal drink. . . . When I suffer, I shall be free in Jesus Christ, and with him shall rise again in freedom. . . . I am God's wheat, to be ground by the teeth of beasts, so that I may be offered as pure bread of Christ." And the reason why Ignatius is willing to face death with such courage is that he will thereby become a witness:

If you remain silent about me, I shall become a word of God. But if you allow yourselves to be swayed by the love in which you hold my flesh, I shall again be no more than a human voice.*

Shortly thereafter, Bishop Polycarp of Smyrna wrote to the Christians in Philippi asking for news regarding Ignatius. The answer from the Philippians has been lost, although it seems certain that Ignatius died as he expected shortly after his arrival in Rome.

The Martyrdom of Polycarp

Although very little is known of Ignatius' martyrdom, there is much more information regarding that of his younger friend, Polycarp, when his time came almost half a century later. It was the year 155, and the policy that Trajan had outlined for Pliny was still in effect. Christians were not sought out; but if they were accused and they refused to worship the gods, they had to be punished.

We know of events in Smyrna through a writer who claims to have witnessed them. It all began when a group of Christians was brought before

---

*Ignatius, *Romans* 1.2–2.1.

the authorities, and all of them refused to worhip the gods. Under the cruelest of tortures they remained firm, we are told, because "resting in Christ they scorned the pains of the world." When Germanicus, an elderly Christian, was brought to trial, he was told that he should take into account his old age and recant, rather than submit to torture and death. To this he responded that he had no desire to continue living in a world where the injustices that he had just seen took place. And, to show how deeply he meant his words, he called the beasts to come to him and kill him. This act of courage further aroused the anger of the mob, who began to shout: "Death to the atheists!" (that is, those who had no visible gods) and "Bring Polycarp!"

When the old bishop learned that he was being sought, he followed the advice of the flock, and hid for several days. But after having changed to another hiding place, and still having been discovered, he decided that his arrest was the will of God, refused to flee any further, and calmly awaited those who came after him.

The proconsul who presided at his trial tried to persuade him, urging him to think about his advanced age and worship the emperor. When Polycarp refused, the judge ordered him to cry: "Out with the atheists!" To this Polycarp responded by pointing at the crowd around him and saying: "Yes. Out with the atheists!" Again the judge insisted, promising that if he would swear by the emperor and curse Christ he would be free to go. But Polycarp replied: "For eighty-six years I have served him, and he has done me no evil. How could I curse my king, who saved me?"

Thus the dialogue went on. When the judge threatened him with burning him alive, Polycarp simply answered that the fire that the judge could light would last only a moment, whereas the eternal fire would never go out. Finally, we are told that after he was tied to the post in the pyre, he looked up and prayed out loud: "Lord Sovereign God . . . I thank you that you have deemed me worthy of this moment, so that, jointly with your martyrs, I may have a share in the cup of Christ. . . . For this . . . I bless and glorify you. Amen."*

Many years earlier, Ignatius of Antioch had advised young bishop Polycarp regarding his duties as bishop and the need to be firm in his faith. Now Polycarp showed himself a worthy hearer of Ignatius' advice, and a follower of his example.

One significant note in this entire account is that Polycarp fled and hid when he learned that he was being sought. We are also told in the same account that a certain Quintus, who offered himself as a martyr, weakened at the last moment and abandoned the faith. This was important for those early Christians, who believed that martyrdom was not something that one chose, but something for which one was chosen by God. Those who were

*Martyrdom of Polycarp 14.

so chosen were strengthened by Christ, who suffered with them, and for that reason were able to stand firm. Their firmness was not of their own doing, but of God. On the other hand, those who ran forward and offered themselves for martyrdom—the "spontaneous"—were false martyrs, and Christ would desert them.

But not all Christians agreed with the author of the *Martyrdom of Polycarp.* Throughout the entire period of persecutions, there were occasional spontaneous martyrs. And, when they remained firm ʳo the end, they found the approval of many. This may be seen of another document of the same time, the *Apology* of Justin Martyr, where we are told that at a Christian's trial two others came forth in his defense, and all three died as martyrs. In telling this story, Justin does not give the slightest indication that the martyrdom of the two "spontaneous" was less valid than that of the one originally accused.

Persecution under Marcus Aurelius

Marcus Aurelius, who became emperor in A.D. 161, was one of the most enlightened minds of his age. He was not, like Nero and Domitian, enamored with power and vainglory. On the contrary, he was a refined man who left behind a collection of *Meditations,* written for his private use, which are one of the literary masterpieces of the time. There he expresses some of the ideals with which he tried to rule his vast empire:

Think constantly, both as a Roman and as a man, to do the task before you with perfect and simple dignity, and with kindness, freedom, and justice. Try to forget everything else. And you will be able to do so if you undertake every action in your life as if it were the last, leaving aside all negligence and the opposition of passion to the dictates of reason, and leaving aside also all hypocrisy, egotism, and rebelliousness against your own lot.*

Under such an emperor, it could be expected that Christians would enjoy a period of relative peace. And yet, the same emperor who expressed such lofty ideals of government also ordered that Christians be persecuted. In the only reference to Christianity in his *Meditations,* the emperor praises those souls that are ready to abandon their bodies when the time comes, rather than cling to life, and then goes on to say that this attitude is praiseworthy only when it is the outcome of reason, "and not of obstinacy, as is the case with Christians."

Furthermore, as a child of his age, this enlightened emperor was also a superstitious man. He constantly sought the advice of seers, and before every significant undertaking sacrifices had to be offered. During the early years of

Meditations 2.5.

his reign, there seemed to be an endless string of invasions, floods, epidemics and other disasters. Soon the explanation arose that Christians were to be blamed, for they had brought the wrath of the gods upon the Empire. It is impossible to know for certain that the emperor believed this explanation; but, in any case, he gave his full support to the persecution, and favored the revival of the old religion. Perhaps, like Pliny, what he found most objectionable in Christians was their stubbornness.

One of the most informative documents from this time is the one that tells of the martyrdom of the widow Felicitas and her seven sons. Felicitas was one of the consecrated widows, that is, women who devoted all their time to work for the church, which in turn supported them. Her work was such that some pagan priests decided to put an end to it by accusing her before the authorities. When the prefect tried to persuade her, first with promises and then with threats, to abandon her faith, she answered that he was wasting his time, for "while I live, I shall defeat you; and if you kill me, in my death I shall defeat you all the more." He then tried to persuade her sons. But she encouraged them to stand firm, and none of them flinched before the worst threats. Finally, the record of the inquest was sent to Marcus Aurelius, who ordered that they should die in different sections of the city —probably to appease various gods.

Another martyr during this persecution was Justin, perhaps the best Christian scholar of the time, who had founded in Rome a school where he taught what he called "the true philosophy," that is, Christianity. He had recently bested a famous pagan philosopher in a public debate, and there are indications that it was this philosopher who accused him. In any case, Justin died as a martyr in Rome, although the "acts" of his martyrdom are much later, and therefore the details are questionable.

Further insight into this persecution come to us through a letter that the churches of Lyons and Vienne, in Gaul, sent to their fellow Christians in Phrygia and Asia Minor. It seems that at first all that was done in those cities was to forbid Christians to visit public places. But then the mob began following them on the streets, shouting at them and pelting them. Finally, several Christians were arrested and taken before the governor to be tried. There a certain Vetius Epagathus came forth from among the mob and offered to defend the Christians. Asked if he was one of them, he said that he was, and was then added to the group of the accused.

The writers of the letter explain that persecution had appeared unexpectedly, "like a bolt of lightning," and that this was the reason why many were not prepared. Some of them weakened and "left the womb of the church like abortive ones."

The rest, however, stood firm, and this in turn increased the wrath of the governor and the mob. Torture was ordered. A certain Sanctus, when tortured, simply answered, "I am a Christian." The more he was tortured, the more he persisted in saying nothing but these words. Moved by this and

A Mosaic depicting the legend of forty martyrs who froze to death.

many other signs of courage, some who had earlier denied the faith returned
to confess it and die as martyrs. We are not told how many died, but the letter
does say that the place where Christians were being held was so full that some
died of suffocation before the executioners could get to them.

   These are only a few examples of what took place under the reign of the enlightened Marcus Aurelius. There are several other accounts of martyr-doms still extant. One must suppose that the accounts that have survived tell only a partial story of what actually took place, not only in Rome, but throughout the Empire.

Towards the End of the Second Century

Marcus Aurelius died in A.D. 180, and was succeeded by Commodus, who had begun to rule jointly with him eight years earlier. Although Commodus did not issue any edicts against persecution, the storm abated during his reign, and the number of martyrs was relatively low. After the death of Commodus, there was a period of civil war, and Christians were once again ignored in favor of more pressing matters. Finally, in A.D. 193, Septimius Severus became master of the Empire. At first, Christians were able to live in peace under his reign. But eventually he too added his name to the growing list of those who had persecuted the church. However, since this was early in the third century, we shall return to it at another point in our narrative.

In summary, during the entire second century, Christians were in a precarious position. They were not constantly persecuted. Sometimes they were persecuted in some areas of the Empire, and not in others. Since the general policy of the Empire was that outlined by Trajan—Christians were not to be sought, but, if brought before the authorities, they must be forced to recant or be punished—the good will of their neighbors was very important. If any believed the evil rumors about them, they would be accused, and persecution would break out. For this reason it was very important to show that those rumors were untrue, and to give pagans a better and more favorable understanding of Christianity. This was the task of the apologists, to whom we now turn.

7/The Defense of the Faith

We do not seek to flatter you, . . . but request that you judge on the basis of a proper and thorough investigation.

JUSTIN MARTYR

Throughout the second century, and well into the third, there was no systematic persecution of Christians. It was illegal to be a Christian; but those who followed the new faith were not sought out by the authorities. Persecution and martyrdom depended on local circumstances, and particularly on the good will of neighbors. If for any reason someone wished to harm a Christian, all that had to be done was to present an accusation. Such may well have been the case with Justin, who seems to have been accused by his rival, Crescentius. At other times, as in Lyons and Vienne, it was the mob, fired by all sorts of rumors about Christians, that demanded that they be arrested and punished.

Given such circumstances, Christians felt the need to refute rumors and misconceptions regarding their beliefs and practices. Even if their arguments did not convince others of the truth of Christianity, something very tangible would be gained if false reports were dispelled. Such was the task of some of the ablest Christian thinkers and writers, known as the "apologists"—that is, defenders. Some of their arguments have had continued usage through the centuries.

Base Rumors and Lofty Criticism

Many of the rumors that the apologists sought to dispel were based on a misunderstanding of Christian practice or teaching. Thus, for instance, Christians gathered every week to celebrate what they called a "love feast." This was done in private, and only the initiates (those who had been baptized) were admitted. Furthermore, Christians called each other "brother" and "sister," and there were many who spoke of their spouses as their "sister"

Communion was the central act of early Christian worship. Here it is shown in a painting from a catacomb.

or "brother." Joining these known facts, imagination drew a picture of Christian worship as an orgiastic celebration in which Christians ate and drank to excess, put the lights out, and vented their lusts in indiscriminate and even incestuous unions.

Communion also gave rise to another rumor. Since Christians spoke of being nourished by the body and blood of Christ, and since they also spoke of him as a little child, some came to the conclusion that, as an initiation rite, Christians concealed a newborn in a loaf of bread, and then ordered the neophyte to cut the loaf. When this was done, they all joined in eating the warm flesh of the infant. The new initiate, who had unwittingly become the main perpetrator of the crime, was thus forced to remain silent.

Some even claimed that Christians worshiped an ass. This was an old rumor about Judaism that was now extended to include Christians, and thus make them an object of mockery.

Such notions—and many other similar ones—were fairly easy to refute, for it sufficed to show that Christians followed principles of conduct that were not compatible with such wild imaginings.

Much more difficult to refute was the criticism of a number of cultured pagans who had taken the trouble to learn about Christianity and claimed that it was intellectually wanting. Although it attacked Christianity on numerous counts, this criticism boiled down to a main point: Christians were an ignorant lot whose doctrines, although preached under a cloak of wisdom, were foolish and even self-contradictory. This seems to have been a common attitude among the cultured aristocracy, for whom Christians were a despicable rabble.

During the reign of Marcus Aurelius, one such intellectual, Celsus, wrote a refutation of Christianity called *The True Word.* There he expressed the feelings of those who, like him, were wise and sophisticated:

In some private homes we find people who work with wool and rags, and cobblers, that is, the least cultured and most ignorant kind. Before the head of the household, they dare not utter a word. But as soon as they can take the children aside or some women who are as ignorant as they are, they speak wonders. . . . If you really wish to know the truth, leave your teachers and your father, and go with the women and the children to the women's quarters, or to the cobbler's shop, or to the tannery, and there you will learn the perfect life. It is thus that these Christians find those who will believe them.*

At about the same time, the pagan Cornelius Fronto wrote a treatise against Christians that unfortunately has been lost. But the Christian writer Minucius Felix may be quoting him when he puts the following words in the mouth of a pagan:

If you still have even a modicum of wisdom or shame, cease searching the heavenly regions, and the goals and secrets of the universe. It is enough that you watch where you walk. This is especially true of people such as you, who lack education and culture, and are crude and ignorant.**

Thus, the enmity against Christianity on the part of many cultured pagans was not a purely intellectual matter, but was deeply rooted in class prejudice. The cultured and sophisticated could not conceive the possibility that the Christian rabble could know a truth hidden to them. Their main objection was that Christianity was a religion of barbarians who derived their teaching, not from Greeks or Romans, but from Jews, a primitive people whose best teachers never rose to the level of Greek philosophers. If anything good is to be found in Jewish Scripture—they said—that is because the Jews copied it from the Greeks.

Furthermore—the argument went on—the Jewish and Christian God is ridiculous. They claim on the one hand that God is omnipotent, high above every creature. But on the other hand they depict God as a busybody who is constantly delving into human affairs, who goes into every home listening to what is said and even checking what is being cooked. This is sheer contradiction and nonsense.

In any case, the worship of this God destroys the very fiber of society, because those who follow this religion abstain from most social activities, claiming that participation in them would be tantamount to worshiping false gods. If such gods are indeed false, why fear them? Why not join in their worship like sensible people, even if one does not believe in them? The truth of the matter is that Christians, while claiming that the gods are false, continue fearing them as true.

As to Jesus, it should suffice to remember that he was a criminal condemned by Roman authorities. Celsus even claims that Jesus was the illegitimate son of Mary with a Roman soldier. If he was truly Son of God, why

*Origen, *Against Celsus* 3.55.
**Octavius* 12.

did he allow himself to be crucified? Why did he not destroy all his enemies? And, even if Christians could answer such questions, Celsus asks further:

What could be the purpose of such a visit to earth by God? To find out what is taking place among humans? Does He not know everything? Or is it perhaps that He knows, but is incapable of doing anything about evil unless He does it in person?*

Also, these Christians preach—and truly believe—that they will rise again after death. It is on the basis of that belief that they face death with an almost incredible obstinacy. But it makes no sense to leave this life, which is certain, for the sake of another, which is at best uncertain. And the doctrine itself of a final resurrection is the high point of Christian nonsense. What will happen to those whose bodies were destroyed by fire, or eaten by beasts or by fish? Will God scour the world after bits and pieces of each body? What will God do with those parts of matter that have belonged to more than one body? Will they be given to their first owner? Will that leave a gap in the risen bodies of all later owners?

Such arguments, and many others like them, could not be set aside by a mere denial. It was necessary to offer solid refutation. This was the task of the apologists.

The Main Apologists

The task of responding to such criticism resulted in some of the most remarkable theological works of the second century, and continued for many years thereafter. At this point, however, it will suffice to deal with the apologists of the second century and the beginning of the third.

Probably the earliest surviving apology is that addressed To Diognetus, whose unknown author—perhaps a certain Quadratus mentioned by ancient historians—seems to have lived early in the second century. Shortly thereafter, before A.D. 138, Aristides wrote an apology that has recently been rediscovered. But the most famous of the early apologists was Justin, to whose martyrdom reference was made in the preceding chapter. Justin had lived through a long spiritual pilgrimage, from school to school, until he found in Christianity what he called "the true philosophy." Three of his works are extant: two apologies—which are really two parts of a single work —and a Dialogue with Trypho, a Jewish rabbi. One of Justin's disciples, Tatian, wrote An Address to the Greeks, and at about the same time Athenagoras composed a Plea for the Christians and a treatise On the Resurrection of the Dead. Later in the century, Theophilus, bishop of Antioch, wrote Three Books to Autolycus, which dealt with the doctrine of God, the interpretation of Scrip-

---

*Origen, Against Celsus 4.3.

ture, and Christian life. All these apologies of the second century were written in Greek, as was also the refutation *Against Celsus,* which Origen wrote in the third century.

In Latin, the two earliest apologies are *Octavius,* by Minucius Felix, and Tertullian's *Apology.* To this day, scholars are not agreed as to which of these two apologies was written first, although it is clear that whoever wrote the later one was indebted to his predecessor.

By reading all these apologies, historians can see what were the main objections that pagans raised against Christianity, as well as the manner in which the most cultured members of the Church responded to them, and how Christian theology developed in the very act of responding to pagan objections.

Christian Faith and Pagan Culture

Since they were accused of being uncultured barbarians, Christians were forced to take up the issue of the relationship between their faith and pagan culture. All Christians agreed that the worship of the gods, and everything related to that worship, must be rejected. This was the reason why they abstained from many civil ceremonies, in which sacrifices and vows were made to the gods. This, together with pacifist convictions, also led many Christians to the conclusion that they could not be soldiers, for the military were required to offer sacrifices to the emperor and the gods. Likewise, there were many Christians who objected to the study of classical literature, where the gods played an important part, and where all sorts of immorality was ascribed to them. To be a Christian required a commitment to the sole worship of God, and any deviation from that commitment was a denial of Jesus Christ, who in the final judgment would in turn deny the apostate.

While all agreed on the need to abstain from idolatry, not all agreed on what should be a Christian's attitude toward classical pagan culture. This included the work and thought of philosophers such as Plato, Aristotle, and the Stoics, whose wisdom has been admired by many to this day. To reject all this would be to set aside some of the highest achievements of the human intellect; to accept it could be seen as a concession to paganism, an inroad of idolatry into the church.

Therefore, on the question of the value of classical culture, Christians took two opposite tacks. Some insisted on a radical opposition between Christian faith and pagan culture. Typical of this attitude was Tertullian, who summarized it in a famous phrase: "What does Athens have to do with Jerusalem? What does the Academy have to do with the Church?"* What

---
Prescription against Heretics 1.7.

prompted him to write these lines was his conviction that many of the heresies that circulated in his time were the result of attempts to combine pagan philosophy with Christian doctrine.

But even apart from the question of possible heresy, there were those who gloried in the "barbarian" origin of Christianity, over against the claims of classical culture and philosophy. Such was the case of Tatian, Justin Martyr's most famous disciple, whose *Address to the Greeks* is a frontal attack to all that the Greeks considered valuable, and a defense of the "barbaric" Christians. Because Greeks called all those who did not speak like them "barbarians," Tatian began by pointing out to them that they were not in agreement as to how Greek was to be spoken, for each region had its own dialect. Furthermore, argued Tatian, these people who claim that their tongue is the greatest of human creations have also invented rhetoric, which is the art of selling words for gold to the highest bidder, and which thus results in the defense of untruth and injustice.

All that the Greeks have that is of any value—so said Tatian—they have taken from barbarians: they learned astronomy from the Babylonians, geometry from the Egyptians, and writing from the Phoenicians. And the same is true of philosophy and religion, since the writings of Moses are much older than those of Plato, and even than those of Homer. Therefore, any agreement between that culture which is supposedly Greek and the religion of the Hebrew and Christian "barbarians" is the result of the Greeks having learned their wisdom from the barbarians. And what makes matters worse is that the Greeks, in reading the wisdom of the "barbarians," misunderstood it, and thus twisted the truth that the Hebrews knew. In consequence, the supposed wisdom of the Greeks is but a pale reflection and caricature of the truth that Moses knew and Christians preach.

If this is what Tatian says about the best of classical culture, one can imagine what he has to say about the pagan gods. Homer and the other Greek poets tell shameful things about them, such as adultery, incest, and infanticide. How are we to worship such gods, clearly inferior to us? Finally, Tatian adds, let it not be forgotten that many of the statues that the pagans worship are in fact representations of prostitutes whom the sculptors used as models. Thus, the very pagans who say that Christians belong to the lower social strata are in fact worshiping people of the lower classes!

But not all Christians took the same stance. On becoming a Christian, Justin did not cease being a philosopher, but rather took upon himself the task of doing "Christian philosophy"; and a major part of that task as he saw it was to show and explain the connection between Christianity and classical wisdom. Thus, he did not share Tatian's negative attitude toward philosophy. But this does not mean that he was willing to compromise his faith or that he was lacking in conviction, for when the time came for him to stand up for his faith he did so with courage, and is therefore known as "Justin Martyr."

Justin claimed that there were several points of contact between Christianity and pagan philosophy. The best philosophers, for instance, spoke of a supreme being from which every other being derives its existence. Socrates and Plato affirmed life beyond physical death; and Socrates showed the strength of that affirmation by the manner in which he died. Plato knew that there are realities beyond those of the present world, and thus posited another world of eternal realities. Justin claimed that the philosophers were basically correct on all these points, although he did not always agree on the manner in which they understood them—for instance, in contrast to the philosophers, Christian hope is not based on the immortality of the soul, but rather on the resurrection of the body. But in spite of such differences, Justin insisted that there were in the philosophers glimpses of truth that could not be explained as mere coincidence.

How, then, can one explain this partial agreement between the philosophers and Christianity? For Justin, the answer is to be found in the doctrine of the Logos. This is a Greek word that means both "word" and "reason." According to a tradition of long standing in Greek philosophy, the human mind can understand reality because it shares in the Logos or universal reason that undergirds all reality. For instance, if we are able to understand that two and two make four, the reason for this is that both in our minds and in the universe there is a Logos, a reason or order according to which two and two always make four. The Fourth Gospel affirms that in Jesus the Logos or "Word" was made flesh. Thus, according to Justin, what has happened in the

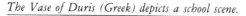

The Vase of Duris (Greek) depicts a school scene.

incarnation is that the underlying reason of the universe, the Logos or Word of God, has come in the flesh.

According to the Fourth Gospel, this Logos is "the true light that enlightens" everyone. This means that, even before the incarnation, he is the source of all true knowledge. Paul had already said (1 Cor. 10:1–4) that the ancient Hebrews' faith rested on none other than Christ, who had been revealed to them even before the incarnation. Now Justin added that there were also among the pagans those who knew the same Logos, however dimly. Whatever truth there is in the writings of Plato was granted to him by the Logos of God, the same Logos who was incarnate in Jesus. Therefore, in a way, Socrates, Plato, and the other sages of antiquity "were Christians," for their wisdom came from Christ. This is not to say, however, that the incarnation was not needed, for those philosophers of old knew the Logos "in part," whereas those who have seen him in his incarnation know him "fully."

What Justin thus did was to open the way for Christianity to claim whatever good it could find in classical culture, in spite of its having been pagan. Following his inspiration, there soon were other Christians who tried to build further bridges betwen their faith and ancient culture. But their work, and the dangers inherent therein, will be seen elsewhere in this narrative.

The Arguments of the Apologists

Justin's use of the doctrine of the Logos provided a basic framework within which Christians could claim whatever they wished from the rich lode of classical culture. There still remained to refute the various objections raised against Christianity. Although it is impossible to list here all such refutations, some examples will give a general idea of the nature of the arguments of the apologists.

When accused of being atheists, because they had no visible gods, Christians responded that in that case many of the greatest philosophers and poets were also atheists. To support that statement it sufficed to quote the ancient writers who had affirmed that the gods were human inventions, and that their vices were worse than those of their worshipers. Aristides suggested that such gods had been invented precisely in order to give full rein to human vice. Also, a common argument was that the idols, often made of gold and precious stones, had to be guarded against thieves. How can a god that must be protected provide any protection? How can a god made by human hands be above humans?

To the objections raised against the final resurrection, the apologists respond by having recourse to divine omnipotence. If God made all bodies out of nothing, why would it be impossible for the same God to create them anew, even after they have been dead and scattered?

To the accusations that Christians are immoral, the apologists respond that this is not true, and that it is rather the pagans who are immoral. How can anyone believe that our worship is orgiastic and incestuous, when the rules of our conduct are such that even evil thoughts must be cast aside? It is the pagans who tell such things of their gods, and even practice them under the guise of worship. How can anyone believe that we eat children, when we reject every form of bloodshed? It is the pagans who leave their unwanted children exposed to the elements, to die of cold and hunger.

Finally, Christians were accused of being subversive, for they refused to worship the emperor and thus destroyed the very fiber of society. The apologists answered that it was true that they refused to worship the emperor or any other creature, but that in spite of this they were loyal subjects of the Empire. What the emperor needs—they said—is not to be worshiped, but to be served; and those who serve him best are those who pray for him and for the Empire to the only true God.

In conclusion, the writings of the apologists witness to the tensions in which early Christians lived. While rejecting paganism, they had to deal with the fact that paganism had produced a valuable culture. While accepting the truth to be found in the philosophers, they insisted on the superiority of Christian revelation. While refusing to worship the emperor, and even while persecuted by the authorities, they continued praying for the emperor and admiring the greatness of the Roman Empire. These tensions were admirably expressed in the address *To Diognetus:*

Christians are no different from the rest in their nationality, language or customs. . . . They live in their own countries, but as sojourners. They fulfill all their duties as citizens, but they suffer as foreigners. They find their homeland wherever they are, but their homeland is not in any one place. . . . They are in the flesh, but do not live according to the flesh. They live on earth, but are citizens of heaven. They obey all laws, but they live at a level higher than that required by law. They love all, but all persecute them.*

---

*To Diognetus 5.1–11.

8/The Deposit of the Faith

*Error never shows itself in its naked
reality, in order not to be discovered. On the
contrary, it dresses elegantly, so that the
unwary may be led to believe that it is more
truthful than truth itself.*

IRENAEUS OF LYONS

The many converts who joined the early church came from a wide
variety of backgrounds. This variety enriched the church and
gave witness to the universality of its message. But it also resulted
in widely differing interpretations of that message, some of which
threatened its integrity. The danger was increased by the syncretism of the
time, which sought truth, not by adhering to a single system of doctrine, but
by taking bits and pieces from various systems. The result was that, while
many claimed the name of Christ, some interpreted that name in such a
manner that the very core of his message seemed to be obscured or even
denied.

Gnosticism

Of all these differing interpretations of Christianity, none was as dangerous,
nor as close to victory, as was gnosticism. This was not a well-defined organization in competition with the church; rather, it was a vast and amorphous
movement that existed both within and outside the church. When it incorporated the name of Christ and other items from the Judeo-Christian tradition
into its diverse systems, it did so in such terms that the rest of Jews
and Christians felt that some crucial elements of their faith were being
denied.

The name "gnosticism" derives from the Greek word *gnosis,* which
means "knowledge." According to the Gnostics, they possessed a special,

mystical knowledge, reserved for those with true understanding. That knowledge was the secret key to salvation.

Salvation was the main concern of the Gnostics. Drawing from several sources, they came to the conclusion that all matter is evil, or at best unreal. A human being is in reality an eternal spirit (or part of the eternal spirit) that somehow has been imprisoned in a body. Since the body is a prison to the spirit, and since it misguides us as to our true nature, it is evil. Therefore, the Gnostic's final goal is to escape from the body and this material world in which we are exiled. The image of exile is crucial for gnosticism. The world is not our true home, but rather an obstacle to the salvation of the spirit.

How, then, is the origin of the world and of the body to be explained? Gnosticism affirmed that originally all reality was spiritual. The supreme being had no intention of creating a material world, but only a spiritual one. Thus, a number of spiritual beings were generated. Gnostic teachers did not agree as to their exact number, with some systems positing 365 such spiritual beings or "eons." In any case, one of these eons, far removed from the supreme being, fell into error, and thus created the material world. According to one system, for instance, Wisdom, one of the eons, wished to produce something by herself, and the resulting "abortion" was the world. That is what the world is in gnosticism: an abortion of the spirit, and not a divine creation.

But, since this world was made by a spiritual being, there are still "sparks" or "bits" of spirit in it. It is these that have been imprisoned in human bodies and must be liberated through gnosis.

In order to achieve that liberation, a spiritual messenger must come to this world, to waken us from our "dream." Our spirits are "asleep" within our bodies, being driven by the impulses and passions of the body, and someone must come from beyond to remind us who we really are and to call us to struggle against our incarceration. This messenger brings the gnosis, the secret knowledge and inspiration necessary for salvation. Above us are the heavenly spheres, each ruled by an evil power whose aim is to impede our progress to the spiritual realm. In order to reach the spiritual "fullness," we must break through each of those spheres. The only way to do this is to have the secret knowledge that opens the way—much like a spiritual password. The heavenly messenger has been sent precisely to give us that knowledge, without which there is no salvation.

In Christian gnosticism—one should always remember that there were also non-Christian Gnostics—that messenger is Christ. What Christ has then done is to come to earth in order to remind us of our heavenly origin, and to give us the secret knowledge without which we cannot return to the spiritual mansions.

Since Christ is a heavenly messenger, and since body and matter are evil, most Christian Gnostics rejected the notion that Christ had a body like ours.

A Gnostic gem with a serpent and a secret word. Many Gnostics saw in the serpent a symbol of opposition to the evil god of creation.

Some said that his body was an appearance, a sort of ghost that miraculously seemed to be a real body. Many distinguished between the heavenly "Christ" and the earthly "Jesus." In some cases, this was coupled with the notion that Jesus did have a body, but that this was of a "spiritual matter," different from ours. Most denied the birth of Jesus, which would have put him under the power of the material world. All these notions are various degrees of what the rest of the church called "docetism"—a name derived from a Greek word meaning "to seem," for all these doctrines implied, in one way or another, that the body of Jesus appeared to be fully human, but was not.

According to several Gnostic teachers, not all human beings have a spirit. Some are purely carnal, and thus are irreparably condemned to destruction when the physical world comes to an end. On the other hand, the imprisoned sparks of the spirit within those whom the Gnostics call "spiritual" will necessarily be saved and return to the spiritual realm.

Meanwhile, how is this life to be lived? At this point, Gnostics gave two divergent answers. Most declared that, since the body is the prison of the spirit, one must control the body and its passions and thus weaken its power over the spirit. But there were also some who held that, since the spirit is by nature good and cannot be destroyed, what we are to do is to leave the body to its own devices and let it follow the guidance of its own passions. Thus, while some Gnostics were extreme ascetics, others were libertines.

Gnosticism was a serious threat to Christianity throughout the second century. The main leaders of the church tenaciously opposed it, for they saw in it a denial of several crucial Christian doctrines, such as creation, incarnation, and resurrection. For that reason, the church at large devised methods to combat it. But before we turn to those methods, we must pause to look at another teacher whose doctrines, similar to gnosticism yet different from it, were seen as a particular threat.

Marcion

Marcion, whose father was bishop of Sinope in Pontus, knew Christianity from an early age. But he had a profound dislike towards both Judaism and the material world. He thus developed an understanding of Christianity that was both anti-Jewish and anti-material. About A.D. 144 he went to Rome, where he gathered a following. But eventually the church at large came to the conclusion that his doctrines contradicted several fundamental points in Christian doctrine. He then founded his own church, which lasted for several centuries as a rival to the orthodox church.

Since Marcion was convinced that the world is evil, he came to the conclusion that its creator must be either evil or ignorant. But instead of positing a long series of spiritual beings, like the Gnostics did, Marcion proposed a much simpler solution. According to him, the God and Father of Jesus is not the same as Jehovah, the God of the Old Testament. It was Jehovah that made this world. The Father's purpose was that there be only a spiritual world. But Jehovah, either through ignorance or out of an evil intent, made this world and placed humankind in it—a theme that one finds in many Gnostic writings as well.

This means that the Hebrew Scriptures are indeed inspired by a god, although this is Jehovah, and not the Supreme Father. Jehovah is an arbitrary god, who chooses a particular people above all the rest. And he is also vindictive, constantly keeping an account on those that disobey him, and punishing them. In short, Jehovah is a god of justice—and of an arbitrary justice at that.

Over against Jehovah, and far above him, is the Father of Christians. This God is not vindictive, but loving. This God requires nothing of us, but rather gives everything freely, including salvation. This God does not seek to be obeyed, but to be loved. It is out of compassion for us, Jehovah's creatures, that the Supreme God has sent his Son to save us. But Jesus was not really born of Mary, since such a thing would have made him subject to Jehovah. Rather, he simply appeared as a grown man during the reign of Tiberius. Naturally, at the end there will be no judgment, since the Supreme God is absolutely loving, and will simply forgive us.

All this led Marcion to set the Hebrew Scriptures aside. If the Old Testament was the word of an inferior god, it should not be read in the churches, nor used as the basis of Christian instruction. In order to fill this gap, Marcion compiled a list of books that he considered true Christian Scriptures. These were the epistles of Paul—according to Marcion, one of the few who had really understood Jesus' message—and the Gospel of Luke. All other ancient Christian books were plagued by Jewish views. As to the many quotations from the Old Testament in Luke and Paul, Marcion explained them away as interpolations—the handiwork of Judaizers seeking to subvert the original message.

Marcion posed an even greater threat to the church than did the Gnostics. Like them, he rejected or radically reinterpreted the doctrines of creation, incarnation, and resurrection. But he went beyond them in that he organized a church with its own bishops and its own scripture. For a number of years, this rival church achieved a measure of success, and even after it was clearly defeated it lingered on for centuries.

The Response: Canon, Creed, and Apostolic Succession

Marcion's list was the first attempt to put together a "New Testament." When early Christians spoke of "Scripture," what they meant was the Hebrew Scriptures, usually in the Greek version known as the Septuagint. It was also customary to read in church passages from one or several Gospels, as well as from the epistles—particularly Paul's. Since there was no approved list, different Gospels were read in different churches, and the same was true of other books. But Marcion's challenge required a response, and thus the church at large began to compile a list of sacred Christian writings. This was not done in a formal manner, through a council or special meeting. What actually happened was that a consensus developed gradually. While very soon there was general agreement as to the basic books to be included in the canon of the New Testament, it took a long time to come to an absolute consensus on every minor detail.

There was no question, except among Gnostics and Marcionites, that the Hebrew Scripture was part of the Christian canon. This was important as a proof that God had been preparing the way for the advent of Christianity, and even as a way of understanding the nature of the God who had been revealed in Jesus Christ. Christian faith was the fullfilment of the hope of Israel, and not a sudden apparition from heaven.

As to what is now called the "New Testament," the Gospels were the first to attain general recognition. It is important to note that those early Christians decided to include more than one Gospel in their canon. At a later time, many have pointed out the inconsistencies among the four Gospels in matters of detail. The early Christians were well aware of these differences, and that was precisely the reason why they insisted in using more than one book. They did this as a direct response to the challenge of Marcion and gnosticism. Many Gnostic teachers claimed that the heavenly messenger had trusted his secret knowledge to a particular disciple, who alone was the true interpreter of the message. Thus, various Gnostic groups had a book that claimed to present the true teachings of Jesus. Such was, for instance, the Gospel of Saint Thomas. Marcion used the Gospel of Luke, from which he had deleted all references to Judaism or to the Hebrew Scriptures. In response to this situation, the church at large sought to show that its doctrines were not based on the supposed witness of a single apostle or Gospel, but on the consensus of the entire apostolic tradition. The very fact that the various Gospels differed in matters of detail, but agreed on the basic issues at stake, made their agreement a more convincing argument. Against Marcion's expurgated Gospel of Luke, the church offered the consensus of a number of Gospels—sometimes three, and sometimes four, since the Fourth Gospel was somewhat slower in gaining universal acceptance. Against the secret traditions and private interpretations of the Gnostics, the church had recourse to an open tradition, known to all, and to the multiplicity of the witness of the Gospels.

Next to the Gospels, the book of Acts and the Pauline epistles enjoyed early recognition. Thus, by the end of the second century, the core of the canon was established: the four Gospels, Acts, and the Pauline epistles. On the shorter books that appear towards the end of the present canon, there was no consensus until a much later date; but there also was little debate. The book of Revelation, widely accepted by the third century, was questioned after the conversion of Constantine, for its words about the prevailing culture and the Empire seemed too harsh. It was in the second half of the fourth century that a complete consensus was achieved as to exactly which books ought to be included in the New Testament, and which ought not to be included.

Another element in the church's response to heresies was what we now call the "Apostles' Creed." The notion that the apostles gathered before beginning their mission and composed this creed, each suggesting a clause, is pure fiction. The truth is that its basic text was put together, probably in Rome, around the year 150. It was then called "symbol of the faith." The word "symbol" in this context did not have the meaning that it has for us today; rather, it meant a means of recognition, such as a token that a general gave to a messenger, so that the recipient could recognize a true messenger. Likewise, the "symbol" put together in Rome was a means whereby Christians could distinguish true believers from those who followed the various heresies circulating at the time, particularly gnosticism and Marcionism. Any who could affirm this creed were neither Gnostics nor Marcionites.

One of the main uses of this "symbol" was in baptism, where it was presented to the candidate in the form of a series of three questions:

Do you believe in God the Father almighty?

Do you believe in Christ Jesus, the Son of God, who was born of the Holy Ghost and of Mary the virgin, who was crucified under Pontius Pilate, and died, and rose again at the third day, living from among the dead, and ascended unto heaven and sat at the right of the Father, and will come to judge the quick and the dead?

Do you believe in the Holy Ghost, the holy church, and the resurrection of the flesh?

Two things stand out in reading these questions. The first is that we have here the core of what later came to be called the "Apostles' Creed." The second is that this creed has been built around the Trinitarian formula that was used in baptism. Since one was baptized "in the name of the Father, of the Son, and of the Holy Ghost," these questions were posed as a test of true belief in the Father, the Son, and the Holy Ghost.

Closer scrutiny clearly shows that this early creed is directed against Marcion and the Gnostics. First of all, the Greek word *pantokrator,* usually translated as "almighty," literally means "all ruling." What is meant here is that there is nothing, and certainly not the material world, which falls outside of God's rule. The distinction between a spiritual reality that serves God and a material reality that does not is rejected. This world, its matter and its physical bodies, are part of the "all" over which God reigns.

The creed's most extensive paragraph is the one dealing with the Son. This is because it was precisely in their Christology that Marcion and the Gnostics differed most widely from the church. First of all, we are told that Jesus Christ is the "Son of God." Other ancient versions say "Son of the same" or "His Son," as does our present Creed. The important point here is that Jesus is the Son of the God who rules over this world and over all reality. The birth "of Mary the virgin" is not there primarily in order to stress the virgin birth—although, quite clearly, that is affirmed—but rather to affirm the very fact that Jesus was born, and did not simply appear on earth, as Marcion and others claimed. The reference to Pontius Pilate is not there to put the blame on the Roman governor, but rather to date the event to insist on the fact that it was a historical, datable event. And docetism is further denied by declaring that Jesus "was crucified . . . died, and rose again." Finally, it is affirmed that this same Jesus will return "to judge," a notion that Marcion would never accept.

The third clause, although less explicit because the needs of the time did not require it to be extensive, also shows the same concern. The "holy church" is affirmed because, over against the Gnostics with their many schools, and Marcion with his own church, Christians were beginning to underscore the authority of the church. And the "resurrection of the flesh" is a final rejection of any notion that the flesh is evil or of no consequence.

Although the canon of the New Testament and the incipient Creed were valuable instruments in the struggle against heresy, the debate finally came to the issue of the authority of the church. This was important, not simply

The final judgment, a traditional theme of Christian teaching and art, was denied by Marcion, who held that God did not judge.

because someone had to decide who was right and who was wrong, but because of the very nature of the issues at stake. All agreed that the true message was the one taught by Jesus. The Gnostics claimed that they had some secret access to that original message, through a succession of secret teachers. Marcion claimed that he had access to that message through the writings of Paul and Luke—which, however, had to be purged of what did not agree with Marcion's views regarding the Old Testament. Over against Marcion and the Gnostics, the church at large claimed to be in possession of the original gospel and the true teachings of Jesus. Thus, what was debated was in a way the authority of the church against the claims of the heretics.

At this point, the notion of apostolic succession became very important. What was argued was simply that, had Jesus had some secret knowledge to communicate to his disciples—which in fact he did not—he would have entrusted that teaching to the same apostles to whom he entrusted the church. If those apostles had received any such teaching, they in turn would have passed it on to those who were to follow them in the leadership of the church. Therefore, were there any such secret teaching, it should be found among the direct disciples of the apostles, and the successors of those disciples, the bishops. But the truth of the matter is that those who can now—that is, in the second century—claim direct apostolic succession unanimously deny the existence of any such secret teaching. In conclusion, the Gnostic claim that there is a secret tradition, and that they have been entrusted with it, is false.

In order to strengthen this argument, it was necessary to show that the bishops of the time were indeed successors of the apostles. This was not difficult, since several of the most ancient churches had lists of bishops linking them with the apostolic past. Rome, Antioch, Ephesus, and others had such lists. Present-day historians do not find such lists absolutely trustworthy, for there are indications that in some churches—Rome among them—there were not at first "bishops" in the sense of a single head of the local church, but rather a collegiate group of officers who sometimes were called "bishops" and sometimes "elders." But in any case, be it through actual bishops or through other leaders, the fact remains that the orthodox church of the second century could show its connection with the apostles in a way in which Marcion and the Gnostics could not.

Does this mean that only churches that could show such apostolic connections were truly apostolic? Not so, since the issue was not that every church could prove its apostolic origins, but rather that they all agreed on the one faith, and could jointly prove that this faith was indeed apostolic. At a later date, the idea of apostolic succession was carried further, with the notion that an ordination was valid only if performed by a bishop who could claim direct apostolic succession. When first developed, late in the second century, the principle of apostolic succession was inclusive rather than exclusive: over against the closed and secret tradition of the Gnostic teachers, it offered an open and shared tradition that based its claim, not on a single favorite disciple of Jesus, but on the witness of all the apostles.

The Ancient Catholic Church

This was the original meaning of the phrase "catholic church." The word "catholic" means "universal," but it also means "according to the whole." To separate itself from the various heretical groups and sects, the ancient church began calling itself "catholic." This title underscored both its universality and the inclusiveness of the witness on which it stood. It was the church "according to the whole," that is, according to the total witness of all the apostles. The various Gnostic groups were not "catholic" because they could not claim this broad foundation. Indeed, those among them who claimed apostolic origins did so on the basis of a hypothetical secret tradition handed down through a single apostle. Only the church "catholic," the church "according to the whole," could lay claim to the entire apostolic witness. Ironically, through an evolution that took centuries, debates regarding the true meaning of "catholic" came to be centered on the person and authority of a single apostle—Peter.

9/The Teachers of the Church

*Ours is the great Teacher of all wisdom,
and the whole world, including Athens and
Greece, belongs to Him.*
CLEMENT OF ALEXANDRIA

During the early decades of the life of the church, most of what Christians wrote addressed a concrete problem or specific issue. This is true, for instance, of the Pauline epistles, each of which was prompted by particular circumstances, and in none of which Paul attempts to discuss the entire body of Christian doctrine. After the apostolic age, the same was true for a while. The various writers of that period whose work has been preserved are given the joint title of "apostolic fathers," and each of their writings deals with very specific issues. This is the case of the epistles of Ignatius of Antioch, to which we have already referred. Likewise, late in the first century, Clement of Rome wrote an *Epistle to the Corinthians,* prompted by problems similar to those which Paul had already addressed in his letters to the same church. The *Didache* or *Teaching of the Twelve Apostles*—not really written by them, but by an unknown Christian at an uncertain time and place—is a manual of discipline giving guidelines for Christian life and worship. The *Shepherd* of Hermas, written by a brother of the bishop of Rome in the middle of the second century, deals mostly with the forgiveness of sins after baptism. In summary, all the writings of the so-called apostolic fathers deal with a single issue, and none of them seeks to expound the totality of Christian doctrine. The same is true of the apologists who wrote in the second half of the second century. Most of their writings deal with the issue of persecution. And none of them looks at the totality of Christian doctrine.

But towards the end of the second century the challenge of Marcion and the Gnostics required a different response. The heretics had created their own systems of doctrine, and to this the church at large had to respond by having some of its teachers offer equally cogent expositions of orthodox belief. Precisely because the speculations of the heretics were vast in scope, the response of Christian teachers was equally vast. This gave rise to the first writings in which one can find a fairly complete exposition of Christian truth. These are the works of Irenaeus, Clement of Alexandria, Tertullian, and Origen.

Irenaeus of Lyons

Irenaeus was a native of Asia Minor—probably Smyrna—where he was born around A.D. 130. There he was a disciple of Polycarp, of whose martyrdom we have already told in an earlier chapter. Throughout his life, Irenaeus was a fervent admirer of Polycarp, and in his writings he often speaks of an "old man"—or a presbyter—whose name is not given, but who is probably Polycarp. In any case, unknown reasons led Irenaeus to migrate to Lyons, in what today is southern France. There he became a presbyter, and as such was sent to Rome with a message for the bishop of that city. While he was in Rome, persecution broke out in Lyons and nearby Vienne—these are the events discussed in chapter 5—and bishop Photinus perished. Upon his return to Lyons, Irenaeus was elected bishop of the church in that city.

Irenaeus was above all a pastor. He was not particularly interested in philosophical speculation nor in delving into mysteries hitherto unsolved, but rather in leading his flock in Christian life and faith. Therefore, in his writings he did not seek to rise in great speculative flights, but simply to refute heresy and instruct believers. Only two of his works survive: the *Demonstration of Apostolic Faith,* and the *Refutation of the So-called Gnosis*—also known as *Against Heresies.* In the first of these, he instructs his flock on some points of Christian doctrine. In the latter, he seeks to refute gnosticism. In both, his goal is to expound the faith that he has received from his teachers, without adorning it with his own speculations. Therefore, the writings of Irenaeus are an excellent witness to the faith of the church towards the end of the second century.

Irenaeus, who sees himself as a shepherd, also sees God as above all a shepherd. God is a loving being who creates the world and humankind, not out of necessity nor by mistake—as Gnostics claimed—but out of a desire to have a creation to love and to lead, like the shepherd loves and leads the flock. From this perspective, the entirety of history appears as the process whereby the divine shepherd leads creation to its final goal.

The crown of creation is the human creature, made from the beginning as a free and therefore responsible being. That freedom is such that it allows us to become increasingly conformed to the divine will and nature, and thus to enjoy an ever-growing communion with our creator. But, on the other

The theme of shepherding, drawn from both the Bible and the stories of Orpheus, was common in Christian teaching and art.

hand, the human creature was not made from the beginning in its final perfection. Like a true shepherd, God placed the first couple in Eden. They were not mature beings, but were rather "like children," with their own perfection as such. This means that God's purpose was that human beings would grow in communion with the divine, eventually surpassing even the angels.

The angels are above us only provisionally. When the divine purpose is fulfilled in the human creature, we shall be above the angels, for our communion with God will be closer than theirs. The function of angels is similar to that of a tutor guiding the first steps of a prince. Although the tutor is temporarily in charge of the prince, eventually the prince will rule even the tutor.

Humankind is to be instructed, not only by the angels, but also by the "two hands" of God: the Word and the Holy Spirit. Led by those two hands, humans are to receive instruction and growth, always with a view to an increasingly close communion with God. The goal of this process is what Irenaeus calls "divinization"—God's purpose is to make us ever more like the divine. This does not mean, however, that we are somehow to be lost in the divine, nor that we shall ever be the same as God. On the contrary, God is so far above us that no matter how much we grow in our likeness to the divine we shall always have a long way to go.

But one of the angels, Satan, was jealous of the high destiny reserved for humankind, and for that reason led Adam and Eve into sin. As a result of sin, the human creature was expelled from paradise, and its growth was thwarted. From that point on, history has unfolded under the mark of sin.

Although the actual course of history is the result of sin, the fact that there is history is not. God always had the purpose that there be history. The situation in paradise, as described in Genesis, was not the goal of creation, but its beginning.

From this perspective, the incarnation of God in Jesus Christ is not the result of sin. On the contrary, God's initial purpose included being united with humankind. In fact, the future incarnate Word was the model that God followed in making humans after the divine image. Adam and Eve were so created that, after a process of growth and instruction, they could become like the incarnate Word. What has happened because of sin is that the incarnation has taken on the added purpose of offering a remedy for sin, and a means for defeating Satan.

Even before the incarnation, and from the very moment of the first sin, God has been leading humanity towards closer communion with the divine. This is why God *curses* the serpent and the earth, but only *punishes* the man and the woman. At the very moment of the Fall, God is working for human redemption.

Israel has an important role in the drama of redemption, for it is in the history of the chosen people that the two "hands of God" have continued their work, preparing humankind for communion with God. Therefore, the Old Testament is not the revelation of a God alien to the Christian faith, but is rather the history of the unfolding redemptive purposes of the same God whom Christians know in Jesus Christ.

At the proper time, when humankind had received the necessary preparation, the Word was incarnate in Jesus Christ. Jesus is the "second Adam" because in his life, death, and resurrection a new humanity has been created, and in all his actions Jesus has corrected what was twisted because of sin. Furthermore, Jesus has defeated Satan, and this in turn has enabled us to live in a new freedom. Those who are joined to him in baptism, and nourished in his body through communion, are also participants of his victory. Jesus Christ is literally the head of the church, which is his body. This body is nourished through worship—particularly communion—and is so joined to its head that it is already receiving the first benefits of Christ's victory. In his resurrection, the final resurrection has dawned, and all who are part of his body will partake of it.

Even at the end, when the Kingdom of God is established, God's task as shepherd will not be finished. On the contrary, redeemed humanity will continue growing into greater communion with the divine, and the process of divinization will go on eternally, taking us ever closer to God.

In conclusion, what we find in Irenaeus is a grand vision of history, so that the divine purposes unfold through it. The focal point of that history is the incarnation, not only because through it God's word has straightened the twisted history of humankind, but also because from the very beginning the union of the human with the divine was the goal of history. God's purpose is to be joined to the human creature, and this has taken place in a unique way in Jesus Christ.

Clement of Alexandria

The life story and the interests of Clement of Alexandria were very different from those of Irenaeus. Clement was probably born in Athens, the city that had long been famous for its philosophers. His parents were pagans; but young Clement was converted in unknown circumstances, and then undertook a vast search for a teacher who could give him deeper instruction in the Christian faith. After extensive travels, he found in Alexandria a teacher who satisfied his thirst for knowledge. This was Pantenus, of whom little is known. Clement remained in Alexandria, and when his teacher died Clement took his place as the main Christian instructor in Alexandria. In 202, when Septimius Severus was emperor, persecution broke out, and Clement had to leave the city. He then traveled along the Eastern Mediterranean—particularly Syria and Asia Minor—until his death in A.D. 215.

Alexandria, where Clement spent most of his career, was the most active intellectual center of the time. Its Museum, or temple of the muses, with the adjacent library, was similar to our modern universities, in that it was a meeting place for scholars in various fields. Furthermore, because it was also a trade center, Alexandria was a meeting place, not only for scholars and philosophers, but also for charlatans and adventurers. Therefore, the syncretistic spirit of the time reached its high point in that city at the mouth of the Nile.

It was in that context that Clement studied and taught, and therefore his thought bears the mark of Alexandria. He was not a pastor, like Irenaeus, but rather a thinker and a searcher; and his goal was not so much to expound the traditional faith of the church—although he did hold that faith—as to help those in quest of deeper truth, and to convince pagan intellectuals that Christianity was not the absurd superstition that some claimed it to be.

In his *Exhortation to the Pagans,* Clement shows the gist of his theological method in making use of Plato and other philosophers. "I seek to know God, and not only the works of God. Who will aid me in my quest? . . . How then, oh Plato, is one to seek after God?" Clement's purpose in the passage is to show his pagan readers that a good part of Christian doctrine can be supported by Plato's philosophy. Thus, pagans will be able to approach Christianity without taking for granted, as many supposed, that it is a religion for the ignorant and the superstitious.

Plato and his disciples, as seen in a mosaic from Pompeii.

But the reason why Clement calls on Plato is not only that it is convenient for his argument. He is convinced that there is only one truth, and that therefore any truth to be found in Plato can be no other than the truth that has been revealed in Jesus Christ and in Scripture. According to him, philosophy has been given to the Greeks just as the Law has been given to the Jews. Both have the purpose of leading to the ultimate truth, now revealed in Christ. The classical philsophers were to the Greeks what the prophets were to the Hebrews. With the Jews, God has established the covenant of the Law; with the Greeks, that of philosophy.

How can one see the agreement between Scripture and the philosophers? At first sight, there seems to be a great distance between the two. But Clement is convinced that a careful study of Scripture will lead to the same truth that the philosophers have known. The reason for this is that Scripture is written allegorically or, as Clement says, "in parables." The sacred text has more than one meaning. The literal sense ought not to be set aside. But those who are content with it are like children who are content with milk, and never grow to adulthood. Beyond the literal sense of the text there are other meanings that the truly wise must discover.

There is a close relationship between faith and reason, for one cannot function without the other. Reason builds its arguments on first principles, which cannot be proven, but are accepted by faith. For the truly wise, faith is the first principle, the starting point, on which reason is to build. But Christians who are content with faith, and do not use reason to build upon it, are again like a child who is forever content with milk.

Clement contrasts such people, who are satisfied with the rudiments of faith, with the wise person or, as he says, the "true Gnostic." Those who are wise go beyond the literal meaning of Scripture. Clement himself sees his task, not as that of a shepherd leading a flock, but rather as that of the "true Gnostic" leading others of similar interests. Naturally, this tends to produce an elitist theology, and Clement has often been criticized on this account.

It is not necessary to say a great deal about the actual content of Clement's theology. Although he sees himself as an interpreter of Scripture, his allegorical exegesis allows him to find in the sacred text ideas and doctrines that are really Platonic in inspiration. God is the Ineffable One about which one can only speak in metaphors and in negative terms. One can say what God is not. But as to what God is, human language can do no more than point to a reality that is beyond its grasp.

This Ineffable One is revealed to us in the Word or Logos, from which the philosophers as well as the prophets received whatever truth they knew, and which has become incarnate in Jesus. On this point, Clement follows the direction set earlier by Justin. The main difference is that, while Justin used the doctrine of the Logos to show to pagans the truth of Christianity, Clement uses the same doctrine to call Christians to be open to the truth in philosophy.

In any case, Clement's importance does not lie in the manner in which he understands one doctrine or another, but rather in that his thought is characteristic of an entire atmosphere and tradition that developed in Alexandria and that would be of great significance for the subsequent course of theology. Later in this chapter, when discussing Origen, we shall see the next step in the development of that theological tradition.

Tertullian of Carthage

Tertullian was very different from Clement. He seems to have been a native of the North African city of Carthage. Although he spent most of his life there, it was in Rome that he was converted to Christianity when he was about forty years old. Having returned to Carthage, he wrote a number of treatises in defense of the faith against the pagans, and in defense of orthodoxy against various heresies. He either was a lawyer or had been trained in rhetoric, and his entire literary output bears the stamp of a legal mind. In an earlier chapter, we have quoted his protest against the "unjust sentence" of Trajan, ordering that Christians should not be sought out, but should be punished if brought before the authorities. Those lines read like the argument of a lawyer appealing a case before a higher court. In another work, *On the Witness of the Soul,* Tertullian places the human soul on the witness stand and, after questioning it, comes to the conclusion that the soul is "by nature Christian," and that if it persists in rejecting Christianity this is due to obstinacy and blindness.

The treatise where Tertullian's legal mind shines is *Prescription against the Heretics.* In the legal language of the time, a *praescriptio* could mean at least two things. It could be a legal argument presented before the case itself was begun, in order to show that the trial should not take place. If, even before the actual case was presented, one of the parties could show that the other had no right to sue, or that the suit was not properly drawn, or that the court had no jurisdiction, the trial could be canceled. But the same word had a different meaning when one spoke of a "long-term prescription." This meant that if a party had been in undisputed possession of a property or of a right for a certain time, that possession became legal, even if at a later time another party claimed it.

Tertullian uses the term in both senses, as if it were a case of a suit between orthodox Christianity and the heretics. His aim is to show, not simply that the heretics are wrong, but rather that they do not even have the right to dispute with the church. To this end, he claims that Scriptures belong to the church. For several generations the church has used the Bible, and the heretics have not disputed its possession. Even though not all of Scripture belonged originally to the church, by now it does. Therefore, the heretics have no right to use the Bible. They are latecomers who seek to change and to use what legally belongs to the church.

In order to show that Scripture belongs to the church, it suffices to look at the various ancient churches where Scripture has been read and interpreted in a consistent manner since the times of the apostles. Rome, for instance, can point to an uninterrupted line of bishops joining the present time—the late second century—to the apostles Peter and Paul. And the same is true of the church in Antioch as well as of several others. All these apostolic churches agree in their use and interpretation of Scripture. Furthermore, by virtue of their very origin the writings of the apostles belong to the apostolic churches.

Since Scripture belongs to the church, the heretics have no right to base their argument on it. Here Tertullian uses the term "prescription" in the other sense. Since heretics have no right to interpret Scripture, any argument with them regarding such interpretation is out of place. The church, as the rightful owner of Scripture, is the only one that has the right to interpret it.

This argument against the heretics has repeatedly been used against various dissidents throughout the history of Christianity. It was one of the main arguments of Catholics against Protestants in the sixteenth century. In Tertullian's case, however, one should note that his argument is based on showing a continuity, not only of formal succession, but also of doctrine, through the generations. Since this continuity of doctrine was precisely what was debated at the time of the Reformation, the argument was not as powerful as in Tertullian's time.

But Tertullian's legalism goes beyond arguments such as this. His legal mind leads him to affirm that, once one has found the truth of Christianity, one should abandon any further search for truth. As Tertullian sees the matter, a Christian who is still searching for further truth lacks faith.

You are to seek until you find, and once you have found, you are to believe. Thereafter, all you have to do is to hold to what you have believed. Besides this, you are to believe that there is nothing further to be believed, nor anything else to be sought.*

This means that the accepted body of Christian doctrine suffices, and that any quest for truth that goes beyond that body of doctrine is dangerous. Naturally, Tertullian would allow Christians to delve deeper into Christian doctrine. But anything that goes beyond it, as well as anything coming from other sources, must be rejected. This is particularly true of pagan philosophy, which is the source of all heresy, and is nothing but idle speculation.

Miserable Aristotle, who gave them dialectics! He gave them the art of building in order to tear down, an art of slippery speech and crude arguments, . . . which rejects everything and deals with nothing.**

In short, Tertullian condemns all speculation. To speak, for instance, of what God's omnipotence can do is a waste of time and a dangerous occupation. What we are to ask is not what God could do, but rather what is it that God has in fact done. This is what the church teaches. This is what is to be found in Scripture. The rest is idle and risky curiosity.

This, however, does not mean that Tertullian does not use logic against his adversaries. On the contrary, his logic is often inflexible and overwhelming, as in the case of the *Prescription.* But the strength of his arguments is not so much in his logic as in his rhetoric, which sometimes leads him to sarcasm. For instance, in writing against Marcion he tells his opponent that the God of the church has made this entire world and all its wonders, whereas Marcion's god has not created a single vegetable. And then he goes on to ask,

---

Prescription against Heretics 8.
**Ibid. 7.

what was Marcion's god doing before its recent revelation? Is the divine love that Marcion touts an affair of the last minute? Thus, through a unique combination of mordant irony and inflexible logic, Tertullian became the scourge of heretics and the champion of orthodoxy.

Yet, around the year 207, that staunch enemy of heresy, that untiring advocate of the authority of the church, joined the Montanist movement. Why Tertullian took this step is one of the many mysteries of church history, for there is little in his own writings or in other contemporary documents that speaks directly of his motives. It is impossible to give a categorical answer to the question of why Tertullian became a Montanist. But it is possible to note the affinities between Tertullian's character and theology, on the one hand, and Montanism on the other.

Montanism is named after its founder, Montanus, who had been a pagan priest until his conversion to Christianity in A.D. 155. At a later time he began prophesying, declaring that he had been possessed by the Holy Spirit. Soon two women, Priscilla and Maximilla, also began prophesying. This in itself was not new, for at that time, at least in some churches, women were allowed to prophesy. What was new, and gave rise to serious misgivings, was that Montanus and his followers claimed that their movement was the beginning of a new age. Just as in Jesus Christ a new age had begun, so was a still newer age beginning in the outpouring of the Spirit. This new age was characterized by a more rigorous moral life, just as the Sermon on the Mount was itself more demanding than the Law of the Old Testament.

The rest of the church opposed Montanist preaching not because they prophesied, but because they claimed that with them the last age of history had dawned. According to the New Testament, the last days began with the advent and resurrection of Jesus, and with the giving of the Holy Spirit in Pentecost. As years went by, this emphasis on the last days being already here was progressively forgotten, to the point that in the twentieth century many find it surprising. But in the second century the conviction of the church was very much alive, that the last days had already begun in Jesus Christ. Therefore to claim, as the Montanists did, that the end was beginning then, with the giving of the Spirit to Montanus and his followers, was to diminish the significance of the events of the New Testament, and to make of the Gospel one more stage in the history of salvation. These were the consequences of Montanism that the church could not accept.

Tertullian seems to have been attracted by Montanist rigorism. His legal mind sought after perfect order, where everything was properly done. In the church at large, in spite of all its efforts to do the will of God, there were too many imperfections that did not fit Tertullian's frame of mind. The only way to explain the continuing sin of Christians was to see the church as an intermediate stage, to be superseded by the new age of the Spirit. Naturally, such dreams were doomed to failure, and some ancient writers tell us that toward the end of his days Tertullian was sufficiently disappointed with

Montanism to found his own sect—which those ancient writers call the "Tertullianists."

Even after he became a Montanist, Tertullian continued his campaign against doctrinal error. Probably the most significant of the works that he wrote during this period is his brief treatise *Against Praxeas,* where he coined formulas that would be of great importance in later Trinitarian and Christological debates.

Little or nothing is known of Praxeas. Some scholars believe that there never was such a person, and that "Praxeas" is none other than Calixtus, the bishop of Rome, whom Tertullian prefers to attack under a fictitious name. Whoever Praxeas was, it is clear that he was influential in the church of Rome, and that there he had sought to explain the relationship between Father, Son, and Holy Ghost in a manner that Tertullian found inadmissible. According to Praxeas, the Father, the Son, and the Holy Ghost were simply three modes in which God appeared, so that God was sometimes Father, sometimes Son, and sometimes Holy Ghost—at least, this is what may be inferred from Tertullian's treatise. This is what has been called "patripassianism" (the doctrine that the Father suffered the passion) or "modalism" (the doctrine that the various persons of the Trinity are "modes" in which God appears).

Since Praxeas had also curtailed Montanist influence in Rome, Tertullian opens his treatise with typical mordancy: "Praxeas served the Devil in Rome in two ways: expelling prophecy and introducing heresy, evicting the Spirit and crucifying the Father."*

But he then moves on to explain how the Trinity is to be understood. It is in this context that he proposes the formula "one substance and three persons." Likewise, when discussing how Jesus Christ can be both human and divine, he speaks of "one person" and "two substances" or "natures," the divine and the human. The manner in which he explains the meaning of the terms "person" and "substance" is drawn mostly from their legal use. Later theologians would explicate the same words in metaphysical terms. In any case, it is significant that, in both the Trinitarian and the Christological questions, Tertullian coined the formulas that would eventually become the hallmark of orthodoxy.

For all these reasons, Tertullian is a unique personality in the story of Christianity. A fiery champion of orthodoxy against every sort of heresy, in the end he joined one of the movements that the church at large considered heretical. And, even then, he produced writings and theological formulas that would be very influential in the future course of orthodox theology. Furthermore, he was the first Christian theologian to write in Latin, which was the language of the western half of the Empire, and thus he may be considered the founder of Western theology.

Against Praxeas 1.

Origen of Alexandria

Clement's greatest disciple, and the last of the four Christian teachers to be considered in this chapter, was Origen. In contrast with Clement, Origen was the son of Christian parents. His father suffered martyrdom during the persecution of Septimius Severus—the same persecution that forced Clement to leave the city. Origen, who was still a young lad, wished to offer himself for martyrdom. But his mother hid his clothes and he was forced to remain at home, where he wrote a treatise on martyrdom addressed to his imprisoned father.

Shortly thereafter, when Origen was still in his late teens, the bishop of Alexandria, Demetrius, entrusted him with the task of training catechumens—that is, candidates for baptism. This was a very serious responsibility, and young Origen, whose genius was exceptional, soon became famous. After teaching catechumens for a number of years, he left that task to some of his best disciples, and devoted himself entirely to running a school of Christian philosophy that was very similar to those founded by the great classical philosophers. There he lectured, not only to Christians who came from afar to listen to him, but also to enlightened pagans drawn by his fame, such as the mother of the emperor and the governor of Arabia.

For a number of reasons, including jealousy, conflict arose between Demetrius and Origen. The final result was that the latter had to leave his native city and settle at Caesarea, where he continued writing and teaching for another twenty years

Finally, during the persecution of Decius (discussed in the next chapter), Origen had the opportunity to show the strength of his faith. Given the nature of that persecution, Origen was not put to death, but was tortured to such a point that he died shortly after having been released. He died at Tyre, when he was about seventy years old.

Origen's literary output was enormous. Since he was aware of the manner in which diverse versions of Scripture differed, he compiled the *Hexapla.* This was an edition of the Old Testament in six columns: the Hebrew text, a Greek transliteration from the Hebrew—so that a reader who did not know that ancient language could at least have some idea of its pronunciation—and four different Greek translations. To this was added an entire system of symbols indicating variants, omissions, and additions. Besides this great scholarly work, Origen wrote commentaries on many books of the Bible, the already cited apology *Against Celsus,* and a great systematic theology called *De principiis—On First Principles.* Part of this great literary production was achieved through dictation, and it is even said that at times he would simultaneously dictate seven different works to as many secretaries.

The spirit of Origen's theology is very similar to that of his teacher,

Clement. It is an attempt to relate Christian faith to the philosophy that was then current in Alexandria, Neoplatonism. He was aware of the danger of abandoning Christian doctrine in favor of the teachings of the philosophers, and thus declared that "nothing which is at variance with the tradition of the apostles and of the church is to be accepted as true." This tradition includes first of all the doctrine that there is only one God, creator and ruler of the universe, and therefore the Gnostic speculations regarding the origin of the world are to be rejected. Secondly, the apostles taught that Jesus Christ is the Son of God, begotten before all creation, and that his incarnation is such that, while becoming human, he remained divine. As to the Holy Ghost, Origen declares that apostolic tradition is not entirely clear, except in affirming that the Spirit's glory is no less than that of the Father and the Son. Finally, the apostles taught that at a future time the soul will be rewarded or punished according to its life in this world, and that there will be a final resurrection of the body, which will rise incorruptible.

However, once these points have been affirmed, Origen feels free to rise in great speculative flights. For instance, since the tradition of the apostles and of the church gives no details as to how the world was created, Origen believes that this is a fair field of inquiry. In the first chapters of Genesis there are two stories of creation, as Jewish scholars knew even before the time of Origen. In one of these stories, we are told that humankind was created after the image and likeness of God, and that "male and female created He them." In the second, we are told that God made Adam first, and then formed Eve out of Adam's rib. In the Greek version of the first narrative, the verb describing God's action is "to create," whereas in the second it is "to form" or "to shape." What is the meaning of these differences? Modern scholars would speak of the joining of separate traditions. But Origen simply declares that there are two narratives because there were in fact two creations.

According to Origen, the first creation was purely spiritual. What God first created were spirits without bodies. That is why the text says "male and female"—that is, with no sexual differences. This is also why we are told that God "created," and not that God "formed."

God's purpose was that the spirits thus created would be devoted to the contemplation of the divine. But some of them strayed from that contemplation and fell. It was then that God made the second creation. This second creation is material, and it serves as a shelter or temporary home for fallen spirits. Those spirits who fell farthest have become demons, while the rest are human souls. It was for these human souls—fallen preexistent spirits— that God made the bodies we now have, which God "shaped" out of the earth, making some male and some female.

This implies that all human souls existed as pure spirits—or "intellects," as Origen calls them—before being born into the world, and that the reason why we are here is that we have sinned in that prior, purely spiritual existence. Although Origen claims that all this is based on the Bible, it is clear

A medieval relief showing Adam and Eve driven from Paradise.

that it is derived from the Platonic tradition, where such ideas had been taught for a long time.

In the present world, the Devil and his demons have us captive, and therefore Jesus Christ has come to break the power of Satan and to show us the path we are to follow in our return to our spiritual home. Furthermore, since the Devil is no more than a spirit like ours, and since God is love, in the end even Satan will be saved, and the entire creation will return to its original state, where everything was pure spirit. However, since these spirits will still be free, there is nothing to guarantee that there will not be a new fall, a new material world, and a new history, and that the cycle of fall, restoration, and fall will not go on forever.

In evaluating all of this, one has to begin by marveling at the width of Origen's mental scope. For this reason, he has had fervent admirers at various times throughout the history of the church. One must also acknowledge that

Origen proposes all of this, not as truths to be generally accepted, nor as something that will supersede the doctrines of the church, but as his own tentative speculations, which ought not to be compared with the authoritative teaching of the church.

However, once this has been said, it is also important to note that on many points Origen is more Platonist than Christian. Thus, for instance, Origen rejects the doctrines of Marcion and of the Gnostics, that the world is the creation of an inferior being; but then he comes to the conclusion that the existence of the physical world—as well as of history—is the result of sin. At this point there is a marked difference with Irenaeus, for whom the existence of history was part of the eternal purpose of God. And when it comes to the preexistence of souls, and to the eternal cycle of fall and restoration, there is no doubt that Origen strays from what Christianity has usually taught.

10/Persecution in the Third Century

The present confession of the faith before the authorities has been all the more illustrious and honorable because the suffering was greater. The struggle intensified, and the glory of those who struggled grew with it.

CYPRIAN OF CARTHAGE

In the last years of the second century, the church had enjoyed relative peace. The Empire was involved in civil wars and in defending its borders against barbarian inroads, and therefore had paid scant attention to Christians. Trajan's old principle, that Christians were to be punished if they refused to worship the emperor and the gods, but that they ought not to be sought out, was still in force. Therefore, whatever persecution there was was local and sporadic.

In the third century, things changed. Trajan's policy was still valid, and therefore the threat of local persecution was constant. But over and beyond that there were new policies that deeply affected the life of the church. The emperors who created and applied these policies were Septimius Severus and Decius.

Persecution under Septimius Severus

Early in the third century, the reigning emperor, Septimius Severus, had managed to put an end to a series of civil wars that had weakened the Empire. But even so, it was not easy to govern such a vast and unruly domain. The "barbarians" who lived beyond the borders of the Rhine and the Danube were a constant threat. Within the Empire there were dissident groups, and there was always the danger that a legion might rebel and name its own emperor, thus precipitating a new civil war. Faced by such difficulties, the emperor felt the need for religious harmony within his territories, and thus settled on a policy of promoting syncretism. He proposed to bring all his subjects together under the worship of *Sol invictus*—the Unconquered Sun —and to subsume under that worship all the various religions and philosophies then current. All gods were to be accepted, as long as one acknowledged the Sun that reigned above all.

This policy soon clashed with the seeming obstinacy of two groups that refused to yield to syncretism: Jews and Christians. Septimius Severus then decided to stop the spread of those two religions, and thus outlawed, under penalty of death, all conversions to Christianity or to Judaism. This was in addition to the still existing threat of Trajan's legislation.

The net result was an increase in local persecutions like those of the second century, to which now was added a more intensive persecution aimed directly at new converts and their teachers. Therefore, the year 202, when the edict of Septimius Severus was issued, is a landmark in the history of persecutions. One tradition affirms that Irenaeus suffered martyrdom in that year. It was also at that time that a group of Christians, including Origen's father, were killed in Alexandria. Since Clement was a famous Christian teacher in that city, and since the imperial edict was particularly directed against those who sought new converts, he had to seek refuge in areas where he was less known.

The most famous martyrdom of that time is that of Perpetua and Felicitas, which probably took place in 203. It is possible that Perpetua and her companions were Montanists, and that the account of their martyrdom comes from the pen of Tertullian. In any case, the martyrs were five catechumens —that is, five people who were preparing to receive baptism. This agrees with what is known of the policies of Septimius Severus. These five people —some of whom were in their teens—were charged, not with being Christians, but with having been converted recently, and thus disobeying the imperial edict.

The heroine of the *Martyrdom of Saints Perpetua and Felicitas* is Perpetua, a young and well-to-do woman who was nursing her infant child. Her companions were the slaves Felicitas and Revocatus, and two other young men whose names were Saturninus and Secundulus. A great deal of the text of the *Martyrdom* is placed on the lips of Perpetua, and some scholars believe that she may actually have spoken most of these words. When Perpetua and her companions were arrested, her father tried to persuade her to save her life by abandoning her faith. She answered that, just as everything has a name and it is useless to try to give it a different name, she had the name of Christian, and this could not be changed.

The judicial process was a long and drawn-out affair, apparently because the authorities hoped to persuade the accused to abandon their faith. Felicitas, who was pregnant when arrested, was afraid that her life would be spared for that reason, or that her martyrdom would be postponed and she would not be able to join her four companions. But the *Martyrdom* tells us that her prayers were answered, and that in her eighth month she gave birth to a girl who was then adopted by another Christian woman. Seeing her moan in childbirth, her jailers asked how she expected to be able to face the beasts in the arena. Her answer is typical of the manner in which martyrdom was interpreted: "Now my sufferings are only mine. But when I face the beasts there will be another who will live in me, and will suffer for me since I shall be suffering for him."*

The account then tells us that the three male martyrs were the first to be put in the arena. Saturninus and Revocatus died quickly and bravely. But no beast would attack Secundulus. Some of them refused to come out to him, while others attacked the soldiers. Finally, Secundulus himself declared that a leopard would kill him, and so it happened.

Perpetua and Felicitas were told that they would be attacked by a ferocious cow. Having been hit and thrown by the animal, Perpetua asked to be able to retie her hair, for loose hair was a sign of mourning, and this was a joyful day for her. Finally, the two bleeding women stood in the middle of the arena, bid each other farewell with the kiss of peace, and died by the sword.

Shortly thereafter, for reasons that are not altogether clear, persecution abated. There were still isolated incidents in various parts of the Empire, but the edict of Septimius Severus was not generally enforced. In 211, when Caracalla succeeded Septimius Severus, there was a brief persecution; but this again did not last long, and was mostly limited to North Africa.

The next two emperors, Elagabalus (218–222) and Alexander Severus (222–235), pursued a syncretistic policy similar to that of Septimius Severus. But they did not attempt to force Jews and Christians to accept syncretism, or to stop seeking converts. It is said that Alexander Severus had on his private altar, jointly with his various gods, images of Christ and Abraham. His mother, Julia Mammea, went to hear Origen lecture in Alexandria.

Under Emperor Maximin there was a very brief persecution in Rome. At that time the church in that city was divided, and the two rival bishops, Pontianus and Hippolytus, were sent to work in the mines. But again the storm passed, and it was even rumored—with little basis in fact—that Philip the Arabian, who ruled from 244 to 249, was a Christian.

In short, during almost half a century, persecution was rare, while the number of converts to Christianity was large. For this entire generation of Christians, the martyrs were worthy of great admiration, but they had lived in times past, and those evil times were not likely to be repeated. Every day

---

Martyrdom of Perpetua and Felicitas 5.3.

Decius believed that Rome must return to her gods.

there were more Christians among the aristocracy, and the ancient rumors about Christian immorality had little credence among the masses. Persecution was a past memory, both painful and glorious.

Then the storm broke out.

Under Decius

In 249, Decius took the imperial purple. Although Christian historians have depicted him as a cruel person, the truth is that Decius was simply a Roman of the old style, whose main goal was to restore Rome to her ancient glory. There were several factors contributing to the eclipse of that glory. The barbarians beyond the borders were increasingly restless, and their incursions into the Empire were growing more and more daring. There was a serious economic crisis. And the ancient traditions associated with the classical times of Roman civilization were generally forgotten.

To a traditional Roman such as Decius, it seemed obvious that one of the reasons for all this was that the people had abandoned the ancient gods. When all adored the gods, things went better, and the glory and power of Rome were on the increase. By neglecting the gods, Rome had provoked their displeasure, and had been itself neglected by them. Therefore, if Rome's ancient glory was to be restored, it was necessary to restore also its ancient religion. If all the subjects of the Empire would worship the gods, perhaps the gods would once again favor the Empire.

This was the basis of Decius' religious policy. It was no longer a matter of rumors about Christian immorality, nor of punishing the obstinacy of those who refused to worship the emperor. It was rather an entire religious campaign for the restoration of ancestral religion. What was at stake, as Decius saw it, was the survival of Rome itself. Those who refused to worship the gods were practically guilty of high treason.

Given these circumstances, Decius' persecution was very different from the earlier ones. The emperor's purpose was not to create martyrs, but apostates. Almost fifty years earlier, Tertullian had declared that the blood of the martyrs was a seed, for the more it was spilled the greater the number of Christians. The exemplary deaths of Christians in those early years had moved many who had witnessed them, and therefore persecution seemed to encourage the spread of Christianity. If, instead of killing Christians, they were forced to recant, this would be a victory for Decius' goal of restoring paganism.

Although Decius' edict has been lost, it is clear that what he ordered was not that Christians as such ought to be persecuted, but rather that the worship of the gods was now mandatory throughout the Empire. Following the imperial decree, everyone had to offer sacrifice to the gods and to burn incense before a statue of Decius. Those who complied would be given a certificate attesting to that fact. Those who did not have such a certificate would then be considered outlaws who had disobeyed the imperial command.

The imperial decree found Christians unprepared for the new challenge. Those generations that had lived under constant threat of persecution were now past, and the new generations were not ready for martyrdom. Some ran to obey the imperial command: Others stood firm for a while, but when brought before the imperial authorities offered the required sacrifice to the gods. Still others obtained fraudulent certificates without actually worshiping the gods. And there was a significant number who resolved to stand firm and refuse to obey the edict.

Since Decius' goal was to promote the worship of the gods, rather than to kill Christians, those who actually died as martyrs were relatively few. What the authorities did was to arrest Christians and then, through a combi-

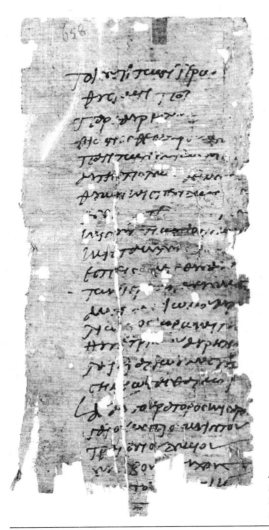

A fragment of a certificate from the time of Decius, attesting that the bearer had complied with the imperial edict.

nation of promises, threats, and torture, to try to force them to abandon their faith. It was under this policy that Origen was imprisoned and tortured. And Origen's case found hundreds of counterparts throughout the Empire. This was no longer a sporadic or local persecution, but one that was systematic and universal. As proof of the widespread application of the imperial decree, certificates of having sacrificed have survived from some rather remote parts of the Empire.

One of the results of this persecution was that a new title of honor appeared within the church, that of the "confessors." Until that time, practically all who were taken before the authorities and remained firm had become martyrs. Those who offered sacrifice to the gods and to the emperor were apostates. Due to the policies established by Decius, there were now those who remained firm in their faith, even in the midst of cruel torture, but who never received the crown of martyrdom. Those who had confessed the faith in such circumstances were then given the title of "confessors," and were highly respected by other Christians.

Decius' persecution was brief. In A.D. 251, Gallus succeeded him, and his policies were set aside. Six years later Valerian, a former companion of Decius, began a new persecution. But he fell prisoner to the Persians, who took him in captivity, and the church enjoyed another forty years of relative peace.

The Question of the Lapsed: Cyprian and Novatian

In spite of its brief duration, the persecution under Decius was a harsh trial for the church. This was due, not only to the fact itself of persecution, but also to the problems that had to be faced after it.

In short, the great question before the church was what to do about the "lapsed"—those who, in one way or another, had weakened during the persecution. There were several complicating factors. One was that not all had fallen in the same manner nor to the same degree. The case of those who ran to offer sacrifice as soon as they were told of the imperial decree was hardly the same as that of those who purchased fraudulent certificates, or those others who had weakened for a moment, but had then reaffirmed their faith and asked to rejoin the church while the persecution was still in progress.

Given the great prestige of the confessors, some thought that they were the ones with authority to determine who among the lapsed ought to be restored to the communion of the church, and how. Some confessors, particularly in North Africa, claimed that authority, and began restoring some of the lapsed. This met with the opposition of many bishops who claimed that only the hierarchy had the authority to restore the lapsed, and that only it could do so in a uniform and just manner. Still others were convinced that both the confessors and the bishops were showing too much leniency, and that the lapsed ought to be treated with greater rigor.

In the debate surrounding this question, two people played crucial roles: Cyprian and Novatian.

Cyprian had become a Christian when he was about forty years old, and shortly thereafter had been elected bishop of Carthage. His favorite theologian was Tertullian, whom he called "the master." Like Tertullian, he was trained in rhetoric, and he could easily overwhelm his opponents with his arguments. His writings are among the best Christian literature of the time.

Cyprian, who had become a bishop shortly before the persecution, thought that his duty was to flee to a secure place with other leaders of the church, and continue guiding the flock through an extensive correspondence. As was to be expected, many interpreted this decision as an act of cowardice. The church of Rome, for instance, had lost its bishop in the persecution, and the clergy of that city wrote to Cyprian questioning his decision. He insisted that he had fled for the good of his flock, and not out of cowardice. As a matter of fact, his valor and conviction were amply proven a few years later, when he offered his life as a martyr. But meanwhile his own authority was questioned, and there were many who claimed that the confessors of Carthage, who had suffered for their faith, had more authority than he did, particularly when it came to the question of the restoration of the lapsed.

Some of these confessors thought that the lapsed should be readmitted directly, with no other requirement than their own declaration of repentance. Soon some of the presbyters, who had other reasons for disliking their bishop, joined the confessors, and the outcome was a schism that divided the church in Carthage and throughout the neighboring areas. Cyprian then called a synod—that is, a gathering of the bishops of the region—which decided that those who had purchased or otherwise obtained certificates without actually having sacrificed would be immediately readmitted to the communion of the church. Those who had sacrificed would only be readmitted on their deathbeds, or when a new persecution gave them the opportunity to prove the sincerity of their repentance. Those who had sacrificed and showed no repentance would never be readmitted. All these actions were to be taken by the bishops, and not by confessors. These decisions ended the controversy, although the schism continued for some time.

The main reason why Cyprian insisted on the need to regulate the readmission of the lapsed into the communion of the church was his own understanding of the church. The church is the body of Christ, and will share in the victory of its Head. Therefore, "outside the church there is no salvation," and "no one can have God as Father who does not have the church as mother." By this he did not mean that one had to be in total agreement with the hierarchy of the church—he himself had his own clashes with the hierarchy of Rome. But he did believe that the unity of the church was of supreme importance. Since the actions of the confessors threatened that unity, Cyprian felt that he had to reject those actions and to insist on the need for a synod to decide what was to be done with the lapsed.

Besides this, Cyprian was an admirer of Tertullian, whose writings he studied assiduously. Tertullian's rigorism had an influence on Cyprian, and he revolted against the idea of restoring the lapsed too easily. The church was to be a community of saints, and the idolaters and apostates had no place in it.

Novatian was more rigorous than Cyprian. He clashed with the bishop of Rome, Cornelius, because in his opinion the lapsed were being readmitted too easily. Years earlier, there had been in the same city a similar conflict between Hippolytus, a noted theologian, and bishop Calixtus, because the latter was willing to forgive those guilty of fornication who repented, and Hippolytus insisted that this should not be done. At that time the result was a schism, so that there were two bishops in Rome. In the case of Novatian's protest the result was the same. As in so many other cases, the issue was whether purity or forgiving love should be the characteristic note of the church. The schism of Hippolytus did not last long, but the Novatianist schism did continue for several generations.

The significance of these episodes is that they show that the restoration of the lapsed was one of the main concerns of the Western church from a very early date. The question of what should be done about those baptized Christians who sinned divided the Western church repeatedly. It was out of that concern that the entire penitential system developed. Much later, the Protestant Reformation was in large measure a protest against that system.

11/Christian Life

*. . . not many of you were wise according
to worldly standards, not many were
powerful, not many of noble birth; but . . .
God chose what is weak in the world to
shame the strong.*

I COR. 1:26–27

When telling the story of Christianity, one must always remember that the sources themselves are not a fair representation of all that was taking place. Since most of the surviving documents deal with the work and thought of the leaders of the church, or with persecution and conflicts with the state, there is always the tendency to forget that these writings present only a partial picture. Furthermore, when one attempts to reconstruct the rest of the picture, one is faced with an almost total lack of sources, and must be content with piecing together bits of information.

The Social Origins of Early Christians

The complaint of the pagan writer Celsus was quoted earlier: Christians were ignorant folk whose teaching took place, not in schools nor in open forums, but in kitchens, shops, and tanneries. Although the work of Christians such as Justin, Clement, and Origen would seem to belie Celsus' words, the fact remains that, in general, Celsus was telling the truth. Wise scholars among Christians were the exception rather than the rule. It is significant that in his apology *Against Celsus* Origen does not contradict Celsus on this score. From the perspective of cultured pagans such as Tacitus, Cornelius Fronto, and Marcus Aurelius, Christians were a despicable rabble.

They were not entirely wrong, for there are indications that the vast majority of Christians during the first three centuries belonged to the lower echelons of society. According to the witness of the Gospels, Jesus spent most of his time with poor, ill, and despised people. Paul, who belonged to a higher social class than most of the earliest disciples, does say that the majority of Christians in Corinth were ignorant, powerless, and of obscure birth. The same is generally true during the first three centuries of the life of the church. Although there were Christians of relatively high rank, such as Domitilla and Perpetua, it is likely that for each of these there were hundreds of Christians of humbler status and less instruction.

It was mostly out of this rank and file that legends and writings arose with a very different tone from that of Justin and the other Christian scholars. Foremost among these writings are some of the apocryphal gospels and some of the "acts" of various apostles and of the Virgin. The miraculous plays a central role in these writings, even to the point of the ridiculous. Thus, for instance, in one of the apocryphal Gospels young Jesus amuses himself by breaking the water jars of his playmates, and throwing the pieces into a well. When they burst into tears, saying that their parents will punish them for having broken the jars, Jesus orders the water to return the broken jars, and these come up unscathed. Or, when Jesus wishes to be atop a tree, he does not climb like other boys. He simply orders the tree to bend down to him, sits on it, and tells the tree to return to its original position.

However, this naive credulity should not lead one to underestimate those common Christians. A comparison of their theology with that of more cultured Christians does not always favor the latter. Thus, for instance, the active, sovereign, and just God who is depicted in many of these writings is closer to the God of Scripture than is the ineffable and distant One of Clement of Alexandria. Furthermore, while the great apologists made every effort to prove to the authorities that their faith was not opposed to imperial policies, there are indications that some common Christians were well aware that there was an unavoidable clash between the goals of the Empire and the divine purpose. When one of these Christians was taken before imperial authorities, we are told that he refused to acknowledge the authority of the emperor, and declared that Christ was "my Lord, the emperor over all kings and all nations." Finally, while some of the more cultured Christians tended to spiritualize Christian hope, in the faith of the common people there was still the vision of a Kingdom that would supplant the present order, of a new Jerusalem where God would wipe away the tears of those who were suffering under the social order of the Empire.

Christian Worship

Worship was one point at which Christians of all social classes had a common experience. As we reconstruct that experience, we must rely mostly on documents left behind by Christian leaders. But, since common Christians

This shrine, found in a relatively humble house in Herculaneum, attests to the presence of Christians there in the first century.

partook of the same services, here we have a rare glimpse at the life of all Christians.

We are told in the book of Acts that from the very beginning the early church had the custom of gathering on the first day of the week for the breaking of bread. The reason for gathering on the first day of the week was that this was the day of the resurrection of the Lord. Therefore, the main purpose of this service of worship was not to call the faithful to repentance, or to make them aware of the magnitude of their sins, but rather to celebrate the resurrection of Jesus and the promises of which that resurrection was the seal. This is why Acts describes those gatherings as happy occasions: "they partook of food with glad and generous hearts, praising God for having favor with all the people" (Acts 2:46–47). Those early communion services did not focus their attention on the events of Good Friday, but rather on those of Easter. A new reality had dawned, and Christians gathered to celebrate that dawning and to become participants in it.

From that time, and throughout most of its history, the Christian church has seen in communion its highest act of worship. Only at a relatively recent date has it become common practice in many Protestant churches to focus their worship on preaching rather than on communion.

Besides the well-known but scant data offered by the New Testament, it is possible to reconstruct early Christian worship by piecing together information from a number of extant documents. Although these writings come from different times and places, and therefore there are differences and inconsistencies in what they tell us, it is possible to draw from them a general picture of the typical service of communion.

The most remarkable characteristic of those early communion services was that they were celebrations. The tone was one of joy and gratitude, rather than sorrow and repentance. In the beginning, communion was part of an entire meal. Believers brought what they could, and after the common meal there were special prayers over the bread and the wine. However, by the beginning of the second century the common meal was being set aside, perhaps for fear of persecution, or in order to quell the rumors about orgiastic "love feasts." Although the celebration then became more symbolic, the original tone of joy remained.

At least since the second century, there were two main parts in a communion service. First there were commented readings of Scripture, with prayers and hymn singing. Since at that time it was almost impossible for an individual Christian to possess a copy of Scripture, this first part of the service was almost the only way in which believers came to know the Bible, and therefore it was rather extensive—sometimes lasting for hours. Then came the second part of the service, communion proper, which opened with the kiss of peace. After the kiss, the bread and wine were brought forth and presented to the one presiding, who then offered a prayer over the elements. In this prayer, often lengthy, the saving acts of God were usually recounted, and the power of the Holy Spirit was invoked over the bread and the wine. Then the bread was broken and shared, the common cup was passed, and the meeting ended with a benediction. Naturally, although these were the common elements in a typical communion service, in various places and circumstances other elements could be added.

Another common characteristic of these early communion services was that only those who had been baptized could attend. People coming from other congregations were certainly welcome, as long as they were baptized Christians. Sometimes, converts who had not yet received baptism were allowed in the early part of the service—the readings, sermons, and prayers —but were sent away at the time of communion proper.

Another early custom was to gather for communion at the tombs of the

faithful. This was the function of the catacombs. Some authors have drama-
tized the "church of the catacombs," depicting them as secret places where
Christians gathered in defiance of the authorities. This is at best an exaggeration. The catacombs were cemeteries whose existence was well known to the
authorities, for Christians were not the only ones with such subterranean
burial arrangements. Although on occasion Christians did use the catacombs
as hiding places, the reason why they gathered there was not that they feared
the authorities, but rather that many heroes of the faith were buried there,
and Christians believed that communion joined them, not only among themselves and with Jesus Christ, but also with their ancestors in the faith.

This was particularly true in the case of martyrs. As early as the middle
of the second century, it was customary to gather at their tombs on the
anniversary of their deaths, and there to celebrate communion. Once again,
the idea was that they too were part of the church, and that communion
joined the living and the dead in a single body. It was this practice that gave
rise to saints' days; these usually celebrated, not their birthday, but the day
of their martyrdom.

More frequently than in catacombs or cemeteries, Christians gathered
in private homes. There are indications of this in the New Testament. Later,
as congregations grew, some houses were exclusively devoted to divine
worship. Thus, the oldest Christian church, found in the excavations of
Dura-Europos and built before A.D. 256, seems to have been a private
dwelling that was converted into a church.

Another consequence of the growth of congregations was that it soon
became impossible for all Christians in a particular city to gather together for
worship. The unity of the body of Christ was so important that it seemed that
something was lost when in a single city there were several congregations.
In order to preserve and symbolize the bond of unity, the custom arose in
some places to send a piece of bread from the communion service in the
bishop's church—the "fragmentum"—to be added to the bread to be used
in other churches in the same city. Also, in order to preserve and symbolize
the unity of Christians all over the world, each church had a list of bishops
of other churches, both near and far, for whom prayer was to be made during
communion. These lists were usually written on two writing tablets hinged
or strung together, as was then customary for such notes and for some official
communications. These sets of tablets were called "diptychs," and at a later
date the deletion of someone's name from a church's diptychs became a
matter of grave importance. Just as the bond of unity was sealed by the
inclusion of a name, that bond was broken by deleting a name.

At the beginning, the Christian calendar was rather simple and was
basically a weekly calendar. Every Sunday was a sort of Easter, and a day of
joy; and every Friday was a day of penance, fasting, and sorrow. Rather early,
for reasons that are not altogether clear, Wednesday also became a day of
fasting. Once a year there was a very special Sunday, the day of resurrection,

the greatest of Christian celebrations. Unfortunately, Christians were not in agreement as to when the great day was to be celebrated, for some thought it should be set in accordance with the Jewish Passover, while others believed that it should always be celebrated on a Sunday. By the second century there were bitter debates about the matter. To this day, although for other reasons, not all churches agree on the manner in which the date of Easter Sunday is to be determined. Part of what took place at Easter was the baptism of new converts, and the renewal of the vows of baptism by those who were already Christian. In preparation for these events, there was a time of fasting and penance. This is the origin of our present-day Lent. Pentecost, a feast of Jewish origin, was also celebrated by Christians from a very early date.

The earliest feast day in connection with the birth of Jesus was January 6, Epiphany, the day of his manifestation. This was originally the celebration of the birth itself. Later, particularly in some areas of the Latin West, December 25 began to take its place. This latter date was actually a pagan festival which, after the time of Constantine, was preempted by the celebration of Christmas.

Baptism was, besides communion, the other great event of Christian worship. As has already been said, in order to partake of communion one had to be baptized. In Acts we are told that people were baptized as soon as they were converted. This was feasible in the early Christian community, where most converts came from Judaism or had been influenced by it, and thus had a basic understanding of the meaning of Christian life and proclamation. But, as the Church became increasingly Gentile, it was necessary to require a period of preparation, trial, and instruction prior to baptism. This was the "catechumenate," which, by the beginning of the third century, lasted three years. During that time, catechumens received instruction on Christian doctrine, and were to give signs in their daily lives of the depth of their conviction. Finally, shortly before being baptized, they were examined and added to the list of those to be baptized.

Usually baptism was administered once a year, on Easter Sunday. Early in the third century it was customary for those about to be baptized to fast on Friday and Saturday, and to be baptized very early Sunday morning, which was the time of the Resurrection of Jesus. The candidates were completely naked, the men separated from the women. On emerging from the waters, the neophytes were given white robes, as a sign of their new life in Christ (see Col. 3:9–12 and Rev. 3:4). They were also given water to drink, as a sign that they were thoroughly cleansed, both outside and inside. Then they were anointed, thus making them part of the royal priesthood; and were given milk and honey, as a sign of the Promised Land into which they were now entering.

After all the candidates were baptized, the entire congregation went in procession to the meeting place, where the neophytes partook of communion for the first time.

Baptism was usually by immersion. The *Teaching of the Twelve Apostles,* a document of uncertain date, prefers that it be done in "living"—that is, running—water. But where water was scarce it could be administered by pouring water three times over the head, in the name of the Father, the Son, and the Holy Spirit.

To this day, scholars are not in agreement as to whether the early church baptized infants. By the early third century, there are indications that sometimes the children of Christian parents were baptized as infants. But all earlier documents, and many later ones, provide such scant information that it is impossible to decide one way or the other.

The Organization of the Church

It is clear that early in the second century there were in the church three distinct positions of leadership: bishop, presbyter—or elder—and deacon. Some historians have claimed that this hierarchy is apostolic in origin. But the truth is that the extant documents would seem to point in an opposite direction. Although the New Testament does refer to bishops, presbyters, and deacons, these three titles do not appear together, as if they were three clearly defined functions that always existed together. Actually, the New Testament would seem to indicate that the organization of local churches varied from place to place, and that for a certain time the titles of "bishop" and "elder" were interchangeable. There are also some historians who are inclined to believe that some churches—Rome included—were not led by a single bishop, but rather by a group of leaders who were called either "bishops" or "presbyters."

As has already been explained, the emphasis on the authority of bishops and on apostolic succession was a part of the response of the church to the challenge of heresies in the late second and early third centuries. As the church became increasingly Gentile, the danger of heresies was greater, and this in turn led to a greater stress on episcopal authority.

The place of women in the leadership of the early church deserves special attention. It is clear that by the end of the second century the leadership of the church was entirely masculine. But the matter is not quite as clear in earlier times. Particularly in the New Testament, there are indications that women also had positions of leadership. Philip had four daughters who "prophesied"—that is, who preached. Phoebe was a female deacon in Cenchreae, and Junias was counted among the apostles. What actually seems to have taken place is that during the second century, in its efforts to combat heresy, the church centralized its authority, and a by-product of that process was that women were excluded from positions of leadership. But still in the early years of the second century, governor Pliny informed Trajan that he had ordered that two Christian "female ministers" be tortured.

When speaking of women in the early church, mention should be made of the particular role of widows. The book of Acts says that the primitive church helped support the widows in its midst. This was in part an act of obedience to the repeated Old Testament injunction to care for the widow, the orphan, and the sojourner. But it was also a matter of practical necessity, for a widow deprived of means of support either had to remarry or to seek refuge with her children. In either case, if the new husband or the child was not a Christian, the widow would be severely limited in her Christian life. Therefore, it soon became customary for the church to support its widows, and to give them particular responsibilities. In an earlier chapter, the story was told of a widow whose ministry was such that she enraged the pagans, and therefore became a martyr. Other widows devoted themselves to the instruction of catechumens. Eventually, the word "widow" changed its meaning within the church and came to mean, not a woman whose husband had died, but any unmarried woman who was supported by the community and who in turn performed some particular functions within it. Some were women who chose to remain unmarried in order to perform their ministry. It is then that one begins to read such strange phrases as "the virgins who are called widows." Eventually, this would give rise to feminine monasticism, which developed earlier than its masculine counterpart.

Missionary Methods

The enormous numerical growth of the church in its first centuries leads us to the question of what methods it used to achieve such growth. The answer may surprise some modern Christians, for the ancient church knew nothing

An early Christian marriage ceremony. The caption reads, "May you live in God."

of "evangelistic services" or "revivals." On the contrary, in the early church worship centered on communion, and only baptized Christians were admitted to its celebration. Therefore, evangelism did not take place in church services, but rather, as Celsus said, in kitchens, shops, and markets. A few famous teachers, such as Justin and Origen, held debates in their schools, and thus won some converts among the intelligentsia. But the fact remains that most converts were made by anonymous Christians whose witness led others to their faith. The most dramatic form taken by such witness was obviously that of suffering unto death, and it is for this reason that the word "martyr," which originally meant "witness," took on the meaning that it has for us. Finally, some Christians were reputed for their miracles, which also won converts.

The most famous of these workers of miracles was Gregory Thaumaturgus—a name that means "wonderworker." He was from the region of Pontus, and had been converted through the learned witness of Origen. But upon returning to Pontus and becoming bishop of Neocaesarea, his great evangelistic success was due, not to his theological arguments, but to the miracles that he was said to perform. These were mostly miracles of healing, but we are also told that he could control the course of a river in flood, and that the apostles and the Virgin appeared to him and guided his work. Gregory was also one of the first to use a missionary method that has appeared again and again in later times: he substituted Christian festivals for the old pagan ones, and made sure that the Christian celebrations outdid the others.

Another surprising fact about the early expansion of Christianity is that, after the New Testament, very little is said of any missionaries going from place to place, like Paul and Barnabas had done. It is clear that the enormous spread of the Gospel in those first few centuries was not due to full-time missionaries, but rather to the many Christians who traveled for other reasons —slaves, merchants, exiles condemned to work in the mines, and the like.

Finally, one should note that Christianity spread mainly in the cities, and that it penetrated the rural areas slowly and with much difficulty. It was long after Constantine that Christianity could claim most of the rural population of the Empire.

The Beginnings of Christian Art

Since at first Christians gathered in private homes, it is not likely that there were in their meeting places many decorations or symbols alluding to the Christian faith. If there were any, they certainly have not survived. But as soon as Christians began having their own cemeteries—the catacombs—and

A Roman mosaic of Christ. Note the "Chi Rho" monogram behind his head.

their own churches—such as the one in Dura-Europos—Christian art began to develop. This early art is found mostly in simple frescoes—paintings on walls—in catacombs and churches, and in the carved sarcophagi—stone coffins—in which some of the wealthier Christians were buried.

Since communion was the central act of worship, scenes and symbols referring to it are most frequent. Sometimes what is depicted is the celebration itself, or the Lord's Supper in the upper room. In other cases there is simply a basket with fish and bread.

The fish was one of the earliest Christian symbols, and for that reason appears frequently in communion scenes as well as in other contexts. The significance of the fish, apart from its connection with the miraculous feeding of the multitudes, was that the Greek word for fish—*ichthys*—could be used as an acrostic containing the initial letters of the phrase: "Jesus Christ, Son of God, Savior." For this reason the fish appears, not only in representative art, but also in some of the most ancient Christian epitaphs. Thus, for instance, the epitaph of Abercius, bishop of Hierapolis towards the end of the second century, says that faith nourished Abercius with "a fresh water fish, very large and pure, fished by an immaculate virgin" (Mary, or the church?). And other similar epitaphs speak of "the divine race of the heavenly fish," and "the peace of the fish."

Other scenes in primitive Christian art refer to various biblical episodes: Adam and Eve, Noah in the ark, water coming out of the rock in the desert, Daniel in the lions' pit, the three young men in the fiery furnace, Jesus and the Samaritan woman, the raising of Lazarus, and so forth. Generally, what one finds is very simple art, more allusive than realistic. For example, Noah is often depicted as standing in a box that is hardly large enough to keep him afloat.

In conclusion, the ancient Christian church was composed mostly of humble folk for whom the fact of having been adopted as heirs of the King of Kings was a source of great joy. This was expressed in the joy of their worship, in their art, in their life together, and in their valiant deaths. The daily life of most of these Christians took place in the drab routine in which the poor in all societies must live. But they rejoiced in the hope of a new light that would destroy the dark injustice and idolatry of their society.

12/The Great Persecution and the Final Victory

I am concerned only about the law of God, which I have learned. That is the law which I obey, and in which I shall overcome. Besides that law, there is no other.

THELICA, MARTYR

After the persecutions of Decius and Valerian, the church enjoyed a long period of relative peace. Early in the fourth century, however, the last and worst persecution broke out. The reigning emperor was Diocletian, who had reorganized the Empire and brought renewed prosperity. Part of Diocletian's reorganization had consisted in placing the government on the shoulders of a team of four emperors. Two of these had the title of "augustus": Diocletian himself in the East, and Maximian in the West. Under each of them there was a junior emperor with the title of "caesar": Galerius under Diocletian, and Constantius Chlorus under Maximian. Thanks to Diocletian's political and administrative gifts, this division of power worked quite well as long as he held ultimate authority. Its main purpose, however, was to ensure an orderly process of succession; for Diocletian planned that a "caesar" would succeed his "augustus," and that then the remaining emperors would appoint someone to fill the vacancy left by the promoted caesar. Diocletian hoped that this would avert the frequent civil wars that racked the Empire over the question of succession. As we shall see, this hope proved futile.

In any case, under Diocletian's administration the Empire was enjoying relative peace and prosperity. Apart from recurring skirmishes on the borders, only Galerius had to undertake significant military campaigns, one along the Danube and another against the Persians. Of the three emperors,

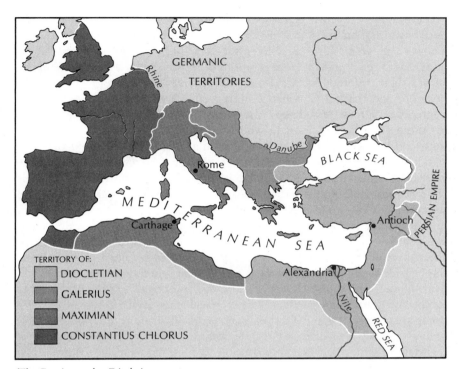

The Empire under Diocletian

it seems that only Galerius had given any indication of enmity towards Christianity. Both Diocletian's wife, Prisca, and their daughter, Valeria, were Christians. The peace of the church seemed assured.

The first difficulties probably appeared in the army. There was no general agreement among Christians regarding military service, for, while most church leaders of the time said that Christians should not be soldiers, there were many believers in the legions. In any case, around A.D. 295 a number of Christians were condemned to death, some for refusing to join the army, and others for trying to leave it. Galerius saw this attitude of Christians towards military service as a serious danger, for it was conceivable that at a critical moment the Christians in the army would refuse to obey orders. Therefore, as a measure required for military morale, Galerius convinced Diocletian that all Christians should be expelled from the legions. Diocletian's edict did not order any further penalty for Christians besides expulsion from the ranks of the military. But in some areas, probably due to an excess of zeal on the part of some officers who did not wish to see their ranks thinned, there were attempts to force Christian soldiers to deny their faith. The result was a number of executions, all of them in the army of the Danube, under the command of Galerius.

After these events, Galerius seems to have been increasingly predisposed against Christians, and in 303 he finally convinced Diocletian to issue a new edict against Christians. Even then, the purpose was not to kill Christians, but to remove them from positions of responsibility within the Empire. It was then ordered that Christians be removed from every government position, and that all Christian buildings and books be destroyed. At the beginning, there were no sterner measures. But soon the conflict grew worse, for there were many Christians who refused to turn over their sacred writings, and in such cases they were tortured and condemned to death.

Then fire broke out twice in the imperial palace. Galerius accused the Christians of having set it, seeking revenge for the destruction of their churches and the burning of their books. Some Christian writers of the period suggest that Galerius himself was responsible for the fires, which he had set in order to blame the Christians. Whatever the case may be, Diocletian's fury was not slow in coming, and it was decreed that all Christians in the imperial court must offer sacrifice before the gods. Prisca and Valeria complied, but the Grand Chamberlain Dorotheus and several others suffered martyrdom. Throughout the Empire churches and sacred writings were being set to the torch, and there were areas where overzealous officials followed the emperor's example and put Christians to death. The only area where there seems to have been a slight respite was the territory under the rule of Constantius Chlorus, where persecution was limited to tearing down some church buildings—at least, this is what we are told by historian Eusebius, who wished to present Constantius in the best possible light.

The situation grew worse. There were disturbances in some areas, and Diocletian became convinced that Christians were conspiring against him. He then decreed, first, that all the leaders of the churches be arrested and, somewhat later, that all Christians must offer sacrifice to the gods.

Thus was unleashed the most cruel of all the persecutions that the ancient church had to endure. Following the example of Decius, efforts were made to encourage Christians to abandon their faith. Accustomed as they were to the relative ease of several decades, many Christians succumbed. The rest were tortured with refined cruelty, and eventually killed in a variety of ways. A number were able to hide, and some of these took the sacred books with them. There were even a few who crossed the border into Persia—thus seeming to confirm the worst suspicions as to their lack of loyalty.

While all this was taking place, Galerius aspired to the supreme position within the Empire. In 304 Diocletian became ill and, although he survived, he felt weak and tired. Galerius went to him and, first with entreaties and finally with threats, induced him to abdicate. He also secured Maximian's abdication by threatening to invade his neighbor's territories with his clearly superior army. In 305 both Diocletian and Maximian abdicated, while Galerius and Constantius Chlorus took the title of augustus. The two caesars under them, Severus and Maximinus Daia, were Galerius' inept creatures.

The Diocletian persecution was the most cruel
that the ancient Church had to endure.

These arrangements, however, were not well received by many in the legions, where the sons of Constantius and Maximian, Constantine and Maxentius, were very popular. Constantine was a hostage in Galerius' court to insure the loyalty of Constantius Chlorus. But he escaped and joined his father. When the latter died, the troops refused to obey the designs of Galerius and proclaimed Constantine as their augustus. Meanwhile, Maxentius had taken Rome, and Severus, who ruled in the ancient capital, committed suicide. Galerius invaded the territories held by Maxentius. But his troops began to pass over to his rival's side, and he was forced to return to the eastern portion of the Empire, where his support was stronger. Finally, in desperation, Galerius appealed to Diocletian, asking him to come out of retirement and establish order. But Diocletian declared that he was quite happy growing cabbages in his retirement, and refused to resume the government of the Empire, although he was willing to lead the necessary negotiations among the various rivals. The final result was a very unstable arrangement, which included the appointment of a new augustus, Licinius. By then the claimants to various parts of the Empire were too numerous to list here, and further civil wars were clearly inevitable. Meanwhile Constantine, the son of Constantius Chlorus, was simply biding his time and strengthening his position in his territories in Gaul and Great Britain.

In the midst of such political chaos, persecution continued, although its impact depended on the policies set by each emperor in each region. In the West, most of the territory was under the effective control of Constantine and Maxentius, and neither of these two emperors enforced the decrees against Christians, which they saw as the work of their rival, Galerius. Galerius and his main protégé, Maximinus Daia, continued persecuting Christians. Maximinus sought to perfect the policies of Galerius by having Christians maimed and put to work in stone quarries. But then many of the condemned began organizing new churches in their places of punishment, and Maximinus had them killed or deported anew. The lists of martyrs grew longer and longer, and there seemed to be no end in sight.

Then help came from an unexpected quarter. Galerius became ill with a painful disease and, perhaps convinced by those Christians who said that this was a punishment from God, grudgingly decided to change his policy. On April 30, A.D. 311, he proclaimed:

With all the laws which we have decreed for the good of the state, we have sought to restore the ancient rules and traditional discipline of the Romans. We have particularly sought to have Christians, who had abandoned the faith of their ancestors, return to the truth. . . . After the promulgation of our edict ordering all to return to the ancient customs, many obeyed for fear of danger, and we were forced to punish others. But there are still many who persist on their opinions, and we are aware that they neither worship nor serve the gods, nor even their own god. Therefore, moved by our mercy to be benevolent towards all, it has seemed just to us to extend to them our pardon, and allow them to be Christians once again, and once again gather in their assemblies, as long as they do not interfere with public order.

In another edict we shall instruct our magistrates regarding this matter.

In return for our tolerance, Christians will be required to pray to their god for us, for the public good, and for themselves, so that the state may enjoy prosperity and they may live in peace.*

Such was the edict that ended the most cruel persecution that the church had to suffer from the Roman Empire. Soon prisons were opened, and forth came a multitude of people bearing the marks of torture, but thankful for what they saw as an intervention from on high.

Galerius died five days later, and Christian historian Lactantius, who made it a point to show that those who persecuted Christians died horrible deaths, declared that his repentance came too late.

---

*Eusebius of Caesarea, *Church History* 8.17.6–10.

The Empire was then divided among Licinius, Maximinus Daia, Constantine, and Maxentius. The first three recognized each other, and declared Maxentius to be an usurper. As to their policies towards Christians, Maximinus Daia was the only one who soon began anew the persecution that Galerius had stopped.

But a great political change was about to take place, which would put an end to persecution. Constantine, who during the previous intrigues and civil wars had limited his intervention to diplomatic maneuvering, began a campaign that would eventually make him master of the Empire. Suddenly, when least expected to do so, Constantine gathered his armies in Gaul, crossed the Alps and marched on Rome, Maxentius' capital. Taken by surprise, Maxentius was unable to defend his strongholds, which were rapidly occupied by Constantine's troops. All that he could do was to collect his army before Rome, and there fight the invader from Gaul. Rome itself was well-defended, and if Maxentius had chosen the wiser course, and remained behind the city walls, perhaps history would have taken a different turn. But instead, he consulted his augurs, who advised him to present battle.

According to two Christian chroniclers who knew Constantine, on the eve of the battle he had a revelation. One of our sources, Lactantius, says that it was in a dream that Constantine received the command to place a Christian symbol on the shields of his soldiers. The other chronicler, Eusebius, says that the vision appeared in the sky, with the words, "in this you shall conquer." In any case, the fact remains that Constantine ordered that his soldiers should use on their shield and on their standard or *labarum* a symbol that looked like the superimposition of the Greek letters chi and rho. Since these are the first two letters of the name, "Christ," this *labarum* could well have been a Christian symbol. Although eventually Christians saw in this the great moment of Constantine's conversion, historians point out that even after this event Constantine continued worshiping the Unconquered Sun. In truth, Constantine's conversion was a long process, to which we shall return in the next chapter.

In any case, the important fact is that Maxentius was defeated, and that as he fought on the Milvian bridge he fell into the river and drowned. Constantine thus became master of the entire western half of the Empire.

Once his campaign had begun, Constantine moved rapidly. After the battle of the Milvian bridge, he met with Licinius at Milan, and there concluded an alliance with him. Part of what was agreed there was that the persecution of Christians would stop, and that their churches, cemeteries, and other properties would be returned to them. This agreement, commonly known as the "Edict of Milan," marks the date usually given for the end of persecutions (A.D. 313), although in truth Galerius' edict was much more important, and even after the "Edict of Milan" Maximinus Daia continued his policy of persecution. Eventually, through a series of steps that shall be told in the next chapter, Constantine became sole emperor, and persecution came to an end.

Whether this was in truth a victory, or the beginning of new and perhaps greater difficulties, will be the theme of many of the chapters to follow. Whatever the case may be, there is no doubt that the conversion of Constantine had enormous consequences for Christianity, which was forced to face new questions. What would happen when those who called themselves servants of a carpenter, and whose great heroes were fisherfolk, slaves, and criminals condemned to death by the state, suddenly saw themselves surrounded by imperial pomp and power? Would they remain firm in their faith? Or would it be that those who had stood before tortures and before beasts would give way to the temptations of an easy life and of social prestige? These questions were the burning issues that the Christian church had to face in the next period of its history.

Suggested Readings

Henry Bettenson, ed. *Documents of the Christian Church.* London: Oxford, several editions.

E. C. Blackman. *Marcion and His Influence.* London: S.P.C.K., 1948.

Virginia Corwin. *St. Ignatius and Christianity in Antioch.* New Haven: Yale, 1960.

E. R. Dodds. *Pagan and Christian in an Age of Anxiety.* Cambridge: University Press, 1968.

W. H. C. Frend. *The Early Church.* Philadelphia: J. B. Lippincott, 1966.

Justo L. González. *A History of Christian Thought,* Vol. I. Nashville: Abingdon, 1970.

Edgar J. Goodspeed. *A History of Early Christian Literature.* Chicago: University of Chicago Press, 1966. Revised and enlarged by Robert M. Grant.

R. P. C. Hanson. *Tradition in the Early Church.* London: SCM, 1962.

Hans Jonas. *The Gnostic Religion.* Boston: Beacon Press, 1958.

Josef A. Jungman. *The Early Liturgy to the Time of Gregory the Great.* London: Darton, Longman & Todd, 1959.

Hans Lietzmann. *The Beginnings of the Christian Church.* London: Lutterworth, several editions.

Hans Lietzmann. *The Founding of the Church Universal.* London: Lutterworth, several editions.

Jaroslav Pelikan. *The Christian Tradition,* Vol. I. Chicago: University of Chicago Press, 1971.

Robert B. Workman. *Persecution in the Early Church.* London: Epworth Press, reprint, 1960.

PART II

THE IMPERIAL CHURCH

Chronology

Emperors	Bishops of Rome*	Events**
(306–337) Constantine	Sylvester (314–335)	Edict of Milan (313)
		Arian controversy begins
		Pachomius' first foundation (324)
		Council of Nicea (325)
		Constantinople founded (330)
	Marcus (335–336)	
Constantine II (337–340)	Julius (337–352)	
Constantius II (337–361)		
Constans (337–350)	Liberius (352–366)	Arianism at its apex
Julian (361–363)	*Felix II (353–365)*	Pagan reaction
Jovian (363–364)		
Valentinian I (364–375)		
Valens (364–378)	Damasus (366–383)	†Eusebius of Caesarea and
	Ursinus (366–367)	Athanasius (373)
Gratian (375–383)		Battle of Adrianople (378)
Valentinian II (375–392)	Siricius (384–399)	†Basil the Great (379)
		†Macrina (380)
Theodosius (379–395)		Council of Constantinople (381)
Maximus (383–388)		
		†Gregory of Nazianzus (389)
Eugenius (392–394)		†Gregory of Nyssa (395?)
Arcadius (395–408)		†Martin of Tours and
Honorius (395–423)	Anastasius (399–401)	Ambrose (397)
	Innocent (401–417)	†John Chrysostom (407)
Theodosius II (408–450)		
		Fall of Rome (410)
	Zosimus (417–418)	
		†Jerome (420)
		†Augustine (430)

*Bishops whom the Roman church does not recognize are in italics.
**Dagger (†) indicates that year given is year of death.

13/Constantine

*The eternal, holy and unfathomable
goodness of God does not allow us to
wander in darkness, but shows us the way
of salvation. . . . This I have seen in
others as well as in myself.*

CONSTANTINE

We have left Constantine at the moment when, after defeating Maxentius at the Milvian bridge, he joined Licinius in ordering the end of persecution. Although we have already indicated that eventually he became sole ruler of the Roman Empire, it now remains to follow the process by which he achieved that goal. The question of the nature and sincerity of his conversion must also be discussed. But what is of paramount importance for the story of Christianity is not so much how sincere Constantine was, or how he understood the Christian faith, as the impact of his conversion and his rule both during his lifetime and thereafter. That impact was such that it has even been suggested that until the twentieth century the church has lived in its "Constantinian era," and that we are now going through a crisis connected with the end of that long era. Whether or not this is true is a question to be discussed when our narrative comes to the twentieth century. In any case, Constantine's religious policies had such enormous effect on the course of Christianity that all of Part II may be seen as a series of reactions and adjustments in response to those policies.

From Rome to Constantinople

Long before the battle at the Milvian bridge, Constantine had been preparing to extend the territories under his rule. To that end, he took great care to develop a strong base of operations in Gaul and Great Britain. He spent over five years strengthening the borders along the Rhine, where the barbarians

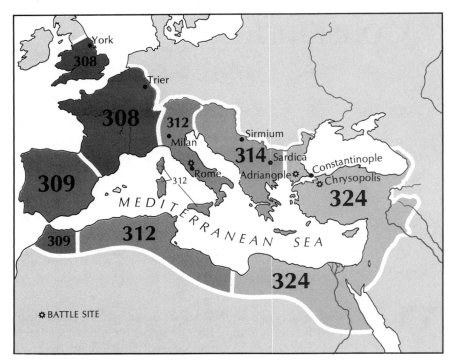

Constantine's Advancing Power

were a constant threat, and courting the favor of his subjects by his just and wise government. This did not make him an ideal ruler. His love of luxury and pomp was such that he built a grandiose and ornate palace in his capital city—Trier—while neglecting public works to such an extent that the drainage system of the nearby fields failed, and the vineyards that were the backbone of the local economy were flooded. Yet, he seems to have had that rare gift of rulers who know just how far they can tax their subjects without losing their loyalty. By securing the borders against barbarian incursions, Constantine won the gratitude of many in Gaul. Frequent and extravagant shows in the circus gained the support of those who prefered violence and blood—the barbarian captives thus sacrificed were so many that a chronicler of the times affirms that the shows lost some of their interest because the beasts grew tired of killing.

An astute statesman, Constantine challenged his rivals one at a time, always protecting his flanks before making the next move. Thus, although his campaign against Maxentius seemed sudden, he had been preparing for it, both militarily and politically, for many years. His military preparations were such that in his campaign against Maxentius he committed only one-fourth of his resources, thus making sure that during his absence there would not be a major barbarian invasion, or a revolt in his own territories. In the field of diplomacy, he had to make sure that Licinius, who was Maxentius' neigh-

Constantine would leave his mark on the Christian Church for more than a thousand years.

bor to the east, would not take advantage of Constantine's campaign to invade and lay claim to some of Maxentius' territories. In order to preclude that possibility, Constantine offered his half-sister Constance in marriage to Licinius, and he may also have made a secret agreement with his future brother-in-law. This would seem to cover his flank. But even then, he waited until Licinius was involved in a conflict with Maximinus Daia before launching his own invasion of Italy.

The victory at the Milvian bridge gave Constantine control of the western half of the Empire, while the East was still partitioned between Licinius and Maximinus Daia. A less astute statesman would have immediately moved against Licinius—for it seems that at this time Constantine had already decided that he would eventually go to war with him. But Constantine knew how to bide his time. As he had done earlier in Gaul, he now devoted his efforts to consolidate his power in his new territories. His meeting with Licinius in Milan seemed to strengthen their alliance, and forced Licinius to direct his efforts against their common rival, Maximinus Daia. Thus, while Constantine gathered further resources, Licinius was forced to spend his in a war with Maximinus. At Milan, Constantine further joined Licinius to his interests by fulfilling the promise of marrying him to Constance.

The two allies were still at Milan when news arrived that Maximinus had invaded Licinius' territories and taken the city of Byzantium. It appears that he knew that war was inevitable, and had decided to strike first. But Licinius moved rapidly, and Maximinus was still near Byzantium—later Constantinople, and now Istanbul—when his enemy appeared before him with a smaller army and defeated him. Maximinus was forced to flee, and died shortly thereafter.

The Empire was then divided between Licinius, who ruled over the entire area east of Italy, including Egypt, and Constantine, who controlled Italy as well as western Europe and North Africa. Since the two emperors were related by marriage, there was hope that the civil wars had come to an end. But the truth was that both Licinius and Constantine sought to rule the whole Empire, which, in spite of its vastness, was too small for both of them. For a while, each of the two rivals devoted himself to consolidate his power and to prepare for the inevitable conflict.

Finally, hostilities broke out. A conspiracy to murder Constantine was discovered, and the ensuing investigation implicated a relative of Licinius who had fled to his kinsman's territories. Licinius refused to send his relative to Constantine to be executed, and eventually declared war on Constantine. Although Christian historians have usually laid all the blame for this conflict on Licinius, the truth is that Constantine wished to go to war with his brother-in-law, but was able to make his rival appear as the aggressor.

Constantine then invaded Licinius' territories. Two battles were indecisive, but Constantine proved to be the better strategist by taking Byzantium. Since Licinius was on the European side of his territories, and Byzantium controlled communications with Asia, where the main body of his resources was, Licinius was effectively cut from those resources and had to sue for peace.

Once again, Constantine showed that he was an able statesman and a patient man. He had a good chance of crushing Licinius by refusing to make peace. But to do this he would have to lead his armies far from the base of

Licinius was Constantine's brother-in-law and his main rival.

his power, and there was always the possibility that Licinius would gain the upper hand by a maneuver similar to Constantine's own taking of Byzantium. He therefore was content with taking most of Licinius' European territories.

This took place late in 314, and a period of peace followed. Once again, Constantine used that time to consolidate his power in the newly conquered territories. Instead of residing in the West, he established his headquarters in Sirmium—in what is now Yugoslavia—and later in Sardica—now Sofia. Both cities were in the recently conquered territories, and thus Constantine was able to keep an eye on Licinius and to strengthen his rule over the area.

The truce lasted until 322, although there was an ever-increasing tension between the two emperors. The main reason for conflict was still the ambition of both men, which found expression in the question of what titles and honors were to be given to their sons. But by the time war finally broke out, the question of religious policy had also become a bone of contention.

Licinius' religious policy needs to be clarified, for after Constantine's victory some Christian writers, in order to justify his actions against Licinius, made the latter appear in a bad light. For a number of years after the Edict of Milan, Licinius took no measures against Christians. Actually, a contemporary Christian writer, in telling the story of Licinius' victory over Maximinus Daia, makes it sound very similar to Constantine's victory over Maxentius—including a vision. But Christianity in Licinius' territories was divided over a number of issues, and such divisions led to public disorders. When Licinius used his imperial powers to assure peace, there were groups of Christians that considered themselves wronged, and who began thinking of Constantine as the defender of the true faith, and as "the emperor whom God loved." Licinius was not a Christian, but there are indications that he feared the power of the Christian God; and therefore, when he learned that his subjects were praying for his rival, he felt that this was high treason. It was then that he took measures against some Christians, and this in turn gave Constantine to opportunity to present himself as the defender of Christianity against Licinius the persecutor.

In 322, Constantine invaded Licinius' territories, using the pretext that he was in pursuit of a band of barbarians who had crossed the Danube. Licinius interpreted this, rightly or wrongly, as an intentional provocation, and prepared for war by gathering his troops at Adrianople, where he awaited Constantine's somewhat smaller armies.

Contemporary chroniclers affirm that Licinius feared the magical power of Constantine's *labarum,* and that he ordered his soldiers to avoid looking at the Christian emblem, and not to direct a frontal attack against it. If this is true, it must have demoralized his troops. In any case, after a long and bloody battle, Constantine's smaller army won the day and Licinius fled to Byzantium.

Licinius hoped to be able to hold Byzantium indefinitely, for his fleet was stronger than Constantine's, and he could always receive reinforcements by sea. But his admiral was inexperienced, and most of his fleet was wrecked by a storm. Fearful of being completely cut off from the rest of his territories, Licinius then crossed to Asia Minor. Constantine followed him there, and after a series of defeats Licinius lost heart. His wife Constance—probably accompanied by Bishop Eusebius of Nicomedia, who will have an important role to play as our story unfolds—went in his name to her brother Constantine, who promised to spare Licinius' life in exchange for his abdication. After many years of planning and warring, Constantine was master of the entire Roman Empire. Shortly thereafter, Licinius was murdered. Some chroniclers claim that he was conspiring against Constantine; others hint that Constantine either ordered his death or at least approved of it.

Constantine would reign for the next thirteen years, until his death in 337. Compared with the previous civil wars, this was a period of rebuilding and prosperity. But there was always political uneasiness, and quite a few people were condemned to death for real or supposed conspiracies against the emperor—among them his oldest son, Crispus, who had commanded his father's fleet in the war against Licinius.

Constantine had not sought absolute power for the mere pleasure of it. He also dreamed, like Decius and Diocletian before him, of restoring the ancient glory of the Empire. The main difference was that, whereas Decius and Diocletian had sought that end through a restoration of paganism, Constantine believed that it could best be achieved on the basis of Christianity. Some of the staunchest opponents of this policy were in Rome, particularly in its Senate, where the members of the old aristocracy bemoaned the eclipse of their ancient gods and privileges. Several years before his final struggle with Licinius, Constantine had clashed with the interests of the Roman Senate. Now, as absolute master of the Empire, he set out on a bold course: he would build a "New Rome," an impregnable and monumental city, which would be called Constantinople—that is, "city of Constantine."

It may well have been during his campaign against Licinius that Constantine became aware of the strategic value of Byzantium. That city was at the very edge of Europe, where it almost touched Asia Minor. Thus, it could serve as a bridge between the European and the Asiatic portions of the Empire. Furthermore, if properly fortified, Byzantium would control the Bosporus, through which all shipping had to pass in its way from the Mediterranean to the Black Sea. A peace treaty made with Persia several decades earlier was about to expire, and the emperor felt the need to establish his headquarters near the Eastern border. But at the same time the Germanic tribes on the Rhine were always a threat, and therefore it would not be wise for the emperor to settle too far from the West. For all these reasons, Byzantium seemed the ideal location for the new capital. Constantine's choice—for which he took no credit, claiming that he was following instructions from God—proved to be most wise, for the city that he founded would play a strategic role for centuries to come.

But ancient Byzantium was too small for the grandiose dreams of the great emperor. Its walls, built during the reign of Septimius Severus, were scarcely two miles long. Aping the ancient legend of Romulus and Remus and the founding of Rome, Constantine went to the fields far beyond the ancient walls, and with his lance marked the route that the new walls should follow. This was done amid great ceremonies in which both Christians and pagan priests took part. When those who followed the emperor, seeing him walk far into the countryside, asked him how far he intended to go, he is said to have answered: "As far as the One who walks ahead of me." Naturally, Christians in his entourage would have understood these words to refer to their God, whereas pagans would have taken them to mean one of their gods, or perhaps the Unconquered Sun. By the end of the ceremonies, Constantine had set aside a vast area, capable of holding a teeming multitude.

Construction began immediately. Since the materials and skilled artisans available were not enough to meet Constantine's timetable, statues, columns, and other such things were brought from various cities. Constantine's agents scoured the Empire in search of anything that could embellish the new capital. Years later, Jerome would say that Constantinople was dressed in the nakedness of the rest of the Empire. A number of statues of pagan gods were taken from their ancient temples and placed in such public places as the hippodrome, the public baths, or the squares. Thus used as mere ornaments, the ancient gods seemed to be losing their old power.

Many signs of ancient Constantinople can still be seen in modern Istanbul.

Perhaps the most famous statue thus taken to Constantinople was the image of Apollo said to be the work of Phidias, one of the best sculptors of all time. This was placed in the middle of the city, atop a huge stone column brought from Egypt, and which was reputed to be the largest such monolith in the world. To make it even taller, the column was placed on a marble pedestal that was over twenty feet high. The entire monument measured approximately 125 feet from top to bottom. But the statue itself no longer represented Apollo, for a new head, that of Constantine, had been placed on it.

Other great public works were the basilica of Saint Irene—that is, holy peace—the hippodrome, and the public baths. Also, a great palace was built for the emperor, and the few noble families that agreed to move from Old Rome were given replicas of their ancestral mansions.

All this, however, did not suffice to populate the new city. To that end, Constantine granted all sorts of privileges to those who came to live there, such as exemption from taxes and from military service. Soon it became customary to give free oil, wheat, and wine to the citizens of Constantinople. The result was that the city grew at such an incredible rate that a century later, under Theodosius II, it was necessary to build new walls, for the population had outgrown the ones that in Constantine's time had seemed excessively ambitious.

As will be seen in future chapters of this history, Constantine's decision to found a new capital had important consequences, for shortly thereafter the western portion of the Empire—old Rome included—was overrun by the barbarians, and Constantinople became the center that for a thousand years kept alive the political and cultural inheritance of the old Empire. Since its capital was in ancient Byzantium, this eastern Roman Empire was also called the Byzantine Empire.

From the Unconquered Sun to Jesus Christ

The nature of Constantine's conversion has been the subject of many debates. Shortly after the events told in this chapter, there were Christian authors—one of whom we shall meet in the next chapter—who sought to show that the emperor's conversion was the goal towards which the history of the church and of the Empire had always been moving. Others have claimed that Constantine was simply a shrewd politician who became aware of the advantages to be drawn from a "conversion."

Both interpretations are exaggerated. It suffices to read the documents of the time to become aware that Constantine's conversion was very different from that of other Christians. At that time, people who were converted were put through a long process of discipline and instruction, in order to make certain that they understood and lived their new faith, and then they were baptized. Their bishop became their guide and shepherd as they sought to discover the implications of their faith in various situations in life.

Constantine's case was very different. Even after the battle of the Milvian bridge, and throughout his entire life, he never placed himself under the direction of Christian teachers or bishops. Christians such as Lactantius— tutor to his son Crispus—formed part of his entourage. Hosius, bishop of Cordova, became for a time his liaison with other ecclesiastical leaders. But Constantine reserved the right to determine his own religious practices, and even to intervene in the life of the church, for he considered himself "bishop of bishops." Repeatedly, even after his conversion, he took part in pagan rites in which no Christian would participate, and the bishops raised no voice of condemnation.

The reason for this was not only that the emperor was both powerful and irascible, but also that, in spite of his policies favoring Christianity, and of his repeated confession of the power of Christ, he was not technically a Christian, for he had not been baptized. In fact, it was only on his deathbed that he was baptized. Therefore, any policy or edict favoring Christianity was received by the church as the action of one who was friendly or even inclined to become a Christian, but who had not taken the decisive step. And any religious or moral deviations on Constantine's part were seen in the same light, as the unfortunate actions of one who, while inclined to become a Christian, was not one of the faithful. Such a person could receive the advice and even the support of the church, but not its direction. This ambiguous situation continued until Constantine's final hour.

On the other hand, there are several reasons why Constantine cannot be seen as a mere opportunist who declared himself in favor of Christianity in order to court the support of Christians. First of all, such a view is rather anachronistic, for it tends to see Constantine as a forerunner of modern politicians. At that time, even the most incredulous did not approach religious matters with such a calculating attitude. Secondly, if Constantine had been such an opportunist, he chose a poor time to seek the support of Christians. When he put the Chi-Rho on his *labarum,* he was preparing to go to battle for the city of Rome, center of pagan traditions, where his main supporters were the members of the old aristocracy who considered themselves oppressed by Maxentius. Christians were stronger, not in the West, where the battle was to be fought, but in the East, to which Constantine would lay claim only years later. Finally, it should be pointed out that whatever support Christians could give Constantine was of doubtful value. Given the ambivalence of the church toward military service, the number of soldiers in the army, particularly in the West, was relatively small. Among the civilian population, most Christians belonged to the lower classes, and thus had scarce economic resources to put at the disposal of Constantine. After almost three centuries of tension with the Empire, it was impossible to predict what would be the attitude of Christians before such an unexpected thing as a Christian emperor.

The truth is probably that Constantine was a sincere believer in the power of Christ. But this does not mean that he understood that power in the same way in which it had been experienced by those Christians who had died for it. For him, the Christian God was a very powerful being who would support him as long as he favored the faithful. Therefore, when Constantine enacted laws in favor of Christianity, and when he had churches built, what he sought was not the goodwill of Christians, but rather the goodwill of their God. It was this God who gave him the victory at the Milvian bridge, as well as the many that followed. In a way, Constantine's understanding of Christianity was similar to Licinius', when the latter feared the supernatural power of his rival's *labarum*. The difference was simply that Constantine had laid claim to that power by serving the cause of Christians. This interpretation of Constantine's faith is supported by his own statements, which reveal a sincere man whose understanding of the Christian message was meager.

This did not prevent the emperor from serving other gods. His own father had been a devotee of the Unconquered Sun. While not denying the existence of other gods, the worship of the Unconquered Sun was addressed to the Supreme Being, whose symbol was the sun. During most of his political career, Constantine seems to have thought that the Unconquered Sun and the Christian God were compatible—perhaps two views of the same Supreme Deity—and that the other gods, although subordinate, were nevertheless real and relatively powerful. Thus, on occasion, he would consult the oracle of Apollo, accept the title of High Priest that had traditionally been the prerogative of emperors, and partake of all sorts of pagan ceremonies without thinking that he was thus betraying or abandoning the God who had given him victory and power.

Besides, Constantine was a shrewd politician. His power was such that he could favor Christians, build churches, and even have some images of gods moved to Constantinople to serve as ornaments in his dream city. But if he had attempted to suppress pagan worship, he would soon have had to face an irresistible opposition. The ancient gods were far from forgotten. Christianity had made very little progress among the old aristocracy and the rural masses. There were in the army many followers of Mithra and other gods. The Academy of Athens and the Museum of Alexandria, the two great centers of learning of the time, were devoted to the study of ancient pagan wisdom. An imperial decree could not undo all this—not yet, anyway. And in any case the emperor himself, who saw no contradiction between the Unconquered Sun and the Incarnate Son, was not inclined to issue such a decree.

Given these circumstances, Constantine's religious policy followed a slow but constant process. It is likely that this process responded both to the demands of political realities and to Constantine's own inner development, as he progressively left behind the ancient religion and gained a better understanding of the new one. At first, he simply put an end to persecution and ordered that confiscated Christian property be returned. Shortly thereafter he gave new signs of favoring Christianity, such as donating to the church the Lateran palace in Rome, which had belonged to his wife, or putting the imperial posts at the service of bishops traveling to attend the Synod of Arles in 314. At the same time, he sought to keep good relations with those who followed the ancient religions, and most especially with the Roman Senate. The official religion of the Empire was paganism, and as head of that Empire Constantine took the title of Supreme Pontiff or High Priest, and performed the functions that corresponded to that title. On coins minted as late as 320 one finds the names and symbols of the ancient gods, as well as the monogram for the name of Christ—the ☧ that Constantine had used for the first time at the Milvian bridge.

The campaign against Licinius gave Constantine occasion to appear as the champion of Christianity. He was now moving into the territories where, for quite a time, the church had counted the greatest number of adherents. Thus, after defeating Licinius, Constantine was able to appoint a number of Christians to high positions in government. Since his tensions with the Roman Senate were growing, and that body was promoting a resurgence of paganism, Constantine felt increasingly inclined to favor Christianity.

In A.D. 324 an imperial edict ordered all soldiers to worship the Supreme God on the first day of the week. This was the day on which Christians celebrated the resurrection of their Lord. But it was also the day of the Unconquered Sun, and therefore pagans saw no reason to oppose such an edict. A year later, in 325, the great assembly of bishops that was later to be known as the First Ecumenical Council gathered at Nicea.* That assembly was called by the emperor, who once again put the imperial posts at the disposal of the traveling bishops.

The founding of Constantinople was a further step in that process. The very act of creating a "New Rome" was an attempt to diminish the power of the ancient aristocratic families of Rome, who were mostly pagan. And the raiding of pagan temples for statues and other objects with which to embellish the new capital was a blow to paganism, many of whose ancient shrines lost the gods that were objects of local devotion. At the same time, the building of new and sumptuous churches contrasted with the sacking of the old temples.

In spite of all this, almost to his dying day Constantine continued functioning as the High Priest of paganism. After his death, the three sons who succeeded him did not oppose the Senate's move to have him declared a god. Thus the ironic anomaly occurred, that Constantine, who had done so much to the detriment of paganism, became one of the pagan gods.

---

*See the Appendix for a list of all the Ecumenical Councils, with dates and primary decisions.

The Impact of Constantine

Constantine's impact on the life of the church was such that it was still felt as late as the twentieth century. But there were also more immediate consequences of his reign and policies, changes in the life of the church that became apparent almost immediately.

Obviously, the most immediate consequence of Constantine's conversion was the cessation of persecution. Until then, even at times of relative peace, Christians had lived under the threat of persecution, and what was for many the hope of martyrdom. After Constantine's conversion, that threat and that hope dissipated. The few pagan emperors who reigned after him did not generally persecute Christians, but rather tried to restore paganism by other means.

One of the results of the new situation was the development of what may be called an "official theology." Overwhelmed by the favor that the emperor was pouring on them, many Christians sought to show that Constantine was chosen by God to bring the history of both church and Empire to its culmination, where both were joined. Typical of this attitude was church historian Eusebius of Caesarea—not to be confused with Eusebius of Nicomedia—who will be the subject of the next chapter.

Others took the opposite tack. For them, the fact that the emperors declared themselves Christian, and that for this reason people were flocking to the church, was not a blessing, but rather a great apostasy. Some who tended to look at matters under this light, but did not wish to break communion with the rest of the church, withdrew to the desert, there to lead a life of meditation and asceticism. Since martyrdom was no longer possible, these people believed that the true athlete of Christ must continue training, if no longer for martyrdom, then for monastic life. The fourth century thus witnessed a massive exodus of devoted Christians to the deserts of Egypt and Syria. This early monastic movement will be the subject of Chapter 15.

Others with a negative reaction to the new state of affairs felt that the best course was simply to break communion with the church at large, now become the imperial church, which was to be considered sinful and apostate. To these we shall turn in Chapter 16.

Among those who remained in the church, withdrawing neither into the desert nor into schism, there was a great deal of intellectual activity. As in every such period, there were some who proposed theories and doctrines that the rest of the church felt it had to reject. Most important of these was Arianism, which gave rise to bitter controversies regarding the doctrine of the Trinity. In Chapter 17 we shall discuss these controversies up to the year 361, when Julian became emperor.

Julian's reign marked the high point of another attitude towards Constantine's conversion: pagan reaction. Chapter 18 will deal with that reign and the attempt to revitalize paganism.

Most Christians, however, reacted to the new situation with neither total acceptance nor total rejection. Most church leaders saw the new circumstances as offering unexpected opportunities, but also great dangers. Thus, while affirming their loyalty to the emperor, as most Christians had always done, they insisted that their ultimate loyalty belonged only to God. Such was the attitude of the great "fathers" of the church—a misnomer, for there were also some "mothers" among them. Since both danger and opportunity were great, these leaders faced a difficult task. Perhaps not all their decisions and attitudes were correct; but, in any case, this was an age of giants who would shape the church for centuries to come.

However, before we turn to the various reactions to Constantine's conversion, we must pause to considered the impact of that conversion on worship, which is the point at which most rank and file Christians probably felt that impact most directly.

Until Constantine's time, Christian worship had been relatively simple. At first, Christians gathered to worship in private homes. Then they began to gather in cemeteries, such as the Roman catacombs. By the third century there were structures set aside for worship. The oldest church that archaeologists have discovered is that of Dura-Europos, which dates from about A.D. 250. This is a fairly small room, decorated with very simple murals.

After Constantine's conversion, Christian worship began to be influenced by imperial protocol. Incense, which was used as a sign of respect for the emperor, began appearing in Christian churches. Officiating ministers, who until then had worn everyday clothes, began dressing in more luxurious garments. Likewise, a number of gestures indicating respect, which were normally made before the emperor, now became part of Christian worship. The custom was also introduced of beginning services with a processional. Choirs were developed, partly in order to give body to that procession. Eventually, the congregation came to have a less active role in worship.

Already in the second century, it had become customary to commemorate the anniversary of a martyr's death by celebrating communion where the martyr had been buried. Now churches were built in many of those places. Eventually, some came to think that worship was particularly valid if it was celebrated in one of those holy places, where the relics of a martyr were present. In consequence, some began to unearth the buried bodies of martyrs in order to place them—or part of them—under the altar of one of the many churches that were being built. Others began claiming revelations of martyrs who had not been known, or who had been almost forgotten. Some even said that they had received visions telling them where a particular martyr was buried—as in the case of Ambrose and the supposed remains of Saints Gervasius and Protasius. Eventually, the relics of saints and of New Testament times were said to have miraculous powers. Empress Helena, the mother of

Constantine, gave special impetus to this entire development when, in a pilgrimage to the Holy Land, she thought she had discovered the very cross of Christ. Soon this cross was said to have miraculous powers, and pieces of wood claiming to come from it were found all over the Empire.

While these developments were taking place, many leaders of the church viewed them with disfavor, and tried to prevent superstitious extremes. Thus, a common theme of preaching was that it was not necessary to go to the Holy Land in order to be a good Christian, and that the respect due to the martyrs should not be exaggerated. But such preaching was unequal to the task, for people were flocking into the church in such numbers that there was little time to prepare them for baptism, and even less to guide them in the Christian life once they had been baptized.

The churches built in the time of Constantine and his successors contrasted with the simplicity of churches such as that of Dura-Europos. Constantine himself ordered that the church of Saint Irene—Holy Peace—be built in Constantinople. Helena, his mother, built in the Holy Land the Church of the Nativity and another one on the Mount of Olives. Similar churches were built in the major cities of the Empire, sometimes by imperial command, and sometimes simply following the example of the new capital. This policy continued under Constantine's successors, most of whom sought to perpetuate their memory by building great churches. Although most of the churches built by Constantine and his first successors have been destroyed, there is enough evidence to have a general idea of their basic plan—which in any case was copied in a number of later churches that still stand.

Some of these churches had an altar in the center, and their floor plan was polygonal or almost round. But most of them followed the basic rectangular plan of the "basilica." This was an ancient word which referred to the great public—or sometimes private—buildings whose main part was a great room divided into naves by two of more rows of columns. Since these structures provided the model for church buildings during the first centuries after Constantine's conversion, such churches came to be known as "basilicas."

In general, Christian basilicas had three main parts: the atrium, the naves, and the sanctuary. The atrium was the entryway, usually consisting of a rectangular area surrounded by walls. In the middle of the atrium was a fountain where the faithful could perform their ablutions—ritual washing—before entering the main part of the building. The side of the atrium abutting the rest of the basilica was called the narthex, and had one or more doors leading to the naves.

The naves were the most spacious section of the basilica. In the middle was the main nave, set aside from the lateral ones by rows of columns. The roof of the main nave was usually higher than the rest of the building, so that on the two rows of columns separating it from the other naves there were tall walls with windows that provided light. The lateral naves were lower and usually narrower than the main one. Since there were normally two or four rows of columns, some basilicas had a total of three naves, and others had five—although there were some basilicas with up to nine naves, very few had more than five.

Towards the end of the main nave, near the sanctuary, there was a section reserved for the choir, usually fenced in. On each of the two sides of this section there was a pulpit, which was used for the reading and exposition of Scripture as well as for the main cantor during the singing of the Psalms.

The sanctuary was at the end of the nave, with the floor at a higher level. It ran on a direction perpendicular to the nave, and was somewhat longer than the rest of the basilica was wide, thus giving the entire floor plan the shape of a cross or T. In a place near the middle of the sanctuary was the altar, where the elements were placed for the celebration of communion.

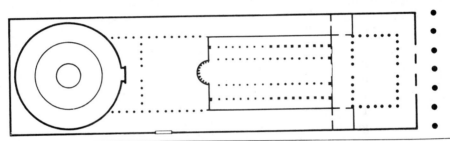

The floor plan of the Constantinian Church of the Holy Sepulchre is typical of the basilica, with rows of columns creating several naves (in this case, five). Note also the apse and atrium.

The back wall of the sanctuary, directly behind the main nave, was semicircular, thus forming the apse—a concave space behind the altar. Against the wall of the apse there were benches for the officiating ministers. If it was the main church of a bishop, amid these benches there was a chair for the bishop, the "cathedra"—which gave rise to the word "cathedral." On some occasions, the bishop would preach seated on the cathedra.

The inside of the basilica was richly adorned with polished marble, lamps and tapestries. But the characteristic medium of Christian art during that period—and long thereafter in the Eastern church—was the mosaic. Walls were covered with pictures made of very small colored pieces of stone, glass, or porcelain. Usually these mosaics represented scenes from the Bible or from Christian tradition. Sometimes there was also a mosaic of the person who had paid for the building, and this person is often depicted in the act of presenting a small replica of the basilica. Naturally, the main wall to be decorated was that of the apse. This usually was a great mosaic representing either the Virgin with the Child on her lap, or Christ seated in glory, as supreme ruler of the universe. This depiction of Christ, known as the "pantokrator"—that is, universal ruler—shows the impact of the new political situation on Christian art, for Christ is depicted as sitting on a throne, very much like a Roman emperor.

Near the basilica stood other buildings. The most important of these was the baptistry. This was usually round or polygonal, and was large enough to accommodate several dozen people. In its center was the baptismal pool, into which one descended by a series of steps. Here baptism was celebrated, normally by immersion or by pouring. (Actually, these were the normal ways of administering baptism at least until the ninth century. Baptism by dabbing water on the head had been practiced long before that, but usually only in extreme conditions of poor health, deathbed baptisms, or scarcity of water. It was in the colder areas of western Europe, in the ninth century, that this alternate form of baptism became more common. In Italy baptism by immersion was continued until the thirteenth century, and the Eastern churches—Greek, Russian, and so forth—still baptize by immersion.)

In the middle of the baptistry a great curtain separated the room in two, one side for men and the other for women; for in the fourth century one still descended to the waters naked, and was given a white robe on rising from them.

All this serves to illustrate what was taking place as a result of Constantine's conversion. The ancient church continued its traditional customs. Communion was still the central act of worship, celebrated every Sunday. Baptism was still by immersion, and kept a great deal of its ancient symbolism. But changes brought about by the new situation could be seen everywhere. Thus, the great question that the church faced at this time was to what degree and how it should adapt to the changed circumstances. All were agreed that some measure of adaptation was necessary. All were also agreed that such adaptation should not relinquish the traditional faith of the church. The disagreement rested on exactly what it meant to be obedient in a new age while remaining faithful to an old message.

14/Official Theology: Eusebius of Caesarea

Looking westward or eastward, looking over the whole earth, and even looking at heaven, always and everywhere I see blessed Constantine leading the same Empire.

EUSEBIUS OF CAESAREA

Eusebius of Caesarea was in all probability the most learned Christian of his time. He was also one of the most ardent admirers of Constantine and his work, as may be seen in the words quoted above; and for this reason he has sometimes been depicted as a spineless man who allowed himself to be swept by the glitter of imperial power. But things are not so simple when one considers his entire career.

Eusebius was born around the year 260, most likely in Palestine, where he spent most of his early years. He is known as Eusebius "of Caesarea" because, although it is not certain that he was born there, it was in that city that he spent most of his life and that he served as bishop. Practically nothing is known of his parents, and it is impossible to determine whether he grew up in a Christian home or was converted as a youth.

In any case, the person who left a deep impression on Eusebius was Pamphilus of Caesarea. Pamphilus was a native of Berytus—now Beirut, in Lebanon—who had studied in Alexandria under Pierius, a famous teacher who was carrying on Origen's work in that city. After holding some important posts in Berytus, Pamphilus went to Caesarea, probably at the request of the bishop of that city. The church of Caesarea had kept Origen's library, and Pamphilus spent long hours working with it and adding to it. In this task he was aided by several others who were moved by Pamphilus' intellectual curiosity and profound faith. One of those captivated by the scholar from Berytus was young Eusebius, who acknowledged his debt by calling himself "Eusebius of Pamphilus."

Pamphilus, Eusebius, and several others spent several years working as a team, probably living in the same room and pooling their economic resources. Eventually, the disciple outdid the master, and Eusebius traveled far and wide in quest of documents regarding Christian origins. During that period of joint work, Pamphilus and Eusebius wrote several works, although most of them have now been lost.

But their peaceful and scholarly life would come to an end. It was still the time of persecutions, and the threat that had always loomed on the horizon now became the storm of the great persecution under Diocletian. By June of 303, the persecution made itself felt in Caesarea, in the first martyrdom in many years. From then on, the storm grew worse. In 305 Maximinus Daia, a bitter enemy of Christianity, achieved imperial rank. Two years later, Pamphilus was arrested. But then there was a lull in the storm, and the great Christian scholar simply remained in prison for more than two years before being condemned to death. During that time, he and Eusebius collaborated on a five-book *Defense of Origen,* to which Eusebius added a sixth book after his teacher's martyrdom.

Eusebius himself was not arrested. Why this was so is not clear. At least on two occasions he left the city, and one may suppose that part of his reason for doing so may have been to avoid arrest. At that time, most Christians held that there was no shame in hiding during a time of persecution, for martyrdom was something for which one had to be chosen by God. In any case, Eusebius did not suffer personally during the persecution, although his teacher and many of his companions died as martyrs.

In the midst of such evil times, Eusebius carried on with what would become his most important work, his *Church History.* This work, which he later revised, is of great importance for later church historians. Without it, a great deal of the story that we have been telling would have been lost. It was Eusebius who collected, organized, and published practically all that is now known of many persons and episodes in the life of the early church. Without him, our knowledge of the early history of Christianity would be reduced by half.

Finally, in 311, things began to change. First came the edict of Galerius. Then Constantine defeated Maxentius, and Constantine and Licinius, meeting at Milan, put an end to persecution. From the point of view of Eusebius and his surviving companions, what was taking place was a direct intervention by God, something similar to the events of Exodus. From then on Eusebius—and probably a vast number of other Christians whose opinions were not set down in writing—began looking upon Constantine and Licinius as the instruments of the divine design. When hostilities finally broke out between the two Emperors, Eusebius was convinced that Licinius had become insane and begun to persecute Christianity. Constantine, and he alone, remained as God's chosen instrument.

A few years before Constantine became sole emperor, Eusebius had been elected bishop of Caesarea. This was a great responsibility, for persecution had disbanded his flock, which he now had to gather and organize anew. Furthermore, the bishopric of Caesarea had jurisdiction, not only over the church in the city itself, but also over the rest of Palestine. Now become a pastor and administrator, Eusebius had little time for his literary and scholarly pursuits.

He had been bishop of Caesarea for a number of years when a new storm came to break the peace of the church. This was not a matter of persecution by the government, but rather a bitter theological debate that threatened to rend the church asunder: the Arian controversy. Since this will be the subject of a later chapter, it is not necessary to discuss it here. Let it suffice to say that Eusebius' role in the controversy was not beyond reproach. The reason for this, however, was not that he was a hypocrite or an opportunist. It was rather that Eusebius never fully understood what was at stake. For him, the peace and unity of the church were of prime importance. Therefore, although at

"Canon tables," first devised by Eusebius, were an ancient form of Gospel parallels.

first he seemed to be inclined towards Arianism, at the Council of Nicea he took an opposite stance, only to waver again once the Council had disbanded. Since he was a famous bishop and scholar, many looked to him for direction, and his confusion—which was probably shared by many of lesser intellectual gifts—did little to bring the controversy to a happy conclusion.

Eusebius had met Constantine years before, when the future emperor visited Palestine with Diocletian's court. In Nicea, at the time of the Council, he saw the emperor seeking the unity and well-being of the church. On a number of other occasions he had interviews and correspondence with the emperor. Probably he came to know the ruler best when Constantine and his court went to Jerusalem for the dedication of the newly built Church of the Holy Sepulchre. The festivities on that occasion were part of the celebration of the thirtieth anniversary of Constantine's reign. The Arian controversy was still boiling, and the bishops gathered for the great dedication—first at Tyre and then at Jerusalem—were deeply interested in it, as was also the emperor. Eusebius, as bishop of the principal city in the area, played an important part in the proceedings, and delivered a speech in praise of Constantine. This speech, still extant, is one of the reasons why some accuse him of sheer flattery. But, when judged in terms of what was then customary in such situations, Eusebius' speech appears rather moderate in its praise of the emperor.

In any case, Eusebius was neither a close friend nor a courtier of Constantine. He spent most of his life in Caesarea and the surrounding area, busy with ecclesiastical affairs, while Constantine spent his time either in Constantinople or in other parts of the Empire. The contacts between the two were brief and intermittent. Since Eusebius was admired by many of his colleagues, the emperor cultivated his support. And, since Eusebius was convinced that, after the great trials of his earlier years, Constantine had been raised up by God, he did not hesitate to support the emperor. Furthermore, it was after Constantine's death in 337 that Eusebius wrote his lines of highest praise for the ruler who had brought peace to the church. Therefore, his actions are not so much those of a flatterer as those of a rather uncritical, but grateful, man.

Eusebius' gratitude, however, went far beyond its most obvious expressions in words of praise. His understanding of what had taken place in the person of Constantine left a mark on his entire work, and particularly in the way in which he understood the history of the church up to his time. The final draft of his *Church History* did not simply seek to retell the various events in the earlier life of the church. It was really an apology that sought to show that Christianity was the ultimate goal of human history, particularly as seen within the context of the Roman Empire. Similar notions had appeared earlier, when Christian writers in the second century declared that all truth comes from the same Logos who was incarnate in Jesus Christ. According to such authors as Justin and Clement of Alexandria, both philosophy and the

Hebrew Scriptures were given as a preparation for the Gospel. Also circulating was the idea that the Empire itself, and the relative peace that it brought to the Mediterranean basin, had been ordained by God as a means to facilitate the dissemination of the Christian faith. Others, such as Irenaeus, had held that the entirety of human history from the time of Adam and Eve had been a vast process by which God had been training humankind for communion with the divine. What Eusebius then did was to bring together these various ideas, showing them at work in the verifiable facts of the history of both the church and the Empire. The history that thus resulted was no mere collection of data of antiquarian interest, but rather a further demonstration of the truth of Christianity, which is the culmination of human history.

The Arch of Constantine is one of the few remaining monuments of Constantine's reign.

In support of that thesis, Constantine's conversion was the keystone. According to Eusebius, the main reason for persecution was that Roman authorities did not see that Christianity was the crowning touch on the best Roman traditions. Faith and the Empire, like faith and philosophy, were not really incompatible. On the contrary, the Christian faith was the culmination of both philosophy and the Empire. Therefore, Constantine's religious policies were important for Eusebius' understanding of history, not simply because they were advantageous for the church, but for much deeper reasons. The new situation was living and convincing proof of the truth of the Gospel, to which all human history pointed.

This theological perspective made it very difficult for Eusebius to take a critical stance towards the events of his time. He seems to have been aware of some of Constantine's shortcomings, especially his irascible and sometimes even bloodthirsty temperament. But in order not to weaken his argument, Eusebius simply remains silent about such things.

The importance of all this is not merely in what Eusebius says or does not say about Constantine. Far beyond that, Eusebius' work is an indicator of the degree to which, even unwittingly, Christian theology was being shaped by the new circumstances, even to the point of abandoning some of its traditional themes.

Three examples should suffice to illustrate the manner in which theology was being accommodated to fit the new situation. First of all, it is clear that, in the New Testament as well as in the early church, it was affirmed that the Gospel was first of all good news to the poor, and that the rich had particular difficulty in hearing it and receiving it. Actually, one of the theological issues that caused some concern for earlier Christians was how it was possible for a rich person to be saved. But now, beginning with Constantine, riches and pomp came to be seen as signs of divine favor. The next chapter will show that the monastic movement was in part a protest against this accommodating understanding of the Christian life. But Eusebius—and the thousands of others for whom he probably spoke—does not seem to have been aware of the radical change that was taking place as the persecuted church became the church of the powerful, nor of the dangers involved in that change.

Likewise, Eusebius described with great joy and pride the ornate churches that were being built. But the net result of those buildings, and of the liturgy that evolved to fit them, was the development of a clerical aristocracy, similar to the imperial aristocracy, and often as far from the common people as were the great officers of the Empire. The church imitated the uses of the Empire, not only in its liturgy, but also in its social structure.

Finally, the scheme of history that Eusebius developed led him to set aside a fundamental theme of early Christian preaching: the coming Kingdom of God. Although Eusebius does not go as far as to say so explicitly, in reading his works one receives the impression that now, with Constantine and his successors, the plan of God has been fulfilled. Beyond the present political order, all that Christians are to hope for is their own personal transference into the heavenly kingdom. Since the time of Constantine, and due in part to the work of Eusebius and of many others of similar theological orientation, there was a tendency to set aside or to postpone the hope of the early church, that its Lord would return in the clouds to establish a Kingdom of peace and justice. At later times, many groups that rekindled that hope were branded as heretics and subversives, and condemned as such.

Although Eusebius illustrates the changes that were taking place, this is not to say that he was solely responsible for them. On the contrary, the entire history of the period would seem to indicate that Eusebius, although more articulate than most, was simply expressing the common feeling among

Christians, for whom the advent of Constantine and of the peace he brought about was the final triumph of Christianity over its enemies. Those Christians were not able to express their opinions with Eusebius' elegance and erudition; but they were the ones who, step by step, shaped the church in the years to come. Eusebius is not the creator of what we have called "official theology," but rather the mouthpiece of the thousands of Christians who, like him, were overawed by God's mercy in finally delivering the church from persecution. But not all Christians regarded the new circumstances with like enthusiasm, as the next chapters will amply show.

15/The Monastic Reaction

Monks who leave their cells, or seek the company of others, lose their peace, like the fish out of water loses its life.
ANTHONY

The new situation of the church after Constantine's peace was not equally received by all. Over against those who, like Eusebius of Caesarea, saw the more recent events as the fulfillment of God's purposes, there were those who bewailed what they saw as the low level to which Christian life had descended. The narrow gate of which Jesus had spoken had become so wide that countless multitudes were hurrying past it—some seemingly after privilege and position, without caring to delve too deeply into the meaning of Christian baptism and life under the cross. Bishops competed with each other after prestigious positions. The rich and powerful seemed to dominate the life of the church. The tares were growing so rapidly that they threatened to choke out the wheat.

For almost three hundred years, the church had lived under the constant threat of persecution. All Christians were aware of the possibility that some day they would be taken before Roman authorities, and there placed before the awesome choice between death and apostasy. During the prolonged periods of quiet in the second and third centuries, there were those who forgot this; and when persecution did arrive, they proved too weak to withstand the trial. This in turn convinced others that security and comfortable living were the greatest enemies of the church, and that these enemies proved stronger during periods of relative peace. Now, when the peace of the church seemed assured, many of these people saw that very assurance as a snare of Satan.

How was one to be a true Christian in such circumstances? When the church joins the powers of the world, when luxury and ostentation take hold of Christian altars, when the whole of society is intent on turning the narrow path into a wide avenue, how is one to resist the enormous temptations of the times? How is one to witness to the Crucified Lord, to the One who had nowhere to lay his head, at a time when many leaders of the church live in costly homes, and when the ultimate witness of martyrdom is no longer possible? How to overcome Satan, who is constantly tempting the faithful with the new honors that society offers?

Many found an answer in the monastic life: to flee from human society, to leave everything behind, to dominate the body and its passions, which give way to temptation. Thus, at the very time when churches in large cities were flooded by thousands demanding baptism, there was a veritable exodus of other thousands who sought beatitude in solitude.

The Origins of Monasticism

Even before Constantine's time, there had been Christians who, for various reasons, had felt called to an unusual style of life. Reference has already been made to the "widows and virgins"—that is, to those women who chose not to marry, and to devote all their time and energies to the work of the church. Some time later Origen, following the Platonic ideal of the wise life, made arrangements to live at a mere subsistence level, and led a life of extreme asceticism—it is said that he even took literally the word of Christ about those who have made themselves "eunuchs for the Kingdom." Also, although gnosticism had been rejected by the church, its influence could still be felt in the widely held notion that there was a fundamental opposition between the body and the life of the spirit, and that therefore in order to live fully in the spirit it was necessary to subdue and to punish the body.

Thus, monasticism has roots both within the church and outside of it. From within the church, monasticism was inspired by Paul's words, that those who chose not to marry had greater freedom to serve the Lord. This impulse towards celibacy was often strengthened by the expectation of the return of the Lord. If the end was at hand, it made no sense to marry and to begin the sedentary life of those who are making plans for the future. At other times, there was an additional reason for celibacy: since Christians are to witness to the coming Kingdom, and since Jesus declared that in the Kingdom "they neither marry nor are given in marriage," those who choose to remain celibate in the present life are a living witness to the coming Kingdom.

A number of outside influences also played a part in the development of Christian monasticism. Several schools of classical philosophy held that the body was the prison or the sepulchre of the soul, which could not be truly free as long as it did not overcome the limitations of the body. Stoic doctrine, very widespread at the time, held that passions are the great enemy of true wisdom, and that the wise devote themselves to the perfecting of their souls and the subjugation of their passions. Several religious traditions in the

From the beginning, many monastics were women;

Mediterranean basin included sacred virigins, celibate priests, eunuchs, and others whose lifestyle set them apart for the service of the gods. From all these sources, as well as from Scripture, Christian monasticism drew its ideals.

The First Monks of the Desert

Although there were early monastics throughout the Roman Empire, it was the desert—especially the Egyptian desert—that provided the most fertile soil for the growth of monasticism. The very word "monk" derives from the Greek *monachos,* which means "solitary." One of the driving motivations for the early monks was the search for solitude. Society, with its noise and its many activities, was seen as a temptation and a distraction from the monastic goal. The term "anchorite," which soon came to mean a solitary monk, originally meant "withdrawn" or "fugitive." For these people, the desert was attractive, not so much because of its hardship, but rather because of its inaccessibility. What they sought was not burning sands, but rather an oasis, a secluded valley, or an abandoned cemetery, where they would not be disturbed by others.

It is impossible to tell who was the first monk—or nun—of the desert. The two that are usually given that honor, Paul and Anthony, owe their fame to two great Christian writers—Jerome and Athanasius—who wrote about

and some of them served as models for men as well as other women.

them, each claiming that his protagonist was the founder of Egyptian monasticism. But the truth is that it is impossible to know—and that no one ever knew—who was the founder of the movement. Monasticism was not the invention of an individual, but rather a mass exodus, a contagion, which seems to have suddenly affected thousands of people. In any case, the lives of Paul and Anthony are significant, if not as those of founders, certainly as typical of the earliest forms of monasticism.

Jerome's life of Paul is very brief, and almost entirely legendary. But still, the nucleus of the story is probably true. Towards the middle of the third century, fleeing persecution, young Paul went to the desert, where he found an old abandoned hiding place for counterfeiters. There he passed the rest of his life, spending his time in prayer and living on a diet that consisted almost exclusively of dates. According to Jerome, Paul lived in such conditions for almost a century, and his only visitors during that time were the beasts of the desert and the elderly monk, Anthony. Although this may be somewhat exaggerated, it does point to the ideal of solitude that was so important to the early monastics.

According to Athanasius, Anthony was born in a small village on the left shore of the Nile, the son of relatively wealthy parents. When they died, Anthony was still young, and his inheritance was sufficient to permit a comfortable life both for him and for his younger sister, for whom he now took responsibility. His plans were simply to live off his inheritance, until a reading of the Gospel in church made such an impact that he felt compelled to change his life. The text that day was the story of the rich young ruler, and

The Egyptian desert was the favorite dwelling place of anchorites and other monastics.

the words of Jesus were very clear to Anthony, who was relatively rich: "If you would be perfect, go, sell what you possess and give to the poor, and you will have treasure in heaven" (Matt. 19:21). In response to those words, Anthony disposed of his property and gave the proceeds to the poor, reserving only a portion for the care of his sister. But later he was moved by the words of Jesus in Matthew 6:34: "do not be anxious about tomorrow." He then disposed even of the small reserve fund that he had kept for his sister, placed her under the care of the virgins of the church, and left for the desert.

Anthony spent his first years of retreat learning the monastic life from an old man who lived nearby—which shows that Anthony was not the first Christian anchorite. These were difficult times for the young monk, for often he missed the pleasures he had left behind, and began to feel sorry for having sold all his goods and withdrawn to the desert. When he was thus tempted, Anthony had recourse to stricter discipline. Sometimes he would fast for several days; at other times he would limit his food to a single meal a day, after sunset.

After several years, Anthony decided that it was time to leave his elderly teacher and the other neighboring monks from whom he had learned monastic discipline. He then went to live in a tomb in an abandoned cemetery, where he subsisted on bread, which some kind souls brought him every few days. According to Athanasius, at this time Anthony began having visions of demons that accosted him almost continuously. At times, his encounter with these demons was such that it resulted in a physical struggle that left him sore for days.

Finally, when he was thirty-five years old, Anthony had a vision in which God told him not to fear, for he would always be able to count on divine aid. It was then that Anthony decided that the tomb in which he lived was not sufficiently distant from society, and mover farther into the desert. He found an abandoned fort where he now fixed his residence. Even there the demons followed him, and the visions and temptations continued. But Anthony was now convinced that he had God's help, and the struggle became more bearable.

However, it was not only demons that pursued the monastic athlete. He was pursued by other monks who were desirous to learn from him the discipline and wisdom of prayer and contemplation. And he was also pursued by the curious and the ailing, for by then he was becoming famous as a saint and a worker of miracles. Again and again the elderly anchorite withdrew to desolate places, but he was repeatedly found by those who sought him. He finally gave up this struggle and agreed to live near a number of disciples, on condition that they would not visit him too frequently. In exchange, Anthony would visit them periodically and talk with them about monastic discipline, the love of God, and the wonders of contemplation.

On two occasions, however, Anthony did visit the great city of Alexandria. The first was when the great persecution broke out under Diocletian, and Anthony and several of his disciples decided to go to the city in order to offer up their lives as martyrs. But the prefect decided that such ragged and disheveled characters were not worthy of his attention, and the would-be martyrs had to be content with speaking words of encouragement to others.

Anthony's second visit to Alexandria took place many years later, during the Arian controversy. The Arians claimed that the holy hermit had sided with them, and against Athanasius, and Anthony decided that the only way to undo such false rumors was to appear in person before the bishops gathered in Alexandria. According to Athanasius, the elderly monk, who had to speak in Coptic because he knew no Greek—and who probably was also illiterate—spoke with such wisdom and conviction that he confounded the Arians.

Finally, towards the end of his days, Anthony agreed to have two younger monks live with him and take care of him. He died in 356, after instructing his two companions to keep the place of his burial secret and to send his cloak—his only possession—to bishop Athanasius in Alexandria.

Both Paul and Anthony went to the desert before the time of Constantine—and even then, there were others already there. But when Constantine came to power, the life which these hermits had led became increasingly

For a long time, Anthony was tempted in such a way that his strife seemed a physical struggle with demons.

popular. Some travelers who visited the region declared, with obvious exaggeration, that the desert was more populated than some cities. Others speak of twenty thousand women and ten thousand men leading the monastic life in a single area of Egypt. No matter how exaggerated these figures may be, the fact to which they point is certain: those who fled society for the withdrawn life of the hermit were legion.

Their life was extremely simple. Some planted gardens, but most of them earned their living weaving baskets and mats that they then traded for bread and oil. Apart from the ready availability of reeds, this occupation had the advantage that while weaving one could pray, recite a psalm, or memorize a portion of Scripture. The diet of the desert consisted mostly of bread, to which were occasionally added fruit, vegetables, and oil. Their belongings were limited to the strictly necessary clothing, and a mat to sleep on. Most of them frowned on the possession of books, which could lead to pride. They taught each other, by heart, entire books of the Bible, particularly the Psalms and books of the New Testament. And they also shared among themselves edifying anecdotes and pearls of wisdom coming from the most respected anchorites.

The spirit of the desert did not fit well with that of the hierarchical church whose bishops lived in great cities and enjoyed power and prestige. Many monks were convinced that the worst fate that could befall them was to be made a priest or a bishop—it was precisely at this time, and partly as a result of the changes brought about after Constantine's conversion, that Christian ministers began to be called "priests." Although some monks were ordained, this was done almost always against their will or in response to repeated entreaties from a bishop of known sanctity, such as Athanasius. This in turn meant that many anchorites would go for years without partaking of communion, which from the very beginning had been the central act of Christian worship. In some areas, churches were built in which the nearby hermits gathered for Saturday and Sunday. On Sunday, after communion, they would often have a common meal, and then part for another week.

On the other hand, this sort of life was not free of temptations. As years went by, many monks came to the conclusion that, since their life was holier than that of most bishops and other leaders of the church, it was they, and not those leaders, who should decide what was proper Christian teaching. Since many of these monks were fairly ignorant and prone to fanaticism, they became the pawns of others of more education, power, and cunning, who used the zeal of the desert hosts to their own ends. In the fifth century, this came to the point where rioting monks would seek to impose by force and violence what they considered to be orthodox doctrine.

Pachomius and Communal Monasticism

The growing number of people withdrawing to the desert, and the desire of most of them to learn from an experienced teacher, gave rise to a new form of monastic life. Anthony was repeatedly compelled to flee from those who sought his help and guidance. Increasingly, solitary monasticism gave way to a communal form of the monastic life. Those who lived in such communities still called themselves "monks"—that is, solitary—but by this they meant, not that they lived completely alone, but that they lived in solitude from the world. This form of monasticism is called "cenobitic," a name derived from two Greek words which mean "communal life."

As in the case of solitary monasticism, it is impossible to name the founder of cenobitic monasticism. Most probably it appeared simultaneously in various places, brought about, not so much by the creative genius of one person, as by the pressure of circumstances. The completely solitary life of the early monastics was not well suited for many who went to the desert, and thus was cenobitic monasticism born. However, although not its founder, Pachomius deserves credit as the organizer who most contributed to its final shape.

Pachomius was born around A.D. 286, in a small village in southern Egypt. His parents were pagans, and he seems to have known little about Christianity before being taken from his home and forced to join the army. He was very saddened by his lot, when a group of Christians came to console him and his companions. The young recruit was so moved by this act of love that he vowed that, if he somehow managed to leave the military, he too would devote himself to serve others. When quite unexpectedly he was allowed to leave the army, he sought someone to instruct him in the Christian faith, and to baptize him. Some years later he decided to withdraw to the desert, where he asked an old anchorite to be his teacher.

For seven years young Pachomius lived with the anchorite, until he heard a voice commanding him to move. His old teacher helped him build a shelter, and there Pachomius lived by himself until his younger brother, John, joined him. Together, the two brothers devoted themselves to prayer and contemplation.

But Pachomius was not satisfied, and he constantly asked God to show him the way to better service. Finally, he had a vision in which an angel told him that he was to serve humankind. Pachomius rejected the vision, declaring that he had come to the desert to serve God, not humans. But the message was repeated and Pachomius, perhaps remembering his early vows when he was a soldier, decided to change the direction of his monastic life.

With his brother's help, he built a large enclosure, sufficient for a number of monks, and recruited what would be the first members of the new community. Pachomius hoped to teach them what he had learned of prayer and contemplation, and also to organize a community in which all would help each other. But his recruits had not been properly selected, discipline broke down, and eventually Pachomius expelled the lot.

He then began a second attempt at communal monasticism. Pachomius' earlier attempt had failed because his recruits said that he was too demanding. In this new attempt, rather than relaxing his discipline, he was more rigorous. From the very beginning, he demanded that any who wished to join the community must give up all their goods and promise absolute obedience to their superiors. Besides, all would work with their hands, and none would be allowed to consider any task unworthy of them. The basic rule was mutual service, so that even those in authority, in spite of the vow of absolute obedience which all had made, had to serve those under them.

The monastery that Pachomius founded on these bases grew rapidly, to the point that during his lifetime nine such communities were established, each with several hundred monks. Meanwhile Mary, Pachomius' sister, founded similar communities for women.

Each of these monasteries was encircled by a wall with a single entrance. Within the enclosure there were several buildings. Some of them, such as the church, the storehouse, the refectory, and the meeting hall, were used in common by the entire monastery. The rest were living quarters in which monks were grouped according to their responsibilities. Thus, for instance, there was a building for the gatekeepers, who were responsible for the lodging of those who needed hospitality, and for the admission and training of those who requested to join the community. Other such buildings housed the weavers, bakers, cobblers, and so forth. In each of them there was a common room and a series of cells, one for every two monks.

The daily life of a Pachomian monk included both work and devotion, and Pachomius himself set an example for the rest by undertaking the most humble tasks. For the devotional life, Paul's injunction to "pray without ceasing" was the model. Thus, while the bakers kneaded the bread, or the cobblers made shoes, all sang psalms, recited passages of Scripture, prayed either aloud or in silence, meditated on a biblical text, and so forth. Twice a day there were common prayers. In the morning the entire community gathered to pray, sing psalms, and hear the reading of Scripture. In the evening they had a similar service, although gathered in smaller groups, in the common rooms of the various living quarters.

The economic life of Pachomian communities was varied. Although all lived in poverty, Pachomius did not insist on the exaggerated poverty of some anchorites. At the tables there was bread, fruit, vegetables, and fish—but never meat. What the monks produced was sold in nearby markets, not only in order to buy food and other necessary items, but also in order to have something to give the poor and any sojourners who came by. In each monastery there was an administrator and an aide, and these had to render periodic accounts to the administrator of the main monastery, where Pachomius lived.

Since every monk had to obey his superiors, the hierarchical order was clearly defined. At the head of each housing unit there was a superior, who in turn had to obey the superior of the monastery and his deputy. And above the superiors of the various monasteries were Pachomius and his successors, who were called "abbots" or "archimandrites." When Pachomius was about to die, his monks vowed obedience to whomever he would choose as his successor, and thus was established the custom that each abbot would name the person to succeed him in absolute command of the entire organization.

This abbot's authority was final, and he could name, transfer, or depose the superiors of all the communities in the entire system.

Twice a year, all Pachomian monks gathered for prayer and worship, and to deal with any issues necessary for the good order of the communities. The organization was also kept together by frequent visits to all monasteries by the abbot or his representative.

Pachomius and his followers never accepted ecclesiastical office, and therefore there were no ordained priests among them. In order to partake of communion, they visited a nearby church on Saturdays, and on Sundays a priest would visit the monastery and celebrate communion.

In the women's communities, life was organized in a similar fashion. The abbot—Pachomius and his successors—ruled these communities as well as those for men.

Those who wished to join a Pachomian community simply appeared at the gate of the enclosure. This was not easily opened to them, for before being admitted to the gatekeepers' house candidates were forced to spend several days and nights at the gate, begging to be let in. Thus, they were required to show both the firmness of their resolve and their humility and willingness to obey. When the gate was finally opened, the gatekeepers took charge of the candidates, who lived with them for a long period, until they were considered ready to join the community in prayer. Then they were presented to the assembly of the monastery, where they sat at a special spot until a place was found for them in one of the houses, and a role assigned to them in the ongoing life of the monastery.

A surprising fact about the entire process of admission to the Pachomian communities is that many of the candidates who appeared at the gates and were eventually admitted had to be catechized and baptized, for they were not Christians. This gives an indication of the enormous attraction of the desert in the fourth century, for even pagans saw in monasticism a style of life worth pursuing.

The Spread of the Monastic Ideal

Although the roots of monasticism are not to be found exclusively in Egypt, that was the region where the movement gained most momentum in the fourth century. Devout people from different regions went to Egypt, some to remain there and others to return to their countries with the ideals and practices they had learned in the desert. From Syria, Asia Minor, Italy, and even Mesopotamia, pilgrims went to the land of the Nile and on their return spread the story and the legends of Paul, Anthony, Pachomius, and countless others. Throughout the eastern portion of the Empire, wherever there was a suitable place, a monk fixed his abode. Some exaggerated the ascetic life by ostentatious acts, such as spending their lives atop a column in a ruined temple. But others brought to the church a sense of discipline and absolute dedication that were very necessary in the seemingly easy times after Constantine.

However, those who most contributed to the spread of the monastic ideal were not the anchorites who copied the ways of the Egyptian desert and sought secluded places where they could devote themselves to prayer and meditation, but rather a number of bishops and scholars who saw the value of the monastic witness for the daily life of the church. Thus, although in its earliest times Egyptian monasticism had existed apart and even in opposition to the hierarchy, eventually its greatest impact was made through some of the members of that hierarchy.

Several of those who thus contributed to the spread of monasticism were of such importance that we shall deal with them in later chapters. But it may be well to point out here their significance for the history of monasticism. Athanasius, besides writing the *Life of Saint Anthony*, repeatedly visited the monks in the desert, and when he was persecuted by imperial authority he found refuge among them. Although he himself was not a monk, but a bishop, he sought to organize his life in such a way that it would reflect the monastic ideals of discipline and renunciation. When exiled in the West, he made known to the Latin-speaking church what was taking place in the Egyptian desert. Jerome, besides writing the *Life of Paul the Hermit*, translated Pachomius' *Rule* into Latin, and he himself became a monk—although an unusually scholarly one. Since Jerome was one of the most admired and influential Christians of his time, his works and his example had a significant impact on the Western church, which thus became more interested in the monastic spirit. Basil of Caesarea—known as Basil the Great—found time in the midst of all the theological debates in which he was involved to found monasteries where time was given both to devotion and to the care of the needy. Answering questions addressed to him by monks, he wrote a number of treatises which, although not originally intended as monastic rules, eventually were quoted and used as such. Augustine, the great bishop of Hippo, partly owed his conversion to reading Athanasius' *Life of Saint Anthony*, and lived as a monk until he was forced to take a more active role in the life of the church. Even then, he organized those who worked with him into a semi-monastic community, and thus provided inspiration for what would later be called the "Augustinian canons."

But the most remarkable example of the manner in which a saintly and monastic bishop contributed to the popularity of the monastic ideal was Martin of Tours. The *Life of Saint Martin*, written by Sulpitius Severus, was one of the most popular books in western Europe for centuries and was one of the most influential elements in the shaping of western monasticism.

Martin was born around A.D. 335 in Pannonia, in what is now Hungary. His father was a pagan soldier, and during his early years Martin lived in various parts of the Empire—although the city of Pavia, in northern Italy, seems to have been his most frequent place of residence. He was very young when he decided to become a Christian, against his parents' will, and had his name included in the list of catechumens. His father, in order to tear him apart from his Christian contacts, had him enrolled in the army. It was the time when Julian—later known as "the Apostate"—led his first military campaigns. Martin served under him for several years. During this period, an episode took place that ever since has been associated with the name of Martin.

Martin and his friends were entering the city of Amiens when an almost naked and shivering beggar asked them for alms. Martin had no money for him, but he took off his cape, cut it in two, and gave half to the beggar. According to the story, later in his dreams Martin saw Jesus coming to him, wrapped in half a soldier's cape, and saying: "Inasmuch as you did it to one of the least of these my brethren, you did it to me." This episode became so well known, that ever since Martin is usually represented in the act of sharing his cape with the beggar. This is also the origin of the word "chapel" —for centuries later, in a small church, there was a piece of cloth reputed to be a portion of Martin's cape. From that piece of cape—*capella*—the little church came to be called a "chapel," and those who served in it, "chaplains."

Shortly after the incident at Amiens, Sulpitius Severus tells us, Martin was baptized, and two years later he was finally able to leave the army. He then visited the learned and saintly bishop Hilary of Poitiers, who became a close friend. Several different tasks and vicissitudes took him to various parts of the Empire, until finally he settled just outside the city of Tours, near Poitiers. There he devoted himself to the monastic life, while the fame of his sanctity spread through the region. It was said that God performed great works through him, but he always refused to count himself as anything more than an apprentice in the Christian life.

When the bishopric of Tours became vacant, the populace wanted to elect Martin to that position. The story goes that some of the bishops present at the election opposed such an idea, arguing that Martin was usually dirty, dressed in rags, and disheveled, and that his election would damage the prestige of the office of bishop. No agreement had been reached when it was time to read the Bible, and the person assigned for that task was nowhere to be found. Then one of those present took the book and began reading where it fell open: "By the mouth of babes and infants, thou hast founded a bulwark because of thy foes, to still the enemy and the avenger" (Psalm 8:2). The crowd took this to be a direct message from heaven. Martin, the filthy and unseemly man whom the bishops scorned, had been chosen by God to silence the bishops. Without further ado, Martin was elected bishop of Tours.

But the new bishop was not ready to abandon his monastic ways. Next to the cathedral, he built a small cell where he devoted all his free time to

*The story that Martin divided his cloak with a beggar, and that
Christ then appeared to him in the form of a beggar, became a
common theme in Christian art.*

the monastic life. When his fame was such that he could find no peace in that cell, he moved back to the outskirts of the city, and from there he would carry on his pastoral tasks.

When Martin died, many were convinced that he was a saint. His fame and example led many to the conviction that a true bishop ought to be like him. Thus, the monastic movement, which at first was in great measure a protest against the wordliness and the pomp of bishops, eventually left its imprint on the idea itself of the episcopate. For centuries—and in some quarters to the present time—it was thought that a true bishop should approach the monastic ideal as much as possible. In that process, however, monasticism itself was changed, for whereas those who first joined the movement fled to the desert in quest of their own salvation as years went by monasticism would become—particularly in the West—an instrument for the charitable and missionary work of the church.

16/The Schismatic Reaction: Donatism

What is debated between the Donatists and us is, where is to be found this body of Christ which is the church? Are we to seek the answer in our own words, or in those of the Head of the body, our Lord Jesus Christ?

AUGUSTINE OF HIPPO

Whereas those who followed the monastic way of life expressed their dissatisfaction with the new order by withdrawing to the desert, others simply declared that the church at large had been corrupted, and that they were the true church. Of several groups with similar views, the most numerous was that of the Donatists.

The Donatist controversy was one more instance in which the church was divided over the question of the lapsed and how they ought to be restored. After each period of violent persecution, the church had to face the issue of what to do with those who had yielded their faith, but who now sought to be restored to the communion of Christians. In the third century, this had resulted in the schism of Novatian in Rome; and in North Africa, Cyprian, bishop of Carthage, had to defend his episcopal authority against those who held that the confessors were the ones who should determine how the lapsed were to be restored. Now, in the fourth century, the debate over the restoration of the lapsed became particularly virulent in North Africa.

The persecution had been very violent in that region, and the number of those who had yielded was great. As in other cases, those who had yielded had not done so to the same degree. Some bishops avoided further persecution by handing over to the authorities heretical books, and leading them to believe that these were Christian Scriptures. Others turned in the genuine

Scriptures, claiming that in so doing they were avoiding bloodshed, and that this was their responsibility as pastors. Many, both clergy and lay, succumbed to imperial pressure and worshiped the pagan gods—indeed, the number of the latter was such that some chroniclers state that there were days when the pagan temples were full to overflowing.

On the other hand, there were many Christians who remained firm in their faith, and as a result suffered imprisonment, torture, and even death. As earlier, those who survived imprisonment and torture were called "confessors," and were particularly respected for the firmness of their faith. In Cyprian's time, some of the confessors had been too ready to readmit the lapsed, without any consultation with the authorities of the church. Now, after Constantine's conversion, a significant number of confessors took the opposite tack, insisting on greater rigor than the church was applying. These more demanding confessors claimed that the lapsed were not only those who had actually worshiped the gods, but also those who had handed the Scriptures to the authorities. If changing a tittle or a jot in Scriptures was such a great sin, argued the confessors, is it not an even greater sin to turn the sacred text over to be destroyed? Thus some bishops and other leaders were given the offensive title of "traditores"—that is, those who had handed over or betrayed.

Such was the state of affairs when, shortly after the end of persecution, the very important bishopric of Carthage became vacant. The election fell on Caecilian. But he was not popular with the rigorist party, which elected Majorinus as his rival. In these elections there were intrigues and unworthy maneuvers on both sides, so that each was justified in claiming that his rival's election had been irregular. When Majorinus died shortly after being made rival bishop of Carthage, his party elected Donatus of Casae Nigrae, who became their leader for almost half a century, and from whom the movement eventually derived the name of "Donatism."

Naturally, the rest of the church was profoundly disturbed by this schism in North Africa, for it was possible to acknowledge only one bishop of Carthage. The bishops of Rome and of several other important cities declared that Caecilian was the true bishop of Carthage, and that Majorinus and Donatus were usurpers. Constantine, who was greatly interested in keeping together the church so that it could help unify his Empire, followed the lead of these bishops, and sent instructions to his officers in North Africa, that they should acknowledge only Caecilian and those in communion with him. This had important practical consequences, for Constantine was issuing legislation in favor of Christianity, such as tax exemption for the clergy. On the basis of his instructions to North Africa, only those in communion with Caecilian could enjoy these benefits—or receive any of the gifts that Constantine was offering to the church.

What were the causes of the Donatist schism? The foregoing is only the outward history of its beginnings. But in truth the schism had theological, political, and economic roots.

Carthage, now in ruins, was the center of Roman rule and church life in North Africa.

The theological justification, and immediate cause of the schism, had to do with the issue of what was to be done with those who yielded during a time of persecution. According to the Donatists, one of the three bishops who had consecrated Caecilian was a traditor—that is, had delivered Scriptures to the authorities—and therefore the consecration itself was not valid. Caecilian and his party responded by claiming, first, that the bishop was not a traditor and, secondly, that even had he been one, his action in consecrating Caecilian would still have been valid. Thus, besides the factual question of whether or not this particular bishop—and others in communion with Caecilian—had yielded, there was the further issue of whether an ordination or consecration performed by an unworthy bishop was valid. The Donatists declared that the validity of such an act depended on the worthiness of the bishop performing it. Caecilian and his followers responded that the validity of the sacraments and of other such acts cannot be made to depend on the worthiness of the one administering them, for in that case all Christians would be in constant doubt as to the validity of their own baptism or of the communion of which they partook. Since it is impossible to know the inner state of the soul of a minister offering such sacraments, there would be no way to dispel doubt regarding their validity.

The Donatists, on their part, insisted that Caecilian, whose consecration had been flawed by the participation of a traditor, was not really a bishop, and that for that reason all those whom he ordained were false ministers, whose sacraments had no validity. Furthermore, those other bishops of whose consecration there was no doubt had sinned by joining in communion with people such as Caecilian and his party. For that reason, their sacraments and ordinations were no longer valid.

Given the two positions, if a member of Caecilian's party decided to join the Donatists, a new baptism was required, for the Donatists claimed that a baptism administered by their opponents was not valid. But, on the other hand, those who left the Donatist party were not rebaptized by Caecilian and his followers, for they claimed that baptism was valid regardless of the worth of the one administering it.

These were the main theological issues involved in the debate. But when one reads between the lines of the documents of the time, one becomes aware that there were other reasons for conflict that were often hidden by the theological debates. Thus, it appears that among the Donatists there were some who had delivered the Scriptures to the authorities, and even some who had made an entire inventory of all the objects that the church used in worship, in order to give that inventory to the authorities. Yet, these people were accepted among the Donatists. Furthermore, one of the first leaders of Donatism was a certain Purpurius, who had murdered two nephews. Thus, it is difficult to believe that the real reason for the enmity of the Donatists towards the rest of the church was their concern for purity.

The Birthplace of Donatism

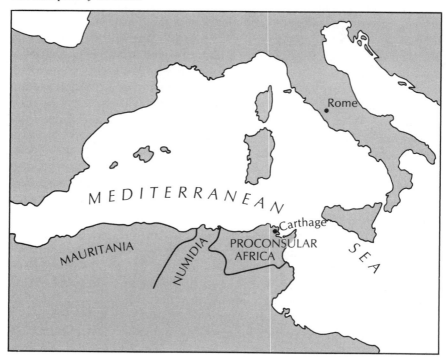

It is a fact that the two parties soon separated along social and geographical lines. In Carthage and its immediate surroundings—Proconsular Africa—Caecilian and his followers were strong. But further west, in Numidia and Mauritania, the Donatists were very popular. Numidia and Mauritania were agricultural areas. A great deal of their produce was exported to Italy through Carthage. The net result was that the Carthaginians, with less labor and risk, gained more than those who actually raised the crops. Furthermore, Numidia and Mauritania were much less romanized than Carthage and the area around it. Many in the less romanized areas retained their ancestral language and customs, and saw Rome and everything connected with it as a foreign and oppressive force. In Carthage, on the other hand, there was a strongly latinized class of landowners, merchants, and military officers, and it was this class that reaped most of the benefits of trade and other contacts with Italy. For these people, good relations with Rome as well as with the rest of the Empire were of paramount importance. But in Carthage itself, as well as in its outlying districts, there was a numerous lower class whose feelings were similar to those of the Numidians and Mauritanians.

Long before the advent of Constantine, Christianity had made significant inroads in Numidia and among the lower classes of Proconsular Africa—also, to a lesser degree, in Mauritania. The new faith of these converts was a power even the Empire could not overcome. At the same time, a smaller number of members of the romanized classes of Carthage had embraced Christianity. This brought into the Christian community some of the tensions of the rest of society. But at that time those who were converted—particularly those of the higher classes—had to break many of their social contacts, and therefore the tensions within the church were not as great as they could have been.

This situation changed drastically with the advent of Constantine and the peace of the church. Now one could be both a good Roman and a good Christian. Following the lead of the Emperor, the romanized classes flocked to the church. Others from the same social strata who had been converted earlier saw this as a positive development, for their earlier decision was now corroborated by other important people. But Christians from the lower classes tended to see the new developments as a process of corruption of the church. What these Christians had always hated in the Roman Empire was now becoming part of the church. Soon the powerful—those who controlled politics and the economy—would also control the church. It seemed necessary to resist that process, and to remind the newly converted powerful that when they were still worshiping pagan gods, the supposedly ignorant Numidians, Mauritanians, and others knew the truth.

All this may be seen in the various stages of the conflict. Caecilian was elected with the support of the romanized Christians of Carthage. His election was opposed by the lower classes in Proconsular Africa, and by almost all the people and clergy of Numidia. When he had hardly had time to study the issues debated, Constantine decided that Ceacilian's party represented the legitimate church. The same was decided by the bishops of the great Latin cities—and eventually by those of Greek cities. On the other hand, the Donatists were quite willing to accept the support of those members of the Numidian clergy who had weakened during the persecution.

This does not mean that from its origins Donatism was consciously a political movement. The early Donatists were not opposed to the Empire, but to "the world"—although for them many of the practices of the Empire were wordly. They repeatedly sought to persuade Constantine that he had erred in deciding in favor of Caecilian. Even as late as the reign of Julian, during the second half of the century, some Donatists hoped that Roman authorities would see the error of their ways, and come to their support.

Around the year 340, there appeared among the Donatists a group called "circumcellions"—a name of debatable origin, which probably means that they had their headquarters in martyrs' shrines. They were mostly Numidian and Mauritanian Donatist peasants who resorted to violence. Although sometimes they have been depicted as no more than bandits masquerading as people driven by religious motives, the truth is that they were religious to the point of fanaticism. They were convinced that there was no death more glorious than those of the martyrs, and that now that persecution in the old style had ended, those who died in battle against the perverters of the faith were also martyrs. In some cases, this quest of martyrdom reached such a pitch that people commited mass suicide by jumping off cliffs. This may well be fanaticism; but it is not opportunistic hypocrisy.

The circumcellions became an important factor in the schism. Sometimes the Donatist leaders in the towns tried to disassociate themselves from this radical party. But at other times, when they needed activist troops, they appealed to the circumcellions. The time came when many villas and land holdings in secluded places had to be abandoned. The rich and those who represented the Empire did not dare travel though the countryside without heavy escorts. More than once, the circumcellions appeared at the very gates of fortified towns. Credit suffered, and trade almost came to a standstill.

In response, Roman authorities had recourse to force. There were persecutions, attempts to persuade the dissidents, massacres, and military occupation. All to no avail. The circumcellions were the expression of a deep discontent among the masses, and the Empire was unable to stamp out the movement. As we shall see later on, shortly thereafter the Vandals invaded the area, thus putting an end to Roman rule. But even under the Vandals the movement continued. In the sixth century, the Eastern Roman Empire—with its capital in Constantinople—conquered the region. But the circumcellions continued. It was only after the Moslem conquest in the seventh century that Donatism and the circumcellions finally disappeared.

In conclusion, Donatism—particularly its radical branch, the circumcellions—was a response to the new conditions brought about by the conversion of Constantine. While some Christians received the new order with open arms, and others withdrew to the desert, the Donatists simply broke with the church that had now become an ally of the Empire. The serious theological questions they had raised about the nature of the church and the validity of the sacraments would force other Christians, notably Saint Augustine, to deal with these issues.

17/The Arian Controversy and the Council of Nicea

*And [we believe] in one Lord Jesus Christ,
the Son of God, begotten from the Father as
the only-begotten, that is, from the
substance of the Father, God from God,
light from light, true God from true God,
begotten, not made, being of one substance
with the Father . . .*

CREED OF NICEA

From its very beginnings, Christianity had been involved in theological controversies. In Paul's time, the burning issue was the relationship between Jewish and Gentile converts. Then came the crucial debates about Gnostic speculation. In the third century, when Cyprian was bishop of Carthage, the main point in discussion was the restoration of the lapsed. All these controversies were significant, and often bitter. But in those early centuries the only way to win such a debate was by solid argument and holiness of life. The civil authorities paid scant attention to theological controversies within the church, and therefore the parties in conflict were not usually tempted to appeal to those authorities in order to cut short the debate, or to win a point that had been lost in theological argument.

After the conversion of Constantine, things changed. Now it was possible to invoke the authority of the state to settle a theological question. The Empire had a vested interest in the unity of the church, which Constantine hoped would become the "cement of the Empire." Thus, the state soon began to use its power to force theological agreement on Christians. Many of the dissident views that were thus crushed may indeed have threatened the very core of the Christian message. Had it not been for imperial intervention, the issues would probably have been settled, as in earlier times, through long debate, and a consensus would eventually have been reached. But there were many rulers who did not wish to see such prolonged and undecisive controversies in the church, and who therefore simply decided, on imperial authority, who was right and who should be silenced. As a result, many of those involved in controversy, rather than seeking to convince their opponents or the rest of the church, sought to convince the emperors. Eventually, theological debate was eclipsed by political intrigue.

The beginning of this process may be seen already in the Arian controversy, which began as a local conflict between a bishop and a priest, grew to the point that Constantine felt obliged to intervene, and resulted in political maneuvering by which each party sought to destroy the other. At first sight, it is not a very edifying story. But on closer scrutiny what is surprising is not that theological debate became entangled in political intrigues, but rather that in the midst of such unfavorable circumstances the church still found the strength and the wisdom to reject those views that threatened the core of the Christian message.

The Outbreak of the Controversy

The roots of the Arian controversy are to be found in theological developments that took place long before the time of Constantine. Indeed, the controversy was a direct result of the manner in which Christians came to think of the nature of God, thanks to the work of Justin, Clement of Alexandria, Origen, and others. When the first Christians set out to preach their message throughout the Empire, they were taken for ignorant atheists, for they had no visible gods. In response, some learned Christians appealed to the authority of those whom antiquity considered eminently wise, the classical philosophers. The best pagan philosophers had taught that above the entire cosmos there was a supreme being, and some had even declared that the pagan gods were human creations. Appealing to such respected authorities, Christians argued they they believed in the supreme being of the philosophers, and that this was what they meant when they spoke of God. Such an argument was very convincing, and there is no doubt that it contributed to the acceptance of Christianity among the intelligentsia.

But this was also a dangerous argument. It was possible that Christians, in their eagerness to show the kinship between their faith and classical philosophy, would come to the conviction that the best way to speak of God was not that of the prophets and other biblical writers, but rather that of Plato, Plotinus, and the rest. Since those philosophers conceived of perfection as immutable, impassible, and fixed, many Christians came to the conclusion that such was the God of Scripture.

Two means were found to bring together what the Bible says about God and the classical notion of the supreme being as impassible and fixed. These two means were allegorical interpretation of scriptural passages, and the doctrine of the Logos. Allegorical interpretation was fairly simple to apply. Wherever Scripture says something "unworthy" of God—that is, something that is not worthy of the perfection of the supreme being—such words are not to be taken literally. Thus, for instance, if the Bible says that God walked in the garden, or that God spoke, one is to remember that an immutable being does not really walk or speak. Intellectually, this satisfied many minds. But emotionally it left much to be desired, for the life of the church was based on the faith that it was possible to have a direct relationship with a personal God, and the supreme being of the philosophers was in no way personal.

There was another way to resolve the conflict between the philosophical

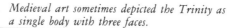

Medieval art sometimes depicted the Trinity as a single body with three faces.

idea of a supreme being and the witness of Scripture. This was the doctrine of the Logos, as developed by Justin, Clement, Origen, and others. According to this view, although it is true that the supreme being—the "Father"—is immutable, impassible, and so on, there is also a Logos, Word, or Reason of God, and this is personal, capable of direct relations with the world and with humans. Thus, according to Justin, when the Bible says that God spoke to Moses, what it means is that the Logos of God spoke to him.

Due to the influence of Origen and his disciples, these views had become widespread in the Eastern wing of the church—that is, that portion of the church that spoke Greek rather than Latin. The generally accepted view was that, between the immutable One and the mutable world, there was the Word or Logos of God. It was within this context that the Arian controversy took place.

The controversy itself began in Alexandria, when Licinius was still ruling in the East, and Constantine in the West. The bishop of Alexandria, Alexander, clashed over several issues with Arius, who was one of the most prestigious and popular presbyters of the city. Although the points debated were many, the main issue at stake was whether the Word of God was coeternal with God. The phrase that eventually became the Arian motto, "there was when He was not," aptly focuses on the point at issue. Alexander held that the Word existed eternally with the Father; Arius argued that the Word was not coeternal with the Father. Although this may seem a very fine point, what was ultimately at stake was the divinity of the Word. Arius claimed that, strictly speaking, the Word was not God, but the first of all creatures. It is important to understand at this point that Arius did not deny that the Word existed before the incarnation. On the preexistence of the Word, all were in agreement. What Arius said was that, before anything else was made, the Word had been created by God. Alexander argued that the Word was divine, and therefore could not be created, but rather was coeternal with the Father. In other words, if asked to draw a line between God and creation, Arius would draw that line so as to include the Word in creation, while Alexander would draw it so as to separate all of creation on one side from the Father and the eternal Word on the other.

Each of the two parties had, besides a list of favorite proof-texts from the Bible, logical reasons that seemed to make the opponents' position untenable. Arius, on the one hand, argued that what Alexander proposed was a denial of Christian monotheism—for, according to the bishop of Alexandria, there were two who were divine, and thus there were two gods. Alexander retorted that Arius' position denied the divinity of the Word, and therefore also the divinity of Jesus. From its very beginning, the church had worshiped Jesus Christ, and Arius' proposal would now force it either to cease such worship, or to declare that it was worshiping a creature. Both alternatives being unacceptable, Arius was proven wrong.

The conflict broke out in public when Alexander, claiming that such was his authority and his responsibility as a bishop, condemned Arius' teachings and removed him from all posts in the church in Alexandria. Arius did not accept this judgment, but rather appealed both to the people of Alexandria and to a number of prominent bishops throughout the eastern portion of the Empire who had been his fellow students in Antioch. Soon there were popular demonstrations in Alexandria, with people marching on the streets chanting Arius' theological refrains. And the bishops to whom Arius had appealed wrote letters declaring that the deposed presbyter was correct, and that it was Alexander who taught false doctrine. Thus, the local disagreement in Alexandria threatened to divide the entire Eastern church.

Such was the state of affairs when Constantine, who had just defeated Licinius, decided to intervene. His first step was to send bishop Hosius of Cordova, his advisor in ecclesiastical matters, to try to reconcile the two parties. When Hosius reported that the dissension could not be resolved by mere amicable entreaties, Constantine decided to take a step that he had been considering for some time: he would call a great assembly or council of Christian bishops from all parts of the Empire. Besides dealing with a number of issues where it was necessary to set standard policies, this great council would resolve the controversy that had broken out in Alexandria.

The Council of Nicea

It was the year 325 when the bishops gathered in Nicea, a city in Asia Minor within easy reach of Constantinople, for what later would be known as the First Ecumenical—that is, universal—Council. The exact number of bishops present is not known—the figure 318, given in ancient chronicles, is doubted by some scholars, since it coincides with the number of those circumcised in Abraham's time—but there were approximately three hundred, mostly from the Greek-speaking East, but also some from the West. In order to understand that event as those present saw it, it is necessary to remember that several of those attending the great assembly had recently been imprisoned, tortured, or exiled, and that some bore on their bodies the physical marks of their faithfulness. And now, a few years after such trials, these very bishops were invited to gather at Nicea, and the emperor covered their expenses. Many of those present knew of each other by hearsay or through correspondence. But now, for the first time in the history of Christianity, they had before their eyes physical evidence of the universality of the church. In his *Life of Constantine,* Eusebius of Cesarea, who was present, describes the scene:

There were gathered the most distinguished ministers of God, from the many churches in Europe, Libya [i.e., Africa] and Asia. A single house of prayer, as if enlarged by God, sheltered Syrians and Cilicians, Phoenicians and Arabs, delegates

Constantine, who was not yet baptized, presided over the Council of Nicea.

from Palestine and from Egypt, Thebans and Libyans, together with those from Mesopotamia. There was also a Persian bishop, and a Scythian was not lacking. Pontus, Galatia, Pamphylia, Cappadocia, Asia, and Phrygia sent their most outstanding bishops, jointly with those from the remotest areas of Thrace, Macedonia, Achaia, and Epirus. Even from Spain, there was a man of great fame [Hosius of Cordova] who sat as a member of the great assembly. The bishop of the Imperial City [Rome] could not attend due to his advanced age; but he was represented by his presbyters. Constantine is the first ruler of all time to have gathered such a garland in the bond of peace, and to have presented it to his Savior as an offering of gratitude for the victories he had won over all his enemies.*

In this euphoric atmosphere, the bishops discussed the many legislative matters that had to be resolved after the end of persecution. They approved standard procedures for the readmission of the lapsed, for the election and ordination of presbyters and bishops, and regarding the order of precedence of various episcopal sees.

But the most difficult issue that the Council had to face was the Arian controversy. On this score, there were several different groups whose positions and concerns had to be taken into account.

There was first of all a small number of convinced Arians, led by

*Eusebius of Caesarea, *Life of Constantine* 3.7.

Eusebius of Nicomedia—this bishop, who played a central role throughout the early years of the controversy, is not to be confused with historian Eusebius of Cesarea. Since Arius was not a bishop, he was not allowed to sit in the Council, and it was Eusebius of Nicomedia who spoke for him and for the position that he represented. This small group was convinced that what Arius taught was so patently correct that all that was needed was a clear exposition of the logic of the argument, and the assembly would vindicate Arius and rebuke Alexander for having condemned his teachings.

In direct opposition to the Arian party, there was another small group of bishops who were convinced that Arianism threatened the very core of the Christian faith, and that therefore it was necessary to condemn it in no uncertain terms. The leader of this group was Alexander of Alexandria. Among his followers was a young man who, being only a deacon, could not sit in the Council, but who would eventually become famous as the champion of Nicene orthodoxy: Athanasius of Alexandria.

Most of the bishops from the Latin-speaking West had only a secondary interest in the debate, which appeared to them as a controversy among eastern followers of Origen. For them, it was sufficient to declare that in God there were, as Tertullian had said long before, "three persons and one substance."

Another small group—probably no more than three or four—held positions approaching "patripassianism," that is, that the Father and the Son are the same, and that therefore the Father suffered the passion. These bishops agreed that Arianism was wrong, but their own doctrines were also rejected in the later course of the controversy, as the church began to clarify what it meant by Trinitarian doctrine.

Finally, the vast majority of those present did not belong to any of these groups. They bemoaned the outbreak of a controversy that threatened to divide the church at a time when persecution had finally come to an end and there were new opportunities and challenges to be met. It seems that at the beginning of the sessions these bishops hoped to achieve a compromise that would make it possible to move on to other matters. A typical example of this attitude was Eusebius of Cesarea, the learned historian whose erudition gained him great respect among his fellow bishops.

From the report of those present, what changed matters was the exposition that Eusebius of Nicomedia made of his own views—which were also those of Arius. He seems to have been convinced that a clear statement of his doctrine was all that was needed to convince the assembly. But when the bishops heard his explanation, their reaction was the opposite of what Eusebius of Nicomedia had expected. The assertion that the Word or Son was no more than a creature, no matter how high a creature, provoked angry reactions from many of the bishops: "You lie!" "Blasphemy!" "Heresy!" Eusebius was shouted down, and we are told that his speech was snatched from his hand, torn to shreds, and trampled underfoot.

The mood of the majority had now changed. Whereas earlier they hoped to deal with the issues at stake through negotiation and compromise, without condemning any doctrine, now they were convinced that they had to reject Arianism in the clearest way possible.

At first the assembly sought to do this through a series of passages of Scripture. But it soon became evident that by limiting itself to biblical texts the Council would find it very difficult to express its rejection of Arianism in unmistakable terms. It was then decided to agree on a creed that would express the faith of the church in such a way that Arianism was clearly excluded. The exact process that was followed is not entirely clear. Eusebius of Cesarea, for reasons that scholars still debate, read the creed of his own church. Constantine suggested that the word *homoousios*—to which we shall return—be included in the creed. Eventually, the assembly agreed on a formula that clearly rejected Arianism:

We believe in one God, the Father Almighty, maker of all things visible and invisible.

And in one Lord Jesus Christ, the Son of God, the only-begotten of the Father, that is, from the substance of the Father, God of God, light of light, true God of true God, begotten, not made, of one substance [homoousios] with the Father, through whom all things were made, both in heaven and on earth, who for us humans and for our salvation descended and became incarnate, becoming human, suffered and rose again on the third day, ascended to the heavens, and will come to judge the living and the dead.

And in the Holy Spirit.

But those who say that there was when He was not, and that before being begotten He was not, or that He came from that which is not, or that the Son of God is of a different substance [hypostasis] or essence [ousia], or that He is created, or mutable, these the catholic church anathematizes.*

This formula, with a number of later additions, and without the anathemas of the last paragraph, provided the basis for what is now called the "Nicene Creed," which is the most universally accepted Christian creed. The "Apostles' Creed," being Roman in origin, is known and used only in churches of Western origin—the Roman Catholic Church, and those stemming from the Protestant Reformation. The Nicene Creed, on the other hand, is acknowledged both by these Western churches and by those of the East—Greek Orthodox, Russian Orthodox, and the like.

When one reads the formula as approved by the bishops at Nicea, it is clear that their main concern was to reject any notion that the Son or Word —Logos—was a creature, or a being less divine than the Father. This may be seen first of all in affirmations such as "God of God, light of light, true God of true God." But it is also the reason why the Creed declares that the Son is "begotten, not made." Note that the Creed began by declaring that

---

*Eusebius of Caesarea, *Epistle to the Caesareans.*

the Father is "maker of all things visible and invisible." Thus, in declaring that the Son is "begotten, not made," he is being excluded from those things "visible and invisible" made by the Father. Furthermore, in the last paragraph, those are condemned who declare that the Son "came from that which is not"—that is, out of nothing, like creation. Also, in the text of the Creed itself, we are told that the Son was begotten "from the substance of the Father."

The key word, however, and the one that was the subject of much controversy, is *homoousios,* which is usually translated as "of the same substance." This was intended to convey that the Son was just as divine as the Father. But it also provided the main reason for later resistance to the Creed of Nicea, for it seemed to imply that there was no distinction between Father and Son, and thus to leave the door open for patripassianism.

The bishops gathered at Nicea hoped that the creed on which they had agreed, together with the clear anathemas appended to it, would put an end to the Arian controversy, and proceeded to sign it. Very few—Eusebius of Nicomedia among them—refused to sign. These the assembly declared to be heretical, and deposed them. But Constantine added his own sentence to that of the bishops, banishing the deposed bishops from their cities. He probably intended only to avoid further unrest. But this addition of a civil sentence to an ecclesiastical one had serious consequences, for it established a precedent for the intervention of secular authority in behalf of what was considered orthodox doctrine.

In spite of what the bishops had hoped, the Council of Nicea did not end the controversy. Eusebius of Nicomedia was an able politician, and we are even told that he was distantly related to the emperor. His strategy was to court the approval of Constantine, who soon allowed him to return to Nicomedia. Since the emperor's summer residence was in Nicomedia, soon Eusebius was able to present his case once again before Constantine. Eventually, the emperor decided that he had been too harsh on the Arians. Arius himself was recalled from exile, and Constantine ordered the bishop of Constantinople to restore him to communion. The bishop was debating whether to obey the emperor or his conscience, when Arius died.

Alexander of Alexandria died in 328, and was succeeded by Athanasius, who as a deacon had been present at the Council of Nicea, and who would now become the champion of the Nicene cause. He soon became so identified with that cause that the subsequent history of the Arian controversy is best told by following Athanasius' life. This will be the subject of Chapter 19, and therefore it is not necessary here to follow the later course of the controversy in any detail. Let it suffice to say that Eusebius of Nicomedia and his followers managed to have Athanasius exiled by order of Constantine. By then, most of the Nicene leaders were also banished. When Constantine finally asked for baptism, on his deathbed, he received the sacrament from Eusebius of Nicomedia.

After a brief interregnum, Constantine was succeeded by three of his sons: Constantine II, Constans, and Constantius II. Constantine II ruled over Gaul, Great Britain, Spain, and Morocco. Constantius' territory included most of the East. And Constans was alotted a strip of land between his two brothers, including Italy and North Africa. At first the new situation favored the Nicene party, for the eldest of Constantine's three sons took their side, and recalled Athanasius and the others from exile. But then war broke out between Constantine II and Constans, and this provided an opportunity for Constantius, who ruled in the East, to follow his pro-Arian inclinations. Once again Athanasius was exiled, only to return when, after the death of Constantine II, the West was united under Constans, and Constantius was forced to follow a more moderate policy. Eventually, however, Constantius became sole emperor, and it was then that, as Jerome said, "the entire world woke from a deep slumber and discovered that it had become Arian." Once again the Nicene leaders had to leave their cities, and imperial pressure was such that eventually even the elderly Hosius of Cordova and Liberius—the bishop of Rome—signed Arian confessions of faith.

Such was the state of affairs when the unexpected death of Constantius changed the course of events. He was succeeded by his cousin Julian, later known by Christian historians as "the Apostate." Profiting from the endless dissension among Christians, the pagan reaction had come to power.

18/The Pagan Reaction: Julian the Apostate

This is how that very humane prince [Constantius] dealt with us, although we were close relatives. Without benefit of trial, he killed six of our common cousins, my father, who was his uncle, another uncle on my father's side, and my older brother.

JULIAN THE APOSTATE

J ulian had many reasons to dislike both Constantius and the Christian faith that the latter professed. At the time of Constantine's death, most of the dead emperor's close relatives had been massacred. The only notable exceptions were the three brothers who inherited the throne, and their cousins Julian and Gallus—an older brother of Julian. The circumstances in which these crimes were committed are not altogether clear, and therefore it may be unfair to lay the blame on Constantius. It is clear that after Constantine's death there was some question as to who would succeed him, and that the army then killed most of his relatives—not in order to set up another dynasty, but rather in order to make sure that power would belong undisputably to Constantine's three surviving sons. Of these, only Constantius was then in Constantinople, where the massacre took place, and for that reason the common opinion was that he had ordered, or at least condoned, the death of his relatives.

Whatever the case may be, Julian was convinced that his cousin was guilty. Julian's father was a half-brother of Constantine, and therefore Julian was a first cousin to the three new emperors. Of Julian's vast family, only he and his half-brother survived. He later declared that Gallus, that half-brother, was spared because he appeared to be mortally ill at the time, and that Julian himself was allowed to live because he was only six years old, and thus was

Julian, known to posterity as "the Apostate," was an able ruler who sought to restore the glories of ancient Rome.

no threat to the throne. It is possible that Constantius himself ordered that these two cousins be allowed to live, for they were too young to lead a rebellion; and if Constantine's three sons died without issue, these younger cousins could provide for an orderly succession to the throne.

Meanwhile, both Gallus and Julian were kept away from the court. While Gallus devoted himself to physical exercise, his younger brother became increasingly interested in philosophical studies. Both were baptized and received Christian instruction, and during their exile from court both were made "readers" of the church.

Eventually, Constantius had to call on Gallus, for in A.D. 350 he had become sole ruler of the Empire, and he had no children who could aid him in government or succeed him to the throne. In 351, Constantius gave Gallus the title of "caesar," that is, of junior emperor, and set vast territories under his rule. But Gallus did not turn out to be an able ruler, and there were rumors that he was conspiring against his cousin. A few years after having made him caesar, Constantius had him arrested and beheaded.

Meanwhile, Julian had continued his philosophical studies in Athens, a city famous as the seat of much of ancient wisdom. There he knew Basil of Caesarea, a devout Christian who would eventually become one of the greatest bishops of his time. It was also there that he became interested in the ancient mystery religions. He had definitively abandoned Christianity, and sought after truth and beauty in the literature and religion of classical Greece.

Constantius decided to set aside the bad experience he had had with

Gallus and called his one surviving relative to share his power, giving him the title of caesar and appointing him to rule in Gaul. No one expected Julian, who had spent his life among books and philosophers, to be a great ruler, and in any case Constantius granted him very little support. But Julian surprised his contemporaries. His administration in Gaul was exemplary. And, when the occasion arose to lead a campaign against the barbarians, he proved that he was an able general and gained great popularity in the army.

All this was not entirely to Constantius' liking, for he feared that Julian might seek possession of the throne. Tension increased between the two cousins. When Constantius, who was preparing a campaign against Persia, called the troops in Gaul to the East, they rebelled and proclaimed Julian "augustus," that is, supreme emperor. As soon as Constantius was free of the Persian threat, he marched against Julian and his rebellious troops. When war seemed unavoidable, and both sides prepared for it, Constantius died. Julian had no difficulty in marching to Constantinople and claiming the rule of the whole Empire. It was the year 361.

Julian's first action was to seek revenge from those most responsible for his misfortunes, and from those who had sought to keep him away from the seat of power. To that end he named a court that was theoretically independent, but that in truth responded to the wishes of the emperor. This court condemned several of his worst enemies to death.

Apart from this, Julian was an able ruler, who managed to set order in the chaotic administration of his vast domains. Yet is is not for such actions that he is most remembered, but rather for his religious policy, which earned him the title by which history knows him: "the Apostate."

Julian's Religious Policy

Julian sought both to restore the lost glory of paganism, and to impede the progress of Christianity. Since the time of Constantine, paganism had lost a great deal of its ancient splendor. Constantine himself had not persecuted paganism, nor sought to force the conversion of pagans. But he had sacked ancient temples in order to obtain works of art with which to decorate his new capital city. Under his sons, there were a number of laws passed favoring Christianity. By the time Julian became sole emperor, the ancient temples were practically empty, and there were pagan priests dressed only in rags, trying to supplement their meagre income in a dozen ways and paying scant attention to the ancient rites.

Julian wished to bring about a total restoration and reformation of paganism. To that end he ordered that everything that had been taken from the temples was to be returned to them. Following the example of the Christian church, he organized the pagan priesthood into a hierarchy similar

Julian pursued his philosophical studies in Athens.

to that which the church had by that time. Thus, he divided his entire Empire into regions, each with an archpriest who was above all the pagan priests in that region. The various archpriests of a region were under the high priest of a province. And these high priests were under a "supreme priest," who was Julian himself. All members of this priestly hierarchy were to lead an exemplary life, and they should be concerned, not only with worship, but also with acts of charity for those in need. While rejecting Christianity, Julian actually learned a great deal from it.

While this vast program of religious renewal was being organized, Julian took more direct steps to restore the ancient worship of the gods. He saw himself as chosen by them to do this work; and therefore, while he waited for the entire Empire to return to its ancient faith, he was committed to render unto the gods the worship and the sacrifices that others did not render. By his order there were massive sacrifices in which the gods were offered hundreds of bulls and other animals at a time. But Julian, who was a wise ruler, was well aware that his restoration of paganism was not as popular as he would have wished. People mocked his new ceremonies, even while participating in them. For that reason it seemed necessary, not only to promote paganism, but also to hinder Christianity, its most powerful rival.

To this end Julian took a series of measures, although in all justice it is necessary to insist that he never decreed persecution against Christians. Although there were Christian martyrs in a number of places, this was due, not to imperial command, but rather to mob actions or to overzealous local officials. Julian himself was convinced that persecution of Christians would not help his cause.

Rather than persecuting Christians, Julian followed a two-pronged policy of hindering their progress and ridiculing them. On the first score, he passed laws forbidding Christians to teach classical literature. Thus, while prohibiting what to him was a sacrilege, he kept Christians from using the great works of classical antiquity to spread their faith, as they had been doing since the time of Justin in the second century. Secondly, Julian set out to ridicule Christians, whom he called "Galileans." With this in mind he wrote a work *Against the Galileans,* in which he showed that he knew the Bible, and mocked both its contents and the teachings of Jesus. He then decided to rebuild the Temple in Jerusalem, not because he felt any particular liking towards Judaism, but rather as a practical rebuttal of the common Christian argument that the destruction of the Temple had been the fulfillment of prophecies in the Old Testament.

All these projects were moving along as rapidly as possible, when death overtook him quite unexpectedly. Julian was leading his troops in a campaign against the Persians when he was fatally wounded by an enemy spear. A famous legend, but one lacking all historical foundation, claims that his last words were: "Thou hast conquered, Galilean!"

19/Athanasius of Alexandria

*The results of the incarnation of the Savior
are such and so many, that anyone
attempting to enumerate them should be
compared to a person looking upon the
vastness of the sea and attempting to count
its waves.*

ATHANASIUS OF ALEXANDRIA

Among those who were present at the Council of Nicea there was a young man, so dark and short that his enemies called him "the black dwarf." This was Athanasius, Alexander's secretary, who would soon become one of the central figures in the controversy, and the champion of Nicene orthodoxy. He was one of the great leaders—or "fathers"—of the fourth century, to whose biographies we now turn as the best way to understand the events of that time.

The Early Years

The time and place of Athanasius' birth are not known, although it is likely that he had rather obscure origins in a small town or village on the shore of the Nile. Since he spoke Coptic, the language of the original inhabitants of the area who had been successively conquered by the Greeks and the Romans, and his complexion was dark, like that of the Copts, it is very likely that he belonged to that group, and that therefore he was a member of the lower classes in Egypt. He certainly never claimed to be of high birth, nor to be well-versed in the subtleties of Greco-Roman culture.

During his early years he was in close contact with the monks of the desert. Jerome affirms that he gave a cloak to Paul the Hermit; and Athanasius himself, in his *Life of Saint Anthony,* says that he used to visit that

Mocked as "the black dwarf," Athanasius was a theological giant.

famous monk and wash the old man's hands. This last detail has led some to venture the suggestion that when he was a child Athanasius served Anthony. Whatever the case may be, there is no doubt that throughout his life Athanasius kept in close contact with the monks of the desert, who repeatedly gave him support and asylum.

From the monks, Athanasius learned a rigid discipline that he applied to himself, and an austerity that earned him the admiration of his friends and even the respect of many of his enemies. Of all the opponents of Arianism, Athanasius was most to be feared. The reasons for this were not to be found in subtlety of logical argument, nor in elegance of style, nor even in political perspicacity. In all these areas, Athanasius could be bested by his opponents. His strong suit was in his close ties to the people among whom he lived, and in living out his faith without the subtleties of the Arians or the pomp of so many bishops of other important sees. His monastic discipline, his roots among the people, his fiery spirit, and his profound and unshakable conviction made him invincible.

Even before the Arian controversy broke out, Athanasius had written two works, *Against the Gentiles* and *On the Incarnation of the Word,* which gave a clue as to the nature of his theology. The speculations of Clement or of Origen are not to be found here. These works show the deep conviction that the central fact of Christian faith, as well as of all human history, is the incarnation of God in Jesus Christ. The presence of God amid humankind, made human: that is the heart of Christianity as Athanasius understands it.

In a memorable passage, he speaks of the incarnation in terms of an imperial visit to a city. The emperor decides on such a visit, and resides in one of the houses of the city. As a result, not only that house, but the entire town, receive a special honor and protection. Bandits stay away from such a place. Likewise, the Monarch of the universe has come to visit our human city, living in one of our houses, and thanks to such a presence we are all protected from the attacks and wiles of the Evil One. Now, by virtue of that visit from God in Jesus Christ, we are free to be what God intends us to be —that is, beings capable of living in communion with the divine.

Clearly, the presence of God in history was the central element in the faith of Athanasius. Therefore, it is not surprising that he saw Arianism as a grave threat to the very heart of Christianity. What Arius taught was that the one who had come to us in Jesus Christ was not truly God, but a lesser being, a creature. Such a notion was unacceptable to Athanasius—as it was also to the monks who had withdrawn to the desert for love of God Incarnate, and to the faithful who gathered to participate in worship under Athanasius' leadership. For Athanasius, for the monks, and for many of the faithful, the Arian controversy was not a matter of theological subtleties with little or no relevance. In it, the very core of the Christian message was at stake.

When Alexander, the bishop of Alexandria, was on his deathbed, all took for granted that he would be succeeded by Athanasius. But the young man, whose purpose was to live in peace offering the sacraments and worshiping with the people, fled to the desert. It is said that, shortly before he died, Alexander asked for his younger friend, probably in order to indicate that he wished him to be the next bishop of Alexandria. But Athanasius was still in hiding. Finally, several weeks after the death of Alexander, and much against his own wishes, Athanasius was made bishop of Alexandria. The year was 328, the same year in which Constantine revoked the sentence banishing Arius. Arianism was regaining ground, and the battle lines were being drawn.

Through Many Trials

Eusebius of Nicomedia and the other Arian leaders knew that Athanasius was one of their most formidable enemies. They soon began to take steps to assure his downfall, circulating rumors that he dabbled in magic, and that he was a tyrant over the Christian flock in Egypt. As a result, Constantine ordered him to appear before a synod gathered at Tyre, where he was to answer to grave charges brought against him. In particular, he was accused of having killed a certain Arsenius, a bishop of a rival group, and having cut off his hand in order to use it in rites of magic. A chronicle with a flair for the dramatic reports that Athanasius went to Tyre as ordered, and after hearing the charges brought against him he brought into the room a man covered in a cloak. After making sure that several of those present knew Arsenius, he uncovered the face of the hooded man, and his accusers were confounded when they realized that it was Athanasius' supposed victim. Then someone who had been convinced by the rumors circulating against the bishop of Alexandria suggested that perhaps Athanasius had not killed Arsenius, but had cut off his hand. Athanasius waited until the assembly insisted on proof that the man's hand had not been cut. He then uncovered one of Arsenius' hands. "It was the other hand!" shouted some of those who had been convinced by the rumors. Then Athanasius uncovered the man's other hand and demanded: "What kind of a monster did you think Arsenius was? One with three hands?" Laughter broke out through the assembly, while others were enraged that the Arians had fooled them.

Free from the accusations made before the synod of Tyre, Athanasius decided to go on to Constantinople in order to present his case before the emperor. Eusebius of Nicomedia had a great deal of influence at court, and Athanasius found it impossible to gain admission to the emperor. He then took bolder steps. One day when Constantine was out for a ride, the tiny bishop of Alexandria simply jumped in front of the emperor's horse, grabbed its bridle, and did not let it go until he had been granted an audience. Perhaps such methods were necessary, given the political situation at court. But they served to convince Constantine that Athanasius was indeed a dangerous and impulsive fanatic. Therefore, he was willing to listen some time later, when Eusebius of Nicomedia told him that Athanasius had boasted that he could stop the shipments of wheat from Egypt to Rome. On the basis of Eusebius' accusation, Constantine sent Athanasius away from Alexandria, banishing him to the city of Trier, in the West.

But shortly thereafter Constantine died—after having been baptized by Eusebius of Nicomedia—and was succeeded by his three sons Constantine II, Constans, and Constantius. The three brothers decided that all exiled bishops—there were a number of them—could return to their sees.

Yet Athanasius' return to Alexandria was not the end, but rather the beginning, of a long period of struggle and repeated exiles. There was an Arian party in Alexandria, and these people now claimed that Athanasius, who had been away, was not the legitimate bishop. The rival claimant, a certain Gregory, had the support of the government. Since Athanasius was not willing to give him the church buildings, Gregory decided to take them by force, and the result was a series of disorders of such magnitude that Athanasius decided that, in order to avoid further violence, it was best for him to leave the city. There were also indications that the authorities blamed him for the disorders. This was confirmed when he reached the port and was refused passage because the governor had forbidden it. Eventually he convinced one of the captains, who smuggled him out of the port and took him to Rome.

Athanasius' exile in Rome was fruitful. Both the Arians and the Nicenes

Constantius II, named after his grandfather Constantius Chlorus, eventually became sole heir to Constantine's empire. A staunch supporter of Arianism, he almost succeeded in stamping out all resistance to it.

had requested support from Julius, the bishop of Rome. Athanasius was able to present the Nicene position in person, and he soon gained the support of the Roman clergy, who took up the Nicene cause against the Arians. Eventually, a synod gathered in the ancient capital declared that Athanasius was the legitimate bishop of Alexandria, and that Gregory was a usurper. Although this did not mean that Athanasius could return to Alexandria immediately, it did signal the support of the Western church for the Nicene cause, and for Athanasius in particular.

After the death of Constantine II, Constans became sole emperor in the West, and he then asked Constantius, who ruled in the East, to permit the return of Athanasius to Alexandria. Since at that particular moment Constantius needed the support of his brother, he granted the request, and Athanasius was able to return to Alexandria.

The mismanagement of Gregory in Alexandria had been such that the people received Athanasius as a hero or a liberator. It is possible that one of the factors involved in this situation was that Gregory and the Arian party represented the more Hellenized higher classes, whereas Athanasius was the man of the people. In any case, he was given a noisy and joyous welcome. Besides the inhabitants of the city, many monks came from the desert to join in the celebrations. With such show of support, Athanasius was free from the attacks of his enemies for approximately ten years. During that time he strengthened his ties with other defenders of orthodoxy, particularly through abundant correspondence. It was also at this time that he wrote a number of treatises against Arianism.

But Emperor Constantius was a convinced Arian, and felt the need to rid himself of this champion of the Nicene faith. As long as Constans lived, Constantius endured the presence of Athanasius, who counted on the support of the western emperor. Then a certain Magnentius tried to usurp power in the West, and Constantius had to use all his resources against this new rival.

Finally, in A.D. 353, Constantius, who now ruled the whole Empire, felt sufficiently secure to unleash his pro-Arian policy. Through threats and the use of force, an increasing number of bishops accepted Arianism. It is said that when Constantius ordered a synod to condemn Athanasius and was told that this was not possible, since the canons of the church did not permit them to condemn someone without a hearing, the emperor responded: "My will also is a canon of the church." On that ominous threat, many of the bishops signed the condemnation of Athanasius. Those who refused were banished.

If the chroniclers of the time are to be believed, Constantius feared the power Athanasius had in Alexandria, and for that reason sought to remove him from that city without actually banishing him. Athanasius received a letter in which the emperor granted him an audience that had never been requested. The bishop answered politely that there must have been an error, for he had not asked for such an honor, and did not wish to waste the emperor's valuable time. Constantius then ordered a concentration of troops in Alexandria. When the legions were in place and any revolt could be crushed, the governor ordered Athanasius, in the name of the emperor, to leave the city. Athanasius responded by showing the old imperial order in which he was given permission to return. There must be a mistake, he told the governor, since the emperor would not contradict himself.

Shortly thereafter, when Athanasius was celebrating communion in one of the churches, the governor ordered the building to be surrounded and suddenly burst into the room leading a group of armed soldiers. There was chaos, and Athanasius ordered the congregation to sing Psalm 136, with the refrain: "For His mercy endureth forever." The soldiers pushed their way through the crowd, while some sang and others sought to escape. The clergy who were present formed a tight circle around Athanasius, who refused to flee until his flock was safe. But at that point he fainted, and somehow the clergy carried him to safety.

From that moment, Athanasius seemed to have become a ghost. He was sought everywhere, but the authorities could not find him. He had taken refuge among the monks of the desert, his faithful allies. These monks had means of communication among themselves, and whenever the officers of the Empire approached the bishop's hideout, he was simply transfered to a safer place.

For five years, Athanasius lived among the monks in the desert. During those five years, the Nicene cause suffered severe setbacks. Imperial policy was openly in favor of the Arians. Several synods were forced to declare themselves for Arianism. Eventually, even Hosius of Cordova and Liberius of Rome, both well advanced in years, were forced to sign Arian confessions of faith. Although many bishops and other church leaders were convinced that Arianism was unacceptable, it was difficult to oppose it when the state supported it so decisively. The high point for Arianism came when a council gathered in Sirmium openly rejected the decisions of Nicea. This was what orthodox leaders called the "Blasphemy of Sirmium."

Unexpectedly, Constantius died and was succeeded by his cousin Julian. Since the new emperor had no interest in supporting either side of the controversy, he simply canceled all orders of exile against all bishops. He was hoping that the two parties would weaken each other while he moved forward in his goal of restoring paganism. One of the consequences of this action was that Athanasius was able to return to Alexandria, where he undertook a much-needed campaign of theological diplomacy.

A Theological Agreement

Athanasius had come to the conclusion that many opposed the Nicene Creed because they feared that the assertion that the Son was of the same substance as the Father could be understood as meaning that there is no distinction between the Father and the Son. Therefore, some preferred not to say "of the same substance," but rather "of a similar substance." The two Greek words were *homoousios* (of the same substance) and *homoiousios* (of a similar substance). The Council of Nicea had declared the Son to be *homoousios* with the Father. But now many were saying that they would rather affirm that the Son was *homoiousios* with the Father.

At an earlier time, Athanasius had insisted on the Nicene formula declaring that those who said "of a similar substance" were as heretical as the Arians. But now the elderly bishop of Alexandria was ready to see the legitimate concern of those Christians who, while refusing Arianism, were not ready to give up the distinction between the Father and the Son.

Through a series of negotiations, Athanasius convinced many of these Christians that the formula of Nicea could be interpreted in such a way as to respond to the concerns of those who would rather say, "of a similar substance." Finally, in a synod gathered in Alexandria in A.D. 362, Athanasius and his followers declared that it was acceptable to refer to the Father, Son, and Holy Spirit as "one substance" as long as this was not understood as obliterating the distinction among the three, and that it was also legitimate to speak of "three substances" as long as this was not understood as if there were three gods. On the basis of this understanding, most of the church rallied in its support to the Council of Nicea, whose doctrine was eventually ratified at the Second Ecumenical Council, gathered in Constantinople in A.D. 381. But Athanasius would not live to see the final victory of the cause to which he devoted most of his life.

Further Trials

Although Julian did not wish to persecute Christians, the news that arrived from Alexandria disturbed him. His efforts to restore paganism were met with the staunch resistance of Athanasius, who by now had become a popular hero. If imperial policy were to succeed in Alexandria, it was necessary to exile its bishop once again. It soon became clear to Athanasius that Julian wanted to remove him not only from Alexandria, but also from Egypt. Athanasius knew that he could not remain in the city, where there was no place to hide, and therefore resolved to seek refuge once again among the monks.

Being aware that Athanasius was planning to hide in the desert, the imperial authorities sought to arrest him. According to some biographers of Athanasius, he was a passenger being carried upstream on the Nile when a faster ship was about to overtake him. "Have you seen Athanasius?" shouted some soldiers from the other ship. "Yes," Athanasius answered quite truthfully. "He is just ahead of you, and if you hurry you shall overtake him." Soon the other ship was lost ahead of Athanasius.

As we have seen, Julian's reign did not last long. He was succeeded by Jovian, who was an admirer of Athanasius. Once again the bishop of Alexandria returned from exile, although he was soon called to Antioch to counsel the emperor. When he finally returned to Alexandria, it seemed that his long chain of exiles had come to an end.

But Jovian died in a few months and was succeeded by Valens, a staunch defender of Arianism. Fearing that the emperor would take measures against the orthodox in Alexandria if he remained in the city, Athanasius resolved to leave once again. It soon became evident, however, that Valens was not eager to tangle with the bishop who had bested both Constantius and Julian. Athanasius was thus able to return to Alexandria, where he remained until death claimed him in A.D. 373.

Although Athanasius never saw the final victory of the cause to which he devoted his life, his writings clearly show that he was convinced that in the end Arianism would be defeated. As he approached his old age, he saw emerge around himself a new generation of theologians devoted to the same cause. Most remarkable among these were the Great Cappadocians, to whom we now turn our attention.

20/The Great Cappadocians

Not for all, my friends not for all is it to philosophize about God, since the subject is neither that simple nor that lowly. Not for all, nor before all, nor at all times, nor on all themes, but rather before some, at some times and with some bounds.

GREGORY OF NAZIANZUS

The region of Cappadocia was in southern Asia Minor, in lands now belonging to Turkey. There lived three church leaders known under the collective title of "the Great Cappadocians." These are Basil of Caesarea, the theologian known as "The Great"; his brother Gregory of Nyssa, famous for his works on mystical contemplation; and their friend Gregory of Nazianzus, a poet and orator, many of whose hymns have become classical in the Greek-speaking church. But before turning our attention to them, justice requires that we deal with another person just as worthy, although often forgotten by historians who tend to ignore the work of women. This remarkable woman was Macrina, the sister of Basil and Gregory of Nyssa.

Macrina

The family in which Macrina, Basil, and Gregory were raised had deep Christian roots that went back at least two generations. Their paternal grandparents had spent seven years hiding in the forests during the Decian persecution. In that exile, they were accompanied by several members of their household, including their two sons, Gregory and Basil. This Gregory, who was to be the uncle of our Cappadocians, later became a bishop. His brother Basil, the father of Macrina and her brothers, became a famous lawyer and teacher of rhetoric. His wife was the daughter of a Christian martyr. Thus, the grandparents of our Cappadocians, both on the maternal and paternal sides, had been Christians, and one of their uncles was a bishop.

Macrina was twelve years old when her parents decided to make arrangements for her marriage, as was then customary. They settled on a young relative who was planning to become a lawyer, and Macrina acquiesced. Everything was ready when the groom died, quite unexpectedly. Thereafter, Macrina refused to accept any other suitor, and eventually vowed herself to celibacy and to a life of contemplation.

Some two or three years before Macrina's engagement, Basil had been born. He was a sickly child whose survival was in doubt for a time. The elder Basil, who had always wanted a son, gave this one the best education available, in the hope that he would continue in his father's footsteps as a lawyer and orator. Young Basil studied first at Caesarea, the main city in Cappadocia; later in Antioch and Constantinople; and finally in Athens. It was in the ancient Greek city that he met Gregory, who would eventually become bishop of Nazianzus, as well as Prince Julian, later dubbed "the Apostate."

After such studies, Basil returned to Caesarea, puffed up in his own wisdom. His studies, as well as his family's prestige, guaranteed him a place of importance in Caesarean society. Soon he was offered a position teaching rhetoric.

It was then that Macrina intervened. She bluntly told her brother that he had become vain, acting as if he were the best inhabitant of the city, and that he would do well in quoting fewer pagan authors and following more of the advice of Christian ones. Basil shrugged aside his sister's comments, telling himself that, after all, she was rather unlearned.

Then tragic news arrived. Their brother Naucratius, who was living in retirement in the country, had died unexpectedly. Basil was shaken. He and Naucratius had been very close. In recent times their paths had diverged, for Naucratius had forsaken worldly pomps, while Basil had devoted himself wholeheartedly to them. The blow was such that Basil changed his life entirely. He resigned his teaching position and all other honors, and he asked Macrina to teach him the secrets of religious life. A short time earlier their father had died, and it was now Macrina who became the strength and consolation of her bereaved family.

Macrina sought to console her family by leading their thoughts to the joys of religious life. Why not withdraw to their holdings in nearby Annesi, and there live in renunciation and contemplation? True happiness is not found in the glories of the world, but in the service of God. That service is best rendered when one breaks all ties with the world. Dress and food must be as simple as possible, and one should devote oneself entirely to prayer. Thus, what Macrina proposed was a life similar to that of the ascetics of the desert.

Macrina, her mother, and several other women withdrew to Annesi while Basil, following the desires of his sister, left for Egypt in order to learn more about the monastic life. Since Basil eventually became the great teacher of monasticism in the Greek-speaking church, and since it was Macrina who awakened his interest in it, it could be said that she was the founder of Greek monasticism.

Macrina spent the rest of her life in monastic retreat in Annesi. Years later, shortly after Basil's death, their brother Gregory of Nyssa visited her. Her fame was such that she was known simply as "the Teacher." Gregory has left a record of that visit in his treatise *On the Soul and the Resurrection.* He opens that work by informing us that "Basil, great among the saints, had departed from this life and gone to God, and all the churches mourned his death. But his sister the Teacher still lived and therefore I visited her." Gregory, however, was not easily consoled on finding his sister suffering from a severe asthma attack on her deathbed. "The sight of the Teacher," he wrote, "reawakened my pain, for she too was about to die."

She let him shed his tears and express his pain, and then consoled him, reminding him of the hope of resurrection. Finally, she died in great peace. Gregory closed her eyes, led the funeral service, and went out to continue the work that his sister and brother had entrusted to him.

Basil the Great

Years earlier, Basil had returned from Egypt, Palestine, and other lands where he had gone to study the monastic life, and had settled near Annesi. He and his friend Gregory of Nazianzus founded a community for men similar to the one Macrina had created for women. He believed that community life was essential, for one who lives alone has no one to serve, and the core of monastic life is service to others. He himself made it a point to undertake the most disagreeable tasks in the community. He also wrote rules to be followed in the monastic life. Since all the legislation in the Greek church regarding monastic life is based on the teachings of Basil, he is usually regarded as the father of Eastern monasticism.

But Basil was to be allowed to live in retirement for only a relatively short time. He had lived as a monk for little more than six years when he was ordained a presbyter against his will. He soon had conflicts with the bishop of Caesarea, and rather than creating greater difficulties decided to return to his monastic community. He remained there until Valens became emperor. Since the new emperor was Arian, the bishop of Caesarea decided to set aside his differences with Basil and call on the holy monk to assist him in the struggle against Arianism.

When Basil arrived at Caesarea, conditions were very difficult. Bad weather had destroyed the crops, and the rich were hoarding food. Basil

Basil, seen here in an eleventh-century fresco,
became the leader of the Nicene party.

preached against such practices, and sold all his properties in order to feed
the poor. If all would take only what they needed, he said, and give the rest
to others, there would be neither rich nor poor.

When the bishop of Caesarea died, the election of his successor became
a focal point for the struggle between the orthodox and the Arians. Basil's
prestige was such that he seemed to be the most likely candidate. The Arian
party found only one point at which Basil was vulnerable: his questionable
health. The orthodox responded that they were electing a bishop, not a
gladiator. Eventually, Basil was elected.

The new bishop of Caesarea knew that his election would lead to conflicts with the emperor, who was Arian. Soon Valens announced his intention
to visit Caesarea. The Nicene party knew from bitter experience in other
cities that Valens used such visits in order to strengthen Arianism.

Many imperial officers arrived at Caesarea in order to prepare Valens' visit. The emperor had ordered them to subdue the new bishop through a combination of promises and threats. But Basil was not easy to subdue. Finally, in a heated encounter, the praetorian prefect lost his patience and threatened Basil with confiscating his goods, with exile, torture, and even death. Basil responded, "All that I have that you can confiscate are these rags and a few books. Nor can you exile me, for wherever you send me, I shall be God's guest. As to tortures you should know that my body is already dead in Christ. And death would be a great boon to me, leading me sooner to God." Taken aback, the prefect said that no one had ever spoken to him thus. Basil answered, "Perhaps that is because you have never met a true bishop."

Finally, the emperor arrived. When he took a bountiful offering to the altar, thus showing his favor to the city, no one went forth to receive it. The emperor had to wait for the bishop, who finally accepted his offering, making it very clear that it was he who was favoring the emperor.

After these events, Basil was able to devote his time to his tasks as a bishop. He was particularly interested in organizing and spreading the monastic life, and in advancing the Nicene cause. Through a vast correspondence and several theological treaties, he made a significant contribution to the final victory of Trinitarian doctrine. But, like Athanasius, he was unable to see that final victory, for he died a few months before the Council of Constantinople confirmed the Nicene doctrine in 381.

Gregory of Nyssa

Basil's younger brother, Gregory of Nyssa, was of a completely different temperament. While Basil was tempestous, inflexible, and even arrogant, Gregory preferred silence, solitude, and anonymity. He had no desire to become the champion of any cause. Although he had a solid education, it was not of the quality of Basil's. For a time, he wanted to be a lawyer and a rhetorician, but he did not embrace these goals with great enthusiasm.

Whereas Basil and his friend Gregory of Nazianzus fervently took up monastic life, Gregory married a young woman with whom he seems to have been very happy. Years later, after his wife died and he took up the monastic life, he wrote a treatise *On Virginity,* whose arguments were characteristic of him. According to him, he who does not marry does not have to suffer the pain of seeing his wife going through childbirth, nor the even greater pain of losing her. For him, the monastic life was a way to avoid the pains and struggles of active life. He became known for his mystical life and for the writings in which he described that life and gave directives for those wishing to follow it.

But the struggles of the time were too urgent and too bitter to pass by a person such as Gregory. His brother Basil forced him to become bishop of Nyssa, which was little more than a village. Valens and the Arians used all their power against the orthodox party. Such strife was too much for Gregory, who went into hiding. But in spite of this, after the death of both Valens and Basil, Gregory became one of the main leaders of the Nicene party. As such he was received by the Council of Constantinople in 381.

Although he was a quiet and humble person, his writings show the inner fire of his spirit. And his careful explications of Nicene doctrine contributed to its triumph in Constantinople.

After that great council, Emperor Theodosius took him as one of his main advisors in theological matters, and Gregory was thus forced to travel throughout the empire, and even to Arabia and Mesopotamia. Although there was great value in this work, Gregory always saw it as a hindrance, keeping him away from the life of contemplation.

Finally, being assured that the Nicene cause was firmly established, Gregory returned to the monastic life, hoping that the world would leave him alone. In this he was so successful that the date and circumstances of his death are not known.

Gregory of Nazianzus

The other Great Cappadocian was Gregory of Nazianzus, whom Basil had met when they were fellow students. Gregory was the son of the bishop of Nazianzus, also called Gregory, and his wife Nona—for at that time bishops were often married. The elder Gregory had been a heretic, but Nona had brought him to orthodoxy. As in the case of Basil, Gregory's family was very devout, to such a point that many of them have later received the title of "saint"—Gregory himself, his parents Gregory the elder and Nona, his brother Caesarius, his sister Gorgonia, and his cousin Amphilochius.

Gregory spent most of his youth in study. After some time in Caesarea, he went to Athens, where he remained some fourteen years, and where he met both Basil and Prince Julian. He was thirty years old when he returned to his home country and joined Basil in the monastic life. Meanwhile, his brother Caesarius had become a famous physician in Constantinople, where he served both Constantius and Julian without letting himself be moved by the Arianism of the former or the paganism of the latter.

Back in Nazianzus, Gregory was ordained a presbyter, although he did not wish it. He fled to Basil's monastic community, where he stayed for some time, but eventually returned to his pastoral duties in Nazianzus. At that point he delivered a famous sermon on the duties of a pastor. He began: "I have been overcome, and I confess my defeat."

From then on, Gregory became more involved in the controversies of the time. When Basil made him bishop of a small hamlet, Gregory felt that

*In a ninth-century manuscript of the sermons of Gregory of
Nazianzus, he and others are depicted fleeing from the Arians.*

his friend had imposed on him, and their friendship was sorely strained. It
was a sad time for Gregory, marked by the deaths of Caesarius, Gorgonia,
Gregory the Elder, and Nona. Alone and bereaved, Gregory left the church
that had been entrusted to him, in order to have time for quiet meditation.
He was in his retreat when the news arrived of the death of Basil, with whom
he had never been reconciled.

Gregory was in shock. But eventually he felt compelled to take a leading
role in the struggle against Arianism, in which Basil had sought his help with
relatively little success. In A.D. 379, he appeared in Constantinople. At that
time Arianism enjoyed the total support of the state, and in the entire city
there was not a single orthodox church. Gregory began celebrating orthodox
services in the home of a relative. When he ventured in the streets, the mob
pelted him. Repeatedly, Arian monks broke into his service and profaned the
altar. But he stood firm, strengthening his small congregation with hymns he
composed, some of which have become classics of Greek hymnody.

Finally, the tide changed. Late in the year 380, Emperor Theodosius
made his triumphal entry into Constantinople. He was an orthodox general,
who soon expelled all Arians from the high positions that they had used to
further their cause. A few days later, the new emperor asked Gregory to visit
the cathedral of St. Sophia with him. It was an overcast day, broken only by
a ray of sunlight that hit on Gregory. Some of those present believed this to
be a sign from heaven and began shouting, "Gregory, bishop, Gregory,
bishop!" Since this fit his policy, Theodosius gave his approval. Gregory,
who did not wish to become a bishop, was finally convinced. The obscure
monk from Nazianzus was now patriarch of Constantinople.

A few months later, the emperor called a council that gathered in

Constantinople and over which Gregory presided, as bishop of the city. This task was not to his liking, for he said that the bishops behaved like a swarm of hornets. When some of his opponents pointed out that he was already bishop of another place, and that therefore he could not be bishop of Constantinople, Gregory promptly resigned the position he had never sought. Nectarius, the civil governor of Constantinople, was elected bishop in his stead, and occupied that position with relative distinction until he was succeeded by John Chrysostom, to whom we shall return.

The Council of Constantinople reaffirmed the doctrine of Nicea regarding the divinity of the Son, and added that the same ought to be said about the Holy Spirit. Thus, it was this council that definitively proclaimed the doctrine of the Trinity. Its decisions, and the theology reflected in them, were in large measure the result of the work of the Great Cappadocians.

As to Gregory, he returned to his homeland, where he spent his time composing hymns and devoted himself to his pastoral duties. When he heard that Theodosius planned to call another council and ask him to preside over it, he flatly refused. He lived away from all civil and ecclesiastical pomp until he died when he was some sixty years old.

21/Ambrose of Milan

God ordered all things to be produced so that there would be common food for all, and so that the earth would be the common inheritance of all. Thus, nature has produced a common right, but greed has made it the right of a few.

AMBROSE OF MILAN

The fourth century, so prolific in great Christian leaders, produced none whose career was more dramatic than Ambrose of Milan.

An Unexpected Election

It was in the year 373 that the death of the bishop of Milan threatened the peace of that important city. Auxentius, the dead bishop, had been appointed by an Arian emperor who had exiled the previous bishop. Now that the see was vacant, the election of a successor could easily turn into a riot, for both Arians and orthodox were determined that one of their number would be the next bishop of Milan.

In order to avoid a possible disorder, Ambrose, the governor of the city, decided to attend the election. His efficient and fair rule had made him popular, and he had reason to hope for higher office in the service of the Empire. But first he must deal wisely with the potentially explosive situation in Milan. Therefore, he appeared at the church, where tempers were beginning to flare, and addressed the crowd. He was trained in the best of rhetoric, and as he spoke calm was restored.

Suddenly, from the midst of the crowd, a child cried, "Ambrose, bishop." This caught the fancy of the crowd, and the insistent cry was heard: "Ambrose, bishop; Ambrose; Ambrose!"

Such an election was not part of Ambrose's plans for his career, and therefore he had recourse to various devices in order to dissuade the people.

When that strategy failed, he repeatedly attempted to escape from the city, but was unsuccessful. Finally, when it became clear that the emperor was gratified with the election of his governor, and would be very displeased if Ambrose insisted on his refusal, he agreed to be made bishop of Milan. Since he was only a catechumen, and therefore was not even baptized, it was necessary to perform that rite, and then to raise him through the various levels of ministerial orders. All this was done in eight days, and he was consecrated bishop of Milan on December 1, 373.

Although Ambrose had not sought the office of bishop, he felt that it was a responsibility to which he must devote his best. To help him in his administrative chores, he called on his brother, Uranius Satyrus, who was governor of another province (their sister Marcellina was also a devout Christian who led a semimonastic life in Rome). He also undertook the study of theology, with the help of a priest who had taught him the basics of Christian doctrine. His keen mind helped him in this undertaking, and soon he was one of the best theologians in the Western church.

Shortly after Ambrose's consecration, the nearby region was ravaged by a band of Goths who had crossed the border with imperial permission but had then rebelled. Refugees flocked to Milan, and there was news of many captives for whom the Goths were demanding ransom. Ambrose's response was to order that funds be raised for the refugees and for ransoming the captives by melting some of the golden vessels and other ornaments the

Ambrose fled in order to avoid being made
bishop of Milan.

church possessed. This created a storm of criticism, particularly among the Arians, who were eager to find him at fault and accused him of sacrilege. Ambrose answered:

It is better to preserve for the Lord souls rather than gold. He who sent the apostles without gold also gathered the churches without gold. The church has gold, not to store it, but to give it up, to use it for those who are in need. . . . It is better to keep the living vessels, than the golden ones.*

Likewise, in writing about the duties of pastors Ambrose told them that true strength consists in supporting the weak against the strong, and that they should invite to their feasts, not the rich who could reward them, but rather the poor who could not.

Among the many who went to listen to him preach, there was a young teacher of rhetoric who had followed a long and tortuous spiritual pilgrimage, and who was so entranced by the bishop's words that he returned to his mother's faith, which he had abandoned many years before. Eventually, the young man, whose name was Augustine, was baptized by Ambrose, who does not seem to have been aware of the exceptional gifts of his convert, who one day would become the most influential theologian for the West since the apostle Paul.

The Bishop and the Throne

The western portion of the Empire was ruled by Gratian and his half-brother Valentinian II. Since the latter was still a child, Gratian was also regent in his domains. Gratian was then killed in a rebellion, and the usurper, Maximus, threatened to take Valentinian's territories. The boy emperor was defenseless, and therefore, in a desperate move, he and his mother Justina sent Ambrose as an ambassador before Maximus. The bishop was successful, and the expected invasion was averted.

In spite of this, relations between Ambrose and Justina were not good. The empress was Arian and insisted on having a basilica where Arian worship could be celebrated. On that point, Ambrose was adamant. He would not have a holy place desecrated by heretical worship, nor would he allow the empress' power to be used to further the Arian cause in Milan. Thus followed a long series of memorable confrontations. At one point, Ambrose and his followers were besieged by imperial troops surrounding a disputed church. While those outside threatened the besieged by the clash of arms. Ambrose rallied his flock by singing hymns that he had composed—for he was also a great writer of hymns. Finally, Justina sought an honorable retreat by de-

*Duties of the Clergy 2.137.

manding that, if not the church, at least its sacred vases be delivered to the emperor. After all, had not Ambrose done as much for a mob of refugees and captives? Again the bishop refused, and answered:

I can take nothing from the temple of God, nor can I surrender what I received, not to surrender, but to keep. In so doing I am helping the emperor, for it is not right for me to surrender these things, nor for him to take them.*

It was in the midst of such confrontations with imperial power that Ambrose ordered that an ancient burial ground under one of the churches be dug up. There two skeletons were found, probably dating from long before the Christian era. But someone remembered hearing as a child about two martyrs, Protasius and Gervasius, and immediately the remains were given those names. Soon rumors were circulating about the miracles performed by the "sacred relics," and the people rallied even more closely behind their bishop.

Eventually, seemingly with the connivance of Justina, Maximus invaded Valentinian's territories. Part of the arrangement was probably that Maximus would rid the empress of the annoying bishop of Milan. But the eastern emperor, Theodosius, intervened and defeated Maximus. When Valentinian was killed, probably by some who sought his power, Theodosius intervened once again, and thus became sole ruler of the Empire.

Theodosius was a Nicene Christian—it was under his auspices that the Council of Constantinople gathered in A.D. 381 and reaffirmed the decisions of Nicea. But in spite of this, and now for other reasons, he clashed with Ambrose on two separate occasions. Both times he had to yield before the firmness of the bishop, although in all fairness one must say that the first time justice was on his side.

The first clash took place when some overzealous Christians in the small town of Callinicum burned a synagogue. The emperor decided that they be punished, and that they also must rebuild the synagogue. Ambrose protested that a Christian emperor should not force Christians to build a Jewish synagogue. After several stormy interviews, the emperor yielded, the synagogue was not rebuilt, and the arsonists were not punished. This was a sad precedent, for it meant that in an empire calling itself Christian, those whose faith was different would not be protected by the law.

The other conflict was different, and in it justice was on Ambrose's side. There had been a riot at Thessalonica, and the commandant of the city had been killed by the rioters. Ambrose, who knew the irascible temperament of the emperor, went to him and counseled moderation. Theodosius seemed convinced, but later his wrath was rekindled, and he decided to make an example of the disorderly city. He sent word that the riot had been forgiven, and then, by his order, the army trapped those who had gathered at the circus

*Sermon against Auxentius 5.

to celebrate the imperial pardon, and slaughtered some seven thousand of them.

Upon learning of these events, Ambrose resolved to demand clear signs of repentance from the emperor. Although the details are not clear, one of Ambrose's biographers tells us that the next time Theodosius went to church, the bishop met him at the door, raised his hand before him, and said, "Stop! A man such as you, stained with sin, whose hands are bathed in blood of injustice, is unworthy, until he repents, to enter this holy place, and to partake of communion."*

At that point, some courtiers threatened violence. But the emperor acknowledged the truth in Ambrose's words, and gave public signs of repentance. He also ordered that from that time on, if he ever decreed that someone be put to death, the execution be delayed for thirty days.

After that clash, relations between Theodosius and Ambrose were increasingly cordial. Finally, when the emperor knew that death was near, he called to his side the only man who had dared to censure him in public.

By then Ambrose's fame was such that Fritigil, queen of the Marcomanni, had asked him to write for her a brief introduction to the Christian faith. After reading it, Fritigil resolved to visit the wise man in Milan. But on her way she learned that Ambrose had died—on April 4, 397, Easter Sunday.

---

*Sozomen, *Church History* 7.25.

22/John Chrysostom

> *How think you that you obey Christ's commandments, when you spend your time collecting interest, piling up loans, buying slaves like livestock, and merging business with business? . . . And that is not all. Upon all this you heap injustice, taking possession of lands and houses, and multiplying poverty and hunger.*
>
> JOHN CHRYSOSTOM

One hundred years after his death, John of Constantinople was given the name by which later ages know him: John Chrysostom —"the golden-mouthed." That was a title he well deserved, for in a century that gave the church such great preachers as Ambrose of Milan and Gregory of Nazianzus, John of Constantinople stood above all the rest, a giant above the giants of his time.

But for John Chrysostom the pulpit was not simply a podium from which to deliver brilliant pieces of oratory. It was rather the verbal expression of his entire life, his battlefield against the powers of evil, an unavoidable calling that eventually led to exile and to death itself.

A Voice from the Wilderness

He was above all a monk. Before becoming a monk he was a lawyer, trained in his native Antioch by the famous pagan orator Libanius. It is said that when someone asked the old teacher who should succeed him, he responded: "John, but the Christians have laid claim on him."

Anthusa, John's mother, was a fervent Christian who loved her child

His contemporaries described Chrysostom as short, with a wide and furrowed forehead and deep-set eyes.

with a deep and possessive love. She was quite happy when her lawyer son, then twenty years of age, asked that his name be added to the list of those training for baptism. Three years later, when he completed the time of preparation that was then required, he was baptized by Bishop Meletius of Antioch. Once again his mother rejoiced. But when he told her that he intended to withdraw from the city and follow the monastic way she was adamant, and made him promise that he would never leave her as long as she lived.

John's way of solving the tension between his monastic vocation and his mother's possessiveness was simply to turn their home into a monastery. There he lived with three like-minded friends until, after his mother's death, he joined the monks in the Syrian mountains. He then spent four years learning the discipline of monastic life, and two more rigorously practicing it in complete solitude. Later, he himself would admit that such life was not the best kind of training for the shepherd's task. "Many who have gone from monastic retreat to the active life of the priest or the bishop are completely unable to face the difficulties of their new situation."*

In any case, when John returned to Antioch after his six years of monastic withdrawal, he was ordained a deacon, and a presbyter shortly thereafter. As such, he began preaching, and soon his fame was widespread throughout the Greek-speaking church.

In 397, the bishopric of Constantinople became vacant, and the emperor ordered that John be taken to the capital city to occupy that prestigious position. But his popularity in Antioch was such that the authorities feared a riot, and therefore kept the imperial decree secret. They simply invited the famous preacher to visit a small chapel in the outskirts of the city, and when he was there they ordered him into a carriage, in which he was forcefully taken to the capital. There he was consecrated bishop early in 398.

Constantinople was a rich town, and one given to luxury and intrigue. The great emperor Theodosius was dead, and the two sons who had succeeded him, Honorius and Arcadius, were indolent and inept. Arcadius, who supposedly ruled the East from his capital city of Constantinople, was in turn ruled by a certain Eutropius, the palace chamberlain, who used his power to satisfy his own ambition and that of his cronies. Eudoxia, the empress, felt humiliated by the chamberlain's power, although in fact it was Eutropius who had arranged her marriage to Arcadius. The intrigues that enveloped everything in that city had also been present in John's elevation to the patriarchal throne, for Patriarch Theophilus of Alexandria had been actively campaigning in favor of a fellow Alexandrine, and John had been given the post through Eutropius' intervention.

The new bishop of Constantinople was not completely aware of all this. From what we know of his character, it is probable that, had he been aware, he would have acted just as he did. The former monk was still a monk, and could not tolerate the manner in which the rich inhabitants of Constantinople sought to wed the Gospel with their own luxuries and comforts.

His first task was to reform the life of the clergy. Some priests who claimed to be celibate had in their homes what they called "spiritual sisters," and this was an occasion of scandal for many. Other clergymen had become rich, and lived with as much luxury as the potentates of the great city. The finances of the church were in a shambles, and the care of the flock was largely unattended. John took all those issues head on. He ordered that the "spiritual sisters" move out of the priests' homes, and that the latter lead an austere life. Church finances were placed under a system of detailed scrutiny. The luxury items that adorned the bishop's palace were sold in order to feed the hungry; and the clergy received orders to open the churches at such times

---

*On the Priesthood 6.

as were convenient not only for the wealthy, but also for those who had to work. Obviously, all these measures gained him both the respect of many and the hatred of others.

But such a reformation could not be limited to the clergy. It was necessary that the laity also be called to lead lives more in accordance with the Gospel mandate. Therefore, the golden-mouthed preacher thundered from the pulpit:

The gold bit on your horse, the gold circlet on the wrist of your slave, the gilding on your shoes, mean that you are robbing the orphan and starving the widow. When you have passed away, each passer-by who looks upon your great mansion will say, "How many tears did it take to build that mansion; how many orphans were stripped; how many widows wronged; how many laborers deprived of their honest wages?" Even death itself will not deliver you from your accusers.*

Return to the Wilderness

The powerful could not abide that voice that challenged them from the pulpit of the church of Saint Sophia—the largest in Christendom. Eutropius, who had made him bishop, expected special favors and concessions. But John was convinced that Eutropius was simply another Christian in need of having the Gospel clearly and unambiguously preached. The result was that Eutropius repented, not of his sin, but rather of his error in having brought the meddlesome preacher from Antioch.

Finally the storm broke out over the right of asylum. Some fled from the tyranny of Eutropius and took refuge in the church of Saint Sophia. The chamberlain simply sent some soldiers after them. But the bishop proved unbending, and did not allow the soldiers into the sanctuary. Eutropius protested before the emperor, but Chrysostom took his cause to the pulpit and for once Arcadius did not bow before the requests of his favorite. After that, the influence of the chamberlain waned, and many attributed this to his clash with the bishop.

Shortly thereafter, a series of political circumstances precipitated Eutropius' downfall. The people were jubilant, and soon there were mobs demanding vengeance against the one who had oppressed and exploited them. The chamberlain's only recourse was to run to Saint Sophia and embrace the altar. When the mob came after him, Chrysostom stood in its way, and invoked the same right of asylum that he had invoked earlier against Eutropius. Thus Chrystostom was led to defend the life of his erstwhile enemy, first against the people, then against the army, and finally against the

*Homily 2.4.

emperor himself. The crisis came to an end when the former chamberlain, not trusting the seemingly weak defenses of the church, fled from his refuge, and was captured and killed by some of the many he had wronged.

But Chrysostom had made many more enemies among the powerful. Eudoxia, the emperor's wife, resented the bishop's growing power. Besides, what was being said from the pulpit of Saint Sophia was not to her liking—it fitted her too well. When Chrysostom described the pomp and the folly of the powerful, she felt the people's eyes staring at her. It was necessary to silence that voice from the wilderness that had brought such wild ravings to the elegant Saint Sophia. With that in mind, the empress made special grants to the church. The bishop thanked her. And continued preaching.

Then the empress had recourse to more direct methods. When Chrysostom had to leave the city in order to attend to some matters in Ephesus, Eudoxia joined Theophilus of Alexandria in plotting against the meddling preacher. Upon his return, Chrysostom found himself the object of a long list of ridiculous charges brought before a small gathering of bishops convened by Theophilus. He paid no attention to them, but simply went about his preaching and his management of the church. Theophilus and his partisans found him guilty, and asked Arcadius to banish him. Prodded by Eudoxia, the weak emperor agreed to that request, and ordered Chrysostom to leave the city.

The situation was tense. The people were indignant. The bishops and other clergy from neighboring towns gathered at the capital, and promised

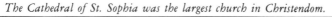

The Cathedral of St. Sophia was the largest church in Christendom.

their support to the bishop. All that he had to do was to give the order, and they would convene as a synod that would condemn Theophilus and his followers. This could be coupled with a popular uprising that would shake the very foundations of the Empire. One word from the eloquent bishop, and the entire conspiracy against him would crumble. Arcadius and Eudoxia were aware of this and made ready for war. But Chrysostom was a lover of peace, and therefore made ready for exile. Three days after receiving the imperial edict, he bid farewell to his friends and followers and surrendered to the authorities.

The populace was not ready to give up without a struggle. The streets were boiling with rumors of mutiny. Arcadius, Eudoxia, and the army did not dare show themselves in public. That night, in what was taken as a sign of divine wrath, the earth quaked. A few days later, in response to the fearful and urgent pleas of Eudoxia, Chrysostom returned to the city and to his pulpit, where he was received with shouts of acclamation.

Although the bishop had returned, the reasons for the conflict were not solved. After a few months of further intrigues, confrontation, and humiliation, Chrysostom received a new order of exile. Once again he refused to heed the advice of his friends, and quietly surrendered to the soldiers who went after him, rather than stirring up a riot that would cause the people further suffering.

But the riot was inevitable. Mobs flocked to Saint Sophia and the surrounding area. The army was ordered to quell the disturbance, and in the ensuing struggle the cathedral and several public buildings nearby caught fire and were destroyed. The cause of the fire was never discovered. But in the inquest, many of Chrysostom's supporters were tortured, and his best-known friends were banished.

Meanwhile, the preacher with the golden mouth was lead to exile in the remote village of Cucusus. Since he lacked a pulpit, he took up the pen, and the world was moved. Innocent, the bishop of Rome, took up his cause, and many followed his example. The emperor's actions were criticized from every quarter, and Theophilus of Alexandria had no support but that of a few timid souls who dared not oppose imperial power. As the controversy became widespread, the little town of Cucusus seemed to have become the center of the world.

Finally, even Cucusus seemed too near a place of exile, and Chrysostom was ordered removed even farther, to a cold and unknown hamlet on the shores of the Black Sea. The soldiers guarding him, being aware that their charge did not have the good will of the crown, paid no attention to his failing health, and during the journey drove him to exertions well beyond his strength. Soon the banished bishop became seriously ill. When he perceived that death was near, he asked to be taken to a small church by the roadside. There he took communion, bid farewell to those around him, and preached his briefest but most eloquent sermon: "In all things, glory to God. Amen."

As we compare the lives of Chrysostom and Ambrose, we see an indication of what would be the future course of the churches in the East as compared with the West. Ambrose faced the most powerful emperor of his time, and won. Chrysostom, on the other hand, was deposed and banished by the weak Arcadius. From then on, the Latin-speaking church of the West would become increasingly powerful, as it filled the vacuum left by the crumbling Empire. In the Greek-speaking East, on the other hand, the Empire would last another thousand years. Sometimes weak, and sometimes strong, this Eastern offshoot of the old Roman Empire—the Byzantine Empire—would zealously guard its prerogatives over the church. Theodosius was not the last western emperor to be humbled by a Latin-speaking bishop. And John Chrysostom was not the last Greek-speaking bishop banished by an eastern emperor.

^{23/}Jerome

*I frankly confess that I get carried away
with indignation. I cannot listen to such
sacrilege with patience.*
JEROME

N one of the great personalities of the fourth century is more
intriguing than Jerome. He is outstanding, not for his sanctity,
like Anthony, nor for his keen theological insight, like
Athanasius, nor for his firmness before the authorities, like
Ambrose, nor even for his preaching, like Chrysostom, but rather for his
titanic and endless struggle with the world and with himself. Although he is
known as "Saint Jerome," he was not one of those saints who are granted
in this life the joy of God's peace. His holiness was not humble, peaceful,
and sweet, but rather proud, stormy, and even bitter. He always strove to
be more than human, and therefore had little patience for those who appeared indolent, or who dared criticize him. Those who suffered his sharp
attacks were not only the heretics of his time, as well as the ignorant and the
hypocritical, but also John Chrysostom, Ambrose of Milan, Basil of Caesarea,
and Augustine of Hippo. Those who disagreed with him were "two-legged
asses." But in spite of this attitude—and perhaps to a large measure because
of it—Jerome earned a place among the great Christian figures of the fourth
century.

He was born around A.D. 348, in an obscure corner of Northern Italy.
By his date of birth, he was younger than many of the great figures of the
fourth century. But it has been aptly said that Jerome was born an old man,
and therefore he soon considered himself older than his contemporaries.
More surprisingly, they came to regard him as an imposing and ancient
institution.

He was an ardent admirer of classical learning, and felt that this love for
an essentially pagan tradition was sinful. His inner turmoil on this score
peaked when, during a serious illness, he dreamt that he was at the final
judgment and was asked: "Who are you?" "I am a Christian," Jerome answered. But the Judge retorted: "You lie. You are a Ciceronian." After that

experience, Jerome resolved to devote himself fully to the study of Scripture and of Christian literature. But he never ceased reading and imitating the style of the classical pagan authors.

He was also obsessed by sex. Upon retiring to the monastic life, he hoped to be rid of that burden. But even there he was followed by his dreams and by the memories of dancers in Rome. He sought to suppress such thoughts by punishing his body, and by an exaggeratedly austere life. He was unkempt, and even came to affirm that, having been washed by Christ, there was no need ever to wash again. And yet that did not suffice. In order to fill his mind with something that would take the place of the pleasures of Rome, he decided to study Hebrew. That language, with its strange alphabet and grammar, seemed barbaric to him. But he told himself that, since the Old Testament was written in it, it must be divine.

Eventually Jerome conceded that he was not made for the life of a hermit. It was probably before three years were up that he returned to civilization. In Antioch he was ordained a presbyter. He was at Constantinople before and during the Council of 381. He returned to Rome, where bishop Damasus, a good judge of human nature, made him his private secretary and encouraged him to further study and writing. It was also Damasus who first suggested to him the project that would eventually take up most of his time, and would become his greatest monument: a new translation of Scripture into Latin. Although Jerome did some work on this project while at Rome, it was mostly left for a later stage in his life.

Meanwhile, he found a great deal of help amidst a group of rich and devout women who lived in the palace of a widow, Albina. Besides Albina, the most prominent members of the group were her widowed daughter Marcella, Ambrose's sister Marcellina, and the scholarly Paula, who—with her daughter Eustochium—would play a leading role in the rest of Jerome's life. The bishop's secretary visited that house regularly, for in its women he found devoted disciples, some of whom became accomplished students of Greek and Hebrew. It was in that company that Jerome felt most free to discuss the scholarly questions that occupied his mind—particularly questions having to do with the text of the Bible.

It is significant that Jerome, who never had any close male friends, and who was obsessed by sex, found such solace in this group of women. Perhaps he felt at ease because they did not dare compete with him. In any case, it was they that came to know the sensitivity that he desperately sought to hide from the rest of the world.

However, Jerome was not a tactful man, and he soon made enemies among the leaders of the church in Rome. When Damasus died, late in 384, Jerome lost his staunchest defender. Siricius, the new bishop, had little use for Jerome's scholarship. When one of Paula's daughters died, Jerome's enemies, whom he had criticized for their comfortable life, claimed that her

Jerome, who had no male friends and who abhorred sex, did, however, find solace in the friendship of St. Paula and her daughter Eustochium.

death was due to the rigors recommended by Jerome. Finally, he decided to leave Rome and go to the Holy Land—or, as he said, "from Babylon to Jerusalem."

Paula and Eustochium followed along a different route, and jointly they went in pilgrimage to Jerusalem. Then Jerome went on to Egypt, where he visited the Alexandrine scholars as well as the desert dwellings of the monks. By 386 he had returned to Palestine, where both he and Paula had decided to settle and devote themselves to the monastic way of life. Their goal, however, was not the extreme asceticism of the desert monks, but rather a life of moderate austerity, spent mostly in study. Since Paula was rich, and Jerome was not lacking in means, they founded two monastic houses in Bethlehem, one for women under Paula's leadership, and another for men under Jerome's supervision. He then pursued further studies of Hebrew, in order to translate the Bible, while he taught Latin to the children of the neighborhood, and Greek and Hebrew to Paula's nuns.

Above all, however, he devoted himself to the work that would be his great literary monument: the translation of the Bible into Latin. By then there were other translations, but these had been done on the basis of the Septuagint—the ancient translation of the Hebrew text into Greek. What Jerome then undertook was a direct translation from the Hebrew. After many years of work, interrupted by a voluminous correspondence and by the calamities that shook the Roman world, Jerome completed this enormous task.

Jerome's version, commonly known as the *Vulgate,* eventually became the standard Bible of the entire Latin-speaking church. But at first it was not as well received as Jerome had wished. The new translation, naturally enough, changed some people's favorite texts, and many demanded to know who had given Jerome authority to tamper with Scripture. Furthermore, many believed the legend that the Septuagint had been the work of seventy-two independent translators who, upon comparing their work, found themselves in total agreement. That legend had long been used to argue that the Septuagint was just as inspired as the Hebrew text. Therefore, when Jerome published a version that disagreed with the Septuagint, there were many who felt that he lacked respect for the inspired Word of God.

Such criticism did not come only from ignorant believers, but also from some very learned Christians. From North Africa, Augustine of Hippo wrote:

I pray you not to devote your energies to translating the sacred books to Latin, unless you do as you did earlier in your translation of the book of Job, that is, adding notes that show clearly where your version differs from the Septuagint, whose authority has no equal. . . . Besides, I cannot imagine how, after so long, someone can find in the Hebrew manuscripts anything which so many translators did not see before, especially since they knew Hebrew so well.*

Epistle 28.2.

At first Jerome did not answer Augustine's letter. When he did answer, he implied that Augustine was simply a young man seeking to make a name for himself by criticizing his elders. While praising the other's learning, he subtly indicated that he was doing Augustine a favor by not pursuing the controversy, for a debate between the two of them would be an unequal contest.

A few months after the death of Eustochium,
Jerome took his last Communion and died.

Although most of Jerome's controversies ended in wounds that never healed, the outcome was different in this particular case. Years later, Jerome felt the need to refute the doctrine of the Pelagians—which will be discussed in the next chapter—and to that end he had recourse to Augustine's works. His next letter to the wise bishop of North Africa expressed an admiration that he reserved for very few.

At first glance, Jerome appeared to be an extremely insensitive person, whose only concern was his own prestige. But in truth he was very different than he appeared, and his rigid facade hid a sensitive spirit. No one knew this as well as did Paula and Eustochium. But Paula died in 404, and Jerome felt alone and desolate. His grief was all the greater, for he was convinced that it was not only his end that approached, but that of an era. A few years later, on August 24, 410, Rome was taken and sacked by the Goths under Alaric's command. The news shook the world. Jerome heard of it in Bethlehem, and wrote to Eustochium:

Who could have believed that Rome, built by the conquest of the world, would fall? That the mother of many nations has turned to her grave? . . . My eyes are dim by my advanced age . . . and with the light that I have at night I can no longer read Hebrew books, which are difficult even during the day for the smallness of their letters.*

Jerome survived for almost ten years. They were years of loneliness, pain, and controversy. Finally, a few months after the death of Eustochium, who had become as a daughter to him, the tired scholar went to his rest.

---

*Commentary on Ezequiel, prefaces to books 2 and 7.

24/Augustine of Hippo

When I thought of devoting myself entirely to you, my God . . . it was I that wished to do it, and I that wished not to do it. It was I. And since I neither completely wished, nor completely refused, I fought against myself and tore myself to pieces.

AUGUSTINE OF HIPPO

T ake up and read. Take up and read. Take up and read." These words, probably shouted by a playing child, floated over the fence of the garden in Milan and struck the ears of a dejected professor of rhetoric who sat under a fig tree and cried: "How long, Lord, how long? Will it be tomorrow and always tomorrow? Why does my uncleanliness not end this very moment?" The child's words seemed to him words from heaven. Shortly before, elsewhere in the garden, he had put down a manuscript he was reading. Now he returned to the spot, took up the manuscript, and read the words of Paul: "Not in reveling and drunkenness, not in debauchery and licentiousness, not in quarreling and jealousy. But put on the Lord Jesus Christ, and make no provision for the flesh, to gratify its desires." Responding to these words, Augustine—for that was the name of the rhetorician—made a decision that he had been postponing for a long time: he devoted himself to the service of God. Soon he abandoned his career as a professor, and set on a course that would eventually make him one of the most influential figures in the entire history of Christianity.

In order to understand the scope and meaning of the experience at the garden of Milan, one must follow Augustine's career to that point.

A Tortuous Path to Faith

Augustine was born in A.D. 354, in the little town of Tagaste, in North Africa. His father was a minor Roman official, who followed the traditional pagan religion. But his mother, Monica, was a fervent Christian, whose constant prayer for her husband's conversion was eventually answered. Augustine does not seem to have been very close to his father, whom he hardly mentions in his writings. But Monica did play an important role—sometimes even an overwhelming one—in the life of her only son.

Both parents were aware of the child's exceptional gifts, and therefore sought for him the best education possible. To that end they sent him to the nearby town of Madaura, and later to Carthage.

Augustine was some seventeen years old when he arrived at the great city that for centuries had been the political, economic, and cultural center of Latin-speaking Africa. Although he did not neglect his studies, he also set out to enjoy the many pleasures that the city offered. Soon he had a concubine who bore him a child. He named the boy Adeodatus—given by God.

As all young men of his time preparing for careers as lawyers or public functionaries, Augustine was a student of rhetoric. The purpose of this discipline was learning to speak and to write elegantly and convincingly. Truth was not at issue. That was left for professors of philosophy.

But among the many ancient works that students of rhetoric must read were those of Cicero, the famous orator of classical Rome. And Cicero, besides being a master of language, was a philosopher. Thus, it was reading Cicero that Augustine came to the conviction that proper speech and style were not sufficient. One must also seek after truth.

That search led the young student to Manicheism. This religion was Persian in origin, having been founded by Mani in the third century. According to Mani, the human predicament is the presence in each of us of two principles. One, which he calls "light," is spiritual. The other, "darkness," is matter. Throughout the universe there are these two principles, both eternal: light and darkness. Somehow—Manicheans explained it through a series of myths—the two have mingled, and the present human condition is the result of that admixture. Salvation then consists in separating the two elements, and in preparing our spirit for its return to the realm of pure light, in which it will be absorbed. Since any new mingling of the principles is evil, true believers must avoid procreation. According to Mani, this doctrine had been revealed in various fashions to a long series of prophets, including Buddha, Zoroaster, Jesus, and Mani himself.

In Augustine's time, Manicheism had spread throughout the Mediterranean basin. Its main appeal was its claim to be eminently rational. Like gnosticism earlier, Manicheism supported many of its teachings on astronom-

No other theologian has been as influential as Augustine.

ical observation. Besides, part of its propaganda consisted in ridiculing the teachings of Christianity, and particularly the Bible, whose materialism and primitive language it mocked.

Manicheism seemed to respond to Augustine's difficulties with Christianity, which centered on two issues. The first was that, from the point of view of rhetoric, the Bible was a series of inelegant writings—some even barbaric —in which the rules of good style were seldom followed, and where one found crude episodes of violence, rape, deceit, and the like. The second was the question of the origin of evil. Monica had taught him that there was only one God. But Augustine saw evil both around and in himself, and had to ask what was the source of such evil. If God was supreme and pure goodness, evil could not be a divine creation. And if, on the other hand, all things were created by the divine, God could not be as good and wise as Monica and the church claimed. Manicheism offered answers to these two points. The Bible —particularly the Old Testament—was not in fact the word of the eternal principle of light. Nor was evil a creation of that principle, but of its opposite, the principle of darkness.

For these reasons, Augustine became a Manichee. But there were always doubts, and he spent nine years as a "hearer," without seeking to join the ranks of the "perfect." When, at Manichean gatherings, he vented some of his doubts, he was told that his questions were very profound, and that there was a great Manichean teacher, a certain Faustus, who could answer them. When the much announced Faustus finally arrived, he turned out to be no better than the other Manichean teachers. Disappointed, Augustine decided to carry on his quest in different directions. Besides, his students at Carthage were an unruly lot, and a career in Rome seemed more promising. But that did not turn out as he had hoped, for his students in the capital city, although better behaved, were slow in paying for his services. He then moved on to Milan, where there was a vacancy teaching rhetoric.

In Milan he became a Neoplatonist. Neoplatonism, very popular at the time, was a philosophy with religious overtones. Through a combination of study, discipline, and mystical contemplation, it sought to reach the ineffable One, the source of all being. The goal of the Neoplatonist was the ecstasy that one experienced when lost in such contemplation. Unlike Manichean dualism, Neoplatonism affirmed that there was only one principle, and that all reality was derived from it through a series of emanations—much like the concentric circles that appear on the surface of the water when hit by a pebble. Those realities that are closer to the One are superior, and those that are more removed from it are inferior. Evil then does not originate from a different source, but consists simply in moving away from the One. Moral evil consists in looking away from the One, and turning one's gaze to the inferior realms of multiplicity. This seemed to answer Augustine's vexing questions as to the origin of evil. From this perspective, one could assert that a single being, of infinite goodness, was the source of all things, and at the same time acknowledge the presence of evil in creation. Evil, though real, is not a "thing," but rather a direction away from the goodness of the One. Also, Neoplatonism helped Augustine to view both God and the soul in less materialistic terms than those he had learned from the Manichees.

There remained another doubt: How can one claim that the Bible, with its crude language and its stories of violence and falsehood, is the Word of God? Providing an answer to this question was the role of Ambrose in Augustine's life. Monica, who was with him in Milan, insisted that he should hear Ambrose's sermons. As a professor of rhetoric, Augustine agreed to attend the services led by the most famous speaker in Milan. His initial purpose was not to hear what Ambrose had to say, but to see how he said it. However, as time went by he found that he was listening to the bishop less as a professional, and more as a seeker. Ambrose interpreted allegorically many of the passages that had created difficulties for Augustine. Since allegorical interpretation was perfectly acceptable according to the canons of rhetoric, Augustine could find no fault in this. But it certainly made Scripture appear less crude, and therefore more acceptable.

By then, Augustine's major intellectual difficulties with Christianity had been solved. But there were other difficulties of a different sort. He could not be a lukewarm Christian. Were he to accept his mother's faith, he would do it wholeheartedly, and he would devote his entire life to it. Furthermore, due to the prevalence of the monastic ideal, and to his own Neoplatonic perspective, Augustine was convinced that, were he to become a Christian, he must give up his career in rhetoric, as well as all his ambitions and every physical pleasure. It was precisely this last requirement that seemed most difficult. As he later wrote, at that time he used to pray: "Give me chastity and continence; but not too soon."

At this point a battle raged within himself. It was the struggle between willing and not willing. He had decided to become a Christian. But not too soon. He could no longer hide behind intellectual difficulties. Furthermore, from all quarters came news that put him to shame. In Rome the famous philosopher Marius Victorinus, who had translated into Latin the works of the Neoplatonists, presented himself at church and made public profession of his faith. Then came news of two high civil servants who, upon reading Athanasius' *Life of Saint Anthony*, had abandoned career and honors in order to follow the hermit's example. It was then, unable to tolerate the company of his friends—or himself—that he fled to the garden, where his conversion took place.

After his conversion, Augustine took the necessary steps to embark on a new life. He requested baptism, which he and Adeodatus received from Ambrose. He resigned from his teaching post. And then, with Monica, Adeodatus and a group of friends, he set out for North Africa, where he planned to spend the rest of his days in monastic retreat. Monica had persuaded Augustine to dismiss his concubine of many years—whose name he does not even mention. The return to Africa was interrupted at the seaport of Ostia, where Monica became ill and died. Augustine was so overcome with grief that it was necessary for him and his companions to remain in Rome for several months.

When they finally reached Tagaste, Augustine sold most of the property that he had inherited, gave some of the money to the poor, and with the rest he settled at Cassiciacum with Adeodatus—who died shortly thereafter—and and a few friends whose goal was mystical contemplation and philosophical inquiry. Their objective was not the extreme rigorism of the monks of the desert, but rather an orderly life, with no unnecessary comforts, and devoted entirely to devotions, study, and meditation.

It was at Cassiciacum that Augustine wrote his first Christian works. They still bore a Neoplatonic stamp, although he was slowly coming to appreciate the difference between Christian teaching and some elements in Neoplatonism. He hoped that the few dialogues he wrote at Cassiciacum would be only the beginning of many years devoted to the "philosophical life."

Minister and Theologian of the Western Church

But this was not to be, for his fame was spreading, and there were some who had other designs for his life. In 391, he visited the town of Hippo in order to talk to a friend whom he wished to invite to join the small community at Cassiciacum. While at Hippo he attended church, and bishop Valerius, who saw him in the congregation, preached about how God always sent shepherds for the flock, and then asked the congregation to pray for God's guidance in case there was among them someone sent to be their minister. The congregation responded exactly as the bishop had expected, and Augustine, much against his will, was ordained to serve with Valerius in Hippo. Four years later, he was made bishop jointly with Valerius, who feared that another church would steal his catch. Since at that time it was forbidden for a bishop to leave his church for another, Augustine's consecration to be a bishop jointly with Valerius guaranteed that he would spend the rest of his days at Hippo. (Although neither Augustine nor Valerius was aware of it, there was also a rule against having more than one bishop in a single church.) Valerius died a short time later, and left Augustine as bishop of Hippo.

As a minister and as a bishop, Augustine sought to retain as much as possible of the lifestyle of Cassiciacum. But now his energies had to be directed less towards contemplation, and more towards his pastoral responsibilities. It was with those responsibilities in view that he wrote most of the works that made him the most influential theologian in the entire Latin-speaking church since New Testament times.

Many of Augustine's first writings were attempts to refute the Manichees. Since he had helped lead some friends to that religion, he now felt a particular responsibility to refute the teachings that he had supported earlier. Since those were the main points at issue, most of these early works dealt with the authority of Scripture, the origin of evil, and free will.

The question of the freedom of the will was of particular importance in the polemics against the Manichees. They held that everything was predetermined, and that human beings had no freedom. Against such views, Augustine became the champion of the freedom of the will. According to him, human freedom is such that it is its own cause. When we act freely, we are not moved by something either outside or inside us, as by a necessity, but rather by our own will. A decision is free inasmuch as it is not the product of nature, but of the will itself. Naturally, this does not mean that circumstances do not influence our decisions. What it does mean is that only that which we decide out of our own will, and not out of circumstance or out of an inner necessity, is properly called free.

This was important in order to be able to solve the difficulties having to do with the origin of evil. Augustine insisted that there is only one God, whose goodness is infinite. How, then, can one explain the existence of evil? By simply affirming that the will is created by God, and is therefore good; but that the will is capable of making its own decisions. It is good for the will to be free, even though this means that such a free will can produce evil. The origin of evil, then, is to be found in the bad decisions made by both human and angelic wills—those of the demons, who are fallen angels. Thus, Augustine was able to affirm both the reality of evil and the creation of all things by a good God.

This, however, does not mean that evil is ever a "thing." Evil is not a substance, as the Manichees implied when speaking of it as the principle of darkness. It is a decision, a direction, a negation of good.

Another movement that Augustine had to refute was Donatism. The reader will remember that this movement centered in North Africa, where Augustine now was a pastor. Therefore, throughout his career Augustine had to deal with the various issues raised by the Donatists. One of these was the question of whether ordinations conferred by unworthy bishops were valid. To this, Augustine responded that the validity of any rite of the church does not depend on the moral virtue of the person administering it. If it were so, Christians would live in constant doubt as to the validity of their baptism. No matter how unworthy the celebrant, the rite is still valid, although obviously the celebrant is at fault. On this point, most of the Western church through the centuries has agreed with Augustine, whose views on the church and on the validity of sacraments became normative in the West.

It was also in trying to deal with the Donatist issue that Augustine developed his theory of the just war. As has already been said, some Donatists—the circumcellions—had turned to violence. The entire movement had social and economic roots of which Augustine was probably not aware. But he was certain that the depredations of the circumcellions must cease. He thus came to the conclusion that a war may be just, but that in order for it to be so certain conditions must be fulfilled. The first is that the purpose of the war must be just—a war is never just when its purpose is to satisfy territorial ambition, or the mere exercise of power. The second condition is that a just war must be waged by properly instituted authority. This seemed necessary in order not to leave the field open to personal vendettas. In later centuries, however, this principle would be applied by the powerful in order to claim that they had the right to make war on the powerless, but that the opposite was not true. Actually, this could already be seen in the case of the circumcellions, who according to Augustine did not have the right to wage war on the state, whereas the state had the right to wage war on them. Finally, the third rule—and the most important one for Augustine—is that, even in the midst of the violence that is a necessary part of war, the motive of love must be central.

It was, however, against the Pelagians that Augustine wrote his most important theological works. Pelagius was a monk from Britain who had become famous for his piety and austerity. He saw the Christian life as a constant effort through which one's sins could be overcome and salvation attained. Pelagius agreed with Augustine that God has made us free, and that the source of evil is in the will. As he saw matters, this meant that human beings always have the ability to overcome their sin. Otherwise, sin would be excusable.

But Augustine remembered his experience of the time when he both willed and did not will to become a Christian. This meant that human will was not as simple as Pelagius made it. There are times when the will is powerless against the hold sin has on it. The will is not always its own master, for it is clear that the will to will does not always have its way.

According to Augustine, the power of sin is such that it takes hold of our will, and as long as we are under its sway we cannot move our will to be rid of it. The most we can accomplish is that struggle between willing and not willing, which does little more than show the powerlessness of our will against itself. The sinner can will nothing but sin.

This does not mean, however, that freedom has disappeared. The sinner is still free to choose among various alternatives. But all these are sin, and the one alternative that is not open is to cease sinning. In Augustine's words, before the Fall we were free both to sin and not to sin. But between the Fall and redemption the only freedom left to us is freedom to sin. When we are redeemed, the grace of God works in us, leading our will from the miserable state in which it found itself to a new state in which freedom is restored, so that we are now free both to sin and not to sin. Finally, in the heavenly home, we shall still be free, but only free not to sin. Again, this does not mean that all freedom is destroyed. On the contrary, in heaven we shall continue to have free choices. But none of them will be sin.

Back to the moment of conversion, how can we make the decision to accept grace? According to Augustine, only by the power of grace itself, for before that moment we are not free not to sin, and therefore we are not free to decide to accept grace. The initiative in conversion is not human, but divine. Furthermore, grace is irresistible, and God gives it to those who have been predestined to it.

In contrast, Pelagius claimed that each of us comes to the world with complete freedom to sin, or not to sin. There is no such thing as original sin, nor a corruption of human nature that forces us to sin. Children have no sin until they, on their own free will, decide to sin.

The controversy lasted several years, and eventually Pelagianism was rejected. It simply did not take into account the terrible hold of sin on human will, nor the corporate nature of sin, which is manifest even in infants before they have opportunity to sin for themselves. Augustine's views, however, did not gain wide acceptance. He was accused of being an innovator. In southern France, where opposition to Augustine was strongest, Vincent of Lerins argued that one should believe only what has been held "always, everywhere, and by all." Many contested Augustine's view that the beginning of faith was in God's action rather than in a human decision. These opponents of Augustine's doctrine of predestination have been called, somewhat inexactly, "Semi-Pelagians." Through a process that took almost a century, Augustine was reinterpreted, so that theologians came to call themselves "Augustinian" while rejecting his views on irresistible grace and predestination. In 529, the Synod of Orange upheld Augustine's doctrine of the primacy of grace in the process of salvation, but left aside the more radical consequences of that doctrine. It was thus that later generations—with notable exceptions—interpreted the teachings of the great bishop of Hippo.

Two of Augustine's writings are particularly significant. The first is his *Confessions*. This is a spiritual autobiography, addressed in prayer to God, which tells how God led him to faith through a long and painful pilgrimage. It is unique in its genre in all ancient literature, and even to this day it witnesses to Augustine's profound psychological and intellectual insight.

The other work worthy of special mention is *The City of God*. The immediate motive impelling Augustine to write it was the fall of Rome in A.D. 410. Since at that time there were many who clung to ancient paganism, soon it was charged that Rome had fallen because she had abandoned her ancient gods and turned to Christianity. It was to respond to such allegations that Augustine wrote *The City of God,* a vast encyclopedic history in which he claims that there are two cities, each built on love as a foundation. The city of God is built on love of God. The earthly city is built on love of self. In human history, these two cities always appear mingled with each other.

But in spite of this there is between the two of them an irreconcilable opposition, a war to death. In the end, only the city of God will remain. Meanwhile, human history is filled with kingdoms and nations, all built on love of self, which are no more than passing expressions of the earthly city. All these kingdoms and nations, no matter how powerful, will wither and pass away, until the end of history, when only the city of God will stand. In the particular case of Rome, God allowed her and her empire to flourish so that they could serve as a means for the spread of the Gospel. But now that this purpose has been fulfilled, God has let Rome follow the destiny of all human kingdoms, which is no more than just punishment for their sins.

Augustine was the last of the great leaders of the Imperial Church in the West. When he died, the Vandals were at the gates of Hippo, announcing a new age. Therefore, Augustine's work was, in a way, the last glimmer of a dying age.

And yet, his work was not forgotten among the ruins of a crumbling civilization. On the contrary, through his writings he became the teacher of the new age. Throughout the Middle Ages, no theologian was quoted more often than he was, and he thus became one of the great doctors of the Roman Catholic Church. But he was also the favorite theologian of the great Protestant reformers of the sixteenth century. Thus, Augustine, variously interpreted, has become the most influential theologian in the entire Western church, both Protestant and Catholic.

25/The End of an Era

*The world goes to ruin. Yes! But in spite
of it, and to our shame, our sins still live
and even prosper. The great city, the
capital of the Roman Empire, has been
devoured by a great fire, and all over
the earth Romans wander in exile.
Churches which once were revered are now
but dust and ashes.*

JEROME

When Augustine died, the Vandals were besieging the city of Hippo. Shortly thereafter, they were masters of the northern coast of Africa, except Egypt. A few years earlier, in A.D. 410, Rome had been taken and sacked by Alaric and his Goths. Even earlier, at the battle of Adrianople in 378, an emperor had been defeated and killed by the Goths, whose troops had reached the very walls of Constantinople. The ancient Empire, or rather its western half, was crumbling. For centuries Roman legions had been able to hold the Germanic peoples behind their borders at the Rhine and the Danube. In Great Britain, a wall separated the romanized area from that which was still in control of the "barbarians." But now the floodgates were open. In a series of seemingly endless waves, barbarian hordes crossed the frontiers of the Empire, sacked towns and cities, and finally settled in areas that had been part of the Roman Empire. There they founded their own kingdoms, many of them theoretically subject to the Empire, but in truth independent. The western Roman Empire had come to an end.

The imperial church, which Constantine had inaugurated, continued existing for another thousand years in the Byzantine Empire. Not so in the West, for it would be a long time before western Europe could once again experience the political unity and relative peace that it had known under

Alaric, king of the Goths, took Rome in A.D. 410. That news produced consternation throughout Europe.

Roman rule. It would also take centuries to rebuild much that had been destroyed, not only in terms of roads, buildings, and aqueducts, but also in terms of literature, art, and knowledge of the physical world. In all these fields, it was the church that provided continuity with the past. She became the guardian of civilization and of order. In many ways, she filled the power vacuum left by the demise of the Empire. Centuries later, when the Empire was resurrected in the West, this was done by action of the church, and it was the pope who crowned the emperor.

Meanwhile, there were new challenges to be met. Many of the invaders were pagan, and therefore the conquered felt the need to teach their faith to their victors. Slowly, through the unrecorded witness of thousands of Christians, the invaders accepted the Christian faith, and eventually from their stock came new generations of leaders for the church.

Others were Arian. Years before, especially when Constantius was emperor and therefore Arianism enjoyed the support of the Empire, a number of missionaries had crossed the Danube and begun a mission among the Goths. Foremost among these missionaries was Ulfilas—whose name means "little wolf"—who invented a way to write the language of the Goths, and translated the Bible into it. At the same time, there were many Goths in Constantinople, serving in the imperial guard, and many of these were converted to Christianity before returning to their country. Since most of this contact had taken place when Arianism was on the upswing, it was to Arianism that the Goths had been converted. Then others of their neighbors followed suit. The result was that, by the time of the great invasions, many of the invaders were Christians (although of the Arian persuasion). This meant that the issue of Arianism, which had been considered virtually dead

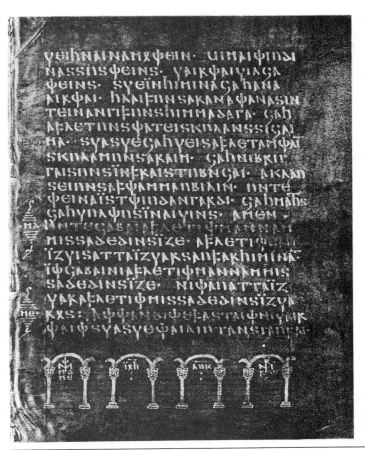

Some fragments of the Gothic version of the Gospels by Ulfilas still survive.

for decades, once again came to the foreground in the West. Eventually, yielding to the influence of those whom they had conquered, all these Arians would accept the Nicene faith. But this was not done without a great deal of struggle and suffering.

Out of all this, a new civilization would arise, one which was heir to classical Greco-Roman antiquity as well as to Christianity and to Germanic traditions. This process took the thousand years known as the Middle Ages, to which we must now turn.

Suggested Readings

Chrysostomus Baur. *John Chrysostom and His Time.* 2 vols. Westminster, Maryland: Newman, 1959, 1960.

Gerald Bonner. *St. Augustine of Hippo: Life and Controversies.* London: SCM, 1963.

Hans von Campenhausen. *The Fathers of the Greek Church.* New York: Pantheon, 1959.

Hans von Campenhausen. *Men Who Shaped the Western Church.* New York: Harper & Row, 1964.

Hermann Doerries. *Constantine the Great.* New York: Harper & Row, 1972.

F. Homes Dudden. *The Life and Times of St. Ambrose.* 2 vols. Oxford: Clarendon, 1935.

W. H. C. Frend. *The Donatist Church: A Movement of Protest in Roman North Africa.* Oxford: Clarendon, 1952.

Robert Payne. *The Fathers of the Western Church.* New York: Viking, 1951.

Robert Payne. *The Holy Fire: The Story of the Fathers of the Eastern Church.* London: Skeffington, 1958.

Marjorie Strachey. *Saints and Sinners of the Fourth Century.* London: William Kimber, 1958.

Helen Waddell. *The Desert Fathers.* Ann Arbor: University of Michigan Press, 1957.

PART III

MEDIEVAL CHRISTIANITY

Chronology

Western Emperors*	Eastern Emperors*	Popes**	Events
Honorius (395–423)	Theodosius II (408–450)	Innocent (401–417) Celestine (422–432)	Fall of Rome (410) †Augustine (430) Council of Ephesus (431)
	Marcian (450–457)	Leo (440–461)	Council of Chalcedon (451) Leo before Attila (453) Vandals sack Rome (455)
	Leo (457–474)		
Romulus Augustulus (475–476)	Zeno (474–491)	Felix III (483–492)	Odoacer ends western empire (476) Henoticon (482)
	Anastasius (491–518)		Clovis is baptized (496)
		Symmachus (498–514)	
	Justin (518–527)	Hormisdas (514–523)	
		John (523–526)	†Boethius (524) †Theodoric (526)
	Justinian (527–565)		Belisarius takes Carthage (533)
		Vigilius (537–555)	II Council of Constantinople (553) Lombards invade Italy (568)
		Pelagius II (579–590)	Conversion of Recared (589)

*Only the names of the most important rulers and popes are included.
**The names of popes not now acknowledged as such by the Roman church are in italics.

Western Emperors*	Eastern Emperors*	Popes**	Events
		Gregory (590–604)	Monte Cassino destroyed (589)
			Augustine in England (597)
	Heraclius (610–641)		Mohammed flees to Medina (622)
		Honorius (625–638)	Mohammed takes Mecca (630)
			†Mohammed (632)
			†Isidore of Seville (636)
			Synod of Whitby (663)
	Constantine IV (668–685)		III Council of Constantinople (680–681)
	Justinian II (685–695; 705–711)	Sergius (687–701)	Moors in Spain (711)
		Gregory II (715–731)	
	Leo III (717–741)	Gregory III (731–741)	
			Battle of Tours (732)
	Constantine V (741–775)	Zacharias (741–752)	
		Stephen II (752–757)	
		Adrian (772–795)	Charlemagne attacks Saxons (772)

Western Emperors*	Eastern Emperors*	Popes**	Events
	Leo IV (775–780) Constantine VI (780–797)		II Council of Nicea (787)
		Leo III (795–816)	
Charlemagne (800–814) Louis the Pious (814–840)	Irene (797–802) Nicephorus (802–811)		
		Nicholas I (858–867)	Norsemen take Paris (845) Photius patriarch (857) Cyril and Methodius in Moravia (863)
Charles the Bald (875–877) Charles the Fat (881–887)			
			King of Bulgaria becomes "czar" (917) Patriarchate of Bulgaria (927)
Henry (933–936) Otto (936–973)			Conversion of Olga of Russia (950)
Otto II (973–983) Otto III (983–1002) Henry II (1002–1024) Conrad II (1024–1039) Henry III (1039–1056)			

Western Emperors*	Eastern Emperors*	Popes**	Events
		Leo IX (1049–1054)	East-West schism (1054)
Henry IV (1056–1106)		Victor II (1055–1057)	
		Stephen IX (1057–1058)	
		Nicholas II (1058–1061)	Hugh abbot of Cluny (1049–1109)
		Alexander II (1061–1073)	Battle of Hastings (1066)
		Gregory VII (1073–1085)	Canossa (1077)
		Urban VI (1088–1099)	Anselm archbishop of Canterbury (1093)
			Council of Clermont (1095)
		Paschal II (1099–1118)	†El Cid (1099)
			Crusaders take Jerusalem (1099)
Henry V (1106–1125)			
		Calixtus II (1119–1124)	Concordat of Worms (1122)
			Abelard condemned (1141)
			Fall of Edessa (1144)
			†Bernard of Clairvaux (1153)
		Alexander III (1159–1181)	†Peter Lombard (1160)
			Fall of Jerusalem (1187)

Western Emperors*	Eastern Emperors*	Popes**	Events
		Innocent III (1198–1216)	
Otto IV (1208–1215)	LATIN EMPIRE (1204–1261)		Battle of Navas de Tolosa (1212) IV Lateran Council (1215)
Frederick II (1215–1250)			†St. Dominic (1221) †St. Francis (1226)
		Gregory IX (1227–1241)	†Bonaventure and Thomas Aquinas (1274) End of crusader presence in Holy Land (1291)
		Celestine V (1294) Boniface VIII (1294–1303)	

Kings of France***	Kings of England***	Popes**	Events
Philip IV (1285–1314)	Edward I (1272–1307)		*Clericis laicos* (1296)
			Unam sanctam (1302)
			Pope's humil- iation at Anagni (1303)
		Benedict XI (1303– 1304)	
		Clement V (1305– 1314)	
	Edward II (1307– 1327)		Beginning of "Babylonian Captivity" (1309)
			Suppression of Templars (1312)
Philip V (1316– 1322		John XXII (1316– 1334)	
Charles IV (1322– 1328)	Edward III (1327– 1377)		†Eckhart (1327)
Philip VI (1328– 1350)		Benedict XII (1334–1342)	Hundred Years' War (1337–1453)
		Clement VI (1342– 1352)	
John II (1350– 1364)			†Occam (1349)
		Innocent VI (1352– 1362)	
Charles V (1364– 1380)		Urban V (1362– 1370)	

***At this point, it is more important to follow the kings of France and England than the emperors.

Kings of France***	Kings of England***	Popes**	Events
	Richard II (1377–1399)	Gregory XI (1370–1378)	End of "Babylonian Captivity" (1377)
		Urban VI (1378–1389)	Great Western Schism (1378)
Charles VI (1380–1422)		*Clement VII* (1378–1394)	Wycliffe condemned at Oxford (1380) †Ruysbroeck (1381) †Wycliffe (1384)
		Boniface IX (1389–1404)	
		Benedict XIII (1394–1423)	
	Henry IV (1399–1413)		Huss rector at Prague (1402)
		Innocent VII (1404–1406)	
		Gregory XII (1406–1415)	
		Alexander V (1409–1410)	Council of Pisa (1409)
		John XXIII (1410–1415)	Huss called to Rome (1410)
	Henry V (1413–1422)		Lollard rebellion (1413–1414) Council of Constance (1414–1418) †Huss (1415)

Kings of France***	Kings of England***	Popes**	Events
		Martin V (1417–1431)	First crusade ag. Hussites (1420)
Charles VII (1422–1461)	Henry VI (1422–1461)		End of Great Schism (1423)
			†Joan of Arc (1431)
		Eugene IV (1431–1447)	Council of Basel (1431–1449)
			Council of Ferrara-Florence (1438–1445)
		Nicholas V (1447–1455)	Fall of Constantinople (1453)
Louis XI (1461–1483)	Edward IV (1461–1483)		
		Sixtus IV (1471–1484)	
			Hans Böhm (1476)
Charles VIII (1483–1498)			

Kings of France***	Kings of England***	Popes**	Events
		Alexander VI (1492–1503)	
	Henry VII (1485–1509)		Columbus in America (1492) †Savonarola (1498)
		Julius II (1503–1513)	
	Henry VIII (1509–1547)		
		Leo X (1513–1521)	

The New Order

> *If only to this end have the barbarians been*
> *sent within Roman borders, . . . that the*
> *church of Christ might be filled with Huns*
> *and Suevi, with Vandals and Burgundians,*
> *with diverse and innumerable peoples of*
> *believers, then let God's mercy be praised*
> *. . . even if this has taken place through*
> *our own destruction.*
> PAULUS OROSIUS

The fall of the western Roman Empire created a number of independent kingdoms, each of which was of great significance for the later history of the church in its territory. It also gave new functions and power to two institutions that had begun to develop earlier: monasticism and the papacy. Finally, new invasions, this time from the southeast, posed new challenges for Christianity. Each of these developments merits separate consideration.

The Barbarian Kingdoms

Although the "barbarians" appeared to the Romans as looters with their minds set on destruction, most of them really aspired to settle within the borders of the Roman Empire, and there to enjoy some of the benefits of a civilization that until then they had only known from afar. Thus, after a period of wandering, each of the major invading bodies settled in a portion of the Empire—some because that was the territory they fancied, and others simply because they had been pushed into that land by other invaders.

The Vandals, who crossed the Rhine in 407, wandered across France and Spain, crossed the Straits of Gibraltar in 429, and took Carthage in 439. By then they were virtual masters of all the northern coast of Africa from the

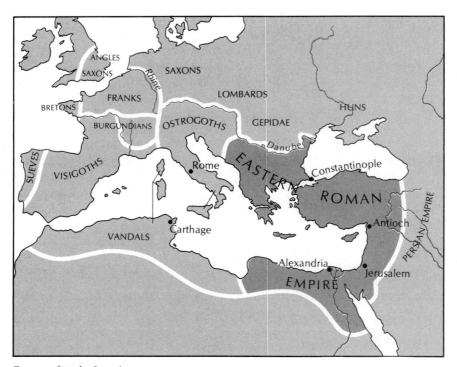

Europe after the Invasions

Straits to the borders of Egypt. They then took to the sea and occupied Sicily, Corsica, and Sardinia. In 455, they sacked the city of Rome, and the destruction they wrought was even greater than that of the Goths forty-five years earlier. Their rule in North Africa was disastrous for the church. They were Arians, and repeated persecutions broke out against both catholics and Donatists. Finally, after almost a century of Vandal rule, the area was conquered by General Belisarius, of the Byzantine Empire. That empire, with its capital in Constantinople, was enjoying a brief renaissance under the leadership of Emperor Justinian, whose dream was to restore the ancient glories of the Empire. The eastern invaders, whom North Africans called "Greeks," brought in still another form of Christianity which, although agreeing in doctrine with that of the western catholics, showed marked differences in terms of culture and daily practices. The net result was that, when the area was conquered by the Moslems late in the seventh century, they found Christianity badly divided, and it eventually disappeared.

The Visigoths—another barbarian group—defeated the Romans at the battle of Adrianople in 378, then swept through the Balkans, and took Rome in 410. By 415 they were in Spain, and they ruled that country until they in turn were overthrown by the Moslems early in the eighth century. The political history of their kingdom was chaotic. Only fifteen of their thirty-four kings died of natural causes or in the field of battle. The rest were either murdered or deposed. They too were Arian, but they did not persecute the orthodox in their territories to the extent that the Vandals did in theirs. Almost two centuries after the conquest, it was clear that the orthodox descendants of the conquered inhabitants were the guardians of ancient culture, and that their participation was necessary in order to provide the kingdom with a measure of stability. This led to the conversion of the Visigoth King Recared (586–601) to Nicene orthodoxy, which he solemnly embraced at a great assembly in Toledo, in A.D. 589. After the king, the vast majority of the nobles became catholic, and Arianism soon disappeared.

The outstanding Christian leader of the entire history of the Visigothic kingdom was Isidore of Seville. He was a scholar who sought to preserve as much as possible of ancient culture. His book *Etymologies* is a veritable encyclopedia that shows the state of knowledge at his time, not only in religious matters, but also in astronomy, medicine, agriculture, and so forth. Although one of the best, it is typical of the writings of the time, for all Isidore could do was to collect and classify the wisdom of the past, with very little by way of original thought. Yet, it was through the works of scholars such as Isidore that the Middle Ages learned of the glories and the wisdom of antiquity.

After the conversion of Recared, the church played the role of legislator for the Visigothic kingdom. In this it provided a measure of order, although in reading the decrees of its councils one cannot but cringe at the injustice and the inequalities that reigned. For instance, a council gathered at Toledo in 633 decreed that priests could only marry with their bishops' permission, and that if any disobeyed, the priest was to be condemned to "do penance for some time," while his wife was to be taken away and sold by the bishop.

The legislation regarding Jews was similar. The same council—whose president was Isidore of Seville, the most enlightened man of his time—decreed that Jews should not be forced to convert to Christianity, but that those who had been forcibly converted earlier would not be allowed to return to the faith of their ancestors, for this would be blasphemy. Furthermore, such converts were forbidden any dealings with Jews who retained their ancient faith, even if they were their closest relatives. And if any of them were found to be observing some of their traditional practices, particularly "the abominable circumcisions," their children were to be taken away from them. Furthermore, any Jew who was found to be married to a Christian woman had to choose between conversion and leaving his wife and children. If the case was reversed, and the wife was Jewish and refused conversion, she had to leave the children with the father.

Even after the conversion of Recared, and in spite of the efforts of the church, the Visigothic kingdom continued to be politically unstable and plagued with violence and arbitrariness. King Recesvinth (649–672), for instance, killed seven hundred of his enemies, and distributed their wives and children among his friends. Finally, under King Roderick (710–711), the Moslems invaded Spain and put an end to Visigothic rule. By then, however, Christianity had become so rooted in the country, that it became the rallying point in the long struggle to reconquer the peninsula from the Moslem Moors.

During most of the fifth century, Gaul was divided between the Burgundians, who were Arians, and the Franks, who were still pagans. The Burgundians, however, did not persecute the catholics, as did the Vandals in North Africa. On the contrary, they imitated their customs, and soon many Burgundians had accepted the Nicene faith of their catholic subjects. In 516, King Sigismund was converted to orthodox Trinitarian doctrine, and soon the rest of the kingdom followed suit.

The Franks (whose country came to be known as "France") were at first an unruly alliance of independent tribes, until a measure of unity was brought by the Merovingian dynasty named after its founder, Meroveus. Clovis, Meroveus' grandson and the greatest of the Merovingian line, was married to a Christian Burgundian princess, and on the eve of a battle promised that he would be converted if his wife's God gave him victory. As a result, on Christmas Day, A.D. 496, he was baptized, along with a number of his nobles. Shortly thereafter, most of the Franks were baptized.

In 534, the Burgundians were conquered by the Franks, and thus the whole region was united. The later Merovingians, however, were weak kings, and by the seventh century the actual government was in the hands of "chamberlains," who in reality were prime ministers. One of these, Charles Martel (that is, "the Hammer") led the Frankish troops against the Moslems, who had taken Spain, crossed the Pyrenees, and threatened the very heart of Europe. He defeated them at the battle of Tours in 732. By then he was virtual king, but did not claim that title. It was his son, Pepin the Short, who decided that the time had come to rid himself of the useless king Childeric III, known as "the Stupid." With the consent of Pope Zacharias, he forced Childeric to abdicate and become a monk. He was then anointed king by Bishop Boniface, who was acting under papal instructions. This was of paramount importance for the later history of Christianity, for Pepin's son, Charlemagne, would be the greatest ruler of the early Middle Ages, one who sought to reform the church, and who was crowned emperor by the pope.

Throughout this process, the role of the church was often compromised. Under powerful kings such as Clovis, ecclesiastical leaders seemed to be content to support and obey the ruler. Soon it became customary for kings to decide who should occupy a vacant bishopric. This was understandable, since extensive holdings of land went with the office of bishop, and therefore a bishop was also a great lord. Shortly before anointing Pepin, Boniface complained to the Pope that the Frankish church was practically in the hands of lay lords, that many of the bishops acted as lords rather than as pastors, and that the notion of a council of bishops gathered to bring order and renewal to the life of the church was unheard of in the Frankish kingdom. Such conditions would continue until the time of Charlemagne.

Great Britain had never been entirely under Roman control. Emperor

Hadrian had built a wall separating the southern portion of the island, which was part of the Roman Empire, from the north, where the Picts and Scots retained their independence. When disaster threatened the Roman possessions on the continent, the legions were withdrawn from Great Britain, and many of the inhabitants left with them. Those who remained were soon conquered by the Angles and the Saxons, who eventually founded the seven kingdoms of Kent, Essex, Sussex, East Anglia, Wessex, Northumbria, and Mercia. All these invaders were pagans, although there always remained a part of the earlier population that retained the Christian faith of Roman times.

Ireland had never been part of the Roman Empire, but Christianity had spread to it before the downfall of the Empire. Although this probably took place through several channels, the spread of Christianity to Ireland is usually attributed to St. Patrick. As a young lad, Patrick had been captured in Great Britain by Irish raiders, and had served as a slave in Ireland. After an adventuresome escape and many other vicissitudes, he had a vision calling him as a missionary to his former captors. Back in Ireland, he met various perils, but eventually his success was great, and the inhabitants were baptized in droves. Soon monasteries were founded, and the learning of antiquity became one of their major interests. Since Ireland was bypassed by the wave of invasions that swept Europe, her monasteries became one of the main sources from which the territories within the ancient Roman Empire regained much of what had been lost during the invasions.

The Irish then began sending missionaries to other countries, most

Germanic traditions were combined with Christian traditions. On this money box there are scenes of the magi and of the hero Wieland.

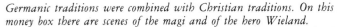

notably to Scotland. The most famous of these missionaries was Columba, who settled on the small island of Iona with twelve companions, probably in A.D. 563. The monastery that they founded there became a center of missions to Scotland, where there soon were several other houses patterned after the Iona community. Eventually, these missions moved south, to territories held by Angles and Saxons.

For reasons that are not altogether clear, there were a number of differences between this Scotch-Irish Christianity and that which had evolved in the former territories of the Roman Empire. Instead of being ruled by bishops, the Scotch-Irish church was under the leadership of the heads of monastic communities. They also differed on the manner in which a number of rites should be performed, and on the date of Easter.

The other form of Christianity had always been present in Great Britain among those who kept the traditions of Roman times, but it gained momentum when Christians on the continent became interested in Great Britain. A biographer of Gregory the Great—to whom we shall return later on in this chapter—records an incident in which young Gregory saw some blond young men who were to be sold as slaves in Rome.

"What is the nationality of these lads?" Gregory asked.

"They are Angles," he was told.

"Angels they are in truth, for their faces look like such. Where is their country?"

"In Deiri."

"De ira (from wrath) they are indeed, for they have been called from wrath to God's mercy. Who is their king?"

"Aella."

"Alleluia! In that land must the name of God be praised."

This dialogue possibly never took place. But it is certain that Gregory was interested in the land of the Angles, and he may have considered going there as a missionary. He became pope in 590, and nine years later sent a mission to the Angles, under the leadership of Augustine, a monk from the same monastery to which Gregory had belonged. When they realized the difficulties that lay ahead, Augustine and his companions considered giving up the enterprise. But Gregory would hear nothing of it, and they were forced to continue. Finally they arrived at the kingdom of Kent, whose king, Ethelbert, was married to a Christian. At first they did not have much success. But eventually Ethelbert himself was converted, and increasing numbers of his subjects followed suit. Augustine then became the first archbishop of Canterbury (the capital of Kent). One by one, the various kingdoms became Christian, and Canterbury became the ecclesiastical capital for all of England.

Soon, however, there were conflicts between those who followed this form of Christianity, and those who belonged to the Scotch-Irish tradition. In Northumbria, we are told that this conflict became serious, for the king followed Scotch-Irish tradition, and the queen held to the Roman one. Since the date for Easter differed, one of them was fasting while the other was feasting. In order to solve the difficulties, a synod was held at Whitby in 663. The Scotch-Irish stood fast on the traditions they said they had received from Columba. The Roman missionaries and their partisans retorted that St. Peter's tradition was superior to Columba's, for the Apostle had received the keys to the Kingdom. On hearing this, we are told, the king asked those who defended the Scotch-Irish position:

"Is it true what your opponents say, that St. Peter has the keys to the Kingdom?"

"Certainly," they answered.

"Then there is no need for further debate. I shall obey Peter. Otherwise, when I arrive at heaven he might close the doors on me and keep me out."

As a result, the synod of Whitby decided in favor of the European tradition, and against the Scotch-Irish. Similar decisions were made throughout the British Isles. But this was not due simply to the naivete of rulers, as the incident at Whitby would seem to imply. It was really the almost inevitable result of the pressure and prestige of the rest of western Christendom, seeking uniformity throughout the church.

In Italy, the barbarian invasions brought a chaotic situation. Although in theory there were emperors in Rome until 476, these in truth were no more than puppets of various Germanic generals. Finally, in 476, Odoacer, leader of the Heruli, deposed the last emperor, Romulus Augustulus, and wrote to Zeno, the emperor at Constantinople, telling him that now the Empire was reunited. At first Zeno was flattered by this, and he even gave Odoacer the title of "patrician." But soon there were conflicts, and the emperor decided to rid himself of the Heruli by inviting the Ostrogoths to invade Italy. This was done, and for a short while Italy was under the rule of the Ostrogoths.

Since the Ostrogoths were Arian, the older population of Italy, which followed the Nicene or catholic faith, looked to Constantinople for support. This in turn made the rulers suspect that their subjects plotted treason. For this reason, the orthodox were often persecuted, although usually not on religious grounds, but rather on charges of conspiracy. It was thus that Boethius, the most learned man of the time, was put in jail by King Theodoric. While in prison he wrote his most famous work, *On the Consolation of Philosophy.* In 524 he was executed, jointly with his father-in-law Symmachus. Two years later, Pope John died in prison. Since then, Boethius, Symmachus, and John were considered martyrs of the Roman church, and the tension between the ancient population and the Ostrogoths grew. Finally, when the Byzantine Empire, under Justinian, had a short period of renewed grandeur, Justinian's general Belisarius invaded Italy and, after twenty years of military campaign, he and others put an end to the kingdom of the Ostrogoths.

But in 568 the Lombards invaded northern Italy, and again threatened the peace of the peninsula, which was now the scene of a constant struggle between the Lombards and the Byzantines. When Constantinople began losing some of the power it had gained under Justinian, there was the danger that the Lombards would overrun the peninsula. Thus, by the middle of the eighth century, the popes, aware that they could expect little help from Constantinople, began to look to the north for help. Thus developed the alliance between the papacy and the Frankish kingdom that would eventually lead to the crowning of Charlemagne as emperor of the West.

In summary, from the fifth to the eighth century western Europe was swept by a series of invasions that brought chaos to the land, and destroyed a great deal of the learning of antiquity. The invaders brought with them two religious challenges that until then could have seemed to be a matter of the past: paganism and Arianism. Eventually, both pagans and Arians were converted to the faith of those whom they had conquered. This was the Nicene faith, also called "orthodox" or "catholic." In the process of that conversion, and also in the effort to preserve the wisdom of ancient times, two institutions played a central role, and thus were strengthened. These two institutions, to which we now turn, were monasticism and the papacy.

Benedictine Monasticism

We have already seen that when the church was joined to the Empire, and thus became the church of the powerful, there were many who found in monasticism a way to live out the total commitment that had been required in earlier times. Although this movement was particularly strong in Egypt and other portions of the eastern Empire, it also found followers in the West. This western monasticism, however, tended to differ from its eastern counterpart on three points. First, western monasticism tended to be more practical. It did not punish the body for the sole purpose of renunciation, but also to train it, as well as the soul, for a mission in the world. Columba and Augustine of Canterbury are examples of this practical bent of western monasticism. Secondly, western monasticism did not place the premium on solitude that was typical in the East. From the beginning, western monasticism sought ways to organize life in community. Finally, western monasticism did not live in the constant tension with the hierarchy of the church that was typical of eastern monasticism. Except in times of extreme corruption of the hierarchy, monasticism in the West has been the right arm of popes, bishops, and other ecclesiastical leaders.

The main figure of western monasticism in its formative years—in many ways, its founder—was Benedict, who was born in the small Italian town of Nursia around A.D. 480. Thus, he grew up under the rule of the Ostrogoths. Since his family belonged to the old Roman aristocracy, he was well aware of the tensions between orthodox and Arian, and the persecutions that the former suffered. When he was about twenty years old, he resolved to become a hermit, and went off to live in a cave. Then followed a period of extreme asceticism, as he sought to overcome the temptations of the flesh. Eventually his fame grew and, as had happened earlier in Egypt with other admired monks, there gathered around him a group of disciples. When the place proved unsuitable for his purposes, Benedict moved the small community to Monte Cassino, a place so remote that there still was a sacred grove, and the local inhabitants continued celebrating ancient pagan worship. Benedict and his followers cut the grove, overturned the pagan altar, and built a monastic foundation in that very place. Shortly thereafter his sister Scholastica settled nearby and founded a similar community for women. Eventually, Benedict's fame was such that the Ostrogoth king went to visit him. But the monk had nothing but harsh words and dire prophecies for the man whom he considered a tyrant.

Benedict's greatest significance, however, was in the *Rule* that he gave to his community. Although fairly brief, this document would determine the shape of monasticism for centuries. Rather than extreme asceticism, what the *Rule* seeks is a wise ordering of the monastic life, with strict discipline, but without undue harshness. Thus, while many of the monks of the desert lived on bread, salt, and water, Benedict prescribed that his monks would have two meals a day, each with two cooked dishes, and at times with fresh fruits and vegetables. Also, each monk was to receive a moderate amount of wine every day. And, in addition to his bed, each monk should also have a cover and a pillow. All this was to be done only in times of abundance, for in times of scarcity monks should be content with whatever was available.

There are, however, two elements of the monastic life that are crucial for Benedict. These are permanence and obedience. The first means that monks are not free to go from one monastery to another as they please. Each monk must remain for the rest of his life in the monastery that he has initially joined, unless ordered to go to another place. The commitment to permanence on the part of Benedictine monks proved one of the sources of the institution's great stability in a time of chaos.

Secondly, the *Rule* insists on obedience. First of all, this means obedience to the *Rule* itself. But the abbot is also to be obeyed "without delay." This means, not only instant obedience, but also that an effort is to be made to make that obedience willing. If what is commanded is impossible, the monk is to explain to the abbot why it is so. If, after such explanation, the superior insists on the command, it is to be obeyed as well as possible. The abbot, however, must not be a tyrant, but is himself subject to God and to the *Rule.* The word "abbot" means "father," and as such should the abbot behave.

An errant monk is to be admonished secretly. If after two such admonitions he does not repent, he is to be reprimanded before the community. The next step is excommunication, which means being barred, not only from

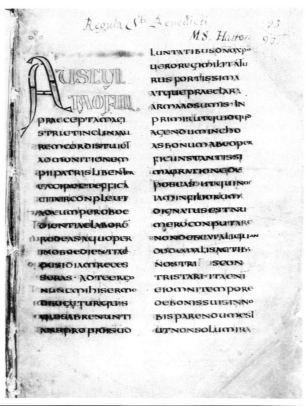

The oldest surviving manuscript of the Rule *of St. Benedict.*

communion, but also from the meals in common and from every contact with the other monks. If he is still unrepentant, he is to be whipped. If even this is to no avail, he is to be sorrowfully expelled from the community. Even then, if he repents, he is to be received again. This, up to three times, for after the third expulsion the monastery will be forever closed to him. In short, the *Rule* is not written for venerable saints, such as the heroes of the desert, but for fallible human beings. This may have been the secret of its success.

The *Rule* also insists on physical labor, which is to be shared by all. Except in exceptional cases of illness or of unique gifts, all will take turns in every task. For instance, there will be weekly cooks, and in order to show that this work is not to be despised, the change of cooks will take place in one of the services of worship. Also, the ill, the elderly, and the very young will receive special consideration in the assignment of tasks. On the other hand, those who come from wealthy families will receive no special treatment on that account. If it is necessary for some reason to establish an order of priority in the monastery, this will be done according to the length of time that each has been part of the community. Thus, whereas poverty for earlier monasticism was a form of private renunciation, Benedict sought to achieve through it the creation of a new order within the community. A monk's poverty welds him to the community, in which all are of equal poverty, and on which all must depend for all their needs.

The core of the monastic life as Benedict conceived it was prayer. Periods were assigned each day for private prayer, but most of the devotions took place in the chapel. There the monks were to gather eight times a day, seven during daytime, and once in the middle of the night, for the Psalmist says: "seven times a day I praise thee" (Ps. 119:164) and "at midnight I rise to praise thee" (Ps. 119:62).

The first gathering for prayer took place in the early hours of dawn, and was followed by seven others. These hours, kept by most monastic houses during the Middle Ages, were called Matins, Lauds, Prime, Terce, Sext, None, Vespers, and Compline. Most of the time at each of these gatherings was devoted to reciting the Psalms and to readings of other portions of Scripture. The Psalms were distributed so that all would be recited in the course of a week. The other readings depended on the time of day, the day of the week, and the liturgical season. As a result, most monks came to know the entire Psalter by heart, as well as other portions of Scripture. Since many of the laity who had the necessary leisure followed similar devotional practices, they too acquired great familiarity with various parts of the Bible, as they appeared in their *Breviaries*—books containing the material to be read at various hours. The eight hours of prayer came to be called "canonical hours," and their celebration the "Divine Office."

Although Benedict himself had little to say about study, soon this was one of the main occupations of Benedictine monks. In order to celebrate the Divine Office, books were needed. Monks became adept at copying both the Bible and other books, and thus preserved them for later generations. Their houses also became teaching centers, particularly for the many children that were placed under their care in order to be trained as monks. And many also served as hospitals and pharmacies, or as hostels where a weary traveler could find shelter.

Eventually, monasteries also had a profound economic impact, for many were established on marginal lands that were brought into production by the labor of the monks. Thus, countless acres were added to the agricultural land of Europe. Furthermore, in a society where the wealthy considered manual labor demeaning, the monasteries showed that the highest intellectual and spiritual achievements could be coupled with hard physical labor.

Although the monastic movement had many followers in western Europe before Benedict's time, it was Benedict's *Rule* that eventually became widespread. In 589, the monastery that Benedict had founded at Monte Cassino was looted and burned by the Lombards. Most of the monks fled to

Rome, taking their *Rule* with them. It was there that Gregory, who would later become pope, came to know them. Soon their *Rule* was followed by many in the city of Rome. Augustine, the missionary to England, took the *Rule* with him to the British Isles. With the support of the papacy, the Benedictine *Rule* spread throughout the Western church. The many monasteries that followed it, although not organized into a formal "order," were united by common practices and ideals.

The Papacy

The second institution which, jointly with monasticism, gave unity and continuity to the Middle Ages was the papacy. The word "pope" simply means "father," and in early times was used to refer to any important and respected bishop. Thus, there are documents refering to "Pope Cyprian" of Carthage, or to "Pope Athanasius" of Alexandria. Whereas in the West it eventually was reserved for the bishops of Rome, in the East it continued to be used with more liberality. In any case, what is important is not the origin of the title "pope," but rather how the bishop of Rome came to enjoy the authority that he had in the Middle Ages, and still has in the Roman Catholic Church.

The origins of episcopacy in Rome are not altogether clear. Most scholars agree that Peter did visit Rome, and that there is at least a very high probability that he died there. But the various lists of the early bishops of Rome, mostly dating from late in the second century, do not agree among themselves. While some claim that Clement was Peter's successor, others name him as the third bishop after the Apostle's death. This has led some scholars to suggest the possibility that in the beginning Rome did not have a single bishop, but rather a "collegiate episcopacy"—a group of bishops who jointly led the church. While such a theory is open to debate, it is clear that during the early centuries the numerical strength of Christianity was in the Greek-speaking East, and that churches such as Antioch and Alexandria were much more important than the one in Rome. Even in the West, the theological leadership of the church was in North Africa, which produced such figures as Tertullian, Cyprian, and Augustine.

It was the barbarian invasions that brought about the great upsurge in the pope's authority. In the East, the Empire continued existing for another thousand years. But in the West the church became the guardian of what was left of ancient civilization, as well as of order and justice. Thus, the most prestigious bishop in the West, that of Rome, became the focal point for regaining a unity that had been shattered by the invasions.

A prime example of this is Leo "the Great," who has been called the first "pope" in the modern sense. Later, we shall see his participation in the theological controversies of the time. In that participation it is clear that Leo's opinion was not generally accepted simply because he was the bishop of

Rome, and that it took a politically propitious moment for his views to prevail. Since those controversies took place mostly in the East, Leo's intervention, although significant, was powerless in the face of imperial opposition, and was accepted only when those in power agreed to it.

In the West, however, things were different. In 452 Italy was invaded by Attila and his Huns, who took and sacked the city of Aquileia. The road to Rome was open to them, for there was no army between them and the ancient capital. The western emperor was weak both in character and in resources, and the East had given indications that it was unwilling to intervene. It was then that Leo left Rome and marched to meet "the Scourge of God." What was said in that interview is not known. Legend has it that Attila saw Saints Peter and Paul marching with the Pope, and threatening the Hun. Whatever was said, Attila decided not to attack Rome, and turned towards the north, where he died shortly thereafter.

Leo was still Bishop of Rome in 455, when the Vandals sacked the city. At that time, he was unable to stop the invaders. But it was he who led the negotiations with the Vandal leader, Genseric, and thus avoided the burning of the city.

Needless to say, these episodes—and others like it—gave Leo great authority in the city of Rome. That he was able to do these things was due both to his personal gifts and to the political situation of the time, when the civil authorities proved incapable of performing their duties. But in Leo's mind there was a deeper reason. He was convinced that Jesus had made Peter and his successors the rock on which the church was to be built, and that therefore the bishop of Rome, Peter's direct successor, is the head of the church. Thus, in Leo's writings one finds all the traditional arguments that would repeatedly be mustered in favor of papal authority.

Leo died in 461 and was succeeded by Hilarius, who had been his close associate, and who continued his policies. But under the next pope, Simplicius, conditions changed. In 476, Odoacer deposed the last western emperor, and thus began in Italy a long period of political chaos. In theory, Italy was now part of the eastern Roman Empire. But there were constant tensions between the popes and the eastern emperors, mostly having to do with the theological controversies to which we shall shortly return. Eventually, this resulted in a schism between East and West that would take several years to heal. This schism was aggravated further by the invasion of Italy by the Ostrogoths. Since they were Arian, tensions between them and the earlier population were unavoidable. By 498, these tensions resulted in the existence of two rival popes, one supported by the Ostrogoths and the other by Constantinople. There were violent riots in the streets of Rome, where the followers of one pope clashed with the followers of the other. At long last, after a series of synods, the conflict was resolved.

The new Pope was Hormisdas (514–523), and under his leadership a series of negotiations finally ended the schism with Constantinople. Meanwhile, the eastern Empire was enjoying its brief resurgence under the leadership of Emperor Justinian. It was then that Belisarius invaded Italy and put an end to the kingdom of the Ostrogoths. But this did not bring a favorable change for the church in Italy, for the emperor and his functionaries tried to impose there a situation similar to that which existed in the eastern Empire, where the church was almost completely subject to the state. The next few popes, for as long as Byzantium held sway, were mere puppets of Justinian and of his empress, Theodora. Those who dared follow an independent policy soon felt the consequences of imperial wrath.

Byzantine power over Italy did not last long. Only six years after the last stronghold of the Ostrogoths had been conquered, the Lombards invaded the area. Had they been united, they would soon have conquered all of it. But after their first victories they broke up into several rival groups, and this slowed their advance. After Justinian's death in 565, Byzantine power began to wane, and Constantinople could no longer maintain a strong army in Italy. Thus, those who had not been conquered by the Lombards, although still technically part of the eastern Empire, were forced to take measures for their defense. In Rome, the popes became responsible for the preservation of the city against the Lombard threat. When Benedict I died in 579, the Lombards were besieging the city. His successor, Pelagius II, saved it by buying the Lombards off. Then, since no help was forthcoming from Constantinople, he turned to the Franks, whom he hoped would attack the Lombards from the north. Although these initial negotiations did not come to fruition, they pointed to the future, when the Franks would become the main support of the papacy.

The next pope, Gregory, was one of the ablest men ever to occupy that position. He was born in Rome around 540, apparently to a family of the old aristocracy. At that time Justinian reigned in Constantinople, and his generals were fighting the Ostrogoths in Italy. Belisarius, Justinian's ablest general, had been recalled to Constantinople, and the war dragged on. The Ostrogoth king, Totila, took the offensive for a short time. In 545, he besieged Rome, which surrendered the next year. At that time, archdeacon Pelagius (later Pope Pelagius II) went out to meet the victorious king and obtained from him a measure of mercy. It is likely that Gregory was at Rome at the time, and witnessed both the sufferings during the siege and Pelagius' intervention on behalf of the city. In any case, the Rome that Gregory knew was a far cry from the ancient glory of the Empire. Shortly after Totila's victory, Belisarius and the Byzantines retook the city, only to lose it again. After years of neglect and repeated sieges, the city was in a grave state of chaos and mismanagement. Many of her ancient monuments and buildings had been destroyed in order to provide stones for repairing the walls. The aqueducts and the system of drainage had fallen into disrepair, and disease was rife.

Little is known of Gregory's early years in this beleaguered city. He may have been an important Roman official before becoming a monk. Some time

This gospel illumination with the symbol of Luke (the winged ox) may be from a copy of the Gospels sent to England by Gregory.

later, Pope Benedict made him a deacon—that is, a member of his administrative council. The next pope, Pelagius II, appointed Gregory his ambassador before the court at Constantinople. There Gregory spent six years, and was often involved in the theological controversies and political intrigues that were constantly boiling in the great city. Finally, in 586, Pelagius sent another ambassador, and Gregory was able to return to his monastery in Rome, where he was made abbot.

At that time the situation in Rome was serious. The Lombards had finally united, and intended to conquer the whole of Italy. Although some resources were sent from Constantinople for the defense of Rome, and although the Lombards were occasionally being attacked from the rear by the Franks, there was great danger that the city would fall.

To make matters worse, an epidemic broke out in Rome. Shortly before, floods had destroyed much of the store of food. Since those who were ill frequently had hallucinations, rumors began circulating. Someone had seen a great dragon emerging from the Tiber. Death was seen stalking the streets. Fire had rained from heaven. Then Pope Pelagius, who with the help of Gregory and other monks had organized the sanitation of the city, the burial of the dead, and the feeding of the hungry, himself became ill and died.

Under such circumstances, there were not many who coveted the empty post. Gregory himself had no wish to become pope, but the clergy and the people elected him. He sought to have his election annulled by writing to the emperor and asking that his appointment not be confirmed—at that time it was customary to request the approval of Constantinople before consecrating the bishop of an important see. But his letter was intercepted. Eventually, although reluctantly, he was made bishop of Rome.

He then set about his new tasks with unbounded zeal. Since there was nobody else to do it, he organized the distribution of food among the needy in Rome, and he also took measures to guarantee the continuing shipments of wheat from Sicily. Likewise, he supervised the rebuilding of the aqueducts and of the defenses of the city, and the garrison was drilled until morale was restored. Since there was little help to be expected from Constantinople, he then opened direct negotiations with the Lombards, with whom he secured peace. Thus, by default, the Pope was acting as ruler of Rome and the surrounding area, which soon came to be known as "Saint Peter's Patrimony." Much later, in the eighth century, someone forged a document, the so-called *Donation of Constantine,* which claimed that the great emperor had granted these lands to Saint Peter's successors.

But Gregory considered himself above all a religious leader. He preached constantly in the various churches in Rome, calling the faithful to renewed commitment. He also took measures to promote clerical celibacy, which was slowly becoming the norm throughout Italy, and which many claimed to follow but did not. Also, as bishop of Rome, Gregory saw himself as patriarch of the West. He did not claim for himself universal authority, as Leo had done earlier. But he took more practical steps, which did in fact increase his authority in the West. In Spain, he was instrumental in the conversion of the Visigothic King Recared to Nicene catholicism. To England, he sent Augustine's mission, which would eventually extend the authority of Rome to the British Isles. His letters to Africa, dealing with the Donatist schism, were not as well received by the local bishops, who wished to guard their independence. He also tried to intervene in the various Frankish territories, seeking more autonomy for the church. But in this he did not succeed, for the Frankish rulers wished to have control of the church, and saw no reason to yield to the pope's entreaties.

However, it is not only for these reasons that Gregory is called "the Great." He was also a prolific writer whose works were very influential throughout the Middle Ages. In these writings, he did not seek to be original or creative. On the contrary, his greatest pride was not to say anything that had not been held by the great teachers of earlier centuries, particularly Saint Augustine. To him, it sufficed to be a disciple of the great bishop of Hippo, a teacher of his teachings. But in spite of such wishes, there was a chasm between Gregory and his admired Augustine. Gregory lived in a time of obscurantism, superstition, and credulity, and to a degree he reflected his age. By making Augustine an infallible teacher, he contradicted the spirit of that teacher, whose genius was, at least in part, in his inquiring spirit and venturesome mind. What for Augustine was conjecture, in Gregory became certainty. Thus, for instance, the theologian of Hippo had suggested the possibility that there was a place of purification for those who died in sin, where they would spend some time before going to heaven. On the basis of these speculations of Augustine, Gregory affirmed the existence of such a place, and thus gave impetus to the development of the doctrine of purgatory.

It was particularly in that which refers to the doctrine of salvation that Gregory mitigated and even transformed the teachings of Augustine. The Augustinian doctrines of predestination and irresistible grace were set aside by Gregory, who was more concerned with the question of how we are to offer satisfaction to God for sins committed. This is done through penance, which consists of contrition, confession, and the actual punishment or satisfaction. To these must be added priestly absolution, which confirms the forgiveness granted by God. Those who die in the faith and communion of the church, but without having offered satisfaction for all their sins, will go to purgatory before they attain their final salvation. The living can help the dead out of purgatory by offering masses in their favor. Gregory believed that in the mass or communion Christ was sacrificed anew (and there is a legend that the Crucified appeared to him while celebrating mass). This notion of the mass as sacrifice eventually became standard doctrine of the Western church —until it was rejected by Protestants in the sixteenth century.

Gregory tells the story of a certain monk who had died in sin. The abbot —Gregory himself—ordered that daily masses be said on behalf of the deceased, whose soul appeared to a brother after thirty days, declaring that he was now free of purgatory, and had moved on to heaven. This and similar stories were not Gregory's invention. They were rather part of the atmosphere and beliefs of the time. But, while earlier Christian teachers had sought to preserve Christian faith free of popular superstition, Gregory readily accepted the stories circulating at his time as if they were simple and direct confirmation of Christian faith.

Under Gregory's successors, the papacy fell on evil days. Constantinople insisted on asserting her authority over Rome. Since at that time, as we shall see in the next chapter, the Eastern church was divided by Christological controversies, the emperors demanded that the popes support their theological positions. Those who refused were treated harshly. Thus, it came about that Pope Honorius (625–638) declared himself a monothelite—that is, a follower of a Christological heresy. When, years later, Pope Martin I disobeyed the emperor's command that there was to be no more discussion of these Christological issues, he was kidnapped and taken to Constantinople. His main supporter, the monk Maximus, had his tongue and his right hand cut off by imperial order, and was also sent into exile. From then on, all the theological controversies with which we shall deal in the next chapter had serious repercussions in Rome, which could not free herself from the overwhelming power of the emperors of Constantinople. During all this time, and until Gregory III (731–741), the election of a pope had to be confirmed by the authorities in Constantinople before the pope could be consecrated as bishop of Rome.

Then the Byzantine fleet was destroyed, and the power of Constantinople in Italy began to wane. The ever present threat of the Lombards forced the popes to find new support elsewhere, and they turned to the Franks. It was for this reason that Pope Zacharias agreed to have Childeric III, "the Stupid," deposed, and Pepin crowned in his stead. Although Zacharias died the same year that Pepin was crowned (752), his successor, Stephen II, collected the debt that Pepin had acquired with the papacy. When the Lombards again threatened, Stephen appealed to Pepin, who twice invaded Italy, and granted to the pope several cities that the Lombards had taken. The protests of the government at Constantinople need not be heeded, and the popes became rulers of a vast portion of Italy. From that point, the alliance between the Franks and the popes grew closer, until Pope Leo III crowned Charlemagne emperor of the West on Christmas Day, A.D. 800.

The Arab Conquests

Early in the seventh century, it seemed that order was about to be restored in most of the ancient Roman Empire. The Arian invaders had embraced Nicene orthodoxy. The Franks, who from the beginning had been converted to that faith, were beginning to unite in Gaul. In the British Isles, the first fruits of Augustine's mission could be seen. The Byzantine Empire still enjoyed many of the results of Justinian's conquests—particularly in North Africa, where the Vandal kingdom had disappeared.

Then something unexpected happened. Out of Arabia, a forgotten corner of the world that had been generally ignored by both the Roman and the Persian empires, a tidal wave of conquest arose that threatened to engulf the world. In a few years, the Persian Empire had vanished, and many of the ancient Roman territories were in Arab hands.

The driving force behind this human avalanche was Mohammed, an Arab merchant who had always had deep religious interests, and who had come in contact with both Judaism and the various Christian sects that existed in Arabia—some of them rather unorthodox. His message, which he claimed had been revealed to him by Gabriel, was that of a single God, both just and merciful, who rules all things and requires obedience from all. It was often presented in rhythmic fashion, like that of the ancient Hebrew prophets. Mohammed claimed that he was not preaching a new religion, but simply the culmination of what God had revealed in the Hebrew prophets and in Jesus, who was a great prophet, although not divine as Christians claimed.

Since polytheism was closely related to their business, the merchants in Mecca opposed the preaching of Mohammed, who took refuge at the nearby oasis where Medina would eventually become a great city. The date of that flight, A.D. 622, is the beginning of the Moslem era, from which years are counted. There he founded the first Moslem community, in which worship, as well as civil and political life, followed the guidelines set out by him. Then he and his followers set out on a military and political campaign that eventually gave them control over Mecca. At that point, Mohammed decreed that his former enemies were forgiven, although all idols must be overthrown. By his death in 632, a goodly part of Arabia was in Moslem hands.

Then leadership passed on to the caliphs—from an Arabic word which means "successor." Under Abu Bakr (632–634), power over Arabia was consolidated, and the Moslems achieved their first victory over the Byzantine armies. Under Omar (634–644) the Arabs invaded Syria. In 635 they took Damascus, and Jerusalem in 638. Two years later, they were masters of the entire region. At the same time, another Moslem army invaded Egypt, founded what would later become Cairo, and took Alexandria in 642. By 647, they were again marching westward along the northern coast of Africa. Meanwhile, a third army invaded the Persian Empire, whose last king died in 651. After that date, with minor setbacks, the Moslems swept through what had been one of the most powerful kingdoms on earth.

During the second half of the century, Moslem advance was somewhat slowed by inner strife, but it continued nonetheless. Carthage fell in 695, and soon many of the inhabitants of North Africa, who had lived through so much strife between catholics, Donatists, Arians, and Byzantines, accepted Islam. By 711, a small band crossed the Straits of Gibraltar—whose name is derived from their leader, Tarik—and found the Visigothic kingdom so weakened that they overran it. Soon all of Spain, except for the extreme northern areas, was under Moslem rule. From there they crossed the Pyrenees and threatened the very heart of western Europe. In 732, they were finally defeated by Charles Martel at the battle of Tours, which marked the end of the first wave of Moslem expansion.

These invasions had enormous significance for Christianity. For one

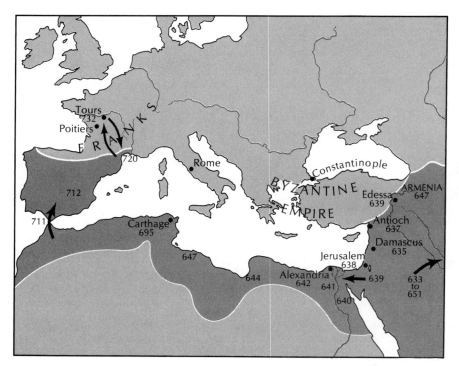

The Arab Conquests

thing, many of the ancient centers of Christianity—Jerusalem, Antioch, Damascus, Alexandria, and Carthage—were now under Moslem rule. In Carthage and the surrounding area, Christianity completely disappeared. In the rest of the vast Arab holdings it was tolerated, but ceased growing, and eventually was content with holding its own.

The Byzantine Empire, which until then had vast territories in the Near East and the northern coast of Africa, was pushed back to what is now Turkey, and to its holdings in Europe. In the next chapter we shall see that many of those within that empire who had dissented from its policies were now under Moslem rule, and therefore the Byzantine emperors no longer felt the need to take their views into account.

But above all, the entire geographic configuration of Christianity changed. Until then, Christianity had developed along the Mediterranean basin. Now, it would find its center along an axis that ran from north to south, including the British Isles, the Frankish kingdom, and Italy. Constantinople would be increasingly alienated from that axis. Therefore it is no coincidence that a few years after the Arab conquests, in A.D. 800, the pope felt inclined to crown Charlemagne emperor of the West, and both he and Charlemagne were ready to ignore the protests that came from Constantinople.

27/Eastern Christianity

When I have no books, or when my thoughts, torturing me like thorns, do not let me enjoy reading, I go to church, which is the cure available for every disease of the soul. The freshness of the images draws my attention, captivates my eyes . . . and slowly leads my soul to divine praise.

JOHN OF DAMASCUS

Although in the last chapter our attention has centered on western Christianity, one must not forget that at the same time there was an eastern branch of the church. For Christians at that time, both East and West, the church was one. Historians, however, can now see that by the early Middle Ages the two branches of the church were drifting apart, and that the final schism, which took place in 1054, was long in the making. Apart from the obvious cultural differences between the Latin-speaking West and the Greek-speaking East, the political course of events produced entirely different situations in the two branches of the church. In the West, the demise of the Empire created a vacuum that the church filled, and thus ecclesiastical leaders—particularly the pope—also came to wield political power. In the East, the Empire continued for another thousand years. It was often beleaguered by foreign invasion or by inner turmoil, but it survived. And its autocratic emperors kept a tight rein on ecclesiastical leaders. This usually led to civil intervention in ecclesiastical matters, particularly in theological debates. Theological discussion came to be tainted with the ever-present possibility of appealing to the emperor to take one's side, and thus crushing an enemy one could not overcome by mere argument. Obviously, many emperors made theological decisions on the basis of political considerations, which led to even greater acrimony. For these reasons, theological controversy became one of the hallmarks of eastern Christianity during the early Middle Ages.

This is not to say that such controversies were not important. The issues at stake were often central to the Gospel. Furthermore, since Christians at that time considered themselves members of the same church, the decisions made in the East, sometimes with little or no western participation, came to be regarded as normative by both East and West. Finally, out of these debates the first permanent schisms developed within Christianity, giving rise to separate churches that still exist.

The Christological Debates to the Council of Chalcedon

The question of the divinity of the Second Person of the Trinity (and of the Holy Ghost) had been settled by the councils of Nicea (325) and Constantinople (381). Although the conversion of some of the barbarians to Arianism and their subsequent invasion of western Europe brought about a brief resurgence of Arianism, this eventually disappeared, and Christians were in basic agreement on Trinitarian doctrine. But there were still other issues that would cause sharp theological disagreement. Foremost among these was the question of how divinity and humanity are joined in Jesus Christ. This is the fundamental Christological question.

On this question, there were in the East two different currents of thought, which historians have conveniently labeled the "Antiochene" and the "Alexandrine"—although not all those who followed the Alexandrine way of thinking were from Alexandria, nor were all the Antiochenes from Antioch. Both sides were agreed that the divine was immutable and eternal. The question then was, how can the immutable, eternal God be joined to a mutable, historical man? At this point, the two schools followed divergent paths. The Alexandrines, like Clement and Origen centuries earlier, stressed the significance of Jesus as the teacher of divine truth. In order to be this, the Savior had to be a full and clear revelation of the divine. His divinity must be asserted, even if this had to be done at the expense of his humanity. The Antiochenes, on the other hand, felt that for Jesus to be the Savior of human beings he had to be fully human. The Godhead dwelt in him, without any doubt; but this must not be understood in such a way that his humanity was diminished or eclipsed. Both sides agreed that Jesus was both divine and human. The question was how to understand that union.

In the West, such questions did not create the same stir. For one thing, after the barbarian invasions, there were other urgent matters that required attention. For another, the West simply revived Tertullian's old formula— that in Christ there were two natures united in one person—and was content to affirm this. Thus, the West played a balancing role between the two factions in the East, and for that reason would come out of the controversies with enhanced prestige.

The first stages of the controversy began even before the Trinitarian issue was settled. One of the defenders of the Nicene position regarding the Trinity, Apollinaris of Laodicea, thought that he could help that cause by explaining how the eternal Word of God could be incarnate in Jesus. This he attempted to do by claiming that in Jesus the Word of God, the Second Person of the Trinity, took the place of the rational soul. Like all human beings, Jesus had a physical body, and this was activated by the same principle that gives life to all human beings. But he did not have a human intellect. The Word of God played in him the role that the intellect or "rational soul" plays in the rest of us.

Although this explanation seemed satisfactory to Apollinaris, soon many began to see flaws in it. A human body with a purely divine mind is not really a human being. From the Alexandrine point of view, this was quite acceptable, for all that was needed was that Jesus really speak as God, and that he have the body necessary to communicate with us. But the Antiochenes insisted that this was not enough. Jesus must be truly human. This was especially important, since Jesus took up humanity so that humankind could be saved. Only if he really became human did he really save us. If any part of what constitutes a human being was not taken up by him, that was not saved by him. Gregory of Nazianzus (one of the Great Cappadocians) put it this way:

If any believe in Jesus Christ as a human being without human reason, they are the ones devoid of all reason, and unworthy of salvation. For that which he has not taken up he has not saved. He saved that which he joined to his divinity. If only half of Adam had fallen, then it would be possible for Christ to take up and save only half. But if the entire human nature fell, all of it must be united to the Word in order to be saved as a whole.*

After some debate, the theories of Apollinaris were rejected, first by a number of leading bishops and local synods called by them, and eventually by the Council of Constantinople in 381—the same council that reaffirmed the decisions of Nicea against Arianism.

The next episode of the Christological controversies was precipitated by Nestorius, a representative of the Antiochene school who became patriarch of Constantinople in 428. There were always political intrigues surrounding that office, for the patriarchate of Constantinople had become a point of discord between the patriarchs of Antioch and Alexandria. The Council of Constantinople had declared that the bishop of Constantinople should have in the East a precedence similar to that which the bishop of Rome had in the West. This was a simple acknowledgment of political reality, for Constantino-

---

*Gregory of Nazianzus, *Epistle* 101.

ple had become the capital of the Eastern Empire. But the bishops of the older churches in Antioch and Alexandria were not content with being relegated to a secondary position. They responded, among other things, by turning the bishopric of Constantinople into a prize to be captured for their own supporters. Since Antioch was more successful at this game than Alexandria, most of the patriarchs of Constantinople were Antiochenes, and therefore the patriarchs of Alexandria regarded them as their enemies—a process we have already seen when dealing with the life of John Chrysostom. For these reasons, Nestorius' position was not secure, and the Alexandrines were looking to catch him at his first mistake.

This happened when Nestorius declared that Mary should not be called *theotokos*—that is, bearer of God—and suggested that she be called *Christotokos*—bearer of Christ. It is difficult for Protestants to understand what was at stake here, for we have been taught to reject the notion that Mary is the "Mother of God," and at first glance this seems to be what is at stake here. But in truth, the debate was not so much about Mary as about Jesus. The question was not what honors were due to Mary, but how one was to speak of the birth of Jesus. When Nestorius declared that Mary was the bearer of Christ, but not of God, he was affirming that in speaking of the incarnate Lord one may and must distinguish between his humanity and his divinity, and that some of the things said of him are to be applied to the humanity, and others to the divinity. This was a typically Antiochene position, which sought to preserve the full humanity of Jesus by making a very clear distinction between it and his divinity. Nestorius and the rest of the Antiochenes feared that if the two were too closely joined together, the divinity would overwhelm the humanity, and one would no longer be able to speak of a true man Jesus.

In order to explain this position, Nestorius declared that in Jesus there were "two natures and two persons," one divine and one human. The human nature and person were born of Mary; the divine were not. What he meant by this is not altogether clear, for the terms "person" and "nature" could be used with different meanings. But his enemies immediately saw the danger of "dividing" the Savior into two beings whose unity consisted in agreement rather than in any real joining together. Soon many others were convinced that Nestorius' doctrines were indeed dangerous.

As was to be expected, the center of opposition to Nestorius was Alexandria, whose bishop Cyril was a much abler politician and theologian than Nestorius. Cyril made certain that he had the support of the West, for which the doctrine of two persons in Christ was anathema, as well as of emperors Valentinian III and Theodosius II, who then called an ecumenical council to be gathered at Ephesus in June 431.

Nestorius' main supporters, John of Antioch and his party, were delayed. After waiting for them for two weeks, the council convened, in spite of the protests of the imperial legate and several dozen bishops. They then dealt with the case of Nestorius and, without allowing him to defend himself, declared him a heretic, and deposed him from his see.

John of Antioch and his party arrived a few days later, and they then convened a rival council, which was much smaller than Cyril's, and which declared that Cyril was a heretic and reinstated Nestorius. In retaliation, Cyril's council reaffirmed its condemnation of Nestorius and added to it the names of John of Antioch and all who had taken part in his council. Finally, Theodosius II intervened, arrested both Cyril and John, and declared that the actions of both councils were void. Then followed a series of negotiations that led to a "formula of union" to which both Cyril and John agreed in 433. It was also decided that the actions of Cyril's council against Nestorius would stand. As to Nestorius, he spent the rest of his life in exile, first in a monastery in Antioch, and then, when he became too embarrassing to his Antiochene friends who had abandoned him, in the remote city of Petra.

Thus, the second episode in the Christological controversies ended with a victory for Alexandria, and with a truce that would not hold for long. In 444, when Dioscorus succeeded Cyril as patriarch of Alexandria, the stage was set for a third and even more acrimonious confrontation, for Dioscorus was a convinced defender of the most extreme Alexandrine positions, and a rather unscrupulous maneuverer.

The storm centered on the teachings of Eutyches, a monk in Constantinople who lacked theological subtlety, and who held that, while the Savior was "of one substance with the Father," he was not "of one substance with us." He also seems to have been willing to say that Christ was "from two natures before the union, but in one nature after the union." Exactly what this meant is not altogether clear. In any case, Patriarch Flavian of Constantinople, whose theology was of the Antiochene tradition, felt that Eutyches' teachings were close to docetism and condemned him. Through a series of maneuvers, Dioscorus had the affair grow into a conflict that involved the entire church, so that a council was called by Emperor Theodosius II, to meet at Ephesus in 449.

When this council gathered, it was clear that Dioscorus and his supporters had taken all the necessary steps to predetermine the outcome. Dioscorus himself had been appointed president of the assembly by the emperor, and given the authority to determine who would be allowed to speak. This council took an extreme Alexandrine stand. When Pope Leo's legates tried to present before the assembly a letter that Leo had written on the subject at hand, they were not allowed to do so. Flavian was manhandled so violently that he died in a few days. The doctrine that there are in Christ "two natures" was declared heretical, as were also all who defended the Antiochene position, even in moderate form. Furthermore, it was decreed that any who disagreed with these decisions could not be ordained.

In Rome, Leo fumed, and called the council a "robbers' synod." But his protests were to no avail. Theodosius II and his court, who apparently had

Ephesus, where the Third Ecumenical Council gathered, was also the site of the council of 449.

received large amounts of gold from Alexandria, considered the matter ended.

Then the unexpected happened. Theodosius' horse stumbled, and the emperor fell and broke his neck. He was succeeded by his sister Pulcheria and her husband Marcian. Pulcheria had agreed earlier with the western position, that Nestorius should be condemned. But she was not an extreme Alexandrine, and felt that the proceedings at Ephesus in 449 had left much to be desired. For this reason, at the behest of Leo, she called a new council, which met at Chalcedon in 451 and which eventually became known as the Fourth Ecumenical Council.

This council condemned Dioscorus and Eutyches, but forgave all others who had participated in the "robbers' synod" of Ephesus two years earlier. Leo's letter was finally read, and many declared that this expressed their own faith. It was a restatement of what Tertullian had declared centuries earlier, that in Christ there are "two natures in one person." Finally, the council produced a statement that was not a creed, but rather a "Definition of faith," or a clarification of what the church held to be true. A careful reading of that "Definition" will show that, while rejecting the extremes of both Alexandrines and Antiochenes, and particularly the doctrine of Eutyches, it reaffirmed what had been done in the three previous great councils (Nicea in 325, Constantinople in 381, and Ephesus in 431):

Following, then, the holy Fathers, we all with one voice teach that it is to be confessed that our Lord Jesus Christ is one and the same God, perfect in divinity, and perfect in humanity, true God and true human, with a rational soul and a body, of one substance with the Father in his divinity, and of one substance with us in his humanity, in every way like us, with the only exception of sin, begotten of the Father before all time in his divinity, and also begotten in the latter days, in his humanity, of Mary the virgin bearer of God.

This is one and the same Christ, Son, Lord, Only-begotten, manifested in two natures without any confusion, change, division or separation. The union does not destroy the difference of the two natures, but on the contrary the properties of each are kept, and both are joined in on person and *hypostasis.* They are not divided into two persons, but belong to the one Only-begotten Son, the Word of God, the Lord Jesus Christ. All this, as the prophets of old said of him, and as he himself has taught us, and as the Creed of the Fathers has passed on to us.

It will be readily seen that this "Definition" does not seek to "define" the union in the sense of explaining how it took place, but rather in the sense of setting the limits beyond which error lies. It is clear that this manner of speaking of the Savior is far distant from that of the Gospels, and has been deeply influenced by extrabiblical patterns of thought. But, given the manner in which the issue was posed, it is difficult to see what else the bishops gathered at Chalcedon could have done in order to safeguard the reality of the incarnation.

The "Definition of faith" soon became the standard of Christological orthodoxy in the entire Western church, and in most of the East—although there were some in the East who rejected it, and thus gave rise to the first long-lasting schisms in the history of Christianity. Some, mostly in Syria and Persia, insisted on a clear distinction between the divine and the human in Christ, and were eventually called "Nestorians." Many others took the opposite tack, rejecting the doctrine of "two natures," and for that reason were dubbed "monophysites"—from the Greek *monos,* one, and *physis,* nature. Very few of these, however, adhered to the teachings of Euthyches. Rather, their concern was that the divine and the human in the Savior not be so divided that the incarnation be rendered meaningless. To this were added political and nationalist considerations which added fire to the theological debates that raged for centuries.

Further Theological Debates

The Chalcedonian Definition did not put an end to Christological debates, particularly in the East. There were many in Egypt who considered Dioscorus a martyr, and believed that Flavian and Leo were heretics. A large number of believers in Syria held similar views. In both cases, their theological objections were also spurred by resentment against the central government in Constantinople, which collected taxes in the provinces and did not return to them proportional benefits. To this were added cultural and ethnic tensions that existed since the time of the first Roman conquest, and had never been resolved. In order to regain the loyalty of these people, the emperors sought theological compromises that would satisfy both them and those who held to the decisions of Chalcedon. It was an impossible task, for the reasons for disaffection were not purely theological. On balance, all that the emperors achieved was further to alienate both the Chalcedonians and the others, and to force the church into endless controversy.

The first to follow this unwise policy was Basiliscus, who had deposed Emperor Zeno, and who in 476 annulled the decisions of Chalcedon and called a new council. But this never met, for Zeno regained the throne and Basiliscus' projects were abandoned. Then Zeno himself published an "edict of union"—*Henoticon*—in 482, in which he simply directed that all should return to what was commonly held before the controversy. But this created a new stir, for many, particularly Pope Felix III, declared that the emperor had no authority to prescribe what was to be believed. Since Zeno had the support of Patriarch Acacius of Constantinople, the dispute resulted in an open breach between the bishops of Rome and Constantinople. This "schism of Acacius" separated East from West until 519, well after the death of both principals. At that time, Emperor Justin and Pope Hormisdas reached an agreement that was in fact a return to the decisions of Chalcedon.

Justin was succeeded by his nephew Justinian, the ablest emperor of the Byzantine Empire, who restored its military glory by reconquering North Africa and Italy, rebuilt Saint Sophia, and codified the entire system of law. But he erred in thinking that he could regain the allegiance of his subjects who rejected the council of Chalcedon by condemning, not the council itself, but the writings of three Antiochene theologians who were particularly distasteful to those who rejected the council. What ensued is usually called "the controversy of the Three Chapters." This created such a stir that eventually Justinian was forced to call a council, which gathered at Constantinople in 553. At Justinian's prodding, the council, which eventually came to be known as the Fifth Ecumenical Council, condemned the Three Chapters. But this did not satisfy those who wished to see the decisions of Chalcedon withdrawn, and therefore Justinian achieved little for all his efforts.

The last emperor who sought to regain the allegiance of those opposed to Chalcedon was Heraclius, early in the seventh century. Patriarch Sergius of Constantinople proposed that, while there are indeed two natures in Christ, there is only one will. Although Sergius' position is not altogether clear, it seems that he meant that in Christ the divine will took the place of the human will. In any case, this was how he was interpreted, and thus the objections raised against his view were similar to those raised earlier against Apollinaris: a man without a human will is not fully human. Sergius' position, which came to be known as "monothelism"—from the Greek *monos,* one, and *thelema,* will—gained the support of Pope Honorius, and long debates ensued. But then came the Arab conquests, which overran Syria and Egypt. Since those were the areas where opposition to Chalcedon was strongest, imperial policy no longer sought to reconcile the anti-Chalcedonians. In 648, Constans II prohibited all further discussion of the will or wills of Christ. Finally, the Sixth Ecumenical Council, gathered at Constantinople in 680–681, condemned monothelism, and declared Pope Honorius to have been a heretic. (Much later, in the nineteenth century, this condemnation of a pope as a heretic came to the foreground in the discussions surrounding the proclamation of papal infallibility.)

In a way, the controversy regarding the use of images was a final episode in the Christological debates. In the early church, there seems to have been no objection to the use of images, for the catacombs and other early places of worship were decorated with paintings depicting communion, baptism, and various biblical episodes. Later, when the Empire embraced Christianity, several leading bishops expressed concern that the masses now flocking to the church would be led to idolatry, and therefore they preached, not against the images themselves, but against their misuse as objects of worship. In the eighth century, several Byzantine emperors took steps against images, and in 754 Constantine V called a council that forbade their use altogether and

Justinian, here shown with his court, led the Empire in a brief revival of its power.

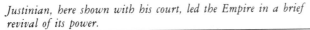

condemned those who defended them. The reasons for this decision are not altogether clear. Certainly, the presence of Islam, with its strong teaching against any physical representation, was a factor. Also, the emperors may have wished to curb the power of the monks, who were almost unanimously in favor of images. In any case, the entire Empire was soon divided between "iconoclasts"—destroyers of images—and "iconodules"—worshipers of images.

A deacon in the Cathedral of St. Sophia reads the decree of 843 that put an end to the iconoclastic controversy.

The iconodules saw their position as a corollary of Christological orthodoxy. If Jesus was truly human, and in him God had become visible, how could one object to representing him? Furthermore, the first maker of images was God, who created humans after the divine image. John of Damascus, who was among those condemned by the council of Constantine V, argued:

To depict God in a shape would be the peak of madness and impiety. . . . But since God . . . became true man . . . the Fathers, seeing that not all can read nor have the time for it, approved the descriptions of these facts in images, that they might serve as brief commentaries.*

The controversy raged for years. The West simply refused to accept the imperial edicts, while the East was rent asunder. Finally, the Seventh Ecumenical Council gathered at Nicea in 787. This assembly distinguished between worship in the strict sense, *latria,* which is due only to God, and a lesser worshipful veneration, *dulia,* which is to be given to images. Although the iconoclasts regained power for a time, in 842 images were definitively restored—an event that many Eastern churches still celebrate as the "Feast of Orthodoxy." In the West, the decisions of the council of 787 were not well received, for the distinction between *latria* and *dulia* was difficult to make in Latin. But eventually the difficulties were overcome, and

On the Orthodox Faith 4.16.

most Christians agreed on the use of images in church, and on the restricted veneration due to them.

The Dissident Churches of the East

Although the various councils came to positions that eventually gained general acceptance in the West and within the borders of the eastern Empire, such decisions were not always well received by churches beyond the confines of the Empire. One of these was the Persian church. Since Persia was a traditional enemy of the Roman Empire, Christians in that nation took pains to show that their faith did not make them foreign agents. When they did not succeed in this, they were cruelly persecuted. In 410, the Persian church organized itself as an autonomous church, under the leadership of the patriarch of Ctesiphon—the Persian capital. When Nestorius was condemned shortly thereafter, a number of theologians of Antiochene inclinations, fearing further reprisals, crossed over to Persia, where they founded a school that eventually became the main center of theological education in Persia. As a result, the Persian church came to hold views that other Christians called "Nestorian." At its high point, this church had flourishing missions in Arabia, India, and even China. But political adversities eventually diminished its numbers, and the few thousand Nestorians who now remain are scattered all over the world.

Armenia was a buffer state between Persia and the Roman Empire, and as such had a turbulent history. The founder of Christianity there was Gregory "the Illuminator," who had been converted while in exile in the Roman Empire, and, after many sufferings and difficulties, converted his relative, King Tiridates III, and baptized him on Epiphany (January 6), A.D. 303. Thus, the rulers of this nation had become Christians before Constantine. Eventually, the rest of the population was converted, and the Bible was translated into Armenian. By 450, when the Persians tried to impose their religion on Armenia, Christianity had become the rallying point of Armenian nationality. This was just before the Council of Chalcedon, and the Armenians hoped that the Roman Empire would come to their aid as fellow Christians. But then Theodosius II, who had promised such aid, died, and his successors Pulcheria and Marcian simply let Armenia be invaded by the Persians. With 1,036 soldiers who fought to the last man, the Armenians defended the mountain passes, hoping that this delay would give the Romans time to intervene. But it was all in vain, and the country was overrun by the Persians. Since it was precisely at that time that Pulcheria and Marcian called the Council of Chalcedon, it is not surprising that the Armenians rejected the decisions of that council. For that reason, they were dubbed "monophysites" —that is, believers in "one nature" in Christ. They in turn declared that those who had gathered at the council were not only traitors, but also heretics.

Under the Persians, the Armenians proved unwilling to give up their religion and traditions, and were granted a measure of autonomy. Then came the Arabs, under whose regime, in spite of sporadic persecution, Armenian Christianity flourished. In the eleventh century, the Turks took the country, and their harshness led many Armenians to emigrate to Asia Minor, where they founded Little Armenia. But eventually this region was also taken by the Turks, who ruled it with an iron hand. Early in the twentieth century, they massacred thousands of Armenians. Entire villages were wiped out. The survivers scattered throughout the world. Meanwhile, the older Armenia continued its traditions, now mostly under Soviet rule.

Ethiopian Christianity had always had strong connections with Egypt. Frumentius and Edessius, the founders of Ethiopian Christianity, had been shipwrecked near the region, captured by the Ethiopians, and eventually set free. But Frumentius went to Alexandria, had Athanasius consecrate him as a bishop, and returned to Ethiopia. After nearly a century of missionary work, mostly from Egypt, the king was converted, and he was soon followed by the rest of the country. When the Council of Chalcedon condemned Dioscorus and other Alexandrines as heretics, Ethiopian Christians followed the example of most Egyptian Christians, and rejected the decisions of the council. Thus they became "monophysite," and to this day remain the largest of the so-called monophysite churches.

Within the borders of the Byzantine Empire, the main strongholds of "monophysism" were Egypt and Syria. In Egypt, opposition to the decisions of the council was coupled with unrest on the part of the people of ancient Egyptian stock, the Copts, who felt exploited and oppressed by the Empire. In the cities, there were many Greek-speaking Christians who felt quite satisfied with the existing order, and who generally accepted the Chalcedonian "Definition of faith." After the Arab conquests, the Coptic Church became the main Christian body in the country. Those who held to Chalcedonian orthodoxy were dubbed "melchites"—that is, "imperial" Christians. Both churches have continued existing side by side until the present day.

Something similar happened in Syria, although the country was more evenly divided between Chalcedonians and "monophysites." The great leader of the latter was Jacob Baradaeus, an indefatigable traveler and organizer, and for that reason their church came to be called "Jacobite."

Eastern Orthodoxy after the Arab Conquests

Although it is obvious that every church thinks of itself as orthodox, that title has become such a hallmark of Eastern Chalcedonian Christianity that it is often called the Orthodox Church.

After the Arab conquests, the Orthodox Church was blocked to the south and east by Islam, and thus its expansion was in a northerly and northwesterly direction. Those areas of Eastern Europe were populated mostly by Slavs, who had invaded them after the Germanic peoples. They occupied most of what is today Poland, the Baltic countries, Russia, Czechoslovakia, Yugoslavia, and Greece. Those who had crossed the Danube were, at least nominally, part of the Byzantine Empire. The rest were divided among many tribes and nations. Then a new group of invaders, the Bulgars, conquered a vast portion of the Danube basin, where they ruled over a mixed population of Slavs and former subjects of the Byzantine Empire.

Such was the situation in 862, when a letter arrived in Constantinople from King Rostislav of Moravia, one of the Slavic kingdoms:

Many Christians have arrived in our midst, some Italian, some Greek, and some German, and they have spoken to us in their different ways. But we Slavs are simple people, and have no one to teach us the truth. . . . Therefore we pray you to send us someone capable of teaching us the whole truth.*

Rostislav was not as naive as he made his letter sound. He feared that the western missionaries in his kingdom would serve as a spearhead for conquest, as had already happened in other areas where missionaries from the Frankish Empire had worked. He was also aware of the rivalry between eastern and western Christians, and his letter was an attempt to use that rivalry to safeguard his kingdom.

In any case, the request was well received in Constantinople, as an opportunity to extend Byzantine influence. In response to Rostislav's request, two brothers, Cyril and Methodius, were sent as missionaries. They had grown up in the Balkans, among Slavs, and therefore already knew something of the language. They had also shown their mettle in a previous mission to Crimea. In Moravia, they were well received. Cyril devised a way to write Slavonic—the Cyrillic alphabet, still used by most Slavic languages —and translated the Bible, several other books, and the liturgy. But they soon ran into opposition from German missionaries, who claimed that the only proper liturgical languages were Latin, Greek, and Hebrew. Finally, Cyril and Methodius went to Rome, where the pope decided in their favor, but put them under his jurisdiction. Thus, for years the Moravian church was torn by a three-way contest between Constantinople, Rome, and the Germans. Finally, in 906, the Hungarians invaded the area, and the kingdom of Moravia disappeared. However, the pioneer work of Cyril and Methodius bore fruit among all the Slavic peoples, some of whom eventually joined western Christianity, while others became Orthodox.

Meanwhile, the Bulgarians had grown strong in the Balkans. They too had been visited by both western and Orthodox missionaries when their king

*Quoted in G. Zananiri, *Histoire de l'église byzantine* (Paris: Nouvelles éditions latines, 1954), p. 185.

Boris decided to become a Christian. After being baptized, Boris requested of Photius, the patriarch of Constantinople, that an archbishop be named for his kingdom. Since Photius asked questions and demanded that certain conditions be met, Boris turned to Pope Nicholas, who sent him two bishops but refused him an archbishop. Finally, Photius' successor to the see of Constantinople did consecrate an archbishop and several bishops to lead the newly formed Bulgarian Orthodox Church. After a brief pagan reaction, Christianity was consolidated under Boris's son Simeon. In 917, Simeon asserted his independence from Byzantium by taking the title of "czar"—emperor—and ten years later a similar action was taken in ecclesiastical matters when the archbishop was given the title of patriarch. Although at first Byzantine authorities took these actions to be a usurpation of power, they eventually were reconciled to them.

The greatest missionary success of the Orthodox Church, however, was the conversion of Russia. Around 950, Queen Olga was converted and baptized by Germanic missionaries. But it was under her grandson Vladimir that Christianity began making significant progress. For reasons that are not altogether clear, Vladimir sent for missionaries, not from the West, but rather from the Byzantine Empire. There is also some question as to how much force he used to induce his subjects to become Christians. His son Yaroslav strengthened the ties with Constantinople, and moved further away from Rome. By 1240, when the Mongols invaded Russia and ruled the country for over two centuries, Christianity was the national bond of unity that allowed Russia to survive as a nation, and eventually to be rid of the invaders. In the sixteenth century, after Constantinople had been taken by the Turks, Russia declared that Moscow was "the Third Rome," her rulers took the imperial title of czars, and the bishop of Moscow that of patriarch.

After the Arab conquests, relations between Rome and Constantinople grew steadily worse. The restoration of the western Empire under Charlemagne meant that the popes no longer needed the support of the Byzantine Empire. And the prolonged controversy over the use of images convinced the West that the Eastern church was a puppet in the hands of the emperor. All this led to what the West called "the schism of Photius" (867). Photius had been made patriarch of Constantinople after a revolution whose leaders had deposed Patriarch Ignatius. Both Photius and Ignatius turned to Pope Nicholas for support, and he took the side of Ignatius. Photius then declared that the entire West was heretical, because it had tampered with the Nicene Creed by including in it the word *Filioque*—"and from the Son." The old Creed said that the Holy Spirit proceeds "from the Father." By adding "and from the Son," so Photius argued, the westerners were tampering both with the Creed itself and with the ancient understanding of the Trinity, which affirms that the Spirit proceeds "from the Father, *through* the Son."

It seems that this alteration of the Nicene Creed arose first in Spain, and from there was taken to France. By Charlemagne's time, the Creed recited in the royal chapel at Aachen included the *Filioque.* When some Frankish monks visiting the East recited the Creed with that clause in it, they created a scandal among the Orthodox, who demanded to know who had given the Franks authority to alter the ancient Creed of the great council. To this were added political rivalries between the ancient Byzantine Empire and the Frankish upstarts, as well as the usual distrust between East and West.

One by-product of this controversy was the resurgence of the Old Roman Creed, now called the Apostles' Creed. The pope, wishing to alienate neither the Byzantines nor the Franks, began using that old, almost forgotten creed instead of the Nicene. Eventually, through the influence of Rome, the Apostles' Creed supplanted the Nicene Creed as the most commonly used among western Christians.

When political circumstances changed in Constantinople, Ignatius was restored as patriarch, and there was an agreement that Photius would be the next patriarch. But the bitterness engendered by the schism continued, and would eventually bear fruit.

The final schism came in the eleventh century. The Bulgarian archbishop, Leo of Ochrid, accused the West of error because it made clerical celibacy a universal rule, and because it celebrated communion with unleavened bread. When the dispute grew, Pope Leo IX sent an ambassador to Constantinople to deal with it. But his choice was most unfortunate. Cardinal Humbert, his legate, knew no Greek and did not care to learn it. He was a zealous reformer whose program included clerical celibacy and the autonomy of the church from civil rulers. To his mind, the Eastern married clergy, and the authority that the Byzantine emperor had over the church, were the very enemies which he had vowed to destroy. He and patriarch Michael Cerularius exchanged insults. Finally, on June 16, 1054, when the patriarch was preparing to celebrate communion, Cardinal Humbert appeared at the cathedral of Saint Sophia, walked to the high altar, and on it placed in the name of the pope—who actually had died shortly before—a sentence of excommunication against "heretic" Michael Cerularius, as well as any who dared follow him. He then walked out, shook the dust from his feet, and set out for Rome. The break between East and West was finally accomplished.

28/Imperial Restoration and Continuing Decay

Let the powerful beware . . . of taking to their own condemnation that which belongs to the church, . . . knowing that ecclesiastical properties are the promises of the faithful, the patrimony of the poor, the price for the remission of sin.

HINCMAR OF REIMS

O n Christmas Day 800, three hundred and four years after the baptism of Clovis, Pope Leo III took a crown in his hands, approached Charles, king of the Franks, and placing the crown on his head exclaimed: "May God grant life to the great and pacific emperor!" Three hundred and twenty-four years earlier, the last emperor of the West had been deposed. In crowning Charles—or Charlemagne, as he came to be called—Leo revived the ancient empire, now reborn under the aegis of the church.

Charlemagne's Reign

When Leo crowned Charlemagne, almost all of western Christendom was under the emperor's rule. The main exceptions were the British Isles and the small area in Spain that the Arabs had never conquered. But even before being crowned emperor, while he was only king of the Franks, Charlemagne had extended his domains beyond the borders of the ancient Roman Empire. This he did through a series of campaigns against the Saxons and their Frisian allies, on the eastern borders of his empire.

The campaigns against the Frisians and Saxons were long and bloody.

Under Charlemagne's leadership, the Western Empire was resurrected.

Repeatedly, Charlemagne invaded their territory and forced them to submit, only to have them rebel again as soon as he was away. Charlemagne resolved to drown the rebellion in blood and in the waters of baptism. Those who proved intractable were slaughtered. The rest were forced to accept baptism. By 784, the Frisians gave up the struggle; a year later, the final resistance of the Saxons was broken, and thousands were forcibly baptized. This was an important step, for many Saxons seem to have believed that in accepting baptism they were forsaking their gods, who in turn would forsake them. Thus, once baptized, one had no god to turn to but the Christian God. In any case, these forced baptisms had such results that soon there were Christian leaders among the Saxons, who then employed similar methods for the conversion of their own neighbors.

Charlemagne also extended his power to the west. His first campaign into Spain was a disaster. He invaded the peninsula because he had been assured of support from some Moslem leaders, and that support never materialized. On the way back, his rearguard was ambushed, probably by Basques, at Roncesvalles—an event that gave rise to the *Chanson de Roland* and to the entire body of literature related to it. Later, Charlemagne's armies did establish a foothold in Spain, conquering the land as far as the river Ebro, and establishing there the province known as the Spanish March. Also, Charlemagne supported the efforts of Alfonso II of Asturias, who was beginning the long process of reconquering the peninsula from the Moors.

As emperor, Charlemagne felt called to rule his people both in civil and in ecclesiastical matters. He appointed bishops just as he named generals, although always seeking men of worth. He also enacted laws ordering that there be preaching in the language of the people, that Sunday be kept as a day of worship and rest, and that tithes be collected as if they were a tax. Monasticism had lost a great deal of its original zeal, with many abbots who viewed their office as a means to riches and power, and Charlemagne decided that the entire institution was in need of reform. This he entrusted to Benedict of Aniane (not to be confused with Benedict of Nursia, who wrote the *Rule*), who had abandoned the court in order to become a monk, and was respected for his wisdom and piety. Benedict of Aniane then brought monasteries in Charlemagne's domains into compliance with the Benedictine *Rule.*

Charlemagne, although not himself an educated man, was a patron of learning. He revived and reformed the schools that already existed, and called to his court deacon Alcuin of York, whom he had met in Italy, and who reintroduced among the Franks the knowledge that had been preserved in British monasteries. From Spain, Charlemagne brought Theodulf, whom he made bishop of Orleans, and who ordered that throughout his diocese there should be a school in every church, and that these were to be open to the poor as well as to the rich. Soon other bishops followed Theodulf's example, and there was a significant revival of learning that was aided by the many scholars who flocked to Charlemagne's domains.

The glory of Charlemagne's empire did not last long after the great emperor's death. His son Louis "the Pious" was a conscientious ruler, but not a good judge of character. He continued the reformation of monasteries under the leadership of Benedict of Aniane. He also ordered that two-thirds of the money received as tithes be given to the poor. And he sought to give the church more autonomy by reverting to the old custom of allowing bishops to be elected by the people and the clergy. But there were many, including some bishops, who took advantage of his longanimity, and the last years of his reign were marred by civil wars in which Louis's sons and their partisans fought each other as well as the emperor. When he died, his possessions were divided among his three sons. Under his grandson Charles "the Fat" of France, who was emperor from 881 to 887, most of the ancient empire was reunited, only to be divided again after Charles' death. To these inner divisions and internecine warfare were added raids and invasions by Norsemen and others.

Also, the Arab conquests had enormous consequences for the economic and political life of western Europe. Before those conquests, there was widespread commerce along the Mediterranean, and even with the Orient. Now the Arabs blocked the way to the Orient and ruled the southern and eastern shores of the Mediterranean. Although there still was some shipping in the Adriatic and on the northern shores of Europe, trade on a large scale was interrupted, and each area had to become more self-sufficient. There came a time when money almost ceased circulating, and gold coins were rare.

Under such circumstances, the main source of wealth was land, rather than money. Kings and other lords often paid for services by granting lands. Thus was feudalism born. This was a hierarchical system, based on the holding of lands, in which each feudal lord, while receiving homage from those who owed their lands to him, paid homage to the greater lord from whom he had received his. At first, grants of land were for a lifetime. But eventually they became hereditary. Since a vassal often held land under various lords, the obligations of vassalage could always be evaded by claiming a conflicting allegiance to another lord. The result of all this was the political and economic fragmentation of western Europe, and the decline of all centralized power, including that of kings.

The church was also affected by this. Since bishoprics and abbeys often had vast holdings of land, bishops, abbots, and abbesses became magnates whose support all sought. Therefore, the question of who had the authority to name those who would fill such positions became one of enormous political significance.

Theological Activity

The revival of learning that Charlemagne had sought bore fruit throughout the ninth century. Wherever there was a strong ruler and a measure of peace, schools flourished, manuscripts were copied, and there was a measure of theological activity. However, during all that time western Europe produced only one systematic thinker of stature, while most theological activity centered on controversies over a single point of doctrine or worship.

The great systematic thinker during the reign of the Carolingians—the dynasty of Charlemagne—was John Scotus Erigena, a native of Ireland who had fallen heir to the knowledge of antiquity that had been preserved in Irish monasteries. Towards the middle of the ninth century, he settled at the court of Charles "the Bald"—one of the three heirs of Louis the Pious—and there came to enjoy great prestige for his erudition. Well-versed in Greek, he translated into Latin the works of the false "Dionysius the Areopagite." In the fifth century, someone had written these works, which were purported to be by the same Dionysius who had heard Paul at the Areopagus. When they were introduced into western Europe during the reign of Charles the Bald, no one doubted their authenticity. Erigena's translation was read as the word of one whose authority was almost apostolic. Since these works expounded a form of Neoplatonic mysticism, soon this was confused with Paul's theology, and the Apostle was read as if he too had been a Neoplatonist.

Erigena's great writing, *On the Division of Nature,* followed along the same lines, and many of his tenets can now be recognized as more Neoplatonic than Christian. However, his tone was so erudite, and his speculation so abstract, that not many read his work, fewer understood it, and no one seems to have become his follower. Later, those few who had taken from Erigena one point or another often found themselves condemned as heretics.

One of the main theological controversies of the Carolingian period centered on the teachings of Spanish bishops Elipandus of Toledo and Felix of Urgel. There remained in Spain many Christians whose ancestors had not fled at the time of the Moslem conquest, and who now lived under Moorish rule. These Christians, the "Mozarabs," kept their ancient traditions of pre-Islamic times, including their form of worship, known as the "Mozarabic liturgy." When Charlemagne began reconquering some of the lands that had previously been under Islamic rule, the Mozarabs clung to their traditions, which the Franks sought to replace by the uses of France and Rome. Thus, there was tension between Franks and Mozarabs even before the controversy broke out.

The conflict began when Elipandus, on the basis of some phrases in the Mozarabic liturgy, declared that, according to his divinity, Jesus was the eternal Son of the Father, but that, according to his humanity, he was son only "by adoption." This led many to call Elipandus and his followers "adoptionists." But there was a vast difference between what Elipandus taught, and true adoptionism. The latter claims that Jesus was a "mere man" whom God had adopted. Elipandus, on the other hand, affirmed that Jesus had always been divine. But he felt the need to insist on the distinction between divinity and humanity in the Savior, and he did this by speaking of two forms of sonship, one eternal and one by adoption. Thus, rather than adoptionism in the strict sense, this was the sort of Christology that earlier theologians of the Antiochene school had held, and whose extreme form was condemned by the Council of Ephesus.

Against these views, others insisted on the close union of the divine and human in Jesus. Beatus of Liebana, for instance, wrote:

Unbelievers could see nothing but a man in the one whom they crucified. And as a man they crucified him. They crucified the Son of God. They crucified God. My God suffered for me. For me was my God crucified.*

Soon the teachings of Elipandus and his follower Felix were condemned both by Frankish theologians and by the popes. Felix was forced to recant, and was kept away from Urgel, where Mozarabic influence was strong. Elipandus, however, was living in Moorish lands, and refused to recant. After the death of both Elipandus and Felix, the controversy subsided.

Meanwhile, however, other controversies had developed in the West. We have already discussed the clash with Constantinople on the interpolation of *Filioque* in the Nicene Creed. Of the many other issues debated among western theologians, the most significant were predestination and the presence of Christ in communion.

The main figure in the controversy regarding predestination was Gottschalk of Orbais, a monk who had carefully studied the writings of Augustine and had come to the conclusion that the church had departed from the teachings of the great bishop of Hippo, particularly in the matter of predestination. For a number of reasons, Gottschalk had made enemies among his superiors, and when he made his views known there were those who were prompt to attack him. Among these were the abbot of Fulda, Rabanus Maurus, and the powerful Bishop Hincmar of Reims. After a debate that involved many distinguished theologians—including John Scotus Erigena— Gottschalk was declared a heretic and imprisoned in a monastery, where he is said to have gone mad shortly before his death.

The other great controversy of the Carolingian period had to do with the presence of Christ in communion. The occasion for the debate was a treatise *On the Body and the Blood of the Lord,* by Paschasius Radbertus, a monk of Corbie who would later be declared a saint. In his treatise, Radbertus declared that when the bread and the wine are consecrated they are transformed into the body and blood of the Lord. They are no longer bread and wine, but the very body that was born of the virgin Mary, and the same blood that ran at Calvary. According to Radbertus, although this transformation takes place mysteriously, and human senses cannot usually perceive it, there are extraordinary cases in which a believer is allowed to see the body and blood of the Lord instead of bread and wine.

When King Charles the Bald read Radbertus' treatise, he had doubts about it, and asked Ratramnus of Corbie to clarify the matter. Ratramnus answered that, although the body of Christ is truly present in communion, this is not the same sort of presence of any other physical body, and that in any case the eucharistic body of Christ is not the same as the historical body of Jesus, which is sitting at the right hand of God.

This controversy shows that, by the Carolingian period, there were some

---

Epistle to Elipandus 1.4.

who held that in communion the bread and wine cease to be such, and become body and blood of Christ. But it also shows that still at that time many theologians took this to be the result of popular exaggeration and inexact use of language. Shortly thereafter, some began to speak of a "change in substance," and finally in the thirteenth century the Fourth Lateran Council (1215) would proclaim the doctrine of transubstantiation.

These are just a sampling of the many controversies that took place during the Carolingian revival of learning. That revival, however, was brief, and its promise was cut short by divisions among the successors of Charlemagne, as well as by new waves of invaders who once again brought fear and chaos to western Christianity.

New Invasions

For a time, Charlemagne and his successors seemed to have brought western Europe out of the confusion created by the Germanic invasions of the fourth and fifth centuries. But in truth those invasions, which had subsided for a while, had not ended, and would start afresh at a time that coincided with the decline of the Carolingian empire.

For centuries, extreme northern Europe had been inhabited by Scandinavians. During the eighth century, these heretofore sedentary people developed the art of shipbuilding to such a point that they mastered the neighboring seas. Their ships, sixty or seventy feet in length and propelled by sail and oars, could carry up to eighty men. In them, the Scandinavians began their expeditions to the rest of Europe, where they were called Norsemen. As the Carolingian empire began to disintegrate, the northern coasts of France became vulnerable to attack, and the Norsemen soon discovered that they could land on them, sack churches, monasteries, and palaces, and return to their lands with booty and slaves. Since they often attacked churches and monasteries in pursuit of the treasures they held, they were taken to be enemies of God.

At first, the Norsemen limited their attacks to the nearby coasts of the British Isles and northern France. But they soon grew more daring, both in reaching farther afield and in settling down as conquerors in new lands. In England, the only one who offered significant resistance was King Alfred the Great of Wessex, but by the eleventh century King Canute of the Danes was master of all of England—as well as of Denmark, Sweden, and Norway. In France, they took and sacked such cities as Bordeaux, Nantes, and even Paris, which they reached in 845. In Spain, they looted the Christian shrine of Santiago de Compostela, as well as the Moslem city of Seville, far south. They crossed the Straits of Gibraltar, and made their presence felt in the Mediterranean. Eventually they settled in Sicily, which they took from the Moslems,

King Canute was master of all England and Scandinavia. Here he places a cross on the altar of a church in England.

and in southern Italy, and founded a kingdom in those lands. Others settled in northern France, in the region that came to be called Normandy. From there, they would cross to England, for a further conquest of that land.

Eventually, the Norsemen became Christians. Many simply took over the faith of those whom they had conquered and among whom they settled. Others, mostly in Scandinavia itself and in distant Iceland, were led to baptism by the example—and sometimes the coercion—of their leaders. By Canute's time, in the first half of the eleventh century, almost all Scandinavians had been baptized.

At about the same time as the Scandinavians invaded from the north, others were coming from the east. These were the Magyars, whom the Latin West called "Hungarians" because they brought memories of the ancient Huns. After settling in what is now Hungary, they repeatedly invaded Germany, and crossed the Rhine more than once. Even distant Burgundy trembled under the hooves of their horses, and into southern Italy they marched, victorious and destructive. Finally, in 933 and 955, Henry the Fowler and his son Otto I of Germany dealt them crushing defeats, and most of their attacks ceased.

The Hungarians assimilated much of the culture of their German neighbors, as well as of the Slavs they had conquered. Missionaries went to Hungary both from Germany and from the Byzantine Empire, and late in the tenth century their king was baptized. The next king, who took the name of Stephen and is generally known as Saint Stephen of Hungary, forced the conversion of all his subjects.

The incursions of Scandinavians and Hungarians made of the tenth century what an historian has called "a dark century of lead and iron." Although towards the end of the century the Empire enjoyed a certain revival under Otto the Great and his immediate successors, it too was an empire of lead and iron. And the papacy, reflecting the times, fell to the lowest depths of its entire history.

Decay in the Papacy

The crowning of Charlemagne put the papacy in an ambiguous position. On the one hand, since the popes seemed to have the right to crown emperors, they enjoyed great prestige beyond the Alps. But, on the other hand, in Rome itself chaos often reigned. Thus, those who had the power to dispose of the empire seemed unable to govern their own city. And this in turn made the papacy an easy prey for the ambitious, one to be had by bribery, deceit, or even violence.

The decline of the papacy was not as rapid as that of the Carolingians. As imperial authority waned, there was a brief period during which the popes were seen as the only source of universal authority in western Europe. For this reason the reign of Nicholas I, which lasted from 858 to 867, was the most outstanding since that of Gregory the Great. His authority was reinforced by a collection of documents, supposedly ancient, which gave popes great power. These documents, the *False Decretals,* were probably forged by members of the lower echelons in the German ecclesiastical hierarchy, who sought to bolster the authority of the pope over their direct superiors. In any case, both Nicholas and the rest of Europe believed that the *Decretals* were genuine, and on that basis he acted with unprecedented energy. He was particularly active in curbing the warring inclinations of the powerful, who often seemed to make war as a sport, while the common folk suffered most of the consequences.

His successor, Hadrian II, followed a similar policy. He clashed with Lothair II, king of Lorraine, whom Nicholas had already reprimanded for marital irregularities. In Monte Cassino, when the king appeared for communion, the pope cursed him and his court. When a terrible epidemic broke out in the king's court, and Lothair was among the dead, the pope's prestige knew no bounds.

But the reign of the next pope, John VIII, saw the first signs of decline. In order to respond to the threat of Moslem invasion, he sought the support of Charles the Fat, as well as of the Byzantines, and found that neither of them would come to his aid. He was murdered in his own palace, and it is said that when the aide who had poisoned him saw that he was slow in dying, he broke the pope's skull with a mallet.

From then on, pope succeeded pope in rapid sequence. Their history is one of intrigues too complicated to follow here, as the papacy became the prize for which the various rival parties in Rome and beyond the Alps fought. Popes were strangled, or died of starvation in the dungeons where they had been thrown by their successors. At times there were two popes, or even three, each claiming to be the one true successor of Saint Peter.

Some instances will suffice to illustrate the mood of the times. In 897 Stephen VI presided over what came to be known as the "Cadaveric Council." One of his predecessors, Formosus, was disinterred, dressed in his papal robes, and exhibited on the streets. Then he was tried, found guilty of a multitude of crimes, and mutilated. Finally, what remained of the body was thrown into the Tiber.

In 904, Sergius III had his two rivals, Leo V and Christopher I, incarcerated and killed. He had come to power with the support of one of the most powerful families of Italy. This family was headed by Theophylact and his wife Theodora, whose daughter, Marozia, was Sergius' lover. Shortly after the death of Sergius, Marozia and her husband Guido of Tuscia captured the Lateran palace and made John X their prisoner, subsequently suffocating him with a pillow. After the brief pontificates of Leo VI and Stephen VII, Marozia placed on the papal throne, with the name of John XI, the son whom she had had from her union with Sergius III. Thirty years after the death of John XI, that papacy was in the hands of John XII, a grandson of Marozia. Later, her nephew became John XIII. His successor, Benedict VI, was overthrown and strangled by Crescentius, a brother of John XIII. John XIV died of either poison or starvation in the dungeon where he had been thrown by Boniface VII, who in turn was poisoned.

For a while, Emperor Otto III was able to determine who would be the pope. His first choice was his own nephew, who became pope at twenty-three years of age, and took the name of Gregory V. Then he named the famous scholar Gerbert of Aurillac, who became Sylvester II and made a valiant but unsuccessful effort to reform the papacy as well as the entire church.

When Otto died, the family of Crescentius—which was also the family of Theophylact, Theodora, and Marozia—once again gained control of the papacy, until the counts of Tusculum gained the upper hand and named

Benedict VIII, John XIX, and Benedict IX. The latter was fifteen years old when he became pope. Twelve years later, in 1045, he abdicated on the basis of having been promised a financial settlement. His godfather, Gregory VI, tried to reform the church, but then Benedict IX withdrew his abdication, and Crescentius' family put forth its own pope, whom they called Sylvester III.

Finally, Henry III of Germany intervened. After an interview with Gregory VI he gathered a council that deposed all three popes and named Clement II. The same council also enacted a series of decrees against ecclesiastical corruption, particularly simony—the practice of buying and selling positions in the church.

Clement II crowned Henry emperor, and died shortly thereafter. Henry then decided to offer the papacy to Bruno, bishop of Toul, already known for his reforming zeal. But Bruno refused to accept the papacy unless he was elected to it by the people of Rome. To that end he left for the ancient capital, in the company of two other monks of similar ideas, Hildebrand and Humbert. As it approached Rome, that small party carried with it the beginnings of a new age for the church.

29/ Movements of Renewal

The story of Martha and Mary in the Gospel shows that the contemplative life is to be preferred. Mary chose the better part . . . But Martha's part, if that is our lot, must be borne with patience.

BERNARD OF CLAIRVAUX

The violence and corruption that followed the decline of the Carolingian empire awakened in many a deep yearning for a new order. The sight of the papacy turned into a bone of contention for petty rivals, bishoprics bought and sold, and the entire life of the church put at the service of the powerful was a scandal for many who took their faith seriously. Given the options open at that time, it was to be expected that most of those who yearned for reform had taken up the monastic life. Thus, it was out of monasteries that a wave of reform arose that conquered the papacy, clashed with the powerful, and was felt even in the distant shores of the Holy Land.

Monastic Reform

Monasticism itself was in need of reformation. Many monasteries had been sacked and destroyed by Norsemen and Hungarians. Those in more sheltered areas became toys for the ambitions of abbots and prelates. The nobles and bishops who were supposed to be their guardians used them for their own ends. Just as the papacy and the episcopacy had become a means of personal aggrandizement, so did the great abbeys. Some became abbots by buying their posts, or even through homicide, and then gave themselves to an easy life on the basis of the abbey's income. The *Rule* of Benedict was generally ignored, and monks who sincerely felt called to the monastic life found that violence was done to their vocation.

In the midst of all this, in 909, Duke William III of Aquitaine founded a small monastery. In itself, this was not new, for such actions had become common on the part of powerful nobles. But several wise decisions and providential circumstances turned that small monastic house into the center of a vast reformation.

In order to lead his new monastery, William called on Berno, a monk who was well known for his steadfast obedience to the *Rule* and for his efforts for the reformation of monasticism. At Berno's request, William set aside for the monastery his own favorite hunting place, Cluny. This, with the necessary lands for the sustenance of the monastery, was deeded over to "Saints Peter and Paul," thus placing the new community under the direct jurisdiction and protection of the pope. Since at that time the papacy was at its nadir, such protection would only amount to forbidding the intervention of nearby bishops and feudal lords, including William himself or his heirs. Also, in order to guarantee that the new monastic foundation did not fall prey to a corrupt papacy, the deed explicitly forbade the pope from invading or otherwise taking what belonged only to the two holy apostles.

Berno ruled at Cluny until 926. Not much is known of those early years,

Thanks to a long series of extraordinarily able abbots, Cluny became the center for a vast renewal of monasticism that eventually made an impact on all of Western Europe.

for Cluny was only one of several monasteries that Berno set out to found or to reform. But after his death the house was led by a series of able and high-minded abbots who turned Cluny into the center of a vast monastic reform: Odo (926–944), Aymard (944–965), Mayeul (965–994), Odilo (994–1049), and Hugh (1049–1109). Six abbots of extraordinary dedication, ability, and length of life ruled Cluny for a total of two hundred years. Under their leadership, the ideals of monastic reform expanded ever farther. The seventh abbot, Pontius (1109–1122) was not of the caliber of the rest. But his successor, Peter the Venerable (1122–1157) regained much of what had been lost in Pontius' time.

At first, the purpose of the monks of Cluny was simply to have a place where they could follow the *Rule* of Benedict in its entirety. But then their horizons widened, and the abbots of Cluny, following Berno's example, set out to reform other houses. Thus there appeared an entire network of "second Clunys," which were directly under the abbot of the main monastery. It was not an "order" in the strict sense, but rather a series of independent monasteries, all under the rule of a single abbot, who normally appointed the prior of each community. This reformation also gained way in women's monastic communities, the first of which, Marcigny, was founded in the eleventh century, when Hugh was abbot of Cluny.

The main occupation of these monks and nuns, as the *Rule* commanded, was the Divine Office, or the celebration of the hours of prayer and Scripture reading that had been set by Benedict. To this the Cluniacs devoted their undivided attention, to such a point that at the height of the movement 138 Psalms were sung in a single day. This was done in the midst of ceremonies that became more and more complicated with the passing years, and therefore the Cluniacs came to spend practically all their time at the Divine Office, neglecting the physical labor that was so important for Benedict. This departure from the *Rule* was justified by arguing that the monks' function was to pray and to praise God, and that they could do this with more purity if they were not soiled in the fields.

At its high point, the reforming zeal of the Cluniacs knew no bounds. After ordering the life of hundreds of monastic houses, they set their sights on the reformation of the entire church. This was the darkest hour of the papacy, when pontiffs succeeded one another with breathtaking frequency, and when popes and bishops had become feudal lords, involved in every intrigue that was brewing. In such circumstances the monastic ideal, as it was practiced at Cluny, offered a ray of hope. Many who were not Cluniacs joined in the goal of a general reformation following the monastic model. In contrast with the corruption that reigned in the highest offices of the church, the Cluniac movement seemed to many a miracle, a divine intervention to bring about a new dawn.

Thus, the goal of ecclesiastical reformation was seen in the eleventh century as an extension of what was taking place in many monastic communities. This was the vision that Bruno of Toul, and his companions Hildebrand and Humbert, took with them on their way to Rome, where Bruno would become pope under the name of Leo IX. Just as Cluny had been able to carry on its great work because it was independent of all civil power, so was the dream of those reformers a church whose leaders would be free from every obligation to civil authorities, be they kings or nobles. Simony (the buying and selling of ecclesiastical posts) was therefore one of the worst evils to be eradicated. The appointment and the investiture of bishops and abbots by nobles, kings, and emperors, although not strictly simony, was dangerously close to it, and must also be forbidden, particularly in those areas whose rulers were not zealous reformers.

The other great enemy of reformation thus conceived in monastic terms was clerical marriage. For centuries, many had practiced celibacy, and there had been earlier attempts to promote it, but never as a universal rule. Now, fired by the monastic example, these reformers made clerical celibacy one of the pillars of their program. Eventually, what had been required only of monks and nuns would also be required of the clergy.

Obedience, another cornerstone of Benedictine monasticism, would also be fundamental to this reformation of the eleventh century. Just as monks owed obedience to their superiors, so must the entire church (in fact, all Christendom) be subject to the pope, who would head a great renewal in which his role would be similar to that of the abbots of Cluny in the monastic reform.

Finally, when it came to poverty, both Cluniac monasticism and the general reformation that it inspired were ambivalent. A good monk should own nothing, and must lead a simple life. The monastery, however, could have property and vast expanses of land. These grew constantly through gifts and inheritance from the faithful who admired the monastic way of life, or who simply wished to earn merit towards their salvation. Eventually, this made it difficult for monks to lead the simple life which the *Rule* required. In the case of Cluny itself, the time came when it and its sister houses were so rich that their monks could spend all their time at the Divine Office and neglect physical labor. Likewise, the reformers criticized the luxurious life of many bishops, but at the same time insisted on the right of the church to its holdings of land and to all the wealth it had accumulated over the centuries. In theory, this was not for the use of the prelates, but for the glory of God and to help the poor. But in truth it hindered the proposed reformation, for it invited simony, and the power that bishops and abbots had as feudal lords led them to be constantly involved in political intrigue.

The wealth that it accumulated was one of the main causes of the decline of the Cluniac movement. Inspired by the holiness of the monks, rich and poor alike made gifts to their monasteries. Cluny and her sister houses adorned their chapels with gold and jewels. Eventually, the simplicity of life that had been Benedict's ideal was lost, and other movements of more recent foundation, and more insistent on poverty, took the place of Cluny. Likewise,

A monastery was a center of learning and worship, as shown in this Spanish manuscript.

one of the main causes of the final failure of the reformation of the eleventh century was the wealth of the church, which made it very difficult for it to set aside the intrigues of the powerful, and take the side of the poor and the oppressed.

Discontent with the ease of Cluny soon gave rise to other movements. Peter Damian, for instance, sought to outdo the Benedictine principle according to which a monk should be content with what is sufficient, and advocated living in extreme need. The next great movement of monastic reform, however, began late in the eleventh century, when Robert of Molesme founded a new monastery at Citeaux. Since the Latin name of this place was *Cistertium,* the movement came to be called "Cistercian." Robert returned to his original monastery, but a community continued existing in Citeaux, and eventually gave rise to a wave of monastic reform similar to that which had been lead earlier by the abbots of Cluny.

The great figure of the Cistercian movement was Bernard of Clairvaux, who was twenty-three years old when he presented himself at Citeaux (in 1112 or 1113) in the company of several relatives and friends, and requested admission to the community. He had decided to join that monastery, and before even presenting himself for admission he had convinced several others to follow him. This was an early indication of his great powers of persuasion, which would eventually be felt throughout Europe and would even send many to the Holy Land. When the number of monks at Citeaux grew too large, he was ordered to found a new community at Clairvaux. This grew rapidly, and soon became a center of reformation.

Bernard was first and foremost a monk. He was convinced that Mary's was a better lot than Martha's, and all he wished to do was to spend his time meditating on the love of God, particularly as revealed in the humanity of Christ. But he soon found himself forced to take on the role of Martha. He was a famous preacher—so much so, that he came to be known as "Doctor Mellifluous," for the words from his mouth were like honey. His fame forced him to intervene as an arbitrator in many political and ecclesiastical disputes. His personality dominated his time, for he was at once the mystic devoted to the contemplation of the humanity of Christ, the power behind and above the papacy (especially when one of his monks became pope), the champion of ecclesiastical reform, the preacher of the Second Crusade, and the enemy of all theological innovation. Bernard's fame gave the Cistercian movement great impetus, and soon it came to play a role similar to that which Cluny had played more than a century before.

This brief overview of the two main movements of monastic reform from the tenth to the twelfth centuries has forced us to move ahead in our story. Therefore, let us return to where we had left our narrative at the end of the previous chapter, to the year 1048, when Odilo was still abbot of Cluny, and rejoin Bruno of Toul and his companions as they made their way to Rome.

Papal Reform

The small band of pilgrims on their way to Rome was headed by Bruno, to whom the emperor had offered the papacy, and who had preferred to enter the city as a pilgrim. If, once there, the people and the clergy elected him, he would accept. But to take the office of pope from the hands of the emperor was dangerously close to simony—or, as Hildebrand had told Bruno, it would mean going to Rome "not as an apostle, but as an apostate."

Another member of the small party was Humbert, who in his monastery in Lotharingia had devoted himself to study and to a constant campaign against simony. This had never been attacked as forcefully as in his treatise *Against the Simoniacs,* which was a blistering attack on the powerful of his time. It was he also who later, in 1054, would lay the sentence of excommunication on the high altar of Saint Sophia, and thus seal the schism between East and West.

The third and most remarkable member of that party was the monk Hildebrand, who while a monk at Rome had met the future pope Gregory VI. As was said at the end of the last chapter, Gregory VI hoped to reform the church. To that end he called Hildebrand to his side. But then a situation developed in which there were three who claimed to be the rightful pope, and Gregory abdicated for the sake of peace and unity. Hildebrand went with him into exile, and it is said that he closed the saintly man's eyes on his deathbed. Two years later, Bruno, on his way to Rome, asked Hildebrand to join him in the task of reformation that lay ahead.

Hildebrand has often been depicted as the ambitious man behind several popes. However, until he felt ready to take power for himself, the sources of the time seem to indicate that in truth he wished nothing more than the reformation of the church. It was apparently on that basis that he supported the work of several popes, until the time came when it seemed that reformation could best be served by accepting the papacy himself, which he took under the name of Gregory VII.

For the time being, however, the man called to be pope was Bruno of Toul, who went to Rome as a barefooted pilgrim in an act of personal devotion. As he crossed northern Italy on his way to Rome, multitudes lined the roads and cheered him, and soon people began to talk of miracles that supposedly had taken place during that pilgrimage. After entering Rome barefooted and being acclaimed by the people and the clergy, Bruno accepted the papal tiara, and took the name of Leo IX.

As soon as he saw himself on Saint Peter's throne, Leo began his work of reformation by calling to his side several people who were known for holding similar ideas. Their program of reformation was based on the promotion of clerical celibacy and the abolition of simony. There was a connection between these two, for in that feudal society the church was one of the few institutions in which there still existed a measure of social mobility. Hildebrand, for instance, was of humble origin, and would eventually become pope. But this social mobility was threatened by the practice of simony, which would guarantee that only the rich would occupy the high offices of the church. If to this was added clerical marriage, those who held high office would seek to pass it on to their children, and thus the church would come to reflect exclusively the interests of the rich and the powerful. Thus, the

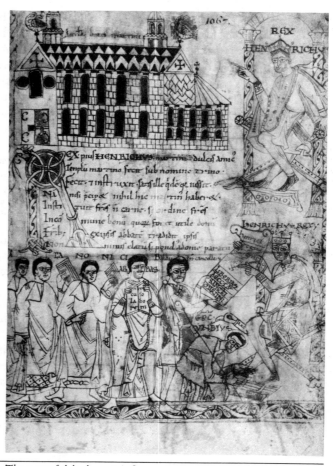

The powerful had great influence in the life of the church. Here King Henry I of France grants an abbey.

movement for reformation by abolishing simony and promoting clerical celibacy had the support of the masses, who seem to have understood that here was an opportunity for wresting from the powerful the control of the church.

After taking a number of reforming measures in Italy, Leo decided that the time had come to carry the movement across the Alps. He went to Germany, where the emperor had already taken some steps against simony, and reaffirmed the emperor's decisions while making it clear that this did not mean that the emperor could rule the life of the church in his domains. While in Germany, he excommunicated Godfrey of Lorraine, who had rebelled against the emperor, and forced him to submit. Then he saved the rebel's life by interceding for him before the emperor.

In France simony was widespread, and Leo sought to put an end to it. With this in mind, he decided to visit that country. Although the king and several prelates let him know that he would not be welcome, Leo went to France and called a council that deposed several prelates who had been guilty of simony. The same council also ordered that married bishops should set their wives aside, but this order was not generally obeyed.

Leo made two grave errors during his pontificate. The first was to take up arms against the Norsemen who had settled in Sicily and southern Italy. Peter Damian urged him to desist, but he marched at the head of the troops, which were defeated by the Norsemen. Captured by those whom he had hoped to conquer, Leo remained a prisoner until shortly before his death. His other error was to send Humbert as his legate to Constantinople. Humbert's rigidity and lack of interest in the concerns of the Byzantines led to the schism of 1054, shortly after Leo's death.

The election of the new pope was a difficult matter. To ask the emperor to select him would be tantamount to the control of the church by the state, which the reformers deplored. To let the Roman clergy and people proceed to the election risked having the papacy fall again in the hands of one of the Italian families who wished to have it as a means to their own political ends. Eventually it was decided that the Romans would elect the new pope, but that this had to be a German—thus making it impossible for any of the various parties in Rome to capture the papacy. The new pope, Victor II, continued Leo's policies. When emperor Henry III found himself in difficulties—Godfrey of Lorraine had rebelled again—the pope went to his aid, and on the emperor's death was entrusted with the care of his young son, Henry IV. Thus for a time Victor held the reins of both church and empire, and the reformation that he advocated progressed rapidly.

After that time, with one exception, there was a succession of reforming popes. That exception led the reformers, under the leadership of Nicholas II, to call the Second Lateran Council, which determined the manner in which popes were to be elected thereafter. The power of election was to rest with the cardinals who also held the title of bishops, who would then seek the consent of the rest of the cardinals, and, finally, of the Roman people. (The origins of the title "cardinal" are obscure, and need not detain us here. By the time of the Second Lateran Council, in 1059, the cardinalate was an ancient institution.) Since the cardinals were committed to reform, and since the popes elected by them would name any new cardinals, the power of the reforming party seemed assured. The next pope, Alexander II, was duly elected by the cardinals and continued the work of reformation, although some of the powerful Roman families, with support from the Germans, set up a rival pope.

When Alexander died, Hildebrand was elected pope, although the order prescribed by the Second Lateran Council was reversed, for it was the people who demanded his election, and the cardinals who agreed. He took the name of Gregory VII, and continued the work of reformation in which he had been engaged for years. His dream was of a world united under the papacy, as one flock under one shepherd. This included, not only western Europe, but also the Byzantine church as well as the lands then under Moslem control. For a while he sought to organize a great military offensive against Islam, with a western front in Spain, and another in the East, where Latin Christians would go to the succor of beleaguered Constantinople. But these plans, as well as his efforts to extend his authority to the East, never came to fruition.

In western Europe, he continued the campaign against simony and the marriage of the clergy. He was most successful in England, where William the Conqueror now ruled. When he was still a papal advisor, Hildebrand had supported William's plans to invade England from Normandy, and now the Conqueror, who in any case was in favor of ecclesiastical reform, supported the pope's campaign against simony. In France, Philip I would not heed Gregory's admonitions. With his support, the French clergy refused to obey Gregory's reforming decrees. Indeed, the two-pronged offensive against simony and clerical marriage was unwise, for it created an alliance between the powerful prelates who profited from ecclesiastical posts, and the many worthy members of the lower clergy who bemoaned simony, but who were married and refused to set their wives aside. By joining the monastic ideal of celibacy to his reformation, Gregory and his friends made it much more difficult for their plans to succeed.

The Papacy and the Empire in Direct Confrontation

Gregory's reforming zeal soon clashed with the interests of Emperor Henry IV. As a young boy, Henry had been under the care of one of the reforming popes, and therefore Gregory believed that he, of all rulers, should support the program of reformation. But Henry felt that the power of bishops and other prelates was such that, for the political survival of the empire, the emperor must be free to appoint those who would support him. The conflict finally broke out when, in response to riots in Milan provoked by extremists who sought to enforce clerical celibacy, Henry deposed the bishop and appointed another in his place. Gregory responded by ordering Henry to appear at Rome by a certain date, and declaring that if he failed to do so he would be deposed and his soul condemned to hell. The emperor, who had recently had significant success and was therefore at the height of his power, responded by calling a council that gathered a few days before the deadline set by the pope, and declared that Gregory was deposed on grounds of tyranny, adultery, and the practice of magic. Then, in the council's name,

Henry sent notification of these decisions "to Hildebrand, not a pope, but a false monk."

Gregory gathered a synod of his supporters, who advised stern measures against the emperor. On the next day, precisely the date for which he had summoned Henry to Rome, Gregory issued his sentence:

In the name of the Father, the Son, and the Holy Ghost, by the power and authority of Saint Peter, and for the defense and honor of the church, I place king Henry . . . under interdict, forbidding him to rule in any of the kingdoms of Germany or Italy. I also free from their oaths any who have sworn or would swear loyalty to him. And I forbid that he be obeyed as king.*

At first, Henry was resolved to continue in the course he had set. But his support began eroding. Many who had other reasons to disobey him now had the pope's sentence as an excuse. The more superstitious began spreading the word that to be near him was to call a curse on oneself. This was given credence when one of his staunchest supporters died unexpectedly. Finally, Henry felt that his only recourse was to appeal to Gregory's mercy. This he would do as privately as possible, and thus set out to meet Gregory in Italy. Gregory was not sure whether the emperor was coming in peace, or rather intended to use violence. His suspicions increased when many in northern Italy received Henry as a hero and rallied to him. But Henry did not wish to gamble his throne on the uncertain outcome of battle, and therefore refused to organize his supporters into an army.

The two finally met at Canossa, where the pope had taken residence because the city was well fortified. Henry had hoped for a private interview where he would make his obeisance before Gregory. But the latter insisted on public penance, and Henry had to beg admission to Canossa, as a penitent, for three days before he was admitted to Gregory's presence. Finally, since it was impossible for one who claimed to be the leader of Christ's disciples to do otherwise, Gregory granted the pardon that Henry begged, and withdrew his sentence against the emperor.

Henry then returned hastily to Germany, where his enemies, encouraged by his difficulties with Gregory, had rebelled. Although Gregory had withdrawn his sentence against Henry, he did nothing to discourage the rebels, who elected their own emperor. The pope's ambiguous posture encouraged civil war, and it soon became clear that Henry would overcome his foes. But Gregory did not trust him, and therefore decided to cast his lot with the usurper. Once again he excommunicated Henry, whose imminent death he also foretold. But this time the emperor's followers did not heed the pope's sentence, and a rival pope, who took the name of Clement III, was elected. Finally, the usurping emperor was killed in battle, and Henry was left as sole master of the empire.

---

*Gregory VII, *Register* 3.10a.

Henry was forced to appear at Canossa to beg Gregory's forgiveness. The third person is Matilda, owner of the castle.

As soon as the ice thawed in the passes through the Alps in the spring of 1081, Henry marched on Rome. Gregory's only possible support were the Normans who ruled in southern Italy, and who had been his allies before. But he had also excommunicated them. He then appealed to Byzantium, but to no avail. At first the Romans defended their city valiantly. But when it became clear that the pope would not negotiate with the invader, they opened the gates of the city, and Gregory had to flee to one of his castles. Henry entered in triumph, and Clement III took possession of the city. Then the Normans intervened, and Henry abandoned the city. The Normans acted as masters of the city, and many citizens were killed, buildings burned, and thousands taken away to be sold as slaves.

Gregory, who had fled to Monte Cassino and then to Salerno, continued thundering against Henry and Clement III. But his words were to no avail. It is said that when he died in 1085 his last words were: "I have loved justice and hated iniquity. Therefore I die in exile."

Before his death, Hildebrand had declared that his successor should be the aged abbot of Monte Cassino. These wishes were followed, and the old man, who had no desire to be pope, was forced to accept. He took the name of Victor III, and was restored to Rome by his allies. But he became ill, and withdrew to Monte Cassino to die in peace.

The reforming party then elected Urban II, who was able to regain the city of Rome and expel Clement III. He is mostly known for having proclaimed the First Crusade—with which we shall deal in the next chapter. But he also continued the policies of Gregory VII. This led him to further conflicts with Philip I of France, whom he excommunicated for having set aside his wife in favor of another. In Germany, he encouraged the rebellion of Henry's son Conrad, who promised that if he were made emperor he would give up any claim to the right to the appointment and investiture of bishops. But Henry reacted vigorously, defeated his son, and had him disinherited by a diet of the empire.

Urban's successor, Paschal II (1099–1118), hoped that the schism would end when Clement III died. But the emperor made certain that another was appointed to take Clement's place, and therefore the schism continued.

Henry IV died in 1106, when he was preparing to wage war against his son Henry, who had also rebelled against him. Paschal was ready to make peace, and declared that all consecrations that had taken place during the previous reign, even under lay appointment and investiture, were valid. But he also made it clear that any future lay investiture was unacceptable, and that any who disobeyed him on this point would be excommunicated. Thus, while clearing the slate, he also threw down the gauntlet for the new emperor.

Henry V waited three years to respond to the pope's challenge. Then he invaded Italy, and Paschal was forced to reach a compromise. What Henry proposed, and Paschal accepted, was that the emperor would give up any claim to the right of investiture of bishops, as long as the church gave up all the feudal privileges that prelates had, and which made them powerful potentates. Paschal agreed, with the sole stipulation that "Saint Peter's patrimony" would remain in the hands of the Roman church. Henry's proposal cut to the heart of the matter, for civil rulers could not afford to give up the right to name and invest bishops as long as these were also powerful political figures. And, if the reformers were consistent on their application of monastic principles to the reform of the church, they should be willing to have the church follow the way of poverty.

But this decision, reasonable though it seemed, was not politically viable. There soon was a violent reaction among prelates who saw themselves deprived of temporal power. Some were quick to point out that the pope had been very liberal with their possessions, but had retained his. Even the high nobility in Germany began to suspect that the emperor, having strengthened his position by stripping the bishops of their power, would turn on them and abolish many of their ancient privileges. Then the people of Rome rebelled against the emperor, who left the city taking as prisoners the pope as well as several cardinals and bishops. Finally, the emperor returned the pope to Rome, and the latter in turn crowned him at St. Peter's—with the doors closed for fear of the populace. The emperor then returned to Germany, where urgent matters required his presence.

In Germany, Henry encountered new difficulties. Many of the high clergy and the nobility, fearing the loss of their power, rebelled. While

Paschal remained silent, many of the German prelates excommunicated the emperor. Then several regional synods followed suit. When Henry protested that by his attitude Paschal was breaking their agreement, the pope suggested that the emperor call a council in order to solve the dispute. This Henry could not do, for he knew that the majority of the bishops, who saw their possessions and power threatened by the emperor's policies, would decide against him. Therefore, he opted for renewed use of force. As soon as the situation in Germany allowed him to do so, he again invaded Italy, and Paschal was forced to flee to the castle of St. Angelo, where he died.

The cardinals then hastened to elect a new pope, lest the emperor intervene in the election. The new pope, Gelasius II, had a stormy and brief pontificate (1118–1119). A Roman potentate who supported the emperor made him a prisoner and tortured him. Then the people rebelled and freed him. But the emperor returned to Rome with his armies, and Gelasius fled to Gaeta. Upon returning to Rome, he was again captured by the same Roman magnate, but he fled and finally fell exhausted in the middle of a field, where some women found him, almost naked and lifeless. He then sought refuge in France, where he died shortly thereafter in the abbey of Cluny.

The decision of Gelasius to flee to France was a sign of the new direction in which papal policy was being forced. Since the Empire had become its enemy, and since the Normans in the south had proven unreliable allies, popes began looking to France as the ally who would support them against the German emperors.

The next pope, Calixtus II (1119–1124), was a relative of the emperor, and both he and his kinsman were convinced that the time had come to end the dispute. After long negotiations, interspersed with threats and even military campaigns, both parties came to an agreement by the Concordat of Worms (1122). It was decided that prelates would be elected freely, according to ancient usage, although in the presence of the emperor or his representatives. Only proper ecclesiastical authorities would henceforth have the right to invest prelates with their ring and crosier, symbols of pastoral authority; but the granting of all feudal rights, privileges, and possessions, as well as of the symbols thereof, would be in the hand of civil authorities. The emperor also agreed to return to the church all its possessions, and to take measures to force any feudal lords holding ecclesiastical property to do likewise. This put an end to this series of confrontations between papacy and empire, although similar conflicts would develop repeatedly through the centuries.

In the end, the program of the reforming popes succeeded. The rule of clerical celibacy became universal in the Western church, and was generally obeyed. For a while, simony almost disappeared. And the power of the papacy continued to grow, until it reached its apex in the thirteenth century.

However, the controversy over the appointment and investiture of prelates shows that the reformist popes, while they insisted on the monastic ideal of celibacy, did not do the same with the ideal of poverty. The question of investitures was important for civil authorities—especially the emperor—because the church had become so rich and powerful that an unfriendly bishop was a political power to be feared. Bishops could afford rich courts and even armies. Therefore, in the interest of self-preservation, rulers had to make sure that those who occupied such important positions were loyal to them. Henry V had pointed to the heart of the matter when he suggested that he was willing to relinquish all claim to the investiture of bishops in his realm, as long as those bishops did not have the power and resources of great feudal lords. As the reformist popes saw matters, the possessions of the church belonged to Christ and the poor, and therefore could not be relinquished to the civil authorities. But in fact those possessions were used for personal profit, and for achieving the ambitious personal goals of bishops and others who in theory were not owners, but guardians.

30/The Offensive against Islam

I say it to those who are present. I command that it be said to those who are absent. Christ commands it. All who go thither and lose their lives, be it on the road or on the sea, or in the fight against the pagans, will be granted immediate forgiveness for their sins. This I grant to all who will march, by virtue of the great gift which God has given me.

URBAN II

Among the many ideals that captivated the imagination of western Christendom during the Middle Ages, no other was as dramatic, as overwhelming, or as contradictory, as was the crusading spirit. For several centuries, western Europe poured her fervor and her blood into a series of expeditions whose results were at best ephemeral, and at worst tragic. What was hoped was to defeat the Moslems who threatened Constantinople, to save the Byzantine Empire, to reunite the Eastern and Western branches of the church, to reconquer the Holy Land, and in doing all this to win heaven. Whether or not this last goal was achieved is not for us to decide. All the others were achieved, but none of them permanently. The Moslems, at first defeated because they were divided among themselves, eventually were united in a common front that expelled the crusaders. Constantinople, and the shadow of her empire, survived until the fifteenth century, but then were swept by the Ottoman Turks. The two branches of the church were briefly reunited by force as a consequence of the Fourth Crusade, but the final result of that forced reunion was greater hatred between East and West. The Holy Land was in the hands of the crusaders for approximately a century, and then returned to Moslem control.

The First Crusade

For centuries, Christians had held the Holy Land in high esteem, and pilgrimages to its holy places had become one of the highest acts of devotion. Those holy places had been in Moslem hands for centuries. But now the rise of the Seljuk Turks, who had become Moslems and were threatening the Byzantine Empire, reminded many of the earlier losses at the time of the Arab conquests. If the West were to save the Byzantines from that threat, it was to be expected that relations between the two branches of the church, broken since 1054, would be restored. Thus, Gregory VII had already envisioned a great western army to save Constantinople and retake the Holy Land. But the time was not yet ripe, and it was Urban II who, at the Council of Clermont in 1095, proclaimed the great enterprise, to which those present responded with cries of "Deus vult"—God wills it.

It was a difficult time in many parts of Europe, where crops had failed and disease ran rampant. Therefore, the call to go to a foreign land as soldiers of Christ was received with enthusiasm by many, both of the lower classes and of the nobility. The apocalyptic dreams that for centuries had been repressed emerged again. Some had visions of comets, angels, or the Holy City suspended over the eastern horizon. Soon a disorganized mob, under the very loose leadership of Peter the Hermit, set out for Jerusalem. Along the way, they fed on the land, on which they fell like locusts, and had to fight other Christians who defended their goods and crops. They also practiced their war against the infidel by killing thousands of Jews. Eventually, most of this initial wave lost their lives, and a few joined the ranks of the more organized crusaders.

The formal crusade was led by Adhemar, bishop of Puy, whom Urban had named his personal representative. Other leaders were Godfrey of Bouillon, Raymond of Saint-Gilles, Bohemund, and Tancred. By various routes, the crusaders converged at Constantinople, where they were well received by Emperor Alexius, and where Peter the Hermit joined them with the remnant of his ragged army. With the help of the Byzantines, they took Nicea, which had been the capital of the Turks—and which the Byzantines entered first, for the emperor feared that the crusaders would sack the city. They then marched on Antioch, and endured many sufferings while crossing Asia Minor. Before the walls of Tarsus, Tancred and Baldwin, Godfrey's younger brother, quarrelled, and Baldwin decided to abandon the enterprise

The siege of Nicea according to a thirteenth-century illustration.

and accept the offer of the Armenians to establish himself as their leader, under the title of count of Edessa. The rest continued their long march to Antioch, to which they finally laid siege.

The siege of Antioch was a difficult enterprise. The besieged had more supplies than the crusaders, who were about to run out of food and had been plagued by desertions, when an Armenian Christian who resided in the city opened a gate to them. At the cry of "God wills it," the crusaders entered the city, while its Turkish defenders sought refuge in the citadel. But four days later a large Turkish army arrived, and the crusaders found themselves besieged while the citadel itself had not yet surrendered to them. Hungry and discouraged, the crusaders began to doubt the wisdom of the entire enterprise.

Then someone said he had a vision, that the Holy Lance with which Christ's side had been pierced lay buried in Antioch. Led by the seer, they dug where he told them. And they found a spear! Convinced that this was the Holy Lance, the crusaders resolved to continue their enterprise. After five days of fasting and prayer, as indicated by the visionary who had told them of the Holy Lance, they sallied against the much larger Turkish army. Their standard was the Holy Lance, and they were possessed of such frenzied zeal that the Turks broke and ran, and the crusaders helped themselves to all the provisions that the Turks had brought with them. They also captured

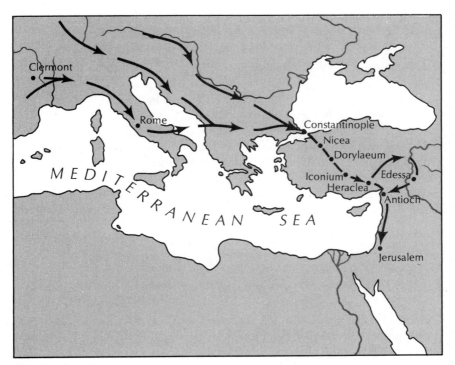

The First Crusade

many women who had been left behind in the Turkish camp, and an eyewitness boasting of the holiness of the Christian army says: "We did nothing evil to them, but simply speared them through."

Bishop Adhemar, the appointed leader of the crusade, had died of fever during the siege, and the army was headless. After much bickering and delay, Godfrey of Bouillon emerged as the new leader, and the army finally caught its first glimpse of the Holy City on June 7, 1099.

Those defending Jerusalem were not Turks, but Fatimite Arabs from Egypt—so named because they claimed descent from Fatima, Mohammed's daughter. Indeed, the reason why the crusaders had achieved their measure of success was that the Moslems were not united. In any case, the garrison in Jerusalem was ready for a long siege, and the surrounding land had been razed, and the wells poisoned, to deny supplies to the besiegers. The crusaders also expected a long siege. But, in early July, they received news of a large Arab army approaching, and came to the conclusion that they had to take the city or withdraw. Since theirs was a religious enterprise, they begged God for support, marching around the city barefooted and singing penitential hymns. A few days later, they attacked the walls. Resistance was strong. But finally a single knight was able to climb to the top of the wall, and there to hold a space where others could follow him. As the breach grew, resistance melted. The defenders fled from the walls, and the crusaders swept into the city that was the goal of their long campaign. It was July 15, 1099.

There followed a horrible bloodbath. All the defenders were killed, as well as many civilians. Women were raped, and infants thrown against walls. Many of the city's Jews had taken refuge in the synagogue, and the crusaders set fire to the building with them inside. According to an eyewitness, at the Porch of Solomon horses waded in blood.

Then the crusaders set out to organize the conquered lands after the fashion of western Europe. Godfrey of Bouillon was made "Protector of the Holy Sepulcher," but his brother Baldwin, who succeeded him in 1100, took the title of King of Jerusalem. The main vassals of this kingdom were Bohemund, Prince of Antioch, Baldwin, Count of Edessa, and Raymond of Toulouse, Count of Tripoli.

Later History of the Crusades

Many of the crusaders now felt that their task was done, and prepared to return home. Godfrey of Bouillon was scarcely able to retain the knights necessary to meet the Moslem army that was already marching on Jerusalem. At Ashkelon, the crusaders defeated the Moslems, and thus the survival of the Latin Kingdom of Jerusalem was assured for a brief span. But reinforcements were sorely needed, and thus it became customary for small bands of armed men to leave Europe for a time of service in the Holy Land. While many of these remained, others simply returned after what amounted to an armed pilgrimage.

The fervor of the crusade also continued among the masses. Repeatedly, there were those who had apocalyptic visions and collected a motley following as they marched towards Jerusalem. There were also those who claimed that, since God valued innocence, children were to play a special role in the entire enterprise. Thus developed several "children's crusades," which were no more than masses of children and adolescents marching eastward, only to die along the way or to be enslaved by those whose territories they crossed.

Since the crusading spirit, and crusading columns, were a constant feature for centuries, it is not altogether correct to speak of the "crusades" as a series of isolated campaigns. But there were high points in the entire enterprise, which are usually called the "Second Crusade," the "Third Crusade," and so on. An outline of these will show some of the later course of the crusading spirit.

The occasion for the Second Crusade was the fall of Edessa, taken by the sultan of Aleppo in 1144. Once again, popular preachers arose who called for the masses to invade the Holy Land. Along the way, some also said, Jews should be exterminated. The preaching of Bernard of Clairvaux was very different, for it sought both to organize an army of relief for the Kingdom of Jerusalem, and to refute the fiery preaching of those who advocated a mad rush to Jerusalem. Finally, under the leadership of Louis VII of France and Conrad III of Germany, and army of almost two hundred thousand left for the Holy land. They were repeatedly defeated by the Turks, and accomplished little.

For a while the Kingdom of Jerusalem grew strong, and under Amalric I it even extended as far as Cairo. But then the Moslems began to regroup and, under the leadership of the sultan of Egypt, Saladin, took Jerusalem in 1187.

The news shook Christendom, and Gregory VIII called for a renewal of the crusading spirit. This Third Crusade was led by three sovereigns: Emperor Frederick Barbarossa, Richard the Lionhearted of England, and Philip II Augustus of France. This too failed. Frederick drowned, and his army dissolved. Richard and Philip achieved nothing but taking Acre after a siege that lasted two years. Philip then returned to Europe, hoping to take advantage of Richard's absence to take some of the latter's lands. Richard himself, on his way home, was captured by the emperor of Germany and kept a prisoner until an enormous ransom was promised.

The Fourth Crusade, called by Innocent III, was an even greater disaster. Its goal was to attack Saladin at his headquarters in Egypt. Instead, it was rerouted to Constantinople, which the crusaders took. They then named Baldwin of Flanders emperor of Constantinople, and thus was founded the Latin Empire of Constantinople (1204-1261). A Latin patriarch of Constantinople was also named, and thus, in theory at least, East and West were reunited. Innocent III, at first incensed by this misuse of the crusade, eventually decided that it was God's way of reuniting the church. But the Byzantines did not accept matters so easily, and continued a long resistance. Finally, in 1261, they retook Constantinople, and ended the Latin Empire. The net result of the entire episode was that the enmity of the Greek East toward the Latin West grew more intense.

The Fifth Crusade, led by the "King of Jerusalem"—the city had been in Moslem hands for a long time—attacked Egypt, and accomplished very little. The Sixth, led by excommunicated emperor Frederick II, had better success than the rest, for the emperor and the sultan came to an agreement granting Jerusalem, Nazareth, and Bethlehem to Frederick, as well as the roads linking those holy places to Acre. Frederick entered Jerusalem and, since no one else would do it, crowned himself King of Jerusalem. The pope who had excommunicated him, Gregory IX, fumed, but Europe rejoiced and called Frederick the "Liberator of Jerusalem." The Seventh and Eighth Crusades, led by Louis IX of France (Saint Louis) were major disasters. The king was captured by the Moslems in the Seventh Crusade, and forced to pay a large ransom. In the Eighth, he died of fever in Tunis. It was the year 1270, and the crusades had run their course.

The Spanish Reconquista

The ancient Visigothic kingdom of Spain had been destroyed by the Moslems in the eighth century, and only small remants of it continued a precarious existence in the region of Asturias, in northern Spain. Later, the Franks established their influence further East. Out of these two foci would come the long struggle against Islam known in Spain as the *Reconquista*—reconquest. Although later legend made this an almost continuous Christian effort against the infidel, the truth is much more complicated, for Christians seem to have fought as much among themselves as against Moslems, and alliances across religious lines were not uncommon.

In the unification of Christian Spain, the "discovery" of the tomb of Saint James played an important role. By the ninth century, this had become one of the main places of pilgrimage for Christians from all over western Europe, and thus the road to Santiago—Saint James—brought northern Spain into constant contact with the rest of western Christendom. Eventually, Saint James became the patron saint of the struggle against the Moslems, and thus came to be known as Santiago Matamoros—Saint James the Moorslayer.

In 1002, the last of the great caliphs of Cordova died, and Moslem lands were soon divided into a multitude of petty kingdoms. It was then that the Spanish Reconquista gained strength. By 1085, the Spanish kingdom of Castile had taken Toledo, the old Visigothic capital. This called forth a reaction from the Moors, who sent reinforcements from North Africa. In 1212, however, the Christian kings joined in defeating the Moors at the battle of Navas de Tolosa, and thereafter the Reconquista marched apace. By 1248, the only Moorish state in the Peninsula was the kingdom of Granada, which survived by paying tribute to the king of Castile. Such would be the situation until 1492, when Granada finally fell to the arms of Ferdinand and Isabella.

Spain and Sicily—the latter taken by the Normans in the eleventh century—were the only areas where the military campaign against Islam was permanently successful.

Consequences of the Offensive against Islam

The most obvious consequence of these various episodes was the increased mistrust and enmity between Christians and Moslems, as well as between Latin and Byzantine Christians. The events of the crusades, and the blood spilled, would not be forgotten easily.

In western Europe, the crusades and the Spanish Reconquista enhanced the power of the papacy. Since it was the popes who called for the crusades, and appointed their leaders, and since they also took a special interest in Spain, the papacy gained further international authority. When Urban II called for the First Crusade, his authority was in doubt, particularly in Germany. By the time of Innocent III, when the Fourth Crusade took Constantinople, the papacy had reached the apex of its power.

The crusades also had an impact on Christian piety. Increased contacts with the Holy Land turned people's attention to the historical narratives of the Bible, and devotion came to center on the humanity of Jesus. Bernard of Clairvaux, the preacher of the Second Crusade, was also a mystic devoted to the contemplation of the humanity of Jesus. Poems and entire books were written about every detail of the passion. For similar reasons, the veneration of relics, which had ancient roots, gained momentum as Europe was flooded with pieces of the True Cross, bones of patriarchs, teeth of biblical figures, and so forth.

The monastic ideal took a new direction with the founding of the military orders. Members of these orders made the traditional vows of obedience, poverty, and chastity. But instead of spending their time in meditation or in study, they were warriors. The order of Saint John of Jerusalem (which

The shape of reliquaries sometimes indicated the nature of the relic kept in them.

later moved its headquarters to Malta), the Templars, and others were founded in the Holy Land. In Spain there were the similar orders of Calatrava, Alcantara, and Santiago. Long after the crusades, these orders continued existing, and some of them held enormous power.

The crusading spirit was also used to combat heresy. In southern France and some sections of Italy, doctrines had spread that were similar to those of the ancient Manichees. It appears that they were imported from Bulgaria, or from the Byzantine Empire, where the sect of the "Bogomils" had long held a Manichean dualism. They were also called "cathars"—a word derived from the Greek for "pure"—or "Albigensians," since they were particularly numerous in the town of Albi, in southern France. Against them, Innocent III called a crusade, and in 1209 ambitious noblemen from northern France invaded the south. Atrocities similar to those that had taken place in Moslem lands were committed, both against Albigensians and against their catholic neighbors who came to their defense. This was an indication that for years to come the crusading ideal would be used in different circumstances, quite apart from the original intent of retaking the Holy Land.

In the field of theology, renewed contact with the Moslem world had far-reaching consequences. Moslem Spain, and to a lesser degree Moslem Sicily, had been centers of learning. In Cordova had been born the greatest Jewish and Moslem philosophers of the Middle Ages, Maimonides and Averroes. They and others had revived a great deal of the philosophy of antiquity, and related it to Jewish and Islamic theological questions. Averroes in particular had written commentaries on Aristotle, and these were so widely used that he came to be known simply as "the Commentator." From Spain and Sicily, the works of these philosophers, as well as of Aristotle himself, were introduced into western Europe, where in the thirteenth century they would give rise to a great deal of philosophical and theological activity.

Finally, there is a complex relationship between the crusades and a series of economic and demographic changes which took place in Europe at approximately the same time. Although it is clear that the crusades contributed to these changes, there were several other contributing factors, and historians are not in agreement as to their relative importance. In any case, the age of the crusades also witnessed the development of cities and of an economy where trade once again became active. Until then, the only important source of wealth was land, and therefore economic power was in the hands of the nobles and prelates who had control of the land. But the development of an economy where trade was increasingly important gave rise to new sources of wealth. This in turn contributed to the growth of cities, where a new class, the bourgeoisie, began to emerge. This class, whose name means precisely "those who live in the city," was formed mostly by merchants whose economic and political power was on the rise. Soon they would be allies of the monarchy against the excessive power of the high nobility; eventually, in the French Revolution, they would overcome both the crown and the nobility.

31/The Golden Age of Medieval Christianity

Just as God established two great luminaries in the heavens, the greater to preside over days, and the lesser to preside over nights, so did he establish two luminaries in the heavens of the universal church. . . . The greater to preside over souls as over days, and the lesser to preside over bodies as over nights. These are pontifical authority and royal power.

INNOCENT III

As the crusades were drawing to a close, Medieval Christianity reached its high point. Once again, this was seen primarily in developments that took place in the two foci of medieval religious life: monasticism and the papacy. And it also found expression in theology and architecture. Therefore, very briefly, we shall turn our attention to each of these in order: the development of mendicant monastic orders, the rising power of the papacy, theological activity, and architecture.

The Mendicant Orders

The growth of cities, trade, and the monetary economy brought about changes that were not always welcome. The monetary economy, for instance, while promoting more specialized production and thus increasing the collective wealth, has the great disadvantage of making economic transactions less direct and human, and of promoting a growing chasm between rich and poor. The growth of cities, and the movement of population that it involved, also made it difficult for the traditional parish ministry to fill the needs of those who flocked to the towns. Thus, it is not surprising that monasticism, which through the ages has shown its enormous adaptability, would take new shapes that both questioned the mores of the monetary economy and responded to the needs of a population on the move. These were the "mendicants"— meaning those who lived by begging.

A forerunner of the mendicant orders was Peter Waldo, a merchant from Lyons who heard the story of a monk who practiced extreme poverty and was moved by it to devote himself to a life of poverty and preaching. He soon gathered a number of followers, but the archbishop forbade their activities. They appealed to Rome, and the theologians appointed to hear their case treated them with derision for their ignorance. In spite of this and despite repeated condemnations, they continued preaching. Persecution then forced them to withdraw to remote valleys in the Alps, where they continued existing until the Protestant Reformation. At that time they were approached by Reformed theologians whose teachings they accepted, and thus became Protestant.

In its early stages, the Franciscan movement was very similar to the Waldensians. Francis, like Peter Waldo, belonged to the merchant class. His true name was Giovanni. But his mother was French, his father had trade relations with France, and he himself was fond of the songs of French troubadours. Therefore, soon friends in his native Assisi called him "Francesco"— the little Frenchman—and by that name he is known to this day.

Like Peter Waldo, Francis had a profound religious experience that led him to embrace a life of poverty. It is said that one day his friends noticed that he was exceptionally happy.

"Why are you so happy?" they asked him.

"Because I have married."

"Whom have you married?"

"Lady Poverty!"

He then gave to the poor all he had. If his parents gave him more, he immediately gave it away. Dressed in rags, he spent his time praising the beauty of poverty to any who would listen, or rebuilding an abandoned chapel, or enjoying the beauty and harmony of nature. His father put him in a cellar and appealed to the authorities. The bishop finally decided that, if Francis was not willing to use wisely of his family's goods, he must give them up. Upon receiving the verdict, he gave up his inheritance, returned to his father the clothes he was wearing, and left naked into the woods, where he lived as a hermit.

Then, late in 1209, he heard the reading of the Gospel (Matt. 10:7–10), where Jesus sent his disciples to preach, taking with them no gold or silver. Until then, he had been concerned almost exclusively with voluntary poverty

*The mystical experiences of St. Francis became a favorite theme of
medieval and Renaissance art.*

and the joy he found in it. Now he saw the possibility of joining poverty with
preaching. His place would not be in quiet solitude, but in the bustle of the
cities, wherever people were, preaching to them, helping the poor and the
sick. Now voluntary poverty was not only a means of self-discipline, but even
more, a means to identify with those who were poor out of necessity.

Led by this new vision, Francis left his retreat and returned to Assisi,
there to preach and to face the insults of his former friends. Slowly, however,
a small following gathered around him, and he and a few others went to
Rome to ask authorization from the pope to found a new monastic order. The
pope was Innocent III—the most powerful man, and one of the wisest, ever
to occupy that position. Innocent was not inclined to grant what Francis
requested. But he was wiser than his predecessors, and, after testing Francis'
mettle, yielded.

Francis returned to Assisi to continue his work with papal approval.
Soon people began flocking to his new "order of lesser brothers"—or Friars
Minor. A sister order for women was founded by Saint Clare, a spiritual sister

of Francis, and became commonly known as the "Clarisses" or "Poor Clares." Franciscans preaching, singing, and begging became a common sight throughout western Europe.

Francis feared that the success of the movement would be its downfall. When his followers began to be respected, he began to fear for their humility. It is said that, when a novice asked him if it was lawful to have a Psalter, he replied: "When you have a Psalter, you will want a Breviary. And when you have a Breviary you will climb to the pulpit like a prelate."

The story is also told of a friar who returned joyful, because someone had given him a gold coin. Francis ordered him to take the coin between his teeth, and bury it in a dung heap, pointing out that such was the best place for gold.

Well aware of the temptations that success placed before his order, Francis made a will forbidding his followers to possess anything, or to appeal to the pope or to anyone else to have the *Rule* that he had given them made less stringent.

At the general chapter of the order that met in 1220, he gave up the leadership of the order, and knelt in obedience before his successor. Finally, on October 3, 1226, he died at a chapel that he had rebuilt in his youth. It is said that his last words were: "I have done my duty. Now, may Christ let you know yours. Welcome, sister Death!"

The founder of the other major mendicant order was Saint Dominic. He was some twelve years older than Francis, but his work as the founder of an order was somewhat later. He was born in the town of Caleruega, in Castile, to an aristocratic family whose tower still dominates the landscape.

After some ten years of study in Palencia, Dominic became a canon of the cathedral of Osma. Four years later, when he was twenty-nine, the chapter of the cathedral resolved to follow the monastic rule of the Canons of Saint Augustine. This meant that the members of the cathedral chapter lived in a monastic community, but without withdrawing from the world nor setting aside their ministry to the faithful.

In 1203, Dominic and his bishop, Diego of Osma, visited southern France. He was moved by the success of the Albigensians, and by the efforts to convert them to catholicism by force. He also noted that the Albigensians' main attraction was the asceticism of their leaders, which contrasted with the easy life of many orthodox priests and prelates. Convinced that there were better means of combating heresy, Dominic set out to preach and teach orthodoxy. This he joined to a disciplined monastic life and rigorous study in order to make use of the best possible arguments against heresy. On the foothills of the Pyrenees he founded a school for noblewomen who were converted from among the ranks of the Albigensians. The archbishop of Toulouse, encouraged by his success, gave him a church in which to preach, as well as a house in which to organize a monastic community.

Shortly thereafter, with the support of the archbishop, he went to Rome in order to request permission from Innocent III to found a new order, with its own rule. The pope refused, for he was concerned over the proliferation of different monastic rules. But he encouraged Dominic to continue his work, and to adopt one of the existing monastic rules. Upon returning to Toulouse, Dominic and his followers adopted the rule of the Canons of Saint Augustine. Then, through further legislation, they adapted that rule to their own needs. They also adopted the rule of poverty and mendicancy, perhaps following the example of early Franciscanism, but certainly as a means to refute the arguments of the Albigensians, who claimed that orthodox Christians were too worldly.

From its very beginnings, the Order of Preachers—for such was the official name of the Dominicans—emphasized study. In this Dominic differed from Saint Francis, who did not wish his friars to have even a Psalter, and who was suspicious of study. The Dominicans, in their task of refuting heresy, must be well armed intellectually, and for that reason their recruits received solid intellectual training. They soon gave to the church some of its most distinguished theologians—although the Franciscans, who entered the theological field somewhat later, were not far behind.

Both mendicant orders spread throughout most of Europe. Soon there were other similar movements, or ancient orders that now followed their example. In general, the later course of the Order of Preachers was much less turbulent than that of the Franciscans.

From the beginning, Dominicans had seen poverty as an argument that strengthened and facilitated their task of refuting heresy. Their main objective was preaching, teaching, and study, and poverty was seen as a means to that end. Therefore, when new circumstances seemed to make it advisable for the order to have property, this was done without major difficulties, and the ideal of living by begging was set aside. Also, since such a step agreed with their original impulse, they soon established a foothold in the universities, which were beginning to blossom at the same time.

The two main centers of theological studies at the time were the nascent universities of Paris and Oxford. The Dominicans founded houses in both cities, and soon had professors teaching in the universities. Before long, such Dominicans as Albert the Great and Thomas Aquinas would bring great prestige to the order in intellectual circles.

Dominicans also tried to convert Moslems and Jews. The most famous preacher among Moslems in the early years was William of Tripoli. Among Jews in Spain, Vincent Ferrer played a similar role. In both cases, however, some of their success was due to the use of force—by the crusaders against Moslems in Tripoli, and by Spanish Christians against Jews in Spain.

The Franciscans also established a foothold in the universities. In 1236, a professor at the University of Paris, Alexander of Hales, joined the Franciscans, and thus the Friars Minor had their first university professor. Before long, there were Franciscan teachers in all the major universities of western Europe.

Following Francis' impulse, his followers preached, not only to Christians, but also to others. Francis himself had always been interested in this, and in 1219 had personally gone to preach in Egypt. The Franciscan John of Montecorvino visited Persia, Ethiopia, and India, and in 1294, after a journey of three years, arrived at Cambaluc—now Beijing. In a few years, he had made several thousand converts. The pope then made him archbishop of Cambaluc, and sent seven other Franciscans to serve under him as bishops. Of these, only three reached their destination. Since Francis had shown keen interest in preaching to the Moslems, his order continued in that effort, and over the years thousands of Franciscans have offered up their lives in it.

In spite of its early success—and perhaps because of it—the order founded by Saint Francis had a stormy history. Francis himself had always feared that his friars would become rich and comfortable. For that reason he ordered absolute poverty, not only for individual friars, but also for the order as a whole. And he nailed down this command by reaffirming it in his will, and forbidding his followers to seek any change in the *Rule* he had given them.

Shortly after the Saint's death, two parties had developed within the order. The rigorists insisted on strict obedience to the Founder's instructions. The moderates argued that changed circumstances required a less literal interpretation of the *Rule,* and that the order ought to be able to accept property given to it for the furtherance of its mission. In 1230, Gregory IX declared that the will of Francis was not binding, and that the order could therefore ask Rome to alter the rule of poverty. In 1245, the order began owning property, although the Holy See held title to it and the Franciscans had only the right to use it. Eventually, even this fiction was abandoned, and the order came to have vast holdings.

While all this was taking place, the rigorists became increasingly alienated from the hierarchy of the church. They saw what was taking place as a great betrayal of Saint Francis. Soon some began saying that the prophecies of Joachim of Fiore, who had lived a generation before Francis, were being fulfilled. Joachim had proposed a scheme of history as consisting of three successive stages: the era of the Father, the era of the Son, and the era of the Spirit. The first, from Adam to Jesus, lasted forty-two generations. Since God loves order and symmetry, Joachim had argued, the era of the Son will last the same number of generations. At thirty years per generation, Joachim came to the date 1260, when the age of the Son would end, and that of the Spirit would begin. During the age of the Son, monks, who are more spiritual than the rest of believers, are heralds of the age of the Spirit.

Since the year 1260 was approaching, it was natural that a number of rigorist Franciscans, alienated as they were from the hierarchy, would adopt Joachim's scheme. The present difficulties, they believed, were but the last struggles before the next age would dawn, when they would be vindicated. Meanwhile, the pope and other leaders of the church were at best believers of a lower sort, and there would soon be no need for them.

Calling themselves "spirituals," those Franciscans set out to preach the theories of Joachim of Fiore. One of their supporters was the minister general of the order, John of Parma; and thus, for a time, it appeared that the Franciscans would follow a path similar to that of the earlier Waldensians, and break with the hierarchical church. But the next minister general, Saint Bonaventure, was able to combine profound piety with strict obedience to the hierarchy, and the "spirituals" lost momentum. The same ideas re-emerged in the fourteenth century among the "Fraticelli"—Italian for "little brothers"—who were ruthlessly persecuted until they disappeared.

One Flock under One Shepherd

The Concordat of Worms (1122) did not end the difficulties of the papacy. In Rome there were still powerful families that sought to capture it for their own purposes, and soon there were once again two claimants to the See of Saint Peter. Europe would have been divided in its allegiance to them had it not been for the decisive support of Bernard of Clairvaux for Innocent II. Having lost Rome to his rival claimant, Innocent sought refuge in France, which declared for him. England and Germany, France's traditional enemies, hesitated in their allegiance. But Bernard convinced both sovereigns to side with Innocent. Eventually, with the support of imperial troops, Innocent was able to return to Rome.

But then the emperor died, and Innocent's relations with his successor deteriorated. Republican ideas were circulating in Italy, and the pope encouraged them in the imperial cities of the north, while the emperor did the same in Rome. A number of imperial cities rebelled, and proclaimed themselves republics. The people of Rome also rebelled, proclaimed a republic, elected a senate, and declared that they would obey the pope's spiritual authority, but not his temporal rule. The next few popes were seldom able to reside in the city. Tension between papacy and empire grew under the next emperor, Frederick Barbarossa (1152–1190), who finally had a series of rival popes elected. But he was unable to impose his policy in Italy, where the rebellious imperial cities, united in a Lombard League, defeated him. After years of struggle, Barbarossa made peace with the pope, at that time Alexander III. The rival pope, Calixtus III, resigned in 1178. Alexander accepted his resignation gracefully, and even appointed him to high ecclesiastical office.

Frederick strengthened his hand by marrying his son Henry to the heir of the throne of Sicily, a traditional ally of the popes. Then Frederick drowned in the Third Crusade, and was succeeded by his son Henry VI, who was both emperor of Germany and king of Sicily. Soon it was clear that Henry sought to control the papacy, and Pope Celestine III excommunicated him. Open warfare seemed inevitable when both the emperor and the pope died.

Since the empire had not yet recovered from the unexpected death of Henry VI, the cardinals were able to elect a new pope without undue pressure. Their choice fell on Lotario de' Conti di Segni, thirty-seven years old, who under the name of Innocent III became the most powerful pope in the history of Christianity.

Henry's widow feared that her infant son, Frederick, would be destroyed by some of those vying for power in Germany, and therefore placed the child under the protection of the pope by declaring the kingdom of Sicily a fiefdom of the papacy. Thus was averted the threat to the papacy which that kingdom had been under Henry VI.

The imperial crown, which Henry had also held, was not hereditary. Rather, the emperor was elected from among the nobles. Young Frederick was obviously too young to be emperor, especially since it was certain that this would not be an easy crown to hold. Those who had supported Henry VI and his house of Hohenstaufen elected Henry's brother Philip. But a rival faction elected Otto IV, who soon had the support of Innocent III. It is clear that Philip had been duly elected. But Innocent declared that he was tainted by his brother's crimes, and that in any case the pope has the authority to determine who is the rightful emperor. The temporal power and the spiritual power, he claimed, have both been instituted by God. They are like the moon and the sun. But, just as the moon receives its light from the sun, so does the emperor receive his power from the pope. On this basis, Innocent declared that Otto was the rightful ruler, and a civil war ensued that lasted ten years, and which ended only when Philip was murdered.

After he was in undisputed control of the Empire, Otto IV broke with the pope who had supported his claim. Once again the main reason for discord was the emperor's effort to increase his power in Italy, and the pope's refusal to allow him to do so. Otto's agents encouraged the republican party in Rome, while he prepared to invade the kingdom of Sicily, which, in theory at least, belonged to the papacy, for young Frederick was Innocent's vassal.

In retaliation, Innocent excommunicated Otto, declared him deposed, and affirmed that the legitimate emperor was young Frederick. With the pope's support, Frederick crossed the Alps, appeared in Germany, and wrested the imperial crown from his uncle. This was a strange victory for both Frederick and Innocent. By supporting Frederick, Innocent had contributed to the restoration of the house of Hohenstaufen, traditional enemies of the papacy. But it was also true that Frederick II, the new emperor, had reached that position on the basis of the papal claim to authority over emperors and kings. Thus, while Innocent acknowledged Frederick, the new emperor had tacitly affirmed that the pope had been within his rights in assuming authority to determine who was the rightful ruler.

Germany was not the only country in which Innocent III intervened.

Indeed, there was hardly a European monarch who did not feel the weight of his authority.

In France, he intervened in the marital life of King Philip Augustus. The king had been widowed and remarried to a Danish princess, but then he had repudiated his second wife and taken a third. Innocent admonished the king to return to his rightful wife, and when Philip refused he placed the entire country under an interdict, forbidding the celebration of sacraments. Philip called a gathering of nobles and bishops, with the hope that they would support him against the pope. But they took the opposite stance, and Philip was forced to leave his third wife and return to the second. The deposed queen died shortly thereafter, suffering from intense depression. The restored queen spent the rest of her life complaining that her supposed restoration was in truth constant torture. In any case, the pope's authority had prevailed over one of the most powerful sovereigns of the time.

In England, the ruler was John Lackland, brother and heir to Richard the Lionhearted. Although John's marital life had been much more disorderly than Philip's, Innocent did not intervene, for at the time he desperately needed England's support in his efforts to establish Otto on the throne of Germany. But later Innocent and John clashed over the question of who was the legitimate archbishop of Canterbury. There were two rival claimants to that see, the most important in England, and both appealed to the pope. Innocent's response was that neither was the legitimate archbishop. Instead, he named Stephen Langton to that post. John Lackland refused to accept the papal decision, and Innocent excommunicated him. When this proved insufficient, Innocent declared John deposed from his throne, released all his subjects from their vows of obedience to him, and called a crusade against him. This was to be under the leadership of Philip Augustus of France, who gladly prepared to obey the pope in this matter. Fearing that many of his subjects were not loyal to him, and that he would not be able to defend his throne, John capitulated and made his entire kingdom a fief of the papacy, as had been done earlier with the kingdom of Sicily.

Innocent accepted John's submission, canceled the crusade that Philip of France was preparing, and thereafter became a staunch supporter of his new ally. Thus, when the English nobility, with the support of Stephen Langton, forced John to sign the Magna Carta, limiting the power of the king vis-à-vis the nobility, Innocent declared that this was a usurpation of power. But all his protests were to no avail.

Innocent also intervened repeatedly in Spain. Pedro II of Aragon, "the Catholic" was forced to turn his kingdom into a fief of the papacy, thus giving credence to Innocent's claim that all lands conquered from unbelievers belonged to the papacy. One of the ironies of history is that this king, known as "the Catholic," died during the crusade against the Albigensians, while supporting the heretics against the crusade proclaimed by Innocent. The kingdoms of Leon and Castile also felt Innocent's hand, for the pope refused to allow the marriage of the King of Leon with the daughter of his first cousin, the King of Castile. And a further irony of history is that one of the sons of that forbidden union, Ferdinand III of Castile and Leon, became a saint of the church.

These are just a few of the many examples of Innocent's far-reaching international policies. His authority was felt in his personal intervention in the affairs of Portugal, Bohemia, Hungary, Denmark, Iceland, and even Bulgaria and Armenia. Although this was done against his wishes, the Fourth Crusade, in taking Constantinople and establishing there a Latin Empire, further extended the reach of his power.

But this was not all. It was during Innocent's reign that the two great mendicant orders of the Franciscans and Dominicans were founded, that the Christian kingdoms of Spain joined to defeat the Moors in the battle of Navas de Tolosa, and that the great crusade against the Albigensians took place. In all of these events, Innocent played a leading role.

Innocent's program for the reformation of the church found expression in the decrees of the Fourth Lateran Council, which gathered in 1215. It was this council that promulgated the doctrine of transubstantiation, which holds that in communion the substance of the body and blood of Christ takes the place of the substance of the bread and wine. This council also condemned the Waldensians, the Albigensians, and the doctrines of Joachim of Fiore. It instituted episcopal inquisition, which meant that every bishop should inquire as to the presence of heresy in his diocese, and destroy it. It determined that no new monastic orders, with new rules, could be founded. It ordered that every cathedral have a school, and that education in such schools be open to the poor. It ordered the clergy to abstain from the theatre, games, hunting, and other such pastimes. It decreed that all the faithful must confess their sins at least once a year. It forbade the introduction of new relics without papal approval. It required all Jews and Moslems in Christian lands to wear distinctive garments that would set them apart from Christians. And it made it unlawful for priests to charge for the administration of sacraments. Since the council accomplished all this, and more, in only three sessions, each of which lasted a single day, it is clear that most of these measures were not the result of the assembly's deliberation, but that they were rather part of a program that Innocent had determined, and which he had the council approve.

For all these reasons, it was under Innocent III that Christendom most nearly approached the ideal of being "one flock, under one shepherd"—the pope. Thus, it is not surprising that his contemporaries came to believe that the pope was more than human, and that by right he had an authority that extended to every human endeavor.

Innocent died in 1216, and for several decades his successors basked in the light of his prestige. Between 1254 and 1273, Germany went through a period of disorder, and eventually it was the papacy, under Gregory X, that restored order by supporting the election of Rudolf of Hapsburg. In return, the new emperor declared that Rome and the papal states were independent of the Empire.

Meanwhile, France's power was increasing, and the popes repeatedly found support in it. Also, the prestige of the mendicant orders was such that many hoped for popes elected from within their ranks. The first Dominican pope was Innocent V, who reigned very briefly in 1276. The first Franciscan was Nicholas IV, who was pope from 1288 to 1292.

When Nicholas died, there was disagreement among the cardinals. Some insisted that the pope should be experienced in wordly matters, a man who understood the intrigues and ambitions of the world; others held to the Franciscan ideal, and sought the election of a candidate embodying it. Finally, the latter group prevailed, and Celestine V was elected. He was a Franciscan of the "spiritual" wing of the order. When he appeared barefooted and riding a donkey, many thought that the prophecies of Joachim of Fiore were coming true. Now was the age of the Spirit beginning, and the church would be led by the humble and the poor. But Celestine decided to abdicate after a brief pontificate. He appeared before the cardinals, shed the papal robes, and sat on the ground, vowing that he would not change his mind.

His successor was a man of entirely different inclinations, who took the title of Boniface VIII (1294–1303). His bull *Unam Sanctam* marked the high point of papal claims to temporal power:

One sword must be under the other, and temporal authority must be subject to the spiritual. . . . Therefore, if earthly power strays from the right path it is to be judged by the spiritual. . . . But if the supreme spiritual authority strays, it can only be judged by God, and not by humans. . . . We further declare, affirm, and define that it is absolutely necessary for salvation that all human creatures be under the Roman pontiff.*

However, as we shall see in the next chapter, such high claims were belied by events, for it was during the reign of Boniface VIII that it became apparent that the power of the papacy was declining.

Theological Activity: Scholasticism

The thirteenth century, which marked the apex of papal power and the birth of the mendicant orders, was also the high point of medieval "scholasticism." This is the name given to a theology that developed in the "schools," and which had its own characteristic methodology. Its early roots grew in monasteries, but in the twelfth century cathedral schools became the center of theological activity, only to be supplanted, early in the thirteenth century, by

---

Corpus of Canon Law 2.1245.

universities. In a way, this is another consequence of the growth of cities. From monasteries, which usually existed apart from centers of populations, theology moved to cathedral schools, that is, to schools connected with churches that had bishops—and therefore usually in cities. Then it centered in universities, which were vast associations of scholars gathered in the principal cities.

The most important forerunner of scholasticism was Anselm of Canterbury. A native of Italy, he had joined the monastery of Bec, in Normandy, in 1060. He was attracted to that particular monastery by the fame of its

Scholarship and the copying of manuscripts had long been a main occupation of monks.

abbot, Lanfranc, who left in 1078 to become archbishop of Canterbury. In 1066, William of Normandy had conquered England, and was now drawing on Normandy for leaders both in ecclesiastical and in civil matters. In 1093, Anselm himself was called to England to succeed Lanfranc as archbishop of Canterbury. He went reluctantly, for he knew that he would soon clash with the king over the question of the relative authority of church and state. (Seventy years later, Thomas Becket, then archbishop of Canterbury, would be murdered at the cathedral for similar reasons.) First under William, and then under his son Henry, Anselm spent most of his career exiled from Canterbury. He made use of those periods of exile, as he had done of his years at Bec, by meditating and writing on theological issues.

Anselm's significance for the development of scholasticism lies in his desire to apply reason to questions of faith. What he sought in doing this was not to prove something which he did not believe without such proof, but rather to understand more deeply what he already believed. This may be seen in the manner in which he dealt with the existence of God and with the motive for the incarnation.

Anselm believed in the existence of God. But he sought to understand more deeply what that existence meant. It was for this reason that he developed in the *Proslogion* what has come to be called "the ontological argument for the existence of God." Briefly stated, Anselm's argument is that when one thinks of God, one is thinking of "that-than-which-no-greater-can-be-thought." The question then is, is it possible to think of "that-than-which-no-greater-can-be-thought" as not existing? Clearly not, for then an existing being would be greater than it. Therefore, by definition, the idea of "that-than-which-no-greater-can-be-thought" includes its existence. To speak of God as not existing makes as much sense as to speak of a triangle with four sides. The exact interpretation, significance, and validity of this argument has been discussed by scholars and philosophers through the ages, and is still discussed. What is important for our purposes, however, is to note the method of Anselm's theology, which applies reason to a truth known by faith, in order to understand it better.

The same is true of Anselm's treatise *Why God Human?* There he explores the question of the reason for the incarnation, and offers an answer that would eventually become standard in western theology. The importance of a crime is measured in terms of the one against whom it is committed. Therefore, a crime against God, sin, is infinite in its import. But, on the other hand, only a human being can offer satisfaction for human sin. This is obviously impossible, for human beings are finite, and cannot offer the infinite satisfaction required by the majesty of God. For this reason, there is need for a divine-human, God incarnate, who through his suffering and death offers satisfaction for the sins of all humankind. This view of the work of Christ, which was by no means the generally accepted one in earlier centuries, soon gained such credence that most western Christians came to accept it as the only biblical one. Again, what is significant here is Anselm's use of reason to seek to understand more fully the incarnation in which he already believes.

Another important forerunner of scholasticism was Peter Abelard. Born in Brittany in 1079, Abelard spent his youth studying under the most famous scholars of his time, finding them wanting, and letting them know his opinion of them. He thus collected some of the many enemies that would make his life a *History of Calamities*—the title of his autobiography. He then went to Paris, where a canon of the cathedral entrusted him with the education of his very gifted niece, Heloise. The teacher and the student became lovers and had a child. Heloise's uncle, outraged, had some ruffians break into Abelard's room and emasculate him. Abelard then withdrew to a life of monastic retreat, but was followed by his many enemies, and by those who were convinced that his bold use of reason was heresy. Foremost among these was the saintly Bernard of Clairvaux, who had him condemned as a heretic in 1141. When Abelard appealed to Rome, he found that Bernard had already closed that door. Thus, towards the end of his career, Abelard looked on his life as a series of calamities. He died in 1142, having been reconciled to the church, and Heloise, who had kept correspondence with him, had his remains moved from Cluny to the monastery of the Paraclete, which he had founded and been forced to leave.

Abelard's main contribution to the development of scholastic theology was the book *Yes and No,* in which he took up 158 theological questions and then showed that various authorities, including the Bible and the ancient Christian writers, did not agree on their answers.

Naturally, such a book aroused great opposition, especially coming from one who was at best suspected of heresy. Abelard's purpose, however, does not seem to have been to discredit the authorities he set against each other, but simply to show that theology must not be content with citing authorities. It was necessary, as he saw matters, to find ways to reconcile such apparently contradictory authorities. Eventually, scholasticism used this method, for the typical scholastic work began by posing a question and then quoting authorities who seemed to support one answer, and other authorities who seemed to support another. What the scholastics did, and Abelard did not do, was then to offer an answer and "solutions" that showed how it was possible for all the authorities quoted to be correct.

The third main forerunner of scholasticism was Peter Lombard, who wrote *Four Books of Sentences.* These were a systematic treatment of theology, dealing in an orderly fashion with the main themes of Christian theology, from the doctrine of God to the last things. Although at first some disagreed with a number of the opinions expressed in it, and sought to have it condemned, it eventually became the basic textbook for the teaching of theology in the universities. This was usually done by commenting on the *Sentences* of Peter Lombard, and therefore the works of major scholastic theologians usually include a *Commentary on the Sentences* written during their years of university teaching.

Besides these forerunners, two developments were significant for the early history of scholasticism. These were the growth of universities and the reintroduction of the teachings of Aristotle into western Europe.

The universities were in part the result of the growth of cities. Students congregated in urban centers, first at the cathedral schools, and then at others, and all these were eventually united in what came to be known as "general studies." Out of these evolved the main universities of Europe. But these were not so much institutions like our modern universities as they were guilds of scholars, both teachers and students, which organized in order to defend the rights of their members, and to certify the level of proficiency achieved by each.

The oldest universities in western Europe date from the late years of the twelfth century; but it was the thirteenth that witnessed the growth of universities as the main centers of study. Although in all of them one could acquire a basic education, soon some became famous in a particular field of study. Those who wished to study medicine tried to go to Montpelier or Salerno, while Ravenna, Pavia, and Bologna were famous for their studies in law. For theology, the main centers were Paris and Oxford.

Those who aspired to become theologians must first spend several years studying philosophy and humanities in the Arts Faculty. Then they entered the Faculty of Theology, where they began as "hearers," and could progressively become "biblical bachelors," "bachelors on the sentences," "formed bachelors," "licensed masters," and "doctors." By the fourteenth century, this process required fourteen years after having completed one's studies in the Faculty of Arts.

Theological academic exercises consisted in commentaries on the Bible or the *Sentences,* sermons, and "disputations." The latter were the academic exercise par excellence. Here a debatable question was posed, and those present and qualified to do so were given opportunity to offer reasons for answering the question one way or the other, usually on the basis of the authority of Scripture or of an ancient writer. Thus was compiled a list of opinions that seemed to contradict each other, similar to Abelard's *Yes and No.* Then the teacher was given time to prepare an answer, for in the next session he had to express his own opinion, and to show that this did not contradict any of the authorities that had been adduced for the opposite view. Eventually, this method was so generalized that the various *Commentaries on the Sentences* followed it, as did Thomas Aquinas in his *Summa Contra Gentiles* and in his *Summa Theologica.*

The other development that made a great impact on scholasticism was the reintroduction of Aristotle into western Europe. From the time of Justin in the second century, most Christian theologians, particularly in the West, had grown accustomed to what was essentially a Platonic or Neoplatonic philosophy. Although some of Aristotle's works were read and used, these had to do mostly with logic, and did not contradict the essentially Platonic world view of early medieval theology. But then the crusades, and especially renewed contacts with Moslems in Spain and Sicily, brought about greater knowledge of Aristotle's philosophy, and it was clear that this differed in many ways from what was generally accepted. Furthermore, since Aristotle's most famous commentator was Averroes, many of the latter's views entered western Europe. This was especially true in the Faculty of Arts of the University of Paris, where there was keen interest in the new philosophy.

Several professors in the Arts Faculty of Paris embraced the new philosophical ideas with enthusiasm. Since they generally read Aristotle through the eyes of the Commentator, Averroes, they have been called "Latin Averroists." There were several elements in their philosophy that profoundly disturbed the theologians. Foremost of these was the insistence on the independence of reason and philosophy from any constraint imposed by faith and theology. The Averroists insisted that the path of reason should be followed to the end, and that if its conclusions somehow differed from those of theology, this was a problem for theologians, and not philosophers, to solve. This position then allowed them to accept a number of doctrines of Aristotle and Averroes that contradicted traditional Christian teaching. For instance, they said that, according to reason, matter is eternal—which contradicted the doctrine of creation out of nothing; and that all souls are ultimately one—which contradicted the Christian doctrine of individual life after death.

Some theologians responded to this challenge by affirming the traditional Platonic and Augustinian outlook. Saint Bonaventure, for instance, who was the most distinguished Franciscan theologian of the thirteenth century, insisted that faith is necessary in order to achieve correct understanding. For example, the doctrine of creation tells us how the world is to be understood, and those who do not set out from that doctrine can easily come to the erroneous conclusion that matter is eternal. Furthermore, all knowledge comes from the Word of God who was incarnate in Christ, and to claim any knowledge apart from him is to deny the very core and source of the knowledge that one claims.

There was, however, another alternative between that of the Averroists and that of traditional Augustinian theology. This was to explore the possibilities that the new philosophy offered for a better understanding of Christian faith. This was the path followed by the two great teachers of the Dominican order: Albert the Great and Thomas Aquinas.

Albert, whose academic career in Paris and Cologne was frequently interrupted by the many tasks assigned to him, made a clear distinction between philosophy and theology. Philosophy operates on the basis of autonomous principles, which can be known apart from revelation, and seeks to discover truth by a strictly rational method. A true philosopher does not seek to prove what the mind cannot understand, even if the question at hand is a doctrine of faith. The theologian, on the other hand, does set out from revealed truths, which cannot be known by reason alone. This does not mean that theological doctrines are less sure. On the contrary, revealed data are always more certain than those of reason, which may err. But it does mean that philosophers, as long as they remain within the scope of what reason can attain, should be free to pursue their inquiry, without having to turn at every step to the guiding hand of theology.

On the question of the eternity of the world, for instance, Albert frankly confesses that as a philosopher he cannot prove creation out of nothing. At best he can offer arguments of probability. But as a theologian he knows that the world was made out of nothing, and is not eternal. What we have here is a case in which reason cannot attain truth, for the object of inquiry is beyond the scope of human reason. A philosopher who claims to prove the eternity of the world, and a philosopher who claims to prove its creation out of nothing, are both poor philosophers, for they ignore the limits of reason.

Albert's most famous disciple was Thomas Aquinas. Born about 1224 in the outskirts of Naples, Thomas was reared in an aristocratic family. All his brothers and sisters eventually came to occupy places of distinction in Italian society. His parents had intended an ecclesiastical career for him, with the hope that he would hold a post of power and prestige. He was five years old when they placed him in the abbey of Monte Cassino, there to begin his education. At fourteen, he began studies at the University of Naples, where he first encountered Aristotelian philosophy. All this was part of the career his parents had planned for him. In 1244, however, he decided to become a Dominican. The new order, still in its early years, was regarded askance by many among the wealthy. Therefore, his mother and brothers—his father had died—tried to persuade him to change his mind. When this failed, they locked him up in the family castle, where they kept him for more than a year while trying to dissuade him through threats and temptations. He finally escaped, completed his novitiate among the Dominicans, and went to study at Cologne under Albert.

Many who knew Thomas in his early years failed to see the genius in him. He was so big and quiet that his fellow students called him "the dumb ox." But slowly his intelligence broke through his silence, and the Dominican order acknowledged his intellectual gifts. He thus came to spend most of his life in academic circles, particularly in Paris, where he became a famous professor.

His literary production was enormous. His two most famous works are the *Summa Contra Gentiles* and the *Summa Theologica*. But he also wrote commentaries on the *Sentences,* on Scripture, and on several works of Aristotle, as well as a number of philosophical and theological treatises. He died in 1274, when he was scarcely fifty years old. His teacher Albert outlived him, and became one of the staunchest defenders of his views.

It is impossible to review here even the salient points of Thomism—the name given to his system. Therefore, we shall limit our discussion to the relationship between faith and reason, which is at the heart of Thomism, and to the arguments for the existence of God, which illustrate the difference between Thomas' theology and that of his predecessors. Finally, a word will be added regarding the significance of Thomas' work.

On the relationship between faith and reason, Thomas follows the path outlined by Albert, but defines his position more clearly. According to him, some truths are within the reach of reason, and others are beyond it. Philosophy deals only with the first; but theology is not limited to the latter. The reason for this is that there are truths that reason can prove, but which are necessary for salvation. Since God does not limit salvation to those who are intellectually gifted, all truth necessary for salvation, including that which can be reached by reason, has been revealed. Thus, such truths are a proper field of inquiry for both philosophy and theology.

One example of how this is applied is the manner in which Thomas deals with the question of the existence of God. It is impossible to be saved without believing that God exists. For that reason, the existence of God is a revealed truth, and the authority of the church suffices to believe in it. No one can plead lack of intelligence, for the existence of God is an article of faith, and even the most ignorant person can accept it on that basis. But this does not mean that the existence of God is a truth beyond the reach of reason. In this case, reason can prove what faith accepts. Therefore, the existence of God is a proper subject for both philosophy and theology, although each arrives at it following its own method. Furthermore, rational inquiry helps us to understand better that which we accept by faith.

That is the purpose of Thomas' "five ways" or arguments for the existence of God. The five ways are parallel, and do not have to be expounded here. Let it suffice to say that each of them starts from the world as it is known through the senses, and then shows that such a world requires the existence of God. The first way, for instance, begins by considering movement, and argues that, since what is moved must have a mover, there must be a prime mover, and this is God.

It is interesting to compare these arguments with Anselm's. Anselm distrusted the senses, and thus starts, not by looking at the world, but by examining the idea itself of God. Thomas' arguments follow the opposite route, for they start with the data known through the senses, and from them move on to the existence of God. This is a clear example of the manner in which Thomas' Aristotelian orientation contrasts with Anselm's Platonist views. Whereas Anselm believed that true knowledge is to be found in the realm of pure ideas, Thomas held that sense perception is the beginning of knowledge.

Thomas' work was of great significance for the further development of theology. This was partly due to the systematic structure of his thought, but above all to the manner in which he joined traditional doctrine with what was then a new philosophical outlook.

As to the systematic character of his work, Thomas' *Summa Theologica* has been compared to a vast Gothic cathedral. As we shall see in the next section of this chapter, the great Gothic cathedrals were imposing monuments in which each element of creation and of the history of salvation had a place, and in which all elements stood in perfect balance. Likewise, the *Summa* is an imposing intellectual construction. Even those who disagree with what Thomas says in it cannot deny its architectural structure, its symmetry, in which each element seems to be in its proper place and balanced with all the others.

But Thomas' significance is even more in his ability to turn a philosophy that many considered a threat into an instrument in the hands of faith. For centuries, western theology—and much of eastern theology as well—had been dominated by a Platonic bias. This had come about through a long process that involved such figures as Justin Martyr, Augustine, Pseudo-Dionysius, and many others. That philosophy had helped Christianity in various ways, particularly in its early struggles with paganism, for it spoke of an invisible Supreme Being, of a higher world that the senses cannot perceive, and of an immortal soul. Yet, Platonism also had its own dangers. By interpreting the Christian faith in Platonic terms, it was possible that Christians would come to undervalue the present world, which according to the Bible is God's creation. It was also possible that the incarnation, the presence of God in a physical human being, would be pushed to the background, for Platonism was not interested in temporal realities—which could be dated and located at a particular time and place—but rather in immutable truth. There was therefore the danger that theologians would pay less attention to Jesus Christ as a historical figure, and more to the eternal Word of God—again conceived in Neoplatonic terms.

The advent of the new philosophy threatened much of traditional theology. For that reason many reacted against it, and the reading and teaching of Aristotelianism were often forbidden. Condemnations of Aristotle often included some theses held by Thomas, and therefore there was a struggle before Thomism was considered an acceptable theological system. But eventually its value was acknowledged, and Saint Thomas—as he came to be known—was recognized as one of the greatest theologians of all time.

Stones That Bear a Witness: Architecture

Medieval churches had two purposes, one didactic and one cultic. Their didactic purpose responded to the needs of an age when books were scarce, and there were not many who could read them. Church buildings thus

The contrast between Romanesque and Gothic architectural styles was marked. Above: Southwell Cathedral, England (Romanesque). Below: Cathedral of Notre Dame, Chartres, France (Gothic).

became the books of the illiterate, and an attempt was made to set forth in them the whole of biblical history, the lives of great saints and martyrs, the virtues and vices, the promise of heaven and the punishment of hell. Today it is difficult for us to read these architectural books. But those who worshiped in them knew their most minute details, in which their parents and grandparents had read for them stories and teachings that they in turn had learned from earlier generations.

The cultic purpose of church buildings centered on the medieval understanding of communion. This was seen as the miraculous transformation of the bread and wine into the body and blood of the Lord, and as the renewal of the sacrifice of Christ. Inasmuch as possible, a church building had to be worthy of such miraculous events, and of the Body of Christ that was reserved in it even after the service. The church was not seen primarily as a building for meeting or even for worship, but as the setting in which the Great Miracle took place. Thus, what a town or village had in mind in building a church was to build a setting for its most precious jewel.

The earlier basilicas evolved into a style of architecture called Romanesque—that is, Roman-like. The main differences were three. First, the sanctuary was elongated, so that while the earlier basilicas had the shape of a "Tau" cross (a T), Romanesque churches tended towards our more common "Latin" cross. This was done mostly because there was a growing distinction between the people who attended services, and the priests and monks who officiated and sang in it. As the number of the latter grew, particularly in monastic chapels, it became necessary to enlarge the sanctuary. Secondly, whereas the earlier churches had wooden roofs, Romanesque buildings had stone roofs. This was done by building a series of semicircular arches. Since in an arch (or in a vault resulting from the juxtaposition of a series of arches) the weight of the structure produces a lateral thrust, it was necessary to build thicker walls, with very few windows, and supported on the outside by heavy buttresses—pillars of stone that added weight to the wall and balanced the outward thrust of the vault. For this reason, Romanesque churches had very little light, and windows were generally limited to the facade and the apse. Thirdly, during the Middle Ages it became customary to add to the churches a belfry, which could be either part of the main structure or a separate building.

Towards the middle of the twelfth century, however, Romanesque began to be supplanted by Gothic. The name "Gothic" was given to this style at a later time, by critics who thought that it was barbaric, something worthy only of the Goths, but has been kept as a designation for an architectural style worthy of appreciation. In spite of the great differences between the two styles, Gothic developed from Romanesque. Therefore, the basic plan of churches continued being the same, and roofs were made by vaults based on the principle of the arch. But Gothic perfected that principle by using pointed

*One of the most famous Gothic cathedrals is Notre Dame in Paris,
whose steeples were never finished.*

arches rather than semicircular ones, and by building the ceilings, not on the
principle of the "barrel vault" used by Romanesque, but rather with
"groined" and "ribbed" vaults whose great advantage was that the weight
rested on columns in the corners, rather than on entire walls. By repeating
the process, long and high roofs could be built without having to place them
on thick walls. But the lateral thrusts of such vaults was enormous, and thus
it became necessary to increase the inward thrust of the buttresses. This was
done, not by simply building heavier ones, but by use of "flying buttresses,"
in which, again using the principle of the arch, a pillar built some distance
from the wall exerted a lateral thrust that balanced the weight of the vault.

Thus, it was possible to erect a building whose main lines were so vertical that it seemed to soar to heaven. This effect was then enhanced by adding towers and spires, and by making the "nerves" of the vaults stand out and run along the columns all the way to the ground.

The entire structure no longer needed the heavy walls of Romanesque buildings, and this in turn made wide spaces available for stained-glass windows that illuminated the building with mysterious light effects, and also served to depict biblical stories, lives of saints, and the like.

The final outcome of these developments was—and still is—impressive. Stone seemed to take flight and rise to heaven. The entire building, inside and out, was a book in which the mysteries of faith and all creation were reflected. Inside, the long naves and slender columns, the multicolored windows, and the play of lights provided a worthy setting for the eucharistic miracle.

The Gothic cathedrals that still dominate the skyline of many cities are the legacy of the Middle Ages to future generations. There were cases, such as that of the cathedral of Beauvais, where the vault collapsed because architects sought to impose on stone an ideal verticality of which it was not capable. Perhaps this too was a symbol of an age when the lofty ideals of Hildebrand, Francis, and others sought to overcome the resistance of human nature.

32/The Collapse

> *It is better to avoid sin, than to flee from death. If you are not ready today, how will you be ready tomorrow? The morrow is uncertain. How do you know that you will live until then?*
>
> KEMPIS

The thirteenth century was the high point of medieval civilization. With Innocent III, the papacy reached the apex of its power. At the same time, the mendicant orders set out to bring the world to Christ, the universities developed impressive theological systems, and in Gothic art even the weight of stone seemed to have been overcome. In theory, Europe was united under a spiritual head, the pope, and a temporal one, the emperor. And, since the crusaders had taken Constantinople, it seemed that the schism between the Eastern and Western branches of the church had been healed.

But in all these elements of unity there were tensions and weak points that would eventually bring down the imposing edifice of medieval Christianity. Already in 1261, the Latin Empire of Constantinople had come to an end, and so had the fictitious union between East and West that the Fourth Crusade had accomplished. During the fourteenth and fifteenth centuries, new economic and political conditions would challenge the papacy and cause it to lose much of its authority. Nationalism, war, plague, corruption, and invasion would shatter the dreams of the thirteenth century, and open the way for the new order of the Modern Age.

New Conditions

The monetary economy, which had been developing during the last two centuries, became a dominant factor towards the end of the Middle Ages. Credit systems, trade, and manufacturing—obviously, in a minor scale by twentieth-century standards—gave increasing power to the bourgeoisie. The interests of this rising class clashed with those of the feudal lords. The frequent petty wars between nobles, the taxes that each imposed on goods crossing their lands, and the desire of the great barons to be self-sufficient, deterred trade and made it less profitable. For the bourgeoisie, a strong centralized government was highly desirable, for this would protect trade, suppress banditry, regulate coinage, and put an end to petty wars. Therefore, the bourgeoisie tended to support the efforts of kings to curtail the power of the high nobility.

Kings also profited from that alliance. Powerful nobles could afford to disobey their monarchs only as long as the latter did not have the resources to raise armies against them. These resources the kings obtained from the bourgeoisie. Thus, during the late Middle Ages, the growth of centralized monarchies went hand in hand with the rising power of bankers and merchants.

Out of this process developed several modern states. France, England, and the Scandinavian countries were the first to be united under relatively strong monarchies. Spain was divided among several Christian kingdoms and the Moslem one in Granada, and was not united until the end of the Middle Ages. Germany and Italy were not united until much later.

Nationalism became a significant factor during this period. Earlier, most Europeans had considered themselves natives of a county or a city. But now there was more frequent talk of a French nation, for instance, and the inhabitants of that nation began having a sense of commonality over against the rest of Europe. This took place even in those areas that were not united under a powerful monarch. Late in the thirteenth century, several Alpine communities rebelled and founded the Helvetic Confederation, which during the following century continued growing, and repeatedly defeated imperial troops sent against them. Finally, in 1499, Emperor Maximilian I had to acknowledge the independence of Switzerland. In Germany, although the country was not united, there were many indications that the inhabitants of the various electorates, duchies, free cities, and the like began to feel German, and to bewail and resent the foreign interventions that German disunity allowed.

Nationalism in turn undermined the papal claims to universal authority. If the popes seemed to lean towards France, as was indeed the case during their residence in Avignon, the English were ready to disobey and even oppose them. If, on the other hand, a pope refused to be a docile instrument of French interests, France simply had a rival pope elected, and all of Europe was divided in its allegiance to two different popes. The net result was that the papacy as an institution lost a great deal of its prestige and authority, and that many began hoping for a reformation of the church that would come from sources other than the popes.

The dominant political and military event of the fourteenth and fifteenth centuries was the Hundred Years' War (1337–1475). Although basically a conflict between France and England, this war so involved the rest of Europe that some historians suggest that it be called the "First European War." Edward III of England claimed the throne of France, held by his first cousin Philip VI, and this, together with the English invasion of Scotland, and France's support for King David of Scotland, led to war. Through a series of alliances, the war soon involved Emperor Louis of Bavaria, the kings of Navarre, Bohemia, and Castile, and innumerable other participants. Repeatedly the English invaded France, won impressive victories in the battlefield —Crecy and Agincourt—and were forced to withdraw for lack of funds. When a peace treaty was signed by both major parties, war broke out in Castile, and soon France and England were at war again. The English gained the upper hand when Charles VI came to the throne of France. The new king gave signs of madness; and, when it became necessary to appoint a regent, two parties developed that eventually went to war. The English took sides in the affair, and again invaded the country. They and their French allies were winning when Charles VI died. His son the Dauphin, whose party had been losing the war, declared that he was now king, and took the name of Charles VII. He was besieged in Orleans, and had little hope of truly becoming the ruler of France, when many of his former enemies decided that, now that his father was dead, they should support him. It was also at that time that he first heard of Joan of Arc, a young woman from the village of Domremy.

Joan of Arc claimed that she had had visions of Saints Catherine and Margaret, and of archangel Michael, ordering her to lead the Dauphin's troops to break the siege of Orleans, and then to have him crowned at Reims, the traditional place where kings of France were crowned. On hearing this, Charles sent for her, seemingly in disbelief, and perhaps to amuse himself. But Joan convinced him to trust her, and she was sent to try to bring into the city supplies that were sorely needed and which were stored in Blois. This she did, somehow crossing the enemy lines. Then she was allowed to lead a sortie against the besiegers, again with incredible success. Rumors circulated in the enemy camp of this young maiden clad in armor who every day came out of the city, and every day took one of their bastions. Finally, the siege was broken, and the enemy withdrew. The "Maid of Orleans"— as she was then called—did not allow the Dauphin's troops to follow the retreating armies, pointing out that it was Sunday, a day for prayer and not for battle. From that point on, the course of the war changed. The French, tired of civil war, flocked to the Dauphin's standards, and Joan was able to accompany him in triumphal march to Reims. This and other cities that had long held out against him opened their gates, and he was finally crowned in the cathedral of Reims, while the Maid of Orleans stood by the altar.

She wished to return to Domremy, but the king would not allow it, and she had to continue fighting until she was captured and sold to the English. Her former allies abandoned her, and it seems that the king did not even try to negotiate for her ransom. The English sold her for ten thousand francs to the bishop of Beauvais, who wished to try her as a heretic and a witch.

The trial took place in Rouen, where she was accused of heresy for claiming to receive orders from heaven, for insisting that these orders were given to her in French, and for dressing as a man. She agreed to sign a recantation, and was condemned to life imprisonment. But then she said that Saints Catherine and Margaret had spoken to her again, and rebuked her for her recantation. In consequence, she was taken to the Old Market Square in Rouen, and burned alive. Her last request to the priest who accompanied her was to hold the crucifix high, and speak the words of salvation loudly, so she could hear them above the roar of the flames. Twenty years later, Charles VII entered Rouen, and ordered an inquiry which, as was to be expected, exonerated her. In 1920, Benedict XV made her a saint of the Roman Catholic Church. But long before that she had become the national heroine of France.

By the time Joan died, in 1431, Charles VII had the upper hand. Soon the civil war in France ended, and by 1453 hostilities between England and France had been reduced to a series of skirmishes. When peace was finally signed, in 1475, all English possessions on the Continent, except Calais, were in French hands. (Calais would become French in 1558.)

This long war had important consequences for the life of the church, as we shall see in the rest of this chapter. Since, during part of the war, the popes resided in Avignon under the shadow of the French, the English came to see the papacy as their enemy. Later, during the Great Schism in which the entire Western church was divided in its allegiance to two rival popes, nations chose their allegiance partly on the basis of alliances and enmities created by the Hundred Years' War—and the war itself made it more difficult to put an end to the Schism. Finally, in France, England, and Scotland, the enduring international conflict strengthened nationalist sentiments, and thus weakened the claims of the papacy to universal authority.

Another event that set the stage for the life of the church in the later Middle Ages was the great plague of 1347. Bubonic plague, we now know, is transmitted by fleas, and black rats act as an intermediary host. Trade had improved greatly, particularly since the Genovese, by defeating the Moors, had opened the Straits of Gibraltar to Christian shipping. Thus, there was constant contact between northern Europe and the Mediterranean, and when plague broke out in the Black Sea, and moved on to Italy, it soon appeared also in northern Europe. In three years the plague swept the entire continent, and decimated the population. According to some estimates, a third of the population died of the plague or of related causes. After those three years, the storm abated, although there were new outbreaks every ten or twelve years.

The plague had far-reaching consequences. Economically, all Europe was disrupted. Entire markets disappeared. Unemployment increased drastically in areas where mortality had not been as high as in the rest of Europe. This in turn created political turmoils, riots, and further economic disruption. It would take Europe several centuries to find a measure of demographic and economic stability.

The plague swept through Western Europe,
killing most of the population of some areas.

The plague also had important religious consequences. Since in the new outbreaks those who died were mostly the young, who had not developed immunities, it seemed that Death had come to prefer younger victims. The nature of the disease itself, which attacked people who seemed perfectly healthy, led many to doubt the rationally ordered universe of earlier generations. Among intellectuals, this led to doubts as to the ability of reason to understand the mysteries of existence. Among the populace, it encouraged superstition. Since death was always at the threshold, life became a preparation for it. Many went on pilgrimage to the Holy Land, to Rome, or to Santiago. Those who were too poor to contemplate such long journeys went on pilgrimage to local shrines. The veneration of relics, and trade in supposed relics, gained momentum—in spite of the prohibitions of the Fourth Lateran Council. Fear was everywhere: fear of the plague, fear of hell, fear of the Supreme Judge, whom many had to face sooner than expected.

For many Jews, the plague brought death by violence. Christians could not understand why the plague seemed to make less headway in Jewish neighborhoods. Today some suggest that there were more cats and fewer rats in those areas, because among Christians cats had been associated with witchcraft. Whatever the case may be, at the time of the plague some came up with the simple explanation that Jews had poisoned the wells from which Christians drank. The result was violence and massacre. It was a time of fear, and fear demanded its victims.

While all this was taking place, Constantinople led a precarious existence. She had been weakened by the Fourth Crusade, and the ensuing period of Latin rule. When the Byzantine Empire was restored, some areas that had become independent from Constantinople during the struggle against the Latin invaders retained their independence. The Byzantine Empire, in spite of its high-sounding name, was little more than the city of Constantinople and its surroundings. The Turkish menace grew, and was stemmed only because the Turks themselves were more concerned with other enemies—the Albanians, Hungarians, and, in the East, the Mongols. In 1422, the Turks besieged Constantinople, but had to abandon the enterprise when they were attacked by other enemies. By mid-century, it was clear that the great dream of Sultan Mohammed II was to take Constantinople and make it the capital of his empire.

The Byzantine emperors had no other option than to appeal to the West. The price that the popes demanded was ecclesiastical reconciliation, and this was achieved at the Council of Ferrara-Florence in 1439. But this did not help the Byzantine Empire, for the Pope was unable to convince western Christians to come to the help of the beleaguered city, and the actions of the council did convince many of the Empire's subjects that their leaders had capitulated before heresy, and should not be defended. In 1443, the patriarchs of Jerusalem, Alexandria, and Antioch rejected the decisions of the council, and thus broke communion with Constantinople. The Russians took a similar position. Thus, Constantinople was friendless, and Constantine XI, who was then emperor, had no option but to continue his plans of union with Rome, and hope that somehow western Europe would come to his help. Late in 1452, after more than four centuries of mutual excommunication, the Roman mass was celebrated in Saint Sophia.

The days of Constantinople were numbered. On April 7, 1453, Mohammed II laid siege to the city. The ancient walls were no match for his artillery, which Christian engineers in search of profit had built. The besieged fought bravely, but the wall crumbled around them. On May 28, there was a solemn service in the cathedral of Saint Sophia. On May 29, the city fell. Emperor Constantine XI Paleologus died in battle. The Turks broke through the walls and the city was sacked for three days and three nights, as the sultan had promised his troops. Then Mohammed II took formal possession of it. In Saint Sophia, the great cathedral of the East, now resounded the name of the Prophet. Constantine's dream of a new Christian Rome had come to an end.

The Papacy under the Shadow of France

The foregoing section has dealt with a series of events that took place during the thirteenth and fourteenth centuries. They were the context in which the church moved in those difficult times. We now return to the end of the thirteenth century, where we left our story in the previous chapter—with the election of Boniface VIII (1294).

There was a marked contrast between the previous pope, Celestine V, and Benedetto Gaetani, who now became Boniface VIII. Celestine had failed because, in his austere simplicity, he was unable to understand the duplicity and intrigues of those with whom he had to deal. Gaetani, on the other hand, was well at home with kings and potentates, and in his diplomatic career had gained a deep understanding of the intrigues that were always brewing in European courts. Both were sincere men who sought to reform the church. But whereas Celestine had tried to achieve that reformation through Franciscan simplicity, Boniface would seek the same end through power politics. Celestine was one of the humblest men ever to occupy the throne of Saint Peter; Boniface, one of the haughtiest.

Not all were happy with Boniface's election. Besides the powerful Colonna family in Italy, who had hoped to capture the papacy, there were the extreme Franciscans or "fraticelli," around whom many rallied in support of Celestine. Among the fraticelli, as well as among some of the lower classes whose only hope was for a new age to dawn, many had come to believe that the election of Celestine had been the beginning of the "age of the Spirit" that Joachim of Fiore had announced. His resignation was a severe blow, and many refused to accept it, claiming that Gaetani had forced it. Others contended that, even if Celestine's resignation was voluntary, the powers of the pope did not include the right to abdicate, and that therefore, even against his own will, Celestine was still pope. When Celestine died, those who held such positions spread the word—probably false, or at least grossly exaggerated—that Boniface had mistreated him, and that this had caused his death.

In spite of such opposition, the early years of Boniface's reign were eminently successful. He felt called to pacify Italy, and in this he succeeded to a great extent. Against the Colonna, his most powerful opponents in Italy, he called a crusade that deprived them of their lands and castles, and forced them into exile. In Germany, Albert of Hapsburg rebelled against Adolf of Nassau and killed him. Boniface called him a rebel and a regicide, and Albert was forced to seek reconciliation under terms that enhanced the prestige of the pope. England and France were threatening to go to war in what proved to be a prelude to the Hundred Years' War, and Boniface resolved to make peace between them. When Philip IV of France and Edward I of England refused to heed his entreaties, he used greater force, and in 1296 issued the bull *Clericis laicos,* forbidding the clergy to make any kind of contribution to the secular power. With this he hoped to bring economic pressure to bear on the two kings, who in turn responded with measures against the clergy and the papacy, and continued their war. This, however, brought no results, for neither side was able to gain a decisive advantage, and finally both kings had to accept Boniface's mediation—although Philip made it clear that he accepted the mediation of the private person Benedetto Gaetani, and not of the pope. Meanwhile Scotland, faced with English invasion, declared herself a fief of the papacy. Although England generally ignored the protection that this was supposed to grant Scotland, Boniface saw in it further confirmation of the universal power of the pope.

Then came the year 1300, which marked the high point of his papacy. He proclaimed a great year of jubilee, promising plenary indulgence to all who visited the tomb of Saint Peter. Rome was flooded with pilgrims who came to render homage, not only to Saint Peter, but also to his successor, who seemed to be the foremost figure in Europe.

But relations with France grew tense. Philip granted asylum and support to Sciarra Colonna, one of Boniface's bitterest enemies. He further challenged the pope by confiscating ecclesiastical lands, and by offering his sister's hand to the emperor whom Boniface had denounced as a usurper and regicide. The correspondence between France and Rome verged on insults. The French ambassador before the papal court was offensive to the pope, and the king complained that Boniface's legate was just as offensive. Early in 1302, a papal bull was burned in the king's presence, and later that year Philip called the Estates General—the French parliament—in order to muster support for his policies toward Rome. It is significant that this session of the Estates General was the first to include, besides the traditional two "estates" of the nobility and clergy, the "third estate" of the bourgeoisie. This assembly sent several communiques to Rome supporting Philip's policies.

Boniface's response was the bull *Unam Sanctam,* which was quoted in the last chapter as the high point of papal claims to universal power, both ecclesiastical and political. He then convoked the French prelates to a meeting in Rome, there to discuss what was to be done with King Philip. The latter issued a decree forbidding all bishops to leave the kingdom without his permission, under penalty of confiscation of all their property. He also hastened to make peace with King Edward of England. The pope, on his part, conveniently forgot that Emperor Albert of Germany was a ususper and a regicide, and made an alliance with him, while he ordered all German nobles to accept him as emperor. At a session of the French Estates General, William Nogaret, one of Philip's closest advisors, accused Boniface of being a heretic, a sodomite, and a false pope. In compliance with the king's wishes, the assembly asked Philip, as "guardian of the faith," to call a council to judge the "false pope." In order to assure himself of the support of the clergy before the council gathered, Philip issued the "Ordinances of Reform," by which he reaffirmed all the ancient privileges of the French clergy.

Boniface's last weapon was that which his predecessors had used against other recalcitrant rulers, excommunication. He gathered his closest advisors in Anagni, his native town, and there prepared a bull of excommunication that was to be issued on September 8. But the French were aware that the confrontation was reaching its climax. Sciarra Colonna and William Nogaret were in Italy making ready for such an occasion, and, drawing on Philip's credit with Italian banks, they organized a small armed band. On September

7, the day before the planned sentence of excommunication, they entered Anagni and kidnapped the pope, while his home and those of his relatives were sacked by mobs.

Nogaret's purpose was to force Boniface to abdicate. But the elderly pope was firm and declared that, if they wished to kill him, "here is my neck, here my head." Nogaret struck him, and then they humiliated him by forcing him to sit backwards on a horse, and thus parading him through town.

Only two of the cardinals who were present at Anagni, Peter of Spain and Nicholas Boccasini, remained firm supporters of the humiliated pope. Finally, Boccasini was able to move some of the people, who reacted against the outrage, freed the pope, and expelled the French and their partisans from the city.

But the evil had been done. Back in Rome, Boniface was no longer able to inspire the respect he had commanded earlier. He died shortly after the episode of Anagni. His enemies circulated rumors that he had committed suicide, when in truth it seems that he died quietly, surrounded by his closest advisors.

In such difficult circumstances, the cardinals hastened to elect Boccasini as the next pope, who took the name of Benedict XI. He was a Dominican of humble origin and sincere piety, who sought to follow a policy of reconciliation. He restored to the house of Colonna the lands that Boniface had confiscated, forgave all the enemies of Boniface, except Nogaret and Sciarra Colonna, and extended an offer of peace to Philip. But this was not enough. Philip insisted on the project of calling a council to judge the dead pope. This Benedict could not accept, for it would be a serious blow to papal authority. On the other side, there were those who accused the new pope of excessive concessions to those who had attacked the papacy. He was thus besieged and criticized by both sides when he died, after a very brief pontificate. Soon the rumor spread that he had been poisoned, and each party accused the other. But there is no proof that Benedict was in fact poisoned.

The election of the next pope was a difficult matter, for each party insisted on one of its members being elected. Finally, through a subterfuge, the pro-French party obtained the agreement of the cardinals on the election of Clement V. This agreement was possible because the new pope, while seemingly taking the side of the defenders of Boniface's memory, had been in contact with the French. A pope elected under such circumstances would not be a model of fortitude or firmness. During his entire reign (1305–1314), Clement V did not visit Rome once. Although the citizenry of Rome insisted on his establishing residence in the city, Philip kept him occupied in France, and therefore under his thumb. During his pontificate, Clement V named twenty-four cardinals, and all but one were French. Furthermore, several of them were his relatives, thus creating and encouraging the nepotistic practices that would be one of the great ills of the church until the sixteenth century.

Clement's defense of Boniface's memory was no more forceful. He refused to agree to the council that the French wished. But the council was not necessary, for little by little Clement undid all that Boniface had done, forgave Nogaret and his companions, and even declared that in the whole affair Philip had acted with "admirable zeal."

The most shameful event of this weak papacy, however, was the arrest and trial of the Templars. This was one of the military orders founded during the crusades, and therefore it had become obsolete. But it was also rich and powerful. At a time when the king was affirming his rule over the ancient nobility, the power and wealth of the Templars were an obstacle to his policy of centralization. Since they were a monastic order, they could not be subjected directly to temporal power, and therefore Philip resolved to accuse them of heresy and force weak Clement to suppress the order in such a manner that most of its wealth would benefit the French treasury.

Unexpectedly, all the Templars who happened to be in France were arrested. Under torture, some were forced to confess that they were in truth a secret order opposed to the Christian faith, that in their worship they practiced idolatry, cursed Christ, and spit on the cross, and that they were sodomites. Although many stood firm under torture, those who broke down and agreed to confess what was required of them were enough to continue legal proceedings against the entire order. Among those who yielded was the grand master of the order, Jacques de Molay, who may have been convinced that the accusations were so preposterous that no one would give them credence.

The Templars hoped that the pope would defend them and protest against the injustice that was being done. But Clement did exactly the opposite. When he received the report from the king's officers as to what the Templars had confessed, he ordered the arrest of all the members of the order who were not in France, and thus precluded any action they might take against their incarcerated brothers. When he learned that the supposed confessions had been obtained through torture, he ordered that this be stopped, declaring that he would judge the Templars, and that the civil authorities had no jurisdiction over them. But the accused remained in prison, and the pope did nothing to free them. The king then accused Clement of being the instigator of the evils that the Templars supposedly practiced, and Clement, yielding once more, agreed to have a council judge the matter.

The council, which Philip and Nogaret had hoped would be malleable to their desires, proved sterner than the pope. Perhaps the bishops were shamed by the weakness of their leader. However, they insisted on hearing the case anew, and on giving the accused an opportunity to defend themselves. Finally, while the council dealt with other matters, Philip and Clement came to an agreement. Instead of trying the Templars for their supposed crimes, the order would be abolished by administrative decision of the pope, and the property it held would be transferred to another military order. The council, no longer having jurisdiction over the case, was dissolved. As to the wealth of the Templars, Philip took most of it by sending the pope an enormous bill for their trial, and insisting that payment for this bill take precedence over any other disposition of the property of the Templars.

Many of the Templars spent the rest of their life in prison. When Jacques de Molay and a companion were taken to the cathedral of Notre Dame in Paris in order to confess publicly their sins and thus silence those who said that a grave crime had been committed, they recanted and declared that all the accusations were lies. That very day they were burned alive.

Clement V died in 1314. His pontificate was a sign of things to come. In 1309 he had begun residing in Avignon, a papal city at the very borders of France. For nearly seventy years, while still claiming to be bishops of Rome, the popes would generally remain in Avignon. This period, often called the "Avignon Papacy" or the "Babylonian Captivity of the Church," was marked, not only by the absence of the popes from Rome, but also by their willingness to serve as tools of French policy.

After Clement's death, the cardinals were unable to reach an agreement as to who would be the next pope. They finally elected a man seventy-two years old, expecting that his pontificate would be brief and that during that time they would be able to reach a consensus. But this pope, who took the name of John XXII, surprised the world with his vitality and the length of his pontificate (1316–1334). With the help of the French, he sought to assert the power of the papacy in Italy, which was therefore involved in constant wars. In order to finance these, as well as his court at Avignon, John developed an elaborate system of ecclesiastical taxes that produced widespread resentment, particularly among those who opposed his pro-French policies.

Benedict XII (1334–1342), while promising the Romans that he would

For several decades the popes resided in Avignon, on the border of France.

return to their city, ordered a great palace to be built in Avignon. He also contradicted his promises to the Romans by having the papal archives moved to Avignon. Since he put all the resources of the papacy at the service of the French crown, and it was the time of the Hundred Years' War, his policies alienated England and the Empire, her main ally. Clement VI (1342–1352) tried to mediate between the French and the English, but it was clear that the latter saw him as a partisan of the former, and therefore his efforts were fruitless. During his pontificate, which was marked by nepotism, the court at Avignon rivaled those of great secular lords in its pomp and luxury. Since this was the time of the plague, many believed that this was divine punishment for the popes' absence from Rome. The next pope, Innocent VI (1352–1362) began making arrangements to return to Rome, but died before this could be accomplished. Urban V (1362–1370) was a man of reforming ideas who led a rigorously disciplined life. He reformed the court at Avignon, sending away those who would not follow his example of austerity. In 1365 he returned to Rome, and was received with great demonstrations of joy. But then he proved unable to hold the loyalty of his Roman subjects, and all over Italy there was such disorder that he decided to return to Avignon. The next pope was Gregory XI (1370–1378), who had been made a cardinal by his uncle Clement VI when he was seventeen years old. It was at the time of his election that Catherine of Siena came forth, calling the pope to return to Rome.

As a young girl, Catherine had joined the "Sisters of the Penance of St. Dominic." This was a very flexible organization whose members continued living at home, but devoted themselves to a life of penance and contemplation. Two years later, she had a vision in which Jesus joined her in mystical marriage, and ordered her to serve others. Then began a second stage in her life, during which she spent a great deal of time helping the poor and the sick. She became famous as a teacher of mysticism, and gathered around her a circle of men and women, many of them more educated than she, whom she taught the principles and practice of contemplation. Several of these disciples were Dominicans who were well versed in theological questions, and from them Catherine learned enough theology to avoid the errors of other mystics who had been condemned by the church.

In 1370, the same year of Gregory's election, she had another mystical experience. For four hours she lay so quietly that her friends thought she had died. But then she woke up, declared that she had had a vision, and set out on a campaign to have the papacy return to Rome. In order to do this, it was necessary to pave the way in Italy, where constant wars made it unsafe for the pope to reside. To that end she began a pilgrimage from city to city, and was received by multitudes who flocked to see her, and among whom stories circulated about her many miracles. All the while she wrote humbly but firmly to the pope, whom she called "our sweet father," but to whom she also complained of "seing God thus offended" by the long stay at Avignon.

Siena, in central Italy, was Catherine's birthplace.

To what degree this influenced Gregory's decisions, it is impossible to know. But in any case on January 17, 1377, amid general rejoicing, Gregory entered Rome. The long period of exile in Avignon had ended.

Catherine died three years after that event. A century later she was made a saint of the Roman Church, and in 1970 Paul VI gave her the title of "doctor of the church"—one of two women who have been so honored.

In summary, the long period of the popes' residence in Avignon had disastrous consequences for the life of the church. Since this was the time of the Hundred Years' War, and the popes were tools of French policies, those countries which were at war with France grew accustomed to seeing the papacy as a foreign power, and in them nationalism was soon joined to resentment against the papacy. Since the court at Avignon, and the constant wars and intrigues in which it was involved, required abundant funds, John XXII and his successors devised means to acquire them. When a position was vacant, its income for one year was to be sent to Rome. If the vacancy lasted longer, the income continued going to Avignon. Therefore, the popes had a vested interest in frequent and unfilled vacancies. This did not benefit the pastoral ministry of the church, which was repeatedly interrupted by frequent and prolonged vacancies. To this was added the sale of ecclesiastical posts—

the very simony that Gregory VII and other advocates of reform had deplored. Since ecclesiastical positions were a good means of income, there were some who held several of them, and who therefore were usually absent from their charges. These evils, usually called simony, pluralism, and absenteeism, were compounded by another practice for which many popes set the example: nepotism—the naming of relatives to positions of power. By the end of the Babylonian Captivity of the Church, there were many who were clamoring for a reformation of the church. Since the papacy itself was in need of reform, this clamor was often joined with attempts to limit the power of the popes, or to redefine it in purely spiritual terms.

The Great Western Schism

Catherine of Siena's dream seemed to have been fulfilled when Gregory XI took the papacy back to Rome. But the political conditions that had produced the "Babylonian Captivity of the Church" had not disappeared. Soon the difficulties were such that Gregory began considering the possibility of returning to Avignon, and probably would have done so had death not interrupted his plans. It was then that a situation developed that was even worse than the Babylonian Captivity.

With the papacy vacant, the people of Rome feared that a pope would

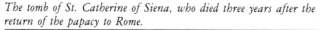

The tomb of St. Catherine of Siena, who died three years after the return of the papacy to Rome.

be elected who would be inclined to return to Avignon, or who at least would
again be willing to serve the interests of France, as had been done by a long
series of popes. There were grounds for such fears, since the French cardinals
vastly outnumbered the Italians, and several of them had indicated that they
preferred Avignon to Rome. There was the possibility that the cardinals
would leave Rome and meet someplace else, perhaps under French protection, to elect a French pope who would be willing to reside in Avignon. The
rumor of a possible flight on the part of the cardinals created a riot. The place
where the conclave was to meet in order to elect a new pope was invaded
by a mob that would not leave until they had searched the entire building
and made certain that there was no way for the cardinals to escape. All the
while, the mob, both in the building and outside, clamored for the election
of a Roman, or at least of an Italian.

Under such circumstances, the conclave did not dare elect a French
pope. After long deliberation, they chose the archbishop of Bari, an Italian,
who took the name of Urban VI. With great pomp, and the participation of
all the cardinals, both French and Italian, Urban was crowned on Easter
Sunday, 1378.

The crowning of Urban VI seemed to be the beginning of a new age.
He was a man of humble origins and austere life, who would clearly undertake the reformation for which so many were calling. But it was also clear
that in this he would clash with the many cardinals who were used to luxury,
and for whom their office was a means to riches and to the aggrandizement
of their families. Even the most cautious and levelheaded pope would find
great difficulty in implementing the much-needed reform.

But Urban was neither cautious nor levelheaded. In his zeal to put an
end to absenteeism, he declared that those bishops who formed part of his
court, and therefore were not in their dioceses, were traitors to Christ and
guilty of perjury. From the pulpit he thundered against the cardinals' ostentatiousness, and then affirmed that a prelate receiving any gift whatsoever was
guilty of simony and should therefore be excommunicated. Trying to wrest
power from the hands of the French, he decided to appoint a vast number
of Italian cardinals, so that they would be the majority. And then he committed the indiscretion of announcing his plan to the French before actually
implementing it.

All this was no more than the reformation that so many wished. But
Urban's actions against the cardinals gave credence to reports that he had
gone mad. His reactions to such reports were such as to make them even
more credible. Also, while claiming that he wished to reform the church, he
continued appointing relatives to positions of importance, thus making himself vulnerable to the charge of nepotism.

An ever-increasing number of cardinals joined the opposition. First the
French, and then many of the Italians, fled from Rome and gathered in
Anagni. There they declared that they had elected Urban under coercion,

and that such an election was not valid. They conveniently forgot that after the election all of them had participated in the coronation, and that they had not raised a single voice of protest. And they also forgot that for several months they had been part of Urban's papal court, without ever expressing any doubts as to the validity of his election.

Urban responded by appointing twenty-six new cardinals from among his staunchest supporters. This would give his partisans the majority in the college of cardinals, and therefore those who had defected declared that cardinals elected by a false pope were not true cardinals, and that it was time to proceed to the proper election of a pope.

Gathered in conclave, the same cardinals—except one—who had elected Urban, and who for some time had served him, elected a new pope whom they declared to be the legitimate successor of Saint Peter. The Italian cardinals who were present abstained from the election, but did not protest.

Thus an unprecedented situation developed. On several earlier occasions there had been more than one claimant to the papacy. But now for the first time there were two popes elected by the same cardinals. One of them, Urban VI, was repudiated by those who had elected him, and had created his own college of cardinals. The other, who took the name of Clement VII, had the support of those cardinals who represented continuity with the past. Therefore, all western Christendom was forced to take sides.

The decision was not easy. Urban VI had been duly elected, in spite of the tardy protests of those who had elected him. His rival, by the very act of taking the name of Clement, announced his inclination to continue the policies of the popes who had resided in Avignon. But it was also true that Urban gave no signs of the wisdom necessary to lead the church in such difficult times, while Clement was an able diplomat—though certainly not a pious man, as even his supporters conceded.

As soon as he was elected, Clement took arms against Urban, and attacked the city of Rome. Being repulsed, he took up residence in Avignon. The result was that there were now two popes, one in Rome and one in Avignon, each with his court and his college of cardinals, and each seeking the recognition of the various courts in Europe.

As was to be expected, France opted for the pope in Avignon, and in this was followed by Scotland, her old ally in the war against England. This in turn meant that England took the opposite tack, for the papacy in Avignon was a threat to her interests. Scandinavia, Flanders, Hungary, and Poland also took the side of Urban. In Germany, the emperor, who was an ally of England against France, followed the same policy, but many of the nobles and bishops who had reason to oppose the emperor declared for Clement. Portugal changed sides repeatedly. Castile and Aragon, at first supporters of Urban, eventually decided in favor of Clement. In Italy, each city and each ruler followed its own course, and the important kingdom of Naples changed its allegiance repeatedly.

Catherine of Siena devoted to Urban's cause the few years she had left. But it was a difficult cause to defend, particularly since Urban decided to create a principality for his nephew, and to that end became involved in a series of senseless wars. When some of his cardinals suggested that he change this policy, he had them arrested, and to this day the manner of their death is not known.

Since the schism was due to conflicting interests that went beyond the existence of two popes, when these died others were elected to continue their line. When Urban died, in 1389, his cardinals named Boniface IX. By taking that name, the new pope indicated that he would follow the policies of Boniface VIII, whose great enemy had been the French crown. But this new Boniface left aside Urban's program of reform, and his papacy gave new impetus to the practice of simony. Indeed, the schism itself encouraged simony, for each of the rival popes was in need of funds in order to compete with his adversary, and the sale of ecclesiastical posts was a convenient way to obtain such funds.

In 1394, the theologians of the University of Paris presented a proposal to the king that outlined three ways in which the schism could be healed: the first was that both popes resign, and a new one be elected; the second, that the question be settled by negotiation and arbitration; the third, that a general council be called to decide on the matter. Of these three solutions, the theologians preferred the first, since the other two would pose the difficult questions of who would be the arbitrator, or who had the authority to call a council. The king, Charles VI, followed the advice of the theologians, and when Clement VII died he asked the Avignon cardinals not to elect a new pope, for he hoped that the pope in Rome could be persuaded to abdicate.

But the schism, created in part by French interests, now had a life of its own. The cardinals in Avignon feared that if they did not have a pope their case would be weakened, and they hastened to elect Spanish cardinal Pedro de Luna, who took the name of Benedict XIII. If the king wished to insist on his solution, and force both popes to resign, he would have to face two parties, each of which had a pope, and not a Roman pope opposed only by a headless college of cardinals in Avignon. Charles VI pursued the new course he had set. His ambassadors tried to persuade the various courts in Europe to pressure both popes into resigning. In France itself, a national council withdrew its obedience from Benedict. French troops then laid siege to Avignon. But Benedict was able to hold out until changing political circumstances forced Charles to abandon his project, and declare himself once again in favor of the papacy in Avignon.

These events showed that Christendom was growing weary, and that if the two rival popes did not end the schism, others would. For these reasons Benedict XIII and the Roman popes—first Boniface IX, then Innocent VII, and finally Gregory XII—began a series of maneuvers to make it appear that they were seeking to end the schism, and that it was the other party that refused to negotiate. These maneuvers came to the point where Benedict XIII and Gregory XII agreed to meet in September 1407. In May of the following year, the meeting had not taken place. The two rivals were only a few miles apart, and Benedict finally went to the appointed meeting place, but Gregory refused to budge.

Before such refusal, and conscious that Europe was growing weary, the Roman cardinals broke with their pope and began their own negotiations with the Avignon party. France then withdrew her support for Benedict and his party, and once again took up the efforts to end the schism. The conciliar movement, which had been developing over the years, was about to see its day.

33/In Quest of Reformation

Therefore, the pope is not the head, nor are the cardinals the whole body of the holy, catholic and universal church. Only Christ is the head, and his predestined are the body, and each is a member of that body.
JOHN HUSS

T he sorry state of the church during the fourteenth and fifteenth centuries gave impetus to various movements of reform, each with its own program. One of these, the conciliar movement, hoped both to heal the schism and to put an end to such corrupt practices as simony and nepotism, without substantially challenging accepted Christian dogma. Others, such as John Wycliffe and John Huss, came to the conclusion that it was not only the life, but also the doctrine of the church that ought to be reformed. Still others vented the apocalyptic expectations that so frequently take hold of the hopes of the poor and the oppressed. To these various movements of reformation we now turn. The reader should note, however, that for the sake of clarity we are not following a strictly chronological order. Thus, while we continue our narrative at the point where we left it in the previous chapter, when Europe was seeking a solution to the Great Schism, we shall then have to return to John Wycliffe, who lived before the heyday of the conciliar movement.

The Conciliar Movement

Back in the fourth century, when Constantine saw the church threatened with schism over the Arian controversy, he had called a council. At other times in the centuries immediately thereafter, other crises had been solved by similar means. Later, as the popes gained power, the councils became instruments for their policies and programs, as we saw in the case of the Fourth

Lateran Council, which endorsed a long series of measures that Innocent III put forth. Now, as the moral authority of the papacy waned through the long decades of the Babylonian Captivity and the ensuing Great Schism, there were many who hoped that a universal council could destroy the great evils of the time, both by restoring unity and by reforming the church. As the conciliar theory developed, its proponents came to hold that a universal council, representing the entire church, had more authority than the pope. If this were the case, then it would seem that the question of who was the legitimate pope could best be settled, not by the popes themselves, who obviously could not agree on the matter, but rather by a council. The great difficulty standing in the way of such a simple solution was the question of who had authority to call a council. If one party or the other convoked the assembly, there was always the danger that the outcome would be prejudiced, and that the schism would not be healed.

This difficulty was solved when the cardinals of both parties, weary of the popes' refusal to negotiate, issued a joint call to a great council that was to gather in Pisa in 1409. Each of the two rival popes then called his own council to pre-empt the one at Pisa, but both failed. While still claiming to be the legitimate pope, each of the two withdrew to a fortified stronghold.

When the council finally gathered in Pisa, it had the support of both colleges of cardinals, as well as of most of the courts of Europe. Rather than trying to determine who was the rightful pope, the council declared that both

The council gathered at Pisa in 1409, seeking to end the schism and decide who was the rightful pope.

were unworthy and that therefore both the legitimate pope—whoever that might be—and his rival were deposed. The council then went on to take measures against simony and other evils, while the cardinals elected Alexander V to take the place of the deposed pope and his rival. Shortly thereafter, convinced that it had put an end to the schism, the council adjourned.

But the situation was now even worse, for the two earlier claimants to the papacy refused to accept the decisions of the council, and therefore now there were three popes. Although Alexander V was acknowledged by most of Europe, each of his two rivals had enough support to insist on his claims. Less than a year after being elected, Alexander died, and the cardinals elected John XXIII to take his place. Neither Alexander nor John was able to end the schism, and political turmoil forced John to flee Italy and seek shelter with Emperor Sigismund of Germany, who then decided that the time had come to call another council to put an end to the schism. (At this point, the reader may be asking, how is it that there was a Pope John XXIII in the fifteenth century, and another Pope John XXIII in the twentieth? The answer is that the Roman Catholic Church accepts as legitimate the line of popes who resided in Rome, that is, Urban VI and his successors. The rival popes in Avignon, as well as the two "Pisan popes" Alexander V and John XXIII, are considered antipopes.)

Since the Hundred Years' War was going against France at that time, Sigismund, the emperor whose refuge Pope John sought, was the most powerful sovereign of Europe. He offered protection to the fugitive pope, on condition that he agree to the convocation of another general council. This was done, and when the council gathered at Constance in 1414 John XXIII expected that the assembly would support him. But it soon became clear that his ambitions and lifestyle were not in agreement with the reformist goals of the council, and that he could not count on the outcome of its sessions. When the council demanded his resignation, John fled. For several months, he was a fugitive. But all his supporters failed him, and he was captured, taken back to Constance, and forced to resign. He was then condemned to prison for the rest of his life, lest he attempt to claim the papacy once more. Shortly thereafter, Gregory XII, the Roman pope, resigned, as he had promised to do if his rivals did likewise. After passing some decrees for the reformation of the church, the council took steps for the election of a new pope. The cardinals present, jointly with a commission named by the council, elected Martin V. As to Benedict XIII, the last of the Avignon line, he took refuge in a fortress where he continued claiming that he was the legitimate pope. But no one paid much attention to him, and when he died in 1423 no successor was elected.

Those who gathered at Constance had hoped, not only to end the schism, but also to begin the long process of ridding the church of heresy and corruption. It was with the first of these in mind that they condemned John Huss—to whom we shall return later in this chapter. However, when it came

The seal of the Council of Basel.

to evils such as simony, pluralism and absenteeism, the council found that it could do little more than issue some fairly general decrees. It therefore resolved to take measures for the continuation of what it had begun, and ordered that similar councils should meet periodically in order to make certain that the reformation that began at Constance would continue.

The next council, called by Martin V as had been ordered at Constance, gathered at Pavia in 1423, and then moved to Siena fleeing from the plague. Attendance was scarce, and once the council had passed a number of minor decrees Martin had no difficulty in having it adjourn.

As the date for the next council (1430) approached, Martin seemed disinclined to convoke it. But he became aware that conciliarism was still strong, and that his failure to call the council would provoke a crisis. He died shortly after the council gathered, this time in Basel, and his successor, Eugene IV, declared it dissolved. But the council refused to adjourn, and there was talk of sitting in judgment of the pope. At that point Emperor Sigismund intervened, and Eugene withdrew the decree of dissolution. By then the council, which at first had attracted little notice, had become the center of attention, and seemed to have gained supremacy over the pope. There were even those who suggested that it should meet indefinitely and rule the church directly.

Then a request for help came from Constantinople, which was threatened by the Turks. In order to secure such help, the Byzantine emperor and the patriarch of Constantinople declared that they were willing to rejoin the Western church and take part in its council, if it would move to a city closer to Constantinople. Eugene seized the opportunity to transfer the council to Ferrara. Most of the council refused to obey, but others, in the hope of ending the centuries-old schism between East and West, joined the pope's council at Ferrara. Thus, it happened that the conciliar movement, which had come to power as a response to schism in the papacy, was itself divided, and there were now two councils and one pope.

The council of Ferrara, which later moved to Florence, gained widespread recognition when, forced by circumstances, the emperor and the patriarch of Constantinople accepted its formula for reunion, which included papal supremacy.

Meanwhile, the council of Basel became more and more radical. One by one, its most distinguished leaders left it and joined the pope's council. What was left of the old council declared Eugene deposed and named Felix V in his stead. Thus, now there were two councils and two popes, and the conciliar movement, which had ended the papal schism, had resurrected it. But the remnant of the council of Basel, and the pope whom it named, made little impact on the life of the church. Eventually, the last members of the council moved to Lausanne, where they finally disbanded. In 1449, Felix V gave up his claim to the papacy. By then, it was clear that the papacy had won, and that from that time councils would be subject to it, and not vice versa.

John Wycliffe

In order not to interrupt our narrative, we have followed the course of the papacy and of the conciliar movement until the middle of the fifteenth century. In the conciliar movement, we have seen a program of reformation addressed mainly at moral and pastoral issues, such as simony and absenteeism. But at the same time there were other movements that sought to reform, not only the life, but also the doctrines, of the church. The two most outstanding leaders of this type of reformation were John Wycliffe and John Huss. Wycliffe lived during the Avignon papacy, and died just as the Great Schism was beginning. Huss, to whom we shall devote the next section of this chapter, died at the Council of Constance.

Little is known of Wycliffe's early years. He spent most of his career at Oxford, where he became famous for his erudition and his unflinching logic —although not for his sense of humor, which he totally lacked. In 1371, he left the university to serve the crown, first as a diplomat, and then as a polemicist. It was the time of the papacy in Avignon, at the service of French interests. Therefore, the English authorities welcomed Wycliffe's arguments on the nature and limits of lordship or dominion. According to him, all legitimate dominion comes from God. But such dominion is characterized by the example of Christ, who came to serve, not to be served. Any lordship used for the profit of the ruler rather than for that of the governed is not true dominion, but usurpation. The same is true of any dominion, no matter how legitimate, which seeks to expand its power beyond the limits of its authority.

Therefore, any supposed ecclesiastical authority that collects taxes for its own benefit, or seeks to extend its power beyond the sphere of spiritual matters, is illegitimate.

Naturally, these views were well received by civil authorities in England, involved as they were in a constant quarrel with the papacy precisely over the questions of taxation and of the temporal authority of popes. But Wycliffe meant every word he said, and soon his logic led him to point out that what he had affirmed regarding the limits of ecclesiastical dominion was also true of civil power. This too must be measured according to the service that it renders its subjects. In consequence, Wycliffe soon lost the support of those who had earlier rejoiced in his forthrightness.

At this time, his position also grew more radical. The scandal of the Great Schism encouraged this, and he began teaching that the true church of Christ is not the pope and his visible hierarchy, but rather the invisible body of those who are predestined to salvation—a point he drew from Saint Augustine of Hippo. Although it is impossible to know exactly who has been predestined, there are indications in the fruits that each produces, and this would seem to indicate that many ecclesiastical leaders are in truth reprobate. Towards the end of his life, Wycliffe declared that the pope was among those who were probably reprobate.

According to Wycliffe, it is true that Scripture is the possession of the church, and that only the church can interpret the Bible correctly. But this church that owns Scripture is the body of all who are predestined, and therefore the Bible ought to be put back in their hands, and in their own language. It was because of this claim that Wycliffe's followers, after his death, saw to it that the Bible was translated into English.

However, the point at which Wycliffe's doctrines aroused most controversy was his understanding of the presence of Christ in communion. The Fourth Lateran Council, in 1215, had affirmed the doctrine of transubstantiation. Wycliffe rejected this because he saw in it a denial of the principle manifested in the incarnation. When God was joined to human nature, the presence of the divinity did not destroy the humanity. Likewise, what takes place in communion is that the body of Christ is indeed present in the bread, but without destroying it. In a "sacramental" and "mysterious" way, the body of Christ is present in communion. But so is the bread.

Since these views contradicted what was then official dogma of the church, Wycliffe was declared a heretic by many at Oxford, where he had returned when his popularity with the civil authorities began to wane. Although he was incarcerated for some time, his prestige was such that he was allowed to continue his studies and his writing.

Finally, in 1381, he retired to his parish at Lutterworth. The fact that he had a parish, and that he had received this from the crown in gratitude for services rendered to it, shows the degree to which the evils that the reformers so deplored had spread throughout the church. Even Wycliffe, an ardent advocate of reform, had financed his life at Oxford with the proceeds of an ecclesiastical appointment. And later, when he was in need of ready cash, he exchanged that appointment for a less productive one, plus a sum of money.

Wycliffe died of a stroke in 1384. Since he died in the communion of the church, he was buried in consecrated ground. But the council of Constance later condemned him, and his remains were disinterred and burned. His ashes were then thrown into the river Swift.

Even while Wycliffe was alive, some of his disciples set out to preach his doctrines. It is not clear that this was done at his instigation, nor even that all who eventually received the name of "Lollards" were in fact Wycliffites. But in any case there was soon a substantial number of people who held beliefs similar to those of Wycliffe, and who set out to translate the Bible into English and to preach their understanding of the Christian faith. The name "Lollards" by which they were known was pejorative, and was derived from a word meaning "mumblers." They were convinced that the Bible belonged to the people and should be returned to them; that pastors should not hold civil offices; and that images, clerical celibacy, pilgrimages, and other such uses were an abomination. They also rejected the doctrine of transubstantiation, and prayers for the dead. In many of these tenets, they were forerunners of the Protestant Reformation.

At first, Lollardism had a significant number of adherents among the nobility, although it soon became a popular movement. At one point, they sought to have Parliament change the laws regarding heresy. But in this they failed, and their situation became precarious. Most of the Lollards among the nobility recanted and returned to the official church. A few persisted, and in 1413 Sir John Oldcastle led an abortive rebellion that led to his capture and execution. The movement then lost most of its support among the gentry. But it continued spreading among the lower classes, where it became more radical. A Lollard conspiracy, discovered in 1431, hoped both to reform the church and to overthrow the government. In spite of constant persecution, Lollardism never disappeared. Early in the sixteenth century, it enjoyed a revival, and many of its followers were condemned to death. Eventually, the Lollard remnant swelled the ranks of Protestants in England. But long before that time, Wycliffe's teachings made an impact on distant Bohemia.

John Huss

Bohemia, in what is now Czechoslovakia, became the home of another reformist movement, which ecclesiastical authorities were not able to suppress. Its leader was John Huss, a famous preacher and scholar who became rector of the University of Prague in 1402. From that prestigious position, and from the pulpit of the nearby chapel of Bethlehem, he advocated a reformation similar to what the conciliarists of his time were proposing. He had no intention of altering the traditional doctrines of the church, but only of restoring Christian life, and particularly the life of the clergy, to its highest ideals.

The writings of Wycliffe had been taken to Bohemia by a number of Czechs who had studied in England—where King Richard II was married to a Bohemian princess. These writings caused a great stir at the university, although at first the debate centered on technical points in Wycliffe's philosophical views. The university was divided between Germans and Czechs, and soon that division was reflected in the positions taken by various teachers vis-à-vis Wycliffe's philosophy, for the Czechs accepted it and the Germans rejected it, mostly claiming that it was outdated. Then some of the German scholars injected into the controversy the question of Wycliffe's orthodoxy, and thus put the Czechs in the difficult position of defending the writings of a man whose theology was questionable, and with whom in any case they did not completely agree. Huss in particular, while defending scholars' rights to read and discuss the works of Wycliffe, disagreed with him on the question of the presence of Christ in communion, and held the traditional doctrine of transubstantiation. Eventually, with the support of the king of Bohemia, the Czechs gained the upper hand, and the German teachers left Prague in order to found their own university at Leipzig. On leaving, they declared that they were doing so because Prague had become a hotbed of heresies, particularly those of Wycliffe. Thus, the debate over Wycliffe's writings contributed to give the rest of the world the impression that the Czechs were heretics.

The Council of Pisa had tried to end the Great Western Schism, with the result that there were now three popes. Bohemia supported the Pisan popes—first Alexander V and then John XXIII. The archbishop of Prague, who had clashed with Huss, obtained a papal decree banning the works of Wycliffe, and also ordering that preaching should take place only in cathedrals, parish churches, and monasteries. Since the chapel of Bethlehem did not fall in any of these categories, the papal decree practically amounted to silencing Huss. After deep soul-searching, Huss decided that he could not obey, and continued preaching. In 1410, he was summoned to Rome to answer for that act of disobedience and for others that followed. He refused to go, and was excommunicated in 1411. But he had the support of the king and the people of Bohemia, and therefore the papal sentence had little effect.

The conflict with the Pisan papacy led Huss to more radical views. First, he came to the conclusion that an unworthy pope is not to be obeyed. He did not question the Pisan popes' legitimacy. What he questioned was their authority when it was clear that they were acting for their own interests, and not for the welfare of the church. He thus came to the conclusion that the Bible is the final authority by which the pope as well as any Christian is to be judged. A pope who does not obey the Bible is not to be obeyed.

So far, Huss had said little that the more radical conciliarists could not accept. But then John XXIII proclaimed a crusade against Naples, mostly for reasons of Italian politics, and determined that the crusade would be financed through the sale of indulgences. Huss, who had bought an indulgence twenty years earlier, by then had come to the conclusion that only God can grant forgiveness, and that to sell what comes only from God is a usurpation. In this particular case, he was also incensed by the notion of a war among Christians being sanctified simply because it suited the pope's ambitions.

The king, who needed Pope John's support, ordered Huss to silence his protest. But by then his views were known, and there were public demonstrations against the exploitation of the Czech people by the papacy. John XXIII excommunicated Huss once again, and this time the reformer, who did not wish to involve the entire nation in the controversy, left Prague and his pulpit, withdrew to the country, and continued writing on the needed reformation. He was there when he received news that a great council was to gather at Constance, and that Emperor Sigismud invited him to defend himself before the assembly, and granted him safe-conduct to attend the council.

The great council promised to be the dawn of a new age for the church, and therefore Huss could not refuse the invitation. Perhaps he would be able to contribute to the great reformation that the council would undertake. Upon arriving at Constance, however, it was clear that John XXIII wished to try him directly, apart from the council. Huss was taken to the papal consistory and ordered to recant his heresy. To this he responded that he would gladly recant if someone could show him that he was a heretic. After that stormy interview, he was treated as a prisoner, first in his own residence, then in the bishop's palace, and finally in cells in various monasteries. The emperor protested against this violation of his safe-conduct. But, when he realized that Huss' cause was not popular, and that he would appear as a supporter of heretics, he prudently washed his hands of the entire affair.

On June 5, 1415, Huss was taken before the council. A few days earlier John XXIII, who had fled the city, had been brought back as a prisoner. There was reason to hope that the council would see Huss as an enemy of John, and dismiss the charges against him. But the council, like the emperor, wished to appear as a stern defender of orthodoxy. Therefore, Huss was in chains when he appeared before the assembly. Its leaders wished to have him submit to the council, and declared that all he had to do was recant his heresies. He insisted that he had never held the doctrines of which they accused him. They retorted that all he had to do was recant. This Huss could not do, for then he would be admitting that he had been a heretic, and that his Czech friends and followers were heretics. Finally, convinced that he could not obtain a fair hearing from those present, he declared: "I appeal to Jesus Christ, the only judge who is almighty and completely just. In his hands I place my cause, since he will judge each, not on the basis of false witnesses and erring councils, but of truth and justice." He was then sent back to prison, where many went to plead with him; for what the leaders of the council sought was a recantation that would affirm the assembly's authority, not a condemnation that would cause many to question its wisdom.

Finally, on July 6, Huss was taken to the cathedral. There he was dressed in his priestly garments, which were then torn from him. His tonsure was erased by shaving his head, which was then covered with a paper crown decorated with demons. On his way to the stake, they led him past a pyre where his books were being burnt. When he was tied to the stake, they gave him a last chance to recant, and once again he refused. He then prayed aloud: "Lord Jesus, it is for thee that I patiently endure this cruel death. I pray thee to have mercy on my enemies." He was heard reciting the Psalms as he died. A few days later his colleague Jerome of Prague, who had been the main proponent of Wycliffe's views in Bohemia and had decided to join Huss at Constance, was also burned. Their executioners gathered the ashes and threw them into the lake, so that nothing would remain of the heresiarchs. But some Czechs took back with them bits of the soil where Huss had died, to serve as a memorial of the crime committed at Constance.

The Bohemians were indignant, and almost unanimously repudiated the

In spite of his safe-conduct, John Huss was condemned as a heretic and burned at the stake.

council. Four hundred and fifty-two noblemen gathered in solemn assembly and announced their agreement with Huss, that an unworthy pope ought not to be obeyed. The council countered by ordering that the University of Prague be dissolved, summoning the rebellious nobles to Constance, and declaring that the King of Bohemia was abetting heresy.

In Bohemia itself, several different groups came together in their opposition to the council. The original Hussites were mostly members of the nobility and the bourgeoisie, but they soon had accepted the support of more radical movements arising from the lower classes. Most notable of these was the "Taborites," an apocalyptic movement that had spread among the peasants even before the time of Huss. The Taborites rejected everything that was not to be found in Scripture, whereas the true Hussites were willing to retain everything except what was explicitly rejected by the Bible. Another movement similar to that of the Taborites, but less radical in its apocalypticism, was that of the "Horebites."

The threat of armed intervention led these various groups to agree to *Four Articles* that would become the basis of Bohemian resistance. The first was that the Word of God was to be preached freely throughout the kingdom. The second, that communion would be given "in both kinds"—that is, that the cup, and not only the bread, was to be given to the laity. This was a conclusion that Huss had reached toward the end of his life, and which soon became one of the main demands of all Hussites. Third, all agreed that the clergy should be deprived of its wealth, and live in "apostolic poverty." Finally, the fourth article stated that gross and public sin, especially simony, would be properly punished.

Then King Wenceslas died, and his legitimate successor was Sigismund, the German emperor who had failed Huss at Constance. The Bohemians demanded that he agree to the *Four Articles,* that he grant freedom of worship, and that he promise not to name Germans to public posts. These conditions Sigismund would not accept, and at his request the pope called a crusade against the Hussites. Sigismund and his troops marched to the vicinity of Prague, but there they were crushed by a Bohemian army whose main contingent was Taborite. The Taborites had been joined by John Zizka, a member of the lesser nobility, who organized them into a fighting force. His main weapon was the peasants' carts, which Zizka armed with blades and turned into fearsome war chariots. In a second battle, the remnants of Sigismund's crusade were utterly destroyed. A year later, in 1421, an army of a hundred thousand "crusaders" fled before Zizka's carts. A third crusade, a year later, dissolved before it even met the enemy. Shortly thereafter Zizka, who had lost his one good eye in a battle in 1421, left the Taborites, who had become too visionary for his tastes, and joined the Horebites. He died of the plague in 1424. But the Bohemians continued the struggle, and defeated two other crusades in 1427 and 1431.

By then, the Council of Basel had come to the conclusion that the

Council of Constance had dealt unwisely with the Bohemian question, and invited the Hussites to attend this new council, in order to settle their differences with the catholics. But the Hussites feared a repetition of the events surrounding the trial and death of Huss, and demanded guarantees that the council considered offensive. Once more, the catholics organized a crusade against Bohemia. And once more they were defeated.

This last defeat finally convinced the catholics that negotiation was necessary. As a result of that negotiation, the church in Bohemia rejoined the rest of western Christendom, but was allowed to retain communion in both kinds as well as certain other elements of the *Four Articles*. Many Hussites, particularly among the nobility, agreed to this, and finally Sigismund was able to become King of Bohemia—although he died sixteen months later.

But not all Bohemians accepted this agreement. Many left the established church, and eventually formed the *Unitas Fratrum*—or Union of Brethren. Their numbers grew rapidly, not only in Bohemia, but also in nearby Moravia. During the Protestant Reformation of the sixteenth century, they established close ties with Protestantism, and for some time it seemed likely that they would become Lutherans. Shortly thereafter, the Hapsburg emperors, staunch supporters of Roman Catholicism, persecuted them. They were dispersed, and the *Unitas Fratrum* almost disappeared. From exile, their bishop John Amos Comenius (1592–1670) encouraged them and interceded on their behalf, hoping that some day the plant that had been so brutally cut would bloom again. These hopes were fulfilled long after his death, for later in our story we shall see the impact of a remnant of the *Unitas Fratrum,* by then called simply "Moravians." Another remnant became one of many churches following Calvinist theology.

Girolamo Savonarola

Late in the spring of 1490, a Dominican friar stood at the gates of Florence. A native of Ferrara, Girolamo Savonarola had spent most of his thirty-three years in study and devotion. This was not his first visit to Florence, where he had lived before. But the Florentines, who admired his biblical scholarship, had not liked his vehement preaching and his "foreign" accent—from Ferrara. Now he was returning at the invitation of Lorenzo de Medici, "the Magnificent," who practically owned Florence, and to whom he had been recommended by the famous scholar Pico della Mirandola.

In the monastery of St. Mark, which he joined, Savonarola began a series of sessions expounding Scripture to his fellow friars. Soon many others were attending the sessions, which were moved from the garden to the church, and the lectures became sermons. By Lent, 1491, his fame was such that he was invited to preach at the main church in Florence. What he said there about the evils of the time, and about the contrast between true Christian life and the love of luxury, offended many among the powerful. Lorenzo de Medici was particularly displeased, and hired another preacher to attack Savonarola. This failed, since the people of Florence took the side of Savonarola, and the other preacher decided to leave for Rome, there to plot against his rival.

When Savonarola was elected prior of St. Mark, some of the friars told him that it was customary on such an occasion to visit Lorenzo and thank him for his support of the monastery. The new prior responded that he owed his post to God, not to Lorenzo, and that therefore he would withdraw and thank God in prayer. Shortly thereafter, he sold a great deal of the property of the convent and gave the proceeds to the poor. He also reformed the inner life of the community, to the point that people commented on the holiness and spirit of service of the friars. Other monastic houses then asked to join in the reformation that had thus begun. Even Lorenzo, when he was about to die, called on the saintly friar to join him at his bedside.

Pietro de Medici, Lorenzo's successor, lost the respect of the Florentines. Charles VIII of France was marching south to claim the crown of Naples. Unwilling or unable to organize the defense of Florence, which lay on Charles' path, Pietro tried to buy him off. The Florentines were incensed, and sent their own embassy, led by Savonarola. Meanwhile, they expelled Pietro from the city. When Charles entered Florence, and made unreasonable demands from it, once again it was Savonarola who intervened, and as a result the Florentines became allies of France.

When Charles and his troops left, Savonarola's prestige was such that the Florentines turned to him for guidance as to their form of government. As he recommended, they established a republic, and took steps to restore the economic life of the city, which had been interrupted. Meanwhile, he also recommended that the gold and silver of the churches be sold in order to feed the poor.

It was at this point that Savonarola's program of reformation reached its high point. Although he has often been depicted as a fanatical and ignorant monk, he believed that study should be at the center of the needed reformation. For that reason, under his leadership the friars in Saint Mark's studied Latin, Greek, Hebrew, Arabic, and Chaldean. But he was also convinced that the luxuries of the time, and all the things that the rich valued so much, were vanity, and that lust for them was at the root of the evils that he deplored. Therefore, under his leadership, there were periodic "burnings of vanities." A great wooden pyramid was built in the main square, and under it were piles of straw and firewood laced with gunpowder. On the steps of the pyramid people then placed their "vanities"—dresses, jewelry, wigs, ostentatious furniture, and the like. Then, in the midst of much singing, processions, and other ceremonies, the entire structure was set on fire. Those great bonfires came to take the place of the carnival, which had been banned.

Savonarola's downfall was brought about by political circumstances. The

Savonarola and two of his associates were burned as heretics, their ashes thrown into the river.

pope—Alexander VI, one of the worst popes ever—made an alliance against France that included much of Italy, Germany, and Spain. It would have been advantageous for Florence to join the pope's party. But Savonarola insisted on keeping the promises made to Charles VIII. The pope responded with a series of harsh measures, first against Savonarola, and then against the entire city. It soon became clear to many Florentines that they were losing a great deal of their trade because their preacher insisted on keeping his word. Opposition to Savonarola and his policies grew among the wealthy. Those who supported him became increasingly convinced that he was a prophet, and demanded miracles of him. When something he had foretold became true, they grew even more enthusiastic. But when he failed to perform the miracles they demanded, they too turned against him.

Finally, a mob invaded St. Mark's. Savonarola refused to defend himself, or to have his friends take up arms against other Florentines in order to save him. He was taken by the mob, tied, beaten, and turned over to the authorities, some of whom had been plotting precisely such an event.

It was now necessary to find something of which to accuse him. He was tortured for several days, and the most his tormentors could make him confess was that it was not true that he could foretell the future—which in any case he had never claimed. The pope sent his legates to participate in the judicial process, and these too tortured Savonarola. All they could obtain was his "confession" that he had planned to appeal to a council. Giving up hope to be able to bring more specific charges against him, the judges finally decided to condemn Savonarola and two of his closest collaborators as "heretics and schismatics," without specifying the nature of their heresy. They were then turned over to the "secular arm" to be executed, for the church must not kill. The only mercy they received was that they were hanged before being burned. All three died valiantly. Their ashes were then thrown into the river Arno, to erase all memory of them. But in spite of this there were many who kept relics of the holy friar. When, years later, Rome was sacked by the Germans, some saw in this the fulfillment of Savonarola's prophecies. At various times since then, and even in the twentieth century, there have been in the Roman Catholic Church those who have argued that the Dominican friar was in fact a saint, and that as such his name should be added to the official list of saints of the church.

The Mystical Alternative

In spite of their many evils, and perhaps in part because of them, the fourteenth and fifteenth centuries were a time when mystics abounded. In Spain, England, and Italy there were remarkable mystics whose works were an inspiration for generations to come. But it was in Germany and the Low Countries, along the borders of the Rhine, that mysticism flourished.

The great teacher of German mysticism was Eckhart von Hochheim, generally known as Meister Eckhart, who lived in the late thirteenth and early fourteenth centuries. His mystical doctrine was essentially Neoplatonic, for its goal was the contemplation of the divine, the ineffable One. According to Eckhart, all words about God are inexact, and therefore, strictly speaking, false. "If I say, 'God is good,' that is not true. I am good. God is not." Declarations such as this were open to misinterpretations, giving the impression that Eckhart lacked respect for the godhead. Actually, his intention was exactly the opposite. What he meant was certainly not that God is evil, but rather that all language about God is analogical, and therefore inexact. In any case, his words show the character of his mystical thought, where he sought to exalt God by showing that no human concept can grasp the divine, and that therefore true knowledge of God is not rational, but intuitive. God is known, not by study or rational argument, but by mystical contemplation in which one is finally lost in the divine.

From all eternity, all creatures are in God. Before the foundation of the world, the ideas of all things that would exist were in the mind of God, the Great Artificer. This too is a characteristic theme of the entire Platonic tradition, and of the Neoplatonic mysticism that Eckhart embraced. On the basis of these views, he declared:

Within that true essence of the godhead, which is beyond all being and every distinction, there I already existed. There I willed myself. There I knew myself. There I wished to create the man I am. For that reason, I am my own cause according to my being, which is eternal, although not according to my becoming, which is temporal.*

This statement, and others like it, led many to consider him a heretic. It was said that he taught that the world and all the creatures were eternal, and that he confused God and the world, thus falling into pantheism—the belief that all creatures are part of the divine. He was especially accused of holding that the soul, or part of it, is not created, but rather eternal. Eckhart protested repeatedly that such charges were based on mistaken interpretations of his teachings. And it is true that he tried to avoid pantheism, as well as the doctrine of the divinity of the soul. But his expressions often left him open to such interpretations. Towards the end of his career, he was formally charged with heresy, and convicted of it. He then appealed to Rome, but died before the case was settled.

Although much of what was said about Eckhart's teachings was an oversimplification or an exaggeration, there is no doubt that there is a vast difference between his Neoplatonic mysticism and the Christocentric mysticism of Bernard of Clairvaux and Francis of Assisi. These two found their inspiration in the contemplation of Jesus as a historical human being, as God incarnate in a particular time and place. Eckhart, on the other hand, was not particularly interested in the historical time or the geographical place of biblical events. "Jerusalem," he said, "is as close to my soul as is the place where I stand right now." What he meant by this is that one finds God through inner contemplation, by "allowing oneself to be carried," and thus coming to God "without intermediaries."

Although during his life he was accused of heresy, after his death Meister Eckhart had many followers, particularly in his own Dominican order. Most famous among these were John Tauler and Henry Suso. These two, although less erudite than their teacher, were able to expound his views in terms that were much more accessible to those who had not been trained in theology. Through their works, Eckhart's mysticism gained widespread acceptance.

Further down along the Rhine lived the Flemish mystic John of Ruysbroeck. Although he probably read Eckhart's works, and on some points followed the German master, Ruysbroeck's mysticism was more practical, and more directly related to everyday life. This was carried further by Ger-

---

*Sermon on Blessed Are the Poor in Spirit.

hard Groote, another Flemish mystic who was greatly influenced by Ruys-broeck.

Ruysbroeck and Groote gave shape and popularity to what came to be known as the "modern devotion." This consisted mainly in a life of disciplined devotion centered on the contemplation of the life of Christ, and on its imitation. The most famous writing of this school is *The Imitation of Christ,* which through the centuries has been one of the most widely read devotional works.

Ruysbroeck and his followers also found it necessary to reject the teachings of the "brethren of the free spirit." These were mystics who claimed that, since they had a direct experience with God, they had no need of intermediaries such as the church or the Bible. Some may even have claimed that, since they were spiritual, they were free to let their bodies follow their own inclinations.

Perhaps Groote's greatest contribution was the founding of the Brethren of the Common Life. He gave up the sinecure from which he, like so many in his time, derived his income, and set out to attack corruption in the church and to call his followers to renewed holiness and devotion. But, in marked contrast with many others who had preached similar reformations, Groote did not call his followers to the monastic life. Rather, he insisted that, unless they had a genuine monastic vocation, they were to continue in their callings, and in them to follow the principles of the modern devotion. In spite of this, eventually many of his disciples did take up the monastic life, taking the rule of the Augustinian canons. But they never lost their interest in the "common life" of those who were not called to monasticism. For that reason the Brethren of the Common Life founded excellent schools where they trained, not only those who were to follow the monastic life, but also many who had other plans for their lives. Those schools stressed both scholarship and devotion, and became centers for the renewal of the church, for most of their alumni were possessed of a critical and reforming spirit. The most famous of these alumni was Erasmus of Rotterdam, who was a leading figure in the sixteenth century.

With few exceptions, German and Flemish mystics avoided enthusiastic excesses. Mystical contemplation as they saw it did not lead to turbulent emotions, but rather to an inner peace. This was to be attained, not through emotional stimulation of passions that waver, but rather through inner and firm intellectual contemplation.

The mystic movement itself was not opposed to the church nor to its hierarchy. Although some of its leaders criticized the abuses of prelates, and above all their ostentatiousness, most of them were content with the inner peace of their devotion, and felt no need to oppose ecclesiastical authorities. But, on the other hand, the mystical impulse itself tended to weaken the authority, not only of corrupt prelates, but of the hierarchical church itself. Indeed, if through direct contemplation one can achieve communion with the divine, such traditional means of grace as the sacraments, preaching, and even Scripture lose their importance. The mystics of the fourteenth and fifteenth centuries rarely reached such radical conclusions. But their teachings were a germ of doubt that in later years would increasingly weaken the authority of the hierarchy.

Popular Movements

Most of the foregoing has dealt with movements of reform among the wealthy and the educated. For obvious reasons, most of the extant sources deal with such movements. The poor and the ignorant do not write books about their dreams, which only find their way into books of history when they explode in violent confrontation with the powerful. But such dreams were numerous among the common folk in the later Middle Ages.

Wycliffe's teachings survived, not so much among the learned at Oxford or the nobles who espoused them, as among the Lollards who went from village to village, preaching a Gospel that contradicted a great deal of what the villagers heard from the authorities of the church. Indeed, it is highly unlikely that such preachers would have been able to find a following among the common people, were it not that the teachings of the Oxford professor came to confirm many of their hopes. The Hussites, at first mostly gentry and scholars, found their greatest support among the Taborites, who probably preceded them, and who derived many of their doctrines, not from Huss, but rather from common religiosity and from the apocalyptic expectations of the poor.

Something similar took place among women. For them, monasticism was practically the only way in which to lead a life free from direct dependence on their fathers, husbands, or sons. Thus, women flocked to orders such as the Franciscans and Dominicans. Soon the male leaders of these orders began to limit the number of women who could be admitted to the feminine branches of the orders. This, however, could not restrain the monastic impulse among women, and some of them began joining in small groups in order to live together in prayer, devotion, and relative poverty. Such women were dubbed "beguines," and their houses, "beguinages." Although the origin of these words is obscure, there is no doubt that it was pejorative, and it probably was somehow connected with heresy, of which such women were often suspected. Although a few bishops supported the movement, others banned it. Late in the thirteenth century, and for years to come, the church enacted laws against this sort of life which, while not part of an order under properly constituted authority, often shamed those who belonged to the official monastic orders. When men took up a similar life, they were called "beghards," and they too became suspect.

Another popular movement was that of the flagellants. They first appeared in 1260, but it was the fourteenth century that saw their numbers swell. Whipping oneself in penance for sin was not new, since it was a common practice in many monastic houses. But now it became a popular craze, with little connection with the hierarchy of the church. Thousands of Christians from all walks of life, convinced that the end was near, or that God would destroy the world if humankind did not show repentance, lashed themselves till the blood flowed.

This was not a momentary or disorderly hysteria. On the contrary, the movement had a rigid and sometimes even ritualistic discipline. Those who wished to join did so for thirty-three-and-a-half days, and during that time owed absolute obedience to their superiors. After that initial period, although they returned home, flagellants were committed to whipping themselves every year on Good Friday.

During the thirty-three days of their obedience, flagellants were part of a group that followed a prescribed ritual. Twice a day they would march in procession to the local church, two by two, while singing hymns. After praying to the Virgin in the church, they would return to the public square, still singing. There they would bare their backs, form a circle, and kneel in prayer. While still kneeling, they resumed their singing, and beat themselves vigorously, until their backs were bloody. Sometimes one of their leaders would preach to them, usually on the sufferings of Christ. After the flagellation they would arise, cover their backs, and withdraw in procession. Besides these two public flagellations every day, there was a third one, to be done in private.

At first the hierarchy saw no danger in the movement. But when the flagellants began speaking of their ritual as a form of penance and as a "second baptism"—as the early church had spoken of martyrdom—they were accused of seeking to usurp the "power of the keys," given only to St. Peter and his successors. In several countries they were persecuted. Eventually, the practice of public flagellation was abandoned. But the movement continued a clandestine existence for several generations.

Another movement that illustrates the mood of the time was led by Hans Böhm. In the village of Nicklashausen, in the diocese of Wurzburg, there was an image of the Virgin that had become a center of pilgrimage. In Lent of 1476, a young shepherd by the name of Hans Böhm began preaching among the pilgrims. Times were bad, for the crops had failed, and the bishop of Wurzburg oppressed the poor with ever higher taxes. At first Böhm preached mostly on the need for repentance. But soon he was moved by the poverty of his hearers, and his message took more radical overtones. He pointed to the contrast between the commands of the gospel and the greed and corruption of the clergy. Then he announced that the day would come when all would be equal, and all would work for a living. Finally, he urged his followers, by then more than fifty thousand, to act in advance of that great day, refusing to pay taxes and tithes. And he set a date when all would march together to claim their rights.

How Böhm intended to do this is not known, for on the eve of the appointed day the bishop's soldiers arrested him and dispersed the crowd with artillery shots. Böhm was burned as a heretic. His followers, however, continued gathering at Nicklashausen. The bishop pronounced an interdict on the entire village. But still they came. Finally, the archbishop of Mainz intervened and ordered that the church in the village be destroyed. Having no leader and no center around which to rally, the movement disbanded. But its echo could be heard for generations.

This was just one among many similar episodes. The last years of the Middle Ages were a time of unrest in which social causes joined with religious dissatisfaction and expectation. Ecclesiastical authorities benefited from the existing order, and usually gave their support to the powerful as they suppressed every movement of protest. In that atmosphere anticlericalism flourished, finding its basic inspiration, not in modern secularizing currents, but rather in ancient hopes of justice.

34/Renaissance and Humanism

*Oh supreme liberality of the Father God!
Oh, most high and marvelous joy of the
human creature, to whom has been granted
to have what it chooses, to be what it
decides!*

PICO DELLA MIRANDOLA

The last centuries of the Middle Ages saw a bifurcation of thought and philosophy. On the one hand, there were those who continued the traditions of scholastic theology; and on the other, there were those who looked back to classical antiquity for guidance and inspiration, and who gave birth to the Renaissance.

The Later Course of Scholasticism

After reaching its high point in Thomas Aquinas, scholastic theology was marked by two characteristics. The first was its constant search for ever subtler questions to pose, and for fine distinctions with which to answer them. This was joined with the development of a dense style and technical vocabulary that were far beyond the reach of the uninitiated. Its second characteristic was the increasing rift between philosophy and theology, between what reason can discover and what is known only through divine revelation.

Saint Thomas and his contemporaries had held that there was a basic continuity between faith and reason. This meant that certain revealed truths —such as the existence of God—could also be reached by the proper use of reason. But shortly after the death of the great Dominican theologian, others began questioning the basic assumption of continuity between faith and reason.

John Duns Scotus, the most famous Franciscan theologian after the time of Bonaventure, was appropriately known as "the Subtle Doctor." This was intended as a sign of respect. But it also points to a characteristic of late medieval theology that would soon turn many intellectuals against it. His subtlety and fine distinctions are such and so many, that his writings can only be understood by those who have spent many years studying the philosophy and theology of the time. Even so, it is clear that Scotus disagreed with those theologians of an earlier generation who believed that doctrines such as the immortality of the soul or divine omnipresence could be proven to be true by the sole and proper use of reason. He did not deny these doctrines. Nor did he deny that they were compatible with reason. What he did deny was that reason could prove them. At most, reason could show that they are possible.

This tendency became clearer in the fourteenth and fifteenth centuries. Typical of the time were William of Occam (c. 1280–1349) and his disciples. Starting from divine omnipotence, they reached the conclusion that human natural reason can prove absolutely nothing regarding God or the divine purposes. Most of them distinguished between God's "absolute" and "ordered" power. Given divine omnipotence, the "absolute" power knows no bounds. Whatever God pleases to do is possible. Nothing is above the absolute power of God—not even reason, nor the distinction between good and evil. Were it not so, one would be forced to declare that God's absolute power is limited by reason, or by the distinction between good and evil. It is only according to the "ordered" power that God acts reasonably, and does what is good. Strictly speaking, one should not say that God always does good, but rather that whatever God does, no matter what it might be, is good. It is God who determines what is good, and not vice versa. Likewise, it is incorrect to say that God has to act reasonably. Reason does not determine God's action. On the contrary, it is the sovereign will of God that determines what is to be reasonable and then, by the "ordered" power of God, acts according to those directives.

This meant that all the traditional arguments whereby theologians had tried to prove that a doctrine was reasonable, or even "fitting," lost their power. Take, for instance, the doctrine of incarnation. Anselm, and practically all theologians after him, had claimed that the incarnation of God in a human being was reasonable, since humankind's debt before God, being infinite, could only be paid by God made human. But theologians in the fourteenth and fifteenth century pointed out that, no matter how reasonable this may seem from our point of view, it is not so if we take into account God's absolute power. By that power, God could have canceled our debt, or simply declared that humans are not sinners, or have counted as meritorious something else, quite apart from the merits of Christ. We are saved by Christ's merits, and this is so, not because it had to be so, nor because the incarnation and passion of Christ were the most fitting means to that end, but simply because God decided that it would be so.

This also means that we are not to delude ourselves into thinking that there is something in the human creature which makes it particularly suited for the incarnation of God. The presence of God in a creature is always a miracle, having nothing to do with our capacity to receive God. For this reason, some of Occam's disciples went so far as to declare that God could have become incarnate in an ass.

All this does not mean that these theologians were unbelievers who enjoyed asking difficult questions for the mere joy of it. On the contrary, all that is known of their lives would seem to indicate that they were devout and sincere believers. Their purpose was to praise the glory of God. The Creator is infinitely above the creature. The human mind cannot fathom the mysteries of God. The divine omnipotence is such that before it all our efforts to understand it must cease.

This was not a disbelieving theology, willing to believe only that which reason could prove. It was rather a theology which, after showing that reason could not reach the depths of God, placed everything in God's hands, and was ready to believe anything that God had revealed. And to believe it, not because it made sense, but because it had been revealed.

This in turn meant that the question of authority was of paramount importance for theologians in the fourteenth and fifteenth centuries. Since reason cannot prove that a doctrine is true or false, one must make such determinations on the basis of infallible authorities. Occam himself believed that both the pope and a universal council could err, and that only the Bible was infallible. But later, as the Great Western Schism gave further impetus to the conciliar movement, many became convinced that a universal council was the final authority to which all opposition must yield. This was why at the Council of Constance the famous theologians Gerson and d'Ailly demanded that John Huss submit to the authority of the council. If he was given the opportunity to argue against the council, the assembly's authority would be jeopardized. And, since the power of reason was as little as they had claimed, there would be no authority left to put an end to the schism, to reform the church, or to determine what doctrines were true.

These late medieval theologians stressed the importance of faith, not only as belief, but also as trust. God has ordered the divine power for our good. Therefore, all of God's promises must be trusted, even though reason might lead us to doubt them. The divine omnipotence is above all our enemies. Those who trust in it will not be put to shame. This theme, typical of the late Middle Ages, would reappear later in Martin Luther.

Yet, no matter how devout these theologians were, their subtleties and their insistence on precise definitions and fine distinctions provoked the reaction of many who deplored the contrast between the complexity of academic theology and the simplicity of the gospel. Part of that reaction was the "modern devotion." The best-known book inspired by it, *The Imitation of Christ,* expressed what was a commonly held opinion:

> What good is it for you to be able to discuss the Trinity with great profundity, if you lack humility, and thereby offend the Trinity?
> Verily, high sounding words do not make one holy and just. But a life of virtue does make one acceptable to God.
> It is better to feel repentance, than to be able to define it.
> Were you to memorize the entire Bible and all the sayings of the philosophers, what good would this be for you without the love of God and without grace?
> Vanity of vanities. All is vanity, except loving God and serving only God.*

In summary, during the last centuries of the Middle Ages scholasticism followed a path that could not but provoke a negative reaction among many devout people who declared that this sort of theology, far from being an aid to piety, was an obstacle to it. With ever-growing urgency, the cry was heard for a return to the simplicity of the Gospel.

The Revival of Classical Learning

While scholastic theology continued along its road of ever-increasing complexity, others sought to revive the glories of classical antiquity. This gave rise to the Renaissance and to its counterpart in the field of literature, humanism. Both these terms, "Renaissance" and "humanism," have been used in so many different ways that they require some clarification.

The very name of "Renaissance," or rebirth, as applied to a historical period, implies a negative judgment on the preceding age. Those who first used it meant it precisely that way. They called the thousand years since the fall of Rome the "Middle Ages," because they saw in them little more than a negative intermission between classical antiquity and their own time. In calling the best medieval art "Gothic," they showed the same prejudice, for the word itself meant that this art was the work of barbaric Goths. Likewise, in giving the name of "Renaissance" to the intellectual and artistic movement that sprang up in Italy and spread to the rest of western Europe in the fourteenth and fifteenth centuries, they vented their prejudice against the centuries immediately preceding them, and claimed that what was taking place was a glorious rebirth of theretofore forgotten antiquity. The truth is that the Renaissance, while drinking from the sources of antiquity, also drew from the centuries immediately preceding it. Its art had deep roots in Gothic; its attitude towards the world was inspired as much by St. Francis as by

---

The Imitation of Christ 1.1.3.

Cicero; and its literature was deeply influenced by the medieval songs of the troubadours. Once this has been said, however, there is still ample reason to call this movement "the Renaissance." Many of its main figures believed that the immediate past, and perhaps even the present, was a period of decadence when compared with classical antiquity, and therefore made every effort to promote a rebirth of ancient civilization.

The ambiguity is even greater in the use of the term "humanism." This is the name given to the tendency to place humans at the center of the universe, and to make them the measure for all things. But "humanism" is also the study of the "humanities"—what today we call "liberal arts." In this last sense, it was employed by many scholars at the end of the Middle Ages and in the sixteenth century, who called themselves "humanists" because they were devoted to the study of liberal arts. It is true that many of them were "humanists" also in the other sense, because their study of classical antiquity produced in them a sense of awe before human creativity. But this was not always the case, for many of the humanists had a profound sense of sin and of the limits of human achievement. Therefore, when in the present chapter we speak of "humanism," this simply means a literary movement that sought to return to the sources of classical literature, and to imitate its style.

The revival of antiquity had many advocates, first in Italy, and then throughout western Europe. One of these advocates was the Italian poet Petrarch, who in his youth had written sonnets in Italian, but later preferred to write in Latin, imitating Cicero's style. He soon had many followers, who also emulated classical letters. Many began copying and circulating manuscripts of ancient Latin authors. Others visited Constantinople, and returned with copies of the works of Greek writers. When Constantinople fell to the Turks in 1453, Byzantine exiles flooded Italy with their knowledge of classical Greek literature. The result was a literary awakening that began in Italy and then spread beyond the Alps.

This interest in antiquity also manifested itself in the arts. Painters, sculptors, and architects sought their inspiration, not in the Christian art of the centuries immediately preceding them, but rather in the pagan art of the classical age. Naturally, they did not entirely abandon their own traditions, and for that reason Gothic art did influence their works. But the ideal of many Italian artists of the Renaissance was to rediscover the classical canons of beauty, and to apply them to their work.

This awakening of interest in classical learning coincided with the invention of the printing press, and this in turn had a profound impact on humanism. At first, the printing press was not seen as a means of popularizing literature. On the contrary, most of the early books printed were difficult to read, and were in either Latin or Greek. Furthermore, typography sought to imitate handwritten books, including the frequent abbreviations that copyists used at the time. For the early humanists, the printing press was an excellent medium for communication among scholars, or for duplicating the writings of antiquity, but not for popularizing their ideas. Those ideas remained the

A page of the Gutenberg Bible. The printing press had a profound impact on humanism.

exclusive property of an intellectual aristocracy. With the exception of Savonarola, the printing press was not used for communication to the masses until the time of the Reformation.

In spite of this, the press did have an impact on the literature of the Renaissance. Books were now more accessible, and scholars became aware of the degree to which various manuscripts of the same work differed. Although earlier generations had been aware of these divergences, all they could do was to be very careful in the copying of manuscripts. But now it was possible to produce several hundreds of copies of a book, without any new errors creeping into them. If a scholar, by comparing several manuscripts, produced a reliable text of an ancient writing, and supervised its printing, that work would be of permanent value, for it would not have to be entrusted again to a multitude of copyists who might introduce new errors. Thus the discipline of "textual criticism" arose, whose purpose was to apply all the resources of historical criticism to the task of restoring the works of antiquity. Soon there were scholars working on "critical editions" of Cicero, Jerome, and the New Testament.

The discovery of the extent to which mistakes had crept into ancient texts led to doubt as to the authenticity of some of the texts themselves. Since the manuscripts were not entirely trustworthy, was it not possible that some of the writings that supposedly were very old were in truth the product of a later age? Some of the most respected documents of the Middle Ages, when measured by the tools of historical research, were found to be spurious. Such was the case with the *Donation of Constantine,* in which the great emperor supposedly gave the popes jurisdiction over the West. The scholar Lorenzo Valla studied this document and came to the conclusion that its style and vocabulary showed that it was much later than the time of Constantine. Likewise, Valla offered strong arguments against the legend according to which the *Apostles' Creed* was composed by the apostles, each contributing a clause.

The consequences of these studies for the life of the church were not as immediate nor as drastic as one might expect. Valla was a secretary to the pope, who does not seem to have minded his studies and conclusions. The reason for this was that the results of such studies were circulated only among an intellectual aristocracy whose members were not interested in influencing the masses with their newly found knowledge. It would take some time for the notion to spread, that Christianity as it now existed was not what it had always been, and that a return to the sources was necessary. This notion would be a contributing factor to the Protestant Reformation.

A New Vision of Reality

Italy was going through a period of prosperity. In its principal cities there were financial resources for erecting great buildings, and for adorning them with works of art. Sculptors, painters, and architects flocked to such places. Since the nobles and the rich bourgeoisie were the patrons of the arts, most of the works of the period did not seek to extol the glories of heaven, but rather of those who paid for them. Therefore art, until recently devoted almost exclusively to religious instruction and to the glory of God, turned its attention to human splendor. In the classical works of Greece and Rome there was an admiration for the human creature that medieval art seemed to have forgotten, and which the painters and sculptors of the Renaissance expressed in paint and stone. The Adam that Michelangelo painted in the Sistine Chapel, receiving from God's finger the power to rule over creation, is very different from the frail Adam of medieval manuscripts. He embodies the Renaissance view of what it means to be fully human, born to create, to leave one's imprint on the world.

The same vision took flesh in Leonardo da Vinci. There were few human activities that this great genius of the Renaissance did not try to master. Although now known mostly as a painter, Leonardo also did significant work and research in engineering, jewelry, ballistics, and anatomy. His goal, which was also the ideal of his time, was to be the "universal man." His grand projects of channeling rivers, constructing new weapons, and building submarines and flying machines, never materialized. Many of his paintings remained unfinished, or did not go beyond the stage of preliminary sketches, which are now valued as great artistic treasures. But in spite of the fragmentary and unfinished nature of his work he became the embodiment and symbol of the "universal man" that was the goal of the Renaissance.

That vision of humanity as having unlimited capabilities, both for good and for evil, was the main theme of Pico della Mirandola, one of the authors

Leonardo da Vinci was the embodiment of many Renaissance ideals.

of the period. According to Pico, we have been given by God all kinds of seeds, so that we can decide which we are to sow within ourselves, and therefore what we are to become. Those who choose the "vegetative" seed, or the "sensitive," will be little more than a plant or a brute. But any who choose the "intellectual" seed, and cultivate it in themselves, "will be angels and children of God." And if, dissatisfied with being creatures, such persons turn towards the center of their own soul, "their spirit, joined with God in its dark solitude, will arise above all these things." All this lead Pico to exclaim, in a strange word of praise that epitomizes the Renaissance view of human potentiality, "Who can help but admire this strange chameleon that we are?"

The Popes of the Renaissance

Although the Renaissance was for Italy a time of great prosperity, it was also a time of upheaval. The "Babylonian Captivity" of the papacy in Avignon, and the Great Schism that followed, had affected her more directly than the rest of Europe. She had been the almost constant battlefield for rival popes, or for nobles and republics that supported one side or the other. At the time of the Renaissance, conflict between the old aristocracy and republican sentiments was constant, and therefore in cities such as Florence and Venice there were repeated upheavals that often led to armed encounters, not only in the cities themselves, but also in the surrounding areas. To this were added the constant intrigues of foreign powers—particularly France and Germany—which vied for influence in the region.

It was within this context of prosperity, intrigues, turmoil, and Renaissance ideals that the papacy existed during the last generations before the Reformation. When we last spoke of the popes, Eugene IV had finally asserted his authority over the Council of Basel. His reign was marked by his efforts to embellish the city of Rome. This was an early indication that the spirit of the Renaissance was taking hold of the papacy. Since then, and until some time after the outbreak of the Protestant Reformation, the goals and ideals of most popes would be those of the Renaissance. Most of them were enthusiasts of the arts, and one of the goals of their reigns was to attract to Rome the best artists, and to adorn the city with palaces, churches, and monuments worthy of her place as the capital of Christendom. Some were profoundly interested in literature, and did much to enlarge the papal library. Others were more like warlords who spent most of their time in military campaigns. Still others sought to increase their power through intrigue and diplomacy. Most of them were carried away by the spirit of the age, as could be seen in their love of pomp, despotic power, and sensual pleasure.

Eugene IV was succeeded by Nicholas V, who spent most of his pontificate (1447–1455) trying to gain for Rome political dominance over other Italian states. His goal was to turn the city into the intellectual capital of Europe, and to that end he sought to attract the best authors and artists. His personal library was reputed to be the best in Europe. He was ruthless with those who opposed his power, and had several of them executed. The fall of Constantinople took place during his reign, and he hoped to use the occasion to promote a great crusade that would enhance his prestige throughout Europe. But in this he failed, for his call went unheeded.

His successor was Calixtus III (1455–1458), the first pope of the Spanish family of Borja—known in Italy as Borgia. All that he took from the ideals of the Renaissance was the dream of becoming a great secular prince. With the pretext that it was necessary to unify Italy in order to resist a possible Turkish attack, he paid more attention to military campaigns than to his priestly duties. During his reign, nepotism reached new heights. One of the many relatives on whom he heaped honors was his grandson Rodrigo, whom he made a cardinal, and who would later become the infamous Alexander VI.

The next pope, Pius II (1458–1464), was the last of the Renaissance popes to take his office seriously. His achievements were not great, but at least he did not turn the papacy into a means to increase his power or that of his family.

Paul II (1464–1471) was an opportunist who, upon learning that his uncle had been made pope (Eugene IV), had decided that an ecclesiastical career was more promising than his current occupation in trade. His main interest was collecting works of art—particularly jewelry and silver. His penchant for luxury became proverbial, and his concubines were publicly acknowledged in the papal court. His main project was the restoration of the monuments of pagan Rome, to which he devoted a great deal of wealth and attention. According to some chroniclers, he died of apoplexy, as a consequence of his excesses.

Sixtus IV (1471–1484) bought the papacy by promising gifts and privileges to the cardinals. During his reign, corruption and nepotism reached new heights. The main thrust of his policy was to enrich his family, particularly his five nephews. One of these, Giuliano della Rovere, would later be pope under the name of Julius II. Under Sixtus, the church became a family business, and all Italy was involved in a series of wars and conspiracies whose sole purpose was to enrich the pope's nephews. His favorite nephew, Pietro Riario, was twenty-six years old when he was made a cardinal, patriarch of Constantinople, and archbishop of Florence. Another, Girolamo Riario, plotted the murder of a member of the Medici family who was killed before the altar while saying mass. When the dead man's relatives took revenge by hanging the priest who had murdered their kinsman, the pope excommuni-

The infamous Borgia pope, Alexander VI.

cated the entire city of Florence and declared war on it. In order to support his intrigues and the enormous expenses of his nephews and their supporters, he imposed a heavy tax on wheat. The best grain was sold to fill the papal coffers, while the Roman populace ate bread of the lowest quality. In spite of all this, posterity has forgotten most of Sixtus' misdeeds, and remembers him mostly for the Sistine Chapel, named after him.

Before his election, Innocent VIII (1484–1492) made a solemn vow not to name more than one member of his family to high office, and to put the Roman see in order. But as soon as he was made pope he declared that, since papal power was supreme, he was not bound by his oath, especially one made under pressure. He was the first pope to acknowledge several of his illegitimate children, on whom he heaped honors and riches. The sale of indulgences became a shameless business proposition, under the management of one of his sons. In 1484 he ordered that Christendom be cleansed of witches, and the result was the death of hundreds of innocent women.

After Innocent's death, Rodrigo Borgia bought the cardinals' votes and became pope under the name of Alexander VI (1492–1503). Under him, papal corruption reached its peak. He was a strong and implacable man, who was said to commit publicly all the capital sins—except gluttony, for his digestion was not good. A chronicler affirms that the people used to say: "Alexander is ready to sell the keys, the altars, and even Christ himself. He is within his rights, since he bought them." While Europe trembled before the threat of the Turks, the pope had secret dealings with the sultan. His concubines, who were legally the wives of others in his court, gave him several children whom he acknowledged publicly. The most famous of these were Cesare and Lucrezia Borgia. Even though the worst stories told about this family are probably untrue, those that are undeniable are still enough to convict the pope of corruption and boundless lust for power. Italy, bathed in blood due to his plots and his wars, was ready to believe the worst of him, and the prestige of the papacy suffered accordingly.

Alexander VI died unexpectedly—some said that he took by mistake a potion that he had prepared for someone else. His son Cesare, who had hoped to take hold of the papacy at his father's death, was in bed suffering from the same disease—or the same poison—and was therefore unable to set his plans in motion. The election thus fell on Pius III, a man of reforming zeal who undertook the difficult task of bringing peace to Italy. But he died after being pope for twenty-six days, and the new pope was a worthy successor of Alexander VI.

Julius II (1503–1513), who had been made a cardinal by his uncle Sixtus IV, took that name to indicate that his model was not a Christian saint, but rather Julius Caesar. Like most of the popes of that period, he was a patron of the arts. It was during his pontificate that Michelangelo finished painting the Sistine Chapel, and Raphael decorated the Vatican with his famous frescoes. But Julius' favorite pastime was war. He reorganized the papal guard, dressed it in colorful uniforms that Michelangelo is said to have designed, and led it to battle. His military and diplomatic abilities were such that some even thought that he might finally achieve the unification of Italy, with Julius as its leader. France and Germany opposed these plans, but Julius defeated them in both diplomacy and the battlefield. In 1513, death put an end to the projects of this pope, whom his contemporaries called "the Terrible."

He was succeeded by a son of Lorenzo the Magnificent, Giovanni de Medici, who took the name of Leo X (1513–1521). Following his father's example, Leo was a patron of the arts. He also tried to consolidate the political and military gains of Julius II. In this he failed, and in 1516 he was forced to sign an agreement with Francis I of France that gave the king enormous authority in French ecclesiastical affairs. His passion for the arts overshadowed any religious or pastoral concerns, and his great dream was to complete the great basilica of St. Peter, in Rome. The financing of that project was one of the purposes of the sale of indulgences that provoked Luther's protest. Thus, the man occupying the papacy when the Protestant Reformation began was unequal to the challenge before him.

Suggested Readings

Aziz S. Atiya. *History of Eastern Christianity.* Notre Dame: University of Notre Dame Press, 1967.

Justo L. González. *A History of Christian Thought,* Vol. 2. Nashville: Abingdon, 1971.

Charles Homer Haskins. *The Renaissance of the Twelfth Century.* New York: Meridian Books, 1957.

Friedrich Heer. *The Medieval World.* New York: New American Library, 1961.

J. Huizinga. *The Waning of the Middle Ages.* New York: Doubleday, n.d.

David Knowles. *From Pachomius to Ignatius: A Study of the Constitutional History of Religious Orders.* Oxford: Clarendon Press, 1966.

Gordon Leff. *Heresy in the Later Middle Ages.* 2 vols. Manchester: Manchester University Press, 1967.

Gordon Leff. *Medieval Thought: St. Augustine to Ockham.* Baltimore: Penguin Books, 1958.

H. St. L. B. Moss. *The Birth of the Middle Ages: 395–814.* Oxford: University Press, 1935.

George Ostrogorsky. *History of the Byzantine State.* New Brunswick: Rutgers University Press, 1957.

Roberto Ridolfi. *The Life of Girolamo Savonarola.* London: Routledge and Kegan Paul, 1959.

R. V. Sellers. *The Council of Chalcedon: A Historical and Doctrinal Survey.* London: S.P.C.K., 1953.

Desmond Seward. *The Hundred Years War.* New York: Atheneum, 1978.

Barbara W. Tuchman. *A Distant Mirror: The Calamitous 14th Century.* New York: Alfred A. Knopf, 1978.

Herbert B. Workman. *The Evolution of the Monastic Ideal.* London: Charles H. Kelly, 1913.

PART IV

THE BEGINNINGS OF COLONIAL CHRISTIANITY

Chronology

Events	Date
†Henry the Navigator	1460
Surrender of Granada; Columbus' first voyage	1492
Vasco da Gama travels to India	1497–1498
Alvares Cabral discovers Brazil	1500
Portuguese settle in Goa	1510
Balboa reaches the Pacific	1513
Ponce de León to Florida; Siege and fall of Tenochtitlan	1521
Capture of Atahualpa	1532
De Soto reaches the Mississippi	1541
†Francis Xavier	1552
Villegagnon settles in Brazil	1555
Portuguese settle in Macao	1557
Jean Ribaut in Florida	1562
†Las Casas	1566
†Luis Beltrán	1581
Ricci in Peking	1601
†Toribio Alfonso de Mogrovejo	1606
†Pedro Claver	1654
Jesuits expelled from Spanish colonies	1767
Tupac Amaru rebellion	1780

NOTE: Since this period coincides chronologically with others discussed in the second volume, the reader may refer to the chronologies in that volume for dates of popes, rulers, and events in Europe.

35/Spain and the New World

Diligently seek to encourage and attract the
natives of said Indies to all peace and
quiet, that they may willingly serve us and
be under our dominion and government,
and above all that they may be converted to
our holy catholic faith.
ISABELLA AND FERDINAND

Towards the end of the Middle Ages, and during the time of the
Protestant Reformation, Spain and Portugal began a process of
expansion that would have enormous consequences for the later
history of the church. Protestant church historians, preoccupied
with the momentous events that were taking place in Europe at the time, often
forget that it was precisely during this period that catholicism enjoyed its most
rapid expansion. The same is true of many catholic historians. Such an omis-
sion, which was perhaps defensible at an earlier time, has become inexcusable
in the twentieth century, after the Second Vatican Council. At that council,
and in the life of the church thereafter, the impact of Roman Catholics from
Latin America, Asia, and Africa has been prominent. Therefore, in order to
understand the course of Roman Catholicism in the twentieth century, it is
necessary to understand the forces that shaped it in those lands.

The Nature of the Spanish Enterprise

When, on October 12, 1492, Christopher Columbus and his companions set
foot on the New World, neither he nor anyone in Europe had the remotest
idea of the significance of that event. But as soon as Ferdinand and Isabella

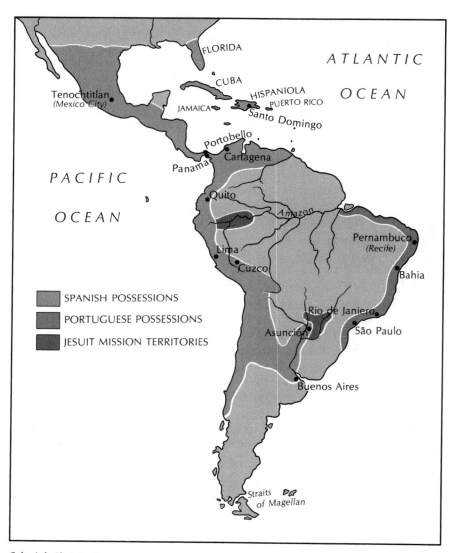

Colonial Christianity

had an inkling of the vast lands and huge sums that could be involved, they took steps to limit Columbus' power. Their reason for doing this was not simple greed, but the experience of long years of struggle to assert their authority in Spain. There, with the help of the bourgeoisie, they were finally managing to curb the power of the potentates, both lay and clerical, who had wrecked the earlier reign of Isabella's brother, Henry IV of Castile. Therefore, they feared the rise of similar magnates in the New World, and their policies were aimed at curbing them. Columbus, as Admiral of the Ocean Sea, Viceroy and Governor General, and as beneficiary of one-tenth of all trade with the New World, would have been able to refuse obedience to the crown, and therefore the sovereigns could not grant him such wealth and power.

In the New World, this usually resulted in the crown enacting laws for the protection of the Indians. Ferdinand and Isabella feared that, if the Spanish conquistadores were not curbed in their exploitation of the Indians, they would become powerful feudal lords with the same independent spirit as the grandees of Spain. This gave rise to constant conflicts between the crown and the Spanish settlers. Repeatedly, laws were enacted in Spain that were not obeyed in the New World. The net result was that the Indians were exploited and decimated, while Spaniards on both sides of the ocean deliberated as to what was the best course to follow.

Religious policies in the new lands followed the patterns that had been established during the Middle Ages. In their wars against the Moors in Spain, Christian Spaniards had drawn on the ideals and principles of the crusades, and now they applied the same principles to the conquest of the Indian "infidels." Also, shortly before the discovery of the New World, Castile had conquered the Canary Islands and Granada, and the popes had granted the crown extraordinary powers over the church in the newly conquered lands. These precedents were now applied in the New World. In a series of bulls from 1493 to 1510, popes Alexander VI and Julius II gave enormous authority to the Spanish crown. The kings of Spain were given the right of "royal patronage"—*patronato real*—over the church in the new lands. As this evolved, it meant that the kings had the right to nominate—and therefore practically to appoint—bishops and other high ecclesiastical officers for the New World. With few exceptions, the crown was also to administer tithes and other offerings, and to be responsible for all the expenses of the church. The result was that the church in Spanish America had very few direct dealings with Rome, and became practically a national church under the leadership of the Spanish kings and their appointees. Although some of the bishops selected by the crown were faithful pastors of their flocks, most of them, especially in later years, were political appointees who had no understanding of, nor concern for, the plight of the masses in Spanish America.

There was, however, another side to the church in the New World. Those who carried out missionary work—usually Franciscans, Dominicans, or Jesuits—lived among the people, and knew their plight. The vows of poverty of these missionaries, and the simplicity of their lifestyle, made it possible for them to live among the Indians, and to see the disastrous results of colonial policies. Thus, the friars became the defenders of the Indians against the depredations of European settlers. The defense of the Indians was taken up by many Dominicans. In the eighteenth century, that defense was one of the factors contributing to the suppression of the Jesuits. And all the while, far above this church that showed concern for the poor, there was the hierarchical church, led by those who owed their posts to their contacts in court.

In the nineteenth century, when the old colonies began their struggle for independence, the church would be divided along similar lines, and for that reason, while most of the bishops were loyalists, many parish priests and friars cast their lot with the rebels. In the latter half of the twentieth century, the revival of Roman Catholicism in Latin America, and the leading role it took in many social struggles, would be due in part to the inroads that the church of the poor was making among the hierarchy.

The Protest

The first open protest against the exploitation of the Indians was a sermon preached in Santo Domingo in 1511 by the Dominican Antonio Montesinos. Local authorities tried to silence him, but his fellow Dominicans rallied to his support, and eventually the dispute reached the court in Spain.

Among those who heard Montesinos was Bartolomé de Las Casas. He had settled in Santo Domingo almost ten years earlier, and at some point had been ordained a priest—probably the first ever to be ordained in the New World. But he was not overly troubled by the exploitation of the Indians. In fact, he himself held several of them in *encomienda*.

The system of *encomiendas*—trusts—was the main abuse against which the Dominicans protested. It was forbidden to enslave the Indians. But, supposedly in order to civilize them and to teach them Christian doctrine, groups of them were "entrusted" to a settler. In exchange for the settler's guidance, the Indians were to work for him. The result was even worse than outright slavery, for those who held trusts—the *encomenderos*—had no investment in the Indians, and therefore no reason to be concerned for their well-being.

Las Casas had an *encomienda* when Montesinos began preaching against this practice. When the debate broke out, he chose to remain silent. Then, on Pentecost 1514, he had a radical change of heart. He gave up his *encomienda,* and from that point on openly declared that Christian faith was incompatible with the exploitation of the Indians by the Spanish. With Montesinos, he traveled to Spain, and convinced authorities to appoint a commission to investigate the matter. When he found that the members of the commission would listen only to the *encomenderos,* he broke with them and returned to Spain. Thus began a long career of repeated crossings of the Atlantic, obtaining in Spain legislation protecting the Indians, and finding in the New World that the authorities were unwilling or unable to apply such legislation. At one point, he tried to set an example of pacific evangelization in Venezuela. But neighboring settlers provoked violence, and finally the Indians rebelled. He then returned to Santo Domingo, where he finally joined the Dominican order. Further travels took him to Central America, Mexico, and again to Spain. He had many sympathizers in the Spanish court, and was made bishop of Chiapas, in southern Mexico. After many clashes with the *encomenderos* in his flock, he resigned and returned to Spain. There he spent thirty-nine years of advocacy for the Indians, partly through direct appeals and partly through his books. He died in 1566, when he was ninety-two years old.

Las Casas' books caused quite a stir, and many came to doubt the morality of the entire Spanish enterprise in the New World. But eventually the vested interests of those who profited from the colonial empire prevailed. In 1552, while Las Casas still lived, his books were banned in Peru. By the middle of the following century, they were included in the Inquisition's list of forbidden books.

Another Dominican who questioned the Spanish enterprise in the New World was Francisco de Vitoria, a professor of theology at the University of Salamanca. Disturbed by the news of the conquest of Peru, and of the atrocities committed by the Spanish, Vitoria gave a series of lectures questioning the right of the Spanish to take the territories of the Indians.

The main result of the protests of Las Casas, Vitoria, and others were the *New Laws of Indies,* enacted by Charles V in 1542. These laws limited the power of the Spanish settlers over the Indians, and outlawed war against any Indians who were willing to live in peace with the Spanish. They were largely ignored in the New World. In Peru, the settlers openly revolted. Eventually, the *New Laws* were forgotten. Throughout the colonial period, however, there were in Spanish America Christians who protested against the exploitation of the Indians, and who devoted their lives to the betterment of their lot.

The Caribbean

In his second voyage, Columbus took with him seven missionaries whose appointed task was to convert the Indians. But when the Spanish arrived at the small fort that Columbus had left in Hispaniola, they found distressing news. Their mistreatment, exploitation, and rape by the Spaniards had provoked the Indians to revolt, and they had destroyed the fort and killed the entire garrison. Columbus ordered the "pacification" of the island, giving his lieutenants instructions to cut the ears and nose of any who would not submit. Soon, however, there were also rebels among the Spaniards. Reports of mismanagement and tyranny in the colony provoked Isabella to action, and Columbus was deposed and taken back to Spain in chains.

Under Columbus' successors, things were no better for the Indians. They were ordered to pay a quarterly tax to the Spaniards in gold or cotton. Those who were unwilling or unable to pay the tax were enslaved. The Indians then took to the mountains, where they were hunted with dogs. As to the missionaries, they seem to have done little more than take some of the sons of Indian chiefs into their homes, there to educate them as Christians. In 1503, orders arrived from Spain that the Indians were to live in their own villages, each with a representative of the Spanish government and a chaplain. This was done in some cases. But then those who were able to work were marched off to mine for gold, and kept away from their families for months. In the end, forced labor, diseases imported by the Spanish, and mass suicides destroyed most of the native population. Similar events took place in Puerto Rico, Cuba, Jamaica, and several of the lesser islands.

The loss of Indian labor led the Spanish to import black slaves. The first arrived from Spain in 1502, but for another few years Indian labor was still too cheap to encourage black slavery. In 1516, Las Casas, in his zeal for the well-being of the Indians, suggested that slaves be imported from Africa. He soon recanted, and became a defender of blacks as well as of Indians. But, by 1553, tens of thousands of Africans were being imported as slaves. It is significant that the few theologians who objected did so, not on the basis of opposition to slavery, but rather because they had doubts as to how the profits should be distributed. In any case, what happened in the Caribbean was repeated throughout the Spanish colonies. Wherever the Indian population was scarce, black African slaves took their place. To this day, blacks are more numerous in areas where the Indian population was low in the sixteenth century.

Mexico

In his march to Tenochtitlan—the capital city of the Aztec empire—Cortez destroyed the idols of the various tribes he visited. He did not do this, however, in the case of the Tlascalans, who were a powerful tribe whose support he needed for the conquest of the Aztec empire. Thus, an odd combination of expediency and fanatical zeal set the tone for Spanish religious policies in Mexico.

Although two priests accompanied the original expedition, these were clearly not enough. Cortez, who in spite of his greed and violence was a sincere catholic, requested from Charles V that mendicant friars, and not secular priests or prelates, be sent to Mexico. His argument was that the friars would live in poverty, and would be able to set a good example for the natives, whereas the secular priests and prelates would live in scandalous luxury and would not be actively interested in the conversion of the Indians. In response to this request, twelve Franciscans went to Mexico. On their arrival, Cortez knelt and kissed their hands. But their task was not easy, for there was great resentment against the Spanish and their religion among the Indians. On the other hand, it seemed clear to the Indians that the Christian God had defeated their own gods, and therefore many Indians, while not forgetting the violence being done against them, rushed to request baptism, thus hoping to gain the support of the powerful Christian God.

Little by little, the twelve original friars, and many others who followed them, gained the respect and even the love of their Indian flock. There were times when the Indians rioted upon learning that their priest was being sent elsewhere, and forced the authorities to change their plans.

There were many conflicts and disputes in the nascent Mexican church. The friars baptized any who wished to receive the holy rite, requesting only that they knew that there is only one God and that Jesus is our redeemer, and that they could recite the Lord's Prayer and the Hail Mary. In some cases, even these minimal requirements were waived. There were reports of missionaries baptizing hundreds in a single day, sometimes merely sprinkling several of them at the same time. The secular priests—that is, those who did not belong to monastic orders—had reason to be jealous of the friars' success, although most of them did little for the instruction of the Indians. In any case, they accused the friars of oversimplifying baptism—not of lowering the requirements, as one might expect, but of omitting certain elements in the administration of the rite itself. Eventually, the dispute was settled by Pope Paul III, who declared that there had been no sin in the previous simplified baptismal rites, but that from that time on certain directives must be followed. But even after this papal intervention there continued being strife between the friars and the seculars for several generations.

The first bishop—and then archbishop—of Mexico was a Franciscan, Juan de Zumárraga. He was convinced that the church was in need of reformation, and that this would be achieved by proper instruction of the faithful and by the development of an educated priesthood. With this in mind, he had a printing press taken to Mexico—the first in the western hemisphere—and with it printed many books for the instruction of the Indians. Among these was included a book whose author Zumárraga did not name, but who was later condemned by the Spanish Inquisition as a Protestant. He also took steps for the founding of the University of Mexico; and he was an ardent defender of the Indians against any who would exploit them, no matter how exalted.

However, like most Christians of his time, this otherwise open-minded bishop had little tolerance for what he considered heresy. In 1536, he was made "apostolic inquisitor" for New Spain—the name then given to Mexico. Between that time and 1543, 131 people were tried for heresy. While most of the accused were Spaniards, thirteen were Indians. The most famous of these was chief Carlos Chichimectecotl, who had studied with the Franciscans, and was accused of worshiping idols, living in concubinage, and lacking respect for priests. He confessed that he lived with his niece. A search of his home produced some idols that he said he kept for historical curiosity. No one had seen him worship them. The case would probably have ended in some minor penalties had not a witness declared that he had heard Chichimectecotl declare that the religion of Christians was doubtful, since many of them were promiscuous drunkards whose priests could not control them. On that basis, he was condemned to be burned at the stake.

Since Chichimectecotl was an educated man, his trial renewed the arguments of those who opposed the education of the Indians. Generally, their argument was not that Indians were incapable of learning. On the contrary, what was said was that if they learned how to read and write they would be able to communicate among themselves from one ocean to the other, and that this would make them dangerous. This fear lay behind the low level of education given to the Indians for several generations. It was also the main reason why even the most progressive Spaniards had doubts about ordaining them. In 1539, a gathering of church leaders under the presidency of Zumárraga opened to Indians the possibility of receiving the four lowest levels of holy orders, but none that had sacramental functions. Even less progressive than the Franciscans, the Dominicans declared that Indians should not be ordained or educated at all. The same spirit prevailed in monasteries. The Franciscans, again the most open-minded in such matters, allowed Indians to live in their monastic communities, and to wear a special brown cassock. But they were not permitted to make vows, nor to become even lay brothers. If any of them was not considered fit by the Spanish Franciscans, they simply expelled him, no matter how long he had been part of the community. In 1588, a royal order opened both priestly orders and monastic vows to Indians. But, in 1636, the king lamented that too many "mongrels, bastards and other defective people" were being ordained.

It is within such a setting that the legend and devotion of the Virgin of Guadalupe must be understood. The legend states that the Virgin appeared to an Indian, Juan Diego, with a message for Zumárraga. The bishop did not believe what the Indian told him, until a series of miracles forced him to believe. As a result, and under direct instructions from the Virgin, a chapel was built at the place of the apparitions. Historians have searched in vain for any indication in the records of Zumárraga and his contemporaries that any part of this story is true. Furthermore, an early Christian chronicler declares that the place where the Virgin supposedly appeared was the very hill where the Indians worshiped a goddess called *Tonantzin,* which means "our mother," and that the Indians simply continued worshiping the old goddess under a new name. But no matter what may be the events behind it, the legend itself is a vindication of the oppressed Indian over against the Spanish bishop. In the end, the bishop had to do what the Indian told him. Ever since, the Virgin of Guadalupe has been more than an object of devotion. She became the symbol and rallying point of Mexican national sentiment against any form of foreign intervention.

The Aztec empire did not include all of present-day Mexico. But its downfall led many of the neighboring states to submit to the Spanish. Towards the south, there were the remnants of the ancient Mayan civilization. Their conquest took years, mostly due to the rugged terrain and the dense vegetation. It was not until 1560 that Spanish lordship over Yucatan was sufficiently established to name a bishop for that area.

After the initial conquest, the Spanish continued moving north in quest

The Virgin of Guadalupe became the rallying point of Mexican national sentiment against all foreign intervention.

of two illusory goals. The first, a sea pass connecting the Atlantic to the Pacific, led them to explore the Gulf of California, for during a long time it was believed that Baja California was an island, and that the Gulf of California somehow joined the Atlantic Ocean. The other chimera was the "Seven Golden Cities" of which some Indian spoke to the Spanish, and which drew them almost directly north, towards New Mexico. At a later time, the threat of French advance from Louisiana, and of the Russians moving down the Pacific Coast, led the Spanish to settle in Texas and in California.

In Baja California, missionaries were more successful than colonizers and explorers. The first who settled in the area, first on the eastern shore of the Gulf of California, and then on the peninsula itself, were the Jesuits. Outstanding among them was Eusebio Francisco Kino, an Italian by birth, who founded a chain of missions extending far beyond the limits of Spanish rule, into present-day Arizona. When he died in 1711, he was planning a mission among the Apaches. But, in 1767, the Jesuits were expelled from all Spanish territories. Some of their missions were entrusted to Franciscans, Dominicans, and others. Many others were simply abandoned.

In California, Franciscan missionaries centered their efforts on Alta California—what is now the state of California. In the eighteenth century, when the authorities organized an expedition to explore and settle the area, the Franciscan Junípero Serra joined it. He then founded a long chain of missions, many far beyond the reach of Spanish protection. In those areas where the Indians had to live under Spanish rule, Serra was a zealous defender of their rights vis-à-vis the Spanish.

But the Franciscans' main thrust was directly north, where conquistadores searched for the fabled Seven Cities. Sometimes with the conquistadores, at other times after them, but most often before them, Franciscans crossed the center of Mexico and entered New Mexico. There the Spanish founded in 1610 the Villa Real de la Santa Fe de San Francisco de Asís— now known simply as Santa Fe. Twenty years later, fifty missionaries were pastors to sixty thousand baptized Indians in New Mexico. The great Indian uprising of 1680 killed some four hundred Spaniards, among whom were thirty-two Franciscans. When the Spanish undertook the reconquest of the area, the Franciscans returned with them.

Spanish expansion from Mexico was also directed westward, across the Pacific. Magellan had visited the Philippines in 1521, and was killed by the natives of that archipelago. Later, a series of expeditions were sent from Mexico. Finally, under the leadership of Miguel López de Legazpi, the conquest of the islands was undertaken in 1565. There the Spanish found many Moslems, whom they called *moros* after the Moors who had ruled Spain for centuries. These, and the Chinese in some of the islands, offered strong resistance. But eventually the entire archipelago was conquered. Once again, policies were followed that were similar to those applied in the western hemisphere, and which provoked great resentment among the original inhabitants of the islands. The Spanish had hoped that these islands would become a stepping stone for missions into the Far East; but they were unwilling to educate the Philippinos, and for that reason this project failed.

Golden Castile

The area that is now Central America and Panama had drawn the attention of Spanish authorities from an early date. Columbus had sailed along its coast, hoping to find a passage to the west. By 1509, the first attempts at conquest and colonization were undertaken. These failed until an adventurer called Vasco Núñez de Balboa overthrew the appointed leader and took charge of the enterprise. In contrast with most other conquistadores, Balboa knew how to establish cordial relationships with the Indians, although he too was capable of atrocities. It seems that the main reason why he befriended the Indians was that he was convinced that this was the best way to obtain gold and women from them. Thanks to Indian help, he was able to send gold to Spain, hoping to legitimize his rule. And with the same help he reached the Pacific Ocean, which he called "South Sea."

Balboa's move in sending gold to Spain backfired. Authorities there decided that this land was too valuable to be entrusted to Balboa, and another leader was appointed for the colony, which was now named Castilla del Oro —Golden Castile. The two men clashed, and eventually the new governor had Balboa executed. His policy was to force the Indians to produce gold. Many were distributed among the colonizers in *encomiendas*. Others were killed because they would not or could not give the Spanish as much gold as they demanded. Finally, most of the Indians fled, and fought as guerillas against the conquistadores. Since there were no crops, food became scarce. More than five hundred Spaniards died, many of them of hunger. The bishop who had been appointed to oversee the church in the colony, as well as the Franciscan missionaries, returned to Spain in protest against the poor management of the colony. It was decades before there was any semblance of order.

Probably the most interesting character in the early history of the church in Central America was father Juan de Estrada Rávago, who was a renegade Franciscan, ambitious conquistador, failed courtier, and benevolent missionary. He was ready to return to Spain, in obedience to a royal decree ordering all renegade friars to leave the colonies, when he learned that a proposed expedition to Costa Rica was in need of funds. He provided them and joined the expedition, of which he eventually became the head. He learned the language of the Indians and, with a single exception, refrained from violence against them. He traveled throughout the area teaching the Christian faith, baptizing people, and building churches. With his own resources he bought clothes, food and seeds for both Indians and settlers. Twelve Franciscans from Mexico joined him, and the church developed rapidly.

By the end of the sixteenth century, most of the original inhabitants of Central America called themselves Christian. But there were still vast areas that the Spanish had not explored, where the Indians kept their ancient religions and government. In supposedly Christianized areas, priests were scarce, and their work was greatly hampered by the resentment provoked by the conquistadores. Golden Castile never produced great amounts of the precious metal, and therefore Spain paid little attention to it.

Florida

From an early date, the Spanish were aware of lands north of Cuba. In 1513, Juan Ponce de León, governor of Puerto Rico, received a royal charter authorizing him to explore and colonize the land of "Bimini," where there was rumored to exist a fountain whose waters restored youth, or at least produced wonderful cures. Ponce's expedition landed in Florida, so named because they took possession in the name of the king on Easter—Pascua Florida. After exploring the coasts both along the Atlantic and in the Gulf, and some violent encounters with the Indians, the expedition returned to Puerto Rico. Several years later, Ponce de León organized a second expedition. But he was wounded by the Indians and withdrew to Cuba, where he died.

Other expeditions fared no better. One in 1528 was wiped out by the Indians. Eight years later, four survivors appeared in Mexico, after having walked halfway across the continent. Hernando de Soto explored the area in 1539 and 1540, but did not attempt to colonize it. Another colonial enterprise undertaken twenty years later was abandoned after two years of hardship and little success.

It was the presence of the French in the area that finally forced the Spanish to invest the resources necessary to take possession of it. In 1562, French settlements were started in Florida and South Carolina under the leadership of Jean Ribaut. To make matters worse from the Spanish point of view, most of the French settlers were Protestants. In reaction to this invasion of lands supposedly granted to Spain by the popes, the Spanish government commissioned Pedro Menéndez de Avilés to destroy the settlements. He attacked the French with a powerful squadron. Many fled inland, where they were eventually killed by the Indians. The Spanish captured the rest, and put 132 men to the sword. Only women and children under fifteen years of age were spared. Ribaut, who was absent at the time, was shipwrecked and surrendered to the Spanish, who executed him and more than seventy others who had survived the shipwreck. Menéndez de Avilés then founded the city of Saint Augustine, which became his center of operations.

Ribaut and his companions were avenged. A Frenchman who was a close friend of Ribaut secretly prepared an expedition that landed at the exact place of the earlier massacre, captured a number of Spaniards, and hanged them. Menéndez de Avilés had declared that he had killed Ribaut and his company, "not as Frenchmen, but as Lutherans." Now the French left a sign that said their victims had been killed "not as Spaniards, but as traitors, thieves, and murderers." Then, before reinforcements could arrive from Saint Augustine, they sailed for France.

From Florida, and now due to the threat of the English, who were showing interest in the New World, the Spanish moved in to Guale (Georgia), Santa Elena (the Carolinas), and Ajacán (Virginia).

In all these lands most of the Spanish were either military or missionaries. These missionaries, mostly Jesuits, with some Franciscans and Dominicans, had to work against enormous difficulties. The Spanish had provoked the hostility of the Indians, and therefore many missionaries were killed as soon as they lacked the protection of Spanish arms. The settlements and missions north of Florida were ephemeral. In 1763, the Spanish ceded Florida to England in exchange for Havana, which the British had taken. Twenty years later, Florida was restored to Spanish rule. Finally, in 1819, it was formally ceded to the United States, which had invaded the area.

Of the ancient Spanish missions in that vast land, nothing remained but the memory, some scattered ruins, and the bones of the missionaries who gave up their lives in a cause that their fellow citizens had made well-nigh impossible.

Colombia and Venezuela

Columbus had visited the coast of South America on his second voyage. The conquest of the coast of present-day Colombia was begun in 1508, but failed. It was begun anew in 1525, with the founding of Santa Marta by Rodrigo de Bastidas. He was convinced that Indians should be treated humanely, and for that reason the other settlers forced him to return to Hispaniola. Then began a wave of terror against the Indians, trying to force them to tell the secret location of El Dorado—another of those incredible fables that the conquistadores believed. With Santa Marta as their base of operations, the Spanish moved west, where they founded Cartagena, and south, where they defeated chief Bogotá and founded the city of Santa Fe de Bogotá.

Very soon after the founding of the first cities, the transplanting of the Spanish church was completed with the establishment of a series of bishoprics and the introduction of the Inquisition. The latter was used almost exclusively against Spaniards, for soon the oppressed Indians and enslaved blacks —they were imported from a very early date—learned that if their masters were about to punish them, all they had to do was to cry, "I deny God," which put them under the somewhat more benevolent jurisdiction of the Inquisition. Eventually, a tacit agreement was reached, that only in extreme cases would the Inquisition intervene against Indians or black slaves. Since by that time the British were making their appearance in the Caribbean, the Inquisition was also used against them, and a number were killed for their Protestant convictions.

The two great Christian figures of this area were Saints Luis Beltrán and Pedro Claver. Luis Beltrán was one of the hundreds of missionaries who

Cartagena, in Colombia, witnessed the work of Sts. Luis Beltran
and Pedro Claver.

sought to bring Christianity to the Indians, and to undo the evil done by the
conquistadores and the settlers. A Dominican, he spent the earlier part of his
career as master of studies in the Dominican house of his native Valencia.
The news from the New World, about the millions who needed someone to
minister to them, moved him, and he decided that he had to find out if he
was called to be a missionary. In 1562, when he was thirty-six years old, he
landed in Cartagena. He repeatedly clashed with the *encomenderos,* and his
preaching about justice often resounded with echos of the Old Testament
prophets. But he was still uncertain about his vocation and finally returned
to Spain, where his piety and holiness gained him many admirers. Luis
Beltrán died in 1581. In 1671, pope Clement X added his name to the official
list of saints of the church—the first with any connection with the New
World.

Pedro Claver, the other great Colombian saint, led a very different life.
He was born in 1580, shortly before Beltrán's death, and from early youth
decided to join the Jesuits and become a missionary to the New World. His
superiors thought that he lacked intelligence, and he was still a novice when
he arrived at Cartagena in 1610. He had ample opportunity to see the
sufferings of black slaves, and therefore when he was finally allowed to make
his final vows in 1622 he added a further vow to his signature: *Petrus Claver,
aethiopum semper servus*—Pedro Claver, forever a servant to blacks.

Since the languages the slaves spoke were too many for him to learn,
he tried to borrow other slaves to serve as his interpreters. But the slavehold-
ers were not willing to lose the labor of these interpreters, and Claver

persuaded his monastery to buy a number of slaves to serve as interpreters. This created friction with his fellow Jesuits, some of whom persisted in treating the slaves as such. Claver insisted that these were brothers in Christ, to be treated as equals. Eventually, by sheer stubbornness, he forced the other Jesuits to agree, at least in theory.

As soon as a slave ship arrived, Claver and his interpreters ran to meet it. Sometimes they were allowed to enter the hold of the ship, but most often they had to wait until the slaves had been transferred to the barracks that would be their temporary homes until they were sold. These quarters were not as cramped as the ships, and slaves were now fed more abundantly, in order to prepare them for auction. Still, many died from the effects of the crossing, or because they refused to eat, fearing that they were being fattened in order to be eaten. Stark naked, the sick and the healthy lay together with the dead on the floor of broken bricks, until Claver and his companions came in and carried out the bodies of the dead. Then they would return with fresh fruit and clothes, and seek out the weakest among the slaves. If these seemed to be seriously ill, Claver would carry them to a small hospital he had built nearby. Then he would return and begin trying to communicate the Gospel to those who were well enough to listen to him.

His methods were dramatic. He gave them water, of which they had not had a sufficient supply since they had boarded their ships, and then explained to them that the waters of baptism quench the thirst of the soul. Getting together a group who spoke the same language, Claver would sit them in a circle, sit among them, and give the only chair to the interpreter, who sat in the center and explained to the bewildered slaves the rudiments of the Christian faith. Sometimes he would tell them that, just as a snake changes its skin as it grows, so must one change one's life at baptism. He would then pinch himself all over, as if he were removing his skin, and explain to them the characteristics of the old life that must be left behind. Sometimes, in order to show their assent, they too would pinch themselves. At other times he explained the doctrine of the Trinity by folding a handkerchief so that three corners could be seen, and then showing that it was a single piece of cloth. This was all done in a warm spirit of friendliness and sometimes even humor.

Claver's concern, which was first shown at the arrival of the slave ships, was evident in many other ways. Since leprosy was a common disease among slaves, and those who had it were simply expelled by their masters, Claver founded a leprosarium where he spent most of his time when there were no slave ships in the bay, or slaves in the barracks waiting to be sold. There he was often seen embracing and trying to console a poor leper whose rotting body made others shy away. Also, during the years of his ministry there were three outbreaks of smallpox in Cartagena, and in all three occasions Claver took upon himself the task of cleaning the sores of infected blacks, who had been cast out to die.

Although his superiors always considered him unintelligent, Claver knew full well how far he could go before the white population of Cartagena would crush his ministry. He never attacked or criticized the whites, but the entire city knew that as he walked along the streets he only greeted blacks and those few whites who supported his work. He soon let it be known that when he heard confessions he would follow an inverse order to that of society, listening first to the slaves, then to the poor, and finally to the children. Those who did not fall in any of these categories would do better to find another confessor.

He found much support among the slaves of Cartagena. On the great festivities of the church, some of these slaves helped him prepare banquets for the lepers, slaves, and beggars of the city. Others took up the ministry of giving decent burial to deceased slaves. Still others visited the sick, gathered fruit for the hungry and for the recent arrivals, collected and mended clothing, and in many other ways ministered to their fellow slaves.

During most of this time, white society in Cartagena paid little attention to this strange Jesuit who spent most of his time among slaves. Those who had anything to do with him mostly tried to dissuade him from his labors, for they feared that giving the slaves a sense of dignity was a dangerous thing to do. His superiors were constantly sending reports to Spain, to the effect that Father Claver had neither prudence nor intelligence.

Towards the end of his days, he was struck by a paralyzing disease and was hardly able to leave his cell. His last outing took him to the pier, where his eyes filled with tears before so much pain that he could no longer assuage. His fellow Jesuits trusted his care to a slave, and Claver had to suffer in his own flesh the consequences of the evil that his race had inflicted upon the black race, for the slave treated him cruelly, letting him lie in his own filth and in many other ways reproducing on his sickbed many of the tortures of the slaves' Atlantic passage.

At the very last moment, Cartagena realized that a saint was about to pass away. The cream of society came to visit him in his cell, and all wanted to carry away a relic. Not even his crucifix was left to the poor Jesuit, for when a marquis declared that he wanted it Claver's superiors ordered him to relinquish it. His death, in 1654, was bemoaned by many who had scorned him while he lived. More than two hundred years later, his name was added to the official list of Catholic saints.

The Four Corners of the Earth: The Inca Empire

The western part of South America was under the control of the Incas. Although the Spanish eventually called their heartland "Perú," the Incas called their empire *Tahuantinsuyu,* which means "the four corners of the world." With borders that are now difficult to determine, this empire included all or part of Peru, Ecuador, Bolivia, Chile, and Argentina—a total of approximately 750,000 square miles.

The conquest of this vast empire was accomplished by Francisco Pizarro through a combination of luck, daring, and treachery. Inca Atahualpa was captured in 1532, but this did not put an end to upheavals and civil wars. While the Indians continued a valiant and spirited resistance, the Spanish fought among themselves. When King Charles of Spain sent a viceroy, the settlers refused to obey him, and it was necessary to bring in reinforcements to quell the rebellion. All the while, Indian resistance continued until as late as 1780. At that time Tupac Amaru, who claimed to be a descendent of the last Inca, led a revolt that gained the support of much of the population—including some poor whites who felt exploited by the Spanish aristocracy.

The role of the church in these events, as in the entire Spanish enterprise in the New World, was twofold. On the one hand, it supported conquest and exploitation. On the other, some of its members raised vigorous voices of protest. A priest who had been instrumental in the betrayal through which Atahualpa was captured was rewarded by being made bishop of Cuzco—the capital of the empire. The enormous wealth of Peru seems to have corrupted even many of the friars, who in other areas were noted for their sacrificial ministry among the Indians. Rumors of licentiousness and greed prompted Spain to send an envoy to investigate the matter. He died mysteriously before he even reached Peru. When it was decided to have separate churches for whites and Indians, there was hardly a voice of protest. Among the Indians, some chiefs killed those who accepted baptism, which had now become a symbol of subjection to the invader. It took many years even for those who were baptized to gain a basic understanding of the Christian faith. Even then, priests paid by the *encomenderos* made certain that this faith was understood in such a way that it made them docile.

In 1581, Toribio Alfonso de Mogrovejo was made archbishop of Lima. This was an enormous archdiocese, for it included what is now Nicaragua, Panama, part of Colombia, all of Ecuador, Peru, Bolivia, Paraguay, and parts of Chile and Argentina. In response to the Protestant Reformation, the Council of Trent—which will be discussed in the next volume—had ordered a number of measures of reform, and Mogrovejo was convinced that these were necessary. In the New World, however, it was not easy to impose the discipline required by Trent. The new archbishop called a provincial synod in order to reform the church. One of the items of business was the corruption of the bishop of Cuzco, which was amply documented. But when the synod gathered, the bishop of Tucumán, a friend of the accused, wrenched the documents from the archbishop's hands and burned them in the oven of a bakery. In spite of such conditions, the archbishop was able to institute some reforms. He also prepared a catechism that was translated into several Indian languages, and which for three hundred years was the main means of Christian instruction in vast areas of Spanish America. He repeatedly clashed

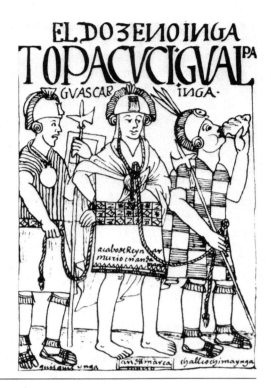

The Spanish conquest was aided by civil war. Here Emperor Huascar is held captive by Atahualpa's troops.

with civil authorities, particularly on the issue of better treatment for the Indians. But he never spoke a word against the fundamental injustice of the regime itself. In 1726, 120 years after his death, his name was added to the official list of Catholic saints.

The Peruvian church produced three others who are now counted among such saints. Saint Rosa of Lima (1586–1617) followed the path of ascetic mysticism, and had experiences of ecstasy. Saint Martin de Porres (1579–1639) entered a Dominican monastery, but was never allowed to become a full member of the order because he was a mulatto. He spent many years taking care of the sick, both human and animals, and planting fruit trees in the countryside, hoping that someday they would help someone who was hungry. Finally, Saint Francisco Solano (1549–1610) was a quiet and humble man who in 1604 was suddenly possessed of an apocalyptic vision, and ran through the streets declaring that Lima had become a new Niniveh, and that God would destroy it in an earthquake if the population did not repent. The message of this new Jonah was heeded, and people flocked to the churches to confess their sins and do penance.

But probably the most remarkable figure of that early period was the Dominican Gil González de San Nicolás, who spent many years as a missionary among the Indians in Chile, and came to the conclusion that the war that was being waged against them was unjust. To attack others with the sole purpose of taking their lands and property, he declared, was a mortal sin, and therefore those who were involved in such activities should be denied the consolation of penance. His preaching found echo among other Dominicans and Franciscans, who refused to grant absolution—and therefore communion —to any who participated in, or profited from, such wars. Civil and ecclesiastical authorities sought an excuse to silence the preacher. Finally, they accused him of heresy, for he had declared that future generations of Spaniards would be punished for the crimes that were taking place, and this was tantamount to affirming that actual sin—and not only original sin—is transmitted from generation to generation. On that basis, the preacher was silenced, and others who had supported him were forced to recant.

La Plata

The territories that are now Argentina, Uruguay, and Paraguay were the last to be occupied by the Spanish. After several unsuccessful settlements, in 1537 they built a fort in what is now the city of Asunción, in Paraguay. Since they were isolated, and knew that they depended on the Indians for their subsistence, the Spanish in Asunción were fairly moderate in their treatment of the Indians. Many of these were gathered in a number of small towns founded by Franciscan missionaries who taught them European methods of agriculture, as well as the rudiments of the Christian faith. One of these missionaries also translated St. Toribio's catechism into Guaraní, the language of the local Indian population.

It was, however, the Jesuits who applied this method most successfully. In many other parts of the Spanish empire, notably in northern Mexico, missionaries had founded towns where Indians lived under their direction. But the common experience was that the proximity of Spanish settlers usually hindered the work of the missionaries, and sometimes even destroyed it. Therefore, rather than follow the Franciscans by organizing Indian villages near Asunción, the Jesuits decided to venture into areas where European influence was barely felt. Roque González, a Jesuit who had grown up in Asunción, and who therefore spoke Guaraní with ease, was the driving force behind these missions. Since he knew the language and customs of the Indians, he was able to defuse a great deal of their hostility, and was thus able to found villages whose inhabitants were there voluntarily, without any coercion by the Spanish.

These towns were actually small theocracies. Although the Indians elected their leaders, they were under the final authority of the missionary, whose word was final, not only in matters of religions and morals, but also in all the practical affairs of the community.

The basic layout of these towns was fairly uniform. In the center there was a big open plaza, where meetings, festivals, and processions took place. Facing it was the church, which included living quarters for the missionary. There were rows of apartments for families, and a separate building for widows and orphans. A large warehouse stored food, seeds, and other common property. Several other buildings housed workshops of all kinds.

Although individuals were allowed to have small private gardens, most property was held in common. This included the vast majority of the land as well as the herds, tools, seeds, and so forth. All had to work a certain number of hours in the common fields, but they also had time of their own that they could devote to their family gardens or to developing and using other skills. In some of these towns, craftsmen became so skilled that they were able to build organs of good quality.

But there were difficulties. Near each town there were other Indians who refused to join, and who constantly invited others to leave or to rebel. It was in one such rebellion that Roque González, the founder of the entire enterprise, was killed. He was declared a saint in 1934. The worst enemies of these missions, however, were whites, both Spanish and Portuguese. The latter, settled in Brazil, feared that Jesuit missions would serve as the vanguard of Spanish penetration. But their main cause of hatred was that the Jesuits did not let them enslave the Indians. The Spanish settlers opposed the Jesuit missions for similar reasons. They felt that, were it not for the Jesuits, all these Indians would be available to work for the Spanish under the system of *encomiendas*.

In 1628, some Portuguese out of Sao Paulo began attacking the Jesuit missions. They would raze villages and carry away their inhabitants to be sold as slaves. In some cases, the Jesuits followed their flocks in their unhappy trek, until the slavers forced them back. The Jesuits then moved their villages farther away from Brazil. But they were soon followed by the slavers, who simply penetrated deeper into the territory.

Given this situation, the Jesuits decided to arm the Indians. Their shops were converted into arms factories, and a standing army was organized under the leadership of one of the Jesuits. Pope Urban VIII excommunicated any who would venture into Jesuit territory to hunt Indians, and King Philip IV declared that the Indians were free, and not subject to slavery. But still the Portuguese came, often with the help of Spanish settlers who wished to destroy the entire enterprise. In 1641, in a pitched battle, the Indians and Jesuits defeated the invaders. Repeated accusations brought against the Jesuits, that they were arming the Indians illegally, found no support in either Rome or Madrid, both of which declared that the Jesuits had the right to arm themselves and their flock, since it was done in self-defense. Under such conditions, the missions flourished, and by 1731 there were more than 140,000 Indians living in them.

But opposition did not cease. It was rumored that the Jesuits hid vast amounts of gold that rightfully belonged to the crown. Repeated investigations found that there was no basis for this charge. Then it was said that the Jesuits aspired to create an independent republic, and even that they already had a "King Nicholas I of Paraguay." Since at that time there were similar accusations circulating in Europe against the Jesuits, and since the house of Bourbon, which ruled in Spain and in several other European lands, was following an anti-Jesuit policy, in 1767 the crown ordered that all Jesuits must leave all Spanish colonies. Upon receiving these orders, the Spanish governor feared rebellions. But the Jesuits encouraged the Indians to accept the new situation, and left in peace.

The plan was that Franciscans and Dominicans would take the place of the Jesuits. But there were similar vacancies throughout the Spanish empire, and there were not enough Dominicans and Franciscans to fill them. Lacking in leadership, many missions disappeared. Civil authorities began exploiting the Indians, and since the new missionaries did little to prevent such abuses the Indians began distrusting them. Soon the Portuguese were again invading the area, hunting slaves. Some Spaniards did likewise. By 1813, the missions were reduced to a third of what they had been, and their decline continued. The missions of Paraguay, a discordant witness at a time when Christianity was used to oppress and exploit the Indians, could not withstand the pressures of boundless greed.

36/The Portuguese Enterprise

If the Indians had a spiritual life and would acknowledge their Creator and their vassalage to Your Majesty and their obligation to obey Christians, . . . men would have legitimate slaves captured in just wars, and would have also the service and vassalage of the Indians in the missions.

MANOEL DE NÓBREGA

Africa

Portugal completed the conquest of her lands from the Moors in the thirteenth century, almost two hundred years before Castile. Since the latter hemmed her in, the only route left for Portuguese expansion was the sea. In the first half of the fifteenth century, Prince Henry the Navigator encouraged the exploration of the west coast of Africa. Under his auspices, and after fourteen unsuccessful attempts, Portuguese sailors weathered Cape Bojador and reached Sierra Leone. There were several goals which inspired this exploration. One was the hope to reach the Orient by sailing around Africa, or by crossing that continent, and thus to circumvent the Moslems who at that time controlled the most direct land routes between Europe and the Far East. Also, vague rumors of the existence of Ethiopia had reached European courts, and there was the hope of finding this Christian kingdom, establishing an alliance with it, and launching a great crusade that would attack the Moslems from two different directions at the same time. Finally, the slave traffic soon became an important factor in the exploration and colonization of Africa.

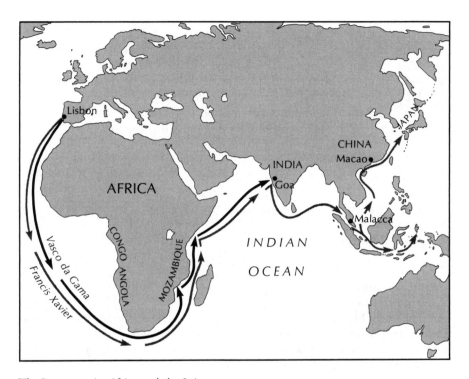

The Portuguese in Africa and the Orient

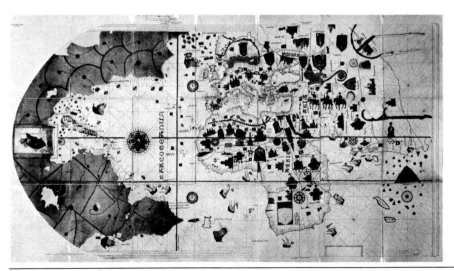

*The Portuguese sailed around Africa and on to the Orient, as this
Portuguese trade map shows.*

In 1487, the first Portuguese explorer rounded the Cape of Good Hope. Ten years later, Vasco da Gama sailed along the east coast of Africa, crossed the Indian Ocean, and returned to Europe with proof that it was possible to establish commercial links with India while circumventing the Moslems.

While these early explorations were taking place, the Portuguese were busily establishing alliances and colonies on the African coast. In 1483, an expedition landed at the mouth of the Congo and learned that this land, and vast territories in the interior of the continent, were ruled by the "Manicongo." Since they hoped to reach Ethiopia by sailing up the Congo, they treated the Manicongo's subjects respectfully. Four Portuguese remained behind, and four Africans were taken as guests to the court of Lisbon. When these returned with stories of the wonders of European civilization, and of their good treatment in Lisbon, the Manicongo decided to become an ally of the Portuguese, who in turn sent missionaries and craftsmen. After a month of Christian preaching, the Manicongo was baptized and took the Christian name of Joao, after the King of Portugal. Portuguese military support in wars against his neighbors convinced the Manicongo that he had made the right choice.

The next Manicongo, Afonso, was even more favorable to the Portuguese and their missionaries. In 1520, after long negotiations, Pope Leo X consecrated Henrique, a brother of Afonso, as bishop of the Congo. On his return to his land, however, the new bishop found that many European clerics paid little attention to his directives. He died in 1530, and two years later the church in the Congo was placed under the jurisdiction of the Portuguese bishop of the nearby island of Sao Tome. The mission begun with such cordial relationships produced ever-increasing friction. After Afonso's death, civil war broke out, in part because many Congolese resented the presence and influence of the Portuguese. The latter intervened militarily, and in 1572 Manicongo Alvaro declared himself a vassal of Portugal. By then resentment and suspicion had replaced the earlier friendly relations.

South of the Congo lay the lands of a ruler known as the "Ngola." These lands—now Angola—were seen from the beginning as a source of slaves. In the Congo, the Manicongo controlled the slave trade. In Angola, through the use of force, Portuguese slavers obtained greater advantages. Eventually, the coast became a Portuguese colony. Although Portugal claimed vast lands in the interior of the continent, those territories, seldom visited by them, were seen mostly as a vast source of slaves, usually taken to the coast by African slavers. Although churches were established, these were mostly for the Portuguese and for a few Africans along the coast. Since there were other lands that appeared more important to Portuguese eyes, the church in Angola was generally entrusted to what amounted to the dregs of Portuguese clergy.

The Portuguese enterprise on the eastern coast of Africa was even more violent. When Vasco da Gama arrived at Mozambique and discovered that many of its inhabitants were Moslem, he bombarded the city. Going on to

Mombasa, he did the same. He finally established an alliance with Malindi, which was a rival of both Mozambique and Mombasa. In 1505, Portugal sent a fleet of twenty-three vessels to India, with instructions to stop along the way and establish Portuguese rule in eastern Africa. In five years, the entire coast was subject to the Portuguese. In 1528, Mombasa gave signs of rebelliousness, and was bombarded for a second time.

The first Portuguese priests arrived at Mozambique in 1506. Their main task was not seeking to convert Africans, but rather to serve as chaplains to the Portuguese garrisons. In 1534, when the bishopric of Goa, in India, was founded, the entire eastern coast of Africa was placed under its jurisdiction.

Although most Portuguese priests remained in posts along the coast, under the shadow of Portuguese cannon, a number of Jesuits and Dominicans did undertake missions to the interior. The most famous of them was the Jesuit Gonzalo de Silveira, who reached Zimbabwe and converted and baptized its king. Some African traders, fearing that the missionary's success would open the way for Portuguese traders, convinced the king that the Jesuit was a spy and a practicer of evil magic. When he learned that the king had resolved to kill him, Silveira decided not to flee, but rather to remain in his post, where he was strangled in his sleep. Like him, there were many missionaries who gave their lives in the next fifty years, and who in doing so gained the admiration of many Africans. But in spite of these martyrs, the vast majority of the clergy showed little concern for the Africans, and in this they were simply reflecting the attitude of Portugal itself, which by now was much more interested in the Far East, and paid little attention to its African colonies.

Towards the Rising Sun

When, after the first discoveries of Columbus, the pope apportioned the entire non-Christian world between Spain and Portugal, the latter received, not only Africa, where Portuguese explorers had been active for some time, but also the entire Orient, which had always been the goal of the exploration of Africa. Upon Vasco de Gama's return, it became clear that the vast territories and teeming populations of India, Japan, and China could not be conquered by Portugal. Since products from the Orient—silk and spices—brought a high price in European markets, Portugal settled on a policy of trade rather than conquest.

In order to make trade with the East truly profitable, the Portuguese must have control of it. This was the purpose of a vast network of military bases that could both serve as refitting stations for Portuguese ships and as guardians of the sea lanes. Having established themselves on both sides of Africa, the Portuguese closed the Red Sea by taking the island of Socotra and other neighboring areas. In India, they took Goa and fortified it. By establishing a base in Ceylon, they controlled shipping around the southern tip of India. Further East, their presence in Malacca closed the way to China to any daring Europeans who would venture that far. Finally, in China itself, Macao served as the channel for all trade with that enormous nation. Many of these places were taken by force. In others, such as Macao, the Portuguese were allowed to settle because the local or national authorities wished to trade with them. But even in those places where their original settlement took place through the force of arms, the Portuguese were interested in trade, not in conquest, and therefore avoided any conflicts that could interrupt trade.

King Joao III of Portugal, having heard of the zeal of the recently founded Jesuit order, requested that six Jesuits be sent to his colonies in the Orient. Loyola, the founder of the order, could only spare two. One of these was Francis Xavier, who upon learning what he was commanded to do took time only to mend his cassock and left for Lisbon. There the king and his court were so impressed with the Jesuits that they insisted that one of them remain in Portugal, and Francis Xavier was sent as the sole missionary to the Orient.

In May of 1542, after a voyage of more than a year, Xavier arrived at Goa, the center of Portuguese operations in the East. He was scandalized by the life of the Portuguese, but soon discovered that all his recriminations were to no avail. He then hit upon a method that became characteristic of him. He would walk along the streets with a bell, inviting children to come with him to church, where he taught them the catechism and the moral teachings of the church. Then he would send them home to share with their parents what they had learned. Little by little, Xavier gained the respect of the adults, who eventually flocked to hear him preach. Then followed scenes of mass penance reminiscent of Florence in Savonarola's time.

But it was not to preach to the Portuguese that Xavier had gone to India. His sojourn in Goa was only an interlude while he prepared for his vaster mission to those who had not heard the name of Christ. Therefore, after spending five months in Goa, Xavier left for the nearby Fishery coast—so named because of its pearl fisheries. This was an area frequently visited by Portuguese traders, and many of the Indians there had accepted Christianity simply because it was the religion of the powerful Portuguese. Xavier took with him two young clergymen who knew the language of the area, and with them as interpreters preached and taught for some time. From neighboring villages came requests that he go and preach to them. Since it was impossible to respond to all such requests, Xavier trained some of his converts, who then traveled about preaching and baptizing.

Most of Xavier's converts, as well as most of those won in other parts of India, belonged to the lower castes. The caste system was deeply ingrained in Indian society, and there was no way to break out of it. People of different castes were not allowed to eat together. Since Christians partook of commu-

Portuguese traders being greeted on their arrival in Japan, by Japanese officials and Franciscan Portuguese missionaries.

nion together, many members of the lower castes believed that if they became Christians this meant that they had joined the caste of the Portuguese. Therefore, conversion and baptism came to have a dimension of social liberation for many converts. But, for the same reason, many members of the higher castes opposed the preaching of Christianity, which they saw as subversive. In many areas there were martyrdoms similar to those of the early years of the church. Xavier himself was attacked in various occasions, and once was wounded by arrows. For a time, he sought to use Portuguese military power to protect his converts. Such military action was ruled out by the Portuguese authorities, not out of pacifist ideals, but rather because it would interrupt trade.

In 1546, leaving others in charge of the work begun in India, Xavier sailed for more distant lands. Three Japanese whom he met in his travels invited him to visit their land. After spending some time back at Goa, Xavier undertook this new mission. In 1549, with the three Japanese converts and two fellow Jesuits, Xavier sailed for Japan. There he was well received, and the number of his converts was such that he was convinced that he had built the foundation of what would soon be a flourishing church. He had no way of knowing that shortly after his death a great persecution would break out, and his newly founded church would almost disappear. (It actually seemed to have been completely destroyed until, three centuries later, Protestant missionaries found that there were about a hundred thousand Christians in Nagasaki and the neighboring area.)

On his return to Malacca, Xavier learned that the Jesuit order had decided to organize a new province that included all territories east of the Cape of Good Hope, and that he had been named its head. These new administrative responsibilities forced him to return to Goa, and to postpone his dream of preaching the Gospel in China.

Finally, in 1552, he sailed for China. Before leaving Goa, he wrote to the King of Portugal: "What encourages us is that God has inspired this thought in us . . . and we do not doubt that the power of God is infinitely superior to that of the king of China." But in spite of such confidence, Xavier was never able to enter China, whose government was averse to any foreign influence. He died on an island at the fringes of the Chinese empire, where he had settled in order to prepare for the day when that vast land would be open to him.

Xavier and his fellow missionaries did not make a clear distinction between European culture and the Christian faith. When their converts were baptized, they were given "Christian"—that is, Portuguese—names, and encouraged to dress in western clothes. Many of these converts actually believed that when they accepted baptism they became subjects of the King of Portugal. For similar reasons, the cultured and the powerful in the various countries that the missionaries visited viewed Christianity as a foreign influence, undermining both traditional culture and the existing social order.

A younger generation of Jesuits, all under Portuguese auspices, but many of them Italians by birth, questioned this identification of Christianity with Portuguese power and culture, and sought ways in which the preaching of the Gospel could be adapted or "accommodated" to the ancient eastern cultures. Most notable among this younger generation were Roberto di Nobili and Matteo Ricci—the first a missionary to India, and the latter to China.

Di Nobili began his missionary career in the Fishery coast, and there became aware that, while many members of the lower castes embraced Christianity as a way to break away from their inferior status, this also meant that those of the higher castes were not willing to listen to a message associated with what they saw as the dregs of society. Therefore, when he was transferred to a different region Nobili decided to follow another method. Arguing that he was of noble birth in his own country, he dressed as a Brahman and took the title of "teacher." He also took up the vegetarian diet of all good Hindus, and learned Sanskrit. By such methods, he gained the respect of many among the higher castes. When some of these were converted, he set them apart in a church of their own, and ordered that no members of the lower castes be allowed to worship with his privileged converts.

Nobili justified these actions claiming that the caste system, although evil, was a cultural matter, and not a religious one. It was necessary to respect the culture of the Hindus, and to preach the Gospel following the lines of

caste. If this were done, he argued, the lower castes would follow the example of their betters, and all would be converted. Such arguments were refuted
by others who pointed out that justice and love are part of the Gospel, and
that to deny these is not to preach true Christianity. Eventually, Nobili's most
extreme propositions were rejected. For a long time, however, there continued existing in India separate churches—or separate areas within a church
—for different castes.

Matteo Ricci followed in China a policy similar to that of Nobili, but less
extreme. China was hermetically closed to any foreign influence, except the
small window for trade provided by Macao. Shortly after Xavier's death, a
Spanish missionary from the Philippines who had tried to visit China had
declared that "with or without soldiers, to try to enter China is like trying
to reach the moon." But, in spite of these difficulties, the Jesuits did not

Matteo Ricci adopted the customs of China.

abandon Xavier's dream. Seeing that China was a highly civilized country that looked upon the rest of the world as barbarians, the Jesuits decided that the only way to make an impact on that vast land was to learn, not only its language, but also its culture. To this end, a group of Jesuits settled at the borders of the Chinese empire, and devoted itself to such studies. Slowly, some Chinese intellectuals in the nearby areas came to the conclusion that these Europeans, unlike the many adventurers who came to China after riches, were worthy of respect. Finally, after protracted negotiations, they were granted permission to settle in the provincial capital of Chaochin, but not to travel to other areas.

Among those who settled in Chaochin was Matteo Ricci, who had become proficient in Chinese language and culture, and who was also a geographer, astronomer, mathematician, and clockmaker. Aware that friendship was an important virtue among the Chinese, he wrote a treatise on that subject, following the canons of Chinese literature, and joining the wisdom of that land with material drawn from western philosophy. Soon people began speaking of "the wise man from the West," and scholars would visit him to discuss astronomy, philosophy, and religion. A map of the world drawn by Ricci, which included vast areas unknown to the Chinese, drew the attention of the court in Peking. His explanations of the movement of heavenly bodies according to complicated mathematical principles gained him even greater respect. Finally, in 1601, he was invited to the imperial court in Peking, where he was given the necessary resources to build a great observatory, and where he remained until his death in 1615.

Ricci's strategy consisted in penetrating into China without necessarily seeking large numbers of converts. He feared that, were he to cause a great religious stir, he and the other missionaries would be expelled from the country, and their work would come to naught. Therefore, he never built a church or chapel, nor did he ever preach to multitudes. It was in his home, in a small circle of friends and admirers who gathered to discuss clockmaking and astronomy as well as religion, that he gained his only converts. When he died, he left a nucleus of believers, all members of the intellectual elite. But, through the years, these in turn converted others, and there eventually was a substantial number of Christians in the country—still led by the Jesuits, who continued serving the court at Peking as its official astronomers.

As in the case of Nobili, Ricci's methods met with objections from other Catholics. In this case, the point at issue was not the caste system, but rather ancestor worship and Confucianism. The Jesuits argued that Confucianism was not a religion, and that there was much in the teachings of Confucius that could be used as a point of entry for the Gospel. As to ancestor worship, they claimed that this was not true worship, but rather a social custom whereby one showed respect for one's ancestors. Their opponents, mostly Dominicans and Franciscans, argued that such worship was in fact idolatry. Another point at issue was which of two possible Chinese words should be used to refer to the Christian God. When the emperor of China learned that this particular dispute had reached Rome, and that the pope was to settle it, he was incensed by the notion that a barbarian who did not know a word of Chinese presumed to teach the Chinese how to speak their own language.

Whereas in China the question of "accommodation" had to do mostly with cultural issues, in India the question posed was whether one can actually claim to preach the Gospel when such preaching is lacking in any word of judgment on human injustice and oppression. Is a Christian faith that accepts the caste system truly Christian? This question, or others like it, would become crucial in later centuries.

Brazil

When the pope partitioned between Spain and Portugal all lands to be discovered, no one knew that the eastern tip of South America reached across the line of demarcation. In 1500, a Portuguese squadron sailing for the Orient gave the coast of Africa a wide berth in order to avoid contrary winds, and accidentally sighted what is now Brazil. After exploring the area, the squadron continued on its way to the Orient, while a ship was sent back to Lisbon with news of the land that had been discovered, seemingly in the middle of the Atlantic. Several preliminary explorations led to the conclusion that the only source of wealth to be found in the area was brazilwood, which could be used for making dyes. King Manoel of Portugal granted the monopoly on brazilwood to a group of Portuguese merchants, whose representatives established trading centers along the coasts. There they traded knives, scissors, needles and the like for brazilwood which the Indians cut and carted to warehouses along the coast.

When brazilwood became more scarce, the Portuguese turned their attention to sugar cane, which could easily be grown in the area. Since at that time sugar demanded very high prices in Europe, there were fortunes to be made in it. The king granted "captaincies" to fifteen of his favorites, giving each fifty leagues of seashore, and as far back inland as Spanish territory began. Only ten of the captaincies were ever settled, and eight of these failed. The two that succeeded were the beginning of the permanent colonization of Brazil.

Growing sugar cane, and processing it into sugar, required abundant cheap labor, and the Portuguese sought to obtain this by enslaving the Indians. In theory, only those Indians who were already slaves of other Indians, and those captured in "just war," could be enslaved by the Portuguese. But soon all sorts of excuses were found for supposedly just wars, and eventually even appearances were cast aside as slavers sailed along the coast, capturing and enslaving any Indians who were unwary enough to allow themselves to be caught. Also, the Portuguese incited wars between different Indian tribes, which would then sell their captives in exchange for tools, knives, and the like.

These methods, however, did not produce sufficient slaves, and many of those captured ran to the jungles at the first opportunity. It was then that the Portuguese began importing slaves from Africa, which lay fairly close across the Atlantic. As the Indian population moved to the interior, died, or was absorbed by the rest, blacks and Portuguese came to be the majority of the people of eastern Brazil.

Reports reaching Lisbon from Brazil were uninspiring. The cruelty and licentiousness of the colonizers provoked a strong reaction. In 1549, with a view both to establishing order and enlarging his coffers, the King of Portugal abolished the captaincies, bought back the land of those who had succeeded, and declared Brazil a royal colony. It was then, with the first governor, that Jesuit missionaries arrived. Their leader was Manoel da Nóbrega, whose words quoted at the beginning of this chapter give a clear indication of how he understood his mission. The first bishop, appointed in 1551, was not much better. He quarreled with the colonizers, and paid no attention to the plight of Indians and Africans. He was returning to Portugal, in order to complain about the settlers, when he was shipwrecked. He and his entire company were eaten by Indians.

The Jesuits founded missions very similar to those of Paraguay, except for one important difference: instead of placing them as far as possible from the settlers, they built them where the Indians could serve in the plantations. The missionaries were grateful for the support of the Portuguese, and in exchange offered the labor of the Indians in what practically amounted to slavery. As one missionary said, "They quake in fear before the governor, and that fear . . . is enough for us to teach them. It helps them to hear the Word of God."

The Indian reaction took the form of a messianic cult that combined Christian elements with others derived from ancient beliefs. When a smallpox outbreak killed thousands of Indians, talk began of a savior whom the Indians called "Santo," who would come and free them from the Portuguese yoke. This new religion, called *santidade,* gained ground both among the Indians under Portuguese tutelage and among those who were still free in the jungle, and served as a bridge between the two groups. Likewise, black slaves developed various combinations of Christianity with their ancestral religions. Both of these movements allowed oppressed blacks and Indians a sense of dignity that official Christianity denied them.

From an early date, the French had competed with the Portuguese in the brazilwood trade, and some of them had hoped to establish a permanent settlement in Brazil. This was attempted in 1555 by Nicholas Durand de Villegagnon, who started a colony on an island in the bay of Guanabara, near present-day Rio de Janeiro. Villegagnon established friendly relations with the Tamoyo Indians, who helped him fortify the island. He also wrote to Calvin, and in response to his request was sent several Protestant pastors to serve those among the settlers who were Protestant. This, and many other issues, created grave difficulties in the settlement, which was eventually wiped out by the Portuguese. The Tamoyo Indians, and a number of French refugees who lived among them, continued resisting for some time. Later the tribe moved inland to escape from the Portuguese. When, late in the sixteenth century, a British adventurer persuaded them to return to the coast and fight for their rights, they were wiped out. Ten thousand of them were killed, and twice that many were captured and sold into slavery.

All told, the early story of Christianity in Brazil, as in so many other lands in that period of colonial expansion, is not an inspiring one. It would be many years before the negative consequences of such inauspicious beginnings could be overcome.

While Spain and Portugal were building vast overseas empires, and planting Roman Catholicism in distant lands, the Protestant Reformation was taking place in Europe. 1521, the year when Luther valiantly stood before Charles V at the Diet of Worms, was also the year when Cortez captured Tenochtitlan. Living as we do, only four centuries after those events, it may be too early to decide which of the two will eventually be of greater significance for the course of Christianity. In any case, in the next volume of this history we shall return to Europe, and resume the narrative of the quest for renewal and reformation, and of those who gave their lives to that quest.

Suggested Readings

Stephen Clissold. *The Saints of South America.* London: Charles Knight, 1972.

Vincent Cronin. *The Wise Man from the West.* New York: Dutton, 1955.

George H. Dunne. *Generation of Giants: The Story of the Jesuits in China in the Last Generations of the Ming Dynasty.* London: Burns & Oates, 1962.

John Hemming. *Red Gold: The Conquest of the Brazilian Indians.* Cambridge, Massachusetts: Harvard University Press, 1978.

Samuel Eliot Morison. *The European Discovery of America: The Southern Vogages, A.D. 1492–1616.* New York: Oxford University Press, 1974.

Stephen Neill. *Colonialism and Christian Missions.* London: Lutterworth, 1966.

J. H. Parry. *The Discovery of South America.* New York: Taplinger, 1979.

The Ecumenical Councils

Number	Date	Name	Primary Decisions
1	325	I Nicea	Condemnation of Arius Son of one substance with Father Creed of Nicea
2	381	I Constantinople	Reiteration of Nicea Divinity of Holy Spirit Condemnation of Apollinaris
3	431	Ephesus	Condemnation of Nestorius Mary *theotokos*—"bearer of God"
4	451	Chalcedon	Condemnation of Eutyches Two natures—divine and human—in Christ
5	553	II Constantinople	Condemnation of "Three Chapters": Theodore of Mopsuestia Theodoret Ibas of Edessa
6	680–681	III Constantinople	Condemnation of monothelism Condemnation of Pope Honorius
7	787	II Nicea	Condemnation of iconoclasts Images worthy of veneration *(dulia)* but not worship *(latria)*
8	869–870	IV Constantinople	Ended schism of Photius
9	1123*	I Lateran	Confirmed Concordat of Worms between Papacy and Empire
10	1139	II Lateran	Compulsory clerical celibacy
11	1179	III Lateran	Determined method of papal election
12	1215	IV Lateran	Transubstantiation Confession and communion at least yearly Condemned Joachim of Fiore, Waldensians, and Albigensians Regulated Inquisition
13	1245	I Lyons	Declared Emperor Frederick II deposed

*In 1054, the church was divided between East and West. After that date, councils listed are only western.

Number	Date	Name	Primary Decisions
14	1274	II Lyons	New regulations for papal elections (basically those employed to the present) Nominal reunion with Constantinople
15	1311–1312	Vienne	Suppression of the Templars
16	1414–1418	Constance	End of Great Schism Condemnation of John Huss Council has authority over pope Plans for reformation and other councils
17	1431–1445	Basel/Ferrara Florence	Nominal reunion with Constantinople, with Armenia, and with Jacobites
18	1512–1517	V Lateran	Condemned schismatic Council of Pisa
19	1545–1563	Trent	Condemned Protestants Authority of Scripture *and* tradition Consolidated Catholic Reformation
20	1869–1870	I Vatican	Papal infallibility
21	1962–1965	II Vatican	Liturgical renewal (use of vernacular) Church responsive to modern world: International economic inequities Nuclear war Religious freedom Openness to other Christians

Index

Credits

Page

9 / Samaria, Palestine; The Bettman Archive.

11 / Wall painting of Judas Maccabeus by Taddeo di Bartolo; Italian, fifteenth century.

13 / Menorah mosaic from Hamman-Lif, Tunisia; third to fifth century A.D.; The Brooklyn Museum, Museum Collection Fund.

15 / The Bettman Archive.

16 / Roman bronze sculpture; The Metropolitan Museum of Art, Gift of Henry G. Marquand, 1897.

19 / Marilyn Silverstone, Magnum Photos, Inc.

21 / The Pierpont Morgan Library.

22 / British Museum, Department of Coins and Medals.

24 / Manuscript illumination of the Apostles (Codex Monacensis Lat. 23338); Bayer. Staatsbibliothek, Munich.

26 / Early Christian ivory plaque; The Metropolitan Museum of Art, Gift of George Blumenthal, 1941.

28 / Detail from the altarpiece of St. Peter by Martin de Soria, 1471-1487. Courtesy, Museum of Fine Arts, Boston, Gift of Robert H. McCormick.

34 / Coin with portrait of Emperor Nero, A.D. 54-68; The American Numismatic Society.

37 / Italian Government Tourist Office.

Page

42 / Princeton University, Department of Art and Archaeology.

47 / Probably Constantinople, ca. A.D. 1300; Dumbarton Oaks, Washington, D.C., courtesy of the Byzantine Collection.

50 / The Bettman Archive.

55 / From Vase of Duris; Kunsthistorisches Museum, Berlin; The Bettman Archive.

60 / Gnostic gem engraved with serpent and the name *Chnoubis;* Agyptisches Museum, Staatliche Museen, Berlin.

65 / The Last Judgment by Andrea Orcogna; Pisa, Italy; The Bettman Archive.

69 / Musée du Louvre, Archives Photographiques.

72 / Pompeiian mosaic of Plato and his pupils; Museo Nazionale, Naples, Italy; The Bettman Archive.

80 / Capital relief from Notre-Dame du Port, Clermont-Ferrand, France, twelfth century; Bildarchiv Foto Marburg.

85 / Decius Addressing the Legions by Peter Paul Rubens, ca. 1617; National Gallery of Art, Washington, D.C.; Samuel H. Kress Collection, 1957.

87 / Greek, A.D. 250; Beinecke Rare Book and Manuscript Library, Yale University.

Page

259 / Mosaic in San Vitale, Ravenna, Italy, A.D. 547; Scala/Art Resource.

260 / Miniature manuscript illustration, mid eleventh century; Princeton University Library, Princeton, N.J.

267 / Gold reliquary in the form of the head of Charlemagne, ca. 1350. Cathedral Treasury, Aachen, Germany; Bildarchiv Foto Marburg.

273 / Tenth century; The British Library.

278 / Bildarchiv Foto Marburg.

281 / The Pierpont Morgan Library, New York City.

284 / Manuscript illumination; The British Library.

288 / Miniature manuscript illustration; Canossa, early twelfth century; The Bettman Archive.

294 / Illumination from *Les Estoires d'Outremer* by William of Tyre, thirteenth century, Bibliothèque Nationale, Paris.

299 / The Bettman Archive.

303 / St. Francis in Ecstasy by Giovanni Bellini; copyright, The Frick Collection, New York City.

312 / Illumination of St. Gregory writing, Add. MS. 39943, The British Library.

320 / The Bettman Archive.

322 / The Bettman Archive.

328 / Miniature illustration from the Toggenburg Bible; Imperial Collection of Vienna; The Bettman Archive.

334 / The Bettman Archive.

336 / Italian Government Travel Office.

Page

337 / Tomb of St. Catherine of Siena, attributed to Isaia da Pisa; Santa Maria sopra Minerva, Rome; Scala/Art Resource.

343 / Italian Government Travel Office.

345 / Seal of the Council of Basel, 1431–1449; Kunsthistorisches Museum, Vienna.

351 / From Ulrich von Reichental's *Chronicle of the Council of Constance;* Bohemian, early fifteenth century; The British Library.

355 / Museo di San Marco, Florence; Alinari/Art Resource.

367 / An illuminated page from a facsimile copy of the Gutenberg Bible, issued ca. 1455. New York Public Library, Rare Book Room.

369 / Self-portrait in red chalk, ca. 1514; Biblioteca Reale, Turin; The Bettman Archive.

372 / Detail of a painting by Pinturicchio, 1492–1503; Vatican Palace, Rome; Alinari/Art Resource.

387 / Courtesy Museum of New Mexico.

392 / The Bettman Archive.

396 / Royal Library, Copenhagen, Denmark.

401 / Facsimile of Juan de Cosa's world map showing Portuguese ports and trade routes in Africa, ca. 1500; The New York Public Library, Map Division.

405 / Painting on a screen, early seventeenth century. Kobe Municipal Museum, Japan.

407 / The Bettman Archive.

To Catherine

Contents

Maps

Preface

This second volume of *The Story of Christianity* could be read by itself, as the history of the course of Christianity from the Reformation to the present. In so doing, however, the reader should be aware that many of the Christian leaders whose views and careers are discussed here would object to such a reading. Loyola and the other leaders of the Catholic Reformation saw themselves as the continuation and defenders of the story told in our first volume. The same is true of Luther, Calvin, Wesley, and most other great Protestant figures, who did not see themselves as innovators any more than did the Catholic theologians.

Except where otherwise noted, quotations from foreign languages are given in my own translation. In some cases where an English translation of the text quoted is readily available, I have so indicated, in the hope that readers may be encouraged to seek and read the texts themselves. In any case, in this volume as in the previous one, I have endeavored to keep footnotes to a minimum, in order to keep the reader's attention on the narrative itself, and not on the scholarly apparatus behind it.

As this book goes to press, I wish to reiterate my gratitude to those mentioned in the preface to the first volume, whose help and support has again proven invaluable. To them I wish to add the staff at Harper & Row in San Francisco, who have made this project their own and have taken an interest in it that I have found both helpful and gratifying. Finally, I wish to thank my readers for the time and interest they have invested in this narrative that is so dear and fascinating to me.

Decatur
January 1984

PART I

THE REFORMATION

Chronology

Popes	Emperors	Castile	Aragon	France	England	Scotland	Events
Alexander VI (1492–1503)		Isabella (1474–1504)	Ferdinand (1479–1516)		Henry VII (1485–1509)	James IV (1488–1513)	Columbus in America (1492)
	Maximilian I (1493–1519)			Louis XII (1498–1515)			
Pius III (1503) Julius II (1503–1513)		Joanna the Mad (1504–1516)			Henry VIII (1509–1547)	James V (1513–1542)	
Leo X (1513–1521)							

Spain

Charles V (the same) Charles I
(1519–1556)   (1516–1556)

Adrian VI
(1522–1523)
Clement VII
(1523–1524)

Paul III
(1534–1549)

Julius III
(1550–1555)

Francis I
(1515–1547)

Henry II
(1547–1559)

Edward VI
(1547–1553)

Mary Stuart
(1542–1567)

Erasmus' New Testament
(1515)
Luther: Ninety-five
Theses (1517)
Diet of Worms (1521)
Loyola at Manresa (1522)

Peasants' war
(1524–1525)
Vienna besieged by
Turks (1529)
Marburg Colloquy
(1529)
Augsburg Confession
(1530)
†Zwingli (1531)
England breaks with
Rome (1534)
Fall of Münster (1535)
Calvin's *Institutes* (1536)
Jesuits approved by pope
(1540)

Council of Trent
(1545–1563)
†Luther (1546)

Popes	Emperors	Spain	France	England	Scotland	Events
Marcellus II (1555)				Mary Tudor (1553–1558)		Peace of Augsburg (1555)
Paul IV (1555–1559)	Ferdinand I (1558–1564)	Philip II (1556–1598)				†Ignatius Loyola (1556)
Pius IV (1559–1565)			Francis II (1559–1560) Charles IX (1560–1574)	Elizabeth I (1558–1603)		Calvin's *Institutes,* final edition (1559)
						†Menno Simons (1561) Wars of religion in France (1562) †Calvin (1564) Uprising in the Netherlands (1566)
Pius V (1566–1572)	Maximilian II (1564–1576)				James VI (1567–1625)	Massacre of St. Bartholomew's day (1572) †Knox (1572)
Gregory XIII (1572–1585)	Rudolph II (1576–1612)		Henry III (1574–1589)			Pacification of Ghent (1576)
Sixtus V (1585–1590)			Henry IV (1589–1610)			†William the Silent (1584) †Mary Stuart (1587)
Urban VII (1590)						

Gregory XIV
(1590–1591)
Innocent IX
(1591)
Clement VIII
(1592–1605)

Philip III
(1598–1621)

Edict of Nantes (1598)

1/The Call for Reformation

The dissolution is such, that the souls entrusted to the clergy receive great damage, for we are told that the majority of the clergy are living in open concubinage, and that if our justice intervenes in order to punish them, they revolt and create a scandal, and that they despise our justice to the point that they arm themselves against it.

ISABELLA OF CASTILE, ON NOVEMBER 20, 1500

As the fifteenth century came to a close, it was clear that the church was in need of profound reformation, and that many longed for it. The decline and corruption of the papacy was well known. After its residence in Avignon, where it had served as a tool of French interests, the papacy had been further weakened by the Great Schism, which divided western Europe in its allegiance to two—and even three—popes. At times, the various claimants to the papal see seemed equally unworthy. Then, almost as soon as the schism was healed, the papacy fell into the hands of men who were more moved by the glories of the Renaissance than by the message of the cross. Through war, intrigue, bribery, and licentiousness, these popes sought to restore and even to outdo the glories of ancient Rome. As a result, while most people still believed in the supreme authority of the Roman see, many found it difficult to reconcile their faith in the papacy with their distrust for its actual occupants.

Corruption, however, was not limited to the leadership in Rome. The conciliar movement, which had sought to end the Great Schism and to reform the morals of the entire church, had succeeded in the first of these goals, but failed in the second. One of the reasons for such failure was that several of the bishops sitting in the councils were themselves among those who profited from the existing corruption. Thus, while the hopeful conciliarist reformers thundered anathemas against absenteeism, pluralism, and simony—the practice of buying and selling ecclesiastical positions—many who sat on the councils were guilty of such practices, and were not ready to give them up.

Such corrupt leadership set the tone for most of the lesser clergy and the monastics. While clerical celibacy was the law of the church, there were many who broke it openly; and bishops and local priests alike flaunted their illegitimate children. The ancient monastic discipline was increasingly relaxed as convents and monasteries became centers of leisurely living. Monarchs and the high nobility often provided for their illegitimate offspring by having them named abbots and abbesses, with no regard for their monastic vocation or lack of it. The learning for which monastic houses had been famous also declined, and the educational requirements for the local clergy were practically nil.

In such circumstances, even the many priests and monastics who wished to be faithful to their calling found this to be exceedingly difficult. How could one practice asceticism and contemplation in a monastery that had become a house of leisure, and a meeting place for fashionable soirées? How could a priest resist corruption in his parish, when he himself had been forced to buy his position? How could the laity trust a sacrament of penance administered by a clergy that seemed to have no sense of the enormity of sin? The religious conscience of Europe was divided within itself, torn between trust in a church that had been its spiritual mother for generations, and the patent failures of that church.

But it was not only at the moral level that the church seemed to be in need of reformation. Some among the more thoughtful Christians were becoming convinced that the teachings of the church had also gone astray. The fall of Constantinople, half a century earlier, had flooded western Europe, and Italy in particular, with scholars whose views were different from those that had become common in the West. The manuscripts these scholars brought with them alerted western scholars to the many changes and interpolations that had taken place in the copying and recopying of ancient texts. New philosophical outlooks were also introduced. Greek became more commonly known among western scholars, who could now compare the Greek text of the New Testament with the commonly used Latin Vulgate. From such quarters came the conviction that it was necessary to return to the sources of the Christian faith, and that this would result in a reformation of existing doctrine and practice.

Although most who held such views were by no means radical, their call for a return to the sources tended to confirm the earlier appeals by reformers

An old world was passing away, and a new one was being born to take its place. In this illustration from one of Galileo's works, he is depicted as discussing the universe with Ptolemy and Copernicus.

such as Wycliffe and Huss. The desire for a radical reformation in the doctrine of the church did not seem so out of place if it was true that such doctrine had changed through the centuries, straying from the New Testament. The many followers those earlier reformers still had in England, Bohemia, and other areas now felt encouraged by scholarship, which, while not agreeing with them in their more radical claims, confirmed their basic tenet: that it was necessary to return to the sources of Christianity, particularly through the study of Scripture.

To this was added the discontent of the masses, which earlier had found expression in apocalyptic movements like the one led by Hans Böhm. The economic conditions of the masses, far from improving, had worsened in the last decades. The peasants in particular were increasingly exploited by the landowners. While some monastic houses and church leaders still practiced acts of charity, most of the poor no longer had the sense that the church was their defender. On the contrary, the ostentatiousness of prelates, their power as landowners, and their support of increasing inequality were seen by many as a betrayal of the poor, and eventually as a sign that the Antichrist had gained possession of the church. The ferment brewing in such quarters periodically broke out in peasant revolts, apocalyptic visions, and calls for a new order.

Meanwhile, the ancient feudal system was coming to an end. First France, and then England and Spain, saw the development of powerful monarchies that forced the nobility to serve the ends of the nation as a whole. The sovereigns of such states felt the need to limit and control the power of the prelates, many of whom were also feudal rulers of vast areas. As France had earlier led in the suppression of the Templars, Spain now felt compelled to bring the ancient military orders, such as Calatrava and Santiago, under royal supremacy; and to that end King Ferdinand was made their grand master. Areas that did not enjoy the same unity, such as the Netherlands and Germany, seethed with nationalist discontent and dreams of union and independence. Latin, which earlier had been a common bond for much of western Europe, was increasingly limited to ecclesiastical and scholarly circles, while the various vernacular languages came to be regarded as equally respectable. Indeed, the fifteenth and sixteenth centuries were the formative period for most of the literary languages of western Europe. Nationalism, which had begun to develop centuries earlier, found expression in these languages, and soon became the order of the day, both in those nations that had achieved political unity and in those that still fretted under feudal disunion and foreign dominance. Such sentiments in turn undermined the ancient dream of "one flock under one shepherd," which now appeared to many as little more than an excuse for foreign intervention.

Other momentous events were also changing the worldview of western Europe. New worlds were being discovered beyond the western horizon. Travel to the Far East was becoming increasingly common. The flat earth around which the sun and the stars revolved became a relic of the past. Great advances were made in medicine, mathematics, and physics. And all this was made readily available to scholars in various areas by means of the printing press, which precisely at that time was coming into its own.

An old world was passing away, and a new one was being born in its place. It was unavoidable that the church too would feel the impact of the new times and that, just as new forms of being human were emerging, new forms of being Christian would also emerge. Exactly how this was to be done, however, was open to debate. Some sought to reform the old church from within, while others lost all hope for such reformation, and openly broke with the papacy. In such an age of turmoil, many sincere Christians went through profound soul searching that eventually led them to conclusions and positions they themselves could not have predicted. Others, equally sincere and devout, came to opposite conclusions. The resulting disagreements and conflict marked the entire age that we now call the Reformation of the sixteenth century.

As the Middle Ages drew to a close, many advocates of reform were convinced that the greatest ill of the church was the obscurantism of what soon would be called the "dark ages." The printing press, the influx of Byzantine scholars, and the rediscovery of the artistic and literary legacy of antiquity gave credence to the hope that the furtherance of scholarship and education would produce the much-needed reformation of the church. If at some point in the past centuries practices had been introduced that were contrary to original Christian teaching, it seemed reasonable to surmise that a return to the sources of Christianity—both biblical and patristic—would do away with such practices.

This was the program of the humanist reformers. In this context, the term "humanist" does not refer primarily to those who value human nature above all else, but rather to those who devote themselves to the "humanities," seeking to restore the literary glories of antiquity. The humanists of the sixteenth century differed greatly among themselves, but all agreed in their love for classical letters. Long before the Protestant Reformation broke out, there was a large network of humanists who carried a vast correspondence among themselves, and who hoped that their work would result in the reformation of the church. Their acknowledged leader, respected by many as the "Prince of Humanists," was Erasmus of Rotterdam.

Erasmus was the illegitimate offspring of a priest and a physician's daughter, and throughout his life felt burdened by his humble origins. Reared in the midst of the bustling commercial activity of Holland, his opinions came to reflect the common values of the bourgeoisie: tolerance, moderation, stability, and so forth. He studied some scholastic theology, but soon came to despise its excessive subtlety and seemingly idle curiosity. He then decided to turn his attention to classical literature, which was enjoying a revival of interest. In a later visit to England, he became part of a circle of humanists interested in the reformation of the church, and these introduced him to the study of Scripture and of early Christian literature, which he saw as captive to the scholastics. It was at that time that he decided to perfect his rudimentary knowledge of Greek, which he soon mastered. Meanwhile, he published the *Enchiridion Militis Christiani—Dagger* (or *Handbook*) *of the Christian Soldier.* There, using military metaphors, he expounded what he took to be the Christian life, and the resources available to the "soldier of Christ."

As a young man, Erasmus had studied under the Brethren of the Common Life, whose "modern devotion" had left a profound imprint on him. Now, joining the humanist spirit to that devotion, he came to describe Christianity as above all a decent, moderate, and balanced life. The commandments of Jesus he saw as similar to the best precepts of Stoicism and Platonism. Their purpose is to subject passion to the rule of reason. This is to be achieved through a fairly ascetic discipline, although this discipline must not be confused with monasticism. The monastic withdraws from the common life of the world; the true "soldier of Christ" trains for practical and daily life in the midst of human affairs. What the church needs, in order to be reformed, is for Christians to practice this discipline, and to abandon the vices of the pagans. In this reference to pagan vices, Erasmus had in mind the evil example set by the popes of the Renaissance, who would rather be compared with Jupiter or with Julius Cesar than with Jesus or St. Peter. He therefore rejected the pomp and the quest for earthly glories that characterized much of the life of the church in his time, and called for greater simplicity of life. This did not mean, however, a mere revival of the monastic spirit. He had much to say against monks and monasteries, which had become havens of idleness and ignorance. But he also rejected the monastic ideal as based on the unacceptable distinction between the precepts of Jesus, which all must obey, and his "counsels of perfection," addressed to monastics in particular. Such distinction, while encouraging some to radical obedience, implied that common Christians were not also "soldiers of Christ," called to complete obedience.

Such obedience Erasmus saw as more important than doctrine. He did believe that doctrines were significant, and he held to traditional Christian orthodoxy on matters such as the incarnation and the Trinity. But he insisted that righteousness was more important than orthodoxy, and he frequently attacked friars who were capable of subtle theological discussions, but whose lives were scandalous.

On the other hand, the true Christian life is one of inwardness. Profoundly influenced by Platonism—and by ancient Christian writers who had suffered the same influence—Erasmus was convinced that the Christian warfare was an inner one. While outward means, such as the sacraments, were important and should not be discarded, their significance was in their inner meaning, in the message they conveyed to the secret heart of the believer. As he would say of baptism, "what good is it to be outwardly sprinkled with holy water, if one is filthy within?"

In short, what Erasmus sought was the reformation of customs, the practice of decency and moderation, an inner devotion shaped by learning and meditation, and a church that encouraged these things. Although his birth was quite humble, he eventually won the admiration of scholars throughout Europe who shared similar hopes, and whose mouthpiece he became. Among his admirers were many in the nobility and even some

IMAGO·ERASMI·ROTERODA
MI·AB·ALBERTO·DVRERO·AD
VIVAM·EFFIGIEM·DELINIATA·

THN·ΚΡΕΙΤΤΩ·ΤΑ·ΣΥΓΓΡΑΜ
ΜΑΤΑ·ΔΗΞΕΙ

·MDXXVI·

*Erasmus, the "prince of humanists," as Albrecht Dürer saw him
in 1526. The Greek inscription declares that his works provide a
better portrait.*

crowned heads. His followers served as secretaries and mentors in some of
the most powerful courts in Europe. The reformation he advocated seemed
to be about to take place.

Then the Protestant Reformation broke out. Spirits were inflamed. Tolerance and moderation became increasingly difficult. It was no longer a matter of reforming customs, or of clarifying some aspects of Christian theology that might have gone astray, but rather of radically shifting some of the fundamental premises of traditional Christianity. Partisans on both sides sought the support of Erasmus, who would rather stay out of a conflict in which passion seemed to have taken the place of reason. Finally, he broke with Luther and his followers, as we shall see later on. But still he refused to support the Catholics in their attacks against Protestants. To the end, he had admirers in both camps, but very few followers. From his study, he continued calling for moderation, for a reformation after the humanist design, and for the ancient virtues of Stoics and Platonists. Few paid heed to him, at least during his lifetime, and he would complain: "I detest dissension, because it goes both against the teachings of Christ and against a secret inclination of nature. I doubt that either side in the dispute can be suppressed without grave loss. It is clear that many of the reforms for which Luther calls are urgently needed. My only wish is that now that I am old I be allowed to enjoy the results of my efforts. But both sides reproach me and seek to coerce me. Some claim that since I do not attack Luther I agree with him, while the Lutherans declare that I am a coward who has forsaken the gospel."* But centuries later, after passions had subsided, both Protestants and Catholics would agree that his were a great mind and a great heart, and that all had something to learn from him.

---

*"Epistle to Laurinus," February 1, 1523.

2/Martin Luther: Pilgrimage to Reformation

Many have taken the Christian faith to be a simple and easy matter, and have even numbered it among the virtues. This is because they have not really experienced it, nor have they tested the great strength of faith.

MARTIN LUTHER

Throughout the history of Christianity, few have been the object of as much debate as Martin Luther has been. Some describe him as the ogre who destroyed the unity of the church, the wild boar that trampled the Lord's vineyard, a renegade monk who spent his life shattering the very foundations of monasticism. For others he is the great hero through whose efforts the preaching of the pure gospel was restored, the champion of biblical truth, the reformer of a corrupt and apostate church. In recent years, however, there has been a growing mutual understanding among Christians of different persuasions. As a result of more balanced studies of Luther, Catholics as well as Protestants have been led to amend opinions that had resulted, not from historical research, but from the heat of polemics. Now few doubt Luther's sincerity, and many Catholic historians affirm that his protest was amply justified, and that he was right on many points of doctrine. On the other hand, few Protestant historians continue to view Luther as the gigantic hero who almost single-handedly reformed Christianity, and whose sins and errors were only of minor importance.

Luther appears to have been an erudite and studious man who was also uncouth and even rude in his manner. Perhaps this helped him express his very profound theological points in a manner that found ready response among the masses. He was sincere in his faith to the point that it became a burning passion within him, and he could also be vulgar in his expression of it. Nothing mattered to him as much as his faith and his obedience to God. Once he became convinced that God wished him to pursue a certain course of action, he followed it to its ultimate consequences. He was clearly not the sort of disciple who, having put a hand to the plow, looks back. His use of language—both Latin and German—was masterful, although he was inclined to underline the importance of a particular point by exaggerating it to the point of distortion. Once convinced of the truth of his cause, he was ready to face the most powerful lords of his time. But the very depth of his conviction, his passionate stance for truth, and his tendency to exaggerate led him to utter expressions and take positions that he or his followers would later regret.

On the other hand, much of Luther's impact was due to circumstances that he neither created nor controlled, and of whose role in the process of reformation he himself was only dimly aware. The invention of the movable type printing press gave his writings a widespread audience they otherwise would not have had—in fact, Luther was the first to make full use of the value of printing as a medium for propaganda, and to write with the printed page in mind. The growing German nationalist sentiment of which he himself partook offered unexpected but very valuable support. Many humanists who hoped for reformation, while disagreeing with many of Luther's tenets and methods, insisted that he should not be condemned without a hearing, as had happened earlier with John Huss. Political circumstances at the outset of the Reformation also prevented Luther's immediate condemnation, and by the time civil and ecclesiastic authorities were ready to intervene it was too late to quiet the storm. On studying Luther's life and work, one thing is clear: the much-needed Reformation took place, not because Luther decided that it would be so, but rather because the time was ripe for it, and because the Reformer and many others with him were ready to fulfill their historical responsibility.

The Long Quest

Luther was born in 1483, in Eisleben, Germany. His father, of peasant origin, had first become a miner and then the owner of several foundries. Young Martin's childhood was not a happy one. His parents were extremely severe, and many years later he would still speak bitterly of some of the punishments he had suffered. Throughout his life he was prey to periods of depression and anxiety, and some scholars suggest that this was due to the excessive austerity of his early years. His first experiences at school were no better, and he later spoke of having been whipped for not knowing his lessons. Although the importance of such early experiences ought not to be exaggerated as the sole explanation for the course of Luther's life, there is no doubt that they left a deep imprint on his character.

In July 1505, when almost twenty-two years of age, Luther joined the Augustinian monastery at Erfurt. Many causes led to this decision. Two weeks earlier, in the midst of a thunderstorm, he had felt overwhelmed by the fear of death and hell, and he had promised St. Anne that he would become a monk. According to his own later explanation, it was his harsh upbringing that took him to the monastery. His father had planned for him a career in law, and had not spared efforts so that he could have the necessary education. But Luther had no desire to become a lawyer, and therefore it is possible that Luther, though not entirely aware of his motives, was interposing a monastic vocation between his father's plans and his own inclinations. Upon hearing of his son's decision, the older Luther was incensed, and took his own good time in forgiving what appeared to him as a betrayal of his lofty goals for his son. Ultimately, however, Luther was led to the monastery by a concern for his own salvation. The theme of salvation and damnation permeated the atmosphere in which he lived. The present life was little more than a preparation and testing for the one to come. It seemed foolish to devote oneself to gaining prestige and riches in the present, through the practice of law, to the detriment of life everlasting. Luther therefore entered the monastery as a faithful child of the church, with the firm purpose of making use of the means of salvation offered by that church, of which the surest was the monastic life of renunciation.

During the year of his novitiate, Luther was convinced that he had made a wise decision, for he felt happy and at peace with God. His superiors promptly recognized his unusual abilities, and decided that he should become a priest. Luther himself later wrote about the overwhelming experience of celebrating his first mass, when he was gripped by terror upon thinking that he was holding and offering nothing less than the very body of Christ. That feeling of terror then became increasingly frequent, for he felt unworthy of God's love, and he was not convinced that he was doing enough to be saved. God seemed to him a severe judge—like his father and his teachers at an earlier time—who, in the final judgment, would ask for an account and find him wanting. In order to be saved from the wrath of such a God, one must make use of all the means of grace offered by the church.

But those means were not sufficient for someone as deeply religious, sincere, and passionate as Luther. Good works and the sacrament of penance were supposed to suffice for the young friar's need to be justified before God. But they did not. Luther had an overpowering sense of his own sinfulness, and the more he sought to overcome it the more he became aware of sin's sway over him. It is mistaken to suppose that he was not a good monk, or that his life was licentious or immoral. On the contrary, he sought to obey his monastic vows to the fullest. He would repeatedly punish his body, as recommended by the great teachers of monasticism. And he went to confession as often as possible. But such practices did not allay his fear of damnation. If for sins to be forgiven they had to be confessed, there was always the horrifying possibility that he might forget some sin, and thus lose the reward after which he was so diligently striving. He therefore spent hours listing and examining all his thoughts and actions, and the more he studied them the more sin he found in them. There were times when, at the very moment of leaving the confessional, he realized that there was some sin that he had not confessed. He would then grow anxious and even desperate, for sin was clearly more than conscious actions or thoughts. It was a condition, a way of being, something that went far beyond the individual sins one could confess to a priest. Thus, the very sacrament of penance, which was supposed to bring relief to his sense of sinfulness, actually exacerbated it, leaving him in a state of despair.

His spiritual advisor then recommended the reading of the great teachers of mysticism. As we have already seen, towards the end of the Middle Ages (partially as a response to the corruption of the church) there was a great upsurge of mystical piety, which offered an alternative path to approach God. Luther resolved to follow that path, not because he doubted the authority of the church, but because that authority, in the person of his confessor, advised him to do so.

Mysticism captivated him for a time—as had been the case earlier with monasticism. Perhaps here he would find the path to salvation. But soon that path became another blind alley. The mystics affirmed that all one had to do was to love God, and that all the rest would follow as a result of that love. This was a word of liberation for Luther, for it was no longer necessary to keep a strict account of all his sins, as he had so eagerly endeavored to do, to be rewarded only by failure and despair. But he soon discovered that loving God was not an easy matter. If God was like his father and his teachers, who had beaten him to the point of drawing blood, how could he love such a God? Eventually, Luther came to the terrifying conclusion that what he felt for God was not love, but hatred!

There was no way out of such difficulties. In order to be saved, one must confess one's sins, and Luther had discovered that, in spite of his best efforts, his sin went far beyond what he could confess. If, as the mystics claimed, it sufficed to love God, this was no great help, for Luther had to acknoweledge that he could not love the just God that demanded an account of all his actions.

At that point his confessor, who was also the superior, took a bold step. Normally, one would suppose that a priest who was going through such a crisis as Luther's should not be made a pastor and teacher for others. But that was precisely what his confessor decided he should be. Centuries earlier, Jerome had found in his Hebrew studies an escape from temptation. Although Luther's problems were different from Jerome's, perhaps study,

This painting by Lucas Cranach (1526), now in the National Museum of Stockholm, is probably the most authentic extant portrait of Luther.

teaching, and pastoral responsibilities would have a similar effect on him. Therefore, Luther was ordered, much against his expectations, to prepare to teach Scripture at the new University of Wittenberg.

Protestant folklore has it that as a friar Luther did not know the Bible, and that it was only at the time of his conversion, or shortly before, that he began to study it. This is false. As a monk who had to follow the traditional hours of prayer, Luther knew the Psalter by heart. Besides, in 1512, after studies that included the Bible, he received his doctorate in theology.

When Luther found himself forced to prepare lectures on the Bible, he began seeing new meanings in it, and the possibility that such meanings would provide an answer to his spiritual quest. In 1513, he began to lecture on the Psalms. Since he had spent years reciting the Psalter, always within the context of the liturgical year—which centers on the main events in the life of Christ—Luther interpreted the Psalms Christologically. When the Psalmist speaks in the first person, Luther took this to be Christ speaking about himself. Therefore, in the Psalter, Luther saw Christ undergoing trials similar to his own. This was the beginning of his great discovery. By itself, it could have led Luther to the commonly held notion that God the Father demands justice, and that it is God the Son who loves us and works for our forgiveness. But Luther had studied theology, and knew that such dichotomy within the Godhead was unacceptable. Therefore, while he found consolation in Christ's sufferings, this did not suffice to cure his anguish and despair.

The great discovery probably came in 1515, when Luther began lecturing on the Epistle to the Romans. He later declared that it was in the first chapter of that epistle that he found the solution to his difficulties. That solution did not come easily. It was not simply a matter of opening the Bible one day and reading that "the just shall live by faith." As he tells the story, the great discovery followed a long struggle and bitter anguish, for Romans 1:17 begins by declaring that, in the gospel, "the righteousness of God is revealed." According to this text, the gospel is the revelation of the rightousness—the justice—of God. But it was precisely the justice of God that Luther found unbearable. How could such a message be gospel, good news? For Luther, good news would have been that God is not just, meaning that God does not judge sinners. But, in Romans 1:17, the good news and the justice of God are indissolubly linked. Luther hated the very phrase "the justice of God," and spent day and night seeking to understand the relationship between the two parts of that single verse, which, after declaring that in the gospel "the justice of God is revealed," affirms that "the righteous shall live by faith."

The answer was surprising. Luther came to the conclusion that the "justice of God" does not refer, as he had been taught, to the punishment of sinners. It means rather that the "justice" or "righteousness" of the righteous is not their own, but God's. The "righteousness of God" is that which is given to those who live by faith. It is given, not because they are righteous, nor because they fulfill the demands of divine justice, but simply because God wishes to give it. Thus, Luther's doctrine of "justification by faith" does not mean that what God demands of us is faith, as if this were something we have to do or achieve, and which God then rewards. It means rather that both faith and justification are the work of God, a free gift to sinners. As a result of this discovery, Luther tells us, "I felt that I had been born anew and that the gates of heaven had been opened. The whole of

Scripture gained a new meaning. And from that point on the phrase 'the justice of God' no longer filled me with hatred, but rather became unspeakably sweet by virtue of a great love."*

The Storm Breaks Loose

Although later events revealed another side to his personality, until this time Luther seems to have been a quite reserved person, devoted to his studies and to his spiritual struggle. His great discovery, while bringing him to a new understanding of the gospel, did not immediately lead him to protest against the church's understanding of Christianity. On the contrary, our friar continued in his teaching and pastoral duties and, although there are indications that he taught what he had recently learned, he did not oppose it to the traditional teaching of the church. Moreover, he himself does not seem to have been aware of the radical contradiction between his discovery and the entire penitential system that was so fundamental to accepted theology and piety.

Through quiet persuasion, Luther brought most of his colleagues at the University of Wittenberg to his way of thinking. When he became convinced that he must challenge traditional views, he composed ninety-seven theses to be debated in an academic setting. In these theses, he attacked several of the main tenets of scholastic theology, and he clearly expected that their publication and debate would cause a stir, allowing him to divulge his great discovery. But, much to his surprise, the theses and the debate on them aroused little interest beyond the university itself. It seemed that the notion that the gospel was entirely other than was commonly thought, which Luther took to be of paramount importance, was received with little more than a great yawn.

Then the unexpected happened. Luther wrote another set of theses, with no expectation that they would have more impact than the previous ones, and the result was such a stir that eventually all of Christendom was involved in its consequences. The reason for this very different reaction was that these other theses—now commonly known as Luther's "Ninety-five Theses"—attacked the sale of indulgences and its theological presuppositions. With little awareness of what he was doing, or whom he was attacking, Luther had spoken against plans for profit designed by very powerful lords and prelates.

The particular sale of indulgences that prompted Luther's protest had been authorized by Pope Leo X, and also involved the economic and political ambitions of the powerful house of Hohenzollern, which aspired to hegemony in Germany. One of the members of that house, Albert of Brandenburg, was already in possession of two episcopal sees, and hoped to

---

*"Preface to the Latin Writings."

acquire the most important archbishopric in Germany, that of Mainz. He began negotiations with Leo X, one of the worst popes of that age of corrupt, avaricious, and indolent popes. The result was an agreement whereby, for the sum of ten thousand ducats, Albert could have what he requested. Since this was a considerable sum, the pope also authorized Albert to announce a great sale of indulgences in his territories, on condition that half of the proceeds be sent to the papal coffers. One of Leo's dreams was to finish building the great Basilica of Saint Peter, begun earlier by Julius II, and for this he needed the funds that he hoped to receive from Albert's sale of indulgences. Thus, the great basilica that is now the pride of Roman Catholicism was one of the indirect causes of the Protestant Reformation.

The man put in charge of the sale of indulgences in Germany was the Dominican John Tetzel, an unscrupulous man who was willing to make scandalous claims for his wares as long as such claims would help sales. Thus, for instance, Tetzel and his preachers were heard announcing that the indulgence that they sold made the sinner "cleaner than when coming out of baptism," and "cleaner than Adam before the Fall," and that "the cross of the seller of indulgences has as much power as the cross of Christ." Those who wished to buy an indulgence for a loved one who was deceased were promised that, "as soon as the coin in the coffer rings, the soul from purgatory springs."*

Pope Leo X raised funds to complete construction of the Basilica of Saint Peter in Rome through the sale of indulgences, against which Luther protested.

---

*Statements of Brother J. Tetzel in defense of indulgences.

Such claims aroused the indignation of many among the learned, who knew that Tetzel and his preachers were misrepresenting the doctrine of the church. Among humanists, who bemoaned the prevailing ignorance and superstition, Tetzel's preaching was seen as another example of the deep corruption of the church. Others who were imbued in the growing German nationalist sentiment saw Tetzel's campaign as one more instance in which Rome was fleecing the German people, exploiting their credulity in order to squander the results in feasts and luxury. But such sentiments were only quietly expressed, and the sale went on.

It was at that point that Luther nailed his famous Ninety-five Theses to the door of the castle church in Wittenberg. His theses, written in Latin, were not calculated to cause a great religious commotion, as he had hoped would be the case with his earlier theses. After that other experience, he seems to have thought that such issues were important only to theologians, and that therefore his new set of theses would not be read or debated beyond academic circles. But these Ninety-five Theses, written with a deep sense of righteous indignation, were much more devastating that the earlier ones. While addressing fewer theological issues, they did evoke a positive response from those who resented the exploitation of Germany by foreign interests —and by Germans such as the Hohenzollerns in connivance with those interests. Also, in concretely attacking the sale of indulgences, Luther was endangering the profit and designs of the pope and of the house of Hohenzollern. And, although his attack was relatively moderate, Luther went beyond the question of the efficacy of indulgences, and pointed to the exploitation that stood at the heart of it. According to Luther, if it is true that the pope is able to free souls from purgatory, he ought to use that power, not for trivial reasons such as the building of a church, but simply out of love, and freely (thesis 82). In truth, the pope should give his money to the poor from whom the sellers of indulgences wring their last coins, and he ought to do this even if it were to require selling the Basilica of Saint Peter (thesis 51).

Luther published his theses on the eve of All Saints, and their impact was such that that date, October 31, 1517, is usually given for the beginning of the Protestant Reformation. Printers soon spread copies of the Ninety-five Theses throughout Germany, both in their original Latin text and in a German translation. Luther himself sent a copy to Albert of Brandenburg, with a very respectful cover letter. Albert sent both the theses and the letter to Rome, asking Pope Leo to intervene. Emperor Maximilian was enraged at the impertinence of the upstart friar, and he too asked Leo to silence Luther. Meanwhile, Luther published an extensive explanation of the theses, clarifying what he had meant in those very brief propositions, but making his attack on indulgences even sharper, and expounding some of the theological stance on which he based his protest.

The pope's response was to ask the Augustinian order to deal with the

The wooden doors of the Castle Church in Wittenberg, on which Luther nailed his Ninety-five Theses, were replaced by metal ones in the nineteenth century. The new doors are inscribed with the text of the famous theses.

matter, for Luther was one of its members. The Reformer was called to the next chapter meeting of the order, in Heidelberg. He went in fear for his life, for he expected to be condemned and burned as a heretic. But he was surprised to find that many of his fellow friars favored his teachings, and that some of the younger ones were even enthusiastic about it. Others saw the dispute between Luther and Tetzel as one more instance of the ancient rivalry between Dominicans and Augustinians, and therefore refused to abandon their champion. Eventually, Luther was able to return to Wittenberg, strengthened by the support of his order, and encouraged by those whom he had won for his cause.

The pope then took a different route. The Diet of the Empire—the assembly of the princes and nobles—was scheduled to meet in Augsburg, under the presidence of Emperor Maximilian. As his legate to that gathering, Leo sent Cardinal Cajetan, a man of vast erudition whose main task was to convince the German princes to undertake a crusade against the Turks, who were threatening western Europe, and to agree to a tax for the support of that enterprise. The fear of the Turkish threat was such that Rome was seeking reconciliation with the Hussites in Bohemia, and was even willing to accept some of the conditions imposed by them. As a secondary task, Cajetan was also instructed to meet with Luther and force him to recant. If the friar proved obstinate, he was to be sent as a prisoner to Rome.

Luther's ruling prince, Frederick the Wise, Elector of Saxony, secured from Emperor Maximilian a safe-conduct for Luther. The latter, however, put little trust in the imperial word, remembering that little more than a century before, under similar circumstances and in violation of an imperial safe-conduct, John Huss had been burned at Constance. But, in spite of this, he went to Augsburg, convinced that he would not die unless God willed it to be so.

The meeting with Cajetan did not go well. The cardinal refused to discuss Luther's teachings, and demanded that he simply recant. The friar, for his part, declared that he was willing to withdraw what he had said, if he could only be convinced that he was wrong. When he learned that Cajetan did not have to debate the issues at stake, because he was armed with the pope's authority to arrest him, Luther secretly left Augsburg at night and returned to Wittenberg, where he issued an appeal to a general council.

During all this time, Luther had been able to count on the protection of Frederick the Wise, Elector of Saxony and therefore lord of Wittenberg. At this point, Frederick felt compelled to protect Luther, not because he was convinced of the truth of the friar's teachings, but simply because justice demanded that he be given a hearing and a fair trial. Above anything else, Frederick wished to be known and remembered as a wise and just ruler. With that end in mind he had founded the University of Wittenberg, many of whose professors now told him that Luther was right, and that he was by no means a heretic. At least until he was duly judged and condemned, Frederick would protect him against the possibility of a crime such as had taken place in the burning of John Huss. Such steadfastness on the elector's part was not easy, for opposition was mounting, and the number and power of those who declared Luther to be a heretic was constantly increasing.

At that point, Maximilian's death left the imperial throne vacant. Since this was an elective honor, it was now necessary to settle on a successor to the dead emperor. The two most powerful candidates were Charles I of Spain and Francis I of France. The accession of either Charles or Francis to the imperial throne was feared by Pope Leo, whose policies would be threatened by the resulting concentration of power in a single person. Charles already had, besides Spain, which was rapidly becoming rich through the gold flowing from its colonial empire, vast hereditary possessions in Austria, the

*Frederick the Wise, Elector of Saxony, was
Luther's staunchest defender. Here he is
depicted with Luther to his right, Melanchthon
to his left.*

Low Countries, and southern Italy. Were the imperial crown to be placed on
his brow, his power would be unrivaled in western Europe. Francis of France,
while not holding as much territory as Charles, also was feared by Leo, for
the union of the French and German crowns would place the papacy once

again under the shadow of France. The pope therefore had to find another candidate worthy of support, not because of his power, but rather by reason of his personal prestige. Given such criteria, the ideal candidate whom the pope could oppose to both Charles and Francis was Frederick the Wise of Saxony, who had earned the respect and admiration of other German princes. Were Frederick to be elected emperor, the resulting balance of power would allow Leo greater influence and independence. Therefore, even before Maximillian's death, the pope had decided to court Frederick, and make him his candidate for emperor.

But Frederick protected Luther, at least until the friar was properly tried and convicted. Therefore, Leo followed a policy of postponing the condemnation of Luther, and seeking better relations both with the Reformer and with his protector. To seek such rapprochement, he sent Karl von Miltitz, a relative of Frederick, as his ambassador to Saxony. As a sign of special papal favor, Miltitz took with him a golden rose for Frederick. Although the pope refrained from sending a similar gift to Luther, he instructed his legate to approach the rebellious monk in a conciliatory attitude.

Miltitz met with Luther, who promised that he would abstain from further controversy as long as his opponents did likewise. This brought about a brief truce, which was broken by John Eck, a professor at Ingolstadt who was incensed by Luther's teachings. Eck was an astute opponent, and therefore instead of attacking Luther, which would have made him appear as having broken the existing peace, he attacked Andreas Bodenstein von Karlstadt, another professor at Wittenberg. Karlstadt had been converted to Luther's position, but he was an impetuous man who was ready to carry his new beliefs to their radical consequences. This in itself made him more vulnerable than Luther to the charge of heresy, and therefore Eck was well advised in challenging Karlstadt to a debate. This was to take place in Leipzig, and was originally billed as a discussion, not of Luther's theses, but of Karlstadt's theology. But the questions posed for debate were clearly those raised by Luther, and therefore the Reformer declared that this was merely a subterfuge to attack him, and that he too would participate in the debate.

This was conducted with the strict formality of an academic debate, and lasted for several days. When Luther and Eck finally confronted each other, it was clear that the former had greater knowledge of Scripture, whereas the latter was more at home in canon law and medieval theology. Eck very ably maneuvered the discussion into his own field of expertise, and finally Luther felt compelled to declare that the Council of Constance had erred in condemning Huss, and that a Christian with the support of Scripture has more authority than all popes and councils against that support. That sufficed. Luther had declared himself in agreement with a heretic who had been condemned by an ecumenical council, and had even dared accuse the council itself of having erred. In spite of the strength of Luther's arguments, which bested Eck at a number of points, it was his rival who won the debate, for he had proven what he had set out to do: that Luther was a heretic and a supporter of the teachings of Huss.

Thus began a new stage in Luther's struggle, marked by more open confrontations and greater dangers. But the Reformer and his followers had made good use of the time granted to them by political circumstances, with the result that throughout Germany, and even beyond its borders, there were increasing numbers who saw in Luther the champion of biblical faith. To those who found themselves in theological agreement with him was added the support of many humanists and German nationalists. The former saw many points of contact between Luther's protest and the reformation that they proposed. The nationalists saw in him the mouthpiece of German outrage in the face of the abuses of Rome.

A few weeks before the Leipzig debate, Charles I of Spain had been elected emperor, to be known thereafter as Charles V. Although Charles owed a debt of gratitude to Frederick the Wise for having supported his candidacy, he was a strictly orthodox man who would not countenance heresy in his lands, and therefore his election bode ill for Luther. Frederick still supported him the more so, since he was becoming increasingly convinced that the Reformer was right. But now the pope had no reason to delay a formal condemnation that had earlier been stayed only for political considerations. In the bull *Exsurge Domine,* in which Leo declared that a wild boar had entered the Lord's vineyard, he ordered all books by Martin Luther to be burned; and he gave the rebellious friar, under penalty of excommunication and being declared anathema, sixty days to submit to Roman authority.

The bull took a long time to reach Luther. As copies of it arrived at various German territories, there were conflicting reactions. In some places, the pope's instructions were obeyed, and there were public burnings of Luther's books. But in other places students and other supporters of Luther chose to burn the works of his opponents. When the bull finally reached Luther, he burned it publicly, together with other books that he declared to be the worst proponents of "popish doctrines." The breach was final, and there was no way to undo it.

It was still necessary to determine the attitude of the emperor and the other German lords, for without their support there was little that Leo could do to silence the Reformer. The political maneuvers that took place in this regard were too complicated to retell here. Let it suffice to say that even Charles V, a convinced Catholic, showed himself willing to use Luther as a threat when he feared that Leo was showing too much favor for his rival, Francis I of France. Eventually, after many comings and goings, it was decided that Luther would appear before the Diet of the Empire to be gathered at Worms in 1521.

At Worms, Luther was taken before the Emperor and several of the great lords of the German Empire. The man in charge of the process showed him a number of books, and asked him if he had indeed written them. After examining them, Luther responded that such was the case, and that he had also written other books besides these. Then he was asked if he still held to what he had declared in those publications, or wished to recant anything. This was a difficult moment for Luther, not so much because he feared imperial power, but rather because he feared God. To dare oppose the entire church and the emperor, whose authority had been ordained by God, was a dreadful act. Once again the friar trembled before the divine majesty, and asked for a day's time in which to consider his answer.

By the next day it was widely known that Luther was to appear before the Diet, and the hall was filled. The emperor's presence at Worms, with a corps of Spanish soldiers who showed little respect for Germans, had irritated the populace as well as many German princes. Once again, Luther was asked to recant. In the midst of a great hush, the friar answered that much of what he had written was basic Christian doctrine, held both by him and by his opponents, and that therefore no one should expect him to repudiate such teachings. At some other points, he continued, his works dealt with the tyranny and injustice that the German people suffered. This too he could not recant, for such was not the purpose of the Diet, and in any case to withdraw such words would result in greater injustice. Third, in his works there were attacks against certain individuals, and points of doctrine that were at issue between him and his opponents. Perhaps, he confessed, some of these things had been said too harshly. But their truth he could not deny, unless someone could convince him that he was in error.

It was not the emperor's purpose to engage in a debate on Luther's teaching, and therefore he was asked once again, "Do you recant, or do you not?" To this Luther responded in German, therefore setting aside the Latin of traditional theological debate: "My conscience is a prisoner of God's Word. I cannot and will not recant, for to disobey one's conscience is neither just nor safe. God help me. Amen."* Then, with a gesture of victory, he left the hall and returned to his quarters.

In burning the papal bull, Luther had challenged Rome. Now, at Worms, he was challenging the Empire. Therefore, he had ample reason to call: "God help me."

---

*Opera 17:580.

3/ Luther's Theology

*The friends of the cross affirm that the cross
is good and that works are bad, for
through the cross works are undone and the
old Adam, whose strength is in works, is
crucified.*

MARTIN LUTHER

At this point in the life of Luther, we must pause to consider his theology, the driving force that would determine much of the rest of his life. By 1521, when he appeared before the Diet of Worms, Luther had come to the main theological conclusions that would characterize the whole of his thought. After that time, he would primarily expand and elaborate on the main points that had led him to his position at Worms. Therefore, this seems to be the best point in our narrative at which to pause and discuss the basic themes of Luther's theology. Earlier, while telling of his personal quest for salvation, we have spoken of the doctrine of justification by faith. But this was by no means the totality of Luther's theology.

The Word of God

As is commonly known, Luther sought to make the Word of God the starting point and the final authority for his theology. As a professor of Scripture, the Bible was for him of paramount importance, and it was in it that he found an answer to his anguished quest for salvation. But this does not mean that he was a rigid biblicist, for what he understood by the "Word of God" was more than the written word in the Bible.

In its primary sense, the Word of God is none other than God. This is supported by the first verses of the Gospel of John, where it is written that "in the beginning was the Word, and the Word was with God, and the Word was

God." The Bible itself declares that, strictly speaking, the Word of God is none other than God the Son, the Second Person of the Trinity, the Word who was made flesh and dwelt among us. Therefore, when God speaks, we are not simply given information; also, and above all, God acts. This is what is meant in the book of Genesis, where the Word of God is a creating force: "God said, let there be . . . and there was." When God speaks, that which is uttered is also created. God's Word, besides telling us something, does something in us and in all creation. That creative and powerful Word was incarnate in Jesus, who is both God's greatest revelation and God's greatest action. In Jesus, God was revealed to us. And also in Jesus God overcame the powers of evil that had us in subjection. God's revelation is also God's victory.

Given this biblical understanding of the Word of God, what makes the Bible the word of God is not that it is infallible, nor that it can serve as a source of authority for theological and religious debate. The Bible is the Word of God because in it Jesus, the Word incarnate, comes to us. Any who read the Bible and somehow do not find Jesus in it, have not encountered the Word of God. This was the reason why Luther, while insisting on the final authority of Scripture, could make deprecating comments about parts of it. The Epistle of James, for instance, seemed to him "pure straw," because he could not find the gospel in it, but only a series of rules of conduct. The book

The act of creation was the subject for the frontispiece of Luther's Bible.

of Revelation also caused him difficulty. Although he was not ready to delete such books from the canon, he openly confessed that it was difficult for him to see Jesus Christ in them, and that therefore they were of little value to him.

This notion of the Word of God as Jesus Christ himself allowed Luther to respond to one of the main objections Catholics raised to his doctrine of the authority of Scripture above the church. They argued that, since it was the church that had determined which books should be included in the canon of Scripture, it was clear that the church had authority over the Bible. Luther responded that it was neither the church that had made the Bible, nor the Bible that had made the church, but the gospel, Jesus Christ, that had made both the Bible and the church. Final authority rests neither in the church nor in the Bible, but in the gospel, in the message of Jesus Christ, who is the incarnate Word of God. Since Scripture gives a more trustworthy witness to that gospel than the pope's corrupt church, or even the best in Christian tradition, the Bible has authority over church, pope, and tradition. This is so, even though it is also true that in the early centuries of Christianity it was the church that recognized the gospel in certain books, and not in others, and thus determined the actual content of the Bible.

The Knowledge of God

Luther agreed with most traditional theology that it is possible to know something about God by purely rational or natural means. Such knowledge includes the fact that God exists, and allows us to distinguish between good and evil. The pagan philosophers of antiquity had it, and it is clear from the laws of ancient Rome that they were able to distinguish between good and evil. Furthermore, the philosophers were able to conclude that there is a single Supreme Being from which all things draw their existence.

But all this is not the true knowledge of God. As Luther would say, one does not get to know God by speculation, like one can get to the roof by climbing a ladder. All human efforts to climb to heaven, and thus to know God, are futile. Such efforts are what Luther calls "a theology of glory." This theology seeks to know the divine being in itself, in its own glory, while ignoring the enormous distance between God and humans. In the final analysis, a theology of glory seeks God in those things that humans consider most valuable and praiseworthy, and that is why it is so concerned with the power of God, the glory of God, and the goodness of God. But this is little more than creating God after our own image, and we deceive ourselves into believing that God's nature is what we would like it to be.

The fact of the matter is that the God of revelation is very different from the God of a theology of glory. God's highest self-disclosure takes place in the cross of Christ, and therefore Luther proposes, instead of a theology of glory, a "theology of the cross." Such theology seeks God, not where we choose, nor as we would like God to be, but in the divine revelation of the cross. There God is seen in weakness, in suffering, at a stumbling block. This means that God acts in a radically different way than we would expect. In the cross, God destroys our preconceived notions of divine glory. When we know God in the cross, we must set aside our previous knowledge of God, that is, all that we thought we knew by means of reason or of the inner voice of conscience. What we now know of God is very different from that other assumed knowledge of a theology of glory.

Law and Gospel

It is in the divine revelation that God is truly known. But, in that revelation, God is made manifest in two ways: law and gospel. This does not mean simply that the law is first, and then the gospel. Nor does it mean that the Old Testament is law, and the New Testament is gospel. Its meaning is much deeper. The contrast between law and gospel shows that God's revelation is both a word of judgment and a word of grace. The two always come together, and one cannot hear of grace without hearing also of judgment.

The doctrine of justification by faith, the message of God's forgiveness, does not imply that God is indifferent to sin. It is not simply that God forgives us because after all our sin is not of great consequence. On the contrary, God is holy, and sin is repugnant to the divine holiness. When God speaks, we are overwhelmed by the contrast between such holiness and our own sin. That is what Luther means by the Word of God as law.

But God also speaks a word of forgiveness—a forgiveness so tied up with the divine holiness that sometimes the same word is both judgment and grace. That forgiveness is the gospel, made all the more joyful and overpowering because the judgment of the law is so crushing. This gospel does not contradict or obliterate the law. God's forgiveness does not deny the gravity of our sin. It is precisely that gravity that makes the gospel such surprising good news.

When we hear that word of pardon, however, the character of the law changes for us. What earlier seemed an unbearable weight now becomes bearable and even sweet. Commenting on the Gospel of John, Luther declares:

At an earlier time there was no pleasure in the law for me. But now I find that the law is good and tasty, that it has been given to me so that I might live, and now I find my pleasure in it. Earlier, it told me what I ought to do. Now I begin to adapt myself to it. And for this I worship, praise, and serve God.*

---

*Sermon on John 1:17.

This constant dialectic between law and gospel means that a Christian is at one and the same time both sinful and justified. The sinner does not cease to be such upon being justified. On the contrary, upon being justified one discovers how deeply sinful one is. Justification is not the absence of sin, but the fact that God declares us to be just even while we are still sinners. The indissoluble bond between gospel and law is paralleled by our own Christian life as both sinners and justified believers.

The Church and Sacraments

Contrary to common belief, Luther was neither an individualist nor a rationalist. During the nineteenth century, when both rationalism and individualism seemed to be the wave of the future, some historians sought to depict Luther as the forerunner of such currents. This was frequently tied to an effort to show that Germany was the mother of modern civilization, of the use of reason, and of individual freedom. In such interpretations, Luther became the great national hero of Germany, the founder of modernity.

But all this is far removed from historical truth. The fact of the matter is that Luther was far from being a rationalist. His frequent references to reason as "dirty" or "a whore" should suffice to prove this point. As to his supposed individualism, this was more characteristic of the Italian leaders of the Renaissance than of the German Reformer; and in any case Luther attached too much importance to the church to be classified as a true individualist.

In spite of his protest against commonly accepted doctrine, and despite his rebellion against the authorities of the Roman church, Luther was convinced that the church was an essential element of the Christian message. His theology was not that of individual and direct communion with God, but rather that of a Christian life to be lived within a community of believers, and this community he frequently called "mother church."

While it is true that all Christians, by virtue of their baptism, are priests, this does not mean—as some later interpreters have said—that one is self-sufficient to approach God for oneself. There is a direct communion with God that all Christians can and should enjoy. But there is also an organic reality within which all communion with God takes place, and that reality is the church. To be priests does not mean primarily that we are our own individual priests, but rather that we are priests for the entire community of belief, and that they are priests for us. Rather than setting aside the need for the community of the church, the doctrine of the universal priesthood of believers strengthens it. It is true that access to God is no longer controlled by a hierarchical priesthood. But we still stand in need of the community of believers, the body of Christ, in which each member is a priest for the rest, and feeds the rest. Without such nourishment, an isolated member cannot live.

Within the life of that church, the Word of God comes to us in the sacraments. For a rite to be a true sacrament, it must have been instituted by Christ, and it must be a physical sign of the promise of the gospel. Applying such criteria, Luther comes to the conclusion that there are only two sacraments: baptism and communion. Other rites and ceremonies that are commonly called sacraments, although perhaps beneficial, ought not to be considered sacraments of the gospel.

Baptism is first of all a sign of the death and resurrection of the believer with Jesus Christ. But it is much more than a sign, for by its power we are made members of the body of Christ. Baptism and faith are closely tied, for the rite itself without faith is not valid. But this does not mean that one must have faith before being baptized, or that infants incapable of faith ought not to be baptized. To come to such a conclusion, Luther declares, would be to fall into the error of believing faith to be a human work, something we must do, and not a free gift of God. In salvation, the initiative is always God's, and this is precisely what the church proclaims in baptizing infants who are incapable of understanding what is taking place. Furthermore, baptism is not only the beginning of the Christian life, but also the foundation and the context in which the entire life of the believer takes place. Baptism is valid, not only when it is received, but throughout life. That is why we are told that Luther himself, when he felt sorely tried, was wont to exclaim, "I am baptized." In his own baptism lay the strength to resist the powers of evil.

Communion is the other Christian sacrament. Luther rejected a great deal of commonly accepted doctrine regarding communion. He was particularly opposed to the celebration of private masses, to the understanding of communion as a repetition of the sacrifice of Calvary, to the notion that there are "merits" in the mass, to the doctrine of transubstantiation, and to the "reservation" of the sacrament—the claim that the body of Christ remains present in the bread even after the celebration of communion is over. But, in spite of his opposition to what he saw as the misuse and misinterpretation of communion, he continued to attach great importance to the sacrament itself, and to the presence of Christ in it. While insisting on the need for the preached Word, he retained the Word made visible in communion as the center of Christian worship.

The question of the manner in which Christ is present in communion gave rise to long debates, not only with Catholics, but also among Protestants. Luther categorically rejected the doctrine of transubstantiation, which he saw as unduly tied to Aristotelian—and therefore pagan—metaphysics. Also, the manner in which the doctrine of transubstantiation had been used had tied it to the theory that the mass was a meritorious sacrifice, and this ran contrary to justification by faith.

On the other hand, Luther was not ready to reduce communion to a mere sign or symbol of spiritual realities. He took the words of Jesus at the institution of the sacrament as very clear and undeniable proof of his physical presence at the sacrament: "this is my body." Therefore, Luther felt compelled to affirm that in communion believers truly and literally partake of the body of Christ. This need not imply, as with transubstantiation, that the bread becomes body, and the wine becomes blood. The bread is still bread, and the wine is still wine. But now the body and blood of the Lord are also in them, and the believer is nourished by that body and that blood through the very act of eating the bread and drinking the wine. Although later interpreters used the term "consubstantiation" to describe Luther's doctrine of the presence of Christ in communion, Luther never used such metaphysical

Communion was of crucial importance for Luther and the entire Lutheran tradition. In this altarpiece, painted by Lucas Cranach the Younger, both Luther and Melanchthon sit at the Last Supper with Jesus, and Frederick the Wise kneels in the foreground.

terms, but would rather speak of the presence of the body of Christ in, with, under, around, and behind the bread and wine.

Not all who opposed traditional doctrine agreed with Luther on these points, and this soon gave rise to conflicts among leaders of the Reformation. Karlstadt, Luther's colleague at the University of Wittenberg who debated Eck at Leipzig, claimed that the presence of Christ in communion was merely symbolic, and that when Jesus said "this is my body" he was pointing to himself, and not the bread. Ulrich Zwingli, who is discussed in Chapter 5, held similar views, although with better arguments. Eventually, the question of how Christ is present in communion became one of the main points at issue in the debates between Lutherans and Reformed.

The Two Kingdoms

Before concluding this brief overview of Luther's theology, a word must be said regarding the relationship between church and state. According to Luther, God has established two kingdoms: one under the law, and the other under the gospel. The state must operate under the law, and its main purpose is to set limits to human sin and its consequences. Without the state, sin would lead to chaos and destruction. Believers, on the other hand, belong to the other kingdom, which is under the gospel. This means that Christians ought not to expect the state to be ruled by the gospel, nor to support orthodoxy by persecuting heretics. Furthermore, there is no reason why Christians should require that the state be ruled by fellow believers in order to obey them. Rulers, as such, must follow the law, and not the gospel. In the kingdom of the gospel, civil authorities have no power. In that which refers to this second kingdom, Christians are not subject to the state, and owe it no allegiance. But one must always remember that believers are at once justified and sinners; therefore, as people who are still sinners, we are under the authority of the state.

In concrete terms, this meant that true faith should not seek to impose itself by means of civil authority, but only through the power of the Word. In the complex realities of power and politics, however, such principles were difficult to follow. Luther repeatedly rejected offers of help from the princes who had embraced his cause, and yet found himself being helped by them. When those who had embraced the Reformation were threatened by Catholic armies, Luther hesitated as to what a proper response would be, but eventually agreed with the Lutheran princes that they were justified in going to war in self-defense.

Luther was not a pacifist. As being under the law, the state can take up arms when circumstances and justice so demand. When the Turks threatened to overrun Christendom, Luther advised his followers to take up arms. And when he became convinced that certain movements, such as the peasant uprisings and anabaptism, were subversive, he declared that civil authorities were under obligation to crush them. He had serious doubts as to the traditional understanding of the relationship between church and state. But his own doctrine of the two kingdoms, on which he sought to base his actions in the political arena, was difficult to apply to concrete situations.

4/An Uncertain Decade

Luther is now to be seen as a convicted heretic. He has twenty-one days from the fifteenth of April. After that time, no one should give him shelter. His followers also are to be condemned, and his books will be erased from human memory.

EDICT OF WORMS

Exile, Unrest, and Rebellion

By burning the papal bull, Luther had challenged the pope's authority. At Worms, by refusing to recant, he challenged that of the emperor. The latter had no intention of allowing a rebellious friar to question his authority, and therefore was ready to take action against Luther, in spite of the safe-conduct Frederick the Wise had obtained for him. But several powerful members of the Diet opposed such action, and Charles was forced to negotiate with them. When the Diet finally acquiesced to the emperor's wishes by promulgating the edict quoted above, Luther was nowhere to be found.

What had happened was that Frederick the Wise, aware the emperor would demand that the Diet condemn Luther, had taken steps to ensure his safety. An armed band, following the elector's instructions, had abducted the reformer and taken him to the castle of Wartburg. Due to his own instructions, Frederick himself did not know where Luther had been hidden. Many thought him dead, and there were rumors that he had been killed by order of the pope or the emperor.

Hidden at Wartburg, Luther grew a beard, sent word to some of his closest friends not to fear for him, and spent his time writing. His most significant work of this period was the German translation of the Bible. The translation of the New Testament, begun at Wartburg, was finished two years later, and the Old Testament took ten years to be completed. But that work was well worth the time spent on it, for Luther's Bible, besides adding impetus to the Reformation itself, shaped the German language and nationality.

While Luther was in exile, his collaborators in Wittenberg continued the work of reformation. Foremost among these were Karlstadt, of whom we have already spoken as a participant at the Leipzig debate, and Philip Melanchthon. The latter was a young professor of Greek whose temperament differed widely from Luther's, but who was firmly convinced of the truth of his older colleague's teachings. Until then, the reformation Luther advocated had not been implemented in the religious life of Wittenberg. Luther's fear of God and of unwarranted innovation were such that he had hesitated to take the concrete steps that would follow from his doctrine. But now, while he was absent, several such steps were taken in rapid succession. A number of monks and nuns left their monastic communities and were married. Worship was simplified, and German was substituted for Latin. Masses for the dead were abolished, as were days of fasting and abstinence. Melanchthon also began to offer communion "in both kinds"—that is, to give the laity the cup as well as the host.

At first, Luther supported these changes. But soon he began to question the excesses that were taking place at Wittenberg. When Karlstadt and several of his followers began tearing down images of saints in churches, Luther recommended moderation. Then three laymen appeared at Wittenberg from neighboring Zwickau, declaring themselves to be prophets. They claimed that God spoke directly to them, and that they therefore had no need of Scripture. Melanchthon was at a loss as to how to respond to such claims, and asked Luther's advice. Finally, the latter decided that what was at stake was nothing less than the gospel itself, and that he must return to Wittenberg. Before taking that step he notified Frederick the Wise of his intentions, making it clear that he was returning to Wittenberg counting, not on Frederick's protection, but on God's.

Although Luther was not one to take such matters into account when it was a question of obedience to God, political circumstances favored him, making it possible for Frederick to keep him hidden at Wartburg, and later allowing him to return to Wittenberg without being arrested and executed. Charles V was determined to stamp out the Lutheran "heresy." But he was threatened by more powerful enemies, and could not allow himself the luxury of alienating those among his German subjects who supported Luther. Charles's most constant rival was Francis I of France. The latter, who in earlier years had been the most influential sovereign in Europe, was not pleased at the rising star of Charles I of Spain, who was also Charles V of the Holy Roman Empire and holder of other vast territories that practically surrounded France. Shortly before the Diet of Worms, the two rivals had clashed in Navarre. (As we shall see later on, it was in that conflict that

Ignatius Loyola received the wound that would eventually turn him into one of the leaders of the Catholic Reformation.) From the year of the Diet—1521—until 1525, Charles was repeatedly at war with Francis. Finally, at the battle of Pavia, the King of France was captured by imperial troops, and the conflict between the two most powerful monarchs in western Europe seemed to have come to an end.

Meanwhile, a few months before the Diet of Worms, Leo X died, and Charles had used his influence to have his tutor, Adrian of Utrecht, elected pope. The new pope, who took the name of Adrian VI and was the last non-Italian pope until the twentieth century, was eager to reform the life of the church, but would brook no deviation from traditional orthodoxy. He implanted austerity of life in Rome, and began a program of reformation that he hoped would respond to the critics of the church and steal Luther's thunder. But Adrian died a year and a half after his election, and his program was abandoned. His successor, Clement VII, returned to Leo's policies, for he too was more interested in the arts and in Italian politics than in ecclesiastical matters. Soon there was serious friction between him and the Emperor, and this prevented the Catholic party from taking coordinated action against the German reformers.

Charles V signed a peace treaty with his prisoner Francis, and on that basis restored him to freedom and to his throne. But the conditions to which Francis had been forced to agree were harsh, and once he was back in France he secured Clement's support against Charles. The latter was eager to destroy Lutheranism and to put an end to the Turkish menace to his eastern borders. Given the nature of these two causes, he hoped to be able to count on the support of France and the papacy. But just as he was preparing his campaign, both Francis and Clement declared war on him.

In 1527, imperial troops, mostly Spanish and German, invaded Italy and marched on Rome. The city could not be defended, and the pope fled to the castle of Sant'Angelo, leaving the city to be sacked by the invaders. Since many of these were Lutheran, the sack of Rome took religious overtones: God was finally punishing the Antichrist. The pope's situation was desperate when, early in 1528, a French army, with English financial support, came to his aid. The imperial troops were forced to withdraw, and would have suffered great losses had not an epidemic forced the French to abandon their pursuit. In 1529, Charles agreed to peace, first with the pope, and then with Francis.

Once again Charles was preparing to take strong measures against the heretics in his German territories, when the Turks, led by Suleiman, marched on Vienna, the capital of Charles's Austrian territories. The fall of Vienna would leave Germany open to Turkish attack, and therefore the emperor and his German subjects set aside their religious differences and joined in a campaign against the Turks. The defenders of Vienna were resolute, and the city stood firm until the advancing German armies forced Suleiman to withdraw.

It was then that, after a prolonged absence, Charles returned to Germany, with the firm intention of stamping out the Lutheran heresy. During the intervening years, however, several important events had taken place. In 1522 and 1523, there had been a rebellion of knights, under the leadership of Franz von Sickingen. The knightly class had seen its fortunes decline for some time, and among the landless and penniless knights nationalist feelings ran high. Many blamed Rome for their ill fortune, and saw Luther as the champion of the German nation. Some, such as Ulrich von Hutten, were also convinced of the truth of Luther's religious teachings, but felt that the reformer was too timid. When they finally rebelled, many claimed that they were doing so in defense of the Reformation, although Luther had done nothing to encourage them. The rebels attacked Trier, but were decisively defeated by the German princes, who took the opportunity to dispossess the lesser gentry of the few lands that still remained in their hands. Sickingen died in battle, and von Hutten fled to Switzerland, where he died shortly thereafter. All this was seen by Luther and his closest colleagues as a great tragedy, proving once again that one should submit to the established authorities.

In 1524, a peasant rebellion broke out. For decades the conditions of the German peasantry had been worsening, and therefore there had been rebellions in 1476, 1491, 1498, 1503, and 1514. But none of these was as widespread nor as devastating as the uprisings of 1524 and 1525. One of the elements making this rebellion particularly virulent was that it took on religious overtones, for many among the peasantry believed that the teachings of the reformers supported their economic demands. Although Luther himself refused to extend the application of his teachings to the political realm in terms of revolution, there were others who disagreed with him on that point. Foremost among these was Thomas Müntzer, a native of Zwickau, whose early teachings were similar to those of the "prophets" from his village who created such a stir in Wittenberg. Müntzer claimed that what was most important was not the written word of Scripture, but the present revelation of the Spirit. In his case such spiritualist doctrine had political consequences, for he felt that those who had been born again by the Spirit should join in a theocratic community, to bring about the Kingdom of God. Luther had forced Müntzer out of Saxony, for he feared the consequences of his teachings. But the fiery preacher returned and joined the peasant rebellion.

Even apart from Müntzer's participation, this uprising had a measure of religious inspiration. In their "Twelve Articles," the peasants made both economic and religious demands. They sought to base their claims on the authority of Scripture, and concluded by declaring that, if any of their demands was shown to be contrary to Scripture, it would be withdrawn. Therefore, although Luther himself could not see any relationship between his doctrines and the rebellion, the peasants themselves did see such relationship.

In any case, Luther was at a loss as to what his attitude should be. Possibly his difficulties were related to his doctrine of the two kingdoms. When he first read the Twelve Articles, he addressed the princes, telling them that what was demanded in them was just, for the peasants were sorely oppressed. But when the uprising broke out, and the peasants took up arms, Luther tried to persuade them to follow a more peaceful course, and finally called on the princes to suppress the movement. Later, when the rebellion was drowned in blood, he urged the victorious princes to be merciful. But his words were not heeded, and it is said that more than 100,000 peasants were killed.

These events had fateful consequences for the Reformation. Catholic princes blamed Lutheranism for the rebellion, and from that time even the most moderate among them took measures against the spread of heresy in their territories. Vast numbers of peasants, convinced that Luther had betrayed them, either returned to the old faith or became Anabaptists.

While Germany was undergoing such turmoil, Catholic moderates throughout Europe were forced to choose sides between Luther and his opponents. The most famous of the humanists, Erasmus, had looked with favor on the early stages of the Lutheran movement, but did not find the resultant discord much to his liking. Controversy and dissension he found to be most repugnant, and therefore he would have preferred to stay out of the debate. But he was too famous to be allowed such a luxury, and eventually was forced to take a stand. Although he had frequently criticized the ignorance and corruption of the clergy, he had never advocated a radical reformation in theology, and therefore, when forced to speak out, he was bound to take the side of Luther's adversaries.

Still, Erasmus preferred to choose his own field of battle. Therefore, instead of attacking Luther on such issues as justification by faith, the mass as a sacrifice, or the authority of the pope, he raised the issue of free will. Luther had been led to affirm the doctrine of predestination both because it was a corollary of justification by faith as a free gift of God, and because he found it amply supported by the authority of Paul and Augustine. It was on this point that Erasmus attacked him, publishing a treatise on free will.

Luther responded by thanking Erasmus for having shown the wisdom to focus his attention on a fundamental issue, and not on peripheral matters such as the sale of indulgences, the relics of the saints, and so on. But then he went on to defend his position with characteristic vehemence. As he saw matters, the notion of free will as held by pagan philosophers and by the moralists of his time did not take into account the enormous power of sin. Sin is such that we are powerless to be rid of it. Only by divine intervention can we be justified and freed from the power of evil. And even then we continue to be sinners. Therefore, when it comes to serving God, our much-vaunted free will can do nothing of itself. It is only by God's initiative—by divine predestination—that we are justified.

The controversy between Luther and Erasmus led many humanists to abandon the Lutheran cause. A few, such as Philip Melanchthon, continued their staunch support of Luther while maintaining cordial relations with Erasmus and his friends. But these were by no means the majority, and therefore the controversy over predestination and free will marked the end of all hope for close collaboration between Lutherans and humanists.

The Diets of the Empire

While all this was taking place, and in the emperor's absence, it was necessary to govern the Empire. Since Charles V had left the country almost immediately after the Diet of Worms, and since that diet's edict against Luther had been the result of imperial pressure, nothing was done to enforce the decree against the reformer. When the Imperial Diet met again at Nuremberg, in 1523, it adopted a policy of tolerance towards Lutheranism, in spite of the protests of the legates of both pope and emperor.

In 1526, when Charles was engaged in his struggles with Francis I of France and Pope Clement VII, the Diet of Spire formally withdrew the edict of Worms, and granted each of the many German states the freedom to choose its own religious allegiance. Austria and many of the southern territories of Germany opted for Catholicism, while others began implementing the Lutheran Reformation. Germany had thus become a religious mosaic.

In 1529, the Second Diet of Spire took a different tack. At that point there was renewed threat of imperial intervention, and princes who until then had been fairly moderate joined the ranks of the staunch Catholics. The result was that the edict of Worms was reaffirmed. This prompted the Lutheran princes to present a formal protest, thus receiving the name of "Protestants."

Charles V finally returned to Germany in 1530, in order to attend the Diet of Augsburg. At Worms, the emperor had refused to listen to Luther's arguments. But now, in view of the turn of events, he requested an orderly exposition of the points at issue. This document, whose main author was Philip Melanchthon, is now known as the "Augsburg Confession." When first drawn, it spoke only for the Protestants of Saxony. But other princes and leaders also signed it, and thus it was the instrument whereby most Protestants presented a united front before the emperor (there were two other minority statements that disagreed on several points with Melanchthon's document). When the signatories of the Augsburg Confession refused to abandon their faith, the emperor was enraged, and ordered that they must recant by April of the following year, or suffer the consequences.

The survival of Protesantism was threatened. If the emperor joined his Spanish resources to those of the German princes, he would easily crush any Protestant prince who refused to recant. The Protestant princes decided that their only hope was to offer a common front. After long hesitation, Luther agreed that it was licit to take up arms in self-defense against the emperor. The Protestant territories then joined in the League of Schmalkald, whose purpose was to resist the imperial edict if Charles sought to impose it by force of arms.

Both sides were making ready for long and cruel war when international events once more forced Charles to postpone action. Francis of France was again preparing for war, and the Turks were planning to avenge their earlier failure before the walls of Vienna. To counteract such powerful enemies, Charles needed a united Germany. These circumstances demanded negotiation rather than war, and finally Protestants and Catholics agreed to the Peace of Nuremberg, signed in 1532. This stipulated that Protestants would be

Emperor Charles V listening to the Augsburg Confession while the rulers who signed it stand around him, each identified by his coat of arms. The scenes in the background represent various Lutheran services. Note that in communion the people are receiving both the bread and the wine, and that blood flows from Christ's side into the chalice.

Augsburg, a city that would play an important role at various times during the Reformation, was the scene of the drafting and signing of Lutheranism's basic document, the Augsburg Confession.

allowed to remain in their faith, but could not seek to extend it to other territories. The imperial edict of Augsburg was suspended, and in return the Protestants offered the emperor their support against the Turks. They also promised not to go beyond what they had declared to be their faith in the Augsburg Confession. Once more, political circumstances favored Protestantism, for it continued advancing into new territories in spite of the agreement of Nuremberg.

5/Ulrich Zwingli and the Swiss Reformation

If the inner man is such that he finds his delight in the law of God because he has been created in the divine image in order to have communion with Him, it follows that there will be no law or word which will delight that inner man more than the Word of God.

ULRICH ZWINGLI

Humanism and nationalism, both contributing factors to the Lutheran reformation even against Luther's intentions, became conscious elements of the reformation Zwingli led in Switzerland.

Zwingli's Pilgrimage

Ulrich Zwingli was born in a small Swiss village in January 1484, less than two months after Luther. After learning his first letters from an uncle, he studied in Basel and Bern, where humanism was thriving. He then went to the University of Vienna, and again to Basel. After receiving the degree of Master of Arts in 1506, he became priest of the village of Glarus. There he continued his humanistic studies, and became proficient in Greek. This combination of priestly duties with humanistic studies was exceptional, for records of the time show that many parish priests in Switzerland were ignorant, and that there were even some who had never read the entire New Testament.

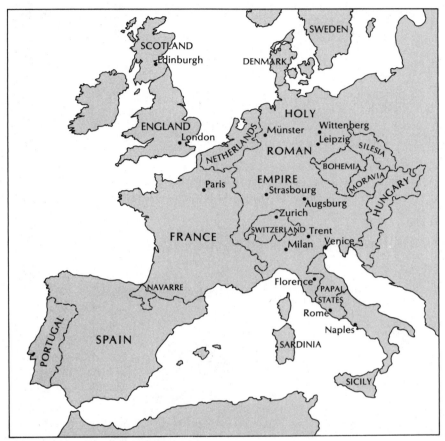

Europe at the Time of the Reformation

In 1512, and again in 1515, Zwingli went on Italian campaigns with mercenary soldiers from his district. The first expedition was successful, and the young priest saw his parishioners looting the conquered region. The outcome of the second was the opposite, and he now had occasion to see the impact of war on the defeated. This convinced him that one of the great evils of Switzerland was that mercenary service destroyed the moral fiber of society. After spending ten years at Glarus, he was made priest of an abbey to which many went on pilgrimage. He soon drew attention upon himself by preaching against the notion that exercises such as pilgrimages could avail for salvation, and declaring that he found nothing in the New Testament in support of such practices.

By the time he became a priest in Zürich in 1518, Zwingli had reached conclusions similar to those of Luther. His route to such conclusions had not been the anguished quest of the German Reformer, but rather the study of Scripture according to the method of the humanists, and his zealous outrage against the superstition that passed for Christianity, against the exploitation of the people by some leaders of the church, and against mercenary service.

Zwingli's preaching, devotion, and learning soon won him the respect of his parishioners in Zürich. When a seller of indulgences arrived, Zwingli convinced the government that he should be expelled from the city before he could peddle his wares. Then Francis I of France, who was at war with Charles V, requested mercenary contingents from the Swiss Confederation,

Ulrich Zwingli, the reformer of Zürich, reached his theological conclusions quite independently from Luther, and by an entirely different route.

and all cantons sent their soldiers— except Zürich. The pope, an ally of Francis, insisted that Zürich had an obligation to the papacy, and prevailed on the government to send mercenary soldiers to serve under Francis. That incident directed Zwingli's attention to the abuses of the papacy, and his attacks against superstition and the unjust use of power became more sharply focused on the papacy.

This was the time when Luther was creating a stir in Germany, daring to oppose the emperor's will at the Diet of Worms. Now Zwingli's enemies spread the word that his teachings were the same as those of the German heretic. Later Zwingli would declare that, even before having heard of Luther's teachings, he had come to similar conclusions through his study of the Bible. Thus, Zwingli's reformation was not a direct result of Luther's; rather, it was a parallel movement that soon established links with its counterpart in Germany. In any case, by 1522, the year after the Diet of Worms, Zwingli was ready to undertake the great task of reformation, and the Council of Government of Zürich was ready to support him in this endeavor.

The Break with Rome

Zürich was under the ecclesiastical jurisdiction of the bishop of Constance, who gave signs of concern over what was taking place in Zürich. When Zwingli preached against the laws of fasting and abstinence, and some of his parishioners gathered to eat sausages during Lent, the suffragan bishop of Constance accused the preacher before the Council of Government. But Zwingli defended his preaching on the basis of Scripture, and he was allowed to continue preaching. Shortly thereafter he expanded the scope of his attacks on traditional Christianity by declaring that priestly celibacy was not biblical, and further declaring that those who commanded it did not follow their own injunctions. Pope Adrian VI, who was aware of the need to reform the church, but was not willing to go as far as Luther and Zwingli demanded, made him tempting offers. But Zwingli refused, insisting on the scriptural base for the reforms he advocated. This led the Council of Government to call for a debate between Zwingli and a representative of the bishop.

At the appointed time, several hundred spectators were present. Zwingli expounded several theses, and defended them on the basis of Scripture. The bishop's representative refused to respond to him, declaring that soon a general council would gather, and that at that time all the matters currently debated would be settled. When he was asked to try to show that Zwingli was wrong, he again refused to do so. Therefore, the Council decided that, since no one had refuted Zwingli's teachings, he was free to continue preaching. This decision marked Zürich's final break with the bishopric of Constance, and therefore with Rome.

From that point, Zürich's reformation marched apace, with the support of the Council of Government. Zwingli's main goal was to restore biblical faith and practice. But in the exact content of this program he differed from Luther, for while the German was willing to retain all traditional uses that did not contradict the Bible, the Swiss insisted that all that had no explicit scriptural support must be rejected. This led him, for instance, to suppress the use of organs in church, for such instruments—as well as the violin, which he played expertly—were not to be found in the Bible. Rapid changes took place in Zürich under Zwingli's direction. Communion in both kinds—the bread and the cup—was offered to the laity. Many priests, monks, and nuns were married. General public education, with no class distinctions, became the norm. And many took it upon themselves to spread Zwingli's ideas to other Swiss cantons.

The Swiss Confederation was not a centralized state, but rather a complex mosaic of different states, each with its own laws and government, that had come together in order to achieve a number of common goals, particularly independence from the German Empire. Within that mosaic, some cantons became Protestant, while others continued in their obedience to Rome and its hierarchy. Religious disagreement, added to other causes of friction, made civil war seem inevitable.

The Catholic cantons took steps to seek an alliance with Charles V, and Zwingli recommended that the Protestant cantons take the military initiative before it was too late. But authorities in the Protestant areas were not ready to be the first to have recourse to arms. When Zürich finally decided that it was time to go to war, the other Protestant cantons disagreed. Then, against Zwingli's advice, economic measures were taken against the Catholic cantons, whom the Swiss Protestants accused of treason for having joined the cause of Charles V, of the hated house of Hapsburg.

In October of 1531, the five Catholic cantons joined in a surprise attack on Zürich. The defenders hardly had time to prepare for combat, for they did not know that they were at war until they saw the enemy's banners. Zwingli marched out with the first soldiers, hoping to resist long enough to allow the rest of the army to organize the defense of the city. In Kappel, the Catholic cantons defeated the army of Zürich, and Zwingli died in battle.

Slightly more than a month later, the Peace of Kappel was signed. The Protestants agreed to cover the expenses of the recent military actions, and in return each canton would have the freedom to make its own choice in matters of religion. From that time, Protestantism was firmly established in several Swiss cantons, while others remained Catholic. The movement of population from one canton to another, seeking freedom for the practice of religion, soon made some cantons staunchly Protestant, and others Catholic.

Zwingli's Theology

Since Zwingli's theology coincided with Luther's on many points, it shall suffice here to show the main points of contrast between the two reformers. The main difference between them resulted from the paths that each followed. While Luther's was that of a tormented soul that finally found solace in the biblical message of justification by faith, Zwingli's was that of the humanist who studied Scripture because it was the source of Christian faith, and humanism encouraged such return to the sources. This in turn meant that Zwingli had a more positive view of the power of reason than did Luther.

A good example of this difference is the manner in which each dealt with the doctrine of predestination. They agreed that predestination was scriptural, and that it was necessary to affirm it as the basis for the doctrine of justification by grace alone. For Luther, the doctrine of predestination was the expression and the result of his experience of knowing himself impotent before his own sin, and therefore finding himself forced to declare that his salvation was not his own work, but God's. In contrast, Zwingli saw predestination as the logical consequence of the nature of God. For the Swiss reformer, the main argument in favor of predestination was that, since God is both omnipotent and omniscient, God knows and determines all things beforehand. Luther would not employ such arguments, but would be content with declaring that predestination is necessary because human beings are incapable a doing anything for their own salvation. He would probably have rejected Zwingli's arguments as the result of reason, and not of biblical revelation nor of the experience of the gospel.

Zwingli's view of original Christianity had been colored by a particular tradition of whose influence he was not aware: the long history of a Neoplatonic interpretation of Christianity that had made its way into Christian theology through the influence of Justin, Origen, Augustine, Dionysius the Areopagite, and others. One element in that tradition is a tendency to undervalue matter, and to contrast it with spiritual reality. This was one of the reasons why Zwingli insisted on a simple form of worship, one that would not lead the believer to the material through excessive use of the senses. Luther, on the other hand, saw the material, not as an obstacle, but as an aid to spiritual life.

The consequences of these diverging views were evident in the two reformers' understanding of sacraments, particularly the eucharist. While Luther held that an inner divine action took place when the outer human action was performed, Zwingli refused to grant such efficacy to the sacraments, for this would limit the freedom of the Spirit. For him, the material elements, and the physical actions that accompany them, can be no more than signs or symbols of spiritual reality.

These diverging views on the sacraments were important for both reformers, for they were part and parcel of the rest of their theology. Therefore, when political circumstances led Landgrave Philip of Hesse to try to bring together the German and Swiss reformers, the question of how Christ is present at communion proved to be an unsurmountable obstacle. This took place in 1529, when under the bidding of Philip the main leaders of the reformation gathered at Marburg: Luther and Melanchthon from Wittenberg, Bucer from Strasbourg, Oecolampadius from Basel, and Zwingli from Zürich. On most issues there was agreement, but not on the meaning and efficacy of communion. Perhaps even there an agreement could have been reached, had Melanchthon not reminded Luther that a compromise with Zwingli on this point would further alienate Catholic Germans whom Luther and his companions still hoped to win for their cause. Some time later, when the break with Catholics was clearly irreversible, Melanchthon himself reached an agreement with the reformers from Switzerland and Strasbourg.

In any case, there is no doubt that the phrase attributed to Luther at the Colloquy of Marburg, "we are not of the same spirit," correctly summarized the situation. Their differences regarding communion were not an unimportant detail in the whole of their theologies, but were rather the result of their divergent views on the relation between matter and spirit, and therefore on the nature of God's revelation.

6/The Anabaptist Movement

Now everybody hopes to be saved by a superficial faith, without the fruits of faith, without the baptism of trial and tribulation, without love or hope, and without truly Christian practice.

CONRAD GREBEL

Both Luther and Zwingli were convinced that, in the course of centuries, Christianity had ceased to be what it was in the New Testament. Luther sought to cleanse it from all that contradicted Scripture. Zwingli went farther, holding that only that which had scriptural foundation should be believed and practiced. But soon there were others who pointed out that Zwingli did not carry such ideas to their logical conclusion.

The First Anabaptists

According to these critics, Zwingli and Luther forgot that, in the New Testament, there is a marked contrast between the church and the society around it. The result was persecution, since Roman society could not tolerate primitive Christianity. Therefore, the compromise between church and state that took place as a result of Constantine's conversion was in itself a betrayal of primitive Christianity. In order to be truly obedient to Scripture, the reformation begun by Luther must go much farther than was allowed by the Reformer. The church must not be confused with the rest of society. Their essential difference is that, while one belongs to a society by the mere fact of being born into it, and through no decision on one's own part, one cannot belong to the true church without a personal decision to that effect. In consequence, infant baptism must be rejected, for it takes for granted that one becomes a Christian by being born in a supposedly Christian society. This obscures the need for a personal decision that stands at the very heart of the Christian faith.

Most of these radical reformers also held that pacifism is an essential element in Christianity. The Sermon on the Mount must be obeyed literally, and any who object that this is impossible simply show their lack of faith. Christians ought not to take up arms to defend themselves, nor to defend their country, even if the Turks threaten it. As was to be expected, such teachings were not well received in Germany, where the Turks were a constant threat, nor in Zürich and the other Protestant areas of Switzerland, where there was always the danger that Protestantism would be crushed by Catholic armies.

These ideas circulated in various seemingly disconnected parts of Europe, including some Catholic countries. But it was in Zürich that they first came to public attention. In that city, there was a group of believers who urged Zwingli to undertake a more radical reformation. These people, who called themselves the "brethren," insisted on the need to found a congregation of true believers, in constrast with the multitudes who called themselves Christian simply because they had been born in a Christian country and had been baptized as infants.

When it finally became apparent that Zwingli would not follow that

Finding himself in agreement with Luther on many points, Zwingli studied the writings of the German reformer. The marginal notes on this copy of one of Luther's works are in Zwingli's handwriting.

The city of Zürich, where Zwingli had led the movement for reformation, was also the birthplace of one of the many Anabaptist groups.

course of action, some of the "brethren" decided that it was time to found such a congregation. George Blaurock, a former priest, asked another of the brethren, Conrad Grebel, to baptize him. On January 21, 1525, at the fountain that stood in the square in Zürich, Grebel baptized Blaurock, who then did the same for several others. They did not then baptize by immersion, for their main concern was not the manner in which the rite was administered, but rather the need for faith before receiving baptism. Later, as they sought to conform to the New Testament, they began baptizing by immersion.

Their enemies soon began calling them "anabaptists," which means "rebaptizers." Such a name was not quite accurate, for the supposed rebaptizers did not hold that one should be rebaptized, but rather that infant baptism was not valid, and therefore the first real baptism takes place when one receives the rite after having made a public confession of faith. In any case, history knows them as Anabaptists, a title which has lost its earlier pejorative connotation.

The Anabaptist movement drew great opposition from Catholics as well as from other Protestants. Although that opposition was usually couched in theological considerations, in fact they were persecuted because they were considered subversive. In spite of their radical views on other matters, both Luther and Zwingli accepted the notion that church and state must live side by side, supporting each other, and both refrained from any interpretation of the gospel that would make it a threat to the established social order. The Anabaptists, without seeking to do so, did threaten the social order. Their extreme pacifism was unacceptable to those in charge of mantaining social and political order, particularly amid the upheavals of the sixteenth century.

Also, by insisting on the contrast between the church and civil society, the Anabaptists implied that the structures of power of that society should not be transferred into the church. Even though Luther's original goals did not intend it, Lutheranism was now supported by the princes who had embraced it, and such princes enjoyed great authority in matters both civil and ecclesiastic. In Zwingli's Zürich, the Council of Government had the final word in religious matters. And the same was true in Catholic lands, where medieval traditions prevailed. This certainly did not preclude repeated clashes between church and state. But there was at least a body of common presuppositions that provided the framework for the solution of such conflicts. All this the Anabaptists undid with their insistence on the church as a voluntary community, totally distinct from the civil community. Furthermore, many Anabaptists were radical egalitarians. In most of their groups women had the same rights as men; and, at least in theory, the poor and the ignorant were as important as the rich and the learned.

All this appeared highly subversive, and therefore Anabaptists had to face severe persecution. In 1525, the Catholic areas of Switzerland began condemning them to death. The following year, the Council of Government of Zürich followed suit. In a few months, persecution spread to the rest of Switzerland. In Germany there was no uniform policy, for each state followed its own course, generally applying to Anabaptists various ancient laws against heretics. In 1528, Charles V ordered that they be put to death on the basis of an ancient Roman law, directed against the Donatists, that established the death penalty for all guilty of rebaptizing. The diet of Spire of 1529— the same in which the Lutheran princes protested and were first called "Protestants"—approved the imperial decree against Anabaptists. The only German prince who followed his conscience and refused to apply the edict was the Landgrave Philip of Hesse. In some areas, including Luther's Electoral Saxony, Anabaptists were accused both of heresy and of sedition. Since one was a religious offense, and the other a crime, both ecclesiastical and civil courts had jurisdiction to judge those accused of being Anabaptists.

The martyrs were many—probably more than those who died during the three centuries of persecution before the time of Constantine. The manner of their death varied from region to region, and even from case to case. With ironic cruelty, many were drowned. Others were burned to death, as

With cruel irony, many Anabaptists were drowned. The drowning of Maria von Monjon, in 1552, is the subject of this engraving by Jan Luiken.

had become customary with heretics centuries earlier. Some were tortured to death, or drawn and quartered. The stories of heroism in such difficult circumstances would fill several volumes. And still, the more fiercely it was persecuted, the more the movement grew.

The Revolutionary Anabaptists

Many of the first leaders of the movement were scholars, and almost all were pacifists. But soon that first generation succumbed to persecution. The movement then became increasingly radical, and became an expression of the popular resentment that had earlier resulted in peasant rebellions. The original pacifism was then forgotten, and hopes of violent revolution took its place.

Even before the heyday of Anabaptism, Thomas Müntzer had brought together some of its tenets with the peasants' hopes for social justice. Now many Anabaptists did likewise. One of them was Melchior Hoffman, a leather-dresser who had been first a Lutheran and then a Zwinglian before becoming an Anabaptist. In Strasbourg, where a measure of tolerance had allowed Anabaptism to become relatively strong, Hoffman began announcing that the Day of the Lord was near. His preaching inflamed the multitudes, who flocked to Strasbourg in the hope that the New Jerusalem would become a reality there. Hoffman himself announced that he would be imprisoned for six months, and that then the end would come. He also rejected the initial Anabaptist pacifism on the grounds that, as the end approached, it would become necessary for the children of God to take up arms against the children of darkness. When he was imprisoned, thus fulfilling the first half of his prediction, even more people went to Strasbourg, there to await a sign from heaven that the time had come to take up arms. But the growing number of Anabaptists in the city provoked repressive measures by the authorities, and in any case Hoffman was still in prison after the predicted day of the Second Coming.

Then someone suggested that the New Jerusalem would not be established in Strasbourg, but rather in Münster. In that city, the existing balance of power between Catholics and Protestants had forced a measure of tolerance, and therefore Anabaptists were not persecuted. There the visionaries went, as did also many others whom intolerable oppression had led to despair. The Kingdom would come soon. It would come in Münster. And then the poor would receive the earth as their inheritance.

Soon the number of Anabaptists in Münster was such that they took over the city. Their leaders were John Matthys, a Dutch baker, and his main disciple, John of Leiden. One of their first steps was to expel the Catholics from the city. The bishop, forced to leave his see, gathered an army and laid siege to the New Jerusalem. Meanwhile, inside the city, there was a growing insistence that everything must conform to the Bible. Moderate Protestants were also expelled. Sculptures, paintings, and all sorts of items connected with traditional belief and worship were destroyed. Outside the city, the bishop killed every Anabaptist that fell into his hands. The defenders, seeing their situation worsen daily as food became increasingly scarce, became more emotional. There were daily claims of visions and revelations. In a military sortie against the bishop, John Matthys was killed, and John of Leiden became the leader of the besieged city. As a result of the prolonged war, and of the constant exodus of males, there were many more women than men. As a remedy, John of Leiden decreed the practice of polygamy, following the example of the patriarchs of the Old Testament.

Although the besieged suffered increasing deprivation, the bishop lacked funds to keep an army in the field. John of Leiden then led his followers in what seemed a successful sortie, and they in response proclaimed him King of the New Jerusalem. But shortly after these events some of the inhabitants of the city, tired of the excesses of the visionaries, opened the gates to the bishop. The King of the New Jerusalem was captured and exhibited throughout the area, jointly with his two principal lieutenants. Then they were tortured and executed.

Thus ended the main outburst of revolutionary Anabaptism. Melchior

Hoffman, forgotten by most, continued in prison, seemingly until his death. For generations, in the church of St. Lambert in Münster, visitors could see the three cages in which the King of the New Jerusalem and his two aides were exhibited.

The Later Anabaptists

The fall of Münster put an end to revolutionary Anabaptism. Soon the explanation given for the tragedy of Münster was the abandonment of pacifism. Like the first Anabaptists, the new leaders of the movement held that the reason why Christians are not willing to follow the precepts of the Sermon on the Mount is not that the precepts are impossible, but rather that they require great faith. Those who really have faith will practice the love that Jesus taught, leaving the consequences in God's hand.

The principal figure in this new generation was Menno Simons, a Dutch Catholic priest who embraced Anabaptism in 1536, the same year that John of Leiden and his cohorts were executed. He joined a Dutch Anabaptist fellowship, and eventually his followers came to be called "Mennonites." Although the Mennonites suffered the same persecution as other Anabaptists, Menno Simons survived, and spent years traveling through Holland and northern Germany preaching his faith and encouraging his followers. He was convinced that pacifism was an essential part of true Christianity, and therefore refused to have anything to do with the revolutionary Anabaptists. He also felt that Christians ought not to offer any oaths whatsoever, and that they should not occupy positions requiring them. But they should obey civil authorities, as long as what is required of them is not contrary to Scripture. Baptism—which he performed by pouring water over the head—should be administered only to adults who confess their faith publicly. Neither that rite nor communion confer grace, but rather are outward signs of what takes place inwardly between God and the believer. Finally, following Jesus' example, Menno and his followers practiced footwashing.

In spite of their refusal to participate in subversive acts, Mennonites were considered subversive by many governments because they would not give oaths or offer military service. For this reason they were scattered throughout eastern Europe, particularly Russia. Later, others left for North America, where they were offered religious tolerance. But, in both Russia and North America, they encountered difficulties, for in both cases the state required that they serve in the armed forces. Thus, in the nineteenth and twentieth centuries, many of them emigrated to South America, where there were still territories where they could live in relative isolation from the rest

Menno Simons, who became an Anabaptist in 1536, was soon one of the movement's most famous leaders. His staunch pacifism was characteristic of most later Anabaptists.

of society. By the twentieth century, Mennonites were the main branch of the old Anabaptist movement of the sixteenth century, and they still insisted on their pacifist stance. But persecution appeared to be mostly a matter of the past, and Mennonites had gained an honored place in society through their social service.

7/John Calvin

> *Let us beware lest our words and thoughts*
> *go beyond what the Word of God tells us.*
> *. . . We must leave to God His own*
> *knowledge, . . . and conceive Him as He*
> *makes Himself known to us, without*
> *attempting to discover anything about His*
> *nature apart from His Word.*
>
> JOHN CALVIN

Without any doubt, the most important systematizer of Protestant theology in the sixteenth century was John Calvin. While Luther was the daring trailblazer for the movement, Calvin was the careful thinker who bound the various Protestant doctrines into a cohesive whole. Also, Luther's tortured quest for salvation and his joyous discovery of justification by faith were such that they always dominated his theology. Calvin, as a theologian of the second generation, did not allow the doctrine of justification to eclipse the rest of Christian theology, and therefore was able to pay more attention to several aspects of Christian faith that Luther had almost ignored—in particular, the doctrine of sanctification.

Calvin's Early Career

Calvin was born in the small town of Noyon, in France, on July 10, 1509. By that time, Luther had delivered his first lectures at the University of Wittenberg. Calvin's father was part of the rising middle class of Noyon, and served as secretary to the bishop and procurator of the cathedral chapter. Through such connections, he obtained for young John the income from two minor ecclesiastical posts, to defray his expenses as a student.

PROMPTE   ET SINCERE ·

IOHANNES · CALVINVS ·
ANNO · ÆTATIS ·53 ·
· B ·

John Calvin, who spent most of his career in Geneva, was without doubt the most important systematizer of Protestant theology in the sixteenth century.

Making use of such resources, and hoping for an ecclesiastical career, young Calvin studied in Paris, where he became acquainted with humanism as well as with the conservative reaction against it. The theological discussion that was then taking place made him familiar with the doctrines of Wycliffe, Huss, and Luther. But, as he declared later, "I was stubbornly tied to the superstitions of the papacy."* In 1528, he received the degree of Master of Arts. His father, who had lost his influence in Noyon, then decided that he should abandon theology and pursue a career in law. With that end in mind, Calvin studied in Orleans and Bourges, under two of the most famous jurists of the time, Pierre de l'Estoile and Andrea Alciati. The former followed the traditional methods for the study and interpretation of law, whereas the latter was an elegant humanist with a reputation for being somewhat pompous. When there was a controversy between the two, Calvin took the side of de l'Estoile. This serves as an indication that, at the very time when he was profoundly imbued in the spirit of humanism, Calvin felt no admiration for the vacuous elegance that characterized some of the most famous humanists.

---

*"Preface to the Commentary on the Psalms," *Opera* 31:22.

The Institutes

How Calvin came to his break with Rome, or the exact date in which this took place, is not known. In contrast to Luther, Calvin wrote little about the inner state of his soul. It seems likely that through the influence of some members of his circle of humanists, and through his study of Scripture and of early Christian times, he came to the conclusion that he must leave the Roman communion, and follow the route of Protestantism.

In 1534, he returned to Noyon and gave up the ecclesiastical posts his father had secured for him, although they were his main source of funds. Whether by that time he had decided to abandon the Catholic Church, or this was only one more step on his spiritual pilgrimage, it is impossible to ascertain. The fact is that in October of that year Francis I, who until then had shown relative tolerance towards Protestants, changed his policy, and in January 1535 Calvin went into exile in Switzerland, in the Protestant city of Basel.

He felt called to spend his time in study and literary labors. What he sought was not to become one of the leaders of the Reformation, but rather to settle in a calm environment where he could study Scripture and write about his faith. Shortly before arriving at Basel, he had written a short treatise on the state of the souls of the dead before the resurrection. What he now hoped to do was to write other such treatises, to help clarify the faith of the church in those confused times.

His main project on this score was a short summary of the Christian faith from a Protestant viewpoint. Until then, most Protestant literature, drawn by the urgency of polemics, had dealt exclusively with the points at issue, and had said little regarding other basic doctrines such as the Trinity, the incarnation, and so on. Thus, he proposed to fill this vacuum with a short manual that he called the *Institutes of the Christian Religion.*

The first edition of the *Institutes* appeared in Basel in 1536 and was a book of 516 pages. It was small in format so that it would fit easily in the wide pockets that were then used, and would therefore be capable of secret circulation within France. It had only six chapters. The first four dealt with the Law, the Creed, the Lord's Prayer, and the sacraments. The last two, more polemical in tone, summarized the Protestant position regarding the "false sacraments" of Rome, and Christian freedom.

The book enjoyed an immediate and surprising success. The first edition, which was in Latin and therefore could be read in different countries, was sold out in nine months. From that point on, Calvin continued working on successive editions of the *Institutes,* and these grew in volume through the years. The controversies of the time, the opinions of various groups that Calvin believed to be in error, and the practical needs of the church contributed to the growth of the work; thus, in order to follow Calvin's theological development and the various controversies in which he was involved, it would suffice to compare the successive editions of the *Institutes*.

Another edition appeared in Strasbourg, also in Latin, in 1539. In 1541, Calvin published in Geneva the first French edition, which became a classic of French literature. From that point on, editions were paired, a French one appearing immediately after one in Latin, as follows: 1543 and 1545, 1550 and 1551, 1559 and 1560. Since the Latin and French editions of 1559 and 1560 were the last to appear during Calvin's lifetime, they constitute the definitive text of the *Institutes*.

That definitive text is far removed from the small handbook on the Christian faith that Calvin published in 1536, for the six chapters of that early edition had become four books with a total of eighty chapters. The first book treats of God and revelation, as well as of creation and the nature of the human creature. The second is concerned with God as Redeemer, and how this is made known to us, first in the Old Testament and then in Jesus Christ. The third shows how, through the Spirit, we can share in the grace of Jesus Christ, and the fruits this produces. Finally, the fourth book deals with the "external means" to that sharing, that is, the church and the sacraments. The entire works shows a profound knowledge, not only of Scripture, but also of ancient Christian literature—particularly the works of Augustine—and of the theological controversies of the sixteenth century. There is no doubt that this was the high point of Protestant systematic theology in the time of the Reformation.

The Reformer of Geneva

Calvin had no intention of following the active lifestyle of the many Protestants who, in various parts of Europe, had become leaders of the Reformation. Although he respected and admired them, he was convinced that his gifts were not those of the pastor or the leader, but rather those of the scholar and author. After a short visit to Ferrara, and another to France, he decided to settle in Strasbourg, where the Protestant cause was victorious, and where there was a theological and literary activity that offered the proper milieu for the work he proposed to do.

But the direct route to Strasbourg was closed by military operations, and Calvin had to make a detour through Geneva. Conditions there were difficult. Some time earlier, the Protestant city of Bern had sent missionaries to Geneva. These missionaries had gained the support of a small nucleus of educated laity who ardently desired the reformation of the church, and also of a powerful sector of the bourgeoisie whose goal was to avoid certain economic and political restrictions that a break with Rome would abolish. The clergy, apparently with little instruction and even less conviction, had simply obeyed the orders of the government of Geneva when it decreed that the mass was abolished, and that the city was now Protestant. All this had taken place just a few months before Calvin's arrival at Geneva, and therefore the Bern missionaries, whose leader was William Farel, now found themselves at the helm of the religious life of the city, and sorely lacking in personnel.

Calvin arrived at Geneva in 1536 with the firm intention of stopping there for no more than a day, and then continuing his journey to Strasbourg. But someone told Farel that the author of the *Institutes* was in town, and the result was an unforgettable interview that Calvin himself later recorded. Farel, who "burned with a marvelous zeal for the advancement of the gospel," presented Calvin with several reasons why his presence was needed in Geneva. Calvin listened respectfully to the other man, some fifteen years older. But he refused to heed Farel's plea, telling him that he had planned certain studies, and that these would not be possible in the confused situation Farel was describing. When the latter had exhausted his arguments, and failed to convince the young theologian, he appealed to their common Lord, and challenged Calvin with a dire threat: "May God condemn your repose, and the calm you seek for study, if before such a great need you withdraw, and refuse your succor and help." Calvin continues his report: "these words shocked and broke me, and I desisted from the journey I had begun."* Thus began his career as the reformer of Geneva.

Although at first Calvin agreed to no more than to lend his aid to the Protestant leaders of the city, particularly Farel, soon his theological insight, his legal training, and his reforming zeal made him the central figure in the religious life of the city. Farel, who until then had been the leader of the Protestant cause, gladly became Calvin's main collaborator and support. But not all were ready to follow the path of reformation that Calvin and Farel laid out. As soon as the two pastors began insisting that the decision to reform the church be taken seriously, many of the bourgeoisie who had encouraged the break with Rome began demurring, while they circulated rumors in other Protestant cities regarding the supposed errors of the Genevan reformers. The conflict finally came to a head on the matter of the right to excommunicate. Calvin insisted that, if religious life was to conform to the principles of reformation, it was necessary to excommunicate unrepentant sinners. The government, then in the hands of the bourgeoisie, refused to allow this, claiming that it was an unwarranted rigorism. The final result was that Calvin, who insisted on his position, was banned from the city. Farel, who was invited to remain, preferred to join his friend in exile rather than serve as an instru-

---

*"Preface to the Commentary on the Psalms," *Opera* 31:26.

ment for the bourgeois in their quest for a religion with many liberties and no obligations.

Calvin saw this as the God-given opportunity to return to the life of writing and scholarship he had projected, and therefore completed his long-interrupted journey to Strasbourg. But once again peace eluded him. There was in the city a large community of exiles who had left France for reason of their faith, and Martin Bucer, the leader of the reformation in Strasbourg, insisted that Calvin should be their pastor. It was then that he produced a French liturgy, as well as French translations of several psalms and other hymns, to be sung by the exiled French community. He also prepared the second edition of the *Institutes,* and he married Idelette de Bure, a widow with whom he was very happy until her death in 1549.

A service in the Calvinist church in Lyons, in 1564, shows the centrality of the pulpit and of preaching in the Reformed tradition.

TEMPLE DE LYON, NOMME PARADIS.

The three years Calvin spent in Strasbourg from 1538 to 1541 were probably the happiest and most peaceful of his life. But, in spite of this, he regretted not having been able to continue his work in Geneva, for whose church he felt deep concern. Therefore, when circumstances changed in the Swiss city, and the new government invited him to return, Calvin agreed without hesitation.

Calvin returned to Geneva in 1541, and one of his first concerns was the preparation of a series of Ecclesiastical Ordinances that the government approved with some modifications. By this action, the government of the church in Geneva was placed mostly in the hands of the Consistory, whose members were the pastors and twelve lay "elders." Since there were five pastors, the lay elders held the majority of the positions in the Consistory. But in spite of this Calvin's personal authority was such that the Consistory usually followed his advice.

During the next twelve years, the Consistory and the government of the city clashed repeatedly, for the ecclesiastical body, following Calvin's promptings, sought to regulate the customs of the citizens—who were also the members of the church—with a severity not always shared by the government. By 1553, the opposition had again come to power, and Calvin's political position was precarious.

It was then that the famous process against Michael Servetus took place. Servetus was a Spanish physician whose physiological studies had made a significant contribution to medical science. But he was also the author of a number of theological treatises in which he argued that the union of church and state after Constantine's conversion was in truth a great apostasy, and that the Council of Nicea, in promulgating the doctrine of the Trinity, had offended God. He had recently escaped from the prisons of the Catholic Inquisition in France, where he was being tried for heresy, and was passing through Geneva when he was recognized. He was arrested, and Calvin prepared a list of thirty-eight accusations against him. Some in Geneva who opposed Calvin took up Servetus' cause, arguing that he had been accused of heresy by Catholics, and that therefore he should be seen as an ally. But the government of the city asked the advice of the various Protestant cantons of Switzerland, and all agreed that Servetus was a heretic, not only by Catholic standards, but also by Protestant ones. This put an end to the opposition, and Servetus was burned to death—although Calvin had argued in favor of a less cruel death by beheading.

Servetus' death was severely criticized, especially by Sebastian Castello, whom Calvin had earlier expelled from Geneva for having interpreted the Song of Songs as a poem of erotic love. Ever since, the burning of Servetus, a noted physician, has become a symbol of the rigid dogmatism of Calvin's Geneva. Undoubtedly, there are grounds for harsh judgment on the proceedings, and particularly on Calvin's role in them. But one should also remember that at that time all over Europe both Protestants and Catholics were acting in similar fashion against those whom they considered heretics. Servetus himself was condemned by the French Inquisition, which had not burned him only because he had escaped.

After Servetus' execution, Calvin's authority in Geneva had no rival. This was especially true since the theologians of all the other Protestant cantons had supported him, while his opponents had found themselves in the difficult position of defending a heretic who had been condemned by both Catholics and Protestants.

In 1559, Calvin saw the fulfillment of one of his fondest dreams in the opening of the Genevan Academy, under the direction of Theodore Beza—who would eventually succeed him as theological leader of the city. In that academy, the youth of Geneva were educated according to Calvinist principles. But its students also included many from various parts of Europe, who later returned to their native lands taking Calvinism with them.

As he saw his end approach, Calvin prepared his will and bid farewell to his closest associates. Farel, who had taken the responsibility of leading the Reformation in nearby Neuchâtel, paid his friend a last visit. Calvin died on May 27, 1564.

Calvin and Calvinism

During Calvin's lifetime, the main issue dividing Protestants—except for the Anabaptists, whom other Protestants considered heretics—was the manner of the presence of Christ in communion. This was the main point of conflict between Luther and Zwingli at the Colloquy of Marburg. On this point, Calvin followed the lead of his friend Martin Bucer, the reformer of Strasbourg, who took an intermediate position between Luther and Zwingli. Calvin affirmed that the presence of Christ in communion is real, although spiritual. This means that such presence is not merely symbolic, nor is communion a mere devotional exercise; rather, there is in it a true divine action for the church that partakes of the sacrament. On the other hand, this does not mean that the body of Christ descends from heaven, nor that it can be present in several altars at the same time, as Luther claimed. Rather, in the act of communion, by the power of the Holy Spirit, believers are taken to heaven and share with Christ in a foretaste of the heavenly banquet.

In 1526, Bucer, Luther, and others had reached the "Wittenberg Concord," which made room for both Luther's and Bucer's views. In 1549, Bucer, Calvin, the main Swiss Protestant theologians, and several others from southern Germany, signed the "Zürich Consensus," a similar document. Also, Luther had been pleased with the publication of Calvin's *Institutes*. Therefore, the difference between Calvin and Luther on the presence of

Christ in communion should not have been an insurmountable obstacle to Protestant unity.

But the followers of the great teachers were less flexible than their masters. In 1552 Joachim Westphal, a Lutheran, published a treatise against Calvin in which he declared that Calvinist views were surreptitiously making their way into traditionally Lutheran territories, and offered himself as the champion of Luther's views on communion. By then Luther had died, and Melanchthon refused to attack Calvin, as Westphal demanded. But the net result was a growing distance between those who followed Luther and those who accepted the Zürich Consensus, who were then called "Reformed" in contraposition to the "Lutherans."

Therefore, during this early period the main characteristic of the "Calvinist" or "Reformed" was not their doctrine of predestination, on which they generally agreed with Lutherans, but rather their understanding of communion. It was in the following century, as we shall see as our story unfolds, that predestination came to be seen as the hallmark of Calvinism. This was not so during the lifetime of Luther and Calvin, for both affirmed the doctrine of predestination.

In any case, due partly to the influence of the Genevan Academy, and partly to the *Institutes,* Calvin's theological influence was soon felt in various parts of Europe. Eventually, a number of churches appeared—in the Netherlands, Scotland, Hungary, France, and so forth—that followed the teaching of the Genevan reformer, and are now known as "Reformed" or "Calvinistic."

8/The Reformation in Great Britain

The universall defection, whereof Saint Paul did prophesy, is easy to be espyed as well in religion as in manners. The corruption of life is evident, and religion is not measured with the playne Worde of God, but by custome, consuetude, will, consent, and determination of men.

JOHN KNOX

Until early in the seventeenth century, Great Britain was divided between the house of Tudor in England, and the Stuart kingdom of Scotland. The two houses were related by blood, and eventually the two kingdoms would be united. But, during the sixteenth century, their relationship was one of enmity and open warfare, and therefore the Reformation followed a different course in each of them. For this reason, in the present chapter we shall deal first with the Reformation in England, and then turn to the Scottish Reformation.

Henry VIII

When the sixteenth century opened, Scotland was an ally of France, and England of Spain, and the hostility between the two great kingdoms on the Continent was reflected in the hostility between the two British kingdoms. In order to strengthen his ties with Spain, Henry VII of England arranged for the marriage of his son and heir, Arthur, to Catherine of Aragon, one of the daughters of Ferdinand and Isabella of Spain. The wedding took place amid great celebrations when the bride was fifteen years old, and it should have sealed the friendship between England and Spain. But Arthur died four months later, and Spain then proposed a union between the young widow and her deceased husband's younger brother, Henry, who was now heir to the English throne. The king of England, eager to retain both the friendship of Spain and the widow's dowry, agreed to the marriage. Since canon law prohibited a man's marriage with his brother's widow, the English representatives in Rome obtained a papal dispensation, and as soon as young Henry was old enough he was married to Catherine.

It was not a happy marriage. In spite of the papal dispensation, there was some doubt as to whether the pope had the power to grant a dispensation from the principle that a man should not marry his brother's widow. This in

Henry VIII, earlier known for his defense of Catholicism against Luther, and in no way a supporter of Protestant doctrine, led the Church of England in its break with Rome.

turn meant that the legality of the marriage itself was also in doubt. The failure of Henry and Catherine to produce a male heir—their only surviving child was princess Mary Tudor—could be interpreted as a sign of divine wrath. The nation had recently suffered the bloodletting of a war of succession, and therefore it seemed imperative that the king have a male heir. But after several years of marriage it was clear that such an heir would not come from Henry's union to Catherine.

Several solutions were proposed. Henry himself suggested that his bastard son, whom he had made Duke of Richmond, be declared legitimate, and made his heir. But such an arrangement would require papal action, and the pope refused to take a step that would alienate Spain. The cardinal who was in charge of these negotiations then suggested that Henry arrange the marriage of Mary with his bastard son. But the King felt that marrying Mary to her own half-brother would only compound the original error of marrying him to his brother's widow. His own solution was to request that Rome annul his own union with Catherine, thus leaving him free to marry another queen who could give him the needed heir. It appears that at the time of the first petition of annulment Henry was not yet enamored of Anne Boleyn, and that therefore he was initially moved by reasons of state rather than of the heart.

Such annulments were not uncommon, and the pope would grant them for various reasons. In this particular case, the argument was that, in spite of the papal dispensation, the marriage between Henry and his brother's widow was not licit, and that therefore it had never been a true marriage. But other factors completely unrelated to canon law were much more weighty. The main consideration was that Catherine was the aunt of Charles V, who at that time had the pope practically under his thumb, and who had received a plea from his aunt to save her from dishonor. The pope, Clement VII, could not invalidate Henry's marriage to Catherine without alienating Charles V. He therefore prolonged the matter as much as possible, and his representatives even suggested that Henry, instead of repudiating his first wife, secretly take a second one. But this was no solution, for the king needed a publicly acknowledged heir. Thomas Cranmer, the king's main advisor in religious matters, suggested that the main Catholic universities be consulted. The most prestigious of these—Paris, Orleans, Toulouse, Oxford, Cambridge, and even those in Italy—declared that Henry's marriage with Catherine was not valid.

From that point on, Henry VIII followed a policy that would eventually lead to a break with Rome. The ancient laws forbidding appeals to Rome were reenacted, thus putting the clergy more directly under the king's authority. He also toyed with the idea of retaining funds that normally went to Rome. By threatening to do so, he forced to pope to name Cranmer archbishop of Canterbury. His conflicts with the papacy did not mean, however, that he felt the least sympathy for Protestantism. In fact, a few years earlier he had published a treatise against Luther that had been acclaimed by Pope Leo X, who conferred on him the title of "defender of the faith." As Henry saw matters, what was needed was not a reformation like the one taking place on the Continent, but rather a restoration of the rights of the crown against undue papal intervention.

But Lutheran ideas, joined now with what still remained of Wycliffe's, were circulating in England, and those who held to them generally rejoiced in the growing distance between their sovereign and the papacy. Wycliffe's program of reformation included the creation of a national church, under the direction of civil authorities, and Henry's policies were inexorably leading in that direction. Such was also the hope of Thomas Cranmer, who envisioned a reformation of the church under royal authority.

The final break took place in 1534, when Parliament, following the dictates of the king, enacted a series of laws forbidding the payment of annates and other such contributions to Rome, ruling that Henry's marriage to Catherine was not a true marriage, and that therefore Mary was not the legitimate heir to the throne, and finally making the king the "supreme head of the Church of England." In order to enforce this last decision, Parliament also declared that any who dared say that the king was a schismatic or a heretic were guilty of treason.

The most notable figure opposing these laws was Sir Thomas More, who had been chancellor of the kingdom and a personal friend of Henry VIII. He refused to swear loyalty to the king as head of the church, and for that reason was imprisoned. There he was visited by one of his daughters, for whom he had secured an excellent humanistic education. She tried to convince him to recant and accept the king's authority over the church, and to that end she listed the names of the many respectable and admired people who had done so. It is said that Thomas More's answer was: "I never intend to pin my conscience to another man's back." At his trial, the ex-chancellor defended his position, saying that he had never denied that the king was the head of the church, but had only refused to affirm it, and that one cannot be condemned for not having said something. But after he had been condemned to death he openly declared that, in order to clear his conscience, he wished it to be clear that he did not believe that a layman such as the king could be the head of the church, nor that any human being had the authority to change the laws of the church. Five days later, he was executed in the Tower of London, after declaring that he died "the king's good servant, but God's first." In 1935, four hundred years after his death, Thomas More's name was added to the official list of saints of the Roman Catholic Church.

What had taken place until then was little more than a schism, with no attempt at reformation, and with no more doctrinal content than was necessary to justify the schism itself. But there were many in England who felt the need for a thorough reformation, and who saw the events of their time as

Thomas More was the most famous of the opponents of Henry's religious policy, and he paid for it with his life.

an opportunity to achieve it. Typical of this attitude was Thomas Cranmer, who supported the king's policies in the hope that they would lead to further and deeper changes.

Henry VIII was essentially conservative on religious matters. He seems to have been a firm believer in most of the traditional teachings of the church, although there is no doubt that his main motivation was political. Therefore, during his reign, the laws having to do with religious matters wavered according to changing political considerations.

Naturally, as soon as he was made head of the church Henry declared his marriage with Catherine void, and regularized the secret marriage with Anne Boleyn that had already taken place. Anne gave him no male heir, but only a daughter, Elizabeth, and eventually Anne was accused of adultery and condemned to death. The king then married Jane Seymour, from whom he finally had a male heir. After Jane's death, Henry tried to utilize his fourth marriage as a way of establishing an alliance with German Lutherans, for he felt threatened by both Charles V and Francis I of France. For that reason he married Anne of Cleves, a sister-in-law of the leading Protestant prince John Frederick of Saxony. But when it became apparent that the Lutherans insisted on their doctrinal positions even though Henry was opposed to them, and that Charles V and Francis I could not agree on a common policy against England, Henry divorced his fourth wife, and ordered that the man who had arranged it be beheaded. The new queen, Catherine Howard, supported the conservative position, and therefore the king's fifth marriage opened a period of difficulties for the advocates of reformation. Henry reached an agreement with Charles V for a joint invasion of France. Since he no longer had to fear the emperor, who had become his ally, he broke all negotiations with German Lutheran leaders. In England, he took steps to make the church conform as much as possible to Roman Catholicism, except in the matter of obedience to the pope. He also refused to restore monasteries, which he had suppressed and confiscated under pretense of reformation, and whose properties he had no intention of returning. But Catherine Howard fell in disgrace and was beheaded, and Charles V, for his own reasons, broke off his alliance with England. The next and last wife of Henry VIII, Catherine Parr, was a supporter of reformation, and the position of those who opposed it was precarious when the king died, early in 1547.

During all the years of Henry's reign, at times with the king's support and at times against his wishes, ideas of reformation had spread throughout the nation. Cranmer had ordered that the Bible be translated into English, and by royal decree a great English Bible had been placed in every church, at a place where all could read it. This was a powerful weapon in the hands of the advocates of reform, who went from place to place drawing attention to those passages in Scripture that supported their teachings and goals. The suppression of monasteries deprived the conservative wing of its staunchest allies. And the humanists, who were both numerous and powerful, saw in the royal policy an opportunity to achieve a reformation without what they considered to be the excesses of German Protestants. The net result was that at the time of Henry's death the advocates of reformation had ample support throughout the kingdom.

Edward VI

Henry was succeeded by his only male heir, Edward, a sickly young man who lived only six more years. The first three years of Edward's reign, under the regency of the Duke of Somerset, were a period of great advance for the cause of the reformers. The cup in communion was restored to the laity, members of the clergy were allowed to marry, and images were withdrawn from the churches. But the most important religious achievement of Somerset's regency was the publication of the *Book of Common Prayer,* whose main author was Cranmer, and which for the first time gave the English people a liturgy in their own language.

After Somerset's regency, the post fell to the Duke of Northumberland, a man of lesser principles than his predecessor, but who for reasons of expediency continued the policies of reformation. During his regency a revised edition of the *Book of Common Prayer* was published. The Zwinglian tendency of this new edition is apparent when one compares the words the minister is to say in offering the bread to the communicants. In the earlier version, the words were: "The body of our Lord Jesus Christ which was given for thee, preserve thy body and soul unto everlasting life." In the new edition, they were: "Take and eat this in remembrance that Christ died for thee, and feed on him in thy heart by faith with thanksgiving." While the first edition could be understood either in a Catholic or in a Lutheran sense, the second clearly drew its inspiration from Zwingli and those who held similar positions. This difference between the two books was an indication of the direction in which things were moving in England. The leaders of the reformist party, who were increasingly inclined towards Reformed theology, had reasons to hope that their cause would win without great opposition.

Mary Tudor

When Edward VI died, the crown went to his half-sister Mary, the daughter of Henry VIII and Catherine of Aragon. Mary had always been a Catholic, for in her experience the movement of reformation had begun with her own dishonor in her youth, when she had been declared an illegitimate child. Furthermore, if Henry had been correct in proclaiming himself head of the church and his marriage to Catherine null and void, Mary was a bastard, and her right to succession was in doubt. Therefore, for reasons both of conviction and of political necessity, Mary was committed to the goal of restoring Roman Catholicism in England. In this task she had the powerful support of her cousin Charles V, and also of a number of conservative bishops who had been deposed during the two previous reigns. But she knew that she must move with caution, and therefore during the first months of her reign she took the time to consolidate her position within England, while she strengthened her ties with the Catholic house of Hapsburg by marrying her cousin Philip of Spain—later Philip II.

However, as soon as she felt herself secure upon the throne, Mary began a series of increasingly repressive measures against Protestants. Late in 1554, England officially returned to obedience to the pope. Most of what had been

*Mary Tudor, nicknamed by the Protestants
"Bloody Mary," restored Catholicism, and
during her reign most of the Protestant leaders
who did not go into exile were condemned to
death*

done during the reigns of Henry and Edward was now undone. The feast days of the saints were restored. Married clergy were ordered to set their wives aside. Finally, open persecution of Protestant leaders became the policy of the kingdom. Almost three hundred of them were burned, while countless others were imprisoned or went into exile. For these reasons, the queen was given the name by which she is known to this day: "Bloody Mary."

The most illustrious of the martyrs during Mary's reign was Thomas Cranmer. Since he was archbishop of Canterbury, his case was sent to Rome, where he was condemned as a heretic and burned in effigy. But the queen's goal was to force the figurehead of the reformist party to recant, thus achieving a moral victory over the Protestants. To that end he was forced to watch from his prison the death of two of his main supporters and close associates in the work of reformation, bishops Latimer and Ridley. Eventually, Cranmer did sign a recantation. To this day historians debate whether he did this out of fear of the pyre, or rather because he had always declared that he would obey his sovereigns. Most probably he himself did not know exactly what his motives were. The fact is that he did recant in writing, and that in spite of this he was condemned to death, as an example to would-be followers. Arrangements were then made for a public recantation before his death. The archbishop was taken to the Church of St. Mary, where a wooden platform had been set up, and after the sermon he was given the opportunity to recant. He began by speaking of his sins and his weakness, and all expected him to conclude by declaring that he had sinned in leaving the Church of Rome. But he surprised his tormentors by withdrawing his words of recantation:

They were written contrary to the truth which I thought in my heart, and written for fear of death, to save my life if it might be. . . . And forasmuch as I have written many things contrary to what I believe in my heart, my hand shall first be punished; for if I may come to the fire it shall first be burned. As for the Pope, I refuse him, for Christ's enemy and antichrist, with all his false doctrine.*

That last act of valor of the elderly man—who did in fact hold his hand in the fire until it was charred—made his earlier wavering be forgotten, and Protestants considered Cranmer the great hero of their cause. Heartened by his example, many insisted on spreading Protestant teachings, and it became increasingly clear that Mary would have to take even harsher measures if Protestantism was to be eradicated.

Elizabeth

Mary died late in 1558, and was succeeded by her half-sister Elizabeth, the daughter of Henry VIII and Anne Boleyn. Charles V had repeatedly suggested that Mary have her half-sister executed, but the bloody queen had not dared go that far, and now her policies were undone by her heir. This was also the time when many who had left the kingdom for religious reasons returned to their homeland, bringing with them Zwinglian and Calvinist ideas they had learned on the Continent. Just as Mary had been a Catholic both out of conviction and out of political necessity, Elizabeth was a Protestant for similar reasons. If the head of the church in England was the pope, and not the king, it followed that the marriage of Henry VIII with Catherine of Aragon was valid, and that Elizabeth, born from Anne Boleyn while Catherine still lived, was illegitimate. Paul IV, who was then pope, indicated

*J. Foxe, *Actes and Monuments of these Latter and Perillous Dayes* (1559), 3:670.

that he was ready to declare Elizabeth a legitimate daughter of Henry, as long as she continued in the Roman communion. But Elizabeth did not even notify him of her elevation to the throne, and recalled the English ambassador to Rome. Although much more politically inclined than Mary, she had been brought up to believe that her father had done right in proclaiming himself head of the Church of England, and she would not waver in that conviction.

Elizabeth was not a Protestant extremist. Her ideal was a church whose practices were uniform, thus uniting the kingdom in common worship, but in which there would also be great latitude for varying opinions. Within that church, there would be no place for either Roman Catholicism or extreme Protestantism. But any moderate form of Protestantism would be acceptable, as long as it participated in the common worship of the Church of England.

Elizabeth's religious policy found expression and support in a new edition of the *Book of Common Prayer.* As an indication of her policy of theological inclusivism, the new book combined the two different formulas that the earlier versions ordered ministers to use in the distribution of the bread. The new text now read as follows:

The body of our Lord Jesus Christ which was given for thee preserve thy body and soul unto everlasting life. Take and eat this in remembrance that Christ died for thee and feed on Him in thy heart by faith with thanksgiving.

Naturally, the purpose of this double formula was to accomodate the divergent opinions of those who believed that communion was simply an act of remembrance, and those who insisted that in it one really partook of the body of Christ.

The same policy may be seen in the "Thirty-nine Articles," promulgated in 1562 in order to serve as doctrinal foundation for the Church of England. Although in them several Catholic doctrines and practices are explicitly rejected, there is no attempt to choose between the various Protestant views. On the contrary, the articles sought to achieve a "via media" in which all but Roman Catholics and the most doctrinaire Protestants could participate. Ever since that time, this has been one of the main characteristics of the Anglican Communion—that is, the Church of England and those derived from it, mostly in former British colonies.

During Elizabeth's reign Catholicism continued a precarious existence in England. Some Catholics took up the cause of Mary Stuart, the exiled queen of Scotland whose career we shall follow in the next section of this chapter. Were Elizabeth to be declared illegitimate, Mary Stuart would be the heir to the English throne. Therefore, she was the focal point of several conspiracies by Catholics, whom the pope had declared free from any obligation of obedience to Elizabeth. Exiled Catholic leaders declared that Elizabeth was a heretical usurper, and plotted her downfall and the elevation of Mary Stuart to the throne of England. Meanwhile, graduates of Catholic seminaries in exile secretly returned to England, where they risked their lives taking the sacraments to the faithful. It was difficult to distinguish between secret meetings for forbidden worship, and conspiracies against the queen and her government. Infiltrated priests and Catholic conspirers against the queen were equally captured and put to death. There was abundant proof of conspiracies against the queen's life, and most of these centered on the hope of crowning Mary Stuart. Whether or not Mary herself inspired such conspiracies is not clear. But in the end she was involved in them, and Elizabeth, after much hesitation, ordered that her cousin be put to death.

The total number of those executed for religious reasons during Elizabeth's reign was approximately the same as those who died under her half-sister Mary Tudor—although it should be remembered that Elizabeth's reign was almost ten times as long as Mary's. In any case, towards the end of Elizabeth's life Catholics were giving indications that they were ready to distinguish between their religious obedience to the pope and their political and civil loyalty to the queen. It was on the basis of this distinction that they would eventually be allowed to practice their religion openly.

It was also towards the end of Elizabeth's reign that the "Puritans" began to grow in numbers. These were people of Calvinist ideas who were called "Puritans" because they insisted on the need to restore the pure practices and doctrines of the New Testament. Since it was at a later time that they became a driving force in English religious life, we shall postpone our discussion of them to another chapter in our story.

The Reformation in Scotland

The kingdom of Scotland, to the north of England, had traditionally followed the policy of seeking the support of France against the English, who frequently invaded its territories. But, in the sixteenth century, the country was divided between those who supported that traditional policy, and those who held that circumstances had changed, and that it was in the nation's best interest to establish closer ties with England. The advocates of the new policy gained a major victory in 1502, when James IV of Scotland married Margaret Tudor, a daughter of Henry VII of England. Therefore, when Henry VIII became king of England, there was hope that the two kingdoms could finally live in peace with each other. James V, the son of James IV and Margaret Tudor, was therefore Henry's nephew, and the latter sought even closer ties by offering James the hand of his daughter Mary. But Scotland decided to return to its traditional alliance with France, and to that end James married the French Mary of Guise. From that point on, the two British kingdoms followed opposite courses, particularly in that which referred to the reformation of the church and relations with the papacy.

While these events were taking place, Protestantism had been making its way into Scotland. From a much earlier date, the doctrines of the Lollards and the Hussites had found followers in the country, and it had been impossible to uproot them. Now Protestantism found a fertile field among those who held to such doctrines. Many Scots who had studied in Germany returned to their homeland, taking with them the ideas and writings of Luther and other reformers. The Scottish Parliament issued laws against those writings, and against those who sought to spread Protestant teachings. The year 1528 saw the first martyrdom of one of these itinerant preachers, and after that time ever increasing numbers were executed. But it was all in vain. In spite of persecution, the new doctrines continued gaining adherents. The spread of Protestantism was particularly noticeable among the nobility, who resented the growing power of the crown and the loss of many of their ancient privileges; and among university students, who constantly read and circulated the smuggled books of Protestant authors.

When James V died in 1542, the heir to the throne was his infant daughter Mary Stuart, and this led to a power struggle. Henry VIII sought to marry the infant queen to his son and heir, Edward—a plan supported by the Protestant Scottish nobles, who were also Anglophiles. The Catholics, Francophiles, wished to see Mary sent to France for her education and married to a French prince. In this they succeeded, thus foiling Henry's plans.

On their part, a group of Protestant conspirators took the castle of St. Andrew, and killed the archbishop. The government, torn by inner conflict, could do little. An army was sent to capture and punish the rebels, but after a short siege the troops were withdrawn, and Protestants throughout the kingdom began considering St. Andrew's the bastion of their faith.

It was then that John Knox entered the scene. Little is known of the early years of this fiery reformer, who soon became the leader of Scottish Protestantism. Born in or about 1515, he studied theology, and was ordained a priest before 1540. He then became a tutor to the sons of two of the noblemen who conspired to take St. Andrew's, and he had also been in contact with George Wishart—a famous Protestant preacher who had died for his faith. When the conspirators took possession of St. Andrew's, he was ordered to take his young charges to the castle. Although he planned to leave for Germany after delivering the young boys, and devote some time to the study of Protestant theology, once he arrived at St. Andrew's he found himself inextricably involved in the events that were shaking the nation. Against his own will, he was made preacher of the Protestant community, and from that time he was the main spokesman for the cause of reformation in Scotland.

The Protestants in St. Andrew's were able to hold out because both England and France were going through difficult times and could not intervene in Scottish affairs. But as soon as France found herself free to send reinforcements to Scotland, the government sent a strong army against the castle, and the Protestants had to surrender. Although this was in violation of the terms of surrender, Knox and several others were condemned to the galleys, where the future reformer spent nineteen months of cruel labor. He was finally released thanks to the intervention of England, where Edward VI now ruled, and where Knox became a pastor.

That English interlude ended when the death of Edward placed Mary Tudor on the English throne, and persecution broke out against Protestantism. Knox then went to Switzerland, where he was able to spend some time in Geneva with Calvin, and in Zürich with Bullinger, Zwingli's successor. He also visited Scotland on two occasions, seeking to strengthen the resolve of the Protestant community.

Meanwhile, important events were taking place in Scotland. Young Mary Stuart had been sent to France, where she enjoyed the protection of her relatives of the house of Guise. Her mother, herself of that family, remained in Scotland as regent. In April 1558, Mary married the heir to the French throne, who slightly more than a year later was crowned as Francis II. Thus Mary, sixteen years old, was both queen consort of France and titular queen of Scotland. But such titles and honors were not all, for she also claimed to be the legitimate queen of England. Mary Tudor had died in 1558, and had been succeeded by her half-sister Elizabeth. But if Elizabeth was illegitimate, as Catholics claimed, the throne belonged to Mary Stuart, great-granddaughter of Henry VII. Therefore, upon Mary Tudor's death, Mary Stuart took the title of queen of England, which made her the avowed enemy of her cousin Elizabeth. In Scotland, the queen mother Mary of Guise ruled as regent. Her pro-Catholic policies forced Protestant leaders to unite and, late in 1557, they made a solemn covenant. Since they promised to serve "the very blessed Word of God, and His congregation," they were known as "Lords of the Congregation." They were aware that their cause was similar to that of English Protestants, and established ties with them. The regent ordered increased persecution against the "heretics," but they persisted in their position, and in 1558 organized themselves into a church. Shortly before that, they had written to Switzerland, asking Knox to return to Scotland.

In his exile, Knox had written a virulent attack against the women who then reigned in Europe: the regent of Scotland, Mary Tudor in England, and Catherine de Medici in France. His work, *The First Blast of the Trumpet against the Monstrous Regiment of Women,* was published at a bad time, for it had scarcely circulated in England when Mary Tudor died and was succeeded by Elizabeth. Although the book was written against her now dead half-sister, Elizabeth resented much of what was said in it, for its arguments based on anti-feminine prejudice could just as well be applied to her. This hindered the natural alliance that should have developed between Elizabeth and John Knox, whose repeated retractions did not suffice to appease the English queen.

Events were not working in favor of the Scottish Protestants. The regent requested troops from France in order to crush the Lords of the Congregation. The latter did achieve some victories over the invaders. But their army, lacking in material resources, could not stay in the field for long. They sent repeated appeals to England, arguing that, if the Catholics were able to crush the Protestant rebellion in Scotland, and that kingdom was thus in the hands of the Catholic faction, and closely tied to France, Elizabeth's crown would be endangered. Knox, who had returned shortly before these events, sustained the Protestants with his sermons and the force of his conviction. Finally, early in 1560, Elizabeth decided to send troops to Scotland. The English army joined the Scottish Protestants, and a long war seemed inevitable. But then the regent died, and the French decided that it was time to sue for peace. As a result, both the French and the English withdrew their troops.

As soon as the immediate danger was past, however, disputes began between Knox and the lords, who until then had supported the cause of reformation. Although other reasons were adduced, at bottom the conflict was economic. The lords sought possession of the riches of the church, while Knox and his supporters wished to employ those resources for establishing a system of universal education, to lighten the load of the poor, and for the support of the church.

In the midst of such struggles, the nobles decided to invite Mary Stuart to return to Scotland and claim the throne she had inherited from her father. Mary had hoped to remain in France as queen of that country, but the death of her husband had deprived her of that honor, and therefore she agreed to the Scottish request. She arrived in Scotland in 1561. Although she never was popular, at first she was content to follow the advice of her bastard half-brother James Stuart, earl of Moray, a Protestant leader who kept her from immediately alienating the other Protestant lords.

Knox himself seems to have been convinced that a clash with the queen was inevitable, and on this she probably agreed with him. From the time of her arrival, Mary insisted on having mass celebrated in her private chapel, and the fiery reformer began preaching against the "idolatry" of the "new Jezebel." The two had a number of increasingly tempestous interviews. But the lords, content with the existing situation, did not follow the preacher in his extremism.

The growing tension with the queen, and with some of the Protestant lords, did not prevent Knox and his followers from organizing the Reformed Church of Scotland, whose polity was similar to later Presbyterianism. In each church elders were elected, as well as a minister, although the latter could not be installed before being examined by the other ministers. The pillars of the new church were the *Book of Discipline,* the *Book of Common Order,* and the *Scots Confession.*

In the end, Mary Stuart was the cause of her own downfall. She had always dreamed of sitting on the throne of England, and in pursuit of that dream she lost first her own throne and then her life. In order to strengthen her claim on the English throne she married her cousin Henry Stuart, Lord Darnley, who also had a distant claim to it. Moray objected to this marriage and to Mary's agreement with Spain to uproot Protestantism in her country, and when his objections went unheeded he rebelled. Mary then called on Lord Bothwell, an able military leader who defeated Moray and forced him to seek refuge in London. Encouraged by this victory, Mary declared that she would soon sit on the throne in London.

Having lost Moray's counsel, Mary's policies became increasingly unwise. She decided that she had made a mistake in marrying Darnley, and let her feelings be known to Bothwell and others. Shortly thereafter, Darnley was murdered, and the main suspect was Bothwell. He was legally exonerated in a trial in which no witnesses for the prosecution were allowed. But this did little to allay suspicion, particularly since Mary married Bothwell a few months later.

The Scottish lords hated Bothwell, and they soon rebelled. When the queen sought to quench the rebellion, she discovered that her troops were not willing to support her cause, and she found herself in the hands of the lords. These then convinced her that they had proof of her participation in Darnley's death, and gave her the choice between abdicating and being tried for murder. She abdicated in favor of her one-year-old son James VI, whom she had had from Darnley, and Moray returned from England as regent of Scotland. Mary managed to escape and to raise an army in support of her cause. But she was defeated by Moray's troops, and her only recourse was to flee to England and seek refuge under her hated cousin Elizabeth.

Romantic imagination has woven many a tale around Mary's captivity and death, making her a martyr in the hands of a cruel and ambitious cousin. The truth is that Elizabeth received her with greater courtesy than was to be expected for someone who for so long had been declaring her illegitimate and trying to take possession of her crown. Although she was a prisoner in the sense that she was not allowed to leave the castle of her residence, there were strict orders that she should be treated as a queen, and she was allowed to choose her own body of thirty servants. But she was the hub of many a conspiracy, most of which included the death of Elizabeth, who was the main obstacle in her path to the English throne and to the restoration of Catholicism in England. Another common element of most of these conspiracies was the invasion of England by Spanish troops in support of Mary's cause. When the third such conspiracy was discovered, with clear proof that Mary was, if not the instigator of the plot, at least a willing participant, she was tried and condemned to death. When she was finally taken before the executioner, she faced death with royal dignity.

In Scotland, Mary's exile did not put an end to the disputes between the various parties. Knox supported the regency of Moray. But there was still significant opposition when the reformer suffered an attack of paralysis and had to withdraw from active life. When he heard of the St. Bartholomew's

Day Massacre of Protestants in France—of which we shall say more in a later chapter—he made a last effort to return to the pulpit, where he told his fellow Scots that they must continue their struggle, lest they suffer a similar fate. He died a few days after this last sermon. By then, it was becoming apparent that Scotland had been won for the Reformed tradition.

9/ Further Developments within Lutheranism

A Christian ruler may and must defend his subjects against every higher authority that seeks to force them to deny the Word of God and practice idolatry.

MAGDEBURG CONFESSION (1550)

The War of Schmalkald

The peace of Nuremberg, signed in 1532, allowed Protestants the free exercise of their faith in their own territories, but prohibited any further expansion of Protestantism. It seems that Charles V thus hoped to contain the advance of the Lutheran heresy, until he could bring together the resources necessary to stamp it out. But such a policy was doomed to failure, for, in spite of the stipulations of Nuremberg, Protestantism continued its expansion.

The political situation of Germany was extremely complex and fluid. Although Charles was emperor, many interests hampered the full exercise of his authority. Even apart from religious matters, there were many who feared the growing power of the house of Hapsburg, whose head Charles was. Some of these were Catholic princes who suspected that Charles would use his opposition to Lutheranism for the aggrandizement of his house, and who therefore were not willing to commit themselves fully to the anti-Protestant crusade Charles hoped to organize. Furthermore, one of the most powerful princes standing in the way of the house of Hapsburg was Philip of Hesse, who was also the leader of the League of Schmalkald. For these reasons, the emperor could not stop the expansion of Protestantism into lands in which it should not have been permitted according to the terms agreed on at Nuremberg.

In 1534, Philip of Hesse wrested the duchy of Württemberg from the Catholics, who had taken possession of it. After diplomatic maneuvers assured him that other Catholic princes would not intervene, Philip invaded the duchy and recalled its exiled duke, who then declared himself for Protestantism. The population of the duchy, that had already given signs of inclination towards Lutheranism, soon took up the religious allegiance of its restored prince.

Another severe blow for German Catholicism was the death of Duke George of Saxony, in 1539. Saxony comprised two separate territories, Ducal Saxony and Electoral Saxony. The latter, under the rule of Frederick the Wise, had been the cradle of Lutheranism. But Ducal Saxony had resisted the new faith, and Duke George had been one of the most bitter enemies of Luther and his followers. At his death, his brother and successor, Henry, declared himself a Protestant, and Luther was invited to preach in the capital, Leipzig, where years earlier he had debated Eck.

In the same year that saw the death of Duke George of Saxony, Brandenburg also became Protestant, and there was even talk that the three ecclesiastical electors, the archbishops of Trier, Cologne, and Mainz, were considering embracing the Protestant faith. This would give Protestants a clear

Emperor Charles V, who was also Charles I of Spain, was firmly convinced of the need to stamp out Protestantism; but various political necessities repeatedly stayed his hand

majority in the electoral college of seven magnates—four lay princes and three archbishops—whose task it would be to choose the next emperor.

Charles's hands were tied, for he was involved in too many conflicts in various parts of the world, and all he could do was to encourage the Catholic princes to form an alliance to rival the League of Schmalkald. This was the League of Nuremberg, founded in 1539. Faced by political realities, Charles also turned to a more conciliatory policy, seeking a rapprochement between Catholics and Protestants. Under this new policy several dialogues took place, but with little or no result. Meanwhile, the League of Schmalkald took over the territories of Henry of Brunswick, the emperor's staunchest ally in northern Germany, and the area became Protestant. Several bishops who were also feudal lords, realizing that the majority of the people in their dioceses leaned towards Lutheranism, turned their possessions into secular states, made themselves into hereditary lords, and declared for Protestantism. Naturally, in such moves there was a great deal of personal ambition. But the fact remained that Protestantism seemed on the verge of overrunning all of Germany, and that for more than ten years the emperor and the pope saw their power and influence diminish.

The printing press soon became one of the main instruments for the spread of Protestantism, as pamphlets circulating from hand to hand carried Protestant ideas to ever wider areas.

Shortly thereafter, however, Protestantism would suffer several severe blows. The first of these was the bigamy of Philip of Hesse. This prince, the leader of the League of Schmalkald, was a sincere man, firmly committed to the Protestant cause. His conscience, however, was deeply troubled because for years he had had no marital life with his wife, and he found it impossible to remain celibate. He was no libertine, but rather a man tormented by his sexual appetites, and by the guilt that he felt at their illicit satisfaction. He consulted the main Protestant theologians, and Luther, Melanchthon, and Bucer—the reformer of Strasbourg—agreed that the Bible did not forbid polygamy, and that Philip could take a second wife without setting the first aside. It was necessary, however, for this to be done in secret, for although polygamy was not a crime in God's eyes, it was such in the eyes of the civil law. This Philip did, and when the secret became public the ensuing scandal put both Philip and his theological advisors in an extremely difficult position. Besides the enormous loss of moral authority these events implied, they also weakened the League of Schmalkald, for many of its members objected to Philip's continuing leadership.

The second blow was the refusal of Duke Maurice of Saxony to join the League. While declaring himself a Protestant, he insisted on carrying out his own independent policy. When Charles explained that he was not opposing Protestantism, but only the rebellion of the Lutheran princes, and promised him special consideration, Maurice decided to believe the emperor, and to take his side against the League of Schmalkald.

The third blow was Luther's death, in 1546. Although he had lost much prestige as a result of the peasant's rebellion and the bigamy of Philip of Hesse, Luther was still the only figure who could unite Protestants under a single banner. His death, shortly after the discovery of Philip's bigamy, left the Protestant party headless both politically and spiritually.

But the most severe blow came from the emperor, who was finally free to turn his attention to Germany, and was eager to avenge the obstinate rebelliousness of the Protestant princes, and the humiliations he had suffered because of them. Profiting from the disarray in the Protestant ranks, and with the support of Duke Maurice, Charles invaded Germany and captured both Philip of Hesse and John Frederick, the son and successor of Frederick the Wise.

The Interim

In spite of his military victory, the emperor knew that it was too late to impose his will on religious matters, and therefore was content with promulgating the "Augsburg Interim," written by a joint commission of Catholic and Protestant theologians. By the emperor's command, all Germans were to obey this Interim, so called because it was to be the law of the land until a general council could be convened to decide on the issues being debated. (The Council of Trent had begun its sessions three years earlier, in 1545; but the pope and the emperor were at odds, and therefore the later refused to accept that council as valid.) Charles hoped to reform the church in Germany, as was already being done in Spain since the reign of his grandmother Isabella —that is, by prosecuting abuse and corruption, encouraging piety and learning, and disallowing any doctrinal divergence. By means of the Interim, he hoped to gain the time necessary to set in motion such a reformation.

But neither Catholics nor Protestants were gratified by this attempt to legislate on matters of conscience. There was general resistance to the Interim. Several Protestant theologians flatly refused to obey it. Those at Wittenberg, led by Melanchthon, finally agreed to a modified version, the "Leipzig Interim." But even this was not acceptable to the majority of Lutherans, who accused Melanchthon and his followers of cowardice. The latter responded by arguing that it was necessary to distinguish between the essential and the peripheral, and that they had made concessions in peripheral matters in order to be able to continue preaching and practicing the essential.

In any case, Charles was unable to exploit the advantages gained by the War of Schmalkald. Many German princes, among them several Catholics, protested against the ill treatment received by Philip of Hesse and John Frederick of Saxony. There were rumors that in order to capture Philip, Charles had made use of means that sullied his honor. The Protestant princes, sharply divided before the war, were drawn together by their opposition to the Interim. Both the pope and the king of France resented Charles's successes and made diplomatic maneuvers to hamper him.

Soon the Protestant princes were conspiring against Charles V. Maurice of Saxony, discontent with the emperor's rewards for his betrayal of the Protestant cause, and fearing the growing power of the house of Hapsburg, joined the conspiracy, which sent an embassy to the king of France in order to secure his support. When rebellion finally broke out, the armies of King Henry II of France invaded Charles's possessions beyond the Rhine. The troops on whose loyalty the emperor could count were not sufficient for combat, and therefore Charles had to flee. Even this was not easy, for Maurice of Saxony had taken possession of several strategic places, and Charles almost fell prisoner to him. After his escape, Charles instructed his armies to retake Metz, which the French had taken. But the French repulsed the attack, and the Protestant princes continued in open revolt. Towards the end of his career, it must have appeared to Charles that his German policy was an almost complete failure.

Charles had increasingly delegated German affairs to his brother Ferdinand, who finally agreed with the rebellious princes to the Peace of Passau. By the terms of this agreement, Philip of Hesse and John Frederick of Saxony were freed, and freedom of religion was granted throughout the Empire.

This freedom, however, had a number of limitations. It did not mean that all subjects were free to choose their own religion, but rather that local rulers could make that decision for themselves and for their subjects, and that the emperor would not insist on the return of Protestant princes to Catholicism. Also, the freedom this treaty granted was only for those who held either to traditional Catholicism or to the Confession of Augsburg. Anabaptists and Reformed were not included in its provisions.

His failure in Germany was one of the motives leading Charles to relinquish his power and seek the peace of the monastery. In 1555, he began to rid himself of his territories, abdicating in favor of his son Philip, first the Low Countries and then his Italian possessions and the throne of Spain. The following year, he formally resigned as emperor and withdrew to the monastery of St. Yuste, in Spain, where he still surrounded himself with imperial pomp, and continued serving as an advisor to his son Philip II of Spain. He died two years later, in September 1558.

The new emperor, Ferdinand I, abandoned his brother's religious policy, and was so tolerant that some Catholics feared that he had secretly become a Protestant. Under his rule, and that of his successor Maximilian II, Protestantism continued expanding to new areas. These included Austria itself, the main hereditary possession of the ancient Hapsburgs. The resulting tensions with Catholic leaders repeatedly broke out in minor political and military clashes. Finally, in the next century, these led to the Thirty Years' War, to which we shall return later.

Scandinavian Lutheranism

While all this was taking place in Germany, Luther's impact was also being felt in neighboring Scandinavia. But, while in Germany the Reformation and the ensuing struggles divided the country and helped the high nobility assert its power over against the monarchy, in Scandinavia it had the opposite effect. There monarchs took up the Reformation as their cause, and its triumph was also theirs.

In theory, Denmark, Norway, and Sweden were a united kingdom. But in truth the king ruled only in Denmark, where he resided. His power in Norway was limited, and nil in Sweden, where the powerful house of Sture, with the title of regents, held sway. Even in Denmark itself royal authority was limited by the power of the aristocracy and of the ecclesiastical hierarchy, who staunchly defended their ancient privileges against every encroachment on the king's part. Since the crown was elective, at the time of each election the magnates, both civil and ecclesiastic, wrung new concessions from those who would be elected. The people, oppressed by great secular and ecclesiastical lords, could do nothing but pay ever-increasing taxes and obey laws designed for the protection of the powerful.

When the Reformation broke out in Germany, the man on the Scandinavian throne was Christian II, who was married to Charles V's sister Isabella. Since the Swedes would not allow him effective power in their land, he appealed to his brother-in-law and to other princes, and with largely foreign troops moved into Sweden and had himself crowned at Stockholm. Although he had vowed to spare the lives of his Swedish enemies, a few days after his coronation he ordered the "massacre of Stockholm," in which the leading aristocrats and ecclesiastics of the country were murdered.

The massacre of Stockholm caused grave resentment, not only in Sweden, but also in Norway and even in Denmark—magnates throughout Christian's territories feared that, after destroying Swedish aristocracy, the king would turn on them. Christian claimed that he sought to free the people of Sweden from the oppression of its own aristocracy. But the treacherous means by which he had disposed of his enemies, and the intense ecclesiastical propaganda against him, soon lost him any popularity he might have had.

Christian then tried to make use of the Reformation as a tool for his own end. Shortly before these events, the first Lutheran preachers had made their way into Denmark, and the people seemed ready to lend them an attentive ear. But again this policy failed, for it exacerbated the prelates' enmity towards the king, while most Protestants preferred to keep their distance from the instigator of the massacre of Stockholm. Eventually, rebellion broke out, and Christian had to flee. He returned eight years later, now with the support of several Catholic rulers from other parts of Europe. He landed in Norway and declared himself the champion of Catholicism. But his uncle and successor, Frederick I, defeated and imprisoned him. He remained in prison the rest of his days—twenty-seven years.

Frederick I was a Protestant, and by that time many among the people and the nobility were of similar persuasion. But, at the time of his election, the new king promised that he would neither attack Catholicism nor use his authority in favor of Protestantism. He realized that it was better to be the true king of a smaller kingdom than the fictitious ruler of a large one, and therefore gave up all claim to the Swedish crown, and allowed Norway to elect its own king. Since the Norwegians elected him, Frederick was able to keep some of the older Scandinavian union, without having to resort to his nephew's tyrannical methods. Also, being able to concentrate on the affairs of Denmark and Norway, he took steps to consolidate the power of the crown in those two kingdoms. In religious matters, he kept the vows he had made at the time of his election. But Protestantism, allowed free rein, made rapid gains. In 1527, it was officially recognized and granted toleration, and by Frederick's death in 1533 most of his subjects were Protestants.

At that point, there was an attempt to impose a Catholic king on the land by means of foreign intervention. But the pretender was defeated, and the new ruler was Christian III, a convinced Lutheran who had been present at the Diet of Worms and who greatly admired Luther both for his doctrines and for his courage. He promptly took measures in support of Protestantism and limiting the power of bishops. He requested from Luther teachers to help him in the work of reformation. Eventually, the entire Danish church subscribed to the Confession of Augsburg.

Meanwhile, events in Sweden were following a similar course. When Christian II sought to impose his authority on that country, among his prisoners was a young Swede by the name of Gustavus Erikson, better known as Gustavus Vasa. The young man escaped, and from his refuge overseas sought to curb the power of Christian. When he learned of the massacre of Stockholm, in which several of his relatives were killed, he secretly returned to his homeland. Working as a journeyman, and living among the people, he confirmed the popular sentiment against Danish occupation. He then proclaimed a national rebellion, and took up arms with a disorganized band of followers from among the common people. As victory followed victory, and one daring feat of arms followed another, his name became legendary. In 1521, the rebels named him regent of the kingdom, and king two years later. A few months after this last proclamation, he entered in triumph in Stockholm, where he was received with shouts of acclamation.

But the royal title carried little authority, for the nobility and the prelates insisted on their ancient privileges. The new king followed a subtle policy of dividing his enemies. At first his harsher measures were directed against the bishops. In every case he distinguished between the powerful who incited rebellion and their followers. When two rebellious bishops were defeated, captured, and condemned to death, the king pardoned all their followers, declaring that they had been misguided. Thus, he drove a wedge between clergy and nobility, and between both of these groups and the majority of the population. The same year as the bishops' rebellion, he convened a national assembly that was attended, not only by prelates and nobles, but also by some from among the bourgeoisie and even the peasantry. When the clergy and the nobility banded together to thwart the king's program of reforms, he simply resigned, declaring that Sweden was not ready for a true king. Three days later, threatened by chaos, the assembly agreed to recall the king and to curb the power of the prelates.

The result of that national assembly, and of Gustavus Vasa's victory, was that the higher clergy lost its political power. From that point on, Lutheran influence was on the increase, and Protestant beliefs were usually joined to royalist convictions. Gustavus Vasa was not a man of profound religious conviction. But by the time he died, in 1560, Sweden was a Protestant country, with a Lutheran ecclesiastical hierarchy, and the monarchy had ceased to be elective in order to become hereditary.

10/The Reformation in the Low Countries

*Let it be known that each of us has two
arms, and that if hunger makes it necessary
we shall eat one to have the strength to
fight with the other.*

A PROTESTANT DEFENDER AT THE SIEGE OF

LEIDEN

I n the Low Countries, as in the rest of Europe, Protestantism gained
adherents from a very early time. In 1523, in Antwerp, the first two
Protestant martyrs were burned. From that point on, there are clear
indications that Protestantism made headway in various areas. But political circumstances were such that this advance of Protestantism soon became involved in the long and bitter struggle for independence.

The Political Situation

Near the mouth of the Rhine, there was a group of territories jointly known
as the "Seventeen Provinces," roughly comprising what are today the Netherlands, Belgium, and Luxemburg. These various territories were under the
lordship of the house of Hapsburg, and therefore Charles V had inherited
them from his father Philip the Fair. Since Charles had been born and raised
in the region, he was well liked by its inhabitants, and under his rule the
Seventeen Provinces grew closer together.

Such political unity, however, was partly fictitious. Although Charles V
encouraged the development of common institutions, throughout his reign
each territory retained many of its ancient privileges and particular form of
government. Cultural unity was also lacking, for between the French-speak-

ing south and the Dutch-speaking north there was an area where Flemish was the common language. The ecclesiastical situation was even more complex, for the jurisdiction of the various bishops did not coincide with political divisions, and some areas were part of bishoprics whose sees were beyond the borders of the Seventeen Provinces.

When Charles V, in a ceremony held at Brussels in 1555, placed the Seventeen Provinces under the rule of his son Philip II, he expected the latter to continue his policies. This was precisely what Philip attempted. But what his father had begun was not easy to continue. The Seventeen Provinces regarded Charles as Flemish, and that was indeed the language in which he always felt most at ease. Philip, on the other hand, had been raised in Spain, and both his language and his outlook were Spanish. In 1556, having received from his father the crown of Spain, he became Philip II, and it was clear that to him this was the most important of his possessions. The Low Countries were put at the service of Spain and her interests. This in turn provoked the resentment of leaders in the Seventeen Provinces, who tenaciously opposed Philip's efforts to complete the unification of the area, and to make it part of the hereditary possessions of the Spanish crown.

Protestant Preaching

Even before the Protestant Reformation broke out, there had been in the Low Countries a strong movement of reformation. This was the birthplace of the Brethren of the Common Life, and of the greatest of humanist reformers, Erasmus of Rotterdam. One of the characteristic themes of the Brethren of the Common Life was the need to read Scripture, not only in Latin, but also in the native language of the people. Therefore, the Protestant Reformation found in the Low Countries a fertile field for its preaching.

Soon Lutheran preachers entered the region, gaining large numbers of converts. Then the Anabaptists, particularly those who followed the teachings of Melchior Hoffman, made great headway. It is noteworthy that the leaders of the "New Jerusalem" in Münster were natives of the Low Countries. While Münster held, many of their countrymen sought to join them, but were intercepted and killed by imperial troops. Then there were several unsuccessful attempts by Anabaptists to gain possession of various cities in the Seventeen Provinces themselves. Finally, there was a great influx of Calvinist preachers from Geneva, France, and southern Germany. Eventually, these Calvinist preachers would be the most successful, and Calvinism would become the main form of Protestantism in the region.

Charles V took stern measures against the spread of Protestantism in these lands. He issued several edicts against Protestantism, and in particular against the Anabaptists. The frequency with which such edicts succeeded each other is proof of their failure to stem the tide of Protestant teaching and conversions. Tens of thousands died for their faith. The leaders were burned, their followers beheaded, and many women were buried alive. But, in spite of such cruel punishments, Protestantism continued its advance. There are indications that towards the end of Charles's reign there was a growing tide of opposition to his religious policies. But Charles was a popular ruler, and in any case most of the people were still convinced that Protestants were heretics who amply deserved their punishment.

Philip, who had never been liked in the Low Countries, increased his unpopularity through a combination of folly, obstinacy, and hypocrisy. When he decided to return to Spain, and to leave the Provinces under the regency of his half-sister Margaret of Parma, he sought to strengthen her authority by quartering Spanish troops in the Low Countries. Such troops had to be supported by the resources of the land. Friction and clashes soon developed between the Spanish soldiers and the native inhabitants of the area, who questioned the need for the presence of foreign troops. Since there was no war requiring their presence, the only possible explanation was that Philip doubted the loyalty of his subjects.

To this was added the appointment of new bishops who were given inquisitorial powers. Undoubtedly, the church in the Seventeen Provinces was in need of reorganization; but Philip's timing and procedure were not wise. Part of the rationale offered for the reorganization of the church was the need to stamp out heresy. Since the inhabitants of the Low Countries knew that in Spain the Inquisition had become an instrument in the hands of royal policy, they feared that the king intended to do the same in their country.

Even worse, Philip and the regent paid scant attention to their most loyal subjects. William, Prince of Orange, who had been a close friend of Charles V, and the Count of Egmont, who had rendered outstanding military service, were made members of the Council of State. But they were not consulted on matters of importance, which were decided by the regent and her foreign advisors. Most hated of such advisors was Bishop Granvelle, whom the natives of the Low Countries blamed for every injustice and humiliation they suffered. After repeated protests, the king recalled Granvelle. But it soon became apparent that the deposed bishop had done no more than obey his master's instructions, and that the offensive policies and practices were dictated by the king himself.

In order to argue their cause, the leaders of the Seventeen Provinces sent the Count of Egmont to Spain. Philip received him with honors and promised a radical change in policy. Egmont returned to his homeland, pleased with the assurances he had received. But he was bitterly disappointed when he opened before the Council the sealed letter Philip had given him, and it clearly contradicted what the king had promised. At the same time, Philip sent instructions to Margaret that the decrees of the Council of Trent

*William, Prince of Orange, led the rebellion of
the Seventeen Provinces.*

against Protestantism be enacted, and that all who opposed them should be
put to death.

The royal orders caused a great stir. The leaders and magistrates of the
Seventeen Provinces were not ready to execute the vast number of their
fellow citizens for whom the king decreed the death penalty. In response to
Philip's commands, several hundred leaders of the nobility and the bourgeoisie joined in a petition to the regent that such policies not be implemented.
Margaret received them, and was showing signs of agitation when one of her
courtiers intervened, telling her that she ought not to heed nor fear "those
beggars."

The Beggars

Those words captured the imagination of the patriots. Since their oppressors called them beggars, that was the name they would give themselves. The leather bag of a beggar became the banner of rebellion. Under that symbol the movement, until then limited to the nobility and the bourgeoisie, took root among the entire population. The standard of rebellion was flaunted everywhere, and the authorities were at a loss as to how to respond.

Before reaching the field of battle, the movement took on religious overtones. There were frequent outdoor meetings, in which Protestantism and opposition to the authorities were preached under the protection of armed "beggars." For fear of greater disturbances, the regent's troops allowed such meetings. Then there were bands of iconoclasts who invaded churches, overturned altars, and destroyed images and other symbols of the old religion. When such a band invaded a church, no one intervened, for many rejoiced secretly while others marveled that heaven did not destroy those who committed such sacrilege.

Finally, the Council of State had to appeal to William of Orange, whose advice it had frequently chided. With the same loyalty with which he had served Charles, and risking his life, William intervened. Thanks to his pleas, and to others who supported him, violence abated, and the iconoclastic wave ceased. This was accomplished, however, only after the Council suspended the Inquisition and allowed a limited freedom of worship. On their part, the beggars promised to refrain from action as long as the government did not seek to impose the Inquisition and other forms of oppression.

But Philip was not a king to be swayed by his subjects' opposition. He had declared, with vehement sincerity, that he had no desire to be "lord of heretics." The old principle that there was no need to keep faith with the unfaithful applied in this situation. While he promised to abide by the agreements reached in the Provinces, and to pardon the rebels, he was raising an army with which to force his will and faith on the Low Countries. William of Orange, who was aware of the king's duplicity, advised his friends, particularly the counts of Egmont and Horn, to join in armed resistance. But they put their trust in the king's promises, and William withdrew to his possessions in Germany.

The storm arrived swiftly. Early in 1567, the Duke of Alba invaded the country with an army of Spanish and Italian troops. The king had given him such powers that the regent became a figurehead, and he was the true ruler. His mission was to drown rebellion and heresy in blood. One of his first steps was to organize a Council of Disturbances, which the people soon dubbed the "Council of Blood." This court was not bound by any legal requirements, for, as Alba explained to Philip, legality would allow only for the conviction of those whose crimes were proven, whereas in this case "matters of state" demanded more drastic measures. Protestants were condemned for their heresy, and Catholics for not having been sufficiently firm in resisting heresy. Even to express a doubt as to the authority of the Council of Disturbances was high treason. The same charge of high treason was brought against any who had opposed the reorganization of the church, or who had declared that the Provinces had rights and privileges that the king could not overturn. Those put to death under such ordinances were so many that chroniclers of the time speak of the stench in the air, and of hundreds of bodies hanging from trees along the wayside. The counts of Egmont and Horn, who had remained in their lands with candid trust and loyalty, were arrested and brought to trial. Since William of Orange was not available, Alba captured his fifteen-year-old son, Philip William, and sent him to Spain. William responded by investing all his financial resources in raising an army, mostly German, with which he invaded the Low Countries. But Alba defeated him repeatedly and, in retaliation, ordered the execution of Egmont and Horn.

Alba seemed to be in full command of the situation when the rebels received support from an unexpected quarter. Orange had granted privateer licenses to a few sailors, in the hope that they would harass Alba's communications with Spain. These "beggars of the sea," at first little more than pirates, achieved a measure of organization, and Philip's naval forces could not contain them. For some time, Elizabeth of England gave them a measure of support, especially by allowing them to sell their prizes in English ports. Eventually, Spain pressured her to change this policy. But by then the beggars of the sea were too strong to be easily suppressed. In a brilliant maneuver, they captured the city of Brill, and after that their repeated success made them a legend and an inspiration to the patriots who resisted on land. Several cities declared themselves in favor of William of Orange, who once again invaded the Provinces, this time with French support. But the French also were dealing in treachery, and William was approaching Brussels when he learned of the Massacre of St. Bartholomew's Day—to which we shall return in the next chapter—and this put an end to all possible collaboration between Protestants and the French crown. Lacking in funds and in every other military support, William was forced to disband his troops, who were mostly mercenary soldiers.

Alba's vengeance was terrible. His armies took city after city, and repeatedly broke the terms of surrender. Prisoners were killed for no other reason than revenge, and several cities that had resisted were put to the torch. Women, children, and the elderly were indiscriminately killed along with the rebels. Soon every rebel stronghold was in Alba's hands.

It was only on the sea that the rebels were still strong. The beggars continually defeated the Spanish, and even captured their admiral. This in turn made it very difficult for Alba to receive supplies and funds for his troops, who therefore began showing signs of mutiny. Tired of the long struggle, and bitter because Spain did not send him the resources he required, Alba asked to be appointed elsewhere.

The new Spanish general, Luis de Zúñiga y Requesens, had the wisdom to exploit the religious differences among the rebels. He sought a separate peace with the Catholics of the southern provinces, thus driving a wedge between them and the Protestants, who were most numerous in the North. Up to that point, the religious question had been only one element among many in what was really a national rebellion against foreign rule. William of Orange, the leader of the uprising, had been a liberal Catholic at least until his exile in Germany, and it was only in 1573 that he declared himself a Calvinist. But Requesens's policies underscored the religious element in the struggle, thus neutralizing the Catholic provinces of the south.

The Protestant cause was therefore desperate. Its only hope seemed to be in the beggars of the sea, while its armies were repeatedly and roundly defeated. The crisis came at the siege of Leiden, an important trading center that had declared itself for Protestantism, and which the Spanish had surrounded. An army sent by William of Orange to break the siege was defeated by the Spanish, and in that battle two of William's brothers were killed. All was lost when William, whose enemies called him "the Silent" or "the Sly," suggested that the dikes be opened, thus flooding the land around Leiden. This implied the destruction of many years of hard work, and the loss of a great deal of arable land. But the citizens agreed. In spite of an incredible shortage of food, the besieged continued their resistance during the four months that it took the sea to reach Leiden. Riding the flood, the beggars of the sea also arrived, shouting that they would rather be Turkish than Popish. Lacking naval support, the Spanish were forced to abandon the siege.

At that point Requesens died. His troops, having neither chief nor pay, mutinied, and set about sacking the cities of the South, an easier prey than those of the North. This served to reunite the inhabitants of the Seventeen Provinces, who, in 1576, agreed to the *Pacification of Ghent*. This was an alliance among the various provinces, making it clear that what was at stake was national freedom, and not religious differences. This agreement was hailed by William of Orange, who had repeatedly argued that religious dogmatism and sectarian intolerance were an obstacle to the unity and freedom of the Provinces.

The next governor was Don John of Austria, an illegitimate son of Charles V, and therefore a half-brother of Philip II. Although he was one of the most admired military heroes of Christendom, for his defeat of the Turks at the battle of Lepanto, he was not allowed to enter Brussels until he had agreed to the stipulations of the *Pacification of Ghent*. But Philip II would not give up the struggle. A new army was sent into the region, and once again the southern provinces abandoned the struggle. Then the northern provinces, against the advice of William of Orange, formed a separate league for the defense of their faith and freedom.

The struggle dragged on for years. Masters of the southern provinces, the Spanish could not conquer those of the North. In 1580, Philip II issued a proclamation promising a reward of 25,000 crowns and a title of nobility to anyone who would kill William the Silent. The latter and his followers responded with a formal declaration that they were independent of all royal authority. But three years later, after several unsuccessful attempts by other parties, an assassin in quest of the reward was able to kill William. (Once again, Philip proved untrue to his word, at first refusing to pay any reward, and then paying only a portion of it.) Philip had hoped that William's death would put an end to the rebellion. But William's son Maurice, then only nineteen years old, proved to be a better general than his father, and led his troops in several victorious campaigns.

In 1607, almost a decade after the death of Philip II, Spain decided that her losses in this struggle were not worth the effort and cost of continuing the war, and a truce was signed. By then, the vast majority of the population in the northern provinces was Calvinist, and many in the North equated their Calvinist faith with their nationalist loyalty, while the southern provinces remained Catholic. Eventually, religious, economic, and cultural differences would lead to the formation of three countries, one Protestant—the Netherlands—and two Catholic—Belgium and Luxemburg.

11/Protestantism in France

O Lord, we cry to you: Will you allow
such crimes to be committed at the expense
of your honor?

ETIENNE DE MAISONFLEUR

A t the dawn of the sixteenth century, no other nation in western
Europe had achieved the degree of national unity and centralization that France had attained. Yet, during the course of that
century, few nations were as bitterly divided as she was. This was
due to the continuing conflict between Protestants and Catholics, which in
France led to long internecine warfare.

Shifting Royal Policies

At the beginning of the reformation, France was ruled by Francis I, the last
great king of the house of Valois. His religious policy was always ambiguous
and hesitant, for he had no desire to see Protestantism enter his territories
and divide them, but he encouraged its spread in Germany, where it was a
thorn in the flesh of his rival Charles V. Thus, although Francis never lent
his support to French Protestants, his attitude towards them varied according
to the dictates of political expediency. When he sought closer ties with the
German Protestants, in order to weaken Charles V, he was constrained to
allow a measure of freedom to those in his own lands who were of the same
persuasion. But, at other times, Protestants were persecuted as vigorously as
they were in other Catholic countries. In spite of such fluctuations, Protestantism gained many adherents in France, particularly among the learned and
the nobility. Those very fluctuations, granting periods of respite followed by
severe persecution, led many French Protestants to exile—John Calvin
among them. From neighboring cities such as Geneva and Strasbourg, these
exiles followed events in their homeland, and were ready to intervene in
them whenever possible.

Meanwhile, in the neighboring kingdom of Navarre—between France and Spain—Francis's sister Margaret of Angouleme, who was married to King Henry of Navarre, encouraged the reform movement. She was a scholarly woman who had supported the French humanist reformers while she was still living in France. Now she offered sanctuary in her court to French Protestant exiles who were fleeing her brother's territories. From Navarre, and from cities just across the French border such as Strasbourg and Geneva, Protestant books were constantly smuggled into France. But in spite of this there is no record of Protestant churches until much later, in 1555.

Francis I died in 1547, and was succeeded by his son Henry II, who continued his father's policies, although his opposition to Protestantism was more constant and cruel. In spite of persecution, it was during Henry's reign that the first Protestant church, mentioned above, was formally organized, following the patterns set forth by the exiled John Calvin. Four years later, when the first national synod gathered, there were churches scattered throughout the nation. That assembly, meeting secretly near Paris, approved a *Confession of Faith* and a *Discipline* for the new church.

Shortly after that gathering, Henry II died of wounds received during

Catherine de Medici was the dominant figure
in France during the reign of her three sons,
Francis II, Charles IX, and Henry III.

a tournament. He left four sons, three of whom would successively inherit the throne—Francis II, Charles IX, and Henry III—and three daughters, among them Margaret of Valois, who would be queen of France after her brothers' death. Their mother was Catherine de Medici, an ambitious woman who sought to rule through her children.

Catherine's projects, however, were hindered by the leaders of the house of Guise. That family, from Lorraine, had become prominent during the reign of Francis I. Later, General Francis of Guise and his brother Charles, cardinal of Lorraine, had been the main advisors of Henry II. And now, since young Francis II was not interested in matters of state, it was these two brothers who ruled in his name. Their power, however, was resented by the older nobility, and particularly by the "princes of the blood," that is, the king's closest relatives.

Among these princes of the blood were Antoine de Bourbon and his brother Louis de Condé. The former had married Jane d'Albret, a daughter of Margaret of Navarre who had followed her mother's religious inclinations and belcome a Calvinist. Her husband Antoine and her brother-in-law Louis then accepted her religion, and thus Protestantism made headway among the highest nobility of the kingdom. Since the house of Guise was staunchly Catholic, and sought to stamp out Protestantism, their struggle with the Bourbons soon took religious overtones. Then a plot was discovered, the Conspiracy of Amboise, whose goal was to take possession of the king and keep him apart from the Guises. Although the plot was not strictly religious in motivation, most of the conspirators were "Huguenots"—a name of uncertain origin given to French Protestants. Among those implicated, and imprisoned by the Guises, was Louis de Condé. And this in turn caused grave misgivings among the nobility, both Catholic and Protestant, who feared that the imprisonment, trial, and conviction of a prince of the blood would be a severe blow to their ancient privileges.

At that point Francis II died unexpectedly. Catherine de Medici quickly intervened and took the title of regent for her ten-year-old son, Charles IX. Since she had been repeatedly humiliated and thwarted by the Guises, one of her first actions was to free Condé and join the Huguenots in their efforts to limit the power of the house of Lorraine—as the Guises were also called. By that time, the Protestants in France were numerous, for there were some two thousand Huguenot churches. Therefore, for reasons of policy rather than conviction, Catherine cultivated the Protestants. Those who were in prison were freed, with a mild admonition to abandon heresy. She then convened a colloquy of Protestant and Catholic theologians that gathered at Poissy in order to seek an agreement. This failed, as was to be expected. But, in 1562, the regent issued the Edict of St. Germain, which granted Huguenots freedom to practice their religion, but forbade their owning places of worship, gathering in synods without a previous permit, collecting funds, supporting an army, and so on. Thus, all that the Huguenots were granted was the right to gather for worship, as long as this took place outside cities, at daytime, and without arms. Catherine hoped by these measures to gain the favor of Protestants, while limiting any political or military power they might have. She wished to make the Huguenots a threat to the house of Lorraine, but not to the unity of the nation or the power of the throne.

The Guises refused to obey this edict, hoping thus to undermine Catherine's authority. Slightly more than two months after the proclamation of the edict, the two Guise brothers, with two hundred armed noblemen, surrounded the stable where a group of Huguenots were worshiping in the village of Vassy, and slew as many as they could.

The massacre of Vassy resulted in the first of a long series of religious wars that ravaged France. After several skirmishes, each side raised an army and took the field—the Catholics under the leadership of the duke of Guise, and the Protestants under Admiral Gaspard de Coligny. The Catholics won most of the battles, but their general was assassinated by a Protestant nobleman; and exactly a year after the massacre of Vassy the two sides agreed to a truce that granted the Huguenots a measure of tolerance. But this was not a lasting peace, for there were two other religious wars between 1567 and 1570.

The Massacre of St. Bartholomew's Day

After prolonged wars, the peace of 1570 offered the promise of lasting peace. Catherine de Medici seemed willing to make concessions to the Protestants, hoping they would help her in her power struggle against the Guises. In 1571, Coligny appeared in court, and he made such a favorable impression on the young king that the latter called him "my father." There were also plans for a marriage between Catherine's daughter Margaret Valois and the Protestant prince Henry Bourbon, Antoine's son. All bode well for the Huguenots, who after long struggles were now able to appear freely at court.

But under sweet appearances other intentions lurked. The new duke of Guise, Henry, was convinced that his father's death had been ordered by Coligny, and was eager for revenge. Catherine herself began to fear the growing influence of the Protestant admiral who had won the king's trust and admiration. Thus developed a plot to be rid of the admiral, who was one of the most upright figures of those turbulent times.

The main Huguenot leaders had come to Paris for the wedding of Henry Bourbon, by then king of Navarre, and the French king's sister Margaret Valois. The ceremony took place, amid great rejoicing and signs of reconciliation, on August 18. The Protestant nobles were lulled into overconfidence by their friendly reception and by the king's obvious good will. Then, as Coligny was returning to his lodgings from the Louvre, someone shot at him from a building owned by the Guise family. He lost a finger from his right hand, and was also wounded on the left arm. But the attempt on his life had failed.

The Huguenot leaders, incensed at such a breach of the king's hospitality, demanded justice. Charles IX took the investigation seriously, and there were indications that the shot had been fired from an arquebus belonging to the Duke of Guise, and that the assassin had fled on a horse from Catherine's stables. Some even suspected that the king's brother, Henry of Anjou—later Henry III—was part of the conspiracy. The indignant king banned the Guises from court, while further inquiries continued.

The conspirators then took drastic measures. Catherine convinced Charles that there was a vast Huguenot plot to wrest the throne from him, and that its leader was Coligny. The king, who had never shown great strength of conviction, believed what he was told, and thus the stage was set for the massacre of Protestants.

On the night of St. Bartholomew's Day, August 24, 1572, with the approval of both Charles IX and Catherine de Medici, the Duke of Guise met with those in charge of keeping order in Paris and gave them detailed instructions, including what dwelling each should attack, and who their victims were to be. He took personal charge of the death of Coligny, who was still convalescing. The admiral was taken by surprise in his bedchamber, where they inflicted several wounds on him. While he was still living, he was thrown out the window to the duke who waited below, and who kicked and killed him. Then his body was horribly mutilated, and what was left was hanged from the gibbet at Montfaucon.

Meanwhile, some two thousand Huguenots met a similar fate. Even at the royal palace, the Louvre, it is said that blood ran down the stairs. The two Protestant princes of the blood, Louis de Condé and Henry Bourbon—

The massacre of St. Bartholomew's Day, August 24, 1572, did not succeed in stamping out Protestantism in France.

the latter king of Navarre and now Charles's brother-in-law—were dragged before the French king, where they saved their lives by denying their faith.

The massacre in Paris was the signal calling to similar events in the provinces. The Duke of Guise had given orders that the massacre should spread to every corner of the kingdom. A few upright magistrates refused to obey, declaring that they were neither executioners nor murderers. But most did obey, and the number of victims reached the tens of thousands.

The news spread throughout Europe. As has been said, William of Orange, who was marching on Brussels with an army he had raised with French support (and who later married one of Coligny's daughters) felt compelled to disband his troops and abandon the campaign. In England, Elizabeth dressed in mourning. Emperor Maximilian II, although a faithful Catholic, expressed horror at the news. But, in Rome and Madrid, there were different reactions. Pope Gregory XIII, while declaring that he deplored the bloodshed, ordered that a Te Deum be sung in celebration of the night of St. Bartholomew, and that the same be done every year in memory of such glorious deeds. Spanish chroniclers affirm that Philip II smiled in public for the first time when he received the news of the massacre, and that he too ordered the singing of a Te Deum and other celebrations.

The War of the Three Henrys

In spite of the many casualties, Protestantism itself had not been stamped out. Lacking in military leaders as a result of the massacre, the Huguenots made themselves strong in La Rochelle and Montauban, cities that had been granted to them by an earlier peace treaty, and declared themselves ready to fight, not only the house of Guise, but also the king himself, whom they now declared to be a traitor and a murderer. Many Catholics, tired of internecine warfare and bloodshed, and convinced that a policy of tolerance was necessary, offered their support. As for Charles IX, it was apparent that he was unable to rule, and the country lived in near chaos until his death in 1574.

The crown then passed to his brother Henry of Anjou—Henry III—one of the authors of the massacre. His mother, Catherine de Medici, had had him elected king of Poland. But, when he received news of his brother's death, he rushed to Paris to claim the French throne, without even bothering to abdicate the Polish one. Like his mother, Henry had no other convictions than those necessary to take and hold power. Therefore, when he decided that it was to his advantage, he made peace with the Protestant rebels, who were granted freedom of worship, except in Paris.

The more belligerent Catholics, led by the Duke of Guise, reacted vigorously. With Spanish support, they declared war on the Huguenots. Eventually Henry III joined them, and thus began another war of religion

—the eighth in a seemingly endless series—that bled the country and solved nothing, for the Huguenots were too weak to defeat the Catholics, and the latter were not strong enough to stamp out Protestantism.

Then events took an unexpected turn. The youngest of the sons of Henry II and Catherine de Medici died, leaving no heir. Since the king himself had no direct heir, the legal succession to the throne now belonged to Henry Bourbon, king of Navarre. This prince, who had been a prisoner in Paris after the massacre of St. Bartholomew's Day, had managed to escape in 1576. He then changed his religion for a fourth time—not the last— declaring himself a Protestant. Although the Huguenots did not find his licentiousness (and that of his wife) to their liking, he had become the center of Protestant resistance. Therefore, as conditions now stood, the legal heir to the crown was a Protestant.

This the Catholic party could not tolerate. It was necessary to find another solution before the king's death left the throne vacant. It was then decided to put forward Henry of Guise as the rightful heir to the throne. A document was supposedly unearthed in Lorraine, showing that the house of Guise was descended from Charlemagne, and that therefore its right to the crown exceeded the claims of the Bourbons and even of the Valois, whose last king Henry III was.

Thus resulted three parties, each headed by a different Henry. The legitimate king, Henry III, was the least worthy and able of the three. The Catholic pretender, Henry of Guise, based his claims on a document that was clearly spurious. The Protestant chief, Henry Bourbon, did not claim the throne itself, but only his right to inherit it.

The war dragged on until Henry of Guise took Paris and had himself proclaimed king. Then Henry III had recourse to the same methods Henry of Guise had earlier employed against the Protestants. Two days before Christmas 1588, by the king's order, Henry of Guise was murdered at the same place where fifteen years earlier he had given instructions for the massacre of St. Barthlomew's day.

This did not put an end to Catholic opposition, however. Very few were ready to trust a king who had repeatedly made use of political assassination. The Catholic rebels simply found new leaders and continued fighting. Soon the king's situation was desperate, and he had no alternative but to flee from Paris and seek refuge in the camp of his erstwhile rival, Henry Bourbon, who at least acknowledged him as the legitimate king.

Henry Bourbon received the king with due respect and granted him asylum, but would not let him determine the policies to be followed. This awkward situation, however, did not last long, for a fanatical Dominican friar, convinced that the king was a tyrant and that in such circumstances regicide was licit, entered the Protestant camp and killed the king.

The death of Henry III did not end the war. Henry Bourbon, who was clearly the legitimate heir, took the name of Henry IV. But French Catholics were not ready to have a Protestant king. In Spain, Philip II was planning to seize the opportunity to make himself master of France. The pope declared that Henry Bourbon's claim to the throne was not valid. For these reasons, the war continued for four more years. Finally, Henry IV decided that the throne would never be his unless he became a Catholic, and therefore once again he changed his religion. Although he probably never said the words attributed to him, "Paris is worth a mass," they clearly express his sentiments. The year after this fifth conversion the new king entered Paris, and thus ended several decades of religious wars.

Although he had become a Catholic, Henry IV did not forget his former comrades in arms. On the contrary, he showed them such loyalty and favor that the more recalcitrant Catholics claimed that he was still a heretic. Finally, on April 13, 1598, he issued the Edict of Nantes, granting the Huguenots freedom of worship in all places where they had had churches by the previous year, except in Paris. He also guaranteed their security by granting them all the fortified towns they had held in 1597.

In spite of his inconstant religious convictions and the licentiousness of his personal life, Henry IV ruled the nation wisely. During his reign, the country prospered, and soon he was respected by many of his former foes. But religious hatred and prejudice had not entirely disappeared, and Henry himself finally fell victim to them in 1610, when his life was ended by a Catholic fanatic who was convinced that the king was still a Protestant heretic, and that God was being served by his death.

12/The Catholic Reformation

On the Cross there hangs the Lord
Of Heaven and earth
And amid the stress of war
Peace comes to birth.

ST. TERESA (TR. E. ALLISON PEERS)

The Protestant movement did not encompass all the strong and varied currents of reformation that were sweeping Europe. Well before Luther's protest, there were many who longed for an ecclesiastical reformation, and who worked towards it. This was particularly true in Spain where, under Queen Isabella and Cardinal Francisco Jiménez de Cisneros, the Catholic Reformation was well under way when Luther was still a young boy.

The Reformation of Spanish Catholicism

When Isabella inherited the crown of Castile in 1474, the church in her lands was in urgent need of reformation. As in the rest of Europe, many prelates were also great lords, more given to war and intrigue than to the spiritual welfare of the faithful. Most of the lower clergy were insufficiently trained, to the point that many were able to do no more than recite the mass. As in other parts of Europe, monasticism was at a low ebb, and some of the larger convents and monasteries had become fashionable places of retreat for the illegitimate children of royalty and nobility.

Isabella was determined to reform the church, and to that end began by securing from the papacy the right to name those who were to fill high ecclesiastical posts. Her husband Ferdinand, the king of neighboring Aragon, obtained similar rights for his territories. But their motivations were very different. Isabella was interested in having the authority to reform the church, whereas Ferdinand saw in the naming of prelates an important political prerogative that would strengthen the crown. Thus, while Isabella was energetically seeking the best candidates to fill vacant posts, Ferdinand filled the vacant archbishopric of Saragossa, his capital, by naming to that post his illegitimate son, who was then six years old.

If Isabella found no support for her program of reformation in her husband Ferdinand, the same was not true of her confessor, Francisco Jiménez de Cisneros. He was an austere Franciscan who had spent ten years in prison for refusing to participate in the corrupt practices of his time. While in prison, he had studied Hebrew and Chaldean, for he was imbued in the scholarly interests of the humanists. Finally, through the recommendation of the reformist bishop of Toledo—who had been chosen by Isabella—he was made confessor to the queen. When the archbishop died, Isabella took the steps necessary to have Jiménez named to the vacant see, the most important in the kingdom. Jiménez refused, and the queen obtained from Pope Alexander VI—who was anything but a reformer—a papal bull ordering the reluctant friar to accept.

Isabella, the great queen of Castile, was a champion of reformation long before Luther's protest. Her program did not include the reformation of doctrine, however, as did Luther's.

The queen and the archbishop set about the reformation of convents and monasteries. They personally visited the most important monastic houses, and those best known for their laxity, calling all to renewed obedience to their monastic vows, reproving those who showed little improvement, and, in some cases, severely punishing those who resisted their entreaties. Protests were sent to Rome. But the pope, while not a reformer, was a politician who understood the need to humor the reformist queen. As a result, her hand was further strengthened, and even the most corrupt among the prelates of her kingdom had to take steps to reform the church.

Jiménez's scholarship, most particularly his great interest in Scripture, was an important element in Isabella's program of reformation. She was convinced that both the church and her kingdom were in need of learned leadership, and therefore encouraged studies. She herself was a scholar, and gathered around herself an impressive array of intellectual men and women. With Ferdinand's support, she encouraged the printing of books, and soon there were printing presses in all the major cities of their kingdoms. In all these projects, Jiménez was an important ally. But his two most significant contributions were the founding of the University of Alcala and the publication of the *Complutensian Polyglot.* The University of Alcala, a few miles from Madrid, soon counted among its alumni several of the most prominent figures in Spanish religious and literary life—Cervantes and Loyola among them. The *Complutensian Polyglot*—named after Complutum, the Latin name for Alcala—was a great multilingual edition of the Bible prepared by the best scholars available: three converts from Judaism prepared the Hebrew text, a Cretan and two Spanish scholars were chiefly responsible for the Greek, and the best Latin scholars in Spain worked on the text of the Vulgate. All these appeared in parallel columns, and the entire work comprised six volumes (the Old Testament in four, the New in the fifth, and a thorough discussion of Hebrew, Chaldean, and Greek grammar in the sixth). Although the work was finished in 1517, it was not officially published until 1520. It is said that when the work was completed, Jiménez rejoiced at "this edition of the Bible that, at this critical time, opens the sacred sources of our religion, from which will flow a much purer theology than any derived from less direct sources." Such a clear affirmation of the superiority of Scripture over tradition, had it been made a few years later, would have led to cries of "Lutheran heresy."

The scholarly interests of Jiménez and Isabella, however, did not lead to tolerance. Studies were to be encouraged as long as they contributed to the reformation of customs and morals, but doctrinal deviation would be severely punished. The Inquisition, normally under papal authority and by that time used mostly as a tool of papal policy, was placed by the pope under the authority of Ferdinand and Isabella. The Dominican friar Tomás de Torquemada, who was known for his uncompromising love for orthodoxy, was appointed to head the Inquisition in Castile, and his name has become famous for the zeal with which he persecuted those whom he considered heretics. These were mostly Jews who had been converted under duress, and who were now accused of "Judaizing."

During Isabella's reign, and with the firm encouragement of Jiménez, the pressure on Jews and "Judaizing" Christians became increasingly severe. Finally, in 1492, it was decreed that all Jews must either accept baptism or leave all territories under Isabella and Ferdinand. Most refused to be baptized, even though it meant exile and the loss of most of their possessions. Although exact figures are not available, it seems that approximately 200,000 Spaniards of the Jewish faith were thus condemned to exile—which many times led to death, capture by pirates, and other such misfortunes.

Shortly before the promulgation of the royal decree against Jews, Granada had fallen to Castilian arms. This was the last Moorish stronghold in the peninsula, and the terms of surrender included freedom for the Moslems to continue practicing their religion. But soon Jiménez and his representatives were seeking the forced conversion of the Moors, who saw no alternative but rebellion. This was drowned in blood. But resistance continued, and eventually it was decreed that all Moors had to choose between baptism and exile. When it became clear that there would be a massive exodus, a new edict was issued, forbidding the Moors from leaving the country, and forcing baptism on them. After such unwilling conversions, the Inquisition was kept busy tracking down those who persisted in their Moslem beliefs. Jiménez, who had been made Inquisitor General, took this task to heart. In 1516, after the death of both Ferdinand and Isabella, he was also made regent, and sought to use his power to force the "converted" Moors to abandon their traditional garb and other customs. But in this he failed, and again the kingdom was shaken by rebellion and bloodshed.

Thus, the scholar who directed the *Complutensian Polyglot,* the patron of books and learning, the reformer of the life of the church, was also the grand inquisitor who would brook no diversity or doctrinal deviation. In this he was typical of most of the Catholic Reformation, which sought to purify the church through austerity, devotion, and scholarship, but at the same time insisted on strict adherence to traditional dogma. The saints and sages of the Catholic Reformation, like Isabella, were pure, devout, and intolerant.

Polemics against Protestantism

Although the Catholic Reformation had begun earlier, the advent of Protestantism gave it a new character. It was no longer a matter of the need to reform the church out of an inner necessity, but also an attempt to respond to those who included doctrine among the things to be reformed. Especially in those areas where Protestantism was a real threat, Catholic reformers felt compelled to respond with both a reformation of custom and a defense of traditional doctrine.

Some of these Catholic leaders were scholars, while others feared that the humanist program was as great a threat as Protestantism. John Eck, the theologian who debated Luther and Karlstadt at Leipzig, was also a conscientious pastor and a scholar who in 1537 published his own German translation of the Bible. On the other hand, James Latomus, rector of the University of Louvain, attacked both Protestants and humanists, arguing that in order to understand Scripture it sufficed to read it in Latin, in the light of the tradition of the church, and that the study of Greek and Hebrew was useless. Eventually, however, it became clear that scholarship was necessary to refute Protestant teachings; and thus appeared a host of theologians and scholars who devoted their efforts to counter Protestant arguments. Foremost among these were Robert Bellarmine and Caesar Baronius.

Bellarmine was the main systematizer of Catholic theological arguments against Protestant claims. For twelve years, beginning in 1576, he held in Rome the newly founded Chair of Polemics, and towards the end of his tenure there he began publishing his great work, *On the Controversies of the Christian Faith,* which he completed in 1593. This became the classical source of arguments against Protestantism. In fact, most of the arguments used to this day are already included in Bellarmine's work. Bellarmine was also one of the participants in the trial of Galileo, which concluded that the notion that the earth moves around the sun is heretical.

Caesar Baronius, on the other hand, was the great Catholic historian. A group of scholars at the University of Magdeburg had begun publishing a vast history of the church in which they sought to show how Roman Catholicism had deviated from original Christianity. Since this work—never completed—devoted a volume to each century, it became generally known as *The Centuries of Magdeburg.* In answer to them, Baronius wrote his *Ecclesiastical Annals.* These works marked the birth of church history as a modern discipline.

New Orders

Although it is true that monastic life had reached a low ebb at the outset of the Reformation, it is also true that there were still many in convents and monasteries who took their vows seriously, and who bemoaned the sad state of monastic life. During the sixteenth century, such longings came to fruition in the reformation of the old orders, as Isabella and Jiménez had advocated, and in the founding of new ones. Among these new orders, some sought to renew the ancient strict observance of monastic vows, whereas others were shaped to respond to the new conditions of the sixteenth century. The most noteworthy new order of the first type was that of the Discalced Carmelites, founded by St. Teresa. The Jesuits, under the leadership of Ignatius Loyola, were foremost among the orders that hoped to respond to the new times with new solutions.

Teresa spent most of her youth in Avila, an ancient walled city perched high in the plateaus of Castile. Her grandfather was a converted Jew who had moved with his family to Avila after having been shamed by the Inquisition in his native Toledo. She had felt attracted to the monastic life from an early age, although she later declared that she also feared it. When she finally joined the Carmelite convent of the Incarnation, just outside Avila, she did so against her father's wishes. There, her wit and charm made her so popular that it became a fad for the aristocracy of the city to visit and exchange pleasantries with her. But she herself was unhappy with this easy style of monasticism, and spent as much time as possible reading books of devotion.

She was dismayed when the Inquisition published a list of forbidden books, which included most of her favorites. She had a vision, in which Jesus told her: "Fear not, for I shall be to you like an open book." From then on, such visions became increasingly frequent. This led her to a prolonged inner struggle, for she had no way of determining whether the visions were genuine or, in her words, "were demon." Her confessors, whom she changed repeatedly, were of little help. One even told her to exorcise the visions with an obscene sign—a thing she could never bring herself to do. Finally, with the help of some learned friars, she came to the conviction that her visions were genuine.

She then felt called, again by a vision, to leave the convent and found another one nearby, there to follow the monastic life with more rigor. Overcoming great opposition from the bishop as well as from other nuns and from the aristocracy of the city, she managed to found her little convent. But this was not enough, for her visions called her to found similar houses throughout Spain. Her enemies accused her of being a gadabout. But she won the respect of bishops and royalty, and eventually the order she founded spread throughout Spain and its possessions. Since her nuns wore sandals instead of shoes, they became generally known as the Discalced ("Barefoot") Carmelites.

She was joined in her efforts by St. John of the Cross, a man so short that, when she met him, St. Teresa is said to have quipped, "Lord, I asked you for a monk and you sent me half of one." Through his work, Teresa's reform resulted in the male branch of the Discalced Carmelites. Thus, Teresa is the only woman in the history of the church to have founded monastic orders for both women and men.

While deeply involved in all the administrative matters related to the convents she founded, Teresa also spent time in mystical contemplation, which often led to visions or to ecstasy. Her many works on the subject have become classics of mystical devotion and, in 1970, Pope Paul VI added her name to the official list of "Doctors of the Church"—an honor she shares with one other woman, St. Catherine of Siena.

While Teresa's reformation was directed to the monastic life and the stricter observance of the ancient rule of the Carmelites, the one led by St. Ignatius Loyola, begun a few years earlier, was intended to respond to the outward challenges the times posed for the church. Ignatius was the scion of an ancient aristocratic family, and had hoped to attain glory through a military career. These dreams were shattered when, at the siege of Pamplona in Navarre, he received a wound that would make him limp for the rest of his life. While still bedridden, and prey to both excruciating pain and bitter disappointment, he turned to the reading of devotional books. This led to a vision he later retold, using the third person to refer to himself:

Lying awake one night, he clearly saw the image of Our Lady with the Holy Child Jesus, and with that vision he received remarkable consolation for a long time, and was left with such repugnance for his former life, and especially for things of the flesh, that it seemed like all the images that had been painted on his soul were erased.*

St. Teresa of Avila, one of the first two women to receive the official title of "doctor of the church," was both a mystic and a reformer of convents and monasteries. Here she is shown in the midst of a mystical experience in which she felt her heart pierced by an arrow.

---

*Autobiography 1.10.

He then went on pilgrimage to the hermitage of Montserrat, where, in a rite reminiscent of the ancient orders of chivalry, he devoted himself to the service of his Lady, the Virgin, and confessed all his sins. Then he withdrew to Manresa, where he intended to live as a hermit. But this did not suffice to calm his spirit, tormented—as Luther's had been earlier—by a profound sense of his own sin. His account of those days is strikingly similar to Luther's:

At that point he came to have much travail with scruples, for, although the general confession he had made at Montserrat had been done with great diligence and in writing, [. . .] it still seemed to him that there were some things that he had not confessed. And this caused him great affliction because, even having confessed those other things, he was not at peace.

Then [. . .] the confessor ordered him not to confess anything of the past, but only those things that were very clear to him. But to him all these things were very clear, and therefore this order was of no benefit to him, and he was still in great travail. [. . .]

When he had such thoughts, very often the temptation came to him with great force, to jump from a big hole in his room, next to the place where he prayed. But then, acknowledging that to kill himself would be a sin, he would cry out, "Lord, I shall do naught to offend thee."*

Such were the torments the future founder of the Jesuits suffered until he came to know the grace of God. He does not tell how this happened. But he does say that "from that day on he was free of those scruples, being certain that our Lord had wished to free him by His mercy."**

At this point, however, the parallelism between Luther and Loyola breaks down, for while the German friar set out on a path that would eventually lead to an open break with the Catholic Church, the Spaniard took an opposite tack. From then on he devoted his life, no longer to the monastic quest for his own salvation, but now to the service of the church and her mission. He first went to the Holy Land, which for centuries had exerted a mysterious attraction on the European soul, hoping to become a missionary to the Turks. But the Franciscans who were already working there feared the complications the fiery Spaniard could create, and forced him to leave. He then decided that he must learn theology in order to serve better. By then a mature man, he joined younger students at the universities of Barcelona, Alcala, Salamanca, and Paris. Soon a small band gathered around him, drawn by his fervent faith and enthusiasm. Finally, in 1534, he returned to Montserrat with his small band, and there all made solemn vows of poverty, chastity, and obedience to the pope.

The initial purpose of the new order was to work among the Turks in the Holy Land. But by the time Pope Paul III gave it his formal approval, in 1540, the threat of Protestantism was such that the Society of Jesus—commonly known as the Jesuits—came to be one of the main instruments of

---

Autobiography 3.22–3.24.
**Autobiography* 3.27.

the Catholic offensive against Protestantism. The Jesuits, however, did not set aside their original missionary commitment, and soon hundreds of them were laboring in the Far East and the New World. As a response to Protestantism, the Society of Jesus was a powerful weapon in the hands of a reformed papacy. Their organization, patterned after the military, enabled them to respond rapidly and efficiently to various challenges and opportunities. Many of them were also scholars who contributed their knowledge to the polemic against Protestantism.

Papal Reformation

When Luther nailed his theses on the Wittenberg door, the papacy was in the hands of Leo X, who was more interested in embellishing the city of Rome, and in furthering the interests of the house of Medici, than in religious matters. Therefore, even those who remained loyal Catholics had little hope that the needed reformation would come from Rome. While some called on lay rulers to put the church's house in order, others revived the earlier conciliarist ideas, and called for a council to discuss both the issues posed by Luther and his followers, and a program for putting an end to corruption and abuse within the church.

The brief pontificate of Adrian VI offered some hope of reformation. He was a man of lofty ideals who did indeed wish to reform the church. But the intrigues of the curia thwarted most of his projects, which in any case were cut short by his unexpected death. The next pope, Clement VII, was a cousin of Leo X, and his policies were similar to those of his kinsman. Although he did succeed in his plans for the beautification of Rome, his pontificate was disastrous for the Roman church, for it was during his time that England declared herself independent of papal authority, and the troops of Charles V took and sacked Rome. Paul III, who succeeded Clement, is an ambiguous figure. He seemed to trust astrology more than theology, and his papacy, like those of his predecessors, was tainted by nepotism—his son was made duke of Parma and Piacenza, and his teenage grandsons were made cardinals. He too wished to make Rome the wealthiest center of Renaissance art, and for that reason continued the systems of exploitation whereby the papacy sought to collect funds from all nations in Europe. But he was also a reforming pope. It was he who gave official recognition to the Jesuits and began using them in missions and in polemics against Protestantism. In 1536, he appointed a distinguished commission of cardinals and bishops to report to him on the need and means of reformation. Their report somehow reached the hands of the enemies of the papacy, and gave Protestants abundant ammunition for their campaign against "Popery." Paul himself, having realized that a significant portion of his income was derived from practices that his own commission had declared corrupt, decided that it was best to let matters continue as they were. He did, however, convoke the council for which so many had been clamoring. It began its sessions at Trent in 1545. The next pope, Julius III, had all the vices of his predecessor, and few of his virtues. Once again nepotism became the order of the day, and the Roman court became a center of games and festivities, in imitation of other courts in Europe. Then Marcellus II, a man with a firm commitment to reformation, became pope. But his sudden death put an end to his pontificate.

Finally, in 1555, Cardinal Giampietro Carafa was elected pope, and took the name of Paul IV. He had been a member of the commission appointed earlier by Paul III, and as soon as he became pope he set out to correct the evils that commission had decried. He was an austere, virtually rigid man, and he tended to equate the need for reformation with strict uniformity in all matters. Under his leadership, the activity of the Inquisition increased to the point of terror; and the *Index of Forbidden Books,* published under his direction, included some of the best Catholic literature. But, in spite of this, Paul IV deserves credit for having cleansed the Roman curia, and for having placed the papacy at the head of the Catholic Reformation. In varying ways and degrees, his was the policy followed by his successors for several generations.

The Council of Trent

The reader will remember that Luther and several other reformers repeatedly appealed to a universal council. During the early years of the Reformation, however, the popes opposed the convocation of such an assembly, for they feared a rebirth of the conciliarist movement, which had claimed supremacy over the Papacy. Therefore, it was only during the reign of Paul III, when the breach between Protestants and Catholics was permanent, that serious consideration was given in Rome to the possibility of calling a universal council. After many difficult and complicated negotiations, it was decided that the council would meet at Trent in December 1545. Charles V had insisted that the council must meet in his territories, and that was the reason for the selection of Trent, an imperial city in northern Italy. Even so, it was attended by few prelates—31 in the first session, and 213 in the last.

Until then, most of the great councils had dealt with a few problems, or with a particular doctrine considered heretical. But the issues posed by Protestantism were of such magnitude, and the church was in such need of reformation, that the council was not content with condemning Protestantism, but felt compelled to discuss every item of theology that the Protestant Reformation had questioned, and also to issue a number of decrees for the reformation of the church. Linking uniformity with orthodoxy, the council also took measures regulating the life and worship of the church.

The Council of Trent, considered by the Roman Catholic Church the nineteenth ecumenical council, had a checkered history. Charles V insisted that it meet within his territories. Later, when relations between Pope Paul III and the emperor grew tense, the pope moved the gathering to the papal states. But the emperor ordered his bishops to remain at Trent, with the result that the council was suspended in 1547. It was reconvened in 1551, and suspended again the following year. In 1555, Paul IV became pope. Although he wished to continue the work of reformation begun by the council, he feared the excessive influence of the Spaniards in the assembly, and therefore refrained from reconvening it. Finally, in 1562, during the pontificate of the next pope, Pius IV, the council gathered again, completing its work in 1563. Therefore, although in theory the council lasted from 1545 to 1563, during most of that time it was in recess.

The decrees of the Council of Trent are too numerous to list here. As measures of reformation, it ordered bishops to reside in their sees, condemned pluralism (the holding of several ecclesiastic offices), listed and defined the obligations of the clergy, regulated the use of such things as relics and indulgences, and ordered the founding of seminaries for the training of the ministry (until that time, there had been no generally accepted regulations or educational requirements for ordination). It also promoted the study of Thomas Aquinas, making his the dominant theology in the Catholic Church. On the other hand, it took measures against Protestantism. In this

The Council of Trent, considered by the Roman Catholic Church the nineteenth ecumenical council, responded to the various issues raised by the Reformation and set the tone for Roman Catholicism for the next four centuries.

vein, it declared that the Latin translation of the Bible, the Vulgate, is authoritative in matters of dogma; that tradition has an authority parallel to that of Scripture; that the sacraments are seven; that the mass is a true sacrifice that can be offered for the benefit of the deceased; that communion in both kinds—that is, with the laity receiving both the bread and the wine—is not necessary; that justification is based on good works done through the collaboration between grace and the believer; and so forth.

In spite of its checkered history, of the scant number of prelates who attended it, and of the resistance of many sovereigns who would not allow its decrees to be published in their territories, the Council of Trent marked the birth of the modern Catholic Church. This was not exactly the same as the medieval church against which Luther protested, for it bore the marks of a reaction against Protestantism. During the next four centuries, that reaction would be such that the Roman Church refused to concede that many of the elements of the Protestant Reformation that the Council of Trent had rejected did have deep roots in Christian tradition. It would be much later, in the twentieth century, that the Catholic church would finally be able to set its own agenda for reformation apart from a reaction to Protestantism.

13/ A Convulsed Age

A mighty fortress is our God,
A bulwark never failing;
Our helper He amidst the flood
Of mortal ills prevailing.
MARTIN LUTHER

The sixteenth century was one of most convulsed periods in the entire history of Christianity. In a few decades, the towering edifice of medieval Christianity collapsed. Salvaging what it could from the debacle, the Council of Trent set the tone for modern Catholicism, while several Protestant confessions arose amid the ruins. The ancient ideal of a single church, with the pope as its visible head—which had never been current in the East—now lost its power also in the West. From that point on, western Christianity was divided among various traditions that reflected great cultural and theological differences.

At the dawning of the sixteenth century, in spite of the corruption that prevailed in many quarters, and of the many voices clamoring for reformation, there was general agreement among Christians that the church was by essence one, and that its unity must be seen in its structure and hierarchy. Indeed, all the main figures of the Protestant Reformation began by holding such an understanding of the church, and very few came to the place where they completely rejected it. Most of the major Protestant leaders did believe that the unity of the church was essential to its nature, and that therefore, although it was temporarily necessary to break that unity in order to be faithful to the Word of God, that very faithfulness demanded that all possible efforts be made to regain the lost unity.

The early sixteenth century also took for granted, as did the Middle Ages before, that the existence and survival of a state demanded religious agreement among its subjects. That notion, which Christians had rejected when they were a minority in the Roman Empire, became prevalent a few decades after the conversion of Constantine. All who lived in a Christian state must be Christians, and faithful children of the church. The only possible exceptions were Jews and, in some areas of Spain, Moslems. But such exceptions were seen as anomalies, and did not protect the followers of those religions from civil disenfranchisement and repeated persecution.

This view of national unity as linked with religious uniformity was at the root of the many wars of religion that shook both the sixteenth and the seventeenth centuries. Eventually, in some areas sooner than in others, the conclusion was reached that religious agreement was not necessary for the security of the state, or that, although desirable, its price was too high. This happened, for instance, in France, where the Edict of Nantes recognized the failure of the previous policy of trying to force all the king's subjects into a single religious mold. In the Low Countries, for different political reasons, leaders such as William the Silent also denied the need for religious uniformity. Thus began a long process whose consequences would be enormous, for one after another the various European states came to adopt a policy of religious tolerance. This eventually led to the more modern idea of the lay state—that is, a state with no religious connections—that was decried by some churches and hailed by others. To these developments we shall return later in our narrative.

The sixteenth century also saw the collapse of the ancient dream of political unity under the Empire. The last emperor who, even in a limited way, could harbor such ilusions was Charles V. After him, the so-called emperors were little more than kings of Germany, and even there their power was limited.

Finally, the conciliarist hope for reformation was also shaken. For several decades, the Protestant reformers hoped that a universal council would prove them right and set the pope's house in order. But exactly the opposite took place. The papacy managed to achieve its own reformation without the help of a council, and by the time the Council of Trent finally assembled it was clear that it would not be a truly international and ecumenical tribunal, but rather a tool in the hands of the papacy.

Devout Christians, both Protestant and Catholic, whose lot it was to live in the sixteenth century saw many of the old certainties crumble around them. Even the discoveries and conquests that were taking place in the New World, Africa, and Asia posed questions that could not be answered within the old parameters. The medieval foundations—the papacy, the Empire, tradition—were no longer solid. As Galileo affirmed, the earth itself was not a fixed point of reference. Social and political commotions were frequent. The ancient feudal system was making way for the early stages of capitalism.

Such was the time of Luther, Erasmus, Calvin, Knox, Loyola, Menno Simons, and the other great reformers. But in the midst of what could have appeared as chaos, these reformers stood firm on their faith in the power of the Word of God. That Word, which had created the worlds out of nothing, was certainly capable of producing the reformation the entire church needed, and to which the Protestant movement was still a preamble. Luther and

*During the sixteenth century the church,
traditionally symbolized by the ark, was tossed
by violent storms.*

Calvin, for instance, always insisted that the power of the Word was such that, as long as the Roman Church continued reading it, and even though the pope and his advisors might refuse to listen to it, there was always in the Roman communion a "vestige of the church," and they therefore awaited the day when the ancient church would once again hearken to the Word, and reforms such as they advocated would take place.

Suggested Readings

Paul Althaus. *The Theology of Martin Luther.* Philadelphia: Fortress, 1966.

Roland H. Bainton. *Erasmus of Christendom.* New York: Charles Scribner's Sons, 1969.

Roland H. Bainton. *Here I Stand: A Life of Martin Luther.* Nashville: Abingdon, 1950.

Roland H. Bainton. *The Reformation of the Sixteenth Century.* Boston: Beacon, 1952.

Ernest Belfort Bax. *Rise and Fall of the Anabaptists.* New York: American Scholar Publications, 1966.

Henry Daniel-Rops. *The Catholic Reformation.* New York: Dutton, 1962.

Gordon Donaldson. *The Scottish Reformation.* Cambridge: University Press, 1960.

Pieter Geyl. *The Revolt of the Netherlands.* New York: Barnes & Noble, 1958.

Justo L. González. *A History of Christian Thought.* Vol. 3. Nashville: Abingdon, 1975.

Arthur James Grant. *The Huguenots.* Hamden, Connecticut: Archon, 1969.

P. E. Hughes. *Theology of the English Reformers.* London: Hodder & Stoughton, 1965.

Franklin H. Littell. *The Free Church.* Boston: Starr King, 1957.

Geddes Macgregor. *The Thundering Scot: A Portrait of John Knox.* London: Macmillan & Co., 1958.

Clyde L. Manschreck. *Melanchthon: The Quiet Reformer.* Nashville: Abingdon, 1958.

John C. Olin. *The Catholic Reformation: Savonarola to Ignatius Loyola.* New York: Harper & Row, 1969.

Jean Horace Rilliet. *Zwingli: Third Man of the Reformation.* London: Lutterworth, 1964.

François Wendel. *Calvin: The Origins and Development of His Religious Thought.* London: Collins, 1965.

PART II

ORTHODOXY, RATIONALISM, AND PIETISM

Chronology

Popes	Emperors	Spain	France	England	Events
Clement VIII (1592–1605)	Rudolf II (1576–1612)	Philip III (1598–1621)	Henry IV (1589–1610)	Elizabeth I (1558–1603)	
				James I (1603–1625)	Gunpowder plot (1605)
Leo XI (1605)					
Paul V (1605–1621)					Founding of Jamestown (1607)
					Evangelical Union in Germany (1608)
					Catholic League in Germany (1609)
	Matthias (1612–1619)		Louis XIII (1610–1643)		
					Synod of Dort (1618–1619)
					Thirty Years' War (1618–1648)

Mayflower pilgrims (1620)

Richelieu's government (1624–1642)

Siege of La Rochelle (1627–1628)
Treaty of Lübeck (1629)
Puritan migration to New World
 (1630–1642)
†Gustavus Adolphus (1632)
Founding of Providence (1636)
Descartes's *Discourse on Method*
 (1637)
Anne Hutchinson in Rhode Island
 (1638)
Long Parliament (1640)
Civil War in England (1642)

Charles I prisoner of Parliament
 (1647)
Treaty of Westphalia (1648)
Charles I beheaded (1649)
Cromwell's Protectorate (1653–1658)
Quakers persecuted in Massachusetts
 (1656)

Charles I
(1625–1649)

Interregnum
(1649–1660)

Charles II
(1660–1685)

Louis XIV
(1643–1715)

Ferdinand II
(1619–1637)

Philip IV
(1621–1665)

Ferdinand III
(1637–1657)

Gregory XV
(1621–1623)
Urban VIII
(1623–1644)

Innocent X
(1644–1655)

Alexander VII
(1655–1667)

Leopold I
(1658–1705)

Popes	Emperors	Spain	France	England	Events
Clement IX (1667–1669)		Charles II (1665–1700)			British take New Amsterdam (1664)
Clement X (1670–1676)					
					King Philip's War (1675–1676)
					Spener's *Pia Desideria* (1675)
Innocent XI (1676–1689)					Bunyan's *Pilgrim's Progress* (1678)
					Founding of Pennsylvania (1681)
					Revocation of Edict of Nantes (1685)
				James II (1685–1688)	
Alexander VIII (1689–1691)				William III (1689–1702)	Tolerance in England (1689)
				and Mary II (1689–1694)	Locke's *Essay* (1690)
Innocent XII (1691–1700)					†George Fox (1691)
Clement XI (1700–1721)		Philip V (1700–1746)			
	Joseph I (1705–1711)			Anne (1702–1714)	
	Charles VI (1711–1740)				
			Louis XV (1715–1774)	George I (1714–1727)	
Innocent XIII (1721–1724)					
Benedict XIII (1724–1730)				George II (1727–1760)	†Francke (1727)
Clement XII (1730–1740)					Founding of Georgia (1733)

Benedict XIV
(1740–1758)

Charles VII
(1742–1745)
Francis I
(1745–1765)

Ferdinand VI
(1746–1759)

Clement XIII
(1758–1769)

Charles III
(1759–1788)

George III
(1760–1820)

Joseph II
(1765–1790)

Clement XIV
(1769–1774)

Louis XVI
(1774–1792)

Pius VI
(1775–1799)

Charles IV
(1788–1808)

Leopold II
(1790–1792)
Francis II
(1792–1806)

Republic

Wesley in Georgia (1736)
Wesley's Aldersgate experience
(1738)

†Zinzendorf (1760)

Captain Cook's voyages (1768–1779)

†Swedenborg (1772)

War of Independence, USA
(1775–1783)
†Voltaire (1778)
Kant's *Critique of Pure Reason* (1781)
Methodist Episcopal Church, USA
(1784)
Tolerance in France (1787)

Taking of the Bastille (1789)

Louis XVI executed (1792)

14/An Age of Dogma
and Doubt

*Our most holy religion is founded on Faith,
not on reason; and it is a sure method of
exposing it to put it to such a trial as it is,
by no means, fitted to endure.*
DAVID HUME

The sixteenth century had been a period of enormous religious
vitality that swept Protestants and Catholics, theologians and rulers, the high and the low. Those who contended on both sides of
the religious struggles of the time were convinced that they were
doing so for religious reasons. Charles V on the Catholic side, and Frederick
the Wise on the Protestant, knew of no higher interest than the cause of
God's truth as they saw it, and subordinated their political and personal
ambitions to that cause. Luther and Loyola lived through years of intense
anguish before reaching the conclusions and attitudes that made them famous. Their actions, and those of their immediate followers, bore the stamp
of those profound religious experiences. Even Henry VIII, whose character
few would praise, seems to have convinced himself that his actions in matters
of religion were guided by a sincere attempt to serve God. Therefore, the
bitter words and even violent actions with which Christians of one persuasion
attacked others were partly due to the firmness of their convictions, and to
the overwhelming experiences that stood at the root of their confessions of
faith.

But, as years went by, there was an increasing number who did not share
the enthusiasm—and often not even the convictions—of earlier generations.
Eventually, even some who were involved in wars of religion gave signs that
political and personal considerations were paramount. Typical was the case
of Henry IV of France, who repeatedly changed his religion in order to save
his life or to achieve his political goals. When he finally attained the throne,

his policy of limited religious tolerance was one of the pillars on which he built modern France.

During the seventeenth and eighteenth centuries, many followed Henry's example. The Thirty Years' War, to which we shall turn in the next chapter, had consequences in Germany similar to those of the earlier wars of religion in France. More and more, German princes and their ministers made use of religion in order to further their political programs. This hindered the political unity of Germany at a time when nationalist sentiment was on the rise, and therefore many Germans came to the conclusion that doctrinal disagreements should not lead to war, and that religious tolerance was a wiser policy.

Partially as a result of all this, and partially as a result of new scientific discoveries, rationalism took hold of Europe. Why be concerned about details of Christian doctrine that produce nothing but quarrels and prejudice, when natural reason, a faculty common to all human beings, can answer the fundamental questions regarding God and human nature? Would it not be much more profitable to construct a "natural religion" on that basis, and to leave matters of detail, and all that can only claim revealed authority, to the credulous and fanatical? Hence, the seventeenth and eighteenth centuries were characterized by doubts regarding the traditional dogmas of both Protestantism and Roman Catholicism.

On the other hand, there were others whose zeal for true doctrine was no less than Luther's, Calvin's, or Loyola's. But this was no longer the time of great theological discoveries, leading along unknown paths. Theologians in the seventeenth and eighteenth centuries zealously defended the teachings of the great figures of the sixteenth, but without the fresh creativity of that earlier generation. Their style became increasingly rigid, cold, and academic. Their goal was no longer to be entirely open to the Word of God, but rather to uphold and clarify what others had said before them. Dogma was often substituted for faith, and orthodoxy for love. Reformed, Lutheran, and Catholic alike developed orthodoxies to which one had to adhere strictly or be counted out of the fold of the faithful.

Not all, however, were content with such orthodoxies. The rationalist option has already been mentioned. Others whose beliefs were not acceptable in their native country migrated to new lands. Some sought an alternative by emphasizing the spiritual dimension of the gospel, sometimes ignoring or even denying its relation to physical and political realities. Still others —the Methodists in England, and the Pietists on the Continent—organized groups of believers who, while not severing their ties with the established churches, sought to cultivate a more intense and personal faith and piety.

From all this follows the outline of this portion of our narrative. We shall deal first with the great religious wars that took place in Germany (chapter 15), France (chapter 16), and England (chapter 17). We shall then turn to the development of orthodoxy within Roman Catholicism (chapter 18),

Of Enuie.

¶ *Where Gods word preached is in place: vnto the people willingly:*
Woe be to them that would deface: for if such cease, the stones will crie.

¶ *The signification.*

*H*E which preacheth in the pulpit, signifieth godly zeale, &
a furtherer of the gospel: and the two which are plucking
him out of his place, are the enemies of Gods word, threat-
ning by fire to cōsume the professors of the same : and that
company which sitteth still, are *Nullifidians*, such as are of no
religion, not regarding any doctrine, so they may bee quiet
to liue after their owne willes and mindes.

ꝝ ho

In this Puritan drawing, a preacher is being pulled from the pulpit by two "enemies of God's word."

Lutheranism (chapter 19), and the Reformed or Calvinist tradition (chapter 20). Chapter 21 will deal with rationalism. In chapter 22 we shall look at those who sought refuge in a spiritualist interpretation of the gospel. German pietism and English Methodism will be the subject of chapter 23. And at the end of this section, chapter 24, we shall look at those who decided to seek an alternative in the new colonies beyond the Atlantic.

15/The Thirty Years' War

*Where, alas, shall we have the liberty to
appear before the Lord in His own house,
without our lives being thereby endangered?*
A PROTESTANT PREACHER IN 1638

The Peace of Augsburg, which put an end to religious wars in Germany in the sixteenth century, could not last. It stipulated that princes or rulers, both Catholic and Protestant, would be free to determine the religion of their territories, and that those of their subjects who wished to do so could migrate to lands whose religion coincided with their own. This agreement, however, included no Protestants but those who subscribed to the Confession of Augsburg; and therefore all others, including Calvinists, were still considered heretics and subject to persecution. Since the freedom to choose their religion was granted only to rulers, many of their subjects were restless and unhappy. Finally, the Peace of Augsburg included the "ecclesiastical reservation," by which it was guaranteed that ecclesiastical territories would remain Catholic even if their bishops became Protestant. For all these reasons, the peace achieved at Augsburg was at best an armistice that would hold only as long as each side felt unable to take military action against the other.

The Storm Gathers

Rudolf II, who had become emperor in 1576, was not trusted by Protestants, for he had been educated in Spain under the Jesuits, and it was said that they still determined many of his policies. He was able to reign in relative peace for thirty years, for he was a weak ruler whose policies in favor of Catholicism were often ignored. Then, in 1606, there were riots in the imperial city of Donauwörth. This city, on the border of staunchly Catholic Bavaria, had opted for Protestantism, and by 1606 the only Catholic nucleus remaining in it was a monastery whose residents were allowed the free exercise of their religion, but only within the monastery itself. But now the monks, perhaps encouraged by the emperor's favor, went out in procession, and the people went at them with clubs and stones, forcing them to withdraw to the monastery. Such incidents were not uncommon at the time, and usually ended with a word of admonition to both sides. In this case, however, more drastic action was taken. More than a year after the event, Duke Maximilian of Bavaria, who felt called to stamp out Protestantism, appeared at Donauwörth with a strong army and set about forcing the conversion of the citizens to Catholicism.

The reaction was not slow in coming. Early in 1608, Protestants banded together in the Evangelical Union. A year later, their opponents organized the Catholic League. The Union, however, did not include all Protestants; therefore, were war to break out, it was clear that the Catholic League would have little trouble crushing the Evangelical Union.

Meanwhile, in nearby Bohemia, events were also leading to a confrontation. This was the land of the ancient Hussites, who had aligned themselves with Reformed Protestantism, and to whom were now added large numbers of German Calvinist immigrants to make the majority of the population heretical in Catholic eyes. Rebellion threatened, and Rudolf's bungling forced him to abdicate. His brother and successor, Matthias, fared no better. His cousin Ferdinand, whom he appointed king of Bohemia, was a staunch Catholic who soon won the distrust of his subjects. When the Royal Council in Prague refused to listen to their objections to the king's policies, the Bohemian Protestants revolted, and threw two of the king's advisors out the window—they were not badly hurt because they fell on a pile of garbage. This episode, known as the "Defenestration of Prague," marked the beginning of the Thirty Years' War, probably the bloodiest and most devastating European war before the twentieth century.

The Course of the War

The Bohemians then called Frederick, elector of the Palatinate, to be their king. The Palatinate, although separated from Bohemia by Catholic Bavaria and other territories, was mostly Reformed, and therefore seemed a natural ally to the Bohemians. Rebellion soon spread east of Bohemia to the neighboring provinces of Silesia and Moravia. Meanwhile, Matthias had died, and his cousin, now emperor Ferdinand II, called on Maximilian of Bavaria and the Catholic League to invade Bohemia. This they did, and dealt the rebels such a crushing blow that they were forced to surrender. Frederick was deposed from both the throne of Bohemia and his hereditary lands in the Palatinate. Bohemia was restored to the same King Ferdinand whom the rebels had repudiated, and the Palatinate went to Maximilian as a reward for

*The Defenestration of Prague marked the beginning of the Thirty
Years' War.*

his services. In both areas Protestants found themselves under persecution.
Several of their leaders were executed, and those with property had it confiscated. In Bohemia, it was decreed that by Easter of 1626 any who were not
ready to become Catholics must leave the country. These and similar measures caused such devastation that, during the thirty years that the war lasted,
the population of Bohemia is estimated to have declined by four-fifths.

The successes of Maximilian caused grave consternation among Protestant powers. To this were added dynastic considerations, for the house of
Hapsburg—which ruled in Spain and had also held the imperial dignity since
the time of Charles V—was feared by other ruling houses. Therefore, late
in 1625, England, the Netherlands, and Denmark joined in a Protestant
League that proposed to invade Germany and restore Frederick—who was
a son-in-law of James I of England—to his lands in the Palatinate. They also
had the support of several German Protestant princes, and even of a few
Catholics who feared the growing power of the Hapsburgs. Meanwhile
Ferdinand II, not content with trusting his empire to the sole defense of
Maximilian and the Catholic League, resolved to raise his own army, which
he placed under the command of Albert of Wallenstein. Therefore, when
Christian IV of Denmark invaded Germany he had to contend with two
armies, Maximilian's and Wallenstein's. Battles and marches once again
ravaged German soil, until Ferdinand II and Christian IV agreed to the

Treaty of Lübeck. The Danes withdrew from Germany, having achieved nothing of great consequence, except to bring further suffering to a land already ravaged by war. Thousands of forced conversions to Catholicism followed.

Then help came from another quarter. In 1611, when he was only seventeen years of age, Gustavus Adolphus had inherited the Swedish throne. This was a poor inheritance, for the Danes then held much of Sweden, and the land was divided among several factions, none of which showed great respect for the crown. But the young king proved an able ruler who slowly reunited his subjects and expelled the Danish invaders. As his power grew, he increasingly turned his attention to the threat that the Hapsburgs would attempt to gain possession of Swedish lands on the Baltic Sea. Since he was also a staunch Lutheran who bewailed the events that were taking place in Bohemia and Germany, he felt compelled to intervene with the

Wallenstein, accused by his enemies of being overly ambitious, was one of the ablest generals of his time.

double purpose of defending the Protestants and defeating the ambitions of the Hapsburgs.

Ferdinand II had disbanded Wallenstein's army, whose leader he feared, and based his power on the support of the Catholic League. Therefore, in 1630, when Gustavus Adolphus invaded Germany, the army facing him in the name of the emperor in truth belonged to the Catholic League. At first the Swedes found little support among German Protestants, who feared the emperor's wrath and in any case did not trust the Swedish invader. But Gustavus Adolphus was a very able general whose repeated victories soon became a legend. His soldiers, in contrast to all the armies who had marched in this protracted war, treated the native population with kindness and respect. While the Swedes were clearly Protestant, they did not force the conversion of Catholics in the areas they conquered. Repeatedly, Gustavus Adolphus made it clear that he did not seek to dismember Germany for Swedish profit. When France offered him financial support in his campaign against the Hapsburgs, he accepted it on condition that it be understood that not a single village in German territory would become French. Eventually, several powerful German Protestant princes came to his support. The Catholic League besieged Magdeburg, hoping that the Swedes would run to its rescue and fall into a trap that had been laid for them. But Gustavus Adolphus saw through their plans, and continued his campaign as he had outlined it. The League then took Magdeburg, whose citizens they massacred, and marched to do battle with the Swedes. In the fields near Leipzig, the League was roundly defeated, and Gustavus Adolphus then sent some of his German allies to invade Bohemia while he marched into southern Germany and threatened Bavaria, the very heart of the Catholic League. By then several Catholic leaders were suing for peace, and many were willing to agree to the terms imposed by the Swedish king: religious tolerance for both Catholics and Protestants, the restoration of its ancient rights to the kingdom of Bohemia, the return of the Palatinate to Frederick, and the expulsion of the Jesuits from the Empire.

Since the Catholic League had failed him, Ferdinand II once again called on Wallenstein, who came to his succor only after having been promised vast rewards. Wallenstein attacked the Protestants who had taken Prague, and forced them to withdraw. Then he joined the remnants of the Catholic League's army, and marched to do battle with the Swedes. They met on the fields of Lützen, where Wallenstein's army was crushed, but Gustavus Adolphus was killed.

The war then degenerated into skirmishes, banditry, and protracted negotiations. The Swedish government was ready for peace; but for their officers and troops, who had spent years on the field, war had become a way of life. Wallenstein was secretly negotiating with the Swedish, the French, and the German Protestants. The emperor had word of this, and Wallenstein and several of his officers were murdered, although it is not certain that this was done by Ferdinand's direct order. The Spanish Hapsburgs sent an army to support their cousins in Germany. The French then became bolder in their support of the Protestants, even though France was then ruled by a cardinal of the Roman Church. Meanwhile, it was the people who suffered in a war whose religious motivations were by then almost forgotten, and had become little more than an excuse in a struggle for power.

The Peace of Westphalia

Eventually, even the most bloodthirsty were tired of war and destruction. Ferdinand II had died in 1637, and his son and successor Ferdinand III, although a sincere Catholic, did not share his father's intolerance. Germans bemoaned seeing their land invaded by foreign troops in support of both sides. Sweden was ready to withdraw its army. France knew that the time had come when the greatest concessions could be obtained. Therefore, after long and complicated negotiations, the Peace of Westphalia, signed in 1648, put an end to the conflict that came to be known as the Thirty Years' War.

France and Sweden profited most from the war, for the former expanded her borders to the Rhine, while the latter received vast lands on the Baltic and the North Sea. Since both France and Sweden wished it, German princes were given greater powers, to the detriment of imperial authority. In religious matters, it was agreed that all—princes as well as their subjects—would be free to follow their own religion, as long as they were Catholics, Lutherans, or Reformed. Buildings and institutions were to revert to the religious confessions that had held them in 1624. And a general amnesty was granted to all who during the war had rebelled against their masters—except in the hereditary possessions of the Hapsburgs.

These were the immediate results of that protracted and cruel war. But there were other consequences that, although not mentioned in the peace agreement, were no less significant. The principles of tolerance of the Peace of Westphalia were not born out of a deeper understanding of Christian love, but rather out of a growing indifference to religious matters. The war had amply shown the atrocities that resulted from attempting to settle religious matters by force of arms. In the end, nothing had been resolved. Perhaps rulers should not allow their decisions to be guided by religious or confessional considerations, but rather by their own self-interest, or by the interests of their subjects. Thus the modern secular state began to develop. And with it there appeared an attitude of doubt regarding matters that previous generations had taken for granted. On what grounds did theologians dare to affirm that they were correct, and that others were mistaken? Could any doctrine be true that produced the atrocities of the Thirty Years'

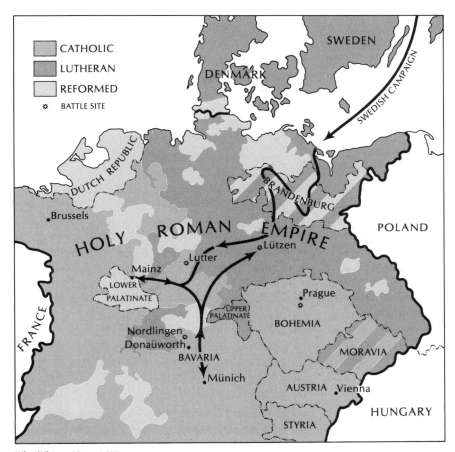

The Thirty Years' War

War? Was there not a more tolerant, more profound, and even more Christian way to serve God, than simply following the dictates of orthodoxy, be it Catholic or Protestant? These were some of the questions posed by the seventeenth and eighteenth centuries, partly as a result of the Thirty Years' War and other similar events.

16/The Church of
the Desert

*A spirit of sanctification, of power, . . .
and above all of martyrdom, while teaching
us to die each day in our inner being, . . .
also prepares and disposes us to offer our
lives with courage in the torture chamber
and on the gallows, if Divine Providence
calls us to it.*

ANTOINE COURT

The assassination of Henry IV by the fanatical Ravaillac, on May 14, 1610, caused great misgivings among French Protestants. Although Henry had declared himself a Catholic for reasons of political convenience, he had proven a faithful friend to his former companions of religion and arms, whose freedom and lives he protected by the Edict of Nantes. They knew that many of their former enemies deplored the peace and tolerance that the deceased king had brought about, and would now seek to undo his policies. Since the new king, Louis XIII, was only eight years old, the government was in the hands of the king's mother, Marie de Medici—the second wife of Henry IV—who felt the need to allay mistrust by confirming the Edict of Nantes. On the basis of that action, the following general assembly of the French Huguenots swore fidelity to the new king.

But Marie gathered around herself a coterie of Italian advisors who understood neither the conditions in France, nor the pain and blood that had been the price for the existing state of affairs. They followed a policy of close collaboration with the Hapsburgs, and particularly with the Spanish branch of that house, which was known for its uncompromising Catholicism and its

hatred of Protestantism. The young king was married to the Spanish princess
Anne of Austria, and his sister, Isabella, to the future Philip IV of Spain. This
provoked several Huguenot uprisings that achieved no more than the death
of their leaders and the loss of a number of Protestant strongholds.

Towards 1622, while Marie de Medici was losing her power, Cardinal
Armand de Richelieu was a rising star in the French court. Two years later,
he had become the king's most trusted advisor. He was a wily politician
whose main goals were the aggrandizement of the French crown and of his
own personal power. Although he was a cardinal of the Church of Rome, his
religious policy was not based on theological or confessional considerations,
but rather on calculations of convenience. Thus, since he was convinced that
the main enemies of the French Bourbons were the Hapsburgs, his interventions in the Thirty Years' War—consisting mostly of undercover financial
support—were in favor of the Protestants and against the Catholic emperor.
The same political considerations, however, led Richelieu to an entirely
different religious policy in France. He had no qualms about dividing Germany by supporting the Protestant party against the Emperor. But in France
the Huguenot party must be destroyed, for they were a cyst within the state.
Again, what most concerned Richelieu was not that the Huguenots were
Protestant heretics, but rather that Henry IV, in order to guarantee their
security, had granted them several fortified cities, and these allowed the

*Although he was a cardinal of the
Roman Church, Richelieu did not
allow religious considerations to affect
his policies and was quite ready to
support Protestantism in his enemies'
lands, if only to embarrass them.*

Huguenots to declare themselves faithful servants of the crown while retaining the ability to rebel and resist if their rights were violated. Richelieu's centralizing policies could not tolerate the existence of such independent power within the French state.

Richelieu's efforts to dissolve the Protestant cyst led to armed action in the siege of La Rochelle, the main Huguenot stronghold. The siege lasted a year, during which the defenders courageously resisted the pick of the French army. When the city finally surrendered, of its 25,000 inhabitants there remained only 1,500 famished and feeble survivors. Then the fortifications of the city were razed and the Catholic mass was celebrated in all its churches. On hearing of this, several other Protestant cities took up arms against the king. But none of them was able to offer as staunch a defense as had La Rochelle, and in many of them the king's troops followed a policy of extermination.

However, what caused Richelieu grave concern was not the existence of Protestants in France, nor the continuation of their life of worship, but simply the political power they had enjoyed. Therefore, once their fortified cities were taken in 1629, he issued an edict of toleration for Protestants, both in religious and in civil matters. Without their military strongholds, the Huguenots were no longer a threat to the crown, and Richelieu had no intention to bleed the country and weaken its economy in a protracted civil war. Having dealt with Protestant political and military power, the cardinal turned his attention to undoing the Hapsburgs; thus, during the last years of his government, the Huguenots enjoyed relative peace.

Richelieu's death, in 1642, was followed by that of the king in the following year. Louis XIV was then five years old, and his mother and regent, Anne of Austria, entrusted affairs of state to Cardinal Jules Mazarin, a former collaborator of Richelieu who continued the policies of his predecessor. Therefore, for several decades after the fall of La Rochelle and the other Protestant cities, French Protestants enjoyed religious tolerance. Although Mazarin's government was marked by repeated conspiracies and rebellions, Protestants were generally not involved in them, and their numbers grew among all social classes. In the countryside there were many Protestants, both among the peasants and among the rural nobility. And in the cities Huguenot intellectuals were accepted into the most distinguished salons.

Louis XIV was twenty-three years old when Mazarin died, and he refused to name a successor to the cardinal. The king, who came to be called "the Sun King," would allow no one to overshadow him. For that reason he clashed with the pope, who sought to intervene in French affairs. Against the centralizing efforts of the papacy of his time, Louis proclaimed and defended the "liberties of the Gallican church"—to which we shall return in chapter 18. But, for exactly the same reasons, he had no patience with heretics or

*Mazarin, Richelieu's successor, changed very
few of the policies followed by the great
cardinal.*

dissidents of any sort, and therefore took strong measures to stamp out
French Protestantism.

The king's measures to achieve the "reunion"—as conversion to Catholicism was called—of Protestants were diverse, and grew sterner with the
passage of time. First there were attempts of persuasion and mild pressure.
Then the king practically offered to buy conversions. The argument was that
Protestant pastors who became Catholic lost their livelihood, and that those
from among the laity who did likewise lost their clients or other means of
support. Therefore, as a means to balance off such losses, money was offered
to any who would be converted. But that policy was not successful, and then
the king had recourse to more severe measures. When, in 1684, France
enjoyed a brief respite in the constant wars in which the Sun King involved
her, the army was used to force the "reunion" of French Protestants. This
policy of violence enjoyed great success, for in some areas tens of thousands
were forcibly converted to Catholicism.

Finally, in 1685, the king issued the Edict of Fontainebleau, abolishing
the provisions of the Edict of Nantes, and making it illegal to be a Protestant
in France. A mass exodus followed immediately, for French Huguenots fled
to Switzerland, Germany, England, the Netherlands, and North America.

Since many of these refugees were artisans and merchants, their departure represented a great economic loss to France—to the point that it has been suggested that the economic disruption caused by the Edict of Fontainebleau was one of the causes leading to the French Revolution.

Officially, there were no more Protestants in France after the Edict of Fontainebleau. In truth, however, many who had been outwardly converted held fast to their previous beliefs, and managed to continue gathering for the celebration of Protestant worship. For many of them, such gatherings were made all the more necessary inasmuch as they bore a heavy burden on their consciences for having denied their faith. Lacking church buildings, they turned to the open fields, or to clearings in the woods. In such places, under cover of night, and all over the country, tens and even hundreds of believers came together periodically to listen to the Word, confess their sins, and break bread. The secret of such gatherings was zealously guarded, and seldom were the agents of the government able to discover the appointed time and place. When they did gain intelligence of such meetings, they waited until all had arrived, and then fell upon the worshipers and arrested them. The men were sent off to row in the galleys, and the women were imprisoned for the rest of their days. Pastors were executed, and children were placed in foster families to be reared as Catholics. In spite of this, the movement continued; and the king's agents were unable to stamp out the "Christians of the desert," as they called themselves.

As often happens in such cases, the movement then developed a radical and visionary wing, claiming that the end of the world was at hand. From his exile in Rotterdam, pastor Pierre Jurieu published a study of the book of Revelation in which he showed that its prophecies were being fulfilled, and that the final victory would take place in 1689. Encouraged by such announcements, some of the Protestants in France became more audacious, and as a result many were killed or condemned to the galleys. But prophetic visions and mystical experiences abounded, and increasing numbers were willing to die for a cause about to be vindicated by God. Some heard voices. Others spoke while in trance. All this made it easier for the authorities to find the recalcitrant Protestants, who were then cruelly tortured. But very few were made to utter the fateful words, "I reunite"—that is, I return to the Catholic Church.

Then this prophetic spirit turned to armed rebellion. This was no longer led by Protestant nobles, as in the earlier wars of religion. The new army "of the desert" was formed mostly by peasants. These peasants still plowed, sowed, and harvested, but during the rest of the time they gathered in armed bands that attacked royal troops. Before marching out they read Scripture, and in the field of battle they sang psalms. Although these rebels never were more than a few hundred, they kept an army of 25,000 men fully occupied. For reasons not altogether clear, the rebels came to be known as "camisards." Since conventional warfare was unable to put the rebels down, the army followed a policy of razing the areas where the camisards operated. About five hundred villages and hamlets were destroyed. But this only served to engross the ranks of the rebels, now reinforced by many who had been left homeless. This struggle continued for many years. By making promises that were not kept, the king's officials were able to stop the rebellion in some areas. But resistance continued until 1709, when the last camisard leaders were captured and executed. By then, their resistance had become legendary in Protestant countries, but no one had given them any significant aid. In 1710, the English finally decided to support them. But by then it was too late, for the last sparks of rebellion had been snuffed out.

Meanwhile, a different group had come to the foreground among French Protestants. These other leaders did not trust apocalyptic visions—which, in any case, had failed to come true—and advocated a return to the Reformed tradition, with worship centered on the clear and careful exposition of Scripture. The outstanding leader of this group was Antoine Court, who in 1715 organized the first synod of the French Reformed Church. He advised that civil authorities should be obeyed in all things, except when they demanded something that was contrary to the Word of God, and this became the official policy of the newly organized church. Ten days after the meeting of that first synod, Louis XIV died, and was succeeded by his five-year-old great-grandson Louis XV. But the death of the Sun King brought no respite to the persecuted Huguenots, for the new government, under the regency of Philippe d'Orleans, continued the religious policies of the previous reign. In spite of this, Court and his followers persisted on the course they had set for themselves. When one of his pastors was imprisoned, Court ordered his followers to refrain from violence as a means to save the man from death. In 1726, a seminary in exile was founded in Lausanne, Switzerland. French candidates for the ministry attended it before returning to their own country, and thus the French Reformed Church began developing a cadre of preachers who were well versed in Scripture and theology. In 1729, Court himself moved to Lausanne, where he became the mentor to an entire generation of clandestine preachers. Although now living in exile, Court visited France repeatedly, encouraging and directing the affairs of the Reformed Church. By the time of his death in 1767, at eighty-three years of age, Reformed Protestantism was firmly rooted in France. But persecution continued until 1787, when the grandson and successor of Louis XV, Louis XVI, finally decreed religious tolerance. During the long period of persecution, thousands of men had been sent to the galleys, and a like number of women had been condemned to life-imprisonment, while only a handful had uttered the words, "I reunite." Two pastors had denied their faith, but countless others had died for their unwillingness to recant. The "church of the desert" had survived.

That struggle, like the Thirty Years' War in Germany, produced in many a profound distrust of dogmas and dogmatism. Among them was

Voltaire, who defended the Protestant cause, not because he felt any sympathy for it, but rather because he considered intolerance to be both absurd and immoral. During those years of persecution and resistance, of horror and glory, the minds were shaped that would later espouse the ideals of the French Revolution.

The Puritan Revolution

*The civil magistrate may not assume to
himself the administration of the Word and
Sacraments . . . yet he hath authority, and
it is his duty to take order, that unity and
peace be preserved in the Church, that the
truth of God be kept pure and entire, that
all blasphemies and heresies be suppressed,
all corruptions and abuses in worship and
discipline prevented or reformed, and all the
ordinances of God duly settled,
administered, and observed.*

WESTMINSTER CONFESSION

I n discussing the Reformation in England, we have seen that Queen
Elizabeth followed an intermediate course between those conservatives
who sought to retain as much as possible of ancient practice and belief,
and the Calvinist Protestants who believed that the entire life and
structure of the church ought to adjust to what they saw as the biblical norm.
During the queen's lifetime, that delicate balance was mantained; but the
tensions inherent in the situation surfaced repeatedly, and only the strong
and decisive intervention of the queen and her ministers was able to restrain
them.

James I

When Elizabeth died in 1603 she left no direct heir, but declared her legitimate successor to be James, the son of Mary Stuart, who was already king

of Scotland. The transition took place without major difficulties, and thus the house of Stuart came to reign in England. The new king—James I of England, but James VI of Scotland—did not find the government of England an easy matter. The English always considered him a foreigner. His plans for the union of the two kingdoms—which eventually came about—won him enemies both in Scotland and in England. Elizabeth's measures in favor of trade were bearing fruit, and therefore the merchant class, which resented the king's policies in support of the nobility and his favorites, was becoming increasingly powerful. But James's greatest conflicts were with those Protestants who thought that the Reformation had not progressed sufficiently in England, and that this was due to the policies of the sovereigns and their advisors. Since neighboring Scotland, from whence the new king had come, had moved further along the road of reformation, English Calvinists felt that the time was ripe for similar changes in their own land.

These more radical Protestants were not organized in a single group, nor did they agree on all matters, and therefore it is difficult to describe them in general terms. They were given the name of "Puritans" because they insisted on the need to "purify" the Church by a return to biblical religion. They opposed many of the traditional elements of worship that the Church of England had retained, such as the use of the cross, certain priestly garments, and the celebration of communion on an altar—whether there ought to be a table or an altar, and where this was to be placed, implied varying interpretations of the meaning of communion and led to long and bitter controversy. They also insisted on the need for a sober life, guided by the commandments of Scripture, and lacking in luxury and ostentation. Since a great deal of the worship of the Church of England appeared to them as needlessly elaborate, this caused further objection to that worship. Many insisted on the need to keep the Lord's Day, devoting it exclusively to religious exercises and to the practice of charity. They were not absolutely opposed to the use of alcohol, for most of them drank moderately, but they were very critical of drunkenness, particularly among ministers of the Church of England. They were also very critical of all that they considered licentious —and this included the theater, not only because immorality was often depicted, but also because of the "duplicity" implicit in acting.

Many Puritans were opposed to bishops. They argued that the episcopacy, at least as it existed in their time, was a later invention, not to be found in the Bible; and that the church ought to look to Scripture as its constitution not only in matters of doctrine, but also in things having to do with its organization and governance. The more moderate among the Puritans simply declared that in the Bible one could find several forms of church government, and that therefore the episcopacy, although perhaps good and useful, was not a matter "of divine right." Others insisted that the New Testament church was ruled by "presbyters," that is, by elders, and that a truly biblical church ought to be so ruled. Still others affirmed that each congregation

*The Puritans insisted on sobriety and frowned on what they called
the "frivolity" of many ecclesiastical and political leaders.*

ought to be independent of all others, and were dubbed "Independents."
Among this latter group were some who believed that baptism ought to be
administered only to believing adults, and who therefore were called "Baptists." Although these various groups disagreed among themselves in many
matters, in general they drew their inspiration from Calvin, Zwingli, and the
other Swiss reformers. Some of the more radical drew on the Anabaptist
tradition.

Meanwhile, the official church was following a parallel but opposite
course. Elizabeth's balance had been achieved by establishing a church whose
theology was moderately Calvinist, while retaining in its worship and governance all that did not clearly and directly contradict its new theology. But this
Elizabethan settlement was difficult to maintain. In order to defend traditional
elements in worship, some began to abandon Calvinist theology. Among the
leading theologians of the Church of England there was such appreciation for
the beauty of worship as it was then practiced that there was little effort to
make it conform to such outside requirements as theology or biblical exegesis. Soon Puritans began to fear that a vast movement was afoot to return to
"Romanism."

All these elements were already present below the surface when James
inherited Elizabeth's crown. From that point on, conflicts that had been latent
for a long time would surface with increasing violence. The Puritans did not

trust the new king, whose mother was none other than Mary Stuart. In truth, James did not favor the Catholics, who had hoped to gain major concessions from him, and were repeatedly disappointed. His ideal was an absolute monarchy such as existed in France. In Scotland, his Presbyterian subjects had not allowed him to reign with the freedom he wished—and was convinced kings deserved—and therefore in England he sought to strengthen the episcopacy as a means to increase his own power. As he is said to have declared, "without bishops, there is no king."

James's personal character did little to increase his prestige. He was a homosexual, and his favorites enjoyed unmerited privileges and power in his court and in his government. While insisting on his right to be an absolute monarch, he wavered between stubborn rigidity and weak flexibility. Although he managed his finances honestly, he was prodigal in spending for superfluous matters, and important projects were hindered for lack of funds. His liberality in granting titles and honors to his friends offended many who had served the crown for a lifetime with little or no reward.

James tried to follow a religious policy similar to that of Elizabeth. Only the Anabaptists were systematically persecuted, for their egalitarian ideas horrified the king. Catholics were seen as loyal to the pope, and therefore as potential traitors. But if the pope was willing to acknowledge James's right to the throne, and to condemn regicide—which some extreme Catholics proposed as a solution to England's religious troubles—the king was willing to tolerate Catholics in his kingdoms. Presbyterians, whom the king had come to hate in Scotland, were tolerated in England, and James even granted them some minor concessions. But the one thing that he would not abandon was the episcopal system of government, for he was convinced—and rightly so—that the bishops were among the most committed and useful supporters of the crown.

The tension between the prelates of the official church and the Puritans grew during James's reign. In 1604, Richard Bancroft, archbishop of Canterbury, had a series of canons approved in which it was affirmed that episcopal hierarchy was an institution of divine origin, and that without it there could be no true church. This implied a rejection of the many Protestant churches on the Continent that had no bishops, and therefore Puritans saw in it a step towards breaking away from Protestant ties in order to reintroduce Catholicism in England. Besides this, several other canons approved on the archbishop's insistence were clearly directed against Puritans.

Parliament was in session, for James had been compelled to call it in order to approve new taxes. The lower chamber, or House of Commons, included many Puritans who now joined with others in an appeal to the king against Bancroft's canons. James called a conference that gathered at Hampton Court, over which he presided. When one of the Puritans made passing reference to a "presbytery," the king declared that there could be no closer connection between the monarchy and a presbytery than that between God and the Devil. All attempts at conciliation failed, and the only result of that meeting was the new translation of the Bible that appeared in 1611, generally known as the King James Version.

That was the beginning of a growing enmity between the House of Commons and the more conservative among the bishops. The latter joined the king in affirming that bishops as well as kings rule by divine right. In 1606, a new series of canons, more staunchly anti-Puritan, was approved by church authorities. The Parliament responded by attacking, not the king or the archbishop, but the more vulnerable of their defenders. Eventually, during the next reign, this growing tension would lead to civil war.

Meanwhile, late in 1605, the "Gunpowder Plot" was discovered. A repressive law against Catholics had been issued the previous year, on the pretext that they were loyal to the pope rather than to the king. It seems that its real purpose was to collect funds, for the authorities used it mostly to impose heavy fines and to confiscate property. In any case, some Catholics decided that it was necessary to be rid of the king. One of them rented a property whose underground storage extended below Parliament's meeting place. The plan was to place several barrels of gunpowder under the meeting room, making it appear that they were full of wine, and blow them up while the king was opening the next session of Parliament. This would kill both the king and the Puritans who now sat in Parliament. But the plot was discovered, and the main conspirators, as well as several whose participation

James I of England, who was also James VI of Scotland, was convinced that the alliance between the crown and the episcopacy was absolutely necessary; he therefore abhorred the presbyterian form of government advocated by many Puritans.

in the plot was never proven, were executed. In some areas, Catholics were hunted down. James himself seems to have attempted to distinguish between the guilty and those who simply happened to be Catholic. But he did take the opportunity to impose more fines and confiscations. Soon thousands of Catholics were in prison.

After the first years of his reign, James tried to rule without convening Parliament. But the authorization of that body was required in order to impose new taxes; and therefore, in 1614, when his financial situation was desperate, James decided to convoke a meeting of Parliament. When the new elections resulted in a House of Commons that was even more intractable than the previous one, James dissolved it and tried to manage only with those tariffs that he had the authority to impose. He was also compelled to borrow from the bishops and the nobility. Then the Thirty Years' War broke out. The deposed elector of the Palatine and King of Bohemia, Frederick, was James's son-in-law. But James did not offer him support, and many English Protestants began declaring that he was a coward and a traitor, while he retorted that he could not intervene in the war for lack of funds. Finally, in 1621, the king called Parliament once again, hoping that the Puritans in the House of Commons would agree to new taxes if they were promised that part of the proceeds would be employed in support of German Protestants. But then it was learned that the king was planning to marry his son and heir to a Spanish princess. Such an alliance with the Hapsburgs was an abomination before the eyes of the Puritans in Parliament, who approved some minor taxes and then insisted on presenting their grievances before the king. The latter responded by dissolving the assembly and arresting several of its leaders. The marriage plans were then abandoned for other reasons, and in 1624 James once again called a meeting of Parliament, only to dissolve it anew without obtaining the funds he required. Shortly thereafter, the king died, and was succeeded by his son Charles.

Charles I

The new king was as convinced as his father had been of the need for a centralized and powerful monarchy, and therefore he too clashed with Parliament. The Puritans were suspicious of the king's intentions for, after the failed negotiations with Spain, Charles had married a sister of King Louis XIII of France. The negotiations leading to this marriage had included concessions to English Catholics, and it was also agreed that the new queen and her court would be free to continue their religious observances. Many Puritans saw in all this a restoration of idolatry, and complained that apostasy had now entered the royal household. Soon some were comparing the queen with Jezebel, although still only in private circles.

Charles inherited his father's conflicts with Parliament, and these came to a head in the trial of Richard Montague, a proponent of the divine right of kings and an enemy of both Puritanism and the parliamentary system. He had published several books on these subjects, and finally, after the publication of one that was particularly offensive to Parliament, the House of Commons brought him to trial and condemned him to a fine and imprisonment. King Charles saved his supporter by making him his personal chaplain, and thus exempt from the authority of Parliament. Talk then began of retaliating by accusing the duke of Buckingham, a minister of the crown, of high treason. The king then dissolved the assembly, and resolved to reign without Parliament. This, however, was not possible, for the king needed funds that only Parliament could vote. But the king was exasperated, and took ever harsher measures. When the archbishop of Canterbury sought to mediate the situation, the king practically deprived him of his powers, and gave them to a commission presided by William Laud, one of the most bitter opponents of Puritanism. Repeatedly, Charles convened Parliament, only to dissolve it when the House of Commons insisted on dealing with their grievances before voting funds. Charles rewarded those among the Commons who supported him by making them lords, thus further depriving himself of what little support he had in the lower chamber. Even the lords began turning against the king, begrudging the honors granted to commoners who had done little more than support him in parliamentary debate. When, in 1629, Charles dissolved the third Parliament of his reign, he was resolved to rule by himself, and it was only eleven years later that he finally felt constrained to convene Parliament anew.

Those eleven years of personal rule brought prosperity to the higher classes. But the rise in prices was much more rapid than the rise in wages, and therefore the majority of the population felt economically oppressed while the powerful were growing richer. In order to obtain the funds he required, Charles made ever greater concessions to the aristocracy, who in turn oppressed the poor. Although the king did show some interest in their plight and took some measures to improve their situation, the fact was that the social and political order caused more suffering than the king's weak measures could alleviate. Increasingly, and particularly in industrial areas, the king and the bishops, who gave his cause religious sanction, were seen as enemies of the people. The Puritans, who attacked the excesses of the crown and of the bishops and the luxury and idolatry of the "new Jezebel," were rapidly gaining in popular support.

In 1633, William Laud was made archbishop of Canterbury. He was enamored with the beauty and stateliness of Anglican worship, and a firm believer in the need for religious uniformity for the good of the state. His measures against the Puritans were both harsh and cruel, including death warrants and orders of mutilation. Enthused by such zealous support, Charles gave Laud full powers in Scotland, where the archbishop tried to impose the

Anglican liturgy. This resulted in a riot that soon became a rebellion. When the General Assembly of the Church of Scotland tried to limit the power of bishops, the king's agents declared it dissolved. But the Assembly refused to obey the royal command, and responded by abolishing the episcopacy and reorganizing the Church of Scotland on a presbyterian basis.

This made war inevitable. The king had neither a sufficiently large army nor the funds to keep one on the field, and turned for support to his Irish subjects, who had strong Catholic sentiments, hoping that the queen's Catholic faith would encourage them to come to his aid. But what he thus achieved was to bring the Scottish Calvinists and the English Puritans closer to each other. In 1640, Charles called a meeting of Parliament hoping to obtain funds for his war against the Scottish rebels. But it soon became clear that many in the Commons were less in sympathy with the king that with his enemies, and Charles dissolved the assembly—thereafter called the "Short Parliament." Encouraged by such a turn of events, the Scots invaded English territory, and the king's troops fled in disorder. Once again, Charles was forced to convene Parliament. Thus began the "Long Parliament," which would be of great importance for the history of England.

The Long Parliament

The years immediately preceeding the first meeting of the Long Parliament had been marred by economic difficulties. Social and economic upheavals, which until then had affected the poor and the proletariat almost exclusively, now began having a negative impact on the bourgeoisie. Therefore, the majority of those elected to the House of Commons of the new Parliament represented those who were discontent with the king's policies, if not for religious motives, then for others of an economic nature. Since many of the nobility had joined the bourgeoisie in investing in mercantile enterprises, many in the House of Lords were willing to join the Commons in limiting the king's power. Thus, the new Parliament proved even more intractable than the previous one. The king had convened it so that it could vote the necessary funds for raising an army and expelling the Scottish rebels from English territory. But the members of Parliament knew that their power resided precisely in the threat of the rebels, and therefore were in no hurry to deal with that issue. First they took a series of measures against those who, in recent years, had sought to destroy Puritanism. Those of Archbishop Laud's victims who still lived were set free, and an indemnization was paid for their suffering. Lord Strafford, one of the king's most loyal ministers, was brought to trial before Parliament and condemned to death, while the king did little or nothing to save him.

Then Parliament took steps to assure that its measures would have

Charles I continued his father's policies and
eventually lost both his throne and his life.

permanent value. In May 1641, it passed a law establishing that the assembly
could not be dissolved by the king without its own agreement. Although that
law deprived him of an important prerogative, the king did not oppose it,
but rather hoped that his problems would be solved by a series of complicated intrigues. When Parliament finally began discussing the matter of funds
to deal with the Scottish rebels, it was discovered that the king had been
negotiating with the invaders, hoping to undo the power of Parliament. A
Catholic rebellion in Ireland was also said to have been instigated by the

queen, supposedly with a view to embarrass Parliament and force it to grant funds to the king for his armies. The sovereigns' duplicity, whether real or fictitious, drew the more radical Protestants into a closer alliance whose goal was to limit the power of the crown.

The bishops, as members of the House of Lords, were Charles's main supporters in Parliament. But the House of Commons began instituting proceedings against some of the bishops, and when the accused tried to attend Parliament the people of London rioted and barred them from the assembly. Encouraged by these events, the more radical members of the House of Commons announced their plans to bring the queen to trial for her supposed participation in the events leading to rebellion in Ireland. Such extreme measures provoked a reaction against the Puritans. Many in the House of Lords were convinced that the time had come to restore order. Time was on the king's side. But he did not have the patience to wait for events to give him the victory, and therefore he hastily accused the leaders of the Commons before the House of Lords. The lords, fearing that some day he might take similar action against them, rejected the accusation. Then the king ordered the arrest of the accused, and Parliament refused to give them up. The following day, a military contingent sent by Charles to arrest those whom he had accused found that Parliament had fled to London, where it was continuing its sessions with the support of the people. Having lost his capital, the king withdrew to his palaces of Hampton Court and Windsor. Meanwhile, in London, the leader of the rebellious Parliament, John Pym, ruled as a "king without a crown." The Commons then proposed a law excluding the bishops from the House of Lords. The higher chamber agreed, the king did not object, and the prelates were therefore expelled. Thus began a process that would progressively exclude from Parliament those opposed to Puritanism, giving the assembly an ever more radical bent. Parliament then ordered that a militia be recruited. Since such troops would be under Parliament's command, the king decided that the time had come for decisive action. He gathered the troops loyal to him, and prepared for battle against Parliament's militia. The conflicts between the throne and Parliament had finally led to civil war.

Civil War

Both sides began building up their armies. Charles found his greatest support among the nobility, while Parliament found its support among those who had most suffered in recent times. The bulk of its army came from the lower classes, to whom were added many merchants and a few noblemen. The king's strength was his cavalry, traditionally the specialty of the nobility;

Parliament's was its infantry and the navy, for which trade was important. At first there were only minor skirmishes, while each party sought outside support: Parliament from the Scots, and Charles from the Catholics in Ireland. Also, threatened by civil war, the various Puritan factions drew closer together.

In its efforts to attract the Scots, Parliament took a series of measures that leaned to Presbyterianism. Not all English Puritans agreed that this was the proper type of church government, but most rejected the episcopacy, considered the king's main ecclesiastical support. Eventually, the episcopacy was abolished—partly because the bishops supported the king, partly for theological reasons, and partly because the confiscation of the bishops' property meant that Parliament could obtain funds without creating new taxes.

Meanwhile, Parliament convoked a body of theologians to advise it in religious matters. This was the famous Westminster Assembly, which included, besides 121 ministers and thirty laymen appointed by Parliament, eight representatives from Scotland. Since the Scots had behind them the strongest army in Great Britain, their influence on the assembly was decisive. In chapter 20 we shall dwell on the theology of the assembly, whose Confession became one of the fundamental documents of Calvinist orthodoxy. For the present, it suffices to say that, although some of its members were "independents"—that is, supporters of the congregational form of government—and others leaned towards episcopacy, the Assembly opted for the Presbyterian form of government, and recommended that Parliament adopt it for the Church of England. There were in Parliament many independents who would have preferred another form of government, but the course of war forced them to join with the Scots in a "Solemn League and Covenant" that committed them to Presbyterianism. This was finally enacted in 1644, and in the following year William Laud—by then archbishop of Canterbury—was executed by order of Parliament.

It was at this time, while Parliament was building up its army, that Oliver Cromwell came to the foreground. He was a relatively wealthy man, descended from one of Henry VIII's advisors. A few years earlier he had become a Puritan, and was now an avid reader of Scripture. He was convinced that every decision, both personal and political, ought to be based on the will of God. This meant that, although he often was slow in coming to a decision, once he had set upon a course he was determined to follow it to its final consequences. Although he was respected by his fellow Puritans, until the time of the Civil War he was known as simply one more member of the House of Commons. However, when he became convinced that armed conflict was inevitable, Cromwell returned to his home, where he recruited a small corps of cavalry. He knew that cavalry was the king's main weapon, and that Parliament would need a similar body. His zeal was contagious, and his small cadre became a mighty body of cavalry, convinced that it was waging holy war, who charged into battle singing psalms. Soon the entire

Oliver Cromwell, at first an obscure member of Parliament, led the rebels to victory and became master of England.

army of Parliament was possessed of similar convictions, and became an irresistible force that crushed the king's army at the battle of Naseby.

That battle was the beginning of the end for the king. The rebels captured his camp, where they found proof that he had been encouraging foreign Catholic troops to invade England. Charles then decided to negotiate with the Scots, hoping to win them with his promises. But the Scots made him a prisoner and eventually turned him over to Parliament. Having thus won the war, Parliament adopted a series of Puritan measures, such as ordering that the Lord's Day be reserved for religious observances, and forbidding frivolous pastimes.

But the Puritans, who had been united in their opposition to the king and his bishops, were deeply divided among themselves. The majority of Parliament by then supported the Presbyterian form of government, which would allow for a national church without bishops. But the Independents were the majority in the army. These Independents did not agree among themselves on many points. But they did agree that a national church with a Presbyterian form of government would deprive them of their freedom to obey the Bible as they understood it. Thus, tension grew between Parliament and its army. In 1646, Parliament tried without success to dissolve the army. More radical groups, such as the "Fifth Monarchy" and the "Levellers," gained ground in the army. Some of them declared that the Lord was about to return, and that it was necessary to transform the social order by establishing justice and equality. Parliament, where the merchant class still had significant power, responded by stricter measures against the army, which in turn responded by declaring that, since it included a wider representation of the people, it was the army, and not Parliament, that had the right to speak for the nation.

At that point the king escaped. He then opened negotiations with the Scots, with the army, and with Parliament, making mutually contradictory promises to all three. He gained the support of the Scots, to whom he promised the establishment of Presbyterianism both in Scotland and in England. Meanwhile, he continued secret negotiation with Parliament. But the Puritan army defeated the Scots, gained possession of the king, and began a purge of Parliament. Forty-five leaders of Parliament were arrested, and many more were kept away from the sessions, while others refused to attend further meetings. What now remained was rightly called by its enemies the "Rump Parliament."

It was this Rump Parliament that then initiated proceedings against Charles, whom they accused of high treason and of having involved the country in civil war. The fourteen lords who dared appear for the meeting of the House of Lords unanimously refused to agree to such proceedings. But the Commons simply continued the trial, and Charles, who refused to defend himself on the grounds that his judges had no legal jurisdiction, was beheaded on January 30, 1649.

The Protectorate

The Scots, fearing the loss of their independence from England, rapidly acknowledged the dead king's son, Charles II, as their ruler. The Irish took the opportunity to rebel. In England itself, the independent Puritans were splintering. Among the more radical, the "Diggers" grew strong. This was a movement that advocated a new social order in which the right to property would be universal. Such preaching threatened the merchant class, which earlier had supported Parliament in its opposition to the king. Meanwhile, the Presbyterians insisted on their project of a national church, which the Independents saw as tyranny. In short, chaos threatened the land.

It was then that Cromwell took the reins of power. Although he had not participated in the purge of Parliament, he approved of its results and, in the name of the Rump Parliament, stamped out first the Irish rebellion and then the royalist outbreak in Scotland. Charles II was forced to flee to the Continent. Then Cromwell decided to do what the king had been unable to do: when the Rump Parliament began discussing a law that would perpetuate its power, Cromwell appeared at the session, expelled the few remaining representatives, and locked the building. Thus, seemingly against his own will, he had become master of the nation. For some time he sought to return to some sort of representative government, but he eventually took the title of "Lord Protector." In theory, he was to rule with the help of a Parliament that would include representatives from England, Scotland, and Ireland. In truth, however, the new Parliament was mostly English, and Cromwell was the real government.

Cromwell then set on a program of reformation of both church and state. Given the prevailing atmosphere, his religious policies were fairly tolerant. Although he was an Independent, he tried to develop a religious system where there was room for Presbyterians, Baptists, and even some moderate advocates of episcopacy. As a true Puritan, he also tried to reform the customs of the land through legislation regarding the Lord's Day, horse races, cockfights, theatre, and so forth. His economic policies favored the middle class, to the particular detriment of the aristocracy, but also in some measure of the poor. Among both the very wealthy and the very poor, opposition to the Protectorate increased.

Cromwell was able to retain control of the country as long as he lived. But his dreams of creating a stable republic failed. Like the kings before him, he was unable to get along with Parliament—even though his partisans forcibly kept his opponents from taking their seats, thus creating a new "rump." Since the Protectorate was obviously temporary, Cromwell was offered the royal crown, but he refused it, still hoping to create a republic. In 1658, shortly before his death, he named his son Richard as his successor. But this younger Cromwell lacked his father's ability, and resigned his post.

The Restoration

The failure of the Protectorate left no alternative but the restoration of the monarchy. Under General Monck's leadership, Parliament recalled Charles II to his father's throne. This brought about a reaction against the Puritans. Although Charles at first sought to find a place for Presbyterians within the national church, the new Parliament opposed such projects, and preferred the traditional episcopacy. Thus, the new government restored both the episcopacy and the *Book of Common Prayer,* and issued laws against dissidents, for whom there was no place in the official church. Such laws, however, were unable to stamp out most of the movements that had emerged during the previous unrest. They continued existing outside the law until, late in that century, toleration was decreed.

In Scotland, the consequences of the restoration were more severe. That country had become staunchly Presbyterian, and now by a royal decree the episcopacy was reinstated, and ministers of Presbyterian persuasion were deposed in favor of others who were willing to preach in support of bishops. This resulted in riots and revolts. Archbishop James Sharp, the foremost prelate of Scotland, was murdered. This brought about the intervention of the English in support of the Scottish royalists, and Presbyterian rebellions were drowned in blood.

On his deathbed, Charles II declared himself a Catholic, thus confirming the suspicions of many of the persecuted Puritans and Scottish Presbyterians. His brother and successor, James II, resolved to restore Roman Catholicism as the official religion of his kingdoms. In England, he sought to gain the support of dissidents by decreeing religious tolerance. But the anti-Catholic feeling of the dissidents was so strong that they would rather have no tolerance if that was necessary to avoid a rebirth of Catholicism. Conditions in Scotland were much worse, and James II—James VII of Scotland—decreed the death penalty for any who attended unauthorized worship, and placed Catholics in positions of power.

After three years under James II, the English rebelled and invited William, Prince of Orange, and his wife Mary, James's daughter, to occupy the throne. William landed in 1688, and James fled to France. In Scotland his supporters held on for a few months, but by the following year William and Mary were firmly in possession of the Scottish crown also. Their religious policy was fairly tolerant. In England, tolerance was granted to any who would subscribe to the Thirty-nine Articles of 1562, and swear loyalty to the sovereigns. Those who refused to swear, called "nonjurors," were granted tolerance as long as they did not conspire against the sovereigns. In Scotland, Presbyterianism became the official religion of the state, and the Westminster Confession its doctrinal norm.

Even after the restoration, however, the Puritan ideal lingered on, and deeply influenced the British ethos. Its two great literary figures, John Bunyan and John Milton, long remained among the most read of English authors. Bunyan's most famous work, generally known by the abbreviated title of *Pilgrim's Progress,* became a popular book of devotion, the subject of much meditation and discussion for generations to come. And Milton's *Paradise Lost* determined the way in which the majority of the English-speaking world read and interpreted the Bible.

18/Catholic Orthodoxy

There is sufficient light for those who wish to see, and sufficient darkness for those of the opposite disposition. Enough clarity to illumine the elect, and enough darkness to keep them humble. Sufficient darkness to blind the reprobate, and sufficient clarity to condemn them and make them inexcusable.

BLAISE PASCAL

The Council of Trent had determined what would be Catholic orthodoxy for the next four centuries, and had also put forth an entire program of reformation. But both that orthodoxy and that reformation had opponents within Catholic ranks. First of all, the Tridentine program of reformation was based on a centralization of power in the papacy, and therefore conflicted with various governments. Second, there were prelates for whom the proposed reformation required sacrifices they were not willing to make. And, finally, there were those who feared that, in its efforts to reject Protestantism, Trent had gone too far, particularly by neglecting Augustine's doctrine of the primacy of grace in human salvation.

Gallicanism and Opposition to Papal Power

Although the Council of Trent had been necessary because the papacy had lacked the will and the power to respond to the challenges of the Protestant Reformation, by the end of its sessions the papacy had gained in prestige and was entrusted with great power over the entire Catholic Church. But this decision on the Council's part was not well received in many European courts. This was a time of growing nationalism and absolute monarchs, and therefore both kings and nationalists opposed the notion of a centralized church under papal authority. Such attitudes were given the name of "Gallicanism"—from "Gaul," or ancient France—because it was in France that they became most powerful. Those who defended the authority of the pope were called "Ultramontanes," for they looked for authority "beyond the mountains"—that is, beyond the Alps.

During the late Middle Ages, when the papacy had existed under the shadow of France, the French monarchy had obtained a number of concessions from the popes, mostly granting the French church a measure of autonomy. Now the French insisted on those ancient "freedoms of the Gallican church," denied by the centralizing edicts of Trent. While some of the Gallicans opposed the centralization of power in the papacy for political reasons, others did so because they were convinced that ecclesiastical authority resided in the bishops, and not in the pope. In any case, the decrees of Trent would not be valid in France until the crown had them promulgated, and this was not easily achieved. Although Henry IV, after protracted negotiations, agreed to the promulgation of the Council's decrees, the French Parliament blocked it. In 1615, five years after the assassination of Henry IV, the decrees had not been promulgated by French civil authorities, and the French clergy, at that time dominated by the Ultramontanes, decided to do it on its own. But the very fact that it had been the French clergy that had decided about the validity of the Council in their country could eventually be used as an argument by the defenders of the "Gallican freedoms."

There were similar movements in other parts of Europe. "Febronianism" was named after Justin Febronius, the pseudonymous author of a book published in 1763 under the title of *The State of the Church and the Legitimate Power of the Roman Pontiff.* This argued that the church is the community of the faithful, and that the bishops, as their representatives, are to rule the church. Therefore, final authority resides in a council of the bishops, and not in the pope. Pope Clement XIII condemned Febronius' work as heretical. But its ideas continued circulating and gaining popularity. Some saw in them a possibility of reuniting Catholics and Protestants by means of a council. Others supported them because they were compatible with their own nationalism. And there were some opulent bishops, lords of vast dioceses, who supported them as a means to evade compliance with the reforms dictated by Rome.

In the imperial court at Vienna, Febronianism took a different turn. The emperor, Joseph II, was a learned and liberal-minded ruler who projected a number of reforms in his territories. He needed the support of the church for such projects; but not of the Tridentine church, which he considered obscurantist and intolerant. Therefore he took over the education of the clergy, closed down those monasteries that he deemed too traditional, founded new churches, and in general carried forth a reformation of the church in the direction he thought best. Other rulers showed an inclination to follow the emperor's example, and the Church of Rome, which had already condemned Febronianism in 1764, also condemend "Josephism" in 1794. But it was not papal condemnation, but rather the French Revolution (to which we shall turn later) that put an end to this and other such movements.

Meanwhile, papal power had suffered a serious blow in the dissolution of the Jesuits. That order, founded precisely to serve as an army to the papacy, was not well regarded by the absolutist monarchs of the eighteenth century. The Jesuits' support of the intolerant policies that led to the Thirty Years' War did not help their popularity. In particular, the house of Bourbon had a profound aversion towards the Jesuits, who had consistently supported their rival house of Hapsburg. Therefore, as the power of the Bourbons waxed, and that of the Hapsburgs waned, the Jesuits found themselves in difficulty. In 1758, an attempt to assassinate Joseph I of Portugal was blamed on the Jesuits. A year later, the Society of Jesus was expelled from Portugal and its colonies, and the crown confiscated its property. In France, also under Bourbon rule, the Society was suppressed in 1764. Three years later, it was expelled from Spain and its colonies by Charles III. Then King Ferdinand IV of Naples followed the example of his father, Charles III of Spain. This led to a concerted effort by the Bourbons to be rid of the Jesuits, not only in their own territories, but throughout the world. Early in 1769, the Bourbon ambassadors in Rome presented to the pope a joint resolution in which they demanded the dissolution of the Jesuits. Finally, in 1773, Pope Clement XIV ordered the Society of Jesus dissolved, thus losing one of the most powerful instruments of papal policy.

Gallicanism, Febronianism, Josephism, and the suppression of the Jesuits show that, while the popes insisted on their universal jurisdiction, in truth they were losing power and authority.

Jansenism

The Council of Trent had categorically condemned the views of Luther and Calvin on grace and predestination; but there were many who feared that, in an extreme reaction against Protestantism, this could lead to a denial of St. Augustine's teachings. Thus arose among Catholics a series of controversies on grace and predestination.

Later in the sixteenth century, the Jesuits at the University of Salamanca, under the leadership of Luis de Molina, affirmed that predestination was based on God's foreknowledge. To this the Dominican Domingo Báñez, one of the best Catholic theologians of the time, responded that such teaching was contrary to Augustine, and therefore ought to be condemned. Each side accused the other before the Spanish Inquisition, the Jesuits declaring that the Dominicans were Calvinists, and the Dominicans claiming that the Jesuits

The enmity of the house of Bourbon led to the expulsion of the Jesuits from France and other Bourbon territories.

were Pelagians. The Inquisition turned the matter over to Rome, and the popes, after long hesitation, simply decided that both accusations were false, and ordered each side to refrain from attacking the other.

Similar controversies at the University of Louvain had greater repercussions. There, Michael Baius proposed theses similar to those of Augustine, arguing that a sinful will can produce no good. In 1567, Pope Pius V condemned seventy-nine theses drawn from Baius' writings. The latter recanted, but continued teaching very similar doctrine. When a Jesuit theologian attacked Baius, the Faculty of Louvain responded by declaring that the Jesuit was a Pelagian. Again, the popes intervened trying to calm the spirits. But Baius' theology continued circulating in Louvain and they resurfaced six decades later, in 1640, in the work of Cornelius Jansenius. His book, *Augustine,* published posthumously, claimed to be no more than a study and exposition of the teachings of that great theologian on the subjects of grace and predestination. But what Jansenius found in Augustine was too similar to the doctrines of Calvin and, in 1643, his theses were condemned by Pope Urban VIII.

This, however, did not put an end to the controversy. In France, the Jansenist torch was taken up by Jean Duvergier, better known as "Saint-Cyran" because he was abbot of a house by that name, and by the nuns of the abbey of Port-Royal. The abbey of Port-Royal, under the leadership of the saintly Mother Angelique, had become a center of devotion and reformation, and Saint-Cyran was well known as a leading figure in that movement. He had been imprisoned by Richelieu, who feared that the religious zeal of these reformers would hinder his political program. Freed in 1643, the same year that the theses of his deceased friend Jansenius were condemned, Saint-Cyran became the champion of Jansenism, and the abbey of Port-Royal its headquarters. Now, however, Jansenism was less a doctrine regarding grace and predestination, and more a movement of zealous religious reform. The Jesuits had proposed the theory of "probabilism," which meant that a probability, no matter how slight, that an action was correct made it morally acceptable. To the French Jansenists this was moral indifferentism, and instead they proposed a life of such discipline and rigor that it was said that the nuns of Port-Royal were "as pure as angels and as proud as demons."

Saint-Cyran died shortly after beeing freed, but the cause was taken up by Antoine Arnauld, Mother Angelique's brother, and by the philosopher Blaise Pascal. From an early age, Pascal had shown his genius, particularly in physics and mathematics. When he was thirty-one, eight years before his death, he was converted to Jansenism. For him this was a profound religious experience that left its mark on the rest of his life. When the Faculty of the Sorbonne condemned Arnauld, he published the first of his twenty "Provincial Letters," purporting to be addressed to the Parisian Jesuits by an inhabitant of the provinces. Their humor and wit soon gained them wide circulation, and they were added to the Index of forbidden books. For a time, it became fashionable among the intelligentsia and the aristocracy of Paris to be a Jansenist.

Then reaction set in. Louis XIV was not a king to tolerate such zeal, which could easily turn into sectarianism. The assembly of the clergy condemned the movement. The nuns of Port-Royal were disbanded. In spite of his Gallicanism, Louis XIV asked the support of Pope Alexander III, who ordered all members of the clergy to repudiate Jansenism. But once again the pendulum swung. Alexander died, his successor proved more lenient, the nuns were allowed to return to Port-Royal, and there was even talk of making Arnauld a cardinal. This, however, was only a brief respite. Eventually, Arnauld was forced into exile, where he died. Louis XIV became increasingly intolerant, and Pope Clement XI reiterated the condemnation of Jansenism. In 1709, the police took possession of Port-Royal and expelled the elderly nuns. Since people still flocked in pilgrimage to the abbey's cemetery, it was ordered dug up, and it is said that the dogs fought over the disinterred remains. In 1713, Clement XI categorically condemned Jansenism in the bull *Unigenitus.*

One of the ablest defenders of Jansenism was Blaise Pascal, whose Provincial Letters *made the Parisian Jesuits the subject of ridicule.*

But Jansenism continued existing, and even grew. By then, however, it had little to do with the teachings of Jansenius, or with the reforming zeal of Saint-Cyran and Angelique, or even with the profound religiosity of Pascal. It was rather a political and intellectual movement closely akin to Gallicanism. Some members of the lower clergy joined the movement as a protest against the opulence of their superiors. Others used it as a means of opposing undue interference of Rome in French affairs. Still others were rationalists who saw in the movement a reaction against dogmatic authority. Eventually, Jansenism disappeared, not because it had been condemned and persecuted, but rather because it had become amorphous.

Quietism

Another major controversy within Catholicism revolved around "Quietism." This doctrine began with the publication in 1675 of the *Spiritual Guide* of the Spaniard Miguel de Molinos. This was a controversial man whom some called a saint, and others a charlatan. His *Spiritual Guide*, and a later *Treatise on Daily Communion,* caused a great stir, for some accused him of heresy, while others claimed that his was the highest form of Christian devotion.

Molinos advocated total passivity before God. A believer is simply to disappear, to die and be lost in God. Any activism, be it of the body or of the soul, must be set aside. Contemplation must be purely spiritual, having nothing to do with any physical or visible means—including the humanity of Christ. The same is true of ascetic discipline, which is another form of activism. When the soul is lost in contemplation of the divine, it must consider nothing else—not even the neighbor.

Such teaching provoked great opposition. Some argued that it was more akin to Moslem mysticism than to the doctrines of the great Christian teachers. Others pointed out that Molinism led to privatism, in which the church has no importance or authority, and in which Christians have nothing to do with political and social life. The Inquisition, asked to judge on the matter, at first supported Molinos. But many confessors protested that this teaching was leading to moral laxity among the faithful. Then rumors circulated that Molinos himself encouraged such laxity among his followers, and that his relations with the women among them were not above reproach.

In 1685, Molinos and several of his followers were arrested by papal order. In his trial before the Inquisition, he refused to defend himself, even from the most absurd accusations. His admirers declared that he was simply practicing the Quietism that he had preached. His accusers said that his silence proved his guilt. When ordered to recant, he did so with such humility that the recantation itself could be interpreted as a sign that he was still true to his beliefs. Although many demanded that he be condemned to death, Pope Innocent XI, not wishing to create a martyr for Quietism, had him imprisoned for the remaining eleven years of his life. In prison, he seems to have continued the life of quiet contemplation that he had advocated.

Quietism penetrated into France, where it was taken up by the widowed Madame Guyon and by her confessor, Father Lacombe. Both were people of profound religious inclinations, given to visions and other mystical experiences. Around them gathered a circle of believers whom they guided in their religious lives. When Madame Guyon published a treatise, *A Short and Simple Means of Prayer,* her fame extended throughout the nation. Then she and her confessor moved to Paris, where their admirers included several women of the highest aristocracy.

But Madame Guyon's doctrines were not above suspicion, for she carried the teachings of Molinos in a more radical direction. She eventually declared that there may be times when, in order to offer God a true sacrifice, one must commit sins one truly despises. Such affirmations, joined with her close collaboration with Lacombe, gave rise to evil rumors, and the archbishop of Paris ordered the priest put in prison, and Madame Guyon placed in a convent. Lacombe was carried from one prison to another, until he lost his mind and died. Madame de Guyon was eventually freed through the intervention of one of the king's favorites.

It was then that Madame Guyon met the young Bishop François Fénelon. He was won over to her teachings, although he never carried them to her extremes. Eventually, the issue of Quietism degenerated into a bitter controversy between Fénelon and one of the greatest French theologians of the time, Jacques Benigne Bossuet. The controversy dragged on, for Bossuet had the support of the king, but Fénelon was a man of admirable piety. Finally, under pressure from Louis XIV, Pope Innocent XII agreed to reject some of Fénelon's theses, although carefully declaring, not that they were wrong, but that they could lead some to error. Upon hearing of the papal decision, Fénelon responded with such humility that in the public mind Bossuet was condemned as an arrogant man who had unnecessarily humiliated a worthy colleague. Fénelon then withdrew to his pastoral duties as Archbishop of Cambray, distributing all his possessions among the poor and leading such an admirable life that he was the probable model for Victor Hugo's saintly but fictitious Monseigneur Myriel, a leading figure in *Les Miserables.*

All these events and controversies show that during the seventeenth and eighteenth centuries Roman Catholicism was reorganizing itself after the crisis of the Reformation. The Council of Trent had strictly defined Catholic orthodoxy, and in theory the Papacy had become the center of ecclesiastical power. In doctrinal matters, the decisions of Trent were inviolable, and therefore all theological controversy took place within the framework of Tridentine orthodoxy. But there were also strong political forces at work against the centralization of ecclesiastical power, thus giving rise to Gallicanism, Febronianism, and Josephism. That opposition to papal power would eventually weaken the Catholic Church and make it more difficult for it to respond to the challenges of the French Revolution.

19/ Lutheran Orthodoxy

I am a Christian, profoundly committed to the Confession of Augsburg in which my parents reared me. And I am also committed to it as a result of my constantly renewed and considered reflexions, and of a daily struggle against every sort of temptation.

PAUL GERHARDT

The reform that Luther advocated and began was doctrinal, and not merely practical. Although he criticized the corruption that had become common in the life of the church, that was not the main point at issue. Luther's reformation began with a theological discovery, and he was always convinced that correct belief was of crucial importance for the church. This did not mean that all had to agree on all points of doctrine. For many years, his main collaborator and closest friend was Philip Melanchthon, who differed from him on many points. Luther himself said that his task was cutting down the trees and removing the great boulders from the field, and that Melanchthon was the more patient man whose task it was to plow and sow. Likewise, although later the differences between Calvin and Luther have been underscored, when the German reformer read the first edition of Calvin's *Institutes* he commented favorably on them. But not all had the same mental amplitude, as became evident in the debates that divided the next generation of Lutherans.

Philippists and Strict Lutherans

After Luther's death, Melanchthon took his place as the main interpreter of Lutheran theology. His systematic exposition of theology, commonly known by the abbreviated title of *Loci theologici,* became the standard textbook for the study of theology among Lutherans, and underwent several editions, each with further revisions by its author. But there were those who thought that Melanchthon was not a faithful exponent of the deceased reformer's theology. The main point of contrast, at the heart of all other differences, was the humanist inclinations of "Master Philip"—as Luther used to call him. When Luther broke with Erasmus and his humanist program of reformation, Melanchthon continued cordial relations with the illustrious scholar. This was partly due to Melanchthon's love of peace. But it was also due to his disagreement with Luther's radical rejection of "dirty reason." For similar reasons Melanchthon, while affirming the doctrine of justification by faith, insisted

The first debates among Lutherans revolved
around the teachings of Melanchthon, whom
some accused of having departed from the
teachings of the deceased reformer.

on the need for good works—although not as a means of salvation, but as a result and witness to it.

These differences between Luther and Melanchthon, exaggerated by some after Luther's death, gave rise to the debate between "Philippists" and "strict Lutherans." The immediate occasion for the conflict was the "Augsburg Interim," an attempt to force Lutherans to agree to a compromise with Catholicism (see chapter 9). None of the Lutheran leaders was enthusiastic about the Interim, and most refused to sign it. But imperial pressure was great, and finally the Wittenberg theologians, headed by Melanchthon, agreed to a modified version of it—the "Leipzig Interim." The strict Lutherans, who had firmly refused to sign the Interim in spite of the displeasure of the emperor, accused the Wittenberg "Philippists" of having forsaken several elements of Luther's teachings. Melanchthon responded by establishing a distinction between the central elements of the gospel and those that are peripheral to it. The latter he called by the Greek name of "adiaphora." The essential must not be abandoned at any cost. The adiaphora, although important, must not be confused with the essential. Therefore, in a situation such as the church was facing at the time, one could be justified in leaving aside some of the secondary elements in order to have the freedom to continue preaching and teaching the essential. The strict Lutherans, under the leadership of Matthias Flacius, responded that, although it may well be true that there are some elements essential to the gospel, and others that are peripheral, there are circumstances that require a clear confession of faith. At such times, some elements that could otherwise be considered peripheral become symbols of the faith itself. To forsake them is to deny the faith. Those who sincerely wish to give clear witness to the faith refuse to yield even on peripheral matters, for fear that their yielding may be construed as surrender. In accepting the Leipzig Interim, Flacius argued, even if the Philippists had yielded only on peripheral matters, they had refused to confess their faith.

Then other issues were added to the debate. The strict Lutherans accused the Philippists of giving too much credit to human participation in salvation. Melanchthon, who had never agreed with Luther's assertions about the "enslaved will," was indeed moving to a position that granted the sinful human will greater freedom, and eventually came to speak of a collaboration among the Spirit, the Word, and human will. Opposing him, the strict Lutherans emphasized the corruption of human nature as a result of sin, and Flacius even came to affirm that the very nature of fallen humankind is corruption. At this time, the strict Lutherans also began insisting on the contrast between Luther and Calvin in their interpretations of the Lord's presence in communion, and insisted that, since Melanchthon's views were akin to Calvin's, the Philippists were in truth Calvinists.

These and similar controversies eventually led to the "Formula of Concord" of 1577. On most of the issues debated, this Formula took an intermediate position. For instance, it declared that while it is true that there are some elements that are not essential to the gospel, in time of persecution one should not abandon even these peripheral matters. But on the matter of communion, the Formula of Concord upheld the strict Lutherans, denying any significant difference between Zwingli's position, clearly rejected by Luther at Marburg, and Calvin's. As a result, from that point on one of the characteristics of Lutheranism was its understanding of communion, expressed in terms of contrast with Calvinism.

The Triumph of Orthodoxy

Whereas the period before the Formula of Concord was marked by the controversies between Philippists and strict Lutherans, the next generations set out to coordinate Luther's teachings with those of Melanchthon. This spirit was already apparent in the Formula of Concord and in its main architect, Martin Chemnitz, whose theology, while it accepted many of the theses of strict Lutheranism, followed a methodology similar to Melanchthon's. For Chemnitz, the task at hand was reconciling the various positions within Lutheranism, while underscoring their difference with Catholicism as well as with other forms of Protestantism.

The theology that evolved out of this program has been called "Protestant scholasticism," and dominated Lutheran thought throughout the seventeenth century and part of the eighteenth. Its main characteristic was its emphasis on systematic thought. Luther never sought to develop a system of theology. Melanchthon did write a short systematic work that soon gained wide recognition. But the theologians of Protestant scholasticism wrote vast systematic works that could be compared with the great summas of medieval scholasticism, both in their size and in their careful distinctions and analyses. For instance, Johann Gerhardt's great work comprised nine volumes that by the second edition had become twenty-three. And, from 1655 to 1677, Abraham Calovius published a systematic theology in twelve volumes.

A second characteristic of Protestant scholasticism that made it similar to medieval theology was its use of Aristotle. Luther had declared that in order to be a theologian one must be rid of Aristotle. But, towards the end of the sixteenth century, there was a renewal of interest in Aristotelian philosophy, and soon most Lutheran theologians were seeking to build their systems on the basis of Aristotelian logic and metaphysics. Some even began using the works of their Jesuit counterparts, who also were doing theology on the basis of Aristotle. Thus, while in its content Protestant scholasticism was radically opposed to Catholicism, in its tone and methodology it was very similar to the Catholic theology of the time.

The third reason why Lutheran theology in the seventeenth century is properly called "scholastic" is that it was mostly the product of the schools. It was no longer, as in the previous century, a theology born out of the life of the church and directed towards preaching and the care of souls, but rather a theology developed in the universities, and addressed to other scholars and university professors.

Although Protestant scholasticism waned towards the end of the eighteenth century, it left two important legacies: its doctrine of scriptural inspiration, and its spirit of rigid confessionalism. Luther had never dealt specifically with the question of the inspiration of Scripture. There is no doubt that he was convinced that the Bible was inspired by God, and that this was the reason why it must be the basis of every theological affirmation. But he never discussed the nature of inspiration. For him, what was important was not the text itself of Scripture, but the divine action to which that text testifies. The Word of God is Jesus Christ, and the Bible is Word of God because it leads to him. But the scholastic Lutherans posed the question of the manner and sense in which the Bible is inspired. The answer that most gave is that the Holy Spirit both told the authors what to write and ordered them to write it. This seemed necessary in order to refute the argument given by some Catholics that the apostles told their disciples some things in writing, and others verbally. According to the Lutheran scholastics, it does not matter whether or not the apostles verbally taught the disciples things that are not written in the Bible, for such teachings—if they did indeed exist—would not have been inspired by God as the Bible was inspired. Only what the Spirit told the apostles and prophets to write is authoritative for the church.

The other important question that the Lutheran scholastics posed about the inspiration of Scripture was to what degree the individuality of the authors determined what they wrote. The most common answer was that the biblical authors were no more than secretaries or copyists for the Holy Spirit. They wrote down, letter by letter, what the Spirit told them. But the Spirit knew the individuality of each author and took it into account. That is the reason why the epistles of Paul, for instance, are different from those of John. All this led to an emphasis on the literal inspiration of Scripture, and even on the divine inspiration of the text as it has been transmitted through the centuries. On this point, it is noteworthy that, while Catholic theologians were arguing that the Vulgate—the ancient Latin translation of the Bible— was divinely inspired, there were Lutheran theologians who denied such inspiration, but who then affirmed that the Holy Spirit had inspired the medieval Jewish scholars who had added vowels to the Hebrew text of Scripture—Old Testament Hebrew had no vowels.

Georg Calixtus and "Syncretism"

The growing rigidity of Lutheran scholasticism was manifest in the controversy surrounding the proposals of Georg Calixtus. He was a convinced Lutheran who believed that, although Lutheran doctrine was the best interpretation of Scripture, this did not suffice to declare all others heretics or false

Christians. He saw a denial of the very spirit of Christianity in the controversies of his time, particularly in the bitter attacks of Christians against other Christians. Therefore, he sought a rapprochement with believers of other confessions, although one that would not lead to the denial of his Lutheran convictions. In order to do this, he made a distinction similar to Melanchthon's between the essential and the secondary. Everything that is in Scripture has been revealed by God, and ought to be believed; but not all is of equal importance. Only that which relates to salvation is fundamental and absolutely necessary. The rest is equally true, and is also important, for otherwise God would not have revealed it. But it is not essential for being a Christian. There is a difference between heresy and error. The former is the denial of something that is essential for salvation. The latter is a denial of another element of revelation. Both heresy and error are evil, and should be avoided. But only heresy is of such gravity as to keep Christians from communion with each other.

How, then, does one distinguish the fundamental from the secondary? On the basis of what Calixtus calls "the consensus of the first five centuries." During those five centuries, Calixtus argued, there was a consensus among Christians. Some positions were condemned as heretical, and we ought to do likewise. But it would be folly to affirm that something that cannot be found in those first five centuries of Christian theology is essential for salvation.

Rejected as a "syncretist" during his lifetime, Georg Calixtus was later hailed as a forerunner of the modern ecumenical movement.

'IR PLVRIM REVEREND AMPLISS ATQ EXEL
LENTISS DN GEORGIVS CALIXTVS SS THEOL DOCT &
Profeis mnchia iulia Celeberr nec non Abbas Coenob Regio
Lothar Dignifsim

Such an assertion would lead to the conclusion that no one was saved during the early centuries of the life of the church!

Again, this does not mean that we are to believe only what can be found in the writings of the first five centuries. On the contrary, we should believe all that Scripture tells us. But lack of belief in something to be found in Scripture and not in the first five centuries of Christian theology is error, not heresy. The doctrine of justification by faith is a case in point. There is no doubt that this doctrine is found in Scripture. But it was not part of the common faith of the first five centuries. Therefore, although it is important, it is not to be required of all, as if any who reject it were heretics. Luther was right in affirming this doctrine, and Lutherans are also right in insisting on its truth. But this does not mean that Catholics are heretics. And the same can be said regarding the differences between Lutherans and Calvinists on the manner of the presence of Christ in communion. Although Calvinists are in error, they are not heretics.

By these arguments, Calixtus hoped to achieve better understanding and mutual appreciation among Christians of different confessions—and for this reason has been rightly called one of the forerunners of the ecumenical movement. But the defenders of Lutheran orthodoxy were not to be swayed. Abraham Calovius emphatically declared that everything that God has revealed in Scripture is absolutely necessary. Anyone who denies or rejects any part of biblical doctrine, no matter how small or seemingly insignificant, denies and rejects none other than God. Other theologians would not go that far, but would point out that, in introducing his theory of the "consensus of the first five centuries," Calixtus had restored to tradition the authority that Luther had denied it. Soon the proposal of Calixtus came to be known as "syncretism," falsely implying that he intended to mix elements from various confessions, or that he believed all confessions to be equally valid. It was only in Poland that Calixtus' proposal was tried out. There, King Wladyslaw IV tried to apply them by opening a dialogue between Catholics and Protestants. But his efforts came to naught, and Georg Calixtus was eventually forgotten.

It was clear that the orthodox theologians of each confession were becoming increasingly entrenched in their positions, as if only those who agreed with them on every point of doctrine properly deserved to be called Christians. Such dogmatism, while bolstering the conviction of some, also gave rise to increasing doubts about the truth of Christianity, or at least about the value of theology and doctrine.

Reformed Orthodoxy

> *Election is the immutable purpose of God*
> *whereby, before the foundation of the world,*
> *he chose, from among the entire human*
> *race, a certain number of people to be*
> *redeemed in Christ.*
> SYNOD OF DORT

During the seventeenth century, the Reformed tradition determined what would thereafter be its orthodoxy. This took place in two solemn assemblies whose pronouncements were seen as the most faithful expression of Calvinism: the Synod of Dort and the Westminster Assembly.

Arminianism and the Synod of Dort

Jacobus Arminius was a distinguished Dutch pastor and professor whose theological training had been thoroughly Calvinistic, and had taken place partly in Geneva, under the direction of Calvin's successor Theodore Beza. Having returned to Holland, he gained wide recognition through his preaching from an important pulpit in Amsterdam. It was due to his good name, and to his fame as a student of the Bible and theology, that the leadership of the church in Amsterdam asked him to refute the opinions of Dirck Koornhert, a theologian who rejected some aspects of Calvin's doctrine, particularly in the matter of predestination. With a view to refuting Koornhert, Arminius studied his writings and compared them with Scripture, with early Christian theology, and with the teachings of several of the major reformers. Finally, after a struggle of conscience, he reached the conclusion that Koornhert was right. Arminius became a professor at the University of Leiden in 1603, and his opinions became a matter of public debate. One of his colleagues, Francis Gomarus, was a firm believer in predestination in the strictest sense, and soon the two clashed. It was thus that Jacobus Arminius, who considered himself a true follower of Calvin, gave his name to Arminianism, the doctrine that many since then have considered the very antithesis of Calvinism.

The issue between Gomarus and Arminius was not whether there is such a thing as predestination. On that point they agreed, for both found abundant biblical references to predestination. They debated the basis on which predestination takes place. According to Arminius, predestination was based on God's foreknowledge of those who would later have faith in Jesus Christ. Gomarus, on the other hand, claimed that faith itself is the result of predestination, so that before the foundation of the world the sovereign will of God decreed who would have faith and who would not. Arminius responded that the great decree of predestination was the one by which God determined that Jesus Christ would be the mediator and redeemer of humankind. That was indeed a sovereign decree, in no way dependent on human response. But the divine decree having to do with the final destiny of each individual was based, not on the sovereign will of God, but rather on divine foreknowledge, by which God knew what each person's response would be to the offer of salvation in Jesus Christ. In almost every other matter, Arminius remained a strict Calvinist. His doctrine of the church and the sacraments, for instance, followed the general lines of Calvin. Therefore, although eventually it was his opponents who came to be known as "Calvinists," the truth is that the entire controversy took place among Calvin's followers. Arminius died in 1609, but his death did not put an end to the debate, for the successor to his chair at Leiden held his opinions, and carried on the controversy with Gomarus.

Political and economic considerations were soon added to the theological issues at stake. Although the struggle for independence from Spain had been long and bitter, and independence was still not assured, there were those in the Netherlands who wished to improve relations with their former oppressor. These were mostly the merchants, who in some cities were a true oligarchy, and who stood to gain from improved trade with Spain. They were staunchly opposed by many of the clergy, who feared that such contacts with Spain would corrupt the doctrinal purity of the Dutch church. Those who did not participate in the prosperity brought about by trade—that is, the lower classes, imbued with patriotism, with Calvinism, and with resentment against the merchants—also opposed such relations. Soon the mercantile oligarchy took the side of Arminius, while their opponents supported Gomarus.

In 1610, the Arminian party issued a document or "Remonstrance," and thereafter were commonly known as "Remonstrants." The document itself contains five articles dealing with the issues under debate. The first article defines predestination in ambiguous terms, for it affirms that God determined before the foundation of the world that those would be saved who believe in Christ. We are not told whether this means, as Arminius taught, that God knew who would believe, and predestined those particular people; or simply that God determined that whoever would later come to believe would be saved—what later came to be called "the open decree of predestination." In any case, this ambiguity is consistent with the final paragraph of the Remonstrance, which declares that this is all that is needed for salvation, and that "it is neither necessary nor useful to rise higher nor to search any deeper." In short, that needless speculation regarding the cause of the divine decree of predestination is to be rejected. The second article affirms that Jesus died for all human beings, although only believers actually receive the benefits of his passion. The third tries to deal with the accusation of Pelagianism, leveled by Gomarus and his supporters against Arminius and his followers. (The reader will remember that Pelagianism was the doctrine that Augustine opposed, which held that humans were capable of doing good on their own.) To make clear that they are not Pelagians, the Remonstrants therefore declare that humans can do nothing good on their own account, and that the grace of God is necessary in order to do good. But the fourth article rejects the conclusion drawn by both Augustine and Gomarus, that grace is irresistible. "As to the manner in which this grace operates, it is not irresistible, for it is written that many resisted the Holy Spirit." Finally, the fifth article discusses whether those who have believed in Christ can fall from grace or not. The Gomarists argued that the power of predestination is such that those who have been predestined to faith cannot lose the grace they have received. The Remonstrants simply responded that biblical teaching on this point is not clear, and that they would need clearer scriptural proof before committing themselves in one direction or the other.

A few years later, political circumstances took a turn against the Remonstrants. Prince Maurice of Nassau—the son and heir of William of Orange —who had refrained from intervening in the debate, took the side of the Gomarists and of those who wished no contact with Spain. Johann van Oldenbarnevelt (or simply Barnevelt), the leading figure in negotiations with Spain, was imprisoned. His friend Hugo Grotius—best known as one of the founders of international law—was also arrested. As part of this reaction against the mercantile party and the Arminians, the Dutch Estates General convoked a great ecclesiastical assembly to put an end to the debate between Gomarists and Remonstrants.

That assembly, known as the Synod of Dort, met from November 1618 to May 1619. In calling it, the Estates General were seeking the support, not only of Dutch Calvinists, but also of those in other parts of Europe. Therefore, invitations were extended to other Reformed churches, and a total of twenty-seven delegates attended from Great Britain, Switzerland, and Germany (the French Huguenots were forbidden to attend by Louis XIII). The Dutch were almost seventy, of which roughly half were ministers and professors of theology, a quarter were lay elders, and the rest were members of the Estates General. The first sessions of the synod were devoted to administrative matters, and also ordered that a new Dutch translation of the Bible be produced. But the main purpose of the gathering was the condemnation of Arminianism, necessary in order to end the strife that was dividing the Netherlands and to secure the support of other Reformed churches. Thus, although the synod did not approve the most extreme theses of Gomarus—who was one of its members—it did agree on the need to condemn Arminianism.

The canons of the Synod of Dort affirmed five doctrines the Remonstrants could not accept, and from that point on those five doctrines have become the hallmark of orthodox Calvinism. The first of these is the doctrine of unconditional election. This means that the election of the predestined is not based on God's foreknowledge of each one's response to the offer of salvation, but only on the inscrutable will of God. The second is limited atonement. The Remonstrants claimed that Christ had died for all humankind. Against them, the Synod of Dort declared that he died only for the elect. Third, the synod affirmed that, although there is still in fallen humans a vestige of natural light, human nature has been so corrupted that that light cannot be properly used. And this is true, not only in that which refers to the knowledge of God and to conversion, but also in things "civil and natural." The fourth basic tenet of Dort is irresistible grace. And, finally, the synod affirmed the perseverance of the saints, that is, that the elect will persevere in grace, and cannot fall from it. Although such perseverance is not the work of the believer, but of God, it should serve to give us trust in our own salvation, and steadfastness in doing good, even though we see the power of sin still active in us. (It has become commonplace among students of theology to remember these five points by thinking of the word "tulip": "T" for total depravity, "U" for unconditional election, "L" for limited atonement, "I" for irresistible grace, and "P" for perseverance of the saints.)

Immediately after the Synod of Dort, severe measures were taken against the Remonstrants. Van Oldenbarnevelt was condemned to death, and Hugo Grotius to life imprisonment—although shortly thereafter, with his wife's help, he managed to escape by hiding in a trunk supposedly full of books. Almost a hundred Arminian ministers were ordered to leave the country, and many others were deprived of their pulpits. Those who insisted on preaching Arminianism were condemned to life imprisonment. The laity who attended Arminian services had to pay heavy fines. Teachers were also required to subscribe to the decisions of Dort. In some places, similar statements were even required of church organists—one of whom was said to have remarked that he did not know how to play the organ according to the canons of Dort.

Maurice of Nassau died in 1625, and after that time measures against the Remonstrants were less rigorous. Finally, in 1631, they were granted official tolerance. They then organized their own churches, many of which continue to this day. The major impact of Arminianism, however, did not take place through these churches, but rather through other groups and movements—particularly the Methodists—that espoused their teachings.

The Westminster Confession

In chapter 17 we told the story of the events leading to the convocation of the Westminster Assembly, postponing the discussion of the theological content of the Westminster Confession until the present chapter, for that confession is one of the clearest and most important examples of the spirit of Calvinist orthodoxy. The Westminster Confession is much more detailed and extensive than the canons of Dort, for it deals with a great variety of themes. Therefore, it cannot be summarized here, and we must be content with pointing to some of the crucial sections that show the agreement of Calvinist orthodoxy in England with its counterpart as seen in the Synod of Dort.

The first chapter deals with the authority of Scripture, the "Supreme Judge" in all religious controversy. Since not all the Bible is equally clear, it states that "the infallible rule of interpretation of Scripture is the Scripture

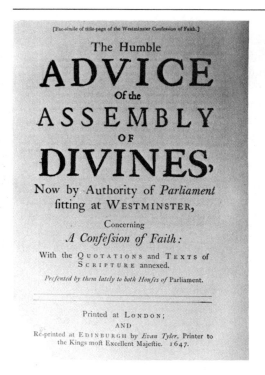

[Fac-simile of title-page of the Westminster Confession of Faith.]

The Humble

ADVICE
Of the

ASSEMBLY
OF

DIVINES,

Now by Authority of *Parliament*
fitting at WESTMINSTER,

Concerning

A Confeſsion of Faith:

With the QUOTATIONS and TEXTS of
SCRIPTURE annexed.

Preſented by them lately to both Houſes of Parliament.

Printed at LONDON;
AND
Re-printed at EDINBURGH by *Evan Tyler,* Printer to
the Kings moſt Excellent Majeſtie. 1647.

The Westminster Confession became one of the foremost documents of orthodox Calvinism, particularly in English-speaking countries.

itself" (1.9). This means that any obscure texts must be interpreted in the light of clearer ones. After discussing the doctrine of the Trinity in traditional terms, the Confession moves on to "God's Eternal Decree," about which it affirms that from all eternity God did "freely and unchangeably ordain whatsoever comes to pass" (3.1). Part of this decree is that some people and angels have been predestined to eternal life, and others to eternal death. Furthermore, this is in no way based on God's foreknowledge of the future actions or responses of individuals.

The Westminster Confession also agrees with Dort that the result of Adam's sin is "this original corruption, whereby we are utterly indisposed, disabled, and made opposite to all good, and wholly inclined to all evil" (6.4). And it also affirms limited atonement in declaring that Christ saves all those whose redemption he also acquired. After sin, human beings have lost all freedom to incline to salvation, which can only result from the "effectual calling" with which God works in the wills of the elect, "determining them to that which is good" (10.1). These elect are justified when the Holy Spirit, at the proper time, applies to them the work of Christ. Then follows sanctification which, although imperfect in this life, is inevitable. Such people "can neither totally nor finally fall away from the state of grace; but shall certainly persevere therein to the end, and be eternally saved" (17.1).

This is then followed by a long series of chapters on the matters being discussed in England at the time of the Puritan revolution, such as the manner in which the Lord's Day is to be observed, whether or not it is lawful to make an oath, the organization of the church, and so forth. But it is clear that the theology of the Westminster Confession is very similar to that of Dort, both in content and in its careful attention to strict orthodoxy. Thus, the study of the canons of Dort and of the Westminster Confession shows the nature of Calvinist orthodoxy in the seventeenth century—and even into the eighteenth. While claiming to be a faithful interpreter of Calvin, it tended to turn the theology of the Genevan Reformer into a strict system that Calvin himself might have had difficulty recognizing. Calvin had discovered in his own life the liberating joy of justification by the unmerited grace of God. For him, the doctrine of predestination was a means of expressing that joy, and the unmerited nature of salvation. But, in the hands of his followers, it became a test of orthodoxy and even of divine favor. At times, they even seemed to confuse doubt regarding the doctrine of predestination with actual reprobation and consequent damnation. There was little left here of the humanist spirit of Calvin, a man who loved literature as an art and who wrote with the elegance and care of a humanist.

21/The Rationalist Option

The reasoning, simple and easy to understand, that geometricians use to reach their most difficult demonstrations had made me think that all that can be encompassed by human knowledge is linked in the same fashion.

RENÉ DESCARTES

Rationalism, an attitude that reached its apex in the eighteenth and nineteenth centuries, was characterized by its interest in the world and by its confidence in the powers of reason. In western Europe, there had been a growing interest in the world of nature since the thirteenth century. That was the time of Albert the Great and Thomas Aquinas, who reintroduced Aristotelian philosophy as a fundamental tool for theology. One of the points of contrast between Aristotelianism and the Platonism that until then had dominated theological thought was precisely that the new philosophy emphasized the importance of sense perception. This meant that the observation of the world could lead to true and significant knowledge, and therefore from the time of Albert the Great—who wrote about animals—there had been a growing interest in the world of nature. The later Middle Ages, with its distrust of speculation, continued the same tendency. In a way, the art of the Renaissance, with its appreciation for the beauty of the human body and of the world, was a further expression of this interst. By the seventeenth century, many thought that the goal of reason was the understanding of the world of nature.

But, parallel to that interest in the world, there appeared—mostly at the time of the Renaissance—a growing confidence in the powers of reason. Often, these two elements were joined in the effort to show the degree to which the order of nature coincides with the order of reason. This may be seen, for instance, in the work of Galileo, who was convinced that the entire natural world was a system of mathematical relations, and that the ideal of knowledge was the reduction of all phenomena to their quantitative expression. Every success of such efforts seemed to confirm the most optimistic expectations of the power of reason.

Descartes and Cartesian Rationalism

These various tendencies led to the philosophy of René Descartes, whose lifetime approximately coincided with the first half of the seventeenth century (1596–1650). His philosophical system was based on a great confidence in mathematical reasoning, joined to a profound distrust of all that is not absolutely certain. He would, therefore, compare his philosophical method to geometry, a discipline that accepts only what is an undeniable axiom, or has been rationally proven.

In applying that method, Descartes felt that he ought to begin by an attitude of universal doubt, thus making sure that, once he found something that could not be doubted, he could be absolutely certain of its truth. He then found that undeniable first truth in his own existence. He could doubt everything, but not that the doubting subject existed. "I think, therefore I am"—in Latin, *cogito, ergo sum*—became the starting point for his philosophy. This "I" whose existence cannot be doubted, however, is only the philosopher as a "thinking thing," for the existence of his body has not been proven, and must still be doubted.

Before proving his own existence as a body, however, Descartes felt that he could prove the existence of God. He found in his mind the idea of a "more perfect being," and since his mind could not produce such an idea, which was above itself, it must have been placed there by God. Therefore, Descartes's second conclusion was that God exists. It was only then, on the basis of the existence of God, and of trust in the divine perfection, that Descartes felt free to move on to prove the existence of the world and of his own body.

Descartes was a profoundly religious man who hoped that his philosophy would be found useful by theologians. But not all agreed with him on this matter. Since it was the time of strict orthodoxies, many theologians feared the challenge of Cartesianism—as his philosophy was called, for his Latin name was Cartesius. The universal doubt that Descartes proposed as his starting point seemed to some no better than crass skepticism. The theological faculties of several universities declared that Aristotelianism was the philosophical system best suited to Christian theology, and there were even those who declared that Cartesianism would necessarily lead to heresy. Dismayed by such criticism, Descartes decided to leave his native France and accepted the invitation of the queen of Sweden to reside in that northern land, where he lived the rest of his days.

French philosopher René Descartes found that,
although he could doubt everything else, he
could not doubt the fact that he was thinking.

But there were others who were enthused by Cartesianism, and saw in it the promise of a theological renewal. In France, those intellectual circles in which Jansenism was in vogue embraced Cartesianism as its philosophical counterpart. Eventually, others among the more orthodox also took up his philosophical system, and the debate regarding the value of Cartesianism continued for a long time.

The main point at which Cartesianism led to further theological and philosophical developments was the question of the relationship between spirit and matter. Descartes had affirmed that humans consist of two parts: one that thinks—*res cogitans*—and one that occupies space—*res extensa*—or, in more traditional terms, soul and body. This was perfectly acceptable to the orthodoxy of the time. The problem, however, was that Descartes had been unable to offer a satisfactory explanation of the manner in which these two relate. When the mind thinks, how are its decisions communicated to the body? When something affects the body, how is this communicated to the soul? Three main solutions were offered to this difficulty: occasionalism, monism, and preestablished harmony. Occasionalism was defended by the Flemish philosopher Arnold Geulincx and by the French priest Nicolas Malebranche. They held that the body and soul do not communicate directly, but only by divine intervention. It is God that moves the body "on occasion" of the soul's decision, and the soul "on occasion" of the body's feelings and requirements. Although the occasionalists argued that this view magnified God's greatness, their position was not generally accepted, for it seemed to blame God for all events and thoughts.

Monism—from the Greek *monos*, "one"—was held by the Dutch Jew Benedictus (or Baruch) de Spinoza. He sought to offer an explanation of reality following a methodology similar to that of mathematics, as Descartes had suggested. He solved the problem of the communication of soul and body—and of the communication of any other substances—by denying that there is more than one substance. Thought and physical extension are not two different substances, but two attributes of a single substance, as "red" and "round" are attributes of a single apple. The same may be said about "God" and the "world," for these are merely different attributes of the one substance which is the universe. Needless to say, these doctrines found little support among orthodox Christians, for whom belief in a God who exists apart from the world was essential.

Finally, the German philosopher and mathematician Gottfried Wilhelm Leibniz suggested "preestablished harmony." In contrast to Spinoza, Leibniz began with the existence of an infinite number of substances, absolutely independent from each other, which he called "monads." These monads, as he said, "have no windows," that is, cannot communicate with each other. Nor does God make them communicate. Rather, from the very beginning, God has created these monads so that they may act in seeming interdependence. The manner in which soul and body communicate is very similar to that in which various clocks in a shop "communicate" among themselves: they do not. Rather, they all work according to the preestablished order set by the clockmaker. If the clockmaker was a good one, it will seem as if all the clocks communicate with each other in order to keep the same time. This solution also met a great deal of opposition for—although such was not Leibniz's intent—it seemed to imply that God had foreordained all things, both good and evil, and that there was no such thing as human freedom.

Empiricism

While these philosophical developments were taking place on the Continent, in Great Britain philosophy was following a different route: "empiricism"— from a Greek word meaning "experience." Its leading figure was Oxford professor John Locke, who in 1690 published his *Essay on Human Understanding*. He had read the works of Descartes, and agreed that the order of the world corresponded to the order of the mind. But he did not believe that there were innate ideas, which one could discover by looking into oneself. On the contrary, he held that all knowledge is derived from experience— both the "outer experience" of the senses, and the "inner experience" by which we know ourselves and the functioning of our minds. This means that the only true knowledge is that based on our three levels of experience: our own selves, whose existence we continually experience; those outer realities that are presently before us; and God, whose existence is proven at each moment by the existence of the self and its experiences. Apart from these three levels, there is no certain knowledge.

But there is another level of knowledge, that of probability, which plays an important role in human life. At this level, we do not apply the strict proofs of reason, but rather those of "judgment." Judgment allows us to surmise that, since we have repeatedly experienced John's existence, it is probable that he continues to exist even when he is not before us. Judgment, although not absolutely certain, is necessary, for it is on its basis that we conduct most of our affairs in life.

Faith is assent to knowledge that is derived from revelation rather than from reason. Therefore, its knowledge, although highly probable, is never certain. Reason and judgment must be used in order to measure the degree of probability of what we are asked to believe by faith. For this reason, Locke opposed the "fanatical enthusiasm" of those who think that all they say is based on divine revelation. For the same reason, he defended religious toleration. Intolerance is born out of the muddled thinking that confuses the probable judgments of faith with the certainty of empirical reason. Besides, toleration is based on the very nature of society. The state does not have the authority to limit the freedom of its citizens in a matter as personal as religion.

In 1695, Locke published a treatise, *The Reasonableness of Christianity*, in which he claimed that Christianity is the most reasonable of religions. According to him, the core of Christianity is the existence of God and faith in Christ as the Messiah. But Locke did not believe that Christianity had added anything of importance to what could in any case have been known by the right use of reason and judgment. In the final analysis, Christianity was little more than a very clear expression of truths and laws that others could have known by their natural faculties.

Deism

Locke's opinions regarding religion reflected a way of thinking that was becoming widespread even before the publication of his works. Tired of the endless squabbles among the partisans of the many sects and movements that appeared in England in the seventeenth century, many sought an understanding of religion that went beyond narrow and quibbling orthodoxy. A common alternative was that of the Deists, or "freethinkers"—called Deists because they rejected what they considered the aberrations of the atheists, and freethinkers in contrast to those who held to the narrow limits of orthodoxy.

The first great figure of Deism was Lord Herbert of Cherbury, who held that true religion must be universal, not only in the sense of calling for the allegiance of all, but also in the sense of being a religion that is natural to all humankind. Such religion is not based on particular revelations, nor on historical events, but rather on the natural instincts of every human being. Its basic doctrines are five: the existence of God, the obligation to worship God, the ethical requirements of such worship, the need for repentance, and reward and punishment, both in this life and in the one to follow. Although there may possibly be divine revelation, any doctrine claiming to stem from it must not contradict these five basic points; and in any case, since such a revelation is given only to part of humanity, there is no reason to expect all to accept it.

Shortly after the publication of Locke's *Essay*, John Toland published what would become one of the classics of Deism, *Christianity not Mysterious, or a Treatise Showing that there Is Nothing in the Gospel Contrary nor Above It, and that no Christian Doctrine Can Be Properly Called a Mystery*; and, in 1730, Matthew Tindal published *Christianity as Old as the World, or the Gospel a Republication of the Religion of Nature*. The very titles of these works suffice to show the nature of Deism, and its effort to show that whatever there is of value in Christianity coincides with "natural religion."

Deism fought on two fronts. On the one hand, it opposed the narrow dogmatism that had taken hold of most branches of Christianity. On the other, it tried to refute the easy skepticism of those who, tired of the quibbling of the theologians, simply abandoned all religion. But many Christians, while not narrowly dogmatic, were uneasy with the manner in which Deism tended to discount the significance of particular historical events and revelation, for this discounted the significance of Jesus Christ. Eventually, however, the most devastating criticism of Deism came not from theologians, but from a Scottish philosopher who showed that "reason" was not as "reasonable" as the Deists and other rationalists believed. His name was David Hume.

David Hume and His Critique of Empiricism

Hume (1711–1776) was a man of boundless optimism who was nevertheless very pessimistic as to the powers of reason. His own optimism made it possible for him to be skeptical about much that the philosophers said, for he would not crumble even if the entire edifice of philosophy came tumbling down. On the contrary, he felt free to allow his intellectual curiosity to lead him wherever it would. Thus, taking as his starting point Locke's empiricism, he came to the conclusion that the scope of true knowledge was much more limited than the rationalists claimed. Indeed, a goodly part of what those

David Hume was the man whom Kant credited with having wakened him from his "dogmatic slumber."

philosophers thought they could affirm on the basis of observation and reason had no such basis, but was simply the result of irrational mental habits. And among such things that the mind takes for granted are such fundamental notions as those of substance and of cause and effect.

The empiricists claimed that only that knowledge that is based on experience was true. But Hume pointed out that no one has ever seen or experienced what we call cause and effect. We have indeed seen, for instance, that a billiard ball arrives at the place where another one is lying. Then we hear a noise and we see the first ball stop and the second one move. If we repeat this experiment several times, we get similar results. And then we say that the movement of the first ball "caused" the movement of the other one. But the truth is that we have not seen any such thing. All that we have seen is a series of phenomena, and our mind has linked them by means of the notion of cause and effect. This last step, taken by any who see a series of phenomena that are seemingly related, has no basis in empirical observation. It is rather the result of our mental habits. Therefore, according to the empiricists' definition, it is not rational knowledge.

The same can be said of the idea of substance. We say, for instance, that we see an apple. But in truth what our senses perceive is a series of attributes: form, color, weight, taste, smell, and so forth. We also perceive that those attributes coincide in one place, and that they seem to cling together, as if something united them. And then our mind, by one of those habits that are not truly rational, declares that all these attributes reside in a substance that we call apple. But, once again, we have not experienced the substance itself. Pure reason does not allow us to affirm that there are such things as substances in which the various attributes that we perceive reside.

This critique of empiricist rationalism put an end to Deism. If the relation of cause and effect is not truly rational, the proof that the Deists use for the existence of God, namely, that someone must have caused this world, is no longer valid. Likewise, notions such as the "soul" and "God" have little meaning if we cannot rationally speak of anything but attributes, and never of substances beyond them.

New Currents in France

Meanwhile, new currents of thought were developing in France and other areas of the Continent. The great figure of this new philosophy was François-Marie Arouet, better known under his pen name, "Voltaire." His political views led to a period of imprisonment in the Bastille, an exile in London, and several years of expatriation in Switzerland. But the more French authorities tried to suppress his teachings, the more he was admired by his fellow citizens. He was an enemy of all fanaticism. Witnessing the persecution of

French Protestants during the last years of Louis XIV's reign, he was convinced that such persecution was wrong and would forever be seen as a stain on the name of the Sun King. When he read Locke's writings on political and religious tolerance, he took up that cause, and devoted his wit and his literary ability to it. But he was not convinced by the optimistic rationalism then in vogue. He commented that Cartesianism was like a good novel, in which all is credible and nothing is true. He also mocked the English Deists for claiming to know about God and the soul more than it is given to human reason to know.

Thus, Voltaire and his followers were rationalists in their own way. His satirical wit—which he also applied to himself—scoffed at all the great systems that were then fashionable. But he did believe in the use of reason as common sense, whose dictates life must follow. Furthermore, he argued that the history of humankind was no more than the history of a progressive understanding of ourselves and our institutions, and our efforts to adjust to that ever-clearer understanding. In particular, this meant progress in the understanding and safeguarding of human rights. Monarchy, although a necessary part of government, was not intended for the benefit of the sovereign, but rather for that of the subjects, whose rights all must respect and defend. By stating and divulging such ideas, Voltaire was one of the forerunners of the French Revolution.

One of Voltaire's contemporaries, Charles Louis de Secondat, Baron de Montesquieu, sought to apply the principles of reason to the theory of government. He thus came to the conclusion that a republic is a better form of government than either despotism, which is based on terror, or monarchy, whose foundation is a prejudice called "honor." Since power corrupts, Montesquieu suggested that government should be exercised by three powers that would balance and limit each other: the legislative, the executive, and the judicial. Thus, by 1748, several decades before the American and French Revolutions, Montesquieu was proposing some of the basic doctrines of those movements.

At about the same time, Jean Jacques Rousseau was expounding other theories that were no less revolutionary. According to him, what we call "progress" is not really such, for what in truth has happened is that humankind has progressively departed from its natural state and fallen into artificiality. In the field of politics, this means that we must return to the original order, whose purpose was to serve the governed by safeguarding justice and freedom. Rulers are in truth employees of the people, and their task is to defend freedom and justice. In the field of religion, Rousseau held that dogmas and institutions are part of the corruption that has characterized the so-called human progress, and that it is necessary to return to natural religion, consisting of belief in God, the immortality of the soul, and the moral order.

Therefore, in various ways, and without agreeing on all matters, these various philosophers gave French rationalism a particular flavor, shunning the speculative flights of other rationalists, and concentrating rather on the social and political implications of reason understood as common sense. By so doing, they were preparing the way for the French Revolution.

Immanuel Kant

The philosophical movements of the seventeenth and eighteenth centuries led to the shattering critique of Immanuel Kant, one of the greatest philosophers of all time. He had been a firm believer in rationalism until, as he later declared, he was awakened from his "dogmatic slumber" by reading Hume. Cartesianism had not been able to overcome the difficulties posed by the problem of the communication of substances. Eventually, the Cartesian theory of innate ideas had led to Leibniz, for whom all ideas were innate, and there was no communication between the mind and other realities. Empiricism, on the other hand, had led to Hume's critique that, if only that knowledge is valid which is acquired through experience, there is no valid knowledge of such fundamental matters as the notion of cause and effect or the idea of substance.

In his *Critique of Pure Reason,* published in 1781, Kant proposed a radical alternative to both systems. According to him, there is no such thing as innate ideas; but there are fundamental structures of the mind, and within those structures we must place whatever data the senses provide us. Those structures are, first of all, time and space; and then twelve "categories," such as causality, existence, substance, and so forth. Time, space, and the twelve categories are not something that we perceive through the senses; rather, they are the structures that our mind has to use in order to organize the sensations that are fed to it by the senses. To make something thinkable, we must place it within the molds of our mental structures. The senses provide a chaotic multitude of sensations. It is only after the mind orders them within the structures of time, space, and the categories that they become intelligible "experiences."

Consequently, the simplistic rationalism of previous generations is no longer possible. In knowledge, what we have is not things as they are in themselves, but rather things as our mind is able to grasp them. Therefore, there is no such thing as purely objective knowledge, and the pure rationality of Cartesians, Empiricists, and Deists is no more than an illusion.

Kant's work also meant that many of the arguments traditionally used in support of Christian doctrine were no longer valid. For instance, since existence is not a datum derived from reality, but rather one of the categories of the mind, there is no way to prove the existence of God or of the soul. Nor can we speak of an "eternity" consisting in the absence of time, since our mind cannot really conceive such a thing. On the other hand, this does not mean an absolute denial of God, the soul, or eternity. What it means is that, if such things are true, reason cannot know them, just as the eye cannot hear and the ear cannot see.

What, then, is one to say about religion? Kant dealt with this subject in several of his works—particularly in his *Critique of Practical Reason,* published in 1788, where he argues that, although pure reason cannot prove the existence of God and the soul, there is a "practical reason" that has to do with the moral life, and whose procedure is different from that of pure reason. This practical reason, whose fundamental principle is "act in such a manner that the rule for your action can be made a universal rule," does know the existence of God as the judge of all action, of the soul and its freedom as the occasion for moral action, and of life after death as the means for rewarding good and punishing evil. All this is very similar to what the Deists had said, and therefore in discussing religious matters Kant did not go much beyond them.

Kant's significance for religion and theology, however, goes far beyond his rather uninspired attempts to ground religion on morality. His philosophical work dealt a deathblow to the easy rationalism of his predecessors, and to the notion that it is possible to speak in purely rational and objective terms of matters such as the existence of God and the future life. After him—as we shall see later, particularly in chapter 28—theologians dealing with the relationship between faith and reason had to take his work into account.

22/The Spiritualist Option

*I was glad that I was commanded to turn
people to that inward light, spirit, and
grace, by which all might know their
salvation, and their way to God; even that
divine Spirit which would lead them into
all Truth and which I infallibly knew
would never deceive any.*

GEORGE FOX

The seemingly endless debates on dogma, and the intolerance of
Christians among themselves, led many to seek refuge in a purely
spiritual religion. Also, excessive emphasis on correct doctrine
worked in favor of the higher classes, who had greater opportunities for education. Those who did not have such opportunities, and who
therefore could not discuss complicated matters of theology, were seen as
children, needing someone to guide them through the intricacies of dogma
in order not to fall into error. Therefore, the spiritualist movement of the
seventeenth and eighteenth centuries attracted both cultured people who had
little use for narrow-minded dogmatism, and others of little or no formal
education who found in the movement an opportunity for expressing themselves. Thus, while some of the founders of spiritualist groups or schools
were relatively unschooled, they soon had among their ranks others of more
education and higher social standing.

Due to the nature of the spiritualist movement, its history is difficult to
trace. The movement produced a multitude of currents and leaders whose
followers and doctrines are so entwined that it is not always possible to
distinguish among them, or to determine who was the originator of a particular idea. Therefore, the simplest way to grasp the nature of the movement
is by turning our attention to three of its main leaders, who are also quite
different among themselves: Boehme, Fox, and Swedenborg.

Jakob Boehme

Jakob Boehme (1575–1624) was born in the German region of Silesia. His parents were staunch Lutherans of humble means. In the midst of that pious family, young Jakob developed a deep faith; but the sermons of that time, long dissertations on theological debates, caused him to lose interest. He was fourteen years old when his father made him apprentice to a cobbler, and that was his occupation for the rest of his life. But, shortly after beginning his apprenticeship, he began having visions; and eventually his master threw him out, declaring that he wanted an apprentice, not a prophet.

Boehme then became a wandering cobbler, traveling from place to place mending shoes. In those travels he came to the conclusion that the leadership of the church had built a veritable "tower of Babel" with its interminable quibbling debates. He therefore determined to cultivate his inner life, and to read all he could find on that subject. Thus he reached a series of conclusions on the nature of the world and of human life, and those conclusions were confirmed in visions and other spiritual experiences. But for some time he kept these convictions and experiences to himself, and was content with his life as a cobbler. When he was about twenty-five years old, he put an end to his wanderings and set up a shop in the town of Goerlitz, where he was able to make a fairly comfortable living.

Although he did not feel called to preach, Boehme was convinced that God had ordered him to write down his visions. The result was the book *Brilliant Dawn,* in which the seer repeatedly asserted that he was writing what God had dictated word for word, and that he was no more than a pen in the hands of God. Boehme did not publish his book, but a manuscript copy reached the local pastor, who accused him before the magistrates. Under threat of deportation, Boehme promised to teach or write no more on religious matters, and for five years kept his promise. But in 1618, impelled by new visions and by some of his admirers, he began writing anew. One of his followers, without his permission, published three of his works, and these also reached the pastor, who once again accused him of heresy. As a result, Boehme was forced to leave Goerlitz.

He then went to the court of the elector of Saxony, where several theologians examined his teachings without reaching a conclusion, for they confessed themselves unable to understand exactly what he meant. Their recommendation was that Boehme be given more time to clarify his ideas. But he would not be granted that time, for he fell ill and decided to return to Goerlitz in order to die there among his friends and followers. He was fifty years old when he died.

The report of the theologians, that they could not understand what he meant, was not simply a subterfuge to avoid pronouncing judgment. The truth is that Boehme's writings are subject to various interpretations. In them, one finds an odd mixture of traditionally Christian themes with others taken from magic, alchemy, occultism, and theosophy. How all this relates is never clear, and the ambiguities are made greater by his use of daring metaphors that are never explained. What does he mean, for instance, by "the eternal womb," or by "the mother of all births"? Are these simply other names for God, or are they intended to convey something else?

In any case, what is important for us at this time is not the exact content of Boehme's teachings, but their basic direction. And this is very clear. It is a reaction against the cold dogmatism of the theologians, and against the seemingly empty liturgy of the church. Against these, Boehme exalted the freedom of the spirit, the inner life, and direct and individual revelation. He declared, for instance, that since "the letter kills," believers ought not to be guided by Scripture, but by the Holy Spirit, who inspired the biblical writers and even now inspires believers. As he said, "I have enough with the book that I am. If I have within me the Spirit of Christ, the entire Bible is in me. Why would I wish for more books? Why discuss what is outside, while not having learned what is within me?"*

Boehme did not have many followers during his lifetime, but his books later gained him many admirers. In England, some of these joined to form a "Boehmenist" movement, some of whose followers clashed with the Quakers of George Fox. Thus, the spiritualist movement, born in part as a protest against the doctrinal debates of traditional theology, was eventually immersed in similar controversies.

George Fox and the Quakers

George Fox (1624–1961) was born in a small English village in the year of Boehme's death. He too was of humble origin, and he too was a cobbler's apprentice. But at nineteen years of age, disgusted at the licentiousness of his fellow apprentices and feeling compelled by the Spirit of God, he quit his occupation and began a life of wandering and attending religious meetings of all sorts, seeking for illumination from on high. He also devoted himself to the study of Scripture, and it was said that he knew it by heart. Fox experienced many inner conflicts, at times despairing of finding truth, and at other times encouraged by religious experiences. Slowly, he came to the conviction that all the various sects that abounded in England were wrong, and their worship was an abomination before God.

If God does not dwell in houses made by human hands, how dare anyone call those buildings where they gather "churches"? They are in truth

---

*Apology to Tilken. 2:298.

4. George Fox Visits Swarthmoor Hall

George Fox, founder of the Quakers, or Friends, differed from other spiritualist leaders in that he paid great attention to the community of believers and to its social obligations.

no more than houses with belfries. Pastors who work for a salary are not real shepherds, but "priests" and "journeymen." Hymns, orders of worship, sermons, sacraments, creeds, ministers—they are all human hindrances to the freedom of the Spirit. Over against all these things, Fox placed the "inner light." This is a seed that exists in all human beings, and is the true way we must follow in order to find God. The Calvinist doctrine of the total depravity of humanity is a denial of the love of God and of the experience of those who love God. On the contrary, there is an inner light in everyone, no matter how dimmed it may be. Thanks to that light, pagans can be saved as well as Christians. This light, however, must not be confused with the intellect or with conscience. It is not the "natural reason" of the Deists, nor a series of moral principles that point to God. It is rather the capability we all have to recognize and accept the presence of God. It is by it that we are able to believe and understand Scripture. Therefore, communication with God through the inner light is previous to any communication by external means.

Although those who were close to him knew something of the fire burning within Fox, for several years he abstained from proclaiming what he was convinced he had discovered regarding the true meaning of faith and Christianity. At that time there were in England many religious sects, and Fox attended all without finding contentment in any. Finally, he felt called by the Spirit to speak out at a Baptist meeting, announcing the inner truths in which he now believed. From that point, such urgings of the Spirit became more frequent. In gatherings of various sects, Fox would declare that he had been ordered by the Spirit to announce his spiritual vision of Christianity. His words were often received with contempt and hostility, and he was repeatedly thrown out of meetings, beaten, and stoned. But such incidents would not stop him, and soon thereafter he was in another "house with a belfry," interrupting the service and proclaiming his message. The number of his followers grew rapidly. At first they called themselves "children of light"; Fox prefered the name of "friends." But those who saw that their religious enthusiasm was such that they would tremble began calling them "quakers," and that was the name by which they became known.

Since Fox and his followers believed that any structure in worship could be an obstacle to the work of the Spirit, the Friends' service of worship took place in silence. Any who felt called to speak or pray aloud were free to do so. When the Spirit moved them, women had the same right to speak as did men. Fox himself did not prepare to speak at such meetings, but simply allowed the Spirit to move him. There were times when many had gathered hoping to hear him speak, but he refused to do so because he did not feel moved by the Spirit. Also, the Quakers did not include in their services the traditional sacraments of baptism and communion, for they feared that physical water, bread, and wine would draw attention away from the spiritual. This was the main reason for their conflict with the Boehmenists, who continued celebrating the sacraments—although calling them "ordinances."

Fox was aware of the danger that his emphasis on the freedom of the Spirit would lead to excessive individualism. Other movements with a similar emphasis have not lasted long, for the exercise of individual freedom has led to the dissolution of the group. Fox avoided this danger by underscoring the importance of community and love. In the Friends' meetings, decisions were not made by majority vote. If an agreement was not reached, the decision was postponed, and the meeting continued in silence until the Spirit offered a solution. If one was not received, the matter was left pending for another occasion.

There were many who disliked the teachings and practices of Fox and the Quakers. Religious leaders resented the manner in which these "fanatics" interrupted their services in order to preach or to read Scripture. The powerful felt the need to teach a lesson to these "Friends," who refused to pay tithes, to swear an oath, to bow before their "betters," or to uncover their head before any but God. The Quakers argued that, since God was addressed in the familiar "Thou," no other being ought to be addressed in the more respectful "You." To many who were used to the submission of their "inferiors," all this seemed disrespectful and an intolerable insubordination.

As a result, Fox was repeatedly beaten, and he spent a total of six years in prison. He was sent to prison for the first time for having interrupted a preacher who declared that the ultimate truth was to be found in Scripture, and arguing that this was not true, for ultimate truth was in the Spirit who had inspired Scripture. On other occasions he was accused of blasphemy, or

*In the Quaker meetings, women as well as men were allowed to
speak whenever the Spirit moved them. This brought ridicule on the
Friends, as shown in this contemporary drawing.*

of conspiring against the government. When the authorities offered to pardon him, he refused, declaring that he was not guilty, and that to accept a
pardon for something he had not done was to lie. On another occasion, when
he was serving six months for blasphemy, he was offered his freedom in
exchange for service in the republican army. He refused, declaring that
Christians ought not to use any other weapons than those of the Spirit, and
had his sentence prolonged by an additional six months. From that point on,
the Friends have been known for their staunch pacifist convictions.

When he was not in prison, Fox spent most of the time in his house in
Swarthmore, and this became the headquarters of the Friends. The rest of
the time he traveled throughout England and abroad, visiting Quaker meetings and taking his message to new areas. First he went to Scotland, where
he was accused of sedition; then to Ireland; later he spent two years in the
Caribbean and North America; and he also made two visits to the Continent.
In all these lands he gained converts, and by the time of his death, in 1691,
his followers were counted by the tens of thousands.

They too were persecuted. They were thrown in jail for vagrancy, blasphemy, inciting to riot, and refusing to pay tithes. In 1664, Charles II issued an edict forbidding unlicensed religious assemblies. Many groups continued gathering in secret. But the Quakers declared that it would be a lie to do so, and therefore simply disobeyed the royal edict. Thousands were then imprisoned, and by the time religious tolerance was granted in 1689, hundreds had died in prison.

The most famous of Fox's followers was William Penn, after whom the state of Pennsylvania is named. His father was a British admiral who tried to secure for him the best education available. While he was a student, young William became a Puritan. Then, while studying in France, he came under the influence of the Huguenots. In 1667, back in England, he became a Quaker. His father, not knowing what to do with so "fanatical" a son, threw him out of the house. Penn continued firm in his convictions, and eventually had to spend seven months in the Tower of London. It is said that at that time he sent word to the king, that the Tower was the worst of arguments to convince him, since, no matter who is right, whoever uses force to seek religious assent is necessarily wrong. Finally, thanks to the intervention of his father and other well-placed friends, he was set free. He then spent several years raising a family, traveling throughout Europe, and writing in defense of the Friends.

His arguments in defense of religious tolerance, however, were not well received. Some even said that he was secretly a Jesuit, and that his true goal was to restore to Roman Catholics the privileges they had lost. It was then that Penn conceived the idea of what he called his "holy experiment." Some friends had spoken to him about New Jersey, in North America. Since the crown owed him a significant amount, and was not willing to pay in cash, Penn was able to obtain from Charles II a grant of land in what is now Pennsylvania. His purpose was to found a new colony in which there would be complete religious freedom. By then other British colonies had been founded in North America. But, with the exception of Rhode Island, all were marked by religious intolerance. In Massachusetts, the most intolerant of the colonies, Quakers were persecuted, condemned to exile, and even mutilated and executed. What Penn now proposed was a new colony in which all would be free to worship according to their own convictions. This seemed bad enough to an intolerant age. But even worse was Penn's plan to buy from the Indians the land that the crown had granted him. He was convinced that the Indians, and not the crown, were the legitimate owners of the land. And he hoped to establish such cordial relations with them that the settlers would have no need to defend themselves by force of arms. The capital of this holy experiment would be called "Philadelphia"—the city of "fraternal love."

No matter how ill-conceived Penn's experiment might have seemed to the more "solid" British citizens, soon there were many people, not only in England, but also in other parts of Europe, willing to take part in it. Many of them were Quakers, and therefore the Friends dominated the political life of the colony for some time. But there were also settlers of many different persuasions. Under the leadership of Penn, who was the first governor of the colony, relations with the Indians were excellent, and for a long time his dream of a peaceful settlement was a reality. Much later, in 1756, another governor declared war on the Indians, and the Quakers resigned their positions in government. But the religious tolerance that was part of Penn's "holy experiment" eventually was imbedded in the Constitution of the United States, as well as in those of many other countries.

Emanuel Swedenborg

George Fox was born in the year of Boehme's death; and Emanuel Swedenborg (1688–1772), to whom we now turn our attention, was born three years before the death of Fox. Therefore, the lives of the three leaders with whom we deal in this chapter span almost the totality of the seventeenth and eighteenth centuries.

Swedenborg's teachings were very similar to those of Boehme and Fox; but in other respects he was very different from them. While the other two were of humble birth, Swedenborg was born in an aristocratic family. And, also in contrast to them, he received the best education available, for he studied at the University of Uppsala, and then spent five years traveling in England, the Netherlands, France, and Germany, always in quest of knowledge. Also, while Fox and Boehme gave signs of their religious restlessness from an early age, young Swedenborg was interested in scientific studies, and it was through these that he began the quest that led him to his religious convictions.

After many years of scientific inquiry, Swedenborg had a vision he said had carried him into the spiritual world, where he had been able to see eternal truths. After that vision he wrote voluminously on the true meaning of reality and of Scripture. According to him, all that exists is a reflection of the attributes of God, and therefore the visible world "corresponds" with the invisible one. The same is true of Scripture, which reflects truths that can only be known by those who have entered the spiritual world.

Swedenborg was convinced that his writings would be the beginning of a new era in the history of the world and of religion. He even claimed that what had taken place when he received his revelations was what the Bible meant when speaking of the second coming of Christ. As was to be expected, such ideas were not well received by the majority of his contemporaries, and therefore the circle of his followers was very small. He himself did not feel called to found a new church, but rather to call the existing one to a new understanding of its nature and message. But in 1784, twelve years after his death, his disciples founded the Church of the New Jerusalem, whose members were never many, but which has survived into the twentieth century. Also, early in the nineteenth century, a "Swedenborgian Society" was founded, whose purpose was the publication and distribution of his writings.

Of the three religious leaders discussed in this chapter, only Fox was able to lead and organize a vast movement. This was partly because he was convinced that the community of believers was necessary for religious life. Also, Fox and his Friends contrasted with most other spiritualists in their interest in social problems, and their active participation in seeking solutions to social ills. But, apart from the case of the Quakers, the spiritualist movement was destined to have little impact on the church and on society at large, for its interests were individualistic and otherworldly. A far greater impact would be made by another movement of protest against both rationalism and cold dogmatism—a movement to which we shall now turn.

23/The Pietist Option

How many rich men are there among the Methodists (observe, there was not one, when they were first joined together) who actually do "deny themselves and take up their cross daily"? Who of you that are now rich, deny yourselves just as you did when you were poor?

JOHN WESLEY

Pietism was a response to the dogmatism of the theologians and the rationalism of the philosophers, both of which it contrasted with the living faith that is at the heart of Christianity. Although, in its strict sense, "Pietism" refers only to the German movement led by Spener and Francke, in this chapter we shall deal also with the similar movements led by Zinzendorf and Wesley.

German Pietism: Spener and Francke

Although many of the elements of what was later called "Pietism" were already circulating in Germany long before his time, Philipp Jakob Spener (1635–1705) has rightly been called the "father of Pietism." He was born and reared in Alsace, in an aristocratic family of deep Lutheran convictions. He studied theology in the best Protestant universities and, after receiving his doctorate, became a pastor in Frankfurt. There he founded groups of Bible study and devotion that he called "colleges of piety." In 1675, five years after beginning this experiment, he published his *Pia desideria,* where he outlined a program for the development of piety. This became the fundamental charter of Pietism.

In this book, Spener turned to the Lutheran doctrine of the universal priesthood of believers, and suggested that there be less emphasis on the differences between laity and clergy, and more on the common responsibility of all Christians. This in turn meant that there should be among the laity a more intense life of devotion and study. To attain this goal, Spener suggested small groups such as his "colleges of piety." As to pastors and theologians, he insisted that candidates should be examined to ascertain that they were "true Christians" of deep personal faith. And he also called on preachers to set aside their polemical and academic tone, for the purpose of preaching is not to show the preacher's knowledge, but rather to call believers to be obedient to the Word of God. In all this there was no attack on the doctrines of the church, for Spener was in total agreement with them. But he insisted that doctrine is not to serve as a substitute for personal faith. While it is true that theological error may have disastrous consequences for the Christian life, it is also true that those who do not go beyond dogma have scarcely penetrated the riches of Christianity. Thus, what he proposed was a new reformation—or at least the completion of what had begun in the sixteenth century and been interrupted by doctrinal debates. Soon many saw in him a new Luther, and from various parts of Germany he received letters thanking him for his inspiration and asking his advice.

All this, however, was not regarded with favor by the leaders of Lutheran orthodoxy. Although Spener did not deviate from Lutheran doctrine, he seemed to discount the fine points of doctrine that orthodoxy had clarified. And he insisted—like Luther before him—on the need to return constantly to Scriptures, and to read them with a spirit of devotion and piety. Furthermore, there was one point at which he seemed to deviate from the Lutheran tradition. Luther, concerned and overwhelmed as he was by the doctrine of justification by faith, had paid scant attention to sanctification. In the struggles of the time, he had insisted that what was important was not the manner of life of the believer, but the grace of God—for it is grace, and not personal sanctity, that justifies. Calvin and the Reformed tradition, while agreeing with Luther on justification, insisted that the God who justifies is also the One who sanctifies, and that God offers to believers the power for holiness of life. On this point, Spener and his followers were closer to Calvin than to Luther. Spener himself had been influenced by Reformed teachers, and was convinced that Lutheranism should lay more emphasis on the need for sanctification. For this reason, many orthodox Lutheran theologians declared that he was in truth a Calvinist.

Spener also made himself vulnerable by his apocalypticism. As has happened so often in difficult times, he became convinced that the prophecies of the book of Revelation were being fulfilled, and that the end was near. Since his predictions did not come true, his enemies could argue that, having erred on that point, he was probably mistaken on others as well.

In a sense, what was at stake in the controversy over Pietism was whether the Christian faith should simply serve to sanction common morality, or should rather call believers to a different sort of life. Orthodox preaching took for granted that God requires of believers nothing more than correct doctrine and a decent life. The Pietists insisted on the contrast between what society expects of its members and what God requires of the faithful. This has always been an uncomfortable challenge for a comfortable church.

Spener's greatest follower was August Hermann Francke, also from a well-to-do Lutheran family. His teachings were similar to Spener's—although he did not agree with the latter's interpretation of current events as those described in Revelation. Even more than Spener, he insisted on the joy of Christian life, which should be a song of praise to God. As a professor at the University of Halle, he also paid more attention to the relationship between Pietism and traditional Lutheran theology. He described his own religious experience as follows:

Suddenly, God heard me. As easily as one turns a hand, my doubts vanished. In my heart I was certain of the grace of God in Jesus Christ. Since then I was able to call God, not only "God," but also "Father." Sadness and anxiety immediately left my heart. And I was suddenly overcome by a wave of joy, such that I praised and magnified God aloud, who had granted me such grace.*

This description of a religious experience, coupled with those of Wesley and others, has led to the false assumption that Pietists insisted on the need for such a personal experience. In fact, in its early stages the movement advocated a living, personal faith, and the manner or time in which one came to it was not of prime importance.

Thousands of Christians embraced the Pietist movement, and joined in small circles or "colleges of piety," even though some theologians accused the movement of being emotional, subjective, and even heretical. Eventually, in spite of such opposition, Pietism left its mark on the entire Lutheran tradition. And, although both Spener and Francke were Lutherans, Pietism also gained adherents among the German Reformed. The outstanding figure of Reformed Pietism was F. A. Lampe (1683–1729), whose hymns, sermons, and books did much to spread the spirit of Pietism. Lampe avoided the technical language that was typical of orthodoxy, and thus won a wide following among the laity, and bitter opposition from academic theologians. But Reformed orthodoxy in Germany did not have the political leverage of Lutheran orthodoxy, and therefore Reformed Pietism did not suffer the political pressures under which its Lutheran counterpart labored—at least, not until it moved into the Netherlands, where Reformed orthodoxy held sway. Later, in North America, the Great Awakening would be an indication of the degree to which Pietism was making inroads into the Reformed tradition.

However, the most significant contribution of Pietism to the story of

---

*Selbstzeugnisse ("Testimonies"), p. 25.

Christianity was the birth of Protestant missions. The reformers of the six-teenth century, involved as they were in a struggle for the survival of Protes-tanitism, paid little attention to the non-Christian world. Some even declared that modern Christians were not called to preach to other nations, since that was a commandment given exclusively to the apostles. At first, the Pietists were not interested in world missions, although they were active in meeting the needs of their fellow Christians by founding schools and institutions to serve orphans, the poor, and others in need. But, in 1707, the King of Denmark, an admirer of the Pietists, decided to send missionaries to his colonies in India. He could find no one in his own possessions to undertake this task, and asked that Francke send him two of his most promising disciples at the University of Halle. These two, Bartholomaeus Ziegenbalg and Hein-rich Plutschau, founded in India the mission of Tranquebar. Their letters and reports, circulated in Germany, awakened great interest among the Pietists. Soon, under Francke's direction, the University of Halle became a center for the training of missionaries. And in Denmark, with the king's support and under Pietist leadership, a school of missions was founded for training mis-sionaries to Lapland and Greenland.

Zinzendorf and the Moravians

Meanwhile, Pietism had also made an impact on the young Count Nikolaus Ludwig von Zinzendorf, whose godfather was Spener. Zinzendorf had been profoundly religious from childhood and would later declare, for that reason, that he had never felt separated from God, and could speak of no experience of conversion. His parents, devout Pietists, sent him to the University of Halle, where he studied under Francke. Later he also went to Wittenberg, one of the main centers of Lutheran orthodoxy, and repeatedly clashed with his teachers. After traveling to other countries, and studying law, he was married and entered the service of the court of Dresden.

It was at Dresden that Zinzendorf first met a group of Moravians who would change the course of his life. These were Hussites who had been forced to leave their native Moravia fleeing persecution, and to whom Zin-zendorf offered asylum in his lands. There they founded the community of Herrnhut, which so attracted Zinzendorf's interest that he resigned his post at Dresden and joined it. Under his direction, the Moravians joined the local Lutheran parish. But there were tensions, for the Lutherans were unwilling to trust the foreigners imbued with Pietism.

In 1731, while in Denmark, Zinzendorf met a group of Eskimos who had been converted by the Lutheran missionary Hans Egede, and this kin-dled in him an interest in missions that would dominate the rest of his life. Soon the community at Herrnhut burned with the same zeal, and in 1732 its first missionaries left for the Caribbean. In a few years, there were Moravian missionaries also in Africa, India, South America, and North America —where they founded the communities of Bethlehem and Nazareth in Pennsylvania, and Salem in North Carolina. Thus, a movement that had begun with two hundred refugees had over a hundred missionaries overseas.

Meanwhile, conflicts with Lutheran authorities in Germany did not abate. Zinzendorf himself had to leave the area, and traveled to North America, where he was present at the founding of the Bethlehem community in 1741. In 1768, a year after Zinzendorf's return, peace was made between the Lutherans and the Moravians, who were acknowledged as true Lutherans. But this was only temporary. Zinzendorf himself had agreed to be made a bishop by the Moravians, who claimed to have the ancient episcopal succession of the Hussites, and this caused further tensions with the Lutherans. Zinzendorf died at Herrnhut in 1760, and shortly thereafter his followers broke with Lutheranism. Although the Moravian church never had a large membership, and soon was unable to continue sending and supporting such a high number of missionaries, its example contributed to the great missionary awakening of the nineteenth century. But perhaps the greatest significance of the movement was its impact on John Wesley and, through him, on the entire Methodist tradition.

John Wesley and Methodism

Late in 1735, and early in 1736, a second Moravian contingent was sailing to the New World hoping to preach to the Indians of Georgia. On shipboard was a young Anglican priest, John Wesley by name, whom Governor Oglethorpe of Georgia had invited to serve as a pastor in Savannah. The young man had accepted, hoping to be able to preach to the Indians, about whose virtues he had unrealistic expectations. All went well during the early days of the crossing, and young Wesley learned enough German to be able to communicate with his Moravian companions. But then the weather turned against them, and the ship was in dire straits. The mainmast split, and panic would have overwhelmed the crew, had it not been for the unbelievable calm of the Moravians, who sang throughout the ordeal. Meanwhile, Wesley, who was also chaplain of the vessel, came to the bitter realization that he was more concerned about himself than about his fellow travelers. After the storm, the Moravians told him that they could behave so bravely because they did not fear death; and the young man began doubting the depth of his own faith.

After reaching Savannah, Wesley asked the Moravian Gottlieb Spangenberg for advice regarding his work as a pastor and as a missionary to the Indians. In his diary, he then left a record of that conversation:

*John Wesley, the founder of Methodism,
combined the religious zeal of the Moravians
with the social activism that had long
characterized the Reformed tradition.*

He said, "My brother, I must first ask you one or two questions. Have you the witness within yourself? Does the Spirit of God bear witness with your spirit, that you are a child of God?" I was surprised, and knew not what to answer. He observed it, and asked, "Do you know Jesus Christ?" I paused, and said, "I know he is the Saviour of the world." "True," replied he; "but do you know he has saved you?" I answered, "I hope he has died to save me." He only added, "Do you know yourself?" I said, "I do."

As a postscript to that conversation, the young Anglican pastor commented: "But I fear they were vain words."*

These experiences left him moved and confused. He had always thought of himself as a good Christian. His father, Samuel Wesley, was an Anglican priest, and his mother Susanna was the daughter of another. She had been

---

*Journal, February 7, 1736.

particularly careful in the religious and moral instruction of her nineteen children. When John was five, fire broke out in the parsonage. The young lad was miraculously saved, and thereafter his mother thought of him as "a brand plucked from the burning" because God had plans for him. At Oxford, he had distinguished himself both as a scholar and as a devout young man. After helping his father in the parish for some time, he had returned to Oxford, where he had joined a religious society founded by his brother Charles and a group of friends. Its members had made a covenant to lead a holy and sober life, to take communion at least once a week, to be faithful in their private devotions, to visit the prisons regularly, and to spend three hours together every afternoon, studying the Bible and books of devotion. Since he was the only ordained priest among them, and he also had exceptional gifts, John Wesley soon became the leader of that group that other students mocked as a "holy club" and "methodists."

That was the story of that young priest who now, in distant Georgia, doubted the depth of his faith. As a pastor, he failed miserably, for he expected his parishioners to behave like the "holy club," and his flock expected him to be content with their attendance at worship. John's brother

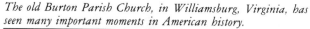

The old Burton Parish Church, in Williamsburg, Virginia, has seen many important moments in American history.

Charles, who was also in Georgia serving under James Oglethorpe, was disappointed with his work, and decided to return to England. But John stayed on, not because he had greater success, but because he would not give up. Then he was forced to leave under a cloud. A young woman whom he had courted had married another. Wesley, deeming the young bride frivolous, denied communion to her, and was sued for defamation. Confused and bitter, he decided to return home, which in any case seems to have been what his parishioners wanted.

Back in England, not knowing what to do, he contacted the Moravians. One of them, Peter Boehler, became his religious advisor. When Wesley came to the conclusion that he lacked saving faith, and that therefore he should cease preaching, Boehler advised him to continue preaching faith until he had it, and once he had it, to continue preaching because he had it. Finally, on May 24, 1738, Wesley had the experience that changed his life:

In the evening I went very unwillingly to a society in Aldersgate Street, where one was reading Luther's preface to the Epistle to the Romans. About a quarter before nine, while he was describing the change which God works in the heart through faith in Christ, I felt my heart strangely warmed. I felt I did trust in Christ, Christ alone for salvation: And an assurance was given me, that he had taken away *my* sins, even *mine,* and saved *me* from the law of sin and death.*

After that experience, Wesley no longer doubted his own salvation. Furthermore, that salvation no longer consumed all his interest. Being assured of it, he could devote all his concern to the salvation of others. As a first step, he visited the Moravian community of Herrnhut. That visit, although greatly inspiring, convinced him that Moravian spirituality was ill-suited to his own temperament and involvement in social issues. Therefore, in spite of his gratitude, he decided not to become a Moravian.

While all this was taking place in Wesley's life, another former member of the "holy club," George Whitefield, had become a famous preacher. A few years earlier he had been moved by an experience similar to Wesley's at Aldersgate, and now divided his time between his parish in Georgia and preaching in England, where he had remarkable success, particularly in the industrial city of Bristol. His preaching was emotional, and when some critics objected to the manner in which he used the pulpit he began preaching in the open, as was often done in Georgia. Since he needed help in Bristol, and in any case would soon have to return to the New World, Whitefield invited Wesley to help him and take charge during his absence.

Although Wesley accepted Whitefield's invitation, the fiery preacher's methods were not entirely to his liking. He objected to preaching in the open. Much later he commented on those early days, declaring that at that time he was so convinced that God wished everything to be done in order,

---

*Journal, May 24, 1738.

that he almost thought it a sin to save souls outside church buildings. Slowly, in view of the results, he reconciled himself to that sort of preaching, although he always deplored the need for it. He was also worried over the response to his preaching. Some people would weep and loudly bemoan their sins, while others would collapse in anguish. Then they would express great joy, declaring that they felt cleansed of their evil. Wesley would have preferred more solemn proceedings. Eventually, he decided that what was taking place in such instances was a struggle between Satan and the Holy Spirit, and that he should not hinder the work of God. In any case, after the early years, such extreme occurrences became less frequent.

Wesley and Whitefield worked together for some time, although slowly Wesley became the main leader of the movement. Eventually, they parted because of theological differences. Both were Calvinists in most matters; but, on the issue of predestination and free will, Wesley departed from orthodox Calvinism, prefering the Arminian position. After several debates, the two friends decided that each would follow his own path, and that they would avoid controversies—an agreement that their followers did not always keep. With the help of the Countess of Huntingdon, Whitefield organized the Calvinist Methodist Church, whose main strength was in Wales.

Wesley had no interest in founding a new denomination. On the contrary, he was an Anglican minister, and throughout his life he remained such. Rather, his purpose was to awaken and cultivate the faith of the masses in the Church of England, as Pietism was doing for German Lutheranism. For that reason he avoided scheduling his preaching in conflict with the services of the Church of England, and he always took for granted that Methodist meetings would serve as preparation to attend Anglican worship and take communion in it. For him, as for most of the church through the centuries, the center of worship was communion. This he took and expected his followers to take as frequently as possible, in the official services of the Church of England.

Although the movement had no intention of becoming a separate church, it did need an organization. In Bristol, the real birthplace of the movement, Wesley's followers were organized into "societies" that at first met in private homes and later had their own buildings. In mockery, people called them "Methodists" and eventually they took this name with pride. When Methodist societies grew too large for the effective care of their members, Wesley followed a friend's suggestion and divided them into "classes," each with eleven members and a leader. These met weekly to read Scripture, pray, discuss religious matters, and collect funds. Since, in order to be a class leader, it was not necessary to be wealthy or educated, this gave significant participation to many who felt left out of the structure of the Church of England. Also, since there were classes for women, under feminine leadership, this also gave women a prominent place in Methodism.

The movement grew rapidly, and Wesley was forced to travel throughout the British Isles, preaching and organizing his followers. When the bishop of Bristol tried to limit his activity, telling him that his itinerant preaching perturbed the order of the parishes, Wesley responded, "The world is my parish." Those words, originally uttered in protest against a rigid ecclesiastical organization, later became the motto of the Methodist missionary enterprise. Meanwhile, however, Wesley and his young movement needed more people to share in the task of preaching. A few Anglican priests had joined the movement—most noteworthy among them was John Wesley's brother Charles, famous for his hymns. It was John Wesley, however, who carried the heaviest burden, preaching several times a day and traveling thousands of miles on horseback every year, until the age of seventy.

These circumstances led to the use of lay preachers. When Wesley heard that layman Thomas Maxfield had been preaching in one of the societies in London, he determined to put a stop to it. But his mother, Susanna, asked him to hear the man before making a decision, and Maxfield so impressed Wesley that he decided that the use of lay preachers was God's answer to the movement's urgent need of preachers. These were not to take the place of the clergy, for they were not to offer communion, and this was the highest form of worship. Their function, like those of the societies, was intended to be parallel and complementary to the sacramental function of the Church of England and its ordained personnel. In any case, among Methodist lay preachers there soon were a number of women—which was not then possible among the ordained clergy.

With all these elements in place, Wesley organized his followers into a "Connection." A number of societies joined to form a "circuit," under the leadership of a "superintendent." As a help in the administration of the Connection, Wesley began the practice of periodic meetings that included both the Anglican clergy who formed part of it, and the lay preachers. This eventually evolved into the "Annual Conference," in which those who were to serve in each circuit were appointed—usually for a period of three years.

In this entire process, conflicts were not lacking. In the early years, there were frequent acts of violence against Methodists. Some of the clergy and the nobility resented the authority the new movement gave to people from the lower classes. Therefore, meetings were frequently interrupted by paid ruffians, and Wesley's life was occasionally in danger. Later, this opposition abated, until it eventually ceased. There were also theological conflicts. Wesley grudgingly broke with the Moravians, whose inclination to quietism he feared and deplored.

But the most significant conflicts were with the Anglican Church, to which Wesley belonged and in which he wished to remain. Until his last days, he reprimanded Methodists who wished to break away from Anglicanism. But the breach was unavoidable. Among the Anglican authorities, some rightly saw the Methodist movement as an indication of their own shortcomings, and therefore resented it. Others felt that the Methodists' breach of order in preaching everywhere, without regard for parish boundaries, was unforgivable. Wesley himself was enough of an Anglican to bemoan the need to do this; but he felt compelled by the urge to reach people whom the church was not reaching.

A difficult legal decision came to make matters more difficult. According to English law, non-Anglican worship services and church buildings were to be allowed, but they must be officially registered as such. This put the Methodists in a difficult situation, for the Church of England did not acknowledge their meetings and buildings. If they registered, this would be a tacit declaration that they were not Anglicans. If they did not, they would be breaking the law. In 1787, after great hesitation, Wesley instructed his preachers to register, and thus the first legal step was taken toward the formation of a separate church. Three years earlier, however, Wesley had taken a step that had more drastic theological implications. For a long time he had been convinced that, in the early church, a "bishop" was the same as a "presbyter" or "elder." This led him to the conviction that all ordained presbyters, including himself, had the power of ordination. But he refrained from employing it to avoid further alienating the leadership of the Church of England. The independence of the United States, however, posed new difficulties. During the War of Independence, most of the Anglican clergy had been loyalists, and after independence most of them had returned to England. This made it difficult—sometimes impossible—for the inhabitants of the new nation to partake of communion. The bishop of London, who supposedly still had jurisdiction over the former colonies, refused to ordain personnel for the United States. Convinced as he was that the celebration of communion was the very heart of Christian worship, Wesley deplored this situation—while he also deplored what he took to be the unwarranted rebellion of Britain's former colonies. Finally, in 1784, he ordained two lay preachers as presbyters for the new country, and made Anglican priest Thomas Coke their "superintendent"—a word that he well knew had the same meaning as the Greek word translated as "bishop." Later, he ordained others to serve also in Scotland and elsewhere. In spite of having taken these steps, Wesley continued insisting on the need not to break with the Church of England. His brother Charles told him that the ordination of ministers for the New World was in itself a break. In 1786, the Conference decided that, in those places where the Anglican churches had no room for all the population, or where their priests were inept, it was permitted to schedule Methodist gatherings in conflict with Anglican worship. Although Wesley refused to acknowledge it, by the time of his death Methodism was clearly becoming a separate church.

The success of Methodism was partly due to the degree to which it responded to new needs resulting from the Industrial Revolution. During the latter half of the eighteenth century, England was undergoing a process of rapid industrialization. This created a mass movement of population to the industrial centers. Such people, uprooted by economic circumstances, tended to lose their connection with the church, whose parish structure was unable to respond to the needs of the new urban masses. It was among those masses that Methodism filled a need and found most of its members.

In North America, a completely different process—the westward movement of settlers—gave rise to an uprooted population lacking traditional ecclesiastic links, and whom the older churches seldom reached. It was among these people that Methodism achieved its greatest success. Officially, North American Methodists became a separate church before their British counterpart. In 1771, Wesley had sent lay preacher Francis Asbury to the colonies. Asbury was the driving force who made sure that Methodism moved westward along with the frontier. When the thirteen colonies declared their independence, Wesley wrote against their rebellion. But American Methodist preachers were mostly colonials who supported the cause of independence, or at least remained neutral. As a result, Methodists in the United States, while still admiring Wesley, were no longer bound by his wishes. It was against those wishes, and in response to the lack of Anglican ministers, that the American movement organized itself into the Methodist Episcopal Church. The name "Episcopal" was the direct result of a conflict with Wesley, who called both himself and Coke "superintendents," but was enraged when he learned that Coke and Asbury—by then also a superintendent—called themselves "bishops." From that point on, American Methodists have had bishops, and English Methodists have not.

Wesley died in 1791. After his death, Methodism underwent a period of inner struggles, mostly revolving around the question of relations with Anglicanism. Eventually, in England as well as in other lands where Methodism had grown strong, Methodist churches were formed that were completely independent of Anglicanism.

24/The Thirteen Colonies

*God requires not a uniformity of religion to
be enacted and enforced in any civil state,
which enforced uniformity, sooner or later,
is the greatest occasion of civil war,
ravishing of conscience, persecution of
Christ Jesus in his servants, and of the
hypocrisy and destruction of millions of
souls.*

ROGER WILLIAMS

The sixteenth century had seen the building of the Spanish and Portuguese empires. In the seventeenth century, however, other powers began building their own empires. Most successful of these was Great Britain, whose colonial expansion began in the seventeenth century and reached its peak in the nineteenth. Among its first overseas enterprises were the thirteen colonies in North America, which would later become the United States.

It is customary to contrast the origin of these colonies with the Spanish ones, and to try to explain their divergent results by those different origins. It is commonly said, for instance, that the Spanish came for gold whereas the British came for religious motives; that the Spanish were cruel with the Indians, but the British tried to live in peace with them; that the Spanish brought the Inquisition, while the British brought religious freedom; that the Spanish came as aristocrats, and became rich on the basis of Indian labor, and that the English came to work the land. Although there is a measure of truth in some of these assertions, historical facts are much more complex.

The economic motivations of the British colonial enterprise were just as strong as those of the Spanish. But the fact was that the Spanish had already conquered the richest empires, and there were no longer treasures as great as those of the Aztecs and the Incas to be had. Therefore, British investors could not hope to become rich by sheer conquest, as Cortez and Pizarro had done, but were forced to set their store on commerce. When it became clear that trade with the Indians would not produce the necessary returns, the colonies turned to agriculture, still with a view to exporting the produce to Europe and thus making a profit for the owners of the colonies. This was done with British labor. Generally, these were not free colonists, cultivating their own land, but indentured labor working the land owned by the colonial company. At first, colonials were not even allowed to own land. As to religious freedom, while it is true that Rhode Island and Pennsylvania led the world in that direction, it is also true that the Pilgrims of New England were no more tolerant than the Spanish Inquisitors. Finally, on the matter of mistreatment of Indians, one must not forget that the destruction of the original population in what eventually became the United States was much more thorough than that perpetrated by the Spanish in their colonies— except in the Caribbean. This had little to do with one nation or the other being more compassionate. Rather, it was a matter of diverse economic circumstances. What the Spanish wanted from the Indians was their labor, and therefore they had no interest in decimating them. What the British wanted was their land; and therefore the most frequent policy toward them, both in the colonial period and after independence, was one of extermination and confinement. In areas where their goal was to obtain land, the Spanish and Portuguese followed the same policy.

It is true that new circumstances in Europe—particularly in Great Britain —led many to migrate to the New World for religious reasons. In speaking of the Puritan Revolution in England, we have seen the great variety of religious persuasions that appeared. Such variety had no place in the policies of governments whose goal was religious uniformity as a means to political stability. Laws demanding religious conformity were more difficult to apply overseas; therefore, religious dissidents hoped for an escape from oppression by migrating to the colonies, or founding new ones. Some of these dissidents were no more tolerant than were the governments from which they were fleeing. But others came to the conclusion that religious tolerance was best, not only as a matter of convenience, but also because it was God's will.

Virginia

The first British colonial ventures in North America failed. In 1584, Sir Walter Raleigh, Queen Elizabeth's favorite, was granted a royal charter for the colonization of North America. He named the area that he hoped to colonize "Virginia," in honor of Elizabeth, the "Virgin Queen." But his two ventures, one in 1585 and another in 1587, did not succeed. The first contingent of settlers returned to England, and the second simply disappeared.

It was in the spring of 1607 that the permanent colonization of Virginia began. In May of that year, 105 settlers landed near the mouth of a river that they named "James" after their new king—Elizabeth had died four years earlier—and founded Jamestown. There was a chaplain among them—the Virginia Company, under whose auspices the enterprise was taking place, hoped to establish the Church of England in the new land, and to offer its services both to the settlers and to the Indians. It was also hoped that the new colony would put a stop to Spanish expansion to the north, feared both for nationalist reasons and for dread of "popery." The colony's main purpose, however, was not religious, but economic. The stockholders of the Virginia Company simply hoped that trade with the Indians, and perhaps agriculture, would yield a handsome profit.

Since the founding of Virginia took place at the high point of Puritan influence in the Church of England, many of the stockholders and settlers believed that the colony should be ruled by Puritan principles. Its early laws required attendance at worship twice a day, the strict observance of the Lord's Day, and stern punishment for profanity and immodest dress. But dreams of a holy commonwealth would have to yield to political realities. King James detested Puritanism, and would not have it in his colony of Virginia. A war with the Indians in 1622 served him as an excuse, and in 1624 he placed the colony under his direct rule. After that time Puritan influence waned. Later Charles I, following James's policy against the Virginia Puritans, took a vast portion of Virginia, created the colony of Maryland, and granted it to a Catholic proprietor. Meanwhile, the colony, at first a marginal enterprise, had found economic success by growing and exporting tobacco. Since this required much labor, by 1619 the colony began importing slaves from Africa. Thus began the slave-holding economy that became characteristic of Virginia and other colonies.

The Puritan Revolution in England made little impact on Virginia. By then the settlers were more interested in growing tobacco and opening new lands for cultivation than in the religious strife in England. Their former Puritanism had lost vigor in the midst of economic prosperity. Particularly, the Puritan valuation of labor had little meaning in a society based on slavery. Therefore, when the Revolution broke out in England, and later when the Stuarts were restored, these events did not shake the colony. Most of the settlers were still members of the Church of England. This was no longer the Puritan Anglicanism of times past, but rather a facile and aristocratic Anglicanism, one easily adapted to the plantation owners, but with little influence on the slaves or on the lower classes of the white population.

The Church of England did little for the conversion of slaves. One of the reasons for this was that there were ancient principles prohibiting Christians from holding fellow believers in slavery, and some insisted that those principles were still valid. Therefore, to avoid difficulties, slaveowners preferred that their slaves not be baptized. In 1667, a law was passed declaring that baptism did not change a slave's condition—another indication of the degree to which established religion was willing to bend to the interests of the powerful. But even then little was done for the conversion of the slaves, since many owners felt that keeping them in ignorance was the best way to be assured of their service and submission.

The adaptation of the church to the interests of the powerful also had consequences among the white population. While the nascent aristocracy remained faithful to Anglicanism, many in the lower classes began turning to dissident movements. Severe measures were taken against them, and hundreds migrated to nearby Catholic Maryland, where there was greater religious freedom. The Quakers also made inroads in Virginia, in spite of laws against them. When George Fox visited the colony in 1762, he rejoiced in finding many Friends, and also noted that, although the movement had been most successful among the lower classes, some of the aristocracy regarded it with favor. Later, through the efforts of Asbury and his preachers, Methodism made great strides—although at that time it still considered itself part of Anglicanism.

Other colonies were founded to the south of Virginia. The Carolinas, granted by the crown to a group of aristocrats and stockholders in 1663, were slow in developing. In order to foster immigration, the proprietors decreed religious freedom, thus attracting many dissidents from Virginia. The society that developed in the Carolinas—particularly in South Carolina—was similar to that of Virginia in its stratification. Again, the higher classes belonged to the Church of England, while many in the lower classes became either Quakers or Baptists. But, even among the white population, most people seem to have had very little contact with any church.

Georgia was founded with two basic purposes. The first was to halt the Spanish, who were moving north from their base in St. Augustine. The second was to serve as an alternative for debtors' prisons. By the beginning of the eighteenth century, there were many religious-minded people in England who sought to better the lot of the disinherited. This movement turned its attention, among other things, to prisons, whose inhuman conditions were the object of repeated attacks in Parliament. One of the leaders of this campaign was military hero James Oglethorpe, who decided that a colony should be founded in North America that could serve as an alternative to the incarceration of debtors. Royal approval was granted in 1732, and the first convicts arrived the following year. To these were soon added others, as well as many religious refugees from other areas. Although Anglicanism was the official religion, it made little impact on the colony. The failure of the Wesleys as Anglican pastors was typical of many others. The Moravians had a measure of success, although their number was never great. Perhaps the most significant religious movement of the early years of the colony was the popular response to George Whitefield's preaching, similar to what was taking place in England. By the time of his death in 1770, he had set his stamp on much of Georgia's religious life. Later, Methodists, Baptists and others harvested what he had sown.

The Northern Puritan Colonies

It was much further north that Puritanism made its greatest impact. There, in what came to be called New England, several colonies were founded whose basic original motivation was clearly religious. The first of these was the Plymouth Plantation, founded by a group of dissidents who had left England for the Netherlands, and then developed the idea of founding in the New World a community based on their religious principles. They came to an agreement with the Virginia Company, which was in urgent need of settlers, and among whose members there was strong Puritan influence. Finally, 101 settlers boarded the *Mayflower* and left for the New World. They reached land much farther north than they had intended, well beyond the limits of Virginia. Therefore, before landing, they decided to organize themselves into a political body—under the king of England, but with the power to govern themselves. In their Mayflower Compact, they committed themselves to obey the "just and equal laws" passed by their own government. Then, after a tentative landing on Cape Cod, they settled at Plymouth. The first months of the new colony were tragic. The population was swept by an epidemic, and only fifty survived. In the spring, however, the Indians taught the settlers how to grow corn; and with that crop, as well as by fishing and hunting, they set by enough stores to see them through the winter. Eventually, they were also able to trade furs for things they needed from Europe, and thus the colony managed to survive.

Shortly after that first settlement, a group of English Puritans, wishing to found in the New World a community more akin to their conscience, organized the Massachusetts Bay Company. They agreed that they would take the Company with them to the New World and establish its headquarters in the colony, thus hoping to avoid undue interference from the English government. When all was ready, more than a thousand settlers began the new colony. Unlike the "pilgrims" of Plymouth, they were not separatists, but simply Puritans who still belonged to the Church of England but who wished for it to follow more closely the practices of the New Testament. Since they saw little hope for this in England, they migrated to America, where they expected to bring their ideals to fruition. This project was rendered all the more necessary by Archbishop Laud's measures against the Puritans. During his persecution, some ten thousand Puritans fled to New England, thus strengthening the colony of Massachusetts Bay, and giving birth to the new colonies of Connecticut and New Haven.

Charles I was preparing to take measures against these growing centers

The Mayflower *"pilgrims" eventually became a symbol of the flight from religious and political oppression into a land of promise.*

of Puritanism when he found himself involved in the civil war that cost him his throne and his life. But the war itself, and the Puritan victory, stopped the migratory wave; for there was now hope of establishing the holy commonwealth, no longer on the distant coasts of an unexplored continent, but in England itself. Although their sympathies were clearly with the Puritan rebels, the colonies remained neutral, and devoted their efforts to increasing their territories and developing their institutions. Therefore, the restoration of the Stuarts was not as severe a blow for them as it was for Puritanism in England. Somewhat later, James II attempted to consolidate several of the northern colonies in the "Dominion of New England." But his fall put an end to this project, and the colonies recovered many of their old privileges, although under new structures of government. It was at this time that religious tolerance was granted, although by royal decision, and not at the request of the settlers.

The Puritan colonies of New England—by then consolidated under the names of Massachusetts and Connecticut—saw a number of theological controversies. The main difficulty was that many of these Puritans, while preserving the custom of baptizing children, insisted on the need of a conversion experience in order to be truly Christian. What, then, was the meaning of baptism? Would it not be better to wait until a person had the experience of conversion, and then administer baptism, as the Baptists claimed? Some found that to be the best solution. But this clashed with the Puritan goal of founding a society that would be guided by biblical principles. A Christian commonwealth is conceivable only if, as in ancient Israel, one becomes a member of it by birth, so that the civil and the religious communities are coextensive. For that reason, it was necessary to baptize the "children of the Covenant," just as in ancient Israel they had been circumcised during infancy. But, on the other hand, if all who were baptized were members of the Covenant, how could purity of life and doctrine be safeguarded? Furthermore, if infants were baptized as "children of the Covenant," what was to be done with infants born of baptized parents who had never had the experience of conversion? Thus, many came to the conclusion that there was a "half-way Covenant," embracing those who, having been baptized, had not been converted. The children of such people were to be baptized, for they were still members of the Covenant. But still only those who had a conversion experience were full members of the church, with power to participate in the process of making decisions. In any case, this controversy gave rise to bitter animosities, and as a result the original optimism of the settlers waned. There was also some debate as to the manner of government of the churches, and the relations among them. Finally, the majority settled on what amounted to congregational rule, although limited by the need for all congregations to agree to a "Confession of Faith" that was a revision of that of Westminster, and which the civil authorities were empowered to safeguard.

One of the most famous episodes of those early years was the trial of the "witches" of Salem, Massachusetts. Before those events, there had been other trials for witchcraft in Massachusetts, and three people had been hanged as a result. But in 1692, on the basis of the idle accusations of some girls, rumors began circulating that witchcraft was widely practiced in Salem, and the rumors eventually led to hysteria. In total, twenty people—fourteen women and six men—were hanged, and several others died in prison. Some confessed that they had practiced witchcraft, and accused others of having been their mentors, thus hoping to save their lives. Eventually, accusations were leveled against respected members of the clergy, wealthy merchants, and even the governor's wife. At that point the authorities decided that it was time to stop the investigations. Twenty years later, the courts of Massachusetts decided that the entire episode had been a gross injustice, and ordered indemnifications to be paid to the families of the victims.

Some of the settlers did show an interest in the evangelization of their Indian neighbors. Remarkable on that score was the Mayhew family, who settled in Martha's Vineyard and worked for the conversion and education of the Indians for five generations—from 1642 until the death of Zacharias Mayhew, in 1806. However, the work that John Eliot began among the Mohicans in 1646 had greater consequences. He was convinced that the Indians were the ten lost tribes of Israel, and that their conversion would bring about the fulfillment of ancient prophecies. He therefore gathered his converts in villages that were ruled according to the law of Moses. There he taught them European agricultural methods and mechanical arts, so that they could sustain themselves. Great stress was also laid on the reading and study of the Bible, which Eliot translated into Mohican after having laboriously learned that language and devised a method for writing it. Eliot himself founded fourteen such villages, and those who followed his inspiration founded many more.

In 1675, some Indians, under the leadership of a chief whom they called King Philip, decided to put an end to the outrages being committed against them, and to the progressive invasion of their lands. In the conflict that ensued, known as "King Philip's War," many of the converted Indians either took the side of the settlers or refrained from fighting. In spite of this, hundreds of them were taken away from their villages and forced to live on an overcrowded island in Boston Bay. Many others were killed by whites who felt that all Indians were enemies. When the settlers finally won the war, the captive Indians and those who surrendered were distributed among the whites—women and children to be their servants, and men as slaves to be sold and shipped as far away as possible. Few traces of Eliot's work were left after these events.

Rhode Island and the Baptists

The intolerance that reigned in the Puritan colonies forced some to abandon them. Most famous among these was Roger Williams, who had arrived in Massachusetts in 1631. After refusing to serve as a pastor in Boston, he declared that the Puritans in the colony erred in granting the civil authorities power to enforce those commandments that had to do with an individual's relations with God. He was convinced that magistrates should be granted authority to enforce only those commandments that had to do with the ordering of society. He also declared that the land the colonies occupied belonged to the Indians, and that the entire colonial enterprise was unjust and illegal. These and other ideas, which at the time seemed radical, made him unpopular in Boston, and he moved to Plymouth. Then he became a pastor in Salem. But when he tried to have his church secede from the rest, the authorities of Massachusetts expelled him. He then settled with a group of friends, first in Plymouth, and then in Narragansett, on lands that he bought from the Indians. There he founded the colony of Providence on the principle of religious freedom.

According to Williams, such freedom was required by the very obligation to worship God. Worship must be sincere, and all efforts to force it actually weaken it. Therefore, in the new colony the rights of citizenship would not be abridged on the basis of one's religious opinions or practices.

These views he expounded in a treatise published in 1644, *The Bloudy Tenent of Persecution for the Cause of Conscience Discussed,* to which one of the main pastors of Massachusetts responded with *The Bloudy Tenent Washed and Made White in the Bloud of the Lambe.*

Meanwhile, others had moved to nearby areas for similar reasons. Late in 1637, prophet Anne Hutchinson was expelled from Massachusetts for, among other reasons, claiming to have received personal revelations. She and eighteen others founded Portsmouth on an island near Providence, also on the basis of religious freedom. Shortly thereafter, a group from Portsmouth founded the community of Newport, at the other end of the same island. All these communities grew rapidly with the influx of Baptists, Quakers, and others from the Puritan colonies. But the only legal claim of these new settlements was based on having bought their lands from the Indians, and many in the nearby colonies spoke of destroying what they considered the sewer of New England. Therefore, Roger Williams traveled to England, and in 1644 obtained from the Long Parliament the legal recognition of the Colony of Rhode Island and Providence Plantations, to be governed as a democracy. After the restoration of the Stuarts, Charles II confirmed the colony's legal rights.

Williams's church in Providence became Baptist. One of its members baptized Williams, who in turn baptized the rest. But Williams himself did not long remain in that church, for his ideas were becoming increasingly radical. His contacts with the Indians, whom he deeply respected, led him to declare that perhaps their religion was as acceptable in the eyes of God as was Christianity, and that in any case they did not have to become Christians in order to be saved. This brought further attacks, not only from the Puritans of Massachusetts, but also from many Baptists in Providence. But he continued moving towards a radical spiritualism that eventually led him to the conclusion that all churches were false, and that Scripture was to be understood in purely spiritual terms.

Meanwhile, the Baptists of Providence were involved in their own controversies. In speaking of the Puritan Revolution in England, we had occasion to speak of the Baptists as one of the many groups that appeared at that time. Although some of their teachings coincided with those of the Anabaptists on the Continent, most Baptists did not derive such ideas from the Anabaptists, but rather from their own study of the New Testament. While in exile in the Netherlands, a number of these Baptists were influenced by Arminianism, which they took with them on their return to England. Others remained in England, and continued sharing in the strict Calvinism that was the backbone of the Puritan movement. Thus, two different groups appeared among the Baptists: the "general" and the "particular." "General Baptists" were those who held, with the Arminians, that Jesus had died for all humankind. "Particular Baptists," on the other hand, held to orthodox Calvinism, affirming that Jesus died only for those who were predestined to be saved. In Providence, some followed the Arminianism of the General Baptists, and others the Calvinism of the Particular Baptists.

The Baptist movement spread throughout the colonies, even though its followers were persecuted in several of them. Entire congregations were expelled from Massachusetts. This did not suffice to stop the supposed contagion, which reached some of the most prestigious members of that society —including the president of Harvard. Slowly, as religious tolerance became more common, Baptist groups surfaced in every colony. At first, most of these were General Baptists. But at the time of the Great Awakening—to which we shall return—there was an upsurge of Calvinism, and in many areas the Particular Baptists far surpassed the others.

Catholicism in Maryland

The main center of Roman Catholicism in the North American British colonies was Maryland. In 1632, Charles I granted Cecil Calvert, Lord Baltimore, rights of property and colonization over a portion of the territories that had earlier been claimed by Virginia. Lord Baltimore was Catholic, and the grant was made to him as part of Charles's policy of seeking Catholic support. Many Catholics in England wished to have a colony where they could live without the restrictions and difficulties they constantly faced in their own country. Since at that time it would have been politically unwise to establish a purely Catholic colony, it was decided that in Maryland there would be religious freedom. Lord Baltimore followed that policy in his instructions to his representatives in Maryland, whom he directed to avoid giving Protestants any excuse to attack the Catholics in the colony.

The first group of settlers arrived in 1634, and its social composition already indicated the prevailing social order in the colony. Approximately one-tenth of the settlers were Catholic aristocrats, and the rest were mostly their Protestant servants. Tobacco culture soon became the mainstay of the economy, giving rise to large and prosperous plantations. The colony was governed by the Catholic landowners, but the majority were Protestants. Repeatedly, whenever the shifting political winds in Britain gave them opportunity, the Protestants sought to take power from the landed Catholic aristocracy. They finally succeeded when James II was overthrown. Anglicanism then became the official religion of the colony, while the rights of Catholics were restricted.

Pennsylvania also had a significant number of Catholics, thanks to the tolerant policies advocated by William Penn. There, as well as in other colonies, Catholicism made significant gains after the Stuart restoration. After the fall of James II in 1688, however, its growth was limited; and throughout the colonial period Catholics remained a minority in each of the thirteen colonies.

The Mid-Atlantic Colonies

The colonies founded between New England and Maryland—New York, New Jersey, Pennsylvania, and Delaware—were not in the beginning a refuge for any particular religious group. We have already spoken of Penn's "experiment" in Pennsylvania. Although the basic inspiration for founding the colony was Quaker, from the very beginning its population comprised people of varied confessions. The same was true of Delaware, which Penn bought from the Duke of York, and which was part of Pennsylvania until 1701.

The political and religious history of New Jersey is complex. In general, however, East New Jersey followed the pattern of the strict New England Puritans, while in the West it was the Quakers who set the tone for the emerging society, and there was religious tolerance. Eventually, however, many of the Quakers of New Jersey became a slaveholding aristocracy whose relations with other Quakers were increasingly strained.

What later became New York was colonized by the Dutch, whose East India Company established its local headquarters in Manhattan, and whose Reformed Church came with them. In 1655, they conquered the rival colony that the Swedes had founded on the Delaware, and they themselves were conquered by the British in 1664. Then the former New Netherland became New York, while the earlier Dutch inhabitants, who in any case were not entirely satisfied with the previous regime, became British subjects. The British brought with them the Church of England, whose only members were the governor and his household and troops. But with the increase of British immigration, the religious composition of the colony approached that of Great Britain.

In short, during the seventeenth and eighteenth centuries, Great Britain founded and expanded a chain of colonies in North America. (In 1759, the British also took the French lands north of the St. Lawrence, but the history of that colony followed a different course.) Religious motivations played an important role in the founding of several of these colonies. Although at first some of them were intolerant of religious diversity, with the passage of time all tended to follow the example of Rhode Island and Pennsylvania, where religious freedom had existed from the beginning and was shown to be a viable option to the religious tensions that had repeatedly bled Europe. At the same time, the practice of slavery, social inequity based on the existence of vast plantations, the exploitation of the Indians and the expropriation of their land, and many similar factors, had dimmed the religious fervor and the hopes for a holy commonwealth that had sparked many of the early settlers.

The Great Awakening

The eighteenth century brought to North America the same Pietistic currents that it brought to Germany and England. Presbyterians, for instance, were divided by a controversy between those who insisted above all on strict adherence to the teachings of Westminster—the Old Side—and those of the New Side, whose emphasis was on the experience of redeeming grace. Although eventually the two sides would come together, for a time the controversy led to schism—a schism that was made more acute due to the great Pietistic wave known as the "Great Awakening."

From an early date, many among the North American colonists had felt that a personal religious experience was of great importance for Christian life. But that feeling became more generalized in a series of events that began in 1734, when the first signs of the Great Awakening appeared in Northampton, Massachusetts. The pastor there was Jonathan Edwards, a staunch Calvinist who had been trained at Yale, and was convinced of the need for a personal experience of conversion. He had been preaching in Northampton for several years, with average results, when his preaching began evoking a response that surprised him. His sermons were not exceptionally emotive, although they did underscore the need for an experience of conviction of sin and of divine forgiveness. In that year of 1734, people began responding to his sermons, some with emotional outbursts, but many with a remarkable change in their lives, and with increased attention to their devotional lives. In a few months, the movement swept the area and reached into Connecticut. Soon it subsided, and after three years its extraordinary signs had almost disappeared. But the memory remained, as well as the hope that it would be rekindled.

Shortly thereafter, George Whitefield visited New England, and his preaching led to many experiences of conversion as well as outward expressions of repentance and joy. Although Edwards was a Congregationalist, he invited the Anglican Whitefield to preach in his church, and it is said that while the visitor preached the pastor wept. This gave the awakening new impetus. The Presbyterian ministers of the New Side, and others of similar inclinations, joined it. While some preachers followed Whitefield's example, traveling throughout the countryside, many local pastors of various traditions —Anglicans, Presbyterians, and Congregationalists—brought new zeal to their pulpits, and extraordinary responses were evoked in their churches also.

Jonathan Edwards was both the leading theologian in the colonies and one of the prominent figures in the Great Awakening.

People wept in repentance for their sins, some shouted for joy at having been pardoned, and a few were so overwhelmed that they fainted.

Such reactions to preaching led the enemies of the Great Awakening to accuse its leaders of undermining the solemnity of worship, and of substituting emotion for study and devotion. It must be said, however, that many of the leaders of the movement were not particularly emotive, that many were scholars, and that in any case the goal of the movement was not worship services marked by continual shows of emotion, but rather a single experience that would lead each believer to greater devotion and more conscientious study of Scripture. This may be seen in Jonathan Edwards's sermons. They are not emotive harangues, but careful expositions of profound theological matters. Edwards believed that emotion was important. But such emotion, including the high experience of conversion, should not eclipse the need for right doctrine and rational worship. The leaders of the Awakening were orthodox Calvinists. It was precisely his Calvinism that led Whitefield to break with Wesley. And Edwards wrote solid and profound defenses of the doctrine of predestination. But, although the movement in its early stages was led by Congregationalists and Presbyterians, in the long run it was the Baptists and Methodists who most profited from it.

At first, the Baptists opposed the movement, calling it frivolous and superficial. But the Awakening led many people to conclusions that were favorable to the Baptists. Indeed, if an experience of conversion had such central importance in Christian life, this raised doubts as to infant baptism.

Therefore, many Congregationalists and Presbyterians, led by the Awakening's emphasis on personal experience, eventually rejected infant baptism and became Baptists. Entire congregations did so.

The Great Awakening also led both Baptists and Methodists to the western frontier. At this time, whites were constantly appropriating Indian lands, and it was the Methodists and Baptists who, imbued with the spirit of the Great Awakening, took up the task of preaching to these western settlers and organizing their religious life. For that reason, these two groups became the most numerous in the newly settled areas. And, as a consequence of that Great Awakening, and of later similar movements, the hope for an "awakening" has become typical of a significant sector of North American Christianity.

Finally, the Great Awakening had political consequences. This was the first movement that embraced the thirteen colonies that would eventually become the United States. Thanks to it, a sense of commonality began developing among the various colonies. At the same time, new ideas were circulating regarding human rights and the nature of government. Those ideas, joined to the growing sense of commonality among the colonies, would produce momentous events.

Suggested Readings

Sydney E. Ahlstrom. *A Religious History of the American People.* Vol. 1. Garden City, New York: Doubleday, 1975.

Carl Bangs. *Arminius: A Study in the Dutch Reformation.* Nashville: Abingdon, 1971.

Frederick C. Copleston. *A History of Philosophy.* Vols. 4–6. London: Burns, Oates and Washburne, 1958–1960.

Rupert E. Davies. *Methodism.* Baltimore: Penguin, 1963.

Herbert H. Henson. *Puritanism in England.* London: Hodder and Stoughton, 1912.

Henry Petersen. *The Canons of Dort.* Grand Rapids: Baker, 1968.

F. Ernest Stoeffler. *German Pietism during the Eighteenth Century.* Leiden: E. J. Brill, 1973.

Henry Van Etten. *George Fox and the Quakers.* New York: Harper, 1959.

PART III

THE NINETEENTH CENTURY

Chronology

Popes	Events
Clement XIV (1769–1774)	Captain Cook's voyages (1775–1779)
Pius VI (1775–1799)	War of Independence, USA (1775–1783)
	Steam engine (1776)
	Tupac Amaru rebellion (1780–1782)
	Kant's *Critique of Pure Reason* (1781)
	Methodist Christmas Conference (1784)
	National Assembly, France (1789)
	Taking of the Bastille (1789)
	Civil Constitution of the Clergy (1790)
	Legislative Assembly, France (1791)
	National Convention, France (1792)
	Particular Baptist Society (1792)
	Louis XVI executed (1793)
	Carey in India (1793)
	Terror in France (1793–1795)
	London Missionary Society (1795)
	British take Ceylon (1796)
	Second Awakening begins (1797)
	Pius VI prisoner of France (1798)
	Roman Republic (1798)
	Consulate, France (1799)
	Founding of Sierra Leone (1799)
	Church Missionary Society (1799)
	Schleiermacher's *Speeches* (1799)
Pius VII (1800–1823)	Cane Ridge revival (1801)
	Louisiana purchase (1803)
	Napoleon emperor (1804)
	British and Foreign Bible Society (1804)
	Independence of Haiti (1804)
	British in Cape of Good Hope (1806)
	Hegel's *Phenomenology of the Spirit* (1807)
	French occupy Rome (1808)

Popes	*Events*
	Joseph Bonaparte King of Spain (1808)
	Mexican independence (1810)
	American Board of Commissioners (1810)
	Independence of Paraguay and Venezuela (1811)
	British-American War (1812–1814)
	Napoleon in Russia (1812)
	Reorganization of the Jesuits (1814)
	Waterloo (1815)
	Independence of River Plate (1816)
	American Bible Society (1816)
	Etsi longissimo (1816)
	Gospel of Matthew in Burmese (1817)
	Independence of Chile (1818)
	James Long in Texas (1819)
	Independence, Peru and Central America (1821)
	Schleiermacher's *Christian Faith* (1821–1822)
Leo XII (1823–1829)	Monroe Doctrine (1823)
	Etsi iam diu (1824)
	Independence of Bolivia (1825)
	American Society for the Promotion of Temperance (1826)
	Panama Congress (1826)
Pius VIII (1829–1830)	Abolition of slavery in Mexico (1829)
	Book of Mormon (1830)
	Comte's *Course of Positive Philosophy* (1830–1842)
Gregory XVI (1831–1846)	
	Boer migration (1835)
	Republic of Texas (1836)
	Abolition of slavery, British Caribbean (1838)
	Opium War (1839–1842)
	Brooke government in Sarawak (1841–1946)
	Livingstone in Africa (1841)

Popes	Events
	Kierkegaard begins his work (1843)
	"Manifest destiny" (1845)
	Methodists and Baptists split over slavery (1845)
Pius IX (1846–1878)	Mexican-American War (1846–1848)
	Liberian independence (1847)
	Famine in Ireland, migration to USA (1847)
	Second Republic in France (1848)
	Communist Manifesto (1848)
	Roman Republic (1849)
	Taiping rebellion (1850–1864)
	Cavour's government in Italy (1852–1861)
	Napoleon III (1852–1870)
	Dogma of Immaculate Conception of Mary (1854)
	Commodore Perry in Japan (1854)
	Holly in Haiti (1855)
	Darwin's *Origin of the Species* (1859)
	Kingdom of Italy (1861)
	Civil War in USA (1861–1865)
	Presbyterians divide over slavery (1861)
	Congregation of Eastern Rites (1862)
	Bismarck chancellor (1862)
	Salvation Army (1864)
	Syllabus of Errors (1864)
	Catholics persecuted in Korea (1865)
	China Inland Mission (1865)
	I Vatican Council (1869–1870)
	Dogma of Papal Infallibility (1870)
	Franco-Prussian War (1870–1871)
	Third Republic in France (1870–1914)
	Moody begins preaching (1872)
	Mary Baker Eddy's *Science and Health* (1875)

Popes	*Events*
Leo XIII (1878–1903)	
	Protestant missionaries in Korea (1884)
	Rerum novarum (1891)
	US Supreme Court approves segregation (1892)
	Five Fundamentals (1895)
	Spanish-American War (1898)
	Boxer rebellion in China (1899–1901)
	Freud's psychoanalysis (1900)
Pius X (1903–1914)	
	Azusa Street revival (1906)
	Pascendi domini regis (1907)
	Belgian Congo (1908)
	Scofield's Bible (1909)
	Japan annexes Korea (1910)
	Methodist Pentecostal Church, Chile (1910)
	World Missionary Conference, Edinburgh (1910)
	Fall of Chinese Empire (1912)
	Assemblies of God (1914)
Benedict XV (1914–1922)	World War I (1914–1918)

25/Political Horizons: The United States

Here ends the 18th Century. The 19th begins with a fine clear morning wind at S.W.; and the political horizon affords as fine a prospect . . . with the irresistible propagation of the Rights of Man, the eradication of hierarchy, superstition and tyranny over the world.
NATHANIEL AMES'S DIARY, DECEMBER 31, 1800

The last years of the eighteenth century, and the first of the nineteenth, brought a series of political changes that shook Europe and the western hemisphere. In general, those changes were the result of the convergence of the new political ideas to which we have already referred (chapter 21) with the economic interests of the growing bourgeoisie. During the second half of the eighteenth century, both in Europe and in the western hemisphere, the economic power of a new class had increased. In France, this new class was the bourgeoisie, which had come into its own with the growth of cities, trade, and industry. In the western hemisphere, riches were based on agriculture and the trade derived from it; and therefore the colonials who owned the land had become a new aristocracy of money. The interests of this aristocracy and of the European bourgeoisie conflicted with those of the older aristocracy of blood. In France, the lower classes were allied with the bourgeoisie in their hatred of the aristocracy, whom they saw as parasites living off the product of their labor. In the New World, the lower classes were also allied with the new aristocracy against the aristocracy of blood, whom they saw as foreigners profiting from the colonies without understanding their dreams and problems. All this resulted in the independence of the United States, the French Revolution, and the independence of Latin America. To each of these events and to its religious consequences we shall devote a separate chapter.

The Independence of the Thirteen Colonies

Since their foundation, the British colonies in North America had enjoyed a measure of autonomy. This was aided by the political and religious convulsions that shook England during the seventeenth century, making it more difficult for the British government to exercise authority overseas. Given these circumstances, many of the colonies had organized their government and their trade as best suited them, and not as best suited the interests of England. In the second half of the eighteenth century, however, the British government began seeking more direct rule in the colonies, and the latter reacted vigorously against this encroachment by royal authorities. There were mainly three factors that precipitated the open conflict. First, the British quartered seventeen regiments in the colonies. Since their defense did not require such military strength, the colonials felt justified in seeing the army as an instrument of repression. Second, taxes were a constant point of friction. The crown decided that the colonies should pay the expenses of government—including the cost of keeping the hated regiments on the field—and to that end decreed a series of taxes. Since even in England the principle that taxes ought to be approved by a representative assembly was of long standing, the colonials felt that they had the same right and that this was being violated. Third, there were conflicts over Indian lands. For both political and moral reasons, British authorities decreed that there would be no more white occupation of areas beyond the Appalachians. This was an unpopular law in the colonies, where poor whites hoped to establish a homestead in lands now forbidden, and speculators of the landed aristocracy had formed companies for the colonization of Indian lands.

For these reasons, tension grew between the colonies and the metropolis. Stricter laws evoked greater defiance. In 1770, British troops fired on a crowd in Boston, and five people were killed. Faced with the threat of these troops now considered foreign, the colonial militia became more active and built up its arsenals. In 1775, when British forces threatened to destroy one of those arsenals, the militia offered resistance, and thus began the War of Independence. On July 4, 1776, more than a year after hostilities had begun, delegates of the thirteen colonies gathered in a Continental Congress in Philadelphia to proclaim their independence from Britain. France and Spain then became allies of the new nation, while England counted on the support of many Indian tribes who feared that the independence of the colonies would result in their own destruction—as did indeed happen. Finally, in 1782, a provisional agreement was reached, confirmed a year later by the Treaty of Paris.

These events profoundly affected North American religion. Many joined the struggle for independence to a rationalist ideology that spoke of Providence as above all a principle of progress. The new nation itself was living proof of human progress. Part of such progress was leaving behind the dogmatic attitude of traditional Christianity, and espousing only "natural religion," or, at best, "essential Christianity." The traditional teachings and practice of Christian churches, except what could be understood in terms of natural reason or common morality, were considered relics of a bygone age, an unnecessary ballast in the ship of progress.

Such ideas became institutionalized in two originally independent movements that were soon entwined: Unitarianism and Universalism. The first was practically contemporary with independence, and made headway mostly in Anglican and Congregationalist circles that were no longer willing to subscribe to traditional orthodoxy. Although the churches that resulted from this movement were called "Unitarian" because they rejected the doctrine of the Trinity, in truth there were many other points of disagreement with orthodoxy. They were rationalists, stressing human freedom and intellectual capabilities in contrast to the orthodox emphasis on divine mystery and human sin. This movement became most influential among the merchant class in New England. Universalism—that is, the doctrine that in the end all will be saved—was introduced in the colonies shortly before their independence by British Methodists who argued that the doctrine of eternal damnation was a denial of God's love. Some Universalist churches were organized in New England after independence. Soon the movement merged with the Unitarians. It was also in these circles that "Transcendentalism" found most of its adherents. This movement, whose most famous representative was Ralph Waldo Emerson, combined rationalism with romanticism. It stressed self-knowledge as a means to understand the universe and its purpose. Like Unitarianism, Transcendentalism gained most of its adepts from among the higher classes, although many of its ideas eventually infiltrated the rest of the nation.

In any case, the most immediate challenge facing the churches in the new nation was the question of their relations with Great Britain. As was to be expected, this issue was most grave for Anglicanism. Since long before independence, many had looked upon Anglican bishops as agents of the crown, and had therefore opposed the naming of bishops for the colonies. During the struggle for independence, there was a high proportion of loyalists among the membership of the Church of England, and eventually many of these emigrated to England or Canada. Finally, in 1783, those Anglicans who remained in the United States became the Protestant Episcopal Church, whose main strength was among the aristocracy.

The United States (1800)

At first Methodism suffered similar reverses, for the same reasons. Wesley was a staunch supporter of the crown, and called on colonial Methodists to obey the royal edicts. After the Declaration of Independence, all English Methodist preachers in the colonies, except Asbury, returned to Great Britain. This did not contribute to Methodist popularity among the patriots. But, thanks to the untiring efforts of Asbury, American Methodism began taking its distinct shape, and new preachers were recruited. Finally, in 1784, at the "Christmas Conference," American Methodism was organized as a church, apart from both Anglicanism and British Methodism. It was also decided that American Methodism would be led by bishops.

Other churches followed different courses. The Baptists grew rapidly, particularly in Virginia and other southern colonies, and from there penetrated the new territories of Tennessee and Kentucky. The Congregationalists, in spite of having gained prestige by their support of independence, made significant gains only in the areas colonized from New England. In general, all denominations spent their best efforts in reorganizing themselves in view of the new situation, and in repairing the damage done by war.

The word that has just been used—"denomination"—points to one of the main characteristics of the Christianity resulting from the North American experience. The word itself indicates that the various "churches" are seen as "denominations," that is, as different names given to Christians. In a religiously pluralistic society where tolerance was necessary for political survival, and in view of the bloodshed that dogmatism had caused elsewhere, North American Protestants tended to think of the church as an invisible reality consisting of all true believers, and of the visible churches or "denominations" as voluntary organizations that believers create and join according to their convictions and preferences.

A practical consequence of this view of the "church" and the "denominations" is that the great debates that have divided North American Protestantism have not been confined to a particular "church," but have crossed "denominational" barriers. Thus, for instance, questions such as slavery, evolution, fundamentalism, liberalism, and racial policies have simultaneously divided several denominations, and the partisans of one position or another have joined across denominational lines.

The Disciples of Christ were born as a response to the denominationalism of American Christianity. The founders of this movement, Thomas Campbell (1763–1854) and his son Alexander (1788–1866), had no desire to found a new church or denomination. Their purpose was to call all Protestant Christians to unity through the proclamation of the gospel in its original purity. Alexander Campbell, who soon became the leader of the movement, combined some of the rationalism common to his age with a profound respect for the authority of the New Testament. Therefore, much of his interpretation of the New Testament was influenced by rationalist views, although his zeal in obeying what he took to be God's commands was unparalleled by the rationalists. With the firm conviction that Christian unity could be achieved by a common return to primitive Christianity as he understood it, Campbell launched a program of reformation that eventually, much against his original designs, led to the formation of a new denomination, the Christian Church (Disciples of Christ). Given the tensions in Campbell's own thought, as well as various later influences, throughout their history the Disciples have included both a rationalist and a conservative wing. But all have been characterized by their interest in Christian unity.

Immigration

The thirteen colonies that later became the United States had been peopled by immigrants, mostly from Great Britain, but also from Germany and other parts of Europe. But late in the eighteenth century, and throughout the nineteenth, there was an unprecedented wave of migration from Europe to the United States. This was due partly to conditions in Europe—the Napoleonic Wars, social upheaval caused by industrialization, the tyranny of various regimes, famine, and so forth—and partly to the vast expansion of land seemingly available to the West of the new nation. At the same time, the slave traffic also took to the United States vast numbers of unwilling immigrants.

Such massive immigration had far-reaching consequences for the shape of Christianity in the United States. The Catholic Church (which, at the time of independence, was a small minority) had, by the middle of the nineteenth century, become the largest religious body in the nation. At first, most Catholics were of English descent. Later came French and Germans. But, around 1846, a great famine began in Ireland lasting several decades, and soon the Irish and their descendents became the largest group within American Catholicism. This in turn created tensions within the Catholic Church, both locally and nationally. At the parish level, each group of immigrants saw the church as a means to preserve its culture and tradition; therefore, each wanted a separate parish. At the national level, there were power struggles between various groups, each wishing to be governed by a hierarchy that understood and represented it. Such tensions would continue well into the twentieth century, and would become more complex as other groups were added to North American Catholicism—Italians, Poles, and others by immigration, the French of Louisiana by purchase, and the Hispanics of Mexico and Puerto Rico by military conquest. Eventually, Catholicism in the United States would be characterized by its cultural diversity and by the degree to which that diversity and the pressure of the surrounding culture have limited the traditional power of the hierarchy.

The growth of Catholicism provoked a strong reaction on the part of some Protestants. In the very early years of the new nation, there was already opposition to unlimited Catholic immigration, on the grounds that democracy was not compatible with the hierarchical understanding of authority of Roman Catholics, and that their growing numbers were therefore a threat to the nation. Later, the Ku Klux Klan would unleash its xenophobic fanaticism, not only against blacks, but also against Catholics and Jews, on the premise that the United States was called to be a white, Protestant, and democratic nation, and that these three characteristics were inseparable. When, in 1864, Pope Pius IX condemned a list of eighty "errors" (see chapter 29) that included several of the fundamental theses of American democracy, there were many in the United States, both conservative and liberal, who saw this as a confirmation of their worst fears regarding the political goals of the Catholic Church. It would take almost another century for the nation to be willing to trust its highest political offices to Roman Catholics.

Lutheranism also grew rapidly through immigration. At first, most Lutheran immigrants were German, but later there were also many Scandinavians. Each of these groups carried its own traditions with it, and for a long time the main item on the agenda of American Lutheranism was the eventual union of the various Lutheran bodies. Other religious groups that grew through immigration were the Mennonites, Moravians, Greek and Russian Orthodox, and Jews. The rich variety of such groups further necessitated the tradition of religious tolerance that had begun centuries earlier in Rhode Island and Pennsylvania.

Many immigrants also brought with them the ideal of a religious community, and thus the American countryside was dotted with small experiments in communal living. From very early times, one of the goals leading Europeans to the colonies of North America was the founding of a new society in a new land. The *Mayflower* Pilgrims were only the first of thousands with similar dreams. Both European immigrants and natives of the United States moved west, seeking places to found ideal communities. The Moravians founded settlements in Pennsylvania that still exist, and similar experiments were undertaken by Mennonites and other Anabaptists in search of a place where they could freely practice their pacifist beliefs. German Pietists founded the community of Ephrata, also in Pennsylvania, and several others nearby and in Ohio. The commonality of goods was a characteristic of many of these settlements. In 1846, the Oneida community went so far as to practice "complex matrimony," in which all adults were married to all others of the opposite sex.

One of the most remarkable of these movements was that of the Shakers, led by Ann Lee Stanley—Mother Ann Lee. For a time they sought to live out their faith in their native England; but social pressure was such that eventually they decided to emigrate to America. In their new homeland, probably in imitation of other neighboring groups, they opted for communal living. Mother Ann Lee claimed that she was the Second Coming of Christ, who had now appeared in feminine form as he had appeared earlier in masculine form. Eventually, all would be saved, and the present community of belief was only the beachhead of that final salvation. Meanwhile, believers must abstain from sex, which is the root of all evil. One of the characteristics of Shaker worship was the important role played by dance. For a few decades, the movement flourished, and several Shaker communities were founded. As experiments in communal living, they were quite successful, for conditions in Shaker communities were usually better than in neighboring areas. But eventually the movement dwindled, lacking both in converts and in new generations.

The Second Great Awakening

Towards the end of the eighteenth century, a Second Great Awakening began in New England. This was not marked by great emotional outbursts, but rather by a sudden earnestness in Christian devotion and living. Attendance at worship increased noticeably, and many spoke of having had an experience of conversion. Nor did this awakening have at first the anti-intellectual overtones of other similar movements. On the contrary, it made headway among some of the most distinguished theologians of New England, and one of its foremost advocates was Timothy Dwight, president of Yale and a grandson of Jonathan Edwards.

That first phase of the awakening resulted in the founding of several societies whose purpose was to make the gospel known. Most important among these were the American Bible Society, founded in 1816, and the American Board of Commissioners for Foreign Missions, founded six years earlier. The latter was the result of a covenant made by a group of students meeting on a haystack, who vowed to devote themselves to foreign missions. When Adinoram Judson, one of the first missionaries sent by the American Board, became a Baptist, many Baptists in the United States set aside some of their extreme congregationalism in order to organize a General Convention whose purpose was to support Baptist missionaries throughout the world. In local churches, women's missionary societies appeared, and some of these would later develop into various feminine organizations. Other societies born during the Second Awakening took up various social causes, such as the abolition of slavery—the American Colonization Society, to which we shall return—and the war against alcohol—the American Society for the Promotion of Temperance, founded in 1826. Women became leaders in the latter cause, to the point that in the second half of the century, under the leadership of Frances Willard, the Women's Christian Temperance Union became the foremost defender of women's rights. Thus, some of the roots of American feminism can be traced to the Second Great Awakening.

Meanwhile, the awakening had moved beyond the limits of New England and of the educated elite, and had made great headway among people of less education and fewer means. Many of these people were moving west, for one of the results of the War of Independence was that the European powers agreed to the expansion of the United States as far as the Mississippi. Many of those who traveled west carried with them the vibrant faith kindled by the Second Awakening. But, since conditions on the frontier were different, the awakening now became more emotional and less intellectual, to the point that it eventually became anti-intellectual.

The Cane Ridge Revival of 1801, in Cane Ridge, Kentucky, marked a significant step in that process. It was originally organized by the local Presbyterian pastor, who announced a great assembly or "camp meeting" for the promotion of a deeper faith. On the appointed date, thousands gathered. In an area where there were few opportunities to gather and celebrate, the pastor's announcement had a resounding success. Many went to Cane Ridge for religious reasons. Others made it an opportunity to gamble and carouse. Besides the pastor who had issued the original invitation, there were several Baptist and Methodist preachers. While some played and others drank, the pastors preached. A critic of the awakening later declared that, at Cane

Ridge, as many souls were conceived as were saved. In any case, the response to the call to repentance was surprising and overwhelming. While some wept and others laughed uncontrollably, others trembled, some ran about, and some even barked. The meeting lasted a week, and since then many have been convinced that such gatherings were the best way to proclaim the gospel. After that time, when the words "evangelism" and "revival" were used, they evoked images of Cane Ridge.

Although the gathering at Cane Ridge had been organized by a Presbyterian, that denomination did not favor the unbridled emotional response that was becoming part of the movement. Soon Presbyterians began taking action against ministers who participated in events such as Cane Ridge. But the Methodists and Baptists took up the idea of celebrating "camp meetings," and these eventually developed into periodic "revivals." Since such revivals became an important part of social life on the frontier, both Methodists and Baptists achieved rapid growth. Another reason for their growth was that they were willing to present the message as simply as possible, and to use preachers with little or no education. While other denominations lacked personnel because they had no educational facilities on the frontier, Methodists and Baptists were willing to use whoever felt called by the Lord. The Methodist vanguard were lay preachers, many of them serving an entire "circuit," always under the supervision of the "Connection" and its bishops. The Baptists made use of farmers or others who made a living from their trade, and who also served as pastors of the local church. When a new area was opened for settlement, there usually was among the settlers a devout Baptist willing to take up the ministry of preaching. Thus, both Methodists and Baptists became strong in the new territories, and by the middle of the century they were the largest Protestant denominations of the country.

Another important consequence of the Second Great Awakening was that it helped break down the strict correspondence between ethnic origin and religious affiliation. Among the new Baptists and Methodists there were German ex-Lutherans, Scottish ex-Presbyterians, and Irish ex-Catholics. Although it was still generally true that denominational allegiance coincided with ethnic origin, after the Second Great Awakening, and especially on the frontier, such correspondence could no longer be taken for granted.

Manifest Destiny and the War with Mexico

Since the first landing of the *Mayflower* Pilgrims, the notion that the British colonies in the New World had been founded with divine assistance, in order to fulfil a providential mission, was commonly accepted. Leaders in the struggle for independence spoke of a new experiment that would lead humankind along paths of progress and liberty. Later immigrants regarded the United States as a Promised Land of freedom and abundance. Such ideas

*During the Second Great Awakening, camp meetings such as this
Methodist one were typical of frontier American Christianity.*

often combined with the conviction that Protestantism was superior to Catholicism, and that the latter was a hindrance to both freedom and progress.
Very early on, England felt that her colonies were threatened by Spanish
Catholics from the South, and by French Catholics from the North; therefore,
she saw such colonies as a Protestant bulwark in the New World. All this was
joined to a racist attitude that took for granted that whites were superior, and
were therefore justified in taking lands away from Indians, and freedom away
from blacks.

These ideas crystalized in the phrase "manifest destiny," coined in 1845.
In 1823, President James Monroe had proclaimed his famous doctrine—that
the United States would not countenence new European ventures in the
western hemisphere—and the destiny of the new nation seemed particularly
manifest in connection with that hemisphere. At about the same time, the
ambassador of Mexico in the United States took note that many people with
whom he spoke in his host country were convinced that the eventual result
of the wars of independence in Spanish America would be that most of the
continent would belong to the United States. When coined in 1845, the
phrase "manifest destiny" referred specifically to western expansion to the
Pacific by occupying Oregon—whose possession was disputed by Great Britain—and all Mexican land directly West of the United States. Since negotiations led to the resolution of the Oregon question, there remained to be
settled the matter of Mexican territory blocking the United States from the
Pacific.

American expansionism had previously played an important role in

Texas. That area, a neglected part of the Mexican state of Coahuila, was invaded in 1819 by James Long, an adventurer who was defeated by the Mexican army. In order to dissuade others from similar adventures, Mexico began allowing people from the United States to settle in Texas, on condition that they be Catholic and that they swear allegiance to Mexico. The net result was a wave of immigration by people who were willing to deny their religion in order to become landowners and who, while nominally Mexican, believed that their race made them naturally superior to the mestizos—people of mixed Indian and European blood—who governed the area in the name of Mexico. One of these immigrants, Stephen Austin, would later declare: "for fifteen years, I have been laboring like a slave to Americanize Texas," and he would add that his enemies were "a population of Indians, Mexicans and renegados, all mixed together, and all the natural enemies of white men and civilization."*

The question of slavery made matters more difficult. Mexico abolished slavery in 1829, and the immigrants of Texas, whose wealth often depended on slavery, responded by conspiring to secede from Mexico and join the United States. Such conspiracies were then aided by those in the United States who had begun to fear the abolitionist movement, and who saw Texas as a possible ally. Others who supported the movement hoped to become rich by speculating on lands the Mexicans would be forced to abandon. At one point, the American ambassador in Mexico tried to bribe a Mexican official by offering him two hundred thousand dollars in exchange for his support for a proposed purchase of Texas.

Finally, war broke out. The Mexican army was more numerous, but the Texan rebels—both immigrants from the United States and discontented Mexicans—were better armed, with more artillery and with rifles whose range was three times that of Mexican muskets. At the mission of El Alamo, in San Antonio, some two hundred rebels resisted an entire Mexican army. After fierce struggle, the last survivors surrendered, and were executed by the Mexicans. "Remember the Alamo" then became the battle cry of the rebels, used in the United States to raise funds and recruit volunteers. The rebels were repeatedly defeated by the larger Mexican army; but, in 1836, Sam Houston took the Mexican headquarters by surprise and captured President Santa Anna, who bought his freedom by agreeing to the independence of the Republic of Texas. The government of Mexico agreed to this, on condition that Texas would remain an independent nation, and not be annexed by the United States—a stipulation to which the latter agreed.

The expansion of the United States to the West, however, could not be stopped by a piece of paper. James K. Polk was elected president in 1844, thus bringing to power those who felt that the nation should continue its

*The Austin Papers, ed. Eugene C. Barker (Washington, D.C.: Government Printing Office, 1919), 3:345, 347.

westward thrust. Even before the new president was sworn in, Texas was made a state of the Union by joint resolution of Congress. The next year produced the phrase "manifest destiny." That destiny—and powerful economic interests hiding behind it—required the conquest of Mexico's northern lands. But there were still many in the United States who opposed such expansion, agreeing with John Quincy Adams's words before the House of Representatives, that in a war with Mexico "the banners of freedom will be the banners of Mexico; and your banners, I blush to speak the word, will be the banners of slavery."* Therefore, it was necessary to make Mexico fire the first shot, and Polk ordered General Zachary Taylor into territory in dispute with Mexico. Years later, Ulysses S. Grant, who as a young lieutenant had been part of that expedition, declared: "We were sent to provoke a fight, but it was essential that Mexico should commence it."** When the Mexican army refused to open hostilities, Taylor was ordered to continue advancing until he drew fire. When Mexico finally offered resistance, Polk obtained from Congress a declaration of war. Grant was convinced that behind all these events stood a conspiracy to increase the number of slaveholding states.

The brief war was concluded by the Treaty of Guadalupe-Hidalgo in 1848, whereby Mexico ceded to the United States, in exchange for fifteen million dollars, more than three million square kilometers—the present states of New Mexico, Arizona, California, Utah, Nevada, and part of Colorado—and agreed to the annexation of Texas by the United States, with the Rio Grande as the border between the two nations. The treaty also guaranteed the rights of Mexicans who decided to remain in the conquered territory. But such rights were soon violated as new settlers moved into the land as if it had no owners, and discrimination against Mexicans as an inferior race became the common practice of the American Southwest.

Before 1848, churches in the United States had been divided in their opinions about the war and the notion of "manifest destiny." Valiant voices of protest were heard against what was seen as naked aggression and as an attempt to reinstitute slavery in lands where it had been banned. But after the war, as settlers rushed to quench their thirst for land, churches joined the westward movement, and soon several denominations were speaking of the "door" that God had opened for the evangelization of Mexicans.

The conquest of these lands had different consequences for Roman Catholicism. The most important was the sudden addition to its membership of a large flock belonging to an entirely different culture from that of the rest of North American Catholics. For several decades, American Catholicism refused to accept that difference, and worked towards the "Americanization" of its new constituency. In 1850, the Catholic Church in the Southwest was

---

*Speech of John Quincy Adams, May 25, 1836 (Washington, D.C.: Gales and Seaton, 1838), p. 119.
**Memoirs, quoted in W. S. McFeely, Grant: A Biography (New York: Norton, 1981), p. 30.

put in the hands of a hierarchy drawn from the East, and the number of Hispanic priests declined rapidly. Mexican-American historians have documented a marked contrast between the older Mexican priests, who lived among the people and served the poor, and the new ones brought from the East, who moved mostly among the English-speaking settlers, and were content with saying mass for the deprived Mexicans. An example of this was the conflict between Father Antonio José Martínez—known among the native population as "el cura de Taos"—and the vicar general for New Mexico, Jean B. Lamy. Although of French background, Lamy served under the diocese of Baltimore, and was a close friend of many of the new citizens of the area—Kit Carson among them. Since 1824, Martínez had headed a seminary in Taos, and most of the older clergy of the area had been trained by him. Although he openly rejected celibacy, many in the area called him a saint, for he devoted his entire life to the care of the poor. When Lamy ordered Martínez and the other Mexican clergy to be more assiduous in collecting the tithes of their flock and sending them to his office, they responded that it was immoral and unchristian to take money from the poor to give to the rich. Lamy excommunicated the refractory priest and his followers, but they continued in their ministry among the Mexicans, serving them as priests and administering the sacraments in open schism with the hierarchy of the church. The movement continued for some years after the death of Martínez, in 1867. As it waned, so did the number of Mexicans offering themselves for the priesthood. It was not until well into the twentieth century that there was in the Southwest a Catholic bishop of Hispanic origin.

Slavery and Civil War

From colonial times, the issue of slavery had troubled the conscience of many. As independence approached, there were those who voiced the opinion that the new nation should be born free of such an evil institution. However, in order to present a common front against Great Britain, such voices were silenced, and the United States, while calling itself the land of the free, continued practicing slavery. Several denominations took a clear stance against it. In 1776, the Quakers expelled from their midst all who insisted on holding slaves. The Christmas Conference in 1784 that organized American Methodist as a separate church also banned slaveholding among its members. And many Baptists, although lacking a national organization that could take similar measures, did take a stance against slavery.

Those early stances, however, were modified with the passage of time. Only the Friends—who in any case were not numerous in the South— remained firm. Methodists as well as Baptists sought to attract the slaveholding whites of the South by moderating their opposition to slavery. By 1843, over a thousand Methodist ministers and preachers owned slaves. Other denominations were equally ambivalent. For instance, in 1818, the General Assembly of the Presbyterian Church, while declaring slavery to be against the law of God, also went on record as opposing its abolition, and deposed a minister for advocating abolition.

At first, antislavery sentiments were equally strong in both North and South. In 1817, the American Colonization Society was founded with the purpose of buying slaves, freeing them, and returning them to Africa. The founding of the Republic of Liberia was largely the result of the Society's work. But such efforts had little impact on slavery in general. Meanwhile, the abolitionist movement was becoming stronger in the North, where slavery was of less economic importance, while the South, whose economic and social system was based on slave labor, took the opposite tack. Soon, many in the South were preaching that slavery was an institution sanctioned by God, and that even blacks profited from it, for by it they had been snatched out of pagan and uncivilized Africa and given the advantages of the gospel. In the North, the abolitionist movement was equally vehement in its conviction that God did not will slavery. Many in the Methodist Church began demanding that the old position of the church against slavery be reasserted. When, in 1844, the Methodist General Conference condemned the bishop of Georgia for holding slaves, the church split, and the following year saw the birth of the Methodist Episcopal Church, South. Something similar happened among Baptists, for when their missionary agency refused to commission a candidate who had been recommended by the Georgia Baptist Convention, on the grounds that he owned slaves, the Southern Baptist Convention was born. In 1861, reflecting the division of the nation, the Southern presbyteries withdrew from the Presbyterian Church and founded their own denomination. These divisions persisted into the twentieth century, when some of them were healed, and others were not. The only major denominations that were able to weather the storm without schism were the Catholics and the Episcopalians.

In 1861, the nation was split, first by the secession of the Confederate States of America, and then by civil war. During the armed conflict, pulpits on both sides defended the justice of their cause. After the war, hatred and prejudice were fostered because—after the period of "Reconstruction," which practically meant northern military occupation—the South became an economic colony of the North. Southern whites were permitted to manage political and social matters as long as they did not interfere with northern economic interests and their investments in the area. Southern whites, unable to vent their anger on the North, turned it towards the black population of the area. Fear of blacks was fostered from many southern pulpits, and when that fear led to the founding of the Ku Klux Klan there were preachers who openly supported its activities. The same hatred and fear of the North also led to anti-intellectualism and conservatism in the southern churches, for most of the great educational centers were in the North, and any ideas coming from them were suspect.

Since southern whites could vent their anger and frustration on blacks, they did so. During Reconstruction, blacks were given positions of responsibility by the northern invaders. But this served only to exacerbate southern white prejudice against them, and as soon as Reconstruction came to an end southern whites moved to restrict the rights and power of blacks. In 1892, the Supreme Court approved segregation, as long as blacks were treated as "separate, but equal." Then the long series of "Jim Crow laws" ensued, effectively excluding blacks from public places, from the right to vote, from good public education, and so forth. Meanwhile, southern white churches continued their racist teachings and practices. Blacks who had formerly attended such churches as slaves were now encouraged to leave them, and this in turn gave rise to various black denominations. Black Baptists formed their own congregations, that later joined in the National Baptist Convention. Black Methodists founded the Colored Methodist Episcopal Church—the C.M.E. Church, later to become the Christian Methodist Episcopal Church. Meanwhile, northern churches—particularly Presbyterians and Methodists —began work among blacks in the South.

But the North was not exempt from prejudice and segregation. Even before the Civil War such attitudes had led to the formation of two black denominations that would later play an important role among freed blacks

Blacks were encouraged to leave white churches and form their own, such as this one in Washington.

in the South: the African Methodist Episcopal Church, and the African Methodist Episcopal Zion Church. The former was founded by Richard Allen, a freedman who had been the first black to be ordained a deacon by North American Methodists. Allen organized in Philadelphia a local church for blacks, but repeated conflicts with the white hierarchy of his denomination eventually led to its separation from the white church and the birth of a new denomination. Five years later, in 1821, similar events in New York led to the creation of the African Methodist Episcopal Zion Church. Both of these denominations played an important role among northern blacks and, after the Civil War, also in the South. They also did important missionary work in Africa.

Soon black churches became one of the principal institutions of black society. Since the only prestigious position to which blacks had relatively free access was the ministry, for a century most black leaders were also pastors. Some black churches advocated submission to present injustice while awaiting a heavenly reward. In others, more radical words of justice and black dignity were heard. But all contributed to the sense of identity and cohesion among blacks that a hundred years later would be the backbone of the struggle for civil rights.

From the Civil War to World War I

The social and economic tensions of earlier decades increased after the Civil War. The South became even more racist and anti-intellectual. In the North, immigration brought about rapid urban growth, and ecclesiastical structures proved unequal to the challenge of that growth, or of the increasing number of blacks who moved to the North seeking better living conditions. In the West, relentless pressure continued to be applied on Indian lands, and Hispanics were the object of discrimination.

In the midst of such diversity, one of the elements contributing to the unity of the nation was the notion that it had a providential role to play for the progress of humankind. Usually that role was understood in terms of racial, religious, and institutional superiority—that is, the superiority of the white race, the Protestant faith, and democratic government based on free enterprise. Thus, late in the century the general secretary of the Evangelical Alliance, Josiah Strong, declared that God was preparing the Anglo-Saxon race for a great moment, "the final competition of races." Then that race, representing "the largest liberty, the purest Christianity, the highest civilization,"* would fulfill its God-given destiny of dispossessing the weaker ones, assimilating others, and moulding the rest, so as to "Anglo-Saxonize" human-

*Quoted in Sydney E. Ahlstrom, *A Religious History of the American People*, vol. 2 (Garden City, New York: Doubleday, 1975), p. 327.

kind. And such sentiments, expressed by one of the leaders of the conservative wing of American Protestantism, were similar to those of the liberal wing, who held that Protestantism and freedom of opinion were the great contribution of the Nordic races against the tyranny and Catholicism of Southern European races, and that therefore people of Nordic origin had the responsibility of civilizing the "backward" races of the rest of the world.

Such notions, however, contrasted with the urban reality of the United States itself, where recent immigrants were exploited and lived in over-crowded conditions, lacking all contact with organized Christianity—particularly in its Protestant form. Protestantism sought to respond to this challenge in various ways. One was the establishment of several organizations whose goal was to serve the urban masses. Most successful among these were the Young Men's Christian Association (YMCA) and the Young Women's Christian Association (YWCA), both imported from England in the mid-nineteenth century. Another Protestant response to the challenge of the new population was the creation of Sunday Schools. At a time when the study of the Bible at home was falling into disuse, and the knowledge of Scripture among the masses was decreasing, Sunday Schools played a very important role. Eventually, there were churches where Sunday School surpassed Sunday worship in importance. In 1872, several large denominations began the practice of agreeing on the Scriptural texts to be used each Sunday, and this in turn was a significant step towards greater understanding and collaboration across denominational lines.

Protestantism also responded to the urban challenge by adapting the old camp meetings to the new situation, and "revivals" became an important element of the urban religious scene. The main figure in the early stages of this development was Dwight L. Moody. Moody was a Chicago shoe sales-man who was moved by the lack of religious life among the masses of that great city. He began by bringing people to the Congregationalist church of which he was a member, but he soon moved on to founding an independent church. He also became involved in the work of the YMCA, where he was noted for his zeal in communicating the gospel to others. It was in 1872, while visiting London in connection with his YMCA responsibilities, that he was first invited to preach. The result was so encouraging that Moody then felt called to preach to the urban masses, first in England, and then in the United States. His method consisted of simple and emotive preaching, calling people to repentance and to accept salvation offered in Jesus Christ. He was convinced that the conversion of the masses would lead to better living conditions in the cities, and therefore he had little to say regarding the conditions and structures that led to so much human misery. But there is no doubt that his message and style were singularly well adapted to the felt needs of the urban masses. Soon he had many imitators, some more successful than others. The revival became part of the American urban landscape.

New denominations also arose as a response to the urban challenge. Within the Methodist tradition, both in England and in the United States, there were many who felt that the Methodist Church had abandoned some basic elements of Wesley's teachings. It was clear that Methodists had been progressively moving towards the middle classes, and paying less attention to the poor, especially the urban poor. Since it was precisely among such people that the movement had achieved its early success, there were many who sought to return to that earlier emphasis. In England, this gave rise to the Salvation Army, founded by Methodist preacher William Booth and his wife Catherine Munford—who was also a preacher, for one of the character-istic notes of the Salvation Army was the equality of the sexes within it. The Army was concerned for both the spiritual and the physical wellbeing of the urban masses, and soon became known for its relief work among the poor, providing food, shelter, work, and so forth. Given the conditions of urban life in the United States, when the Salvation Army was brought over from England it found a fertile field for its work.

There were also several new ecclesiastical bodies born in the United States out of the dissatisfaction of Methodists with the direction their church had taken. These groups wished to return both to the earlier concern for the masses, and to Wesley's teachings on sanctification. This latter emphasis earned the name of "holiness churches," by which they were collectively known. At first, there were many such groups, with no connection among themselves. But slowly they crystalized into several new denominations, of which the most numerous was the Church of the Nazarene, organized in 1908 through the union of several holiness churches. But still, the main strength of the holiness movement was in the hundreds of independent churches, and in others belonging to very small denominations, scattered throughout the country.

At first, worship in many holiness churches was marked by the outpour-ing of the "gifts of the Spirit"—particularly speaking in tongues, miracles of healing, and prophetic utterances. Such practices, eventually abandoned by many holiness churches, reappeared with great vigor in 1906, in the Azusa Street Mission of Los Angeles. Then "Pentecostal fire," starting from that "Azusa Street revival," spread throughout the nation. Since there were in Azusa Street both black and white members, the movement spread to churches of both races. It then moved beyond the limits of the Wesleyan tradition, and was taken up by many Baptists and others. By 1914, the director of a Pentecostal publication called for a great gathering of "believers in the baptism of the Holy Spirit," and out of that gathering emerged the Assemblies of God, the main Pentecostal denomination of the United States. Both the Assemblies and other Pentecostal denominations made significant inroads among the urban masses, and soon moved both to the rural areas and to distant countries, to which they sent numerous missionaries.

Another denomination that took its definitive form after the Civil War, although it had gone through a long process of formation, was the Seventh Day Adventists. Early in the nineteenth century, Vermont Baptist William Miller, by joining data taken from Daniel with other elements from Genesis and the rest of Scripture, had come to the conclusion that the Lord would return in 1843. When that date arrived and passed, most of Miller's followers left him. But a small remnant continued anxiously awaiting the Lord's return. The movement then led a precarious existence until the appearance of prophet Ellen Harmon White. By then, through contacts with Seventh Day Baptists, they had begun keeping the seventh day of the week instead of Sunday. Mrs. White was a superb organizer whose published visions gathered around her the remnants of Miller's followers and many others, who were finally organized into a single body in 1868. Under Mrs. White's leadership, the Adventists took great interest in medicine, dietetics, and missions. By the time Mrs. White died in 1915, the movement had thousands of adherents, both in the United States and in several other nations.

Protestantism in the United States had other challenges to face besides urban growth, and of these the most important was intellectual in character. Europe was constantly sending across the Atlantic, not only immigrants, but also ideas that questioned much that had earlier been taken for granted. Darwin's theory of evolution seemed to contradict the stories of creation in Genesis, and therefore produced quite a stir among the masses. But among theologians a greater challenge was posed by the historical and critical studies that were taking place in Europe. Such studies raised doubts about the historical authenticity of several—if not most—books of the Bible. As a methodological presupposition, all that seemed extraordinary or miraculous was to be rejected. In the same academic circles, great optimism prevailed regarding the human creature and its capabilities. Thanks to evolution and progress, the day was at hand when humans would be able to solve problems until then insoluble, thus bringing in a new age of joy, freedom, justice, peace, and abundance.

Protestant Liberalism was an attempt to couch Christianity in the mold of those ideas, and gained wide acceptance among the intellectual elite in the United States. It was by no means a monolithic movement, for the very idea of "liberalism" implied freedom to think as one saw fit—as long as one did not fall into what liberals called "superstition." But it was a vast wave of thought that many saw as a denial of the Christian faith. In that wave there was a relatively small number of radicals—sometimes called "modernists"— for whom Christianity and the Bible were little more than another religion and a great book among many. But most liberals were committed Christians whose very commitment drove them to respond to the intellectual challenges of their time, in the hope of making the faith credible for modern people. In any case, liberalism in the United States was mostly limited to the Northeast, and to the middle and upper classes, for whom the intellectual issues of the day seemed more pressing that the social conditions of urban laborers. In the South and the West, liberalism had little impact.

The reaction was not slow in coming, for many saw liberalism as a threat to the very core of the Christian faith. At the popular level, probably the issue most discussed was the theory of evolution, and there were even attempts to have courts of law decide on the matter—as late as the last decades of the twentieth century, debate continued as to whether public schools should be allowed to teach the theory of evolution, and as to how this should be done so as not to contradict Scripture. But conservative theologians clearly saw that the question of evolution was only one instance of the threat the new ideas posed to the "fundamentals" of Christianity. Soon the term "fundamentals" became characteristic of the anti-liberal reaction that came to be called "fundamentalism." In 1846, when that movement was beginning to crystalize, the Evangelical Alliance was formed, seeking to join all those who saw liberalism as a denial of the faith. But it was in 1895, at a meeting in Niagara Falls, New York, that the movement listed the five "fundamentals" that could not be denied without falling into the error of liberalism. These were the inerrancy of Scripture, the divinity of Jesus, the Virgin birth, Jesus' death on the cross as a substitute for our sins, and his physical resurrection and impending return. Shortly thereafter, the General Assembly of the Presbyterian Church adopted similar principles. From that point on, and for several decades, the majority of Protestants, particularly in the South, were fundamentalists.

On the other hand, it is significant to note that, while fundamentalism declared itself a defender of traditional orthodoxy, it gave rise to new interpretations of the Bible. Its emphasis on biblical inerrancy and its rejection of many of the conclusions of biblical scholars made it possible to juxtapose texts from different books of Scripture, and thus to develop a number of schemes outlining and explaining God's actions, past, present, and future. The most successful of these schemes were those of the "dispensationalists"—of which there were several. The most popular dispensationalist scheme was developed by Cyrus Scofield, who divided human history into seven "dispensations"—the present one being the sixth. In 1909, the "Scofield Bible" was published, outlining this interpretation of history, and it soon became widely used in fundamentalist circles. Thus, fundamentalism became closely tied with dispensationalism—although many fundamentalists differed from Scofield in matters of detail.

Meanwhile, liberalism was making its most significant contribution in what came to be called the "Social Gospel." This was not the belief of most liberals, who belonged to the urban middle classes, and were scarcely interested in the plight of the poor. But a small core of liberals did devote their efforts to exploring and showing the relationship between the demands of the gospel and the misery in which the urban masses lived. Their leader was Walter Rauschenbush, who was a professor of church history at a Baptist seminary from 1897 until his death in 1918. He insisted that the social and economic life of the nation should conform to the requirements of the gospel, and showed that economic liberalism—the theory that the law of supply and demand suffices to regulate the marketplace—results in great inequity and social injustice. The task of Christians in that context is to seek to limit the unbridled power of runaway capital, and to advocate the enactment of laws that will aid the poor and promote greater justice. The point of contact between the Social Gospel and the rest of liberalism was their common optimism regarding human capabilities and the progress of society. But while other liberals simply trusted the natural progress of humanity and of capitalist society, the proponents of the Social Gospel saw the danger that so-called progress would take place at the expense of the poor.

Both fundamentalism and liberalism reached their apex at a time when the political and economic future of the United States seemed assured. The war with Mexico, the abolition of slavery, and the war with Spain in 1898 seemed to promise that the United States—and the white race that ruled the nation—were destined to lead the world through an era of progress and prosperity. Then World War I broke out, followed by a period of economic distress. How this affected Christianity in the United States is a subject to which we shall return at another point.

New Religions

One of the most remarkable phenomena in the religious life of the United States during the nineteenth century was the birth of several movements that so differed from traditional Christianity that they could well be called new religions. The largest of these were the Mormons, Jehovah's Witnesses, and Christian Science.

During his early years, Joseph Smith, the founder of Mormonism, seemed to be a failure. His parents were poor, rural folk who had moved to New York from Vermont seeking, and failing to find, better economic conditions. Young Joseph was not inclined to labor in the fields, preferring to seek hidden treasures and to claim that he had visions telling him where such treasures could be found. He then declared that an angel named Moroni had appeared to him and had given him a collection of golden tablets written in ancient Egyptian hieroglyphs, as well as two "seer's stones" with which it was possible to read the tablets. Hidden behind a curtain, Smith then dictated his translation of the sacred tablets to others who wrote on the other side of the curtain. The result was the *Book of Mormon,* published in 1830. The book also included the testimony of several witnesses, who affirmed that they had seen the tablets before Moroni took them back.

Shortly after publishing his book, Smith had many followers. Then they were joined by an entire group who had already been practicing communal living, and the Mormons took a similar organization. According to them, their new religion was to Christianity what Christianity was to Judaism: its culmination. Meanwhile, Smith continued having new visions that led him further away from orthodox Christianity. After settling for a time in Ohio, he and his followers moved to Illinois, where they founded an autonomous community, with its own militia, where Smith was eventually called "King of the Kingdom of God." But tensions with the society around them grew, especially when Smith declared himself a candidate for the presidency of the United States. Eventually, an unruly mob lynched the prophet and one of his followers.

The leadership of the movement then fell to Brigham Young, who led the Mormons—more precisely, the Church of Jesus Christ of the Latter Day Saints—to Utah. There they founded an autonomous state, until the United States took possession of the area in 1850, as part of its westward expansion. This produced new conflicts, especially since two years later Young declared that Smith had had a vision, until then kept secret, reinstituting polygamy. In 1857, war broke out between the Mormons and the United States. Eventually and progressively, the Mormons allowed themselves to be shaped by the rest of society, leaving aside their emphasis on visions and community living,

Brigham Young succeeded Joseph Smith, and under his leadership the Mormons reached Utah, where they settled.

and finally, in 1890, officially abandoning polygamy—although it continued to be practiced in secret. Their political influence in Utah was great, and their missionaries soon spread their faith to several other nations.

Jehovah's Witnesses were a result of the manner in which many were reading Scripture, as a book where hidden clues could be found regarding future events and the end of the world. In its early stages, the movement also crystalized some of the resentment of the lower classes against the religious, political, and social establishment. Thus, Charles T. Russell, the founder of the new faith, declared that the three great instruments of Satan were government, business, and the church. He also rejected the doctrine of the Trinity and the divinity of Jesus, and declared that the Second Coming had taken place in 1872, and that the end would be in 1914.

The year 1914 brought World War I, but not the Armaggedon predicted by Russell, who died two years later. He was then succeeded by Joseph F. Rutherford, better known as "Judge Rutherford." It was he who, in 1931, named the movement "Jehovah's Witnesses," and who also organized it into a vast missionary machine, while reinterpreting Russell's teachings after the fiasco of 1914.

Christian Science was the main expression in the United States of a long religious tradition that we have repeatedly encountered in our narrative—when dealing with Gnosticism, Manicheism, Spiritualism, and so forth. In general, that tradition holds that the material world is either imaginary or of secondary importance; that the purpose of human life is to live in harmony with the Universal Spirit; and that Scripture is to be interpreted by means of a spiritual clue, usually unknown to the majority of Christians. The founder of Christian Science, Mary Baker Eddy, suffered repeated illness during her youth. Twice married and widowed, poor and sick, suffering from acute pains that extensive use of morphine could not assuage, she finally went to P. P. Quimby, who claimed that illness was error, and that the knowledge of truth sufficed to cure it. Having been healed by Quimby, she became his disciple and apostle. Several years after Quimby's death, in 1875, she published *Science and Health, with a Key to Scripture.* During her lifetime, this book was published 382 times. In it, Mrs. Eddy used traditional terms of Christian orthodoxy, such as "God," "Christ," "Salvation," "Trinity," and so forth, in a "spiritual" sense that differed from the traditional one—which reminds us of the ancient Gnostic interpretations of Scripture, where words such as "truth" and "life" took a unique meaning. She held that illness was a mental error, the result of a mistaken perspective, and that to heal it one should not make use of physicians or drugs, but rather of the spiritual "science" that Jesus employed, and that she now had rediscovered. Likewise, the knowledge of such science would produce happiness and prosperity—as the middle class of the United States understood those terms.

The Church of Christ, Scientist, was officially founded in 1879, and it soon had followers throughout the nation. Two years later, Mary Baker Eddy founded in Boston a "Metaphysical College," where "practitioners"—not "pastors"—of Christian Science were trained. She then developed a very centralized organization, completely under her control. The church in Boston was declared the "Mother Church," to which all who wished to be members of the Church of Christ, Scientist, had to belong. She also took steps to ensure that no doctrinal deviation would ever find a place in her movement. She declared that the Second Coming of Christ had taken place in the divine inspiration with which her book was written. In order to avoid any variant doctrine, she banned preaching in her churches, placing in its stead prescribed readings of selected texts from the Bible and from her book. These texts, selected and prescribed by Mary Baker Eddy, are still read in worship by her followers, alternately by a man and a woman—for women have always held an important place in the movement.

In spite of the happiness and health that her doctrines promised, the last years of Mary Baker Eddy were filled with pain and anguish. Her physical pain could only be alleviated through increasing doses of morphine, and her spiritual anguish was such that she felt the need to be constantly surrounded by her followers, and thus protected from the waves of "animal magnetism" of her enemies.

This concludes our very brief look at the shape and course of Christianity in the United States during the first century after independence. In this story, the outstanding feature is the seemingly endless series of new "denominations" and movements that divided Christians, and the impact of the social and economic order of the United States on the religion of the nation. Since those years, and the decades that immediately followed them, marked the great age of American expansion, political as well as economic, cultural, and religious, the events and currents that we have just discussed left their mark on the type of Christianity that evolved in many other areas of the globe— a subject to which we shall return in chapter 30.

26/Political Horizons: Europe

There is no religious system or superstition that is not based on ignorance of the laws of nature. The creators and defenders of such folly did not foresee the progress of the human intellect. Being convinced that in their age all was known that would ever be known, . . . they based their dreams on the opinions of their time.

ANTOINE-NICOLAS DE CONDORCET

The last years of the eighteenth century saw far-reaching political and cultural upheavals in Europe. Although such events took place in various countries, the most important were those connected with the French Revolution

The French Revolution

Louis XVI—the king whom we have already mentioned as having decreed tolerance for French Protestants—was neither a good ruler nor a wise politician. During his reign, economic conditions in France grew steadily worse, particularly for the poor, while the expenditures of the king and his court soared. The crown sought funds from the nobility and the clergy, two groups that had traditionally been free of taxes. When they resisted, the king and his ministers called the Estates General. These were the French equivalent of parliament, and were composed of three "estates" or "orders": the clergy, the nobility, and the bourgeoisie. Since the king's purpose was to use the Estates General to overcome the resistance of the clergy and the nobility, his ministers suggested that things be arranged so that the Third Estate—the bourgeoisie—would have more representatives than the other two. Steps were also taken so that the clergy would be represented, not only by bishops and other members of the hierarchy, but also by parish priests whose sympathies would run against the interests of the nobility and the hierarchy. When the assembly finally gathered on May 4, 1789, the Third Estate had more members than the other two together; and among the clergy less than a third were prelates. When the time came to open the sessions, the Third Estate insisted that the assembly should function as a single chamber, with decisions to be made by a simple majority. The clergy and the nobility preferred meeting as three chambers, which would give them two votes against the one of the Third Estate. But the bourgeoisie remained firm. Some priests, resenting the aristocratic leanings of the prelates, joined the Third Estate, and finally these two groups declared themselves a "National Assembly," arguing that they represented the majority of the nation. Two days later the clergy voted to join them.

While all these maneuvers were taking place, the economy continued to worsen, and hunger became even more widespread. Fearing the actions that the National Assembly might take, the government closed its meeting hall and ordered it disbanded. But its members refused to obey, and solemnly swore to continue their sessions until France had a constitution. The king and his advisors responded by moving troops to the outskirts of Paris, and deposing Necker, a Protestant banker and government minister who was very popular among the bourgeoisie and the Paris populace. The people of Paris then expressed their anger in a series of riots that culminated on July 14, 1789, when they took the Bastille, an old fortress that served as a prison for the king's enemies.

From that point on, momentous events followed each other in rapid sequence. The king capitulated before the Third Estate, ordering the other two to join the National Assembly in a new body, the National Constituent Assembly. This group then issued the "Declaration of the Rights of Man and the Citizen," which was to become one of the fundamental documents of democratic movements both in France and in other nations. When the king refused to accept this and other decisions of the Assembly, the populace of Paris mutinied, and from that point on the king and his family were virtual prisoners in the capital city.

Following the principles of its own Declaration, and of the philosophers whose political ideas have been discussed above (chapter 21), the Assembly reorganized the government of the nation, not only in its civil and economic aspects, but also in its religious life. The most important step in this latter direction was the promulgation of the "Civil Constitution of the Clergy," in 1790. For centuries the French church had boasted of its "Gallican liberties" from excessive interference by Rome, placing it under the jurisdiction of French bishops and the French crown. Therefore, the National Constituent Assembly, which thought of itself as the depository of national sovereignty, felt that it had the authority to regulate the life and organization of the Catholic Church in France. Furthermore, some sort of reorganization was necessary, for there were many abuses. The highest positions in the hierarchy, occupied almost exclusively by members of the aristocracy, were not used for shepherding the flock, but rather for the personal benefit of their occupants. Several ancient monasteries and abbeys had become centers of leisurely and luxurious living, and some abbots were known for their courtly and political intrigues. All this was in need of reformation. But there were also many members of the Assembly who were convinced that the church and its faith were remainders of superstitious times now past, and should therefore be destroyed. At the time of the Civil Constitution, those who hoped to see the church disappear were still few, and played only a minor role. But as events unfolded and the Revolution became more extreme, they came to the foreground.

Most of the measures included in the Civil Constitution were intended to reform the church. But what was at issue was the very question of whether the Assembly had the authority to issue such a decree "without consulting the church"—as some put it. It was not clear, however, exactly who was that "church" that should be consulted. Some suggested that a council of all the French bishops be called. But the Assembly knew that such a council would be in the hands of the ecclesiastical aristocracy. Others suggested that the pope be consulted—and indeed, this was the option chosen by the king before sanctioning the Assembly's decree. But this in itself would violate the national sovereignty, and would be a denial of the "Gallican liberties." Pope Pius VI sent word to King Louis XVI that the Civil Constitution was a schismatic document that he would never accept. But the king, fearing the Assembly's reaction, kept this decision secret, and continued trying to convince the pope to change his stance. Under pressure from the Assembly, the king agreed to the Civil Constitution, declaring that his approval was tentative, and depended on the pope's agreement. Finally, the Assembly simply decreed that all who held ecclesiastical office must swear allegiance to the Civil Constitution, and that those who refused would be deposed.

The net result of all this was that the church was divided. In theory, those who refused to swear would suffer no other punishment than loss of their offices. On the basis of the Assembly's own declaration on human rights, they could not be deprived of their freedom of thought, and any who wished to continue having them as priests were free to do so—with the significant difference that those priests who had sworn would be supported by the state, while those who refused to swear would have to be supported by their own followers. In fact, however, those who refused to swear soon became the object of persecution, not on the basis of their religious opinions, but on suspicion of counterrevolutionary activities.

Meanwhile, revolutionary movements were gaining strength in other parts of Europe. Earlier revolutionary attempts in the Low Countries and Switzerland had failed, but monarchs and the high nobility feared that the French movement would spread to other lands. This in turn inspired the French revolutionaries to more extreme measures. In 1791, the National Constituent Assembly was succeeded by the Legislative Assembly, in which there were far fewer voices of moderation. Half a year later, France was at war with Austria and Prussia—thus beginning a long series of armed conflicts that would continue almost without interruption until the end of the Napoleonic Wars in 1815. When the fortunes of war turned against France, the Assembly directed its wrath against the king, who clearly sympathized with the foreign monarchs and aristocrats. At the battle of Valmy, the French were finally able to halt the enemy's advance. The next day, the National Convention took the place of the Legislative Assembly, and on its first session the Convention abolished monarchy and proclaimed the Republic. Four months later, under accusation of high treason, the king was tried, convicted, and executed. This, however, did not put an end to the nation's problems. Under the direction of the bourgeoisie, and with the added burden of war and inner disorder, the national economy was able to do little for the urban poor, and conditions were no better in the countryside. The peasants in the region of La Vendee revolted. Fear of foreign invasion mounted. All this led to a wave of terror where everybody was suspected of conterrevolutionary sentiments, and one after another most of the major figures of the Revolution died at the guillotine.

This was joined to a strong reaction against Christianity, both Catholic and Protestant. The new leaders of the Revolution were convinced that they were the harbingers of a new era in which science and reason would overcome all superstition and religion—which, after all, were nothing but the result of human ignorance. As the new age was being born, the time had come to leave aside the unfounded beliefs of the old. It was on this basis that the French Revolution created its own religion, called first the "Cult of Reason," and later the "Cult of the Supreme Being." By then the Civil Constitution of the Clergy was forgotten, for the Revolution wished to have nothing to do with the church. Even the calendar was changed, giving way to a more "reasonable" one in which weeks had ten days and months were named after conditions of nature in each season—"Thermidor," "Germinal," "Fructidor," and so forth. Great ceremonies were also developed to take the place of religious festivals—beginning with the solemn procession taking Voltaire's remains to the "Pantheon of the Republic." Then temples to Reason were built, and an official list of saints was issued—which included

Jesus, Socrates, Marcus Aurelius, and Rousseau. Other rites were prescribed for weddings, the dedication of children to Freedom, and funerals.

All this would have been merely ridiculous, were it not for the suffering and bloodshed it cost. The promoters of the new religion made use of the guillotine with cruel liberality. Christian worship was supposedly permitted; but any priest who refused to swear before the altar of Freedom could be accused of counterrevolutionary activity and sent to the guillotine. Thus, between two thousand and five thousand priests were executed, as well as several dozen nuns and countless lay people. Many others died in prison. In the end, no distinction was made between those who had sworn allegiance to the Civil Constitution, those who had refused to do so, and Protestants. In fact, French Protestantism—the old "church of the desert"—proved unready for the challenge, and was unable to respond with the same measure of heroism as the Catholics. Although the reign of terror abated in 1795, official government policy continued opposing Christianity. The military victories of the French in Switzerland, Italy, and the Low Countries extended a similar policy to those areas. In 1798, the French invaded the papal lands and captured Pope Pius VI, whom they took to France as a prisoner.

Napoleon Bonaparte, who had been gaining power in the army for some time, became master of France in November 1799. Pius VI had died a few months earlier, still a prisoner of the French. But Napoleon was convinced that the best policy was to seek a measure of reconciliation with the Catholic Church, and therefore opened negotiation with the new pope, Pius VII. It is said—probably with little basis in fact—that Napoleon sent a message to the pope to the effect that he wished to "make him a present of forty million French citizens." Finally, in 1801, the papacy and the French government agreed to a Concordat that provided for the naming of bishops and other prelates in such a way that the interests of both church and state would be safeguarded. Three years later, Napoleon decided that the title of "First Consul" was not enough, and took that of "Emperor" in a coronation ceremony presided over by Pius VII. By then he had also decreed religious freedom for Protestants. Oddly enough, all these difficulties served to increase the authority of the pope over the French church. Until then, French kings and bishops had insisted on the "Gallican liberties," precluding popes from direct intervention in the affairs of the French church. Now the emperor allowed the pope a greater measure of authority on the internal affairs of the French church—as long as papal actions did not interfere with the emperor's policies.

That agreement, however, did not last long, for the ambition of the emperor clashed with the firmness of the pope. As a result, Pius VII saw his lands invaded once again by the French, who made him a prisoner. But even in his captivity the pope remained firm, refusing to countenance Napoleon's actions, and particularly condemning his divorce from Josephine. Pius remained a prisoner until the fall of Napoleon, when he was restored to Rome.

Napoleon was crowned emperor in a ceremony over which Pope Pius VII presided. When Napoleon saw this painting by David, he ordered the painter to alter the pope's gesture, so as to make it more favorable to the emperor.

There he proclaimed a general amnesty for all his enemies, and interceded for Napoleon before the British victors.

The New Europe

The Napoleonic Wars had created chaos throughout Europe. Reigning houses had been overthrown in Spain, Portugal, Italy, the Low Countries, and Scandinavia. After Napoleon's defeat, the main powers that had opposed him—Britain, Austria, Prussia, and Russia—determined the future shape of Europe's political map. The borders of France were set where they had been before the Revolution, and the house of Bourbon was restored in the person of Louis XVIII, a brother of Louis XVI. Most of the monarchs whom Napoleon had deposed were restored to their thrones. João VI of Portugal, who had fled to Brazil, did not immediately return to Lisbon, and when he did so he left the government of Brazil in the hands of his son Pedro. The Netherlands and Belgium were placed under a single monarch. In Sweden, the crown was allowed to remain on the brow of Bernadotte, one of Napoleon's former marshals who had proven to be a wise and popular ruler. It was hoped that these arrangements would bring peace to a continent tired of war. Such hopes were not ill-founded, for—with the exceptions of the Crimean War in 1854–1856 and the Franco-Prussian war in 1870–1871—the rest of the century was a period of relative peace.

But, under the surface of that international peace, social and political tensions led to conspiracies, revolts, and upheavals. One of the main sources of unrest was the quest for national unity among Italians and among Germans. Neither Italy nor Germany had yet achieved its political unity, and in each of those two countries there was a growing sentiment that the time had come for such unity. Those goals were opposed by Austria, whose domains lacked cultural unity and included vast areas of Germany and Italy. Under the direction of the chancellor of Austria, C. L. Metternich, a vast network of international spies and saboteurs developed, with the clear goal of preventing German and Italian unity, and of undermining the various liberal and socialist movements in Europe.

Economic liberalism—not to be confused with theological liberalism—was enthusiastically espoused by the growing mercantile and capitalist bourgeoisie. At the heart of this economic liberalism stood the doctrine of laissez faire—or "let do"—which held that the law of supply and demand sufficed to regulate the marketplace and the entire economic order. According to this theory—in the twentieth century espoused by many who would be called "conservatives"—governments should not intervene by regulating trade or the use of capital. Since at that time the industrial revolution was making its greatest impact on the continent of Europe, it was also a time when capital grew enormously—a growth that the theory of laissez faire did nothing to impede. As to the poor, the theory was that as capital grew and industry developed, their condition too would improve with the general economy. Such economic liberalism—which today would be called conservatism—was often joined to political liberalism, a stance that set great store by universal suffrage (although usually only for males) and constitutional monarchy after the example of the United Kingdom.

The struggle between these ideas and the earlier absolutism had different results in various countries. In Spain, Ferdinand VII restored prerevolutionary absolutism. In France, Louis XVIII showed more prudence by establishing a parliamentary system. In Germany, Prussia became the champion of national unity, while Austria supported the old order. In Italy, some sought national unity under the Kingdom of Piedmont and Sardinia, others hoped to establish a republic, and still others saw the papacy as the center around which national unity should be built. In 1830, Belgium became independent from the Netherlands—a move in which religious sentiments played an important role, for Belgium was Catholic and the Netherlands were Protestant. That same year, republican elements tried to overthrow the French monarchy. Although they did not achieve their goal, they did bring about the downfall of Charles X—a conservative ruler who had succeeded his brother Louis XVIII—and the crowning of Louis Philippe d'Orleans, a ruler of fairly liberal inclinations.

The year 1848 brought new revolutions. There were riots and revolts in Italy, Belgium, Great Britain, Switzerland, and France. Switzerland gained a new constitution. In France, Louis Philippe was overthrown and the Second Republic was proclaimed. This lasted until 1851, when Louis Napoleon, a nephew of the now deceased emperor, took power and proclaimed himself emperor under the name Napoleon III. That same year marked the fall of Metternich in Austria. And—an event practically unnoticed at the time—that was also the year in which Marx and Engels published their *Communist Manifesto.*

The map of Italy began changing shortly after Camillo di Cavour became premier of the Kingdom of Piedmont in 1852. With the help of Napoleon III, Cavour began the vast enterprise of Italian unity. At the time of his death in 1861, the new Kingdom of Italy included the entire peninsula, except the territories of Venice and Rome. The first were annexed in 1866, when Prussia intervened against Austria's continued efforts to keep Italy divided. The story of Rome and the papal states is more complex. In 1849, the revolutionary wave that was sweeping Europe led to the creation of a Roman Republic, and Pope Pius IX had to appeal to Napoleon III to restore him to his papal throne. Under French protection, the papal states were then able to retain a constantly threatened independence. Finally, at the time of the war between France and Germany in 1870, King Victor Emmanuel of Italy took Rome, and thus completed the unification of the peninsula. The king then granted the pope, besides a guaranteed annual

The year 1848 saw many revolts and revolutions, including this riot in Lyons, where workers barricaded themselves against the army.

income, three palaces that would be considered an independent territory—
the Vatican, the Lateran, and Castel Gandolfo. But Pius IX refused, and
the following years brought continued tension between the Vatican and the
Italian government. It was only in 1929 that the papacy finally agreed to
the loss of its extensive holdings, and to an arrangement similar to what
Victor Emmanuel had suggested.

While these events were taking place in Italy, the dominant figure in
Germany was Otto von Bismarck, who had become chancellor of Prussia in
1862. His great achievement consisted in excluding Austria from the German Confederation, and then molding that Confederation into a single nation. After ten years of skilled diplomacy and military conquests, culminating
in the war with France of 1870–1871, Germany was united under Wilhelm
of Prussia. Bismarck's religious policy was directed against Roman Catholicism. That was the religion of the majority in Austria, and therefore the
Prussian chancellor feared that Catholics in his own territories would sympa-
thize with the Austrians. Also, his international policy required that he support the unification of Italy—which Austria opposed—and he therefore was
greatly inconvenienced by Catholics under his rule who insisted that Prussia
should intervene to restore the papal lands to the pope. But, above all, he
was convinced that Catholicism was obscurantist, and that liberal Protestantism was better suited to the great historical mission that Germany would soon
have to fulfill. For these and other reasons, Bismarck took several measures
against Catholicism. Germany broke diplomatic relations with the papacy,
several monastic orders were expelled from the country, and the traditional
subsidies given to the church were cut. In 1880, for reasons of political
expediency, Bismarck changed some of these policies and re-established
relations with the papacy. But these conflicts were one of the factors that
convinced Pius IX—pope from 1846 to 1878—that there was an unavoidable opposition between the Catholic Church and the modern idea of the state
—an issue to which we shall return in chapter 29.

Besides the theological developments and the missionary enterprise that
we shall discuss in chapters 28 and 30, the most significant developments in
European Protestantism during the nineteenth century were those derived
from the growing separation between church and state. After the Reformation of the sixteenth century, in those countries where Protestantism gained
the upper hand, the new church continued relating to the state in the same
manner as had the Catholic church. After the French Revolution, however,
this state of affairs began to change. In the Netherlands, for instance, the
union between the state and the Reformed Church was broken when the
French conquered the land and created the "Batavian Republic," and after
the Restoration the links between church and state were never as strong as
they had been before. In Germany, the quest for national unity led to the
abrogation of many old laws that sought to enforce religious uniformity.
Throughout Europe, political and economic liberalism had similar conse-

quences. This in turn contributed to the growth of "free churches"—that is, those to which one belongs by choice and supports by means of offerings, in contrast to the state churches, supported by state funds. Methodists and Baptists spread throughout Germany and Northern Europe. And, even in the government-related Lutheran and Reformed churches, Pietism made new headway. Pietism led to the formation of several missionary societies, and of others whose purpose was to address the ills of Europe itself. In Germany and other northern lands, "deaconesses" and their organizations did much for the wellbeing of the sick, the elderly, and the poor. In Denmark, Lutheran leader N. F. S. Grundtvig sought to respond to the plight of the rural poor by advocating cooperativism. In general, the lack of state support renewed the zeal of many Protestants in Europe, involving great numbers in the various aspects of the churches' work.

Developments in Great Britain

Throughout the nineteenth century, Great Britain followed a course parallel to that of Europe. There also the industrial revolution made its impact, but much earlier and to an even greater degree. That revolution benefited the middle class and the capitalists, while undermining both the ancient aristocracy and the poor. The rapid growth of cities that resulted from industry and increased trade gave rise to overcrowded slums, and the poor found themselves living and working in conditions of misery and exploitation. Meanwhile, economic and political liberalism made great strides, thus increasing the power of the House of Commons at the expense of the House of Lords. One result of these conditions was a vast wave of migration to the United States, Canada, Australia, New Zealand, and South Africa. Another was the labor movement, which made enormous progress from the beginning of the century, when unions were forbidden by law, to the end of the century, when the Labor Party was a political power. It was also in England, reflecting on the conditions of the London proletariat, that Karl Marx developed many of his economic theories.

All this also influenced the church. At the beginning of the French Revolution, there were in the Church of England many of the evils that had earlier characterized the worst times of the medieval church: absenteeism, pluralism, and the use of ecclesiastical office as a means to further personal and dynastic ambitions. But during the nineteenth century, there was a significant renewal in the Church of England. Aided by a number of reform decrees issued by the government, those who sought a more faithful church came to the foreground. Some of these people of reforming zeal belonged to the "Evangelical" wing of Anglicanism, a group that was profoundly influenced by the Pietism of the Continent and wished to see the Church of

England more closely aligned with the rest of Protestantism. Others, particularly those of the "Oxford Movement," took the opposite tack and came to be known as "Anglo-Catholics." The Oxford Movement emphasized the authority of tradition, apostolic succession, and communion as the center of Christian worship. One of its leaders, John Henry Newman, was converted to Catholicism, and eventually was made a cardinal—although conservative Catholics never quite trusted him. But most of the members of the movement remained within the Church of England, and gave that church a renewed devotional life. Another result of the movement was the rebirth of monasticism within the Church of England, and soon Anglican monks and nuns were trying to meet the needs of the poor and the ill.

However, it was among dissident churches that there was most vitality in England during the nineteenth century. The growth of the middle class brought about an upsurge in the membership of dissident churches. Methodists, Baptists, and Congregationalists gave many signs of vigor, not only in their numerical growth, but also in the many societies that they founded to help the needy, to remedy some of the more blatant social ills, and to take the gospel to the rest of the world. In order to reach the poor and ignorant masses, dissident churches founded Sunday Schools, and these eventually became a common practice among Protestants. Others organized the Young Men's Christian Association (YMCA) and the Young Women's Christian Association (YWCA). Also, a number of new denominations were born—particularly the Salvation Army, founded in 1864 as a means to reach the impoverished and unchurched urban masses.

All these groups, as well as the evangelical wing of Anglicanism, showed great concern for the social ills of the time. The support and inspiration of Methodists, Quakers, and others were important factors in the birth of labor unions, in prison reform, and in legislation regarding child labor. But the most significant accomplishment of British Christians during the nineteenth century was the abolition of slavery in most of the western world. Years earlier, both Quakers and Methodists had condemned slavery. But it was in the nineteenth century, thanks to the effort of William Wilberforce and other committed Christians, that the British government took measures against slavery. In 1806 and 1811, Parliament issued laws forbidding the slave trade. In 1833, freedom was decreed for all slaves in the British Caribbean, and similar laws were later issued for other colonies. At the same time, treaties were sought with other nations, agreeing to end the slave trade. When such treaties were signed, the British navy was given orders to enforce them. Shortly thereafter, most western nations had abolished slavery.

In summary, the nineteenth century brought about great political and economic changes in Europe. In general, Catholicism suffered from those changes more severe blows than Protestantism. Therefore, the nineteenth century was for Catholicism a period of reaction against modern ideas, which

*Protestants in England began several new forms of ministry,
including these centers where the homeless received both shelter and
Christian instruction.*

were usually seen as threats. For Protestantism, on the other hand, the
nineteenth century brought new opportunities. Protestant powers such as
Great Britain and Germany increased their influence in the world. Political
and economic liberalism were closely allied with Protestantism, and were
seen by their adherents as the wave of the future against an outdated and
authoritarian Catholicism. Protestants did take a leading role in the struggle
against social ills, and most notably against slavery. The result was that, while
Roman Catholicism looked upon the new times with extreme caution (see
chapter 29), many Protestants looked upon them with unwarranted optimism
(as we shall see in chapter 28).

27/ Political Horizons: Latin America

The successors of St. Peter have always been our fathers, but war had left us orphans, as a lamb calling in vain for its lost mother. Now the tender mother has sought him and returned him to the fold, and we are given shepherds worthy of the church and of the Republic.

SIMÓN BOLÍVAR

A Panoply of New Nations

The political upheavals that had taken place in Europe and in the British colonies of North America were also felt in Latin America. There had long been in the Spanish and Portuguese colonies a tension between those recently arrived from Europe—the *peninsulares*—and the native descendents of earlier immigrants—the *criollos*. Through the exploitation of Indian and slave labor, the *criollos* had become a relatively wealthy class that felt it understood the affairs of the colonies better than the *peninsulares*, and that they therefore ought to have a hand in running them. But appointments to all significant offices—both civil and ecclesiastic—were made in Europe, and therefore such positions were usually held by *peninsulares*, many of whom had never seen the lands of the New World before they were appointed to rule them. The *criollos*—conveniently setting aside the toil of Indians and black slaves —were convinced that the wealth of the colonies was due to their efforts, and thus resented the authority of the *peninsulares*. Although still faithful subjects of the crown, they deplored the many laws that favored the metropolis at the expense of the colonies. And, since many of them had the necessary means, they often traveled to Europe, from whence they returned imbued with the republican ideas that were sweeping that continent. Thus, the *criollos* played in Latin America a role similar to that of the bourgeoisie in France.

In 1808, Napoleon deposed King Ferdinand VII of Spain, and in his place crowned his own brother Joseph Bonaparte. Spanish resistance to the usurper had its headquarters at Cadiz, where a "junta" or board ruled in the name of the deposed king. Napoleon declared that all Spanish colonies should now obey King Joseph; but he did not have the power to enforce his authority, and local juntas were organized in the New World. While the *peninsulares* insisted that all such juntas should be under the Cadiz government, the *criollos* preferred independent juntas, and their opinion prevailed. Thus, the colonies began ruling themselves, although still in the name of the king. Ferdinand VII was restored in 1814, after Napoleon's defeat. But, instead of showing gratitude for those who had preserved his territories for him, he set out to undo all that the relatively liberal juntas had done. In Spain, he abolished the constitution that the Cadiz junta had issued, and the reaction was such that, in 1820, he was forced to reinstate it. Similar policies in the colonies exacerbated *criollo* resentment against Spanish policies, and soon those who had earlier proven faithful guardians of the king's inheritance rebelled against him. In the River Plate—now Argentina, Paraguay, and Uruguay—the junta simply continued governing the country, until independence was proclaimed in 1816. Three years later, Paraguay declared its independence from both Spain and the River Plate. Uruguay broke away in 1828, becoming an independent nation. Meanwhile, José de San Martín had crossed the Andes and invaded Chile, whose independence was declared in 1818. While these events were taking place in the south, further north Simón Bolívar organized an army that defeated the Spanish and proclaimed the independence of Greater Colombia—now Colombia, Venezuela, and Panama. Then Ecuador joined Greater Colombia, and Bolívar marched to the south, where Peru—now Peru and Bolivia—was also made independent.

Bolívar's dream had been to create a vast republic embracing most of the continent. But such dreams were soon shattered. Greater Colombia broke up into Venezuela, Colombia, and Ecuador. In Peru, the region of "Alto Perú"—high Peru—insisted on its independence, becoming the Republic of Bolívar—now Bolivia. Bolívar's last hopes for a continental confederacy came to nought at the Panama Congress of 1826, where it became clear that local interests—as well as those of the United States—precluded any close collaboration between the new nations. Five years later, a few days before his death, Bolívar expressed his disappointment: "America is ungovernable. Those who have served the revolution have plowed the sea."*

In Mexico, events followed a different course. The *criollos* were planning to grasp power from the *peninsulares* when the conspiracy was discovered, and one of its leaders, Father Miguel Hidalgo y Costilla, decided to make

---

*Simón Bolívar, *Obras completas,* vol. 3 (Havana: Lex, 1950), p. 501.

The nineteenth century brought the independence of most Spanish colonies in the New World, under the leadership of Bolívar and other members of the native aristocracy.

a move before being arrested. On September 16, 1810, he proclaimed Mexican independence, and soon found himself at the head of an unorganized army of sixty thousand Indians and *mestizos*—persons of mixed Indian and Spanish blood. After his capture and execution, Hidalgo was succeeded by *mestizo* priest José María Morelos. Thus, from its very beginnings the new nation had the support and participation of Indians and *mestizos*. For a time, the *criollos* regained power; but later, under the leadership of Benito Juárez, that situation was corrected. Therefore, the Indian and *mestizo* population has played an important role in the political history of Mexico. Central America, originally part of Mexico, proclaimed its independence in 1821, and later broke up into Guatemala, El Salvador, Honduras, Nicaragua, and Costa Rica. (Panama was not originally part of Central America. It belonged to Colombia until 1903, when the United States fostered its independence in order to evade the conditions that Colombia required for the construction of the Canal.)

Brazilian independence also resulted from the Napoleonic Wars. In 1807, fleeing from Napoleon's armies, the Portuguese court took refuge in Brazil. In 1816, João VI was restored to his throne in Lisbon, but showed no inclination to return to Portugal until forced to do so by political circumstances in 1821. He left as regent of Brazil his son Pedro, who later refused to return to Portugal, proclaimed Brazilian independence, and was crowned as Emperor Pedro I of Brazil. In 1825, Portugal recognized the independence of its former colony. Pedro I, however, was not allowed to rule as he wished, and was forced to agree to a parliamentary system of government. In 1889, after the abdication of Pedro's son Pedro II, the republic was proclaimed.

Haiti's independence was the direct result of the French Revolution. As soon as the French Revolution deprived the white population of military support, the blacks, who were the vast majority, rebelled. Independence was proclaimed in 1804, and it was acknowledged by France in 1825. The United States refused to do so until 1862, for until that time slave-holding states feared the example of a nation born out of a slave rebellion.

Looking at all these events as a whole, several common threads appear. Republican ideas from France and the United States provided the ideological framework for revolution and independence in Latin America. But those revolutions usually resulted in power residing in a *criollo* class—or, in the case of Haiti, of military leaders—that paid little attention to the needs of the masses. Vast tracts of land were still in the hands of a few landowners, while the majority of the population had no land. Towards the middle of the nineteenth century, there was great economic development on the basis of foreign capital and the exporting of agricultural products. This in turn fostered even larger holdings of land, and created an alliance between *criollo* landowners and foreign capital. There also appeared in the cities an urban middle class of merchants and government employees who had little power, but whose interests were closely tied to the sort of economic development that was taking place. What was hoped and repeatedly promised was that the development of trade, industry, and education would eventually benefit all social classes, for even the poorest would receive a share of the wealth that was being created. But economic progress required order, and thus dictatorships were often justified.

Throughout the nineteenth century, the great ideological debate in Latin America was between "liberals" and "conservatives." In general, the leaders of both groups belonged to the higher classes. But, while conservative strength was based on the landed aristocracy, liberals found their support among the merchants and intellectuals in the cities. Conservatives feared such notions as freedom of thought and free enterprise. Liberals defended them, both because they were more modern and because they were better suited to the interests of the merchant class. While most conservatives looked to Spain for inspiration, liberals looked to Great Britain, France, and the United States. But neither group was willing to alter the social order so that the lower classes could share in the wealth of the country. The result was a long series of dictatorships (both liberal and conservative), of palace revolutions, and of violent excesses. By the turn of the century, many tended to agree with Bolívar: the continent was ungovernable.

The Church in the New Nations

Throughout the colonial period, the church in Latin America had been under Royal Patronage—*Patronato Real.* This included the virtual naming of bishops by the governments of Spain and Portugal. Therefore, the tensions between *peninsulares* and *criollos* were also felt in the church, whose higher offices were in the hands of *peninsulares,* while *criollos* and *mestizos* formed the bulk of the lower clergy. Although a few bishops supported the cause of Spanish American Independence, most supported the crown, many by means of pastoral letters in which they condemned the rebellion. After independence, most of them had to return to Spain, thus leaving many dioceses vacant. It was impossible to name replacements, for Spain insisted on her ancient rights of Royal Patronage and the new republics could not accept bishops who were named by the crown. The popes wavered in their attitude, for Spain was still one of their main allies in Europe, but the new nations comprised a substantial part of the Catholic flock. Pius VII, in his encyclical *Etsi longissimo* (1816), spoke of the "grave evils of rebellion," and of "our most beloved son in Jesus Christ, Ferdinand, your Catholic king"; eventually, however, he was forced to take a neutral stance. In 1824, Leo XI, in the encyclical *Etsi iam diu,* spoke of the movement for independence as "tares," and of Ferdinand as "our very beloved son Ferdinand, Catholic king of the Spains." In Europe, France, Austria, and Russia joined Spain in opposing the acknowledgment of the new nations that would be implied in naming bishops for them without consulting with Spain. Finally, in 1827, Leo XII decided to name the first bishops for Greater Colombia—and this was the occasion for Bolívar's words quoted at the beginning of this chapter. But this did not put an end to the matter, for Ferdinand broke off relations with Rome, and the pope had to undo much of what he had done. It was only in the next decade that Gregory VII officially acknowledged the existence of the new republics, and named bishops for them. Given the sacramental nature of Catholicism, the lack of bishops meant much more than the mere lack of leaders. Without bishops there could be no ordinations; and without sufficient ordained clergy, much of the sacramental life of the church was interrupted.

The attitude of the lower clergy, mostly *criollos* and *mestizos,* contrasted with that of the bishops. In Mexico, three out of four priests supported the rebellion. Sixteen out of the twenty-nine signatories of the Declaration of

Latin America after Independence

Independence in Argentina were priests. Also, at the beginning of the rebellion there was little popular support for independence, and parish priests did much to gain that support.

For these reasons, the attitude of the new political leadership towards Catholicism was complex. All called themselves Catholic, and the various early constitutions affirmed that Roman Catholicism was the national religion. But tensions with Rome were such that some—particularly in Mexico

—proposed breaking with Rome and creating national churches. Such projects reappeared again and again in later years, whenever the popes seemed inclined to oppose the political interests of a nation.

After independence, the conflict between liberals and conservatives was also reflected in their divergent religious policies. While conservatives wished to continue the ancient privileges of the clergy and the church, liberals opposed many of them. It was then that many native clergymen who had earlier supported independence joined the conservative ranks. The early liberals did not oppose Catholicism as such, but only what they took to be the narrow ideas and practices of a clergy that, while native born, still looked to Spain as the center of the universe. But the constant conflicts between liberals and the leadership of the church led to increased anti-Catholic feelings in liberal ranks.

In the second half of the century, liberalism espoused the positivist philosophy of Comte and therefore became more anti-Catholic. Auguste Comte was a French philosopher, one of the founders of modern sociology, who was convinced that society could and should be reorganized following the dictates of reason. According to him, humanity has gone through three stages of development: the theological, the metaphysical, and the scientific or "positive." Although there are still enclaves of the earlier two stages, Comte argued, we are now in the scientific age, and therefore society must be radically reorganized on the basis of scientific or "positive" principles. The new society to result from that reorganization will make a clear distinction between spiritual authority and temporal power. The latter must be placed on the hands of the capitalists and merchants, who best understand the needs of society. As to spiritual authority, this could well be placed on a new "Catholic Church" without a "supernatural God," and devoted to the "religion of humanity." Such ideas gained wide acceptance among the Latin American bourgeoisie, especially in Brazil, but also in countries such as Argentina and Chile, where ideas from France had often been well received. The result was renewed conflict between liberals and the church, while states became increasingly secular.

The second half of the nineteenth century also brought new waves of immigrants—mostly European, but also Chinese—to the Pacific coast. Such immigration was necessary for the sort of development that the ruling bourgeoisie saw for Latin America. Immigrants provided the labor necessary for industry and commerce, and also served as a balance against the masses of Indians and blacks. In any case, that wave of migration was of great importance for the religious life of the continent. Many of those who hoped to immigrate were Protestants, and therefore several countries felt obliged to grant religious freedom, at first only to such immigrants, and eventually to all. But the most notable consequence of immigration was the enormous growth in the numbers of baptized Catholics for whom the church could provide practically no ministry or religious instruction. As a result, Latin

American Catholicism became more superficial. In great cities such as Buenos Aires and Sao Paulo, most still called themselves Catholics, but few participated in the life of the church.

For a long time, the Catholic hierarchy responded to all this with futile attempts to return to the past. The more widespread the new ideas became, the more vehemently the hierarchy condemned them. Eventually, many Latin American Catholics came to see faith as something to be held independently and even against the authority of the church. Therefore, when Protestantism made its appearance, it found the fields ripe for the harvest.

28/ Protestant Theology

The historical foundation of Christianity as built by rationalistic, by liberal, and by modern theology no longer exists; but this does not mean that Christianity has lost its historical foundation. . . . We modern theologians are too proud of our historical method, too proud of our historical Jesus, too confident in our belief in the spiritual gains which our historical theology can bring to the world.
ALBERT SCHWEITZER

The nineteenth century posed great intellectual challenges for Christianity. While the response of Catholic authorities and theologians was usually to condemn and reject modern ideas, many Protestants sought ways to interpret their ancient faith in terms of the new frame of mind. Therefore, although the challenges were common to both branches of western Christianity, we shall deal with the Protestant response in the present chapter, and with Catholic reactions in the next.

New Currents of Thought

By the beginning of the nineteenth century, the industrial revolution had reached most of Europe—and even some areas of the New World. Its impact went far beyond economic matters, extending to the whole of life. There were mass movements of people seeking employment in industrial centers, or simply leaving lands now devoted to crops to be used for industrial

purposes. The traditional extended family—parents, uncles, aunts, cousins—
was weakened by those movements, and the nuclear family had to bear a
greater burden of responsibility in the transmission of values and traditions.
More people came to see their lives as their private responsibility, and
therefore individualism and preoccupation with the "I" became a common
theme in both philosophy and literature.

The industrial revolution also contributed to the idea of progress.
Throughout most of history, people had thought that the old and tried ideas
and practices were better than most innovations. Even at the time of the
Renaissance and the Reformation, when many new ideas were introduced,
people sought to return to the ancient sources of religion, art, and knowledge. But now people were no longer looking to the past, but to the future.
Applied science had proven able to produce wealth and comfort that did not
exist previously. Future possibilities seemed to have no limit. The leading
classes of society saw the problems created by the industrial revolution as
passing clouds. Applied technology would soon solve them, and then all in
society would benefit from the new order. Since most intellectuals belonged
to those leading classes, these ideas found echo in their teachings and writings. In a sense, even Darwin's theory of evolution was an expression of faith
in progress, applied in this case to the natural sciences. Not only humankind,
but all of nature, is progressing. Progress is part of the structure of the
universe. As is also the case with social progress, this is not an easy advance,
but a harsh struggle in which the fittest survive and, in the very act of
surviving, contribute to the progress of the entire species. This is expressed
in the title of Darwin's book, published in 1859, *On the Origin of Species by
Means of Natural Selection, or the Preservation of Favoured Races in the Struggle for
Life.*

Since progress is such an important element in human life, and even in
the entire universe, the same must be true of history, for what is history but
the progress of the past? The nineteenth century became intensely aware of
the radical changes that had taken place in society through the centuries—
an awareness that was further prodded by increased contact with other cultures, especially in Africa and the Pacific. Thus, the conclusion was reached
that humans had not always been as they are now, for their intellectual and
religious views have also evolved. We have already mentioned Auguste
Comte's theory of a progressive movement from "theology" to "metaphysics," and finally to "science." Such ideas were typical of the nineteenth
century. The result was a series of historical studies that cast doubt on much
of the traditional view of the past. These studies, applied to Scripture and to
early Christianity, produced results that many found incompatible with faith.

Others saw the high social price of the progress brought about by the
industrial revolution. Many Christians sought to respond to the needs of
particular groups. The Sunday School movement was an attempt to reach
those who no longer had much connection with the traditional means of

religious instruction. The Salvation Army, the YMCA, and many similar movements sought to reach the urban masses and alleviate their misery. But the problems and their solutions went far beyond the level of what any charitable institution could do for the disinherited, and many began considering the need for a radical change in the social order. If it was true that there was progress, and that the structure of society had changed through the centuries, why not try to produce further changes in that structure? Comte, often considered one of the founders of modern sociology, proposed precisely such a change—one that placed society in the hands of capitalists and merchants. Such projects were frequently put forth in the nineteenth century. Socialism, in its varying hues, became a common theme of those preoccupied with existing social conditions, including vast numbers of Christians. The failed revolutions of 1848 were partly the result of such ideas and projects.

The socialist author who would eventually become most influential was Karl Marx, whose *Communist Manifesto* was published in 1848. His system went beyond the socialist utopias of the time, for it included an analysis of history and society on the basis of what he called "dialectical materialism." A basic element of that analysis was the notion that ideas, no matter how purely intellectual they might appear, have social and political functions. The dominant class develops an ideology that passes for a purely rational construct, but whose true function is to bolster the existing order. Religion itself is part of that structure of support for the powerful—hence, the oft-quoted dictum that religion is the "opiate of the people." But, Marx continued, history moves on, and its next step will be a vast revolution that will lead first to the "dictatorship of the proletariat," and eventually to a classless society in which even the state will be superfluous—the true Communist society. In any case, although Marx's views would pose a serious challenge to Christians in the twentieth century, during the nineteenth they made relatively little impact.

Late in the nineteenth century, the work of Sigmund Freud posed new challenges. After many years of study in various disciplines, Freud became interested in the manner in which the human mind functions, especially at the subconscious level. On the basis of years of observation, he came to the conclusion that the psyche is moved, not only by that which it consciously knows, but also by other factors that never emerge from the level of the subconscious. This is particularly true of experiences and instincts that the mind suppresses due to social pressure or for some other reason, but never destroys. The instincts of sex and aggression, for instance, remain active no matter how deeply we repress them. This opened new horizons for psychology, but also for theology, which did not always know how to deal with Freud's insights.

Although they lived in the nineteenth century, both Marx and Freud made their greatest impact on the twentieth. But both serve as examples of what was taking place during their time, when scientific reasoning began to be applied beyond the natural sciences in an effort to understand both society and the human mind. It is for this reason that the nineteenth century gave birth to such disciplines as sociology, economics, anthropology, and psychology. It was in the context of those developing disciplines that theologians had to do their work.

Schleiermacher's Theology

We have already seen that Kant's work put an end to the facile rationalism of the eighteenth century. If it is true that "pure reason" reaches an impasse when applied to questions such as the existence of God or life after death, what route can theology follow in dealing with these and other questions of similar importance for religion? If it is true that the structures of thought are in the mind, and do not necessarily correspond to reality, how are we to speak of ultimate realities? There were three possible ways to respond to such questions, and theologians explored all three, as we shall see in this and the following two sections of this chapter.

The first option was to seek a locus for religion other than pure or speculative reason. Kant himself, as we have seen, did this in his *Critique of Practical Reason.* He argued that it is wrong to think that religion is basically an intellectual matter, for in fact religion is grounded, not on the intellect, but on the ethical sense. Human beings are by nature moral, and on the basis of that innate moral sense one can prove the existence of God, the soul, human freedom, and life after death. In a way, Kant thus attempted to salvage something of the Christian rationalism that his *Critique of Pure Reason* had undermined, and to do this by placing religion in a locus other than pure reason.

Early in the nineteenth century, Friedrich Schleiermacher proposed a similar solution, although he gave up the attempt to base religion on reason, be it "pure" or "practical." He was born and raised in the home of a Reformed pastor of Moravian tendencies who placed his son's education in the hands of the Moravians. Although Schleiermacher was Reformed, Moravian Pietism did leave its mark on his theology. In any case, young Schleiermacher went through a period in which the pervading rationalism of his time made it difficult for him to continue holding several of the traditional doctrines of Christianity. He was helped out of that situation by Romanticism. That movement held that there was more to human beings than cold reason, and gained many adepts among the younger generations who felt that rationalism was dehumanizing. Making use of the insights of the Romantics, Schleiermacher began to find his way out of the impasse and doubt in which rationalism had left him. His first major work, *Speeches on Religion to the Cultured among Its Despisers* (1799), was precisely an attempt to show to an audience steeped in Romanticism that religion must still occupy an important place in human life. His main argument was that religion is not a form of knowledge, as both the rationalists and the orthodox believed. Nor is it a system of morality, as Kant implied. Religion is grounded neither in pure nor in practical or moral reason, but rather in *Gefühl*—a German word that is best translated, although not quite accurately, as "feeling."

The *Speeches* did not clarify the content of such "feeling," and Schleiermacher undertook that task in his more mature work, *The Christian Faith*. There he clearly shows that this is not a sentimental "feeling," nor a passing emotion or a sudden experience, but is rather the profound awareness of the existence of the One on whom all existence depends—both ours and that of the world around us. Thus, it is not an undefined or amorphous feeling, for its clear and specific content is our absolute dependence on God. Such "feeling" is not based on rational faculties nor on moral sentiment, but it does have significant consequences both in rational exposition and in ethical responsibility.

This feeling of dependence takes a specific form in each religious community. The purpose of religious bodies is to communicate to others and to future generations their particular constitutive experiences, so that they may share in the same feeling. Schleiermacher himself is interested in the Protestant religious community, which is based on two fundamental historical moments: Jesus and the impact he made on his first disciples, and the Reformation of the sixteenth century.

The function of theology is to explore and expound the implications of that feeling of dependence at three levels: the self, its relations with the world, and its relations with God. Anything that cannot be shown to be related to the feeling of dependence has no place in theology. Let us take, for instance, the doctrine of creation. That doctrine is of paramount importance for the feeling of absolute dependence, for it affirms that all existence depends on God. To deny this would be to deny the dependence that is central to Christian religious feeling. But this does not mean that we have to affirm a particular mode of creation. The creation as told in Genesis may or may not be historically accurate—Schleiermacher himself did not think it was—but in any case this is not a proper matter for theological inquiry, for it has nothing to do with the feeling of dependence. Even if the stories of Moses were true, and had been revealed in some supernatural way, "the particular pieces of information would never be articles of faith in our sense of the phrase, for our feeling of absolute dependence does not gain thereby either a new content, a new form, or clearer definition."* And the same is to be said about other questions such as the existence of angels, of Satan, and so forth. For the same reason, the traditional distinction between the natural and the supernatural should be set aside, not because it opposes modern

---

*Frederich Schleiermacher, *The Christian Faith* (Edinburgh: T. & T. Clark, 1928), p. 151.

science, but rather because that distinction limits our feeling of dependence to those events or places in which the supernatural is made manifest. By thus insisting that religion is different from knowledge, Schleiermacher could interpret the central doctrines of Christianity in such a way that they did not contradict the findings of science.

Schleiermacher's influence was great. At a time when many believed religion to be a matter of the past, people flocked to church when he preached. But he was even more influential over later generations, which appropriately called him the "father of liberalism."

Hegel's System

Another route that remained open after Kant's critique was to agree with him that the mind stamps its seal on all knowledge, but then, instead of seeing this as proof of the limits of reason, to affirm that reason is reality itself. Reason is not something that exists in our minds, and which we then use in order to understand reality. Reason is reality, the only reality there is.

Such was the route followed by G. W. F. Hegel (1770–1831). Hegel began his intellectual career in the field of theology, but later decided that theology was too narrow a field of inquiry, for it was necessary to try to understand, not only religion, but the whole of reality. Reality must be seen, not as a disconnected series of things and events, but as a whole. He proposed that this could be achieved by affirming the identity of reason and reality. It is not simply a matter of reason being able to understand reality, or of reality setting limits to reason. It is rather that reason *is* reality, and that the only reality *is* reason. As he said, "what is rational exists, and what exists is rational."

However, in speaking of "reason" Hegel does not refer to mere understanding, nor to the conclusions of reasoning, but to the process itself of thinking. In thinking, we do not stand before a fixed idea, in order to study it. On the contrary, we pose an idea, examine it so as to surpass it or deny it in favor of another, and finally reach a third idea that includes whatever there was of value in the two previous ones. This process of posing a "thesis," questioning it by means of an "antithesis," and finally reaching a "synthesis," is what Hegel calls "reason." This is, therefore, a dynamic reason, a movement that is constantly advancing. Nor is this reason something that exists only in the human mind. The universal reason—the Spirit, as Hegel sometimes calls it—is the whole of reality. All that exists is that dialectic and dynamic thought of the Spirit.

On that basis, Hegel built an impressive system that included the entirety of history as the thought of the Spirit. The various religions, philosophical systems, and social and political orders are moments in the Spirit's

Hegel developed a philosophical system that soon had thousands of enthusiastic followers, including many who sought to interpret Christianity on the basis of Hegelianism.

thought. In that thought, the past is never lost, but is always surpassed and included in a new synthesis. Thus, the present includes all the past, for it sums it up, and all the future, for the future is the rational development of the present.

Hegel was convinced that Christianity was the "absolute religion." This does not mean that Christianity denies other religions, but rather that it is their culmination—that it sums up the entire process of human religious development. The central theme of religion is the relationship between God and humanity. That relationship reaches its apex in the Christian doctrine of the incarnation, in which the divine and the human are fully united. The union of divine and human, which was implicit in earlier religions, is now made explicit in the incarnation. Likewise, the doctrine of the Trinity is the culmination of the idea of God, for it affirms the dynamic nature of ultimate reality. The dialectic of the Trinity includes three movements. First of all, God is eternal idea, in itself and by itself, even apart from the development of that rational reality that we call creation. This is the "Kingdom of the Father," which is simply God considered apart from any other being. The "Kingdom of the Son" is what we usually call "creation," that is, the world as it exists in time and space, and its culmination is God's incarnation, which shows the ultimate identity between the divine and the human. The "Kingdom of the Spirit" follows this union of the divine and the human, and is made manifest in the presence of God in the community. All this taken together is the "Kingdom of God," which comes to historical fruition in the moral life and in the order of the state—for Hegel had a lofty notion of the state. The result of this, as Hegel saw it, was a philosophy completely free of the narrowness of all dogmatic or partial systems.

This far-reaching scheme of reality found many admirers. It was said that finally humans were able to see reality as a whole. In order to bolster the system, Hegel's followers sought to show how various elements of reality fit in the vast Hegelian system. It was in protest against the popularity of Hegel's system that the Danish philosopher and theologian Søren Kierkegaard facetiously spoke of how all problems would be solved "now that the System is complete; or if not, will be complete by next Sunday." But even among many who did not accept it, Hegel's system forced philosophers and theologians to take history seriously. After Hegel, history would no longer be a secondary matter for those who were concerned with eternal realities, but would be seen rather as the locus in which eternal realities are known. This notion, which has helped later theologians recover much of the biblical perspective, is part of the legacy of Hegel and of the nineteenth century.

Kierkegaard's Work

Søren Aabye Kierkegaard (1813–1855) was one of the most interesting figures of the nineteenth century. Born in a strict Danish Lutheran home that left a deep imprint on him, Kierkegaard had an unhappy youth. His frail and slightly twisted frame made him the object of mockery that he had to suffer throughout his life. But he soon became convinced that his undeniable intellectual gifts meant that he was called to a special mission, and that before that call every other interest must give way. On that basis he broke his engagement with a woman whom he deeply loved. Marriage, he thought, would have made him happy, but would also have prevented him from being the solitary knight of faith that he was called to be. Years later, he would compare that painful decision with Abraham's willingness to sacrifice Isaac; and he would also declare that some of his books were written "because of her."

Kant's critique of rationalism left a third option, different from those followed by Schleiermacher and Hegel: although reason is unable to penetrate ultimate truth, faith can. Kant's "pure reason" can neither prove nor disprove the existence of God; but faith knows God directly. From this perspective, the basis for Christianity is not its reasonableness, nor its place of honor in a system such as Hegel's, nor even a feeling of absolute dependence. Christianity is a matter of faith; of faith in the God whose revelation comes to us in the Scriptures and in Jesus Christ.

Kierkegaard was both a philosopher who had little use for the Hegelianism then in vogue and a Christian of profound conviction who felt called to show the radical nature of Christian discipleship.

But this is not all, for up to this point Kierkegaard has said no more than what has always been said by those who seek in faith a hiding place against the challenges of their time. That kind of "faith," Kierkegaard would say, is not really such; for true faith is never an easy matter, nor is it a means to a tranquil life. On the contrary, faith is always a risk, an adventure that requires the denial of oneself and of all the joys of the faithless. On that basis, Kierkegaard lambasted one of the most famous preachers of his time, declaring that it was ridiculous to speak of a person who had achieved wordly goods by preaching Christianity as a "witness to the truth."

For Kierkegaard, the greatest enemy of Christianity was Christendom, whose purpose it is to simplify the matter of becoming a Christian. Then one is a Christian by simply being neither Jew nor Moslem. But in truth, those who understand Christianity in that fashion are mere pagans. Such "cheap" Christianity, with neither cost nor pain, is like war games, in which armies move and there is a great deal of noise, but no real risk nor pain—and therefore no real victory. What we call "Christianity" is simply "playing at being Christians." And to the mockery of that game many preachers contribute when they seek to make Christianity an easy thing. This is the "crime of Christendom," which plays at Christianity and "takes God for a fool." And the tragedy is that few realize how ridiculous it is to speak of God in such terms.

In response to the tragedy of Christendom, Kierkegaard conceived his calling as "making Christianity difficult." This did not mean that he was to persuade people that Christian faith was wrong. Rather, it meant that he must tell them that what they had heard preached and taught was far from the true faith of Christianity. In other words, in order to be truly Christian, one must become aware of the cost of faith and pay the price. Without that, one may well be a member of Christendom, but not a Christian.

True Christianity has to do with a person's very existence, and not merely with the intellect. It is at this point that Kierkegaard feels compelled to reject the illusions of "the System"—his sarcastic name for Hegel's philosophy. What Hegel and his followers have done is to build an imposing edifice in which there is no place for true human existence—an existence that takes place in anguish, doubt, and despair. They have built a sumptuous mansion and decided to live in the barn, for their building is too good for them. Existence—actual, painful, human existence—is prior to essence, and much more important than it. This emphasis on existence made Kierkegaard the founder of existentialism, although most later existentialists pursued interests very different from his. Existence is a constant struggle, a struggle to become, to be born. In placing existence at the heart of matters, one is forced to abandon, not only Hegelianism, but every other system, and even all hope for a consistent system. Although reality itself may be a system for God, it can never be seen as such from the perspective of one in the midst of existence.

Kierkegaard, however, was interested in a particular form of existence: Christian existence. It too cannot be reduced to a system. The tragedy of Christendom, of easy Christianity, is that existence has ceased to be an adventure and a constant risk in the presence of God, and has become a form of morality or a doctrinal system. Hence, Kierkegaard's great problem, which he sought to pose before all: how to become a true Christian when one has the disadvantage of living in the midst of Christendom.

Christianity and History

The interest in history that characterized the nineteenth century also left its mark on biblical and theological studies. In Tübingen, F. C. Baur (1792–1860) sought to expound the development of theology in the New Testament following Hegel's scheme. Baur and his followers felt that at the very root of the New Testament one finds the conflict between Peter's Judaizing Christianity and the more universal perspective of Paul. The tension between that thesis and antithesis was then resolved in a synthesis that some said was the Fourth Gospel, and others said was second-century Christianity. Baur's basic scheme and its many variants, as well as the general interest in history that existed at the time, led to long and scholarly discussions as to the date and authorship of each book of the Bible. Many looked upon such debates, and their startling conclusions, as a menace to faith. In any case, these debates led to increased refinement in the tools of historical research, and to a better understanding of the Bible and its times.

The study of church history followed a parallel course. The idea that Christian doctrines have in fact evolved through the centuries proved a stumbling block to many. Some insisted that such evolution was only the unfolding of what was already implicit in early Christianity. But others— among them the leading historian Adolph von Harnack (1851–1930)—saw the development of dogma as the progressive abandonment of the faith of the early church, moving away from the teachings *of* Jesus to teachings *about* Jesus. According to Harnack, Jesus taught the fatherhood of God, universal brotherhood, the infinite value of the human soul, and the commandment of love. It was later, through a process that took years, that Jesus and faith in him became the center of the Christian message.

Many of these ideas were derived from one of the most influential theologians of the nineteenth century, Albrecht Ritschl (1822–1889), whom Harnack called "the last of the fathers of the church." Like Schleiermacher, Ritschl responded to Kant's challenge by placing religion in a sphere distinct from pure or cognitive reason. But he thought that Schleiermacher's "feeling of absolute dependence" was too subjective. For him, religion—and Christianity in particular—was neither a matter of rational knowledge nor of subjective feeling, but of practical life. Speculative rationalism he regarded as too cold, not requiring a commitment of faith. Mysticism, on the other hand, he rejected as being too subjective and individualistic. Christianity is practical in that it is lived out in the practical, moral life.

But Christianity is practical also in the sense that it must be based on the factual knowledge of events, and particularly of the event of Jesus. What is of primary importance for the practical life is God's historical revelation in Jesus. When theology forgets this, it falls into either rationalism or mysticism. Against both errors, historical study shows that the center of the teachings of Jesus is the Kingdom of God and its ethics, "the organization of humanity through action based on love." It was this aspect of Ritschl's theology that served as the basis for Rauschenbusch's Social Gospel, of which we have spoken in chapter 25.

The interest of the nineteenth century in history led to the "quest for the historical Jesus." In order to know the true essence of Christianity, it was thought, one must find the factual Jesus hidden behind the faith of the church and even behind the accounts of the gospels. The difficulty in such a quest, however, is that the historian's own values and image of reality are superimposed on any findings. Therefore, by the beginning of the twentieth century, the famous theologian, musician, and missionary Albert Schweitzer concluded that the quest had looked for a man of the nineteenth century, and instead of finding Jesus had found its own image.

The theologians mentioned in this chapter are only a few of many worthy of study, for the nineteenth century was marked by a theological activity rivaled by few other periods. But the few mentioned suffice to give an idea of the great variety of opinions and positions that appeared within Protestantism, and the intellectual vitality reflected in that very variety. Naturally, in that feverish intellectual activity statements were made, and positions taken, that would soon need to be corrected. But the undeniable fact is that the nineteenth century proved that there were in the Protestant ranks many who did not fear the intellectual challenges of their time.

29/Catholic Theology

We are horrified, venerable brethren, at seeing the monstrous doctrines, or rather the enormous errors, that oppress us. They are widely distributed by a multitude of books, pamphlets, and other writings small in size, but great in their evil.

GREGORY XVI

While many Protestant theologians followed the route of liberalism, the Catholic hierarchy tried to keep its theologians from following suit. The main reason for this was the manner in which the new ideas had threatened and damaged the authority of the church.

The Papacy and the French Revolution

The pope at the outset of the French Revolution was Pius VI. Years earlier, in 1775, he had begun his pontificate by issuing a bull in which he attacked the ideas of those philosophers who advocated a new social and political order. Therefore, from the very early days of the Revolution, the pope did all he could to impede its progress. By the time the new French government issued the "Civil Constitution of the Clergy," its tensions with Rome were such that negotiations were almost impossible. In retaliation for the pope's support of conservatism, the French republican government sought to weaken the papacy, and this was one of the reasons for the birth of the "cult of Reason." In Rome itself, French agents undermined the pope's authority by disseminating republican ideas. In 1798, the French army took Rome, proclaimed a republic, and declared that the pope was no longer the temporal ruler of the city. Pius VI died a year later, while virtually a prisoner of the French.

The cardinals then gathered in Venice under the protection of Emperor Francis II of Austria, an enemy of the French Republic, and elected Pius VII. Napoleon's climb to power eased tensions between the new pope and France, and in 1801 an agreement was reached between the two parties. Although Napoleon was not particularly religious, he saw no need to spend his energies in conflicts with the papacy, and Pius VII, having been restored to his see, enjoyed a few years of relative peace. In 1804, he traveled to Paris in order to consecrate Napoleon as emperor—and Napoleon signaled his claim to absolute power by taking the crown from the pope's hand and crowning himself. The following year, the emperor's troops invaded Italy, and in 1808 took the city of Rome. The pope refused to flee, and excommunicated any who did violence to him or to the church. The French took him captive and he was not freed until the fall of Napoleon. He then returned to Rome, where his first official action was to forgive his enemies.

Pius VII died in 1823, two years after Napoleon, and was succeeded by Leo XII. Leo and his successors, Pius VIII and Gregory XVI, were able to reign in peace. But the memory of the French Revolution constantly inclined them towards political and theological conservatism, and they repeatedly blocked attempts by Catholics to lend their support to republican and democratic ideas. The most famous person thus condemned was the French theologian F. R. de Lamennais, who had staunchly resisted Napoleon in his attempts to use the church for his own ends. After a long spiritual pilgrimage, Lamennais came to the conclusion that absolute monarchs would always be tempted to use the church for their own ends, and that therefore Christians ought to foster movements to limit the power of absolute monarchs. This should be done with the support and under the direction of the papacy. As part of this vast political project, the pope should advocate the freedom of the press, for this would be the spearhead of the new order. Lamennais was convinced that if the popes took the lead in such a project, the church would be able to claim its rightful place in the resultant order. Up to that point, Lamennais had been a champion of the church against absolutist governments that would not respect its prerogatives, and Leo XII had even considered making him a cardinal. But when Lamennais began arguing for an alliance between the popes and political liberalism, he lost all support in Rome, where the memory of the French Revolution was still fresh. He went to Rome, hoping to convince the pope of the wisdom of his plan. But Gregory XVI, who was then pope, condemned his ideas in two encyclicals. Lamennais then left the church, taking with him many others of similar ideas.

While this debate was taking place, nationalist sentiment was growing in Italy. A significant faction among Italian patriots hoped that the papacy would provide the center around which a new unified nation would be

The First Vatican Council, under the authoritarian leadership of
Pius IX, marked the high point of tendencies begun at the time of
the Council of Trent. Its most significant action was the declaration
of papal infallibility.

formed. But the papal fear of everything that had the slightest odor of sedition, and their desire to please the very monarchs who sought to keep Italy divided, soon lost the popes all support among Italian nationalists.

Pius IX

The longest pontificate in history, that of Pius IX (1846–1878), was a paradoxical time for the papacy. The greatest of these paradoxes was that, at the same time that the popes were declared infallible, they lost their temporal power. The revolution of 1848 was felt in Rome, where the Republic of Rome was proclaimed in the following year. The pope, expelled from the city, was unable to return until the French intervened in his favor. After his restoration, instead of continuing some of the measures of reformation and liberalization introduced by the republicans, Pius IX tried to rule as an absolute monarch. He also clashed with Cavour, the great statesman of the Kingdom of Piedmont, whose goal was the unification of Italy. Eventually, on September 20, 1870, the troops of the new Kingdom of Italy took the papal states. Although for a long time the popes refused to accept the new reality, those events marked the end of their temporal power, for their sovereignty was now limited to a few palaces that Italy allowed them to keep —particularly the Vatican. At approximately the same time, Bismarck in Germany was taking measures against the power of the church, and other European powers were following his example. Therefore, the pontificate of Pius IX marks the end of the political power of the popes, which had reached its apex in the thirteenth century under Innocent III.

While losing his power, Pius IX insisted on reaffirming it, even if this could be done only in religious matters. Thus, in 1854, he proclaimed the dogma of the Immaculate Conception of Mary. According to that dogma, Mary herself, by virtue of her election to be the Mother of the Savior, was kept pure from all taint of sin, including original sin. This was a question that Catholic theologians had debated for centuries, without reaching a consensus. But the most significant fact from a historical point of view was that, in proclaiming this dogma as the doctrine of the church, Pius IX was the first pope ever to define a dogma on his own, without the support of a council. In a way, the bull *Ineffabilis,* promulgating the dogma of the Immaculate Conception of Mary, was a testing of the waters to see how the world would react. Since the bull did not meet much opposition, the stage was set for the promulgation of papal infallibility.

Meanwhile, the pope did not rest in his struggle against the new political ideas circulating in Europe and America. In 1864, he issued the encyclical *Quanta cura,* accompanied by a *Syllabus of Errors* that listed eighty propositions that Catholics must reject. Some of the errors listed there show the mood of the papacy in the nineteenth century:

13. That the method and principles by which the ancient scholastic doctors developed their theology are not compatible with present needs or with scientific progress.

15. That each person is free to adopt and follow that religion which seems best to the light of reason.

18. That Protestantism is simply a different form of the same Christian religion, and that it is possible to please God in it as well as in the true Catholic church.

21. That the church does not have the power to declare as a dogma that its religion is the only true religion.

24. That the church has no authority to make use of force, nor does it have temporal power . . .

30. That the immunity of the church and of ecclesiastics is based on civil law.

37. That it is lawful to institute national churches, separate and completely independent of the Roman pontiff.

38. That the arbitrary behavior of the popes contributed to the break between the Eastern and western churches.

45. That the entire management of the schools in which youth are educated in a

Christian state, with the sole and partial exception of seminaries, can and should be in the hands of the civil power, in such a manner that no other authority be allowed to intervene in the management of schools, the direction of studies, the granting of degrees, or the selection and certification of teachers.

47. That the good order of civil society requires that public schools, open to children of all classes, and in general all public institutions devoted to the teaching of literature and science, and to the education of youth, be free of all authority on the part of the church, of all its moderating influence, and be subject only to the civil and political authority, so that they may behave according to the opinions of civil magistrates and to the common opinion of the time.

55. That the church ought to be separate from the state, and the state from the church.

77. That in our time it is no longer convenient that the Catholic religion be the only religion of the state, or that every other religion be excluded.

78. That it is therefore praiseworthy that in some Catholic countries the law allows immigrants to practice publicly their own forms of worship.

79. That it is false that, if all religions are granted civil freedom, and all are allowed to express publicly their opinions and ideas, no matter what they may be, this will facilitate moral and mental corruption, and will spread the plague of indifferentism.

80. That the Roman pontiff can and should be reconciled with, and agree to, progress, liberalism, and modern civilization.

Thus, during the last decades of the nineteenth century, the papacy was openly opposed to such innovations as the separation of church and state, freedom of worship, freedom of the press, and public schools under state supervision. At the same time, the pope insisted on his authority, and on the evils that would follow if he was not obeyed. All this reached its high point in the First Vatican Council, still under the direction of Pius IX. In *Pastor aeternus*, the Council promulgated the dogma of papal infallibility:

Therefore faithfully adhering to the tradition received from the beginning of the Christian faith, for the glory of God our Saviour, the exaltation of the Christian religion, and the salvation of Christian people, the sacred Council approving, we teach and define that it is a dogma divinely revealed: that the Roman Pontiff, when he speaks *ex cathedra*, that is, when in discharge of the office of pastor and doctor of all Christians, by virtue of his supreme Apostolic authority, he defines a doctrine regarding faith or morals to be held by the universal Church, by the divine assistance promised to him in blessed Peter, is possessed of that divine infallibility with which the divine Redeemer willed that his Church should be endowed for defining doctrine regarding faith or morals; and that therefore such definitions are irreformable of themselves, and not from the consent of the Church.*

This is the official statement of papal infallibility as the Catholic Church holds it. It is important to note that the text does not say that the pope is always infallible, but only when he speaks "ex cathedra." These words were included in the declaration in order to respond to the objection that Pope

---

*Tr. by H. E. Manning, 1871; quoted in Schaff, *The Creeds of Christendom,* vol. 2 (New York: Harper & Brothers, 1878), pp. 270–71.

Pope Leo XIII.

Honorius, for instance, had been a heretic. The answer to that objection would then be that Honorius, in accepting erroneous doctrine, did not do so "ex cathedra." In any case, of the more than six hundred bishops present, 522 voted in favor, two against, and more than a hundred abstained. (Only once after this proclamation has a pope claimed to be making use of such authority. This was in 1950, when Pius XII promulgated the doctrine of the Assumption of Mary—that is, that at the end of her earthly life Mary was bodily assumed into heaven.)

The promulgation of papal infallibility did not cause the stir that might have been expected. In the Netherlands, Austria, and Germany, some withdrew from the Roman communion and founded the Old Catholic Church. But, in general, protests and criticism were moderate—having lost its political power, the papacy was no longer as formidable as it had once been. In the old struggle between Gallicans and Ultramontanes (see chapter 18), the latter had finally won. But that victory was possible because the papacy had lost much of the power that at an earlier time Gallicans had feared. Papal infallibility was promulgated on July 18, 1870, and on September 20 Rome surrendered before the armies of the Kingdom of Italy. Pius IX declared himself a prisoner of King Victor Emmanuel, and refused to accept the new order. After all, Rome had been lost to the popes many times before, and always someone had intervened to restore it to the papacy. But this time no one intervened, and in 1929 Pope Pius XI finally accepted what had been a fact for more than half a century.

Leo XIII

Pius IX was succeeded by Leo XIII, whose tenure in office was also exceptionally long (1878–1903). Given political conditions in Italy, Leo XIII, who still insisted on his right to temporal authority over Rome and the surrounding area, declared that Catholics should not vote in Italian elections. That prohibition, continued until well into the twentieth century, would in effect deny Catholics the opportunity to participate in the formative years of the Italian nation. But, while following that conservative policy in Italy, Leo saw the need to yield in other fields. Thus, he was able to reach a tacit agreement with Germany, with the result that some of the anti-Catholic policies begun by Bismarck were rescinded. In France, the Third Republic also took anti-clerical measures, but the pope decided it was best to follow a policy of conciliation. In 1892, he even advised the French clergy to abandon their opposition to the republic—even though a few years earlier, in the bull *Immortale Dei,* he had declared democracy incompatible with the authority of the church. Thus, Leo XIII, while acknowledging the need to take into account the new realities and attitudes of modern times, understood papal authority in terms very similar to those of Pius IX, and still kept alive the dream of a Catholic society guided by principles formulated by the Papacy.

This may be seen in the most important document of Leo's pontificate, his bull *Rerum novarum,* issued on May 15, 1891. The subject of that bull was one with which few popes had dealt before: the proper relations between laborers and their employers. The bull shows that Leo is aware of the inequities that have resulted from the contrast between "the enormous fortunes of a few individuals, and the extreme poverty of the masses." Therefore, the time has come "to define the mutual rights and obligations of the rich and the poor, of capital and labor." Such relations have become all the more tragic since labor organizations have disappeared in recent times, and "a small group of very rich people have been able to throw upon the masses of poor laborers a yoke that is little better than slavery itself." Although it is an error to believe that between the rich and the poor there can only be class war, it is true that the defense of the poor merits special attention, for the rich have many ways to protect themselves, while the poor have no other recourse than the protection of the state. Therefore, laws should be such that the rights of the poor are guaranteed. In particular, this refers to the right of every laborer to a salary sufficient to sustain him and his family, without being forced to work beyond a fair limit. All this is to be done because "God seems to lean in favor of those who suffer misfortune."

On the other hand, this does not mean that the opinions of the socialists are correct, for private property is a right established by God, as is also the right of inheritance. Furthermore, the differences that exist in the social order are due, at least in part, to natural differences among human beings. What the pope then asks is, first of all, for the rich to practice charity. This means that no one is under obligation to give to the point of cutting into what is necessary for life, or even for keeping one's state in life. But, having met those needs, "one is obliged to give the needy of what is left." The poor, for their part, ought not to hate the rich, but are rather to remember that poverty is an honorable state, and that the practice of virtue leads to material prosperity.

Leo is well aware that charity and love will not suffice to produce justice, and therefore he calls on all Christians to defend the poor, and urges the formation of labor unions to defend the rights of laborers. Since those rights include fair wages, reasonable hours of work, and the right to practice the Catholic religion without interference, Leo calls for the formation of Catholic labor unions, arguing that in such unions there will not be the hatred and divisions that arise when poverty is unaccompanied by religion. In summarizing its position, the bull declares: "The urgent issue of today is the condition of the working classes. . . . But Christian laborers will easily solve it by forming associations, choosing wise leaders, and following the path that their ancestors have trod with so much profit to themselves and to society."

This encyclical gave new impulse to the many Catholics who were already seeking solutions to the many problems posed by the industrial revolution and growing capitalism. Some whom the bull prodded into action would later come to the conclusion that its solutions were too simplistic. Others would oppose the union movement by pointing out that Leo had encouraged Catholic unions, and not others. Therefore, *Rerum novarum,* while marking the beginning of the modern Catholic trade union movement, is also an indication of Leo's ambivalence before the challenges and requirements of the modern world.

A similar ambivalence could be seen in his attitude towards modern scholarship. Leo did open the archives of the Vatican to historians, for he was convinced that the outcome of historical studies would strengthen the authority of the church. But the bull *Providentissimus Deus,* while admitting the value of historical studies of the Bible, warned against their use to weaken the authority of either the Bible or the church. Therefore, both those who sought greater freedom in the critical study of Scripture and those who opposed them could point to sections in the encyclical that seemed to favor them.

Pius X

The pope who succeeded Leo, and who led the Catholic Church until the beginning of World War I, was Pius X (1903–1914). His policy was much more conservative than Leo's, and drew its inspiration from Pius IX. The result was a growing gulf between the mainstream of modern thought and society on the one hand, and Catholicism on the other. Following the pope's instructions, the Holy Office—the old Inquisition—issued a decree condemning those who had dared apply the new methods of research to Scripture or to theological matters. These were the so-called Modernists, of whom the most famous were the Frenchman A. F. Loissy, the Englishman George Tyrrell, and the German Hermann Schell. Shortly thereafter, in the encyclical *Pascendi Domini gregis,* Pius X confirmed the action of the Holy Office. The net result was that many of the Modernists left the church, while greater numbers of Catholics decided to remain in the church while paying little attention to pontifical directives.

In conclusion, during the period between the French Revolution and World War I, Christianity, both Protestant and Catholic, had to face new political, economic, social, and intellectual circumstances. In general, Protestantism sought means to take those new realities into account, while Catholicism took the opposite tack. Obviously, there were many exceptions to that generalization. One of the net results, however, was that by the time of World War I Protestants and Catholics were as far apart from each other as they had been at any previous time. Protestants looked upon the Catholic Church as a relic of bygone ages, while Catholics were convicted that Protestantism had confirmed its heretical character by capitulating before the challenges of the modern world. As long as such conditions prevailed, there was little hope for a rapprochement between the two branches of western Christianity.

30/Geographic Expansion

Just as the development of improved means
of communication has greatly facilitated the
propagation of the Gospel and the sending
forth of the pure and hopeful influences of
western civilisation, so the drawing together
of the nations and races as a result of these
improvements has made possible the more
rapid spread of influences antagonistic to
Christ's Kingdom.
WORLD MISSIONARY CONFERENCE, EDINBURGH,
1910

The nineteenth century was marked by a geographic expansion comparable only to that of the sixteenth. While the sixteenth century was the great age of Catholic expansion, the nineteenth played a similar role for Protestantism. Although the consequences of that vast enterprise are still not clear, there is little doubt that, from the point of view of the history of Christianity, the most important event of the nineteenth century was the founding of a truly universal church, in which peoples of all races and nations had a part. On the other hand, however, it is necessary to point out that this took place within the context of colonialism and economic imperialism—a framework that also left its stamp on the life of the church.

Colonial Expansion

At the opening of the nineteenth century, one could well have thought that European colonialism had passed its zenith. This was particularly true in the western hemisphere, where European expansion had been most remarkable in previous centuries. The independence of the United States left Britain with no other American colonies than Canada, several islands in the Caribbean, and relatively small holdings in Central and South America. The French lost Haiti, until then their most productive colony. And Spain had to relinquish all its American lands except Cuba and Puerto Rico—both of which she would lose by the turn of the century. The bloodletting of the Napoleonic wars seemed likely to put an end to European hegemony in the world.

But what happened was exactly the opposite. The Napoleonic wars turned Britain's attention towards the colonies held by its enemies. When Napoleon became master of the European continent, Britain was able to survive thanks to her naval superiority. Her most powerful squadrons protected her from invasion, while others sought to intercept trade between Napoleon's Europe—France, Spain, Portugal, and the Netherlands—and her colonies. British citizens learned to expect bad news from the armies that opposed Napoleon on land, and good from the ships that harassed him on the sea. When the wars ended, Britain found herself in possession of several former French and Dutch colonies.

These events coincided with the main reason for colonial expansion in the nineteenth century: the industrial revolution. As technological advances were applied to industrial production, greater capital and wider markets became necessary. For a time, those areas of Europe that had not been industrialized provided the necessary markets. But soon the industrial powers began to look for other outlets, and found them in Latin America and Asia.

In Latin America, these circumstances led to "neocolonialism." The former Spanish colonies had scarcely won their independence when Britain, France, and the United States began competing for control of the new markets. At first, foreign investors were interested mainly in urban markets. But, by 1870, there was a race for control of the agricultural products of the interior. With new industrial and technological developments, what was now needed was not so much new markets as raw materials for industry. Greed then turned its eye to lands that it had scarcely noticed before, and a great deal of foreign capital was invested in railroads, harbors, and processing plants. These investments were made with the consent and support of the ruling *criollos*, whose holdings in land increased enormously in both size and value. Foreign and national capital thus formed an alliance whose interests were best served by the oligarchical governments that it usually supported. Given the power of such an alliance, radical changes in social and political structures were rare.

In Asia, the European industrial revolution had similar consequences, although colonialism usually took its more traditional form of military conquest and overt political domination. At first, the western economic powers were content with opening new markets. But again and again western economic interests, feeling threatened by political developments in the area, by the weakness of the local government, or by another industrial power, forced their nations to intervene militarily and take over the government of the region.

The colonization of black Africa, until then relatively slow, accelerated in the last decades of the century, when Europe burned with imperialistic fever. Many became convinced that, in order to be a power of the first order, a nation had to rule an overseas empire. By then, Britain, France, and the Netherlands had such empires, and now Belgium, Italy, and Germany joined in the mad scramble to claim every corner of the world.

All this was possible thanks to another consequence of industrial development: military might. Western powers had weapons with which they could defeat vastly superior armies. Even such proud and populous nations as China and Japan had to bow before what would otherwise have been second-rate powers. Only a handful of nations in Africa and Asia were able to keep their political independence, and even these were forced to surrender their economic independence. China and Japan, for instance, although never fully conquered by the western powers, were literally forced to open trade with the West. For the first time in history, the world became a vast economic network.

Many in the western world were aware of what was taking place. Some opposed particular colonizing ventures on the grounds that they were contrary to the national interest. Others—mostly Christians of profound convictions—protested against the treatment given to natives of some colonized areas. But, in general, the colonizers were convinced that their enterprise was justified by the benefits the colonized would receive. As they saw matters, God had placed the benefits of western civilization and Christian faith in the hands of white people—both Europeans and North Americans—in order for them to share with the rest of the world. That responsibility was "the white man's burden": to take to the rest of the world the benefits of industrialization, capitalism, democracy, and Christianity.

There were grounds for such visions. Medical science, for instance, reached many remote areas and saved countless lives. Trade and industrial development increased the wealth of many areas, and for that reason gained the support of certain classes among the native populations. But they also produced the dislocation of vast masses who now became landless, the destruction of many of the cultural patterns that had sustained societies for centuries, and growing disparities in living conditions between the rich and the poor throughout the world. In any case, the racial and cultural arrogance that stood at the base of the entire enterprise could not but produce the anticolonial reaction that marked the middle of the twentieth century.

The Missionary Enterprise

The church was deeply influenced by all these circumstances and ideas. The relationship between colonialism and missions, however, was very complex. Although the accusation is often made that missionaries were agents of colonialism, this is not always true, for some opposed it and many criticized various aspects of it. Nor is it always true that missionary work entered through a door opened by colonialism; for, although in many cases missionaries worked in colonized areas, there were many other cases where missionaries reached regions never before visited by white traders or colonizers. Also, many of the colonial authorities and commercial interests opposed missionary work, for they feared that religious conflict would interrupt trade. It is true that the colonial expansion of the West—particularly the Protestant West—coincided with its missionary expansion, and that the two at times aided and at times impeded each other.

One of the most remarkable characteristics of the missionary enterprise during the nineteenth century was the formation of missionary societies. Some of these drew their membership from a single denomination, while others broke confessional barriers. All were voluntary societies, for the churches as institutions did not usually support missions. Forerunners of the movement were the Society for Promoting Christian Knowledge (SPCK), founded in 1698, and the Society for the Propagation of the Gospel in Foreign Parts (SPG), founded in 1701. Both were Anglican, and for some time most of their work was among British expatriates. During the eighteenth century, due to the impact of Pietists, Moravians, and Methodists, several similar societies were founded. But the heyday of missionary societies began late in the eighteenth century, and lasted through the nineteenth. In 1792, thanks to the perseverance of William Carey—often called the "father of modern missions"—the Particular Baptist Society for Propagating the Gospel amongst the Heathen was founded (its name was later shortened to Baptist Missionary Society). Three years later, partly through the example of the Baptists, a group of Methodists, Presbyterians, and Congregationalists founded the London Missionary Society (LMS). The Church Missionary Society, dating from 1799, drew its members from the evangelical wing of the Anglican Church. Other societies were also created with more specific goals, such as the British and Foreign Bible Society, founded in 1804. The movement then spread to other lands, and soon there were Protestant missionary societies in the Netherlands, Switzerland, Denmark, Germany, and several other countries. In France, there were both Protestant and Catholic societies. Congregationalists in the United States founded the American Board of Commissioners for Foreign Missions. When one of its missionaries,

*William Carey, often called "the father of
modern missions," devoted a great deal of his
time to learning the languages of India and
translating the Scriptures into them.*

Adinoram Judson, became a Baptist, a Baptist missionary society was organized to support him and others, and this society eventually gave birth to the
American Baptist Convention.

The emergence of these societies points to another characteristic of the
missionary movement of the nineteenth century: its widespread support. For
centuries before that, most missionary work had taken place with the official
support of a state. But, in the nineteenth century, most western governments
had little or no official relation with the missionary enterprise. For years, the
British East India Company tried to bar missionaries from the lands under
its rule. Most European governments, and the United States, adopted a
neutral—and sometimes slightly hostile—stance towards missionaries and
their goals. In theory at least, missionaries could count on no other protection
than that afforded to their fellow citizens engaged in other endeavors. But
it was at the point of financial support that the contrast was greatest between

the modern missionary movement and its predecessors. Few governments—and few churches—contributed funds to the enterprise. Lacking such civil and ecclesiastical support, those interested in missions had to appeal to the public at large, and hence the growth and proliferation of missionary societies.

In consequence, for the first time in centuries the work of missions captivated the interest of the general membership of churches. Naturally, even then there were many who showed no interest in the matter. But those who wished to do so, from the youngest to the oldest, could make a contribution to the preaching of the gospel in far away lands. Missionary societies, for their part, brought news of what was taking place in the remotest areas of Asia or Africa, and thus became one of the main sources of public information and education regarding other lands and cultures.

Women played an important role in all this. In many denominations, both in the United States and in Europe, women organized their own missionary societies, and collected funds and supplies for work overseas. At first, all missionaries were men—although many were married and took their wives with them. But soon it was shown that women had a great contribution to make overseas. Some feminine missionary societies began sending their own missionaries. Among Catholics, such missionaries were usually nuns, and the work that they did in the mission field was similar to what they did in their homeland—teaching, nursing, care for the aged, and so forth. Among Protestants, women missionaries began taking responsibilities that were forbidden to them at home, such as preaching and organizing churches. (The underlying racism of the times made it acceptable for women to have over the "natives" an authority that sexism denied them in their own lands.) Eventually, the example of these women, and the news of their success, prompted other women in Europe and the United States to demand the opportunity to do the same. Thus, the missionary movement is one of the roots of the feminist movement among western Protestants.

Finally, another important consequence of the missionary movement was the spirit of cooperation that began appearing among various denominations. Rivalries that seemed justifiable in Europe or the United States were a stumbling block for missionary work in India or China. Therefore, many missionaries, and soon their converts also, took steps to lower the barriers separating denominations from each other. Some missionary societies drew their members from more than one denomination. In the mission field, ways were constantly sought to present a common witness and avoid competition. Thus, the ecumenical movement, at least among Protestants, has one of its main roots in the missionary experience of the nineteenth and twentieth centuries.

Asia and Oceania

For centuries, the ancient civilizations of the Far East had fascinated Europe. Medieval books included vague rumors of strange customs and incredible monsters. Then Marco Polo and other travelers brought news of fabulous riches in the courts of China and India. In the sixteenth century, the Portuguese established permanent trading posts in the area, and soon thereafter other European nations began seeking similar footholds. Commerce and its protection often led to military and political conquest, and by the time of World War I there were few countries in Asia and the Pacific that were not under colonial rule. Although not always in agreement with colonial policies, missionaries and the churches they founded were part of that process of European expansion.

In Asia, the area that first felt the impact of the new wave of colonial expansion was the Indian subcontinent—now India, Pakistan, Bangladesh, and Sri Lanka. Christianity had existed there since ancient times, and Catholicism had been introduced in the sixteenth century. Early in the eighteenth century, the first Protestant missionaries had arrived under the auspices of a Danish king profoundly affected by Pietism. But it was in the nineteenth century, with the sudden growth of British influence, that the greatest Protestant missionary advance took place.

The British East India Company had begun its operations in India early in the eighteenth century. A hundred years later, it ruled practically all the eastern coast of the subcontinent. A few years earlier, the British had taken Ceylon. By the middle of the nineteenth century, practically the entire area was under direct or indirect British rule. In 1858, by an act of Parliament, the government of India was taken from the company and placed directly under the British crown.

During its first century in operation, the British East India Company opposed missionary work, for it feared that Christian preaching would produce tensions and riots that would hinder trade. This policy met little opposition in England, where interest in missions was scarce. It was partly as a result of the efforts of William Carey that these conditions changed, and therefore he has properly been called "the founder of modern missions."

Although reared in an Anglican household, William Carey had become a Baptist. A teacher and cobbler by trade, he was fascinated by the news of new lands that Captain Cook was discovering in the Pacific. Joining his faith to his awareness of distant lands, he came to the conviction, unusual in his time, that Christians had the obligation to preach the gospel to those in far countries who had not heard it. After much criticism, he was able to gather a number of like-minded people and thus create the Particular Baptist Society for Propagating the Gospel amongst the Heathen. When the Society proved unable to find someone to send as a missionary, Carey decided to go himself; and, in 1793, he finally landed in Calcutta with his family and a physician who was to accompany him in his labors. The difficulties were many. Characteristically, on one occasion he wrote to his supporters in England that there were obstacles all around, and that therefore there was no alternative but to move ahead with the project! His zeal, and particularly his reports to England, resulted in a new interest in missions, and he was eventually joined by a second contingent of missionaries. Since the British East India Company would not allow the new arrivals to settle in Calcutta, Carey moved his residence to nearby Serampore, and this became the headquarters of the entire enterprise. He and his associates—one of whom was a printer—felt that one of their first tasks was to make the Bible available to the Indian population. Carey had an unusual gift for learning languages, and by his death he had translated the Bible, or part of it, into thirty-five languages. He also devoted his efforts to putting an end to the burning of widows on their husbands' funeral pyres. On both scores he attained remarkable success. Carey's work, and the reports that reached both Britain and the United States, inspired many to emulate him. Many of the missionary societies founded early in the nineteenth century owed their existence to his influence. Increasing numbers of Christians, having heard of Carey's exploits, felt called to similar careers. In 1813, when the charter of the British East India Com-

Carey baptizing his first convert.

pany came up for renewal, Parliament included in the new charter a clause granting missionaries free access to areas under company control.

In India itself, Carey's work did not at first produce great numbers of converts. But towards the end of his career it was clear that a church had been planted in the land, and that others would continue his work. In the next generation, the Scotsman Alexander Duff became famous for his work in education, for he was convinced that the best way for Christianity to enter India was through education. As a result of his work and that of others, by the time India gained its independence a century later many of the leaders of the new nation were either Christians or people profoundly influenced by the Christian faith.

Meanwhile, among the lower classes, there were mass conversions. Protestant missionaries insisted that the caste system that prevailed in India was wrong. In Indian tradition, the very breaking of bread that took place in communion was a breaking of caste. Therefore, many of the "untouchables," and several tribes that had traditionally been excluded from the mainstream of society, found Protestantism a liberating force and joined it. Likewise, many women found in Christianity a word of freedom, and responded by taking positions of responsibility. Most remarkable among them was Ramabai, who traveled to England and the United States, and then returned to India to devote the rest of her life to the education of women. As a result of her work, many women were able to make significant contributions both to the church and to Indian society.

In Southeast Asia, zones of colonial influence were separated by the once powerful kingdom of Siam (now called Thailand). East of it, French colonies appeared—in what was then called French Indochina—while the British took charge of Burma, the area west of Siam. In the French area, Catholic missionaries organized their converts in separate villages where they could live according to Catholic teachings. As a result, the area was divided between Catholic and Buddhist villages until well into the twentieth century. In Burma, the most famous missionary was Adinoram Judson, an American Congregationalist sent by the American Board of Commissioners for Foreign Missions who became a Baptist on his way to the mission field. Following Carey's example, he and his wife translated Scripture into Burmese, Thai, and other languages. They gained few converts, but one of these, Ko Tha Byu, later began a movement of mass conversion among his tribe—the Karens. In Siam, the only land of Southeast Asia that managed to preserve its independence, there were both Catholic and Protestant missionaries. Although their work was hindered by brief periods of persecution, by the end of the century they had succeeded in founding fairly strong churches.

China was the great empire of the Far East. Repeatedly, Christianity had been planted in it, and repeatedly it had disappeared under severe persecution and conditions of isolation. Finally, Ricci and his Jesuit companions had managed to found a small church (see vol. 1, pp 406–409). But then another period of isolationism set in, and by the beginning of the nineteenth century the small Catholic community in China led a precarious existence. Protestant missionaries had dreamed of entering China for a long time. One of Carey's companions had already begun the monumental task of translating the Bible into Chinese. Then the Scotsman Robert Morrison settled in Canton and devoted his life to translating the Bible and other books into Chinese. It took him seven years to gain his first convert, and he never had many. But his example, and the existence of a Chinese translation of Scripture, kept alive the dream of penetrating that vast land with the message of Christianity. The great difficulty, however, was that the Chinese government did not favor the presence of foreigners within its borders. Only a small number of those whom the Chinese considered western barbarians were allowed in certain restricted areas, and it was through these ports that all trade took place.

Then the Opium War broke out (1839–1842). This was one of the most shameful episodes in the history of western colonialism, for the British found themselves going to war against China in defense of the alleged right of British merchants to import opium into China in direct violation of Chinese imperial decrees. The Treaty of Nanking, ending hostilities, granted the British the island of Hong Kong and opened five important ports to British trade. After these events, other powers followed the British example, using their military might to force ever greater concessions from the Chinese. Many of the treaties making such concessions also made provisions for the presence of missionaries in Chinese territory. Some also granted them special protection. Eventually, even Chinese Christians were covered by a number of special provisions. Soon missionaries from various countries and denominations arrived in China, and their initial success was greatly encouraging.

One unexpected by-product of Christian preaching was the rebellion of Taiping—the Heavenly Kingdom. This movement was begun by a schoolteacher who read a number of Christian treatises and decided the time had come to establish the "Heavenly Kingdom of the Great Peace," whose king he would be. In that kingdom, all things would be held in common, there would be equality between the sexes, and there would be laws against prostitution, adultery, slavery, binding of girls' feet, opium, tobacco, and alcohol. In 1850, the movement led to open rebellion, and the troops of the Heavenly Kingdom won several important victories. In 1853, they established the "Heavenly Capital" in Nanking, and even threatened the imperial city of Beijing. Finally, with the help of the western powers, the imperial armies crushed the rebellion. It had lasted fifteen years, and resulted in twenty million deaths.

It was during the Taiping rebellion that J. Hudson Taylor first arrived in China. Forced to return to England by ill health, he devoted his efforts to founding and leading the China Inland Mission, under whose auspices he then returned to China. The purpose of this organization was to evangelize China without introducing the divisions that existed in European and American Protestantism. It accepted missionaries of all denominations, and resulted in hundreds of churches in various areas of the country. Also, it refused to make use of the supposed advantages to be obtained by foreign protection, being aware that the use of such privileges created resentment among the Chinese, and would eventually prove costly.

Taylor's predictions came true. The Boxer rebellion of 1899–1901 was the violent expression of Chinese resentment of foreign intervention. Thousands of missionaries and their converts were killed. The foreign diplomats in Beijing, who had been bickering over the spoils of China, were besieged until a combined western army came to their succor. Eventually, the western powers crushed the rebellion, and the imperial government was forced to make even greater concessions—including the payment of a huge indemnization. Several missionary agencies, having learned the lesson of the rebellion, refused to accept any payments. Eventually, all these upheavals led to the fall of the Empire. In 1911, rebellion broke out, the emperor was forced to abdicate, and the way was open for the creation of the Republic of the United Chinese Provinces. By then, the number of Protestant missionaries was in the tens of thousands, there were flourishing churches in every province, and increasing numbers of Chinese were taking positions of leadership in the church. The future appeared so bright that some western observers began speaking of a conversion of the entire nation similar to what had taken place in the Roman Empire during Constantine's reign.

The nineteenth century saw the founding of many Christian communities in various parts of the world, such as this Chinese congregation standing before its meeting place.

During the first half of the nineteenth century, Japan was entirely closed to all western contact or influence. In 1854, Commodore M. C. Perry of the US Navy forced the Japanese to sign their first commercial treaty with a western power. Then Britain, France, the Netherlands, and Russia followed suit. In 1864, a joint western force put an end to all resistance to foreign influence. The Japanese response was to acknowledge western technological superiority, and to seek to learn as much as possible from the West. By the end of the century, Japan was an industrial and military power capable of defeating the Chinese and Russians; in 1910, it annexed the ancient kingdom of Korea. This process of rapid westernization aided the work of missionaries, who began arriving shortly after Commodore Perry's exploit. Soon there were churches in all the major cities of the nation, and native leadership was produced. It is also interesting to note that Protestant missionaries found in the area of Nagasaki about a hundred thousand people who still retained vestiges of what their ancestors had learned centuries earlier from Francis Xavier and other Jesuit missionaries.

The Japanese had learned Commodore Perry's lesson and, in 1876, they forced Korea to sign its first commercial treaty. Soon, Korea found itself signing similar treaties with the United States (1882), Great Britain (1883), and Russia (1884). This opened the way for the first Protestant missionaries to Korea, Methodists and Presbyterians from the United States who arrived in 1884. Their strategy was to found churches that from the very beginning could be self-supporting, and to develop the native leadership necessary for such churches. The results were astounding. Although Japanese occupation in 1910 created difficulties for the churches, they continued flourishing, and soon Korea had the highest percentage of Christian population of any nation in the Far East except the Philippines.

The Philippines had been conquered and colonized much earlier by the Spanish; and therefore, at the opening of the nineteenth century the population was mostly Catholic. The example of the Spanish American colonies, however, led to increased hopes for independence, which was proclaimed in 1896. Two years later, as a result of the Spanish-American war, Spain ceded the Philippines to the United States. This did not stop the struggle for independence, which continued until the islands were finally made independent in 1946. During the struggle against Spain, the Catholic church was an instrument in the hands of the colonial government, and this gave rise to the Filipino Independent Church—which later was influenced by Protestantism and departed even further from Catholicism. Protestants entered the islands during the period of American occupation, but by 1914 the churches founded by them were still small.

Indonesia, originally colonized by the Portuguese, was mostly in Dutch hands by the beginning of the nineteenth century. The Dutch East India Company, which until 1798 had been in charge of the colonial enterprise, had been inimical to missions. Therefore, it was mostly during the nineteenth century that strong efforts were made to reach the original Indonesian population. Corrupt governments and outright exploitation were strongly criticized by Christians in the Netherlands, and in 1870 a measure of reform was introduced. Meanwhile, in Sarawak, English adventurer James Brooke had established himself as rajah. He and his successors Charles and Vyner Brooke invited missionaries into their territories, hoping that they would improve education and medical services. They also encouraged the immigration of Chinese Christians. Therefore, by the end of the nineteenth century Christianity had made great numeric gains in Indonesia.

To the east and south of these lands were other territories that had been vaguely known to Europeans since the sixteenth century, but which were brought to the attention of Britain by the explorations of Captain James Cook between 1768 and 1779. The largest of these, Australia and New Zealand, were soon colonized by the British, who established in them churches similar to those in their homeland. Both the aboriginal inhabitants of Australia and the Maoris of New Zealand were decimated by European immigrants and the diseases they brought with them, and it fell to the churches to protest against their mistreatment and exploitation. In New Zealand, movements such as the *Hau Hau* and *Ringatu* combined ancient Maori traditions with Christian teachings and a desire for justice and vindication. They had widespread following among the Maoris well into the twentieth century. The smaller islands of the Pacific at first drew the attention of adventurers and dreamers. Then came the missionaries. And finally, in the mad rush for colonies after 1870, the imperial powers entered the scene. By the end of the century, every island was claimed by a foreign power. By then, most of the population of Polynesia was Christian, and there were also churches in almost all the islands of Melanesia and Micronesia. It was only in the remotest regions, such as the interior of New Guinea, that the name of Christ had not been proclaimed.

Africa and the Moslem World

For centuries, Moslem power had blocked European expansion towards the south and the southeast. Beyond the Moslem lands on the North coast of Africa were barren lands, and beyond these were tropical areas deemed unhealthy for Europeans. Therefore, Europe came to see Africa and the Moslem world as obstacles to be overcome before reaching the riches of the East. But during the course of the nineteenth century, that perspective was radically changed. At the beginning of the century, most of the Near East and the north coast of Africa belonged to the Ottoman Empire, whose capital was Istanbul—ancient Constantinople. By the opening of World War I, Great Britain, France, and Italy had control of the North coast of Africa, and the Ottoman Empire was about to disappear. This led many to consider the possibility of beginning missionary work in those areas, and in other traditionally Moslem lands.

However, there were already other Christians in the region—which, after all, had been the birthplace of Christianity. Therefore, the main issue for western missionaries was how their work should relate to those older churches. In general, Roman Catholics sought to bring entire bodies of Eastern Christians into communion with Rome and obedience to the pope. Such groups, while keeping their rites and traditions, in fact became Roman Catholics, and are known as "uniates." In order to deal with issues affecting them in a particular way, the "Congregation of Eastern Rites" was founded in Rome in 1862. Although Roman Catholics also sought to convert Moslems, they had relatively little success. Protestants, on the other hand, often sought to cooperate with the ancient Eastern churches, hoping that such cooperation would bring about a renewal in the life of those churches. This program did achieve a measure of success, but in the end it created tensions within the ancient churches, which then divided. While the conservative wing returned to its older practices, the more progressive one simply became Protestant. It was from such schisms that Protestantism gained the majority of its earliest adherents, although eventually it also began to make converts from the Moslem population. Such work was particularly successful in Egypt, Syria, and Lebanon.

There were few European enclaves in black Africa at the beginning of the nineteenth century. Portuguese rule in Angola and Mozambique did not extend far inland. In 1652, the Dutch had established a colony on the Cape of Good Hope. Shortly thereafter, the French opened a trading post in Senegal. In 1799, the British founded Sierra Leone as a land for freed slaves returning to Africa. That was the extent of European colonization in Africa at the beginning of the century. In sharp contrast, by 1914 the only independent states remaining in the entire continent were Ethiopia and Liberia—and the latter was a creation of the early abolitionist movement in the United States.

The process of colonization was fairly slow in the early nineteenth century. The British took the Cape from the Dutch, who moved north and founded new colonies. In 1820, the first American blacks arrived in Liberia, which became independent in 1847. Meanwhile, missionaries were penetrating into areas never before seen by Europeans, and reporting on the ravishes of the slave trade and the economic resources of the interior of Africa. In 1867, diamonds were found in South Africa. France sought to join its holdings in Algeria with those in Senegal. Germany entered the contest in 1884 by taking possession of Namibia. Leopold II of Belgium, whose powers in his own kingdom were limited, took the colonization of the Congo as a personal enterprise, and in 1908 the area officially became the Belgian Congo. In 1885, the Spanish claimed Rio de Oro and Spanish Guinea. Then

Italy took Eritrea. By then, the rest of the continent had been divided among the British, French, and German.

All these events aroused missionary interest in Europe and the United States. In general, Catholic missions were most successful in Catholic colonies, while Protestants gained more adherents in British and German colonies. Catholics were also hindered by disputes over questions of jurisdiction —Portugal still claimed its ancient rights of patronage over the entire African church, while France and Belgium disputed over the Congo valley. The

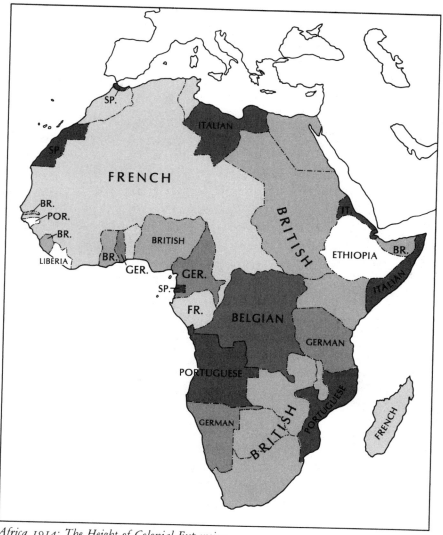

Africa 1914: The Height of Colonial Expansion

most famous of Protestant missionaries to Africa was David Livingstone, whose travels both as a missionary and as a representative of the British government did much to arouse interest in black Africa, and whose reports on the ravages of the slave trade were an important factor contributing to its abolition.

By 1914, not only was most of Africa in colonial hands, but in every one of those territories there were Christian churches. This was true both in the major cities and in the interior of the continent, where churches could be

Africa 1984: The Growth of Independent Nations

found in many remote villages. By then, many of these churches were train-ing their own leadership and extending their work to new areas.

Latin America

The impact of independence on the Catholic Church of Latin America has already been noted in chapter 27. Independence, however, also led to the founding of Protestant churches in every nation of Latin America. At first, this was the result of immigration. The new governments were convinced that they should encourage immigration for a number of reasons. First of all, since their goal was to imitate the industrial development of countries such as Great Britain, it was hoped that immigration from those areas would provide the experienced personnel necessary for such development. Second, there were still vast expanses of untilled, arable land. Immigrants settling on such lands would bring them into production and increase the wealth of the nation. Third, it was necessary to introduce and disseminate ideas contrary to those coming from Spain and still fostered by many in the Catholic Church. Therefore, throughout the entire nineteenth century several Latin American governments encouraged immigration from Europe and the United States.

In the implementation of that policy, it was necessary to remember that many of the prospective immigrants were Protestants who were not willing to abandon their faith. To force them to renounce it would encourage the immigration of unprincipled hypocrites—a bitter lesson that Mexico learned in Texas. Therefore, many governments, even in countries that did not allow such freedom to their own citizens, issued laws guaranteeing freedom of religion to immigrants. Soon, however, they saw the incongruence of such action, and felt compelled to grant their own citizens equal rights. Thus, the policy of encouraging foreign immigration eventually favored the spread of Protestantism among the native population.

Most of the early immigrants came from Europe. Very few came from the United States (if one discounts those who moved into territories taken from Mexico), for it was the time of North American expansion to the West, and there were ample lands to be had in that area without migrating to Latin America. Large numbers of Scots went to Argentina, Uruguay, and Chile, where they could find climates similar to their own, and in many cases better economic conditions than they had at home. Therefore, long before the first Latin Americans were converted to Protestantism, Protestant services were held in English in the major cities of southern Latin America.

A particularly interesting case of mission by immigration was that of James Theodore Holly and his companions, 110 black Episcopalians who emigrated to Haiti from the United States hoping to find greater freedom and to preach the gospel to the Haitians. After eighteen months, forty-three had died of various diseases. Most of the survivors decided to return to the United States or to move on to Jamaica. But Holly and a handful remained and founded a church. In 1876, Holly was consecrated by the Episcopal Church to be the first bishop of the Apostolic Orthodox Church of Haiti—later the Episcopal Church of Haiti.

Immigration eventually led to missions among native Latin Americans. The first missionary to arrive was probably the Scotsman James Thomson, a Baptist representative of the British and Foreign Bible Society who arrived at Buenos Aires in 1818. In the next few years, he visited several countries —from Argentina and Chile to Cuba and Mexico—and then departed for other lands. His work consisted mostly in the distribution of Spanish Bibles and personal discussion with priests and others. It was during the second half of the century that permanent Protestant work began in most countries. The first Protestant sermon in Spanish in Buenos Aires of which there is a record was preached in 1867. At approximately the same time, the Presbyterian Church was beginning work in Chile. In general, it was after 1870 that missionary agencies from the United States began taking an active interest in Latin America.

One of the factors inhibiting such interest, in Europe as well as in the United States, was the presence of Roman Catholicism in the area. To organize missions to Latin America was to declare that Catholics were not Christian, a step that many Protestant agencies and churches were not willing to take. Particularly among Anglicans and Episcopalians, there was strong opposition to missions among Catholics; therefore, the earliest Anglican missions in Latin America worked among Indians in Tierra del Fuego.

By the beginning of the twentieth century, however, Protestant missions had made great strides in Latin America. Most of the early missionaries were concerned, not only with the salvation of souls, but also with physical wellbeing and intellectual development. Therefore, Protestants soon became known for their work in education and medicine. Also, as the prestige of the United States grew, so did the churches that had ties with it. And, while most of the early missionaries had been representatives of the larger denominations, by the beginning of the twentieth century there was an increasing number of missionaries from small conservative denominations.

Schisms in Latin America gave rise to new churches. In both Mexico and Puerto Rico, groups that broke away from the Catholic Church eventually became Episcopalians. In Chile, a small charismatic group expelled from the Methodist Church in 1910 formed the Methodist Pentecostal Church, which soon outgrew the parent body. Thus, by the time World War I broke out in 1914, there were significant numbers of Protestants in every country in Latin America who belonged both to churches that were the direct result of missions, and to others that had been born in Latin America itself.

The Ecumenical Movement

In looking at the entire history of Christianity in the nineteenth century, it may well be that the most significant development that took place during that period was the beginning of a truly universal church. Until then, Christianity had been almost entirely a western religion. By 1914, there were churches in almost every nation of the globe, and these churches were beginning to develop their own leadership as well as their own understanding of what it meant to be Christian in their different contexts. This was the birth of the ecumenical movement in two senses. First of all, the very word "ecumenical" means "pertaining to the entire inhabited earth." Therefore, never before had Christianity been as "ecumenical" as it became in the nineteenth century. Second, if by "ecumenical" one understands that which has to do with the unity of Christians, it is clear that one of the driving forces leading to the modern movement for Christian unity was the missionary movement.

In the United States, where people of different Christian confessions lived next to each other, ecumenical sentiments gained ground as the result of various causes that appealed to people across denominational lines: abolitionism, temperance, fundamentalism, liberalism, and so forth. But even there, since denominational allegiance usually posed no obstacle to the task at hand, divisions were seldom questioned. Perhaps the most serious such questioning was the founding of the Disciples of Christ (see chapter 25).

In overseas missions, however, cooperation became mandatory. Bible translations prepared by missionaries of one denomination were used by others, and it soon became apparent that coordination in such efforts would be good stewardship of limited resources. Also, where such vast lands were waiting to hear the word of the gospel, it made sense to come to some agreement as to what denomination or missionary agency would take responsibility for each area. Most important of all, however, was the difficulty in presenting the gospel to people who had never heard of it when what they saw was a number of competing interpretations of the gospel, each claiming to be true. Divisions that seemed perfectly natural in Europe or the United States made little sense in South India or Japan. Therefore, those who were consumed with a burning zeal for the conversion of the world soon became convinced that Christians of different traditions must work together.

The great forerunner of the ecumenical movement was none other than William Carey, who suggested that an international missionary conference be convened at Capetown in 1810. He hoped that such a conference would bring together missionaries and missionary agencies from all over the world in order to exchange information and coordinate their plans. Since at that time many set great store by their particular traditions, Carey's suggestion fell on deaf ears. It would be exactly a hundred years later that his call would be heeded. Meanwhile, many conferences took place on a smaller scale, both in the sending countries and in the mission field.

Finally, in 1910, the first World Missionary Conference gathered in Edinburgh, Scotland. In contrast to earlier conferences, this one would be attended by official delegates of missionary societies, their numbers to be determined by the proportion of each agency's contribution—in financial terms—to the entire missionary enterprise. It was also stipulated that the conference would deal exclusively with missions among non-Christians, and that therefore there would be no discussion of Protestant missions among Catholics in Latin America, or among the Eastern Orthodox in the Near East. It was also decided that questions of "faith and order" would not be discussed, for it was felt that such discussion could only lead to further alienation. In preparation for the conference, hundreds of people around the world participated in preliminary studies, keeping in contact with the entire picture through correspondence and regional or local conferences. When the conference finally convened, most representatives were British or North American. There was also a significant number of representatives from the rest of Europe. Only seventeen of the participants came from the younger churches —three of them as special guests of the Executive Committee.

The conference fully achieved its basic goal of exchanging information and plans, but its significance was far greater. For the first time, there had been an international conference of such magnitude whose participants were official representatives from missionary societies of various denominations. This in itself paved the way for similar meetings, in which subjects other than missions would be discussed. Second, the conference appointed a Continuation Committee, thereby indicating that a movement had begun that was fully expected to continue. The work of that committee resulted in further studies, conferences, and eventually in the formation of the International Missionary Council. Third, the conference gave international stature to many who would be the leaders of the ecumenical movement in the early decades of the twentieth century—foremost among them Methodist layman John R. Mott. Finally, the conference of Edinburgh was important even in what it excluded, for out of such exclusions developed the Faith and Order movement and the Committee on Cooperation in Latin America. The former would be one of the currents leading to the founding of the World Council of Churches in 1948. In short, the conference of Edinburgh in 1910 was the most important forerunner of the modern ecumenical movement.

Meanwhile, international tensions were increasing, and Christians felt called to gather, not only to discuss ecclesiastical matters, but also to seek ways to preserve international peace. On August 2, 1914, in the city of Constance, a world organization for promoting peace through the churches was founded. That very day World War I exploded.

Suggested Readings

Sydney E. Ahlstrom. *A Religious History of the American People.* 2 vols. Garden City, New York: Doubleday & Company, 1975.

Stewart C. Easton. *The Rise and Fall of Western Colonialism.* New York: Praeger, 1964.

Justo L. González. *A History of Christian Thought,* vol. 3. Nashville: Abingdon, 1975.

Kenneth Scott Latourette. *Christianity in a Revolutionary Age,* vols. 1–3. New York: Harper & Brothers, 1954–1961.

Kenneth Scott Latourette. *A History of the Expansion of Christianity,* vols. 4–6. New York: Harper & Brothers, 1941–1944.

Hugh R. Mackintosh. *Types of Modern Theology: Schleiermacher to Barth.* New York: Charles Scribner's Sons, 1938.

Stephen Neill. *Colonialism and Christian Missions.* London: Lutterworth, 1966.

Claude Welch. *Protestant Thought in the Nineteenth Century.* New Haven, Connecticut: Yale, 1972.

PART IV

THE TWENTIETH CENTURY

Chronology

Popes	Events
Benedict XV (1914–1922)	World War I (1914–1918)
	Russian Revolution (1917)
	Barth's *Commentary on Romans* (1919)
	Prohibition in USA (1919–1933)
	Women's suffrage in USA (1920)
Pius XI (1922–1939)	Mussolini in Rome (1922)
	Founding of *Zwischen den Zeiten* (1522)
	Stockholm Conference (Life and Work) (1925)
	United Church of Canada (1525)
	First six Chinese Catholic bishops (1926)
	Lausanne Conference (Faith and Order) (1927)
	Church of Christ in China (1927)
	Mexico confiscates church property (1927)
	Jerusalem Assembly, International Missionary Council (1928)
	Stock Market Crash (1929)
	Depression (1929)
	H. R. Niebuhr, *The Social Sources of Denominationalism* (1929)
	Aulén, *Christus Victor* (1930)
	Nygren, *Agape and Eros* (1930–1936)
	Spanish Republic (1931)
	Encyclical *Quadragesimo anno,* on social teachings (1931)
	Encyclical *Non abbiamo bisogno,* against Fascism (1931)
	Barth's *Church Dogmatics* (1932–1967)
	Hitler comes to power (1933)
	Vatican concordat with Germany (1933)
	Roosevelt U.S. president (1933)
	Barmen Declaration (1934)
	Civil War in Spain (1936)

Popes	Events
	Encyclicals against Nazism and Communism (1937)
	Oxford Conference (Life and Work) (1937)
	Edinburgh Conference (Faith and Order) (1937)
	War between Japan and China (1937)
	Bonhoeffer, *The Cost of Discipleship* (1937)
	H. R. Niebuhr, *The Kingdom of God in America* (1937)
	Madras Assembly, International Missionary Council (1938)
Pius XII (1939–1958)	Franco's victory in Spain (1939)
	Bonhoeffer, *Life Together* (1939)
	World War II (1939–1945)
	Bultmann's *The New Testament and Mythology* (1940)
	Germany attacks Russia (1941)
	Japan attacks Pearl Harbor (1941)
	Reinhold Niebuhr, *The Nature and Destiny of Man* (1941–1943)
	Fall of Mussolini (1943)
	Encyclical *Divino afflante Spiritu* (1943)
	†Bonhoeffer (1945)
	Germany surrenders (1945)
	Nuclear attack on Hiroshima (1945)
	Independence of Philippines and Indonesia (1945)
	Church of South India (1947)
	Whitby Assembly, International Missionary Council (1947)
	World Council of Churches founded (1948)
	People's Republic of China (1949)
	Dogma of Assumption of Mary (1950)
	War in Korea (1950)
	Encyclical *Humani generis* (1950)

Popes	Events
	Supreme Court against segregation in U.S. public schools (1952)
	Willingen Assembly, International Missionary Council (1952)
	Worker priest movement suspended (1954)
	Evanston Assembly, World Council of Churches (1954)
	†Teilhard de Chardin (1955)
	Conference of Latin American Bishops (CELAM) founded (1955)
	Independence of Ghana (1957)
	Ghana assembly, International Missionary Council (1957–1958)
John XXIII (1958–1963)	
	Pope announces intention to call a council (1959)
	Pope creates Secretariat for Christian Unity (1960)
	Independence of 17 African nations (1960)
	Encyclical *Mater et Magistra* (1961)
	First human in space flight (1961)
	New Delhi Assembly, World Council of Churches. International Missionary Council joins World Council (1961)
	Independence of Algeria (1962)
	Robinson's *Honest to God* (1963)
	Second Vatican Council (1962–1965)
	Moltmann's *Theology of Hope* (1965)
Paul VI (1963–1978)	
	War in Southeast Asia escalates (1965)
	Encyclical *Humanae vitae* (1968)
	†Martin Luther King, Jr. (1968)
	Medellín Assembly, CELAM (1968)

Popes	Events
	Uppsala Assembly, World Council of Churches (1968)
	Astronauts land on the moon (1969)
	Chicago Declaration (1973)
	Fall of Haile Selassie (1974)
	Nairobi Assembly, World Council of Churches (1975)
John Paul (1978)	
John Paul II (1978–)	Puebla Assembly, CELAM (1978)
	Vancouver Assembly, World Council of Churches (1983)

31/ An Age of Drastic Change

We have become conscious of the fact that in the course of some fifteen centuries something like a Christian civilisation has been created, and of the other fact that in our days this Christian civilisation is at stake and its survival is questioned. . . . A new epoch has begun, in which the scholar, the artist, the seer and the saint are replaced by the soldier, the engineer and the man of political power; an epoch which is no more capable of producing real culture, but merely an outward technical civilisation.

EMIL BRUNNER

Throughout the nineteenth century, western civilization had considered itself destined to lead the world into an age of happiness and abundance. The industrial revolution had created wealth and comfort that two centuries earlier would have been considered unattainable. In Asia, Africa, and Latin America, the native populations appeared eager to absorb the ways and wisdom of industrial Europe and the United States. The cause of missions prospered in spite of such setbacks as the Boxer rebellion in China, and there were hopes that in the very near future most of the world's population would be Christian. For almost a century, with minor exceptions, the European powers had lived in peace with each other.

Under the surface, however, were destructive currents that would eventually plunge the world into the most devastating war it had ever known—a war to be followed by revolution, economic upheavals, and an even more destructive conflagration. The relative peace of the nineteenth century in Europe was possible in part because competition among European powers took the form of colonial expansion. While Europe was at peace, war by proxy overseas became a common feature of international policies. By 1914, however, most of the territories of Asia, Africa, and Latin America had been colonized—if not politically, at least economically. Europe then turned its attention to its own southeastern region, the Balkans, where the progressive breakup of the Turkish Empire had created a number of states with unstable boundaries and governments. These lands became the bone of contention among European powers, and it was out of that contention that World War I would emerge. The very technological and industrial progress of which the West boasted would then be seen in its destructive power, for this war provided the occasion for the military use of technology in submarine, aerial, and chemical warfare. The very fact that the industrial powers now controlled distant lands meant that most of the planet was directly or indirectly involved in the conflict. The war, which lasted four years, involved thirty nations and a total armed force of 65 million, of whom almost one-seventh died and more than one-third were wounded in battle. The civilian casualties of the war, although more difficult to assess, were at least as many as the military.

Meanwhile, chaos in Russia had led to revolution. Russia was the one great European power where the liberal ideas of the nineteenth century had made practically no headway. Its autocratic government and landed aristocracy continued ruling the nation as they had centuries earlier. Karl Marx would never have expected Russia, where industrialization had been slow, to become the first country where the revolution he announced would succeed. His expectation was rather that the development of industry and capital would eventually lead to a revolution of industrial workers, and that peasants would not view such a revolution with sympathy. But the war upset his predictions. Nationalist bitterness against a government that appeared unable to win a battle was soon joined to protests in the cities over lack of bread, and in the countryside over lack of land. In March 1917, Czar Nicholas II was forced to abdicate in favor of his brother, who in turn abdicated a few days later. For a short time, the government was in the hands of moderates who hoped for a liberal capitalist republic. But this government's failures in both war and economic policies, and the agitation of V. I. Lenin and his Bolsheviks, lead to the November Revolution of 1917. Lenin immediately moved to set in motion his vast program of social reorganization, nationalizing the land and all banks, and placing factories in the hands of government-controlled trade unions. As part of this program, all church property was also confiscated. Thus, the Russian Church, which had considered itself the "Third Rome" after the fall of Byzantium, now found itself living under conditions similar to those of the Byzantine church after the Turkish invasion. The new government also withdrew from the war, but soon found itself immersed in a its own civil war against counterrevolutionaries who had both international and ecclesiastical support. By the time the Red Army had won the war, the Soviet government was more convinced than ever that the church was its mortal enemy.

In the western hemisphere, the consequences of the war were not as acutely felt. The United States did not enter the war until April 1917 and, although its armed forces suffered heavy casualties, other issues soon demanded national attention. The nation turned inwards, seeking to solve its own problems in isolation from the rest of the world and refusing to join the League of Nations. Two issues with roots in the nineteenth century came to occupy the center of the stage: prohibition and women's suffrage. Prohibition of alcoholic beverages became the law of the land in 1919, less than a year after the end of the war. Women's right to vote was finally granted by the Nineteenth Amendment to the Constitution, in 1920. The 1920s were a decade of economic prosperity, particularly for the wealthy (5 percent of the population received one-third of all personal income). Then came the Great Depression, which led to the election of Franklin D. Roosevelt and the "New Deal." The recovery that took place during Roosevelt's presidency was seen as further proof that the nation was basically sound, and that the Depression had been but a passing phase that had been overcome through hard work and organization. Thus, the first half of the twentieth century in the United States was not marked by the self-doubt and pessimism that was beginning to sweep Europe. In the rest of the hemisphere, the most notable event was the Mexican Revolution, a drawn-out affair, at times quite radical and at other times fairly moderate, which began in 1910 and went on for decades. Here again, there were constant conflicts between the Catholic Church and the revolution. In 1927, as earlier in Russia, all church property was confiscated. Eventually, without returning the confiscated property, the state relented in its most stringent policies against the church.

In Europe, it was hoped that the League of Nations would be able to prevent a repetition of the tragic events of World War I, but the growth of Fascism made such hopes futile. Fascism, which first gained prominence in Italy under the leadership of Benito Mussolini, exploited wounded national pride in order to glorify war, and to turn the entire nation into a totalitarian military machine. Its social doctrines were confused; at first it sided with radical revolutionaries, but eventually it exploited the fear of Communism and joined forces with industrialists in order to create a new aristocracy of power and production. In any case, the dream of national grandeur, and hatred of democracy and political liberalism as the creation of an effeminate bourgeiosie, were characteristic of Fascism in all its stages. As Mussolini put it, "what maternity is to women, that is war to man." Soon the movement spread to other countries. Its German counterpart, the Nazi party, came to power in 1933, and eventually overshadowed Italian Fascism. Through Nazi influence, anti-Semitism became part of the established dogma of international Fascism—and led to the death of millions of Jews in Germany and elsewhere. By 1936, Fascism had at least a measure of power, not only in Italy and Germany, but also in Japan, Poland, Austria, Hungary, Greece, Rumania, and Bulgaria. In 1939, with Franco's victory in the Spanish Civil War, it became firmly established in Spain. Fascist attitudes toward Christianity varied. In Spain, Franco considered the Catholic Church one of his closest allies, and always declared himself her faithful son. Mussolini's attitudes wavered according to various circumstances. Hitler felt that Christianity, with its teachings of universal love and turning the other cheek, was antagonistic to his ultimate goals of conquest and domination—but he sought to use the church to support those goals.

Part of the allure of Fascism was in reviving the dreams of ancient glories. Mussolini promised to restore the Roman Empire. Greek Fascists spoke of a rebirth of Spartan militarism and Byzantine power. Spanish "Falangistas" sought a return to the "golden century" of the Spanish empire. Obviously, these various dreams were mutually contradictory. But what stood behind them—the glorification of war, dread of the free exchange of ideas, a totalitarian nationalism, and opposition to all forms of egalitarianism —united the various Fascist movements in opposition to all that sounded like democracy, liberalism, or pacifism. Italy and Germany joined in an "Axis" to which Japan was later added. Through a Soviet-German agreement, Russian neutrality was assured. A month later, in September, 1939, Europe was at war.

Once again, for the second time in three decades, the entire world was swept into the conflict. At first, the Fascist powers—the "Axis"—made sure that Russia stayed out of the conflict. In fact, Russia took advantage of its friendly relations with the Axis to partition Poland with Germany and to extend her holdings in the Baltic. Soon most of western Europe was in the hands of the Fascists, while their Japanese allies extended their holdings in the Orient. By 1941, with the German invasion of Russia and the Japanese attack on Pearl Harbor, no major power was allowed to remain neutral. Since the Axis had conquered most of Europe, the main fronts of battle were now the Pacific, North Africa, the Russian-German line, and the English Channel. But battles were also being waged in African colonies, in the Near East, and as far as the River Plate. The names of Pacific islands until then unknown in the West became household words. Tribal peoples who lived in relative isolation from the rest of the world now saw their skies criss-crossed by military aircraft, and their lands disputed by nations until then unknown to them. In all, fifty-seven nations declared war on each other.

By the time the smoke subsided and losses were counted, the cost of the war was enormous. In the main belligerent nations, the number of military dead and missing was devastating: one of every 450 inhabitants for the United States, one of every 150 for the United Kingdom, one of every 200 for France, one of every 150 for Italy, one of every 22 for the Soviet Union, one of every 25 for Germany, one of every 46 for Japan, and one of every 200 for China. The total of military personnel killed or missing was more than 15,000,000.* To this must be added the larger number of direct civilian casualties, the millions of Jews killed by the Nazis and their allies, and the incalculable number of those who died of famine or disease as an indirect result of the war.

An uncounted casualty of the war was the optimistic view of the future of western civilization that had prevailed during the nineteenth century. This was the civilization that, through an enlightened combination of Christian values and technical expertise, had been expected to bring about a new age for humankind. This was the civilization that it was the "white man's burden" to share with less fortunate people. And now, through the two most devastating wars the world had ever seen, this civilization had spread death and destruction throughout the world. Its technological prowess had been used to invent the most destructive machines the world had ever known, culminating in the explosion of the first atomic weapon at Hiroshima on August 6, 1945. Germany, the epitome of European civilization, the nation that boasted of its intellectual leadership of the western world, had fallen prey to a demonic fanaticism theretofore unknown among the most primitive tribes of the world.

A direct consequence of all this was the worldwide revolt against colonialism in all its forms. First, the colonial empires of the defeated nations were dismantled. But it soon became clear that even the victors had lost a great deal of prestige as a result of the war. Nationalist movements that had begun decades earlier suddenly took on new life, and in a span of two decades every colonial empire was dismembered. Political independence did not always lead to economic independence, for in many cases an economic neocolonial system was developed to take the place of the old order. But twenty years after the end of the war, it was clear that there were in the younger nations strong movements against economic imperialism. At times, nationalism took the form of a resurgence of ancient non-Christian religions. Some movements sought to change, not only the international economic order, but also the social order of the nation itself, often following a socialist model. The first and largest example of this trend was China, where, partly as a result of the war, the Nationalist government was overthrown by the Communists. Although for some time China was faithful to Russian Communism, she eventually drifted away from links that still smacked of the older tutelage of the

*Encyclopaedia Britannica (1968 ed.), 23: 800.

The birth of the "atomic age" for the first time presented humankind with the ability to destroy itself.

European nations over the rest of the world. Japan followed the opposite tack: committing itself to capitalism and industralization, it sought to compete with the older industrial nations of Europe and North America. Almost all of Africa and the Moslem world became independent of western political rule. Israel and South Africa, two western enclaves in non-Western areas, were hard pressed by their neighbors. Many in the new nations all over the world, as well as the older nations of Latin America, felt that the central agenda for the last decades of the twentieth century was the construction of an economic order less unfavorable to the poorer nations, the restructuring of foreign relations on that basis, and the redistribution of wealth within their own boundaries.

In the midst of all these changes, the older nations of Europe, as well as the United States, often found themselves at a loss. Many in those countries had been taught that the entire colonial and neocolonial enterprise was the result of altruistic motivations and high ideals. From that perspective, the anticolonial reaction was nothing short of bewildering. It could only be explained by the presence of an evil conspiracy leading the "natives" astray, away from their own best interests. This understanding of the anticolonial movement was encouraged by the mentality of the "Cold War." This was the name given to the conflict between capitalist and Communist nations immediately after World War II, and continuing with different degrees of intensity for several decades. As a result of the war, the Soviet Union ruled most of eastern Europe, and Germany was divided between the Federal Republic—West Germany—and the Democratic Republic—East Germany. This area was the scene for much of the activity of the Cold War, including the blockade of Berlin by the Communists, and the building of a wall to prevent citizens of East Berlin from defecting to the West. At times, such as in Korea and Vietnam, the Cold War erupted into open hostilities—although the major powers, fearful of each other's nuclear capabilities, avoided direct military confrontation. Many in the West interpreted the entire anticolonial movement in terms of the Cold War. Since Communists were indeed at work in many revolutionary movements—although not always leading them—it was possible to see the entire anticolonial trend as a vast Communist conspiracy. This interpretation, more popular in the United States than in Europe, had the advantage of explaining how the altruism of the "white man's burden" had led to the virulent anticolonialism of the late twentieth century. But this easy explanation was achieved at the expense of a gross and dangerous oversimplification—one that threatened to alienate the West from the vast majority of humankind.

Meanwhile, similar changes were taking place in the West. People who until recently had seemed content to play a secondary role—particularly blacks and women—suddenly began claiming a share in the process whereby decisions were made. This was not entirely unrelated to the tragedy of two world wars and the clear threat of a third. Indeed, if those in leadership had plunged the world into such debacles, it seemed high time that others be given an opportunity at leadership. During World War II, both blacks and women in the United States had been called to give their best for their country. After the war, they proved unwilling to return to their earlier condition. Both the civil rights movement and the feminist movement were at the same time an attempt to gain greater power for blacks and women, and a criticism of the manner in which white males were running the world.

In all of these situations the church was present. More than any international organization, corporation, or political movement, the church cut across national boundaries, class distinctions, and political allegiances. Indeed, the great legacy of the nineteenth century was that, for the first time in history, a truly universal church had been born. Although some in the twentieth century would see the missionaries of earlier generations as unrealistic dreamers, the truth is that they succeeded, for after their passing they left behind a vast network of Christians of every color and nationality. To such an international church, the issues of the twentieth century were not simple. War, and racial and class strife divided the church—often along lines that had little to do with earlier theological differences. At times it was persecuted; at other times it was used by those with ulterior motives. Amid the perplexities of the twentieth century, its members were often divided, bewildered, and even fearful. And yet, through war, persecution and civil strife, they sought to give witness to the One whose rule of peace and justice shall have no end. That is the story of Christianity in the twentieth century, to which we now turn.

32/ Eastern Christianity

The time has come, when the duty of all Christians in the world is to unite their efforts to fulfill the words of the prophet Isaiah "to change swords into ploughs and spears into sickles," thus proving once more the viability and the permanent actuality of Christianity in the world.

RUMANIAN PATRIARCH JUSTINIAN, 1960

One of the main issues confronted by all Christians in the twentieth century is how to live in the "post-Constantinian era." What is meant by this phrase is that the church can no longer count on the political support that it enjoyed since the times of Constantine. Beginning with the French Revolution, western Christianity has had to face the challenge of secular states that, although not always hostile, tend to ignore it. For Eastern Christianity, on the other hand, that process began when Constantinople fell to the Turks in 1453. It was at that point that we left our narrative of the course of Eastern Christianity, and to it we must now return.

Byzantine Christianity

The support that Christianity had traditionally received from the Byzantine Empire was not an unmixed blessing. It is true that its relation to the Empire gave the Greek Church great prestige, but it is also true that her freedom was greatly limited. While in the West popes were often more powerful than kings, in the East the emperors ruled the church, and patriarchs who did not do their bidding were easily deposed and replaced. When the emperor decided that reunion with Rome was necessary in order to save his empire, that reunion was achieved even against the clear wishes of the vast majority of the Byzantine Church. A year later, in 1453, Constantinople fell to the Turks, and many Byzantine Christians interpreted this event as an act of liberation from a tyrannical emperor who had forced them into a union with heretical Rome.

At first, The Ottoman regime granted a measure of freedom to the church. Mohammed II, conqueror of Constantinople, invited the bishops to elect a new patriarch—the former one had fled to Rome—to whom he granted both civil and ecclesiastical authority over Christians in his territories. In Constantinople itself, half the churches were turned into mosques, but in the other half Christian worship continued with full tolerance from the state. In 1516, the Ottomans conquered Syria and Palestine, and Christians there were also placed under the government of the patriarch of Constantinople. A year later, when Egypt fell to the Turks, the patriarch of Alexandria was given special powers over Christians in Egypt. Although this policy made the patriarchs virtual rulers of a Christian state within the Turkish state, it also meant that a patriarch who did not implement the Sultan's policies was soon deposed.

For several centuries, theological activity in the Greek-speaking church was dominated by western influences and reactions against it. The issues debated in the West during the Protestant Reformation were also discussed in the Greek-speaking church and, in 1629, Cyril Lucaris, patriarch of Constantinople, published a "Confession of Faith" that was clearly Protestant. Although Lucaris was deposed and murdered, his memory was venerated by many—some claiming that the Confession of Faith was spurious. Eventually, in 1672, a synod condemned him "if indeed he was a Calvinist heretic." By the next century, however, the issue was no longer Protestantism; rather, it was western philosophy and science, and the impact they ought to have on Orthodox theology. In the nineteenth century, when Greece became independent of Turkey, this issue took on political overtones. In general, Greek nationalism sided with those who advocated the introduction of western methods of research and scholarship—who also argued that the Greek church, existing now in an independent nation, should be independent from the patriarch of Constantinople. The conservatives, on the other hand, held that commonly received tradition should guide scholarship, and that part of that tradition was subjection to the patriarch of Constantinople, even though he was subject to the Turkish sultan.

During the nineteenth and early twentieth centuries, the Ottoman Empire broke down, and national Orthodox churches were formed, not only in Greece, but also in Serbia, Bulgaria, and Rumania. In each of these areas, the tension between nationalist sentiments and the transnational nature of Orthodoxy was a dominant issue. In the period between the two world wars, the patriarchate of Constantinople recognized the autonomy of the various Orthodox churches, not only in the former Turkish territories in the Balkans, but also in other parts of Europe, such as Estonia, Latvia, and Czechoslovakia. Since most of these territories fell under Russian hegemony after World War II, Soviet religious policies were generally applied in them. Early in the century, the ancient patriarchates of Jerusalem, Alexandria, and Antioch found themselves under Arab rule. At first, these newly formed Arab states existed under the shadow of western powers. At that time, significant numbers of Christians under those patriarchates became either Catholic or Protestant. Then growing Arab nationalism reacted against western power and influence, and the growth of both Protestantism and Catholicism was curbed. By the second half of the twentieth century, the only nation where Orthodox Christianity could still count on something like the traditional union of church and state was Greece.

All of these churches, however, did show signs of vitality. For a time it was feared that the loss of church schools, and the pressure of government propaganda, would keep newer generations away from the church. But the experience of several decades seemed to indicate that the liturgy, traditionally the source of spiritual strength for Orthodox believers, was equal to the task of transmitting the Christian tradition in the midst of hostile states. Although the civil disabilities under which Christians have been placed in several of these states at various times have indeed resulted in a decline in active church participation on the part of those involved in the job market, it is significant that, after retirement, vast numbers return to the church. It is clear that the post-Constantinian period has not spelled the end of those churches that have fallen heir to the ancient Byzantine tradition.

The Russian Church

The fall of Constantinople in 1453 was interpreted by many in Russia as God's punishment for having agreed to reunion with heretical Rome. Eventually, the theory developed that just as Constantinople had replaced Rome as the "second Rome," now Moscow was the "third Rome," the new imperial city whose providential task was to uphold orthodoxy. In 1547, Ivan IV of Russia took the title of "czar" or emperor, by which he meant that he was the successor of the ancient caesars of Rome and Constantinople. Likewise, in 1598, the metropolitan of Moscow took the title of patriarch. To support this self-understanding, the Russian church produced an array of polemical writings against Greeks, Catholics, and Protestants. By the seventeenth century, these notions were so entrenched that an attempt at rapprochement with the Greeks led to schism in Russia.

Czar Alexis I Mikhailovich (1645–1676) saw this rapprochement with Greek Christians as a preliminary step to the conquest of Constantinople, and therefore encouraged Patriarch Nikon to revise the liturgy so as to bring it into agreement with Greek practices. But many in Russia, particularly among the lower classes, reacted violently. They were suspicious of everything foreign, particularly since it appeared that it was the aristocracy that was interested in promoting the new ideas. The result was the schism of the Old Believers, some of whom then joined the peasants in rebellion. This was crushed with great bloodshed, and the peasants' condition of serfdom worsened. The Old Believers continued in existence, although they split over a number of issues—particularly whether to accept priests coming to them from the Orthodox Church, or not to have priests at all. Some were drawn to apocalyptic extremes, and thousands committed suicide as proof of their faith. Eventually, however, the more extreme groups disappeared, and the Old Believers lived on as a minority group within Russia at least until the twentieth century.

Czar Peter the Great (1689–1725) took a different tack. He was not interested in a rapprochement with Greek Christians, but rather with opening his country to western influences. In the life of the church, this led to increased interest in both Catholic and Protestant theology. Those who followed these conflicting schools of thought did not generally abandon their Orthodox faith. Rather, they sought to develop an Orthodox theology using either Catholic or Protestant methodologies. On matters that were open to debate, some followed the Catholic lead, while others took their cue from Protestantism. The Kievan school, whose great figure was Peter Mogila, was associated with Catholic tendencies; while Theophanes Prokopovick and his followers felt that the Protestant critique of tradition ought to be heeded by Russian Orthodoxy. Early in the nineteenth century, the influence of the Enlightment and of Romanticism gave the Prokopovickians the upper hand. But later in the century there was a nationalist reaction, with greater emphasis on the value of the traditionally Russian—the Slavophile movement. The principal figure of this movement was lay theologian Alexis Khomiakov (1804–1860), who applied Hegelian categories to show that the true Orthodox understanding of catholicity—*sobornost*—is a perfect synthesis of the Catholic thesis of the unity of the Church and the Protestant antithesis of the freedom of the gospel.

The Russian Revolution put an end to much of this debate. A different western philosophy, Marxism, had gained the upper hand. In 1918, the church was officially separated from the state, and this was ratified by the constitution of 1936, which guaranteed both "freedom for religious worship" and "freedom for anti-religious propaganda." In 1920, religious teaching in schools was outlawed. Two years earlier, all seminaries were closed. After the death of Patriarch Tikhon in 1925, the Russian Orthodox Church was not allowed to elect his successor until 1943. By then, partly as a result of the war with Germany, the government had decided to recognize the

*Delegation from Russian Orthodox church leaving Vigyan Bhaven
(the Assembly Hall) for the opening procession of the Third
Assembly of the World Council of Churches, New Delhi, India,
1961.*

continued existence of the church. That same year, seminaries were re-opened. Also, permission was granted for the printing of some books and periodicals, and for the manufacture of items necessary for worship.

As in the case of other Orthodox churches under communist rule, the Russian church has found its liturgy capable of supporting the faithful and transmitting the traditions to new generations. Late in the twentieth century, after almost seventy years of communist rule, the Orthodox in the Soviet Union were still some 60 million strong.

Other Eastern Churches

Besides the churches discussed above, there are Orthodox bodies in various parts of the world. Some of these, such as the Orthodox Church of Japan, and those in China and Korea, are the result of the missionary work of the Russian Church. They are fully indigenous, with a membership and clergy that is mostly native, and celebrate the liturgy in the native tongue. Others are the result of what has been called the "Orthodox Diaspora." For a number of reasons—political upheavals, persecution, the search for better living conditions—large numbers of Orthodox have moved to areas distant from their ancestral homeland. Particularly in western Europe and the New World, there are significant numbers of Russians, Greeks, and others for whom their faith and its liturgy are a means of keeping alive traditions and values that would otherwise be lost. Relations among these various bodies pose difficult problems for Orthodoxy, which has always held that there can be no more than one Orthodox church in a given place or area. On occasion, this has put great stress on the bonds of unity within the Orthodox Communion.

But not all churches form part of the Orthodox Communion. Since the time of the Christological controversies in the fifth century, a number of Eastern churches that disagreed with the decisions of the councils had established an independent existence. In the former territories of the Persian Empire, the majority of Christians refused to call Mary "Mother of God," and therefore they were dubbed "Nestorians." These Christians—also known as "Assyrian"—have a long and checkered history. Although for a time in the Middle Ages this church was numerous, and its missions extended into China, in more recent times it has suffered severe persecution, particularly from its Moslem neighbors. Early in the twentieth century, such persecutions decimated its members. Many of the survivors fled to the western hemisphere—including its head, the "catholicos," who sought refuge first in Cyprus and finally in Chicago. At present, their total membership is approximately 100,000 Christians scattered throughout Iraq, Iran, Syria, and the United States.

Those churches that refused to accept the Chalcedonian "Definition of Faith" because it seemed to divide the humanity of Jesus from his divinity are usually called "Monophysites," although such a name does not accurately describe their Christological understanding. The largest of these bodies are the Coptic Church of Egypt and its daughter church, the Church of Ethiopia. The latter was one of the last Eastern churches to receive the active support of the state; but such support ended with the overthrow of Emperor Haile Selassie in 1974. The ancient Syrian Monophysite Church, also known as "Jacobite," is strong in Syria and Iraq. Its head, the Jacobite patriarch of Antioch, resides in Damascus, the capital of Syria. Technically under this patriarch, but in reality autonomous, the Syrian Church in India, which claims to have been founded by St. Thomas, is fully indigenous, and has about half a million members.

As noted earlier, the Armenian Church refused to accept the Chalcedonian Definition of Faith, mostly because it resented the lack of support from the Roman Empire when the Persians invaded Armenia. Their territory was conquered by the Turks, and their staunch refusal to abandon the faith of their ancestors was one of several causes of enmity between them and their

Turkish masters. As the power of the Ottoman Empire waned, that enmity turned to violence. In 1895, and again in 1896 and 1914, thousands of Armenians living under Turkish rule were massacred. Approximately a million managed to escape, and as a result there are presently significant numbers of Armenian Christians in Syria, Lebanon, Egypt, Iran, Iraq, Greece, France, and the western hemisphere. In that portion of Armenia that is now under Soviet control, the church continues an existence similar to that of other churches under Soviet rule.

In the early decades of the twentieth century, the participation of the Eastern churches in the ecumenical movement was rather reserved. They feared that a willingness to discuss issues of "faith and order" would be construed as uncertainty as to their own beliefs, or as a willingness to compromise such beliefs. Therefore, although several of them collaborated with other Christians in practical matters, they refused any official participation in discussions that could be interpreted as attempting to settle matters of faith by negotiation. When the invitation was sent out for churches to attend the First Assembly of the World Council of Churches, to take place in Amsterdam in 1948, most of the Orthodox churches conferred among themselves and decided to abstain. In 1950, the Central Committee of the World Council of Churches issued a statement that allayed most of the misgivings of the Orthodox. After that time, most of the Orthodox churches have become full members of the World Council of Churches. Likewise, the participation of other Eastern bodies has also increased. In this particular context, largely through the agency of the World Council of Churches, there have been significant conversations between those churches that accept the Definition of Chalcedon and those who reject it—Nestorians and Monophysites. In these conversations, it has been found that there is profound agreement between these various bodies, and that many of their disagreements are the results of misunderstanding. Thus, while opening the dialogue between western and Eastern Christianity, the ecumenical movement has also promoted a valuable dialogue among Eastern Christians.

As one looks at these various churches as a whole, two conclusions can be drawn. The first is that these churches, due to their history of having to move with shocking rapidity into the post-Constantinian era, may have significant insights to offer to other Christians who now find themselves living under similar transformations. The other is that western Christians may have underestimated the power of liturgy and tradition, that have allowed these churches to continue their life, and even to flourish, in the most adverse circumstances.

33/ Roman Catholic Christianity

Let us be free of the scandal of having some nations, the majority of whose citizens call themselves Christian, enjoying great riches, while others do not have what is needful and suffer hunger, disease, and all sorts of misery.

SECOND VATICAN COUNCIL

When we last directed our attention to the Roman Catholic Church, in chapter 29, we saw that its reaction to the modern world was mostly one of fear and condemnation. Among the reasons for such reaction were the loss of the Papal States to the new nation of Italy, the fear that the new lay states would hinder the work of the Catholic Church, and the concern that minds would be led astray by modern ideas. In general, the history of the Catholic Church until the pontificate of John XXIII, in the second half of the twentieth century, was a continuation of the policies and attitudes set at the Council of Trent, mostly in reaction against Protestantism. At the same time, there were those within the Catholic Church who felt that such an attitude of condemnation and wholesale rejection of modern trends was a mistake both theological and pastoral. During the earlier part of the twentieth century, such loyal critics would repeatedly express their opinions and alternatives, only to be suppressed or ignored. Therefore, the history of Roman Catholicism during the twentieth century is to a large extent the history of the conflict between those who wished to continue in the direction set at Trent and at the First Vatican Council, and those who wished to see more openness in the Church and a more creative encounter with the challenges of the modern world.

Benedict XV to Pius XII

World War I had just broken out when Pius X died and was succeeded by Benedict XV (1914–1922). He had been made an archbishop by Pius X, whose policies he was determined to continue. Like the previous three popes, he insisted on his right to rule the Papal States, which he claimed Italy had usurped from the Holy See. He directed most of his early efforts to the pursuit of peace; but he was repeatedly rebuffed by the belligerent powers. When peace finally came, and the League of Nations was established, he was not in a position to influence events in any decisive way. After the war he was able to sign concordats with several of the new states that resulted from peace negotiations. In general, he was perceived as more open than his predecessor, but was not a very effective pope.

His successor, Pius XI (1922–1939), was a scholar and an able administrator. He was also acutely aware of the increasing importance of the non-European world, and therefore did all within his power to encourage missionary work and to help churches already established attain maturity. During his pontificate the number of Catholic missionaries doubled, and it was he who consecrated the first Chinese bishops. As we shall see, later in the century this emphasis on the development of Catholicism in other lands would bear significant and unexpected fruit. He was also interested in increasing the activity of the laity, although always under the supervision of the hierarchy. This he outlined in the first of his encyclicals, which set the goals and rules for Catholic Action, the most important Catholic lay organization of the first half of the century.

Although very concerned about the dangers of Communism and its avowed atheistic stance, Pius XI did not manifest the same concern over Fascism, particularly when it posed as Communism's chief enemy. Furthermore, Fascism appealed to the same principles that Pius IX had so strongly advocated in his *Syllabus of Errors:* a hierarchical understanding of society, a strong sense of authority, and a state dedicated to the enforcement of moral standards. Since Italian Fascism in the early stages of its development favored Catholicism, the pope was quite content to work with it. In 1929, his representative and Mussolini signed an agreement that finally resolved the issue of Italian sovereignty over Rome. Italy acknowledged the existence of a sovereign state, "Vatican City," and granted the papacy sovereignty over it, as well as a financial compensation for the loss of other territories. In return, Pius recognized the kingdom of Italy as a legitimate state, with Rome as its capital. Eventually, Pius clashed with Italian Fascism, and he repeatedly condemned Hitler and Nazism in the early stages of their rise to power. But later he weakened his stance against the Nazi regime, and he did support Franco's brand of Fascism in Spain. In Germany, fear of liberalism and Communism had inclined many Catholics towards rising Nazism. In 1933,

Catholic opposition to Hitler collapsed, and the political party led by Mgr. Kaas gave Hitler the necessary majority to take full possession of the government. At about the same time, the bishops gathered at Fulda, and withdrew their earlier harsh words about the dangers of Nazism. In Rome, Pius XI and his secretary of state Cardinal Pacelli—later Pius XII—felt that the time had come to reach an agreement with Hitler, and in a few months a concordat was signed that was seen in international circles as the Vatican's qualified approval of the Nazi regime. It took the pope several years to realize the dangers of Nazism, which for a long time he saw as an acceptable alternative to Communism. Finally, in 1937, he issued two encyclicals, one against Nazism and the other against Communism. The first of these encyclicals, *Mit brennender Sorge,* declared that Nazism was a new form of paganism, and accused Hitler of having disregarded the concordat of 1933. Five days later, the parallel encyclical, *Divini Redemptoris,* condemned Communism, which now caused him grave concern because Russia had increased its antireligious propaganda. Communism was also making rapid progress in Asia, and the pope feared that the Mexican Revolution would lead to another Communist state. In this encyclical, he condemned the Marxist view that religion is a means of oppressing the lower classes, and declared that there could be no grounds for Christian collaboration with it. Meanwhile, the ties developing between Hitler and Mussolini, and repeated clashes with Italian Fascism, caused the pope to prepare a strong speech condemning some of the actions of the Fascist regime in Italy, but he did not yet break relations with it. He was still working on this speech when he died.

The conclave took only one day and three ballots to elect his successor. This was Cardinal Pacelli, who indicated his intention of continuing the policies of Pius XI by taking the name of Pius XII (1939–1958). A man experienced in diplomatic affairs, with a slight penchant to nepotism, and a highly authoritarian and clerical view of the church, Pius XII was also a mystic who spent hours in prayer, an indefatigable worker whose aides often complained that he drove them too hard, and a man of personal magnetism who was much respected by friend and foe alike. The early years of his pontificate were dominated by World War II, which he had tried unsuccessfully to prevent. When war became inevitable, he directed his attention— again to no avail—to keeping Italy out of the conflict, and he also supported a conspiracy to overthrow Hitler. Once war broke out, Pius XII followed a policy of neutrality, hoping that by remaining above the fray he could serve as a mediator at the appropriate time. This neutrality, however, was achieved at the cost of silence in the face of Nazi atrocities against the Jews, a policy for which he has been severely criticized. On this point, even his apologists admit that he was aware of what was taking place in Germany, and defend his policy on the grounds that protests would have achieved little. But such considerations did not keep the pope from denouncing Nazi atrocities against Catholics in Poland—even though the Polish bishops reported that each protest over Vatican Radio was followed by further measures against their

*The position of Pius XII with regard to
Fascism was never clear, and after the war he
was accused of not having spoken against the
atrocities committed by Nazis against Jews.*

flock. On these issues, Pius XII seems to have been simply another exponent
of what had been the basic mood of the papacy since the Council of Trent:
to protect the church at all costs, seeking for it as much freedom and power
as possible, and to subordinate all other issues to this overriding concern. It
is also probable that, while he feared a Nazi victory, he was more concerned
over the growth of Communism, and that in the war between the Axis and
the USSR, his sympathies were with the former. In any case, he did repeatedly insist on the general principles by which nations and governments ought
to be judged, although he refrained from making such judgments himself.

While the pope's reaction to the persecution of Jews in Germany and in the occupied areas of Europe left much to be desired, there were other Catholics who risked life and freedom for the sake of their Jewish brothers and sisters. Pius himself was aware of the clandestine networks that were helping Jews escape from Germany, France, and various countries in eastern Europe. And among the "righteous Gentiles" whom the international Jewish community recognizes as having risen to the challenge of the hour, often to the point of heroism, there are a number of Catholics.

After the war, the pope's international policy was mostly addressed to the threat of Communism. In 1949, he decreed automatic excommunication for any who supported the Communists in whatever country. It was the time of the great imperialistic expansion of Russia, whose orbit of influence soon included most of Eastern Europe. In Asia, after the period of Japanese dominance, China had also become Communist, and at the time it seemed that the Catholic Church in that vast country—as well as all other churches—had been completely crushed. Against this threat, and also hoping to avert future wars, Pius joined the voices calling for a unified Europe. In 1953, he signed a concordat with Franco's regime in Spain—the main surviving bastion of Fascism after the war. His reasons for this were many. The influence of Communists in the government of Spain before the civil war had increased as tension mounted. Catholics who feared Communism saw Franco and his movement as the only alternative, which in turn gave rise to greater anticlericalism. Then the civil war unleashed violent passions, resulting in the deaths of thousands of priests, nuns, and monks. When the dust settled, Franco was in firm control of the nation, and his staunchest allies were the most conservative among the Catholic clergy. Therefore, in the midst of a world in which more and more governments seemed to be turning against the church, the Vatican welcomed Franco and his regime.

The pope's orientation could also be seen in his understanding of the papacy and its teaching and administrative authority. He tended to centralize the government of the church, depriving the national episcopates of much of their initiative. While looking at the ecumenical movement with more favor than his predecessors, in 1950 he placed one more obstacle in that movement's progress by proclaiming the dogma of the Bodily Assumption of Mary into heaven. But, above all, he was extremely suspicious of innovations in the field of theology. In 1950, the bull *Humani generis* reiterated earlier warnings against innovations in theology. Some of the most creative Catholic theologians of the time were silenced, among them several whose writings laid the groundwork for the Second Vatican Council. One of the most creative Catholic thinkers of the twentieth century, Pierre Teilhard de Chardin, was forbidden by the Holy Office from publishing his theological works—they finally appeared after his death, in 1955. In France, some Catholic leaders had sought to penetrate the labor movement through "worker priests," who took employment as common laborers, sometimes without even letting it be known at first that they were priests. Although the movement was criticized by the more conservative elements in French Catholicism, at first it had the support of the Vatican. But when several priests became leaders in the labor movement, and took a stance against capital, the pope withdrew his support. He ordered all worker priests to withdraw from the labor force, and he closed the seminary where most of them were being trained. It was the time of the cold war and the pope, who during World War II had hoped to be a mediator, now found himself drawn into the conflict, seemingly left with with no alternative between Communism and reactionary conservatism.

On the other hand, some of the policies of Pius XII did pave the way for the great changes that took place during the next pontificate. His encyclical of 1943, *Divino afflante Spiritu,* encouraged the use of modern methods of biblical study. Although he later insisted on the need for caution in that enterprise, the biblical studies that had been undertaken would later contribute to the renewal of the church. The reform of the liturgy, which was one of the earliest actions of the Second Vatican Council, had been encouraged by him, albeit with great caution. But, above all, he led the way to the internationalization of the church that eventually made possible the Second Vatican Council. He understood that the age of colonialism had come to an end, and therefore continued his predecessors' policy of strengthening churches outside of Europe. He also encouraged the emancipation of the colonies, to the point that he was criticized as being an enemy of Europe— particularly of France, which for a time was very reluctant to grant independence to its colonies. While insisting on his universal jurisdiction and direct control of all churches, he encouraged the formation of indigenous churches under the leadership of native bishops. Very significant for later developments was the formation, under Vatican auspices, of the Conference of Latin American Bishops (CELAM), the first such official organization on an international and regional basis. He also brought non-Italians into the curia, and internationalized the college of cardinals, which at the time of his death was only one-third Italian. Thus, while he himself was a conservative pope after the fashion of the councils of Trent and Vatican I, he set in motion the machinery that would eventually lead to the Second Vatican Council and to the reformation it espoused.

John XXIII and the Second Vatican Council

The election of the next pope was more difficult than the previous one had been. When the election of Cardinal Roncalli was announced, after the eleventh ballot, many commented that the seventy-seven-year-old cardinal had been elected as a transitional pope, to give the cardinals time to determine the course to follow in the future. But the brief pontificate (1958–1963) of the elderly pope, who took the name of John XXIII, was marked by momentous changes. His very decision to take the name of John, which had been tainted with the bitter memories of the Avignon papacy and the Pisan anti-pope John XXIII, was an indication that the new pope was willing to break new ground. He soon distressed many in the curia, as well as his guards, by his unprecedented visits to the poorer neighborhoods of Rome. Some even voiced fears that he might be too simple a man for the heavy responsibilities that rested on his shoulders. But he was a man of wide experience and profound wisdom, who had shown in delicate posts in Bulgaria, Istanbul, and France that he understood the intricacies of negotiation and diplomacy. Also, by having lived both in Turkish Istanbul and in secularized Paris, he knew to what a degree the church had cut itself off from communication with the world at large. His great task would be to restore that lost communication. And it would be a task requiring all his diplomatic skills, for there were many in the curia and in other high positions in the church who did not share his perception of the situation.

An old man with a vast misson, John XXIII felt the need to move rapidly. Thus, three months after his election he announced his plan to call an ecumenical council. Many in the curia did not approve of the idea. In times past, most councils had been called in order to deal with a pressing issue—usually a heresy thought to be particularly dangerous. Furthermore, after the declaration of papal infallibility by the First Vatican Council, there were those who thought that the age of councils had come to an end, and that henceforth popes should rule the church as absolute monarchs. Indeed, from the time of Pius IX there had been a constant tendency towards further centralization. But Pope John saw matters otherwise. He insisted on calling other bishops "my brother bishops," and on asking their advice rather than commanding them. He was also convinced that the time had come for a total "updating" —in Italian, an *aggiornamento*—of the church, and that this could only be done through the combined wisdom and concerns of the bishops of the entire church.

The preparatory work for the council took more than two years. Meanwhile, the pope issued the encyclical *Mater et Magistra,* which was taken by many Catholic activists in causes of justice as papal approval of their work. Finally, on October 11, 1962, Pope John formally opened the Second Vatican Council. Few expected that this assembly would mark a radical departure from the course the church had followed during the last four hundred years. The documents to be discussed and approved by the council had been prepared by the curia, and in general did little more than reaffirm traditional Catholic doctrine, warning against the dangers of the time. But the pope had also taken steps to lead the council in other directions. The previous year, he had created the Secretariat for the Promotion of Christian Unity, thus indicating his seriousness in the pursuit of a rapprochement with other Christians, and his intention that the council pursue this concern. His opening speech also set a different tone from most of the preparatory documents, for he indicated that it was time for the church to respond to the concerns of the modern world with words of understanding and encouragement, rather than with blistering condemnations. These goals were further aided by the presence of non-Catholic observers—thirty-one at the outset, and ninety-three by the time the Council closed its last session—and especially by the composition of the assembly itself. Indeed, only 46 percent of the prelates present came from western Europe, Canada, and the United States. Fully 42 percent represented Latin America, Asia, and black Africa. More than half of the bishops present came from churches of such limited resources that their living expenses while at the Council had to be covered with funds from the richer churches. Such bishops were deeply concerned with the need to address the plight of the poor, to speak to the non-Christian world, and in general to speak a word of compassion and understanding rather than of self-righteous condemnation. Therefore, the pope's call for the "medicine of mercy" in his opening speech did not fall on deaf ears.

Very soon, it became apparent that the majority of the assembly wished to see vast changes in the life of the church, and particularly in the manner in which it addressed the modern world. The first document to be discussed dealt with liturgy. Of all the documents prepared beforehand, this was the one that proposed most significant changes, for liturgical renewal had been one of the concerns of the previous pope. Even so, the conservative minority sought to block the proposed changes, and those who supported an updating of the liturgy won the day. When the text was returned to the commission that had drafted it, the instructions accompanying it were a clear defeat for the conservatives. From that point on, the documents written by the preparatory commissions were generally returned for rewriting, with instructions for drastic changes.

Pope John did not live to see his council issue its first document, for he died in June 1963. The next pope took the name of Paul, usually associated with the Council of Trent, and some conservatives hoped that he would dissolve the Council, or at least take strong measures to hinder its deliberations. But Paul VI (1963–1978) almost immediately declared his intention that the Council was to continue its work. While there is no doubt that he was more conservative than John XXIII, during the first session of the council he had seen the degree to which Catholic leaders throughout the world felt the need for significant new departures. When the second session opened, on September 29, 1963, he called those present to "build a bridge between the Church and the modern world."

Needing no further encouragement, the Council followed the pope's advice—probably sometimes with more alacrity than Paul VI would have wished. The document on the liturgy, which from the outset had been the most progressive, was approved by the assembly; but the rest were sent back

*The Second Vatican Council turned a new
page in the history of Roman Catholicism.*

to be redrafted along lines more consonant with the church's new openness
to the modern world. The "Constitution on the Sacred Liturgy," the most
tangible result of this second session, soon made its impact felt among the
faithful throughout the world, for it authorized the use of the vernacular
languages to a degree not permitted before. It also declared (38) that

As long as the essential unity of the Roman rite is preserved, in the revision of the
liturgical books steps shall be taken for proper variations and adaptations according
to the needs of various groups, regions, and peoples, particularly in mission territories.

The commissions that then worked on the redrafting of the various
documents were reconstituted, with greater participation of members elected
by the assembly. There were indications that the pope was not happy with

the turn of events, and some even feared that he might declare the Council ended. But Paul VI did not resort to such extreme measures, and the third session of the Council (September 14 to November 21, 1964) again proved that any documents presented before it that did not conform to its reformist spirit would be rejected and returned to commission. The Council issued documents on the church, the Eastern churches, and ecumenism. Many of its members were distressed to see the pope add an "explanatory note" to the document on the church, clarifying that episcopal collegiality was to be understood in terms of the primacy of the pope, and also add some interpolations to the decree on ecumenism—already approved by the assembly—that non-Catholics would find less acceptable than the original document. Also, while many in the Council had been seeking to emphasize the centrality of Christ, and to counteract the extremes to which devotion to Mary could be taken, the pope on his own initiative declared the Virgin to be the "Mother of the Church."

Notwithstanding the implications of these papal actions, when the Council gathered for its fourth and last session (September 14 to December 8, 1965), its members were determined to see its work carried to fruition. There was bitter debate on the document on religious freedom, which conservatives from nations where Catholics were in the majority sternly opposed. But once that last attempt failed, the opposition collapsed, and the rest of the session the more progressive were in complete control of the deliberations. Therefore, with relative ease the Council issued fairly progressive documents on bishops, priests and their formation, the laity, the church and non-Christians, missionary activity, and so forth. Most significant as manifesting a different spirit than had prevailed in Catholicism for centuries were the documents on religious freedom and on the church in the modern world. The former declared that the religious freedom of individuals as well as of groups must be respected, and that all religious groups have the right to organize according to their own principles "as long as the just requirements of public order are not violated." The "Pastoral Constitution on the Church in the Modern World" is the longest document ever issued by a council, and sets a drastically different tone from that followed during the nineteenth century. While insisting on Catholic principles of faith and morality, its shows genuine openness towards the positive aspects of modernity, and deals creatively with such issues as family life, economic and social issues, politics, technology and science, the significance and variety of human cultures, and so forth. In general, its tone is set by its opening statement (1):

The joys and hopes, the griefs and anxieties of people of our time, particularly of those who are poor or in any way afflicted, are the joys and hopes, the griefs and anxieties of Christ's followers. Theirs is a community of people, people who, in union with Christ and with the guidance of the Holy Spirit, move forward towards the Kingdom of the Father and carry the message of salvation intended for all. For this reason this community knows that it is deeply united with humankind and its history.

By the time the Council adjourned, it was clear that the Catholic Church had entered a new epoch in its history. There were still many steps to be taken in implementing the decisions of the Council. In many areas there would be resistance; in others, changes would be rapid, and the Vatican would move to moderate them. In 1968, the pope signaled his conservative inclination by issuing the encyclical *Humanae vitae,* in which he banned all methods of artificial birth control, overruling a papal commission that had recommended the admission of some methods of birth control. After the adjournment of the Council, Paul VI moved slowly, perhaps fearing that too rapid changes could lead to schism or at least to the loss of some of the more conservative members of the Catholic Church. Indeed, such a schism did occur, under the leadership of a conservative bishop. But it did not carry with itself many members, and twenty years after its first session it was clear that the Second Vatican Council had set in motion processes that could not be stopped. An example of this continuing influence was the American bishops' declaration on nuclear war and the arms race, much opposed by some as undue interference on the part of the church in political and military matters. In their declaration, the bishops were simply spelling out the earlier declaration of the Second Vatican Council, that the arms race and the quest for balance in destructive machines can produce no permanent or true peace.

Paul VI died in 1979 and, after the brief pontificate of John Paul I, was succeeded by John Paul II, the first non-Italian pope since the sixteenth century. As a Pole, the new pope had known the struggle of the church under both Germans and Russians, and had no illusions about either Fascism or Communism. His pontificate has been marked by growing tension in Poland between the Communist government and the Catholic Church, encouraged in its resistance by the election of one of its own to the see of Peter. While conservative on issues having to do with the life of the clergy and those with monastic vows, and on matters of personal morality, John Paul II has spoken strong words about the plight of the poor and the injustice of their oppression. He has issued directives against priests holding political office, but has also insisted that the Church should be involved in issues of justice. Therefore, he has been characterized both as conservative and as progressive, depending on the vantage point of each observer.

Theological Developments

The openness of the Second Vatican Council surprised the world, which was not acquainted with the undercurrents of thought in the Catholic Church. But the theological work that led to it had been taking place for half a century. Experiments such as the worker priests were the result of theological stirrings that Rome did not regard with pleasure. But, above all, there were a number of theologians whose Catholic faith was never in doubt, but whose work was either rejected or ignored by the Vatican.

Probably the most original of these theologians was Pierre Teilhard de Chardin. The son of a family of the French aristocracy, at an early age Teilhard decided to join the Jesuits. He was ordained a priest in 1911. When World War I broke out, he refused the rank of captain—which he would have had as a chaplain—and served as a corporal, carrying the wounded in stretchers. When the war ended, he was admitted as a full member of the Society of Jesus, and in 1922 he completed his doctorate in paleontology. He had always been interested in the theory of evolution, not as a denial of creation, but rather as a scientific way of understanding the working of God's creative power. His first writings on the relation between faith and evolution, however, brought swift condemnation from Rome. He was prohibited from publishing further works on theology, and was sent to serve in China, where it was expected that he could do little damage. As an obedient priest, he submitted. The ban, however, did not prevent him from continued writing, as long as he did not publish his manuscripts. Therefore, while pursuing his paleontological work in China, he also continued his theological work, and gave his manuscripts to a few trusted friends. In 1929, he was instrumental in the identification of the Sinanthropus skull, which further confirmed the principle of evolution and brought him acclaim from the scientific community around the world. Still Rome refused to allow him to publish his philosophical and theological works, now circulating among friends in France. Finally, in 1955, after his death, his friends published his works, which immediately won wide attention.

While accepting the general principles of the theory of evolution, Teilhard rejected Darwin's proposal that the "survival of the fittest" is the guiding force behind evolution. Instead, he proposed the "cosmic law of complexity and consciousness," which means that there is a pull in evolution towards the more complex and the more highly conscious. Thus, what we see at any given stage of evolution is a number of organisms that represent different stages or spheres in the evolutionary process. This evolution begins with the "stuff of the universe," which is then organized into the "geosphere"—matter organized into molecules, and molecules into bodies. The next stage is the "biosphere," in which life appears. From this emerges the "noosphere," in which life attains consciousness of itself. At this point, evolution does not end, but rather takes a conscious dimension. Humans as we now know them are not yet the end of the evolutionary process. On the contrary, we are still part of an ongoing evolution, leading to human "hominization." What is characteristic of this new stage is that, as conscious beings, we are involved in our own evolution.

But we are not left without guidance as to what that evolution is to be. The entire process has an "omega point," the converging point of maturation of the entire cosmic process. Indeed, to understand evolution one must not look at it from beginning to end, but rather from end to beginning. It is the end that makes the rest of the process meaningful. And that end, that "omega point," is Jesus Christ. In him a new stage of evolution—the final stage—has appeared: the "Christosphere." Just as humanity and divinity are perfectly united without confusion in Christ, in the end each of us will be perfectly united with God, while also being perfectly ourselves. The church, the body of Christ, is the new historic reality centered in the omega point. Thus, Teilhard combined science with theology and even with a strong mystical inclination. But, in contrast to most mystical tradition, he was a world-affirming mystic.

Even among many who did not accept all of Teilhard's grand cosmic scheme, his influence could be seen. His attempt to look at the evolutionary process "from end to beginning" has encouraged modern theologians, both Catholic and Protestant, to look again at eschatology—that is, at the doctrine of the "last things." For very significant sectors of contemporary theology, eschatology has proven a valuable starting point, rather than an appendix to the rest of theology. Second, Teilhard's emphasis on the continuing evolutionary process, and on our conscious participation in it, has encouraged other theologians to explore the field of human participation in the divine purposes, and to look upon humanity as an active agent in the shaping of history. Finally, his this-worldly mysticism has inspired many to relate their devotional life to their politicial activism.

Henri de Lubac, also a French Jesuit and a friend of Teilhard, is another example of the theology that was developing within the Roman Catholic Church, even against the wishes of the Vatican, during the first half of the twentieth century. Together with Jean Daniélou, de Lubac edited a voluminous series of ancient Christian writings. This sound, scholarly series was also intended for modern audiences, and thus reflected de Lubac's concern that the modern world and Christian tradition be joined in a dynamic and creative tension. He felt that, in recent years, the church had narrowed its understanding of tradition, and had therefore lost a great deal of the dynamism of the entire Christian tradition. When compared with the breadth and catholicity of the earlier tradition, the Catholic theology of his time appeared narrow and stale. Such views, however, were not well received in Rome, and by mid-century he too was silenced. After this ban was lifted, his fellow Jesuits asked him to write a critical study of the work and thought of Teilhard de Chardin, evaluating it in the light of Catholic tradition. He published the first volume of this project in French in 1962, and Rome reacted against it immediately, stopping the project and forbidding the republication and translation of the volume already published. De Lubac was not as inclined to grand cosmic views as was Teilhard; and this, together with his profound knowledge of early Christian tradition, resulted in his having greater impact on Catholic theology. But he too believed that all of humanity has a single goal, and that the whole of history can best be understood from the vantage point of this goal, which is none other than Jesus Christ. The church—not as a juridical organization, but as the mystical body of Christ—is a sacrament in the midst of the world. Although silenced by Rome, de Lubac was much admired by many theologians and progressive bishops, and he was one of the "periti"—that is, experts—whose participation in the Second Vatican Council did much to influence the outcome of that assembly. His very notion of the church as a sacrament in the world stands at the root of the Council's concern that its documents reflect a church open to the world.

Yves Congar, another of the periti at the Second Vatican Council, represented a similar orientation. He had direct personal experience of the harshness of modern life, for in 1939 he was drafted into the French army, and he was a prisoner of war in Germany from 1940 to 1945. A Dominican, he later became Director of the Dominican Monastery in Strasbourg. Like de Lubac, he was convinced that in response to controversy the church had narrowed its own tradition, and thus denied much of the richness of that tradition. He was particularly concerned with the church's self-understanding, and therefore felt the need to go beyond the juridical and hierarchical view of the church that prevailed at his time. For this he drew inspiration from earlier ecclesiologies, in which the image of "people of God" was dominant, and in which the laity were the focus of attention. From that perspective, he showed an openness to other Christians that was unusual among Catholics in the earlier part of the century. Like Teilhard and de Lubac, for a time he was silenced by Rome. But still his influence was widespread, and when the Second Vatican Council was convened he was appointed to be one of its theological mentors. His influence on that assembly can be seen particularly in the documents on the nature of the church, on ecumenism, and on the church in the modern world.

Probably the most influential Catholic theologian of the twentieth century is the Jesuit Karl Rahner, another of the periti at the Second Vatican Council. The son of a German high school teacher, and one of seven siblings —his brother Hugo is also a well-known Jesuit theologian—Rahner has written more than three thousand books and articles. These deal with the most technical matters in theology as well as with everyday questions, such as "why do we pray at night." In all these cases, however, Rahner's method is similar: he affirms both tradition and the modern world, and thus asks of tradition very different questions than are usually asked of it. His purpose is not to solve the mystery of the universe, but rather to clarify the mysterious nature of existence, to bring mystery back to the heart of everyday life. Philosophically, he draws both from Thomas Aquinas and from his professor Martin Heidegger, one of the foremost proponents of existentialism. But he is not particularly interested in philosophy except inasmuch as it helps to clarify Christian teaching. Also, he has done very little popularizing work, but has been content to write mostly for theologians, calling them to a new openness and a renewed interpretation of tradition. For these reasons, although he has repeatedly offered interpretations of tradition that have been at variance with commonly received views, he was never silenced by Rome, as were his French counterparts. Although his influence, both direct and indirect, can be seen in practically all the documents of the Second Vatican Council, it is probably in the understanding of the role of the episcopacy that he had the greatest impact. Indeed, for generations the tendency within Roman Catholicism had been towards greater centralization in Rome, after the model of a monarchical government. Rahner has explored the notion of the episcopate and, without rejecting Roman primacy, has underlined the collegial nature of the episcopacy. This in turn means that the church can be truly catholic—adapting itself to each culture, and not necessarily taking Roman and western European perspectives as the standard of truth. Such a view of catholicity and collegiality stands behind the Council's decisions, not only with reference to the episcopacy itself, but also with reference to the use of the vernacular and the adaptation of the liturgy to various cultures and conditions.

Rahner's judicious combination of sound theological scholarship, the retrieval and reinterpretation of tradition, and an openness to ask new questions of that tradition have also served as a model for more radical theologies —in particular, Latin American theologies of liberation, to which we shall return in our final chapter.

In general, what has taken place in Roman Catholicism during the twentieth century is that, after centuries of refusing to deal with the challenges of the modern world by any other means than confrontation and condemnation, it has opened itself to a dialogue with that world. As a result of that dialogue, Catholics as well as Protestants and even non-Christians have been surprised to find in the Catholic Church an energy that few suspected it had. Long before the Second Vatican Council, theologians whom Rome regarded askance were paving the way for this unexpected development.

34/Protestantism in Europe

Our having grown up forces us to realize where we stand before God. God is teaching us to live as those who can manage without him.

DIETRICH BONHOEFFER

The upheavals of the first half of the twentieth century were felt most strongly in Europe. That continent had been the cradle of much of the optimistic philosophy and theology of the nineteenth century. It had dreamt that under its leadership humankind would see a new day. It had convinced itself that its colonial ventures were a vast altruistic enterprise for the good of the world. European Protestantism had been far more involved in this illusion than its Catholic counterpart, for Catholicism during the nineteenth century had reacted to the modern world with wholesale condemnation, while Protestant liberalism had practically capitulated before the new age. Therefore, when the two world wars and the events surrounding them gave the lie to the dreams of the nineteenth century, Protestant liberalism was shaken to its very foundations. During the nineteenth century, partially as a result of the failure of Catholicism to respond creatively to the challenges of the modern world, skepticism and secularism had become common in France. In the twentieth century, partially as a result of the failure of Liberalism and its optimistic hopes, those areas where Protestantism had been traditionally strong—Germany, Scandinavia, and Great Britain—also witnessed a decided increase in skepticism and secularism. By the middle of the century, its was clear that northern Europe was no longer a stronghold of Protestantism and that other areas of the world had taken the position of leadership in Protestantism that once belonged to it.

World War I and Its Aftermath

By the time war broke out in 1914, many Christian leaders were aware of the increasing tension in Europe, and had taken measures seeking to use the international connections of the churches in order to avert war. When this failed, some of these Christians refused to be carried by nationalist passions, and sought to make the church an instrument of reconciliation. A leader in these efforts was Nathan Söderblom (1866–1931), Lutheran archbishop of Uppsala since 1914, who used his contacts on both sides of the conflict to call for demonstrations of the universal and supranational character of the Christian communion. After the war, his efforts and contacts, as well as his unblemished record as a peacemaker, made him one of the leaders of the early ecumenical movement—to which we shall return.

But Protestantism was sorely lacking in a theology that could help it understand the events of the times, and respond to them. Liberalism, with its optimistic view of human nature and capabilities, had no word for the situation. Söderblom and others in Scandinavia did begin to deal with this lack through a revival of studies on Luther and his theology. During the previous century, German liberal scholarship had depicted Luther as both the forerunner of liberalism and the embodiment of the German soul. Now other scholars, first in Scandinavia and then also in Germany, took a second look at Luther's theology, and discovered there much that was not in agreement with the interpretations of the previous century. Significant landmarks in this movement were Gustav Aulén's *Christus Victor* and Anders Nygren's *Agape and Eros*. Both were characterized by a sense of the power of evil, and of the unmerited grace of God, which contradicted much of what had been said in the previous generation.

The most significant theological response to the challenges of the times, however, was the work of Karl Barth (1886–1968). The son of a Swiss Reformed pastor, Karl Barth had been so intrigued by his confirmation classes in 1901 and 1902 that he decided to study theology. By the time he was ready to begin his theological studies, his father was a professor of church history and New Testament at Berne, and it was under his direction that young Barth planned his studies. After some time at Berne, and an uneventful semester at Tübingen, he went to Berlin, where he was fascinated by Harnack and his grasp of the history of doctrines. Later, as a student in Marburg, he was captivated by the writings of both Kant and Schleiermacher. It was also there that he met Eduard Thurneysen, a fellow student who would be his closest friend throughout his career. Finally, seemingly well equipped with the best liberal theology of his time, Barth became a pastor, first in Geneva—where he took the opportunity for a careful reading of Calvin's *Institutes*—and then in the Swiss village of Safenwil.

Karl Barth was without doubt the most important Protestant theologian of the twentieth century.

Safenwil in 1911 was a parish of peasants and laborers, and Barth became interested in their struggle for better living conditions. Soon he was so involved in the social issues of his parish that he read theology only when preparing sermons or lectures. He became a Social Democrat—a party he joined in 1915—and decided that this movement was, even unknowingly, God's instrument for the establishment of the Kingdom. After all, he felt, Jesus had not come to found a new religion, but to begin a new world, and the Social Democrats were closer to that purpose than a dormant church that was content with its preaching and worship. Then the war shattered both his political hopes and his theology. The new world that the Social Democrats had promised was not forthcoming—at least not in the near future—and the optimism of his liberal mentors seemed out of place in a Europe torn by war. In a conversation with Thurneysen in 1916, the two friends decided that it was time to do theology on a different basis, and that the best way to do this was by returning to the text of Scripture. The next morning, Barth undertook the study of Romans that would shake the theological world.

Barth's *Commentary on Romans,* originally written for his own use and that of a small circle of friends, was published in 1919. There, he insisted on the need to return to faithful exegesis rather than systematic constructions. The God of Scripture—he declared—is transcendent, never an object of human manipulation, and the Spirit that works in us is never something that we possess, but is always and repeatedly a gift of God. Barth also reacted against the religious subjectivism that he had learned from many of his teachers. In this regard, he declared that in order to be saved one must be free of such individual concern, and be a member of the body of Christ, the new humanity.

While readers in Germany and Switzerland poured on his *Commentary on Romans* a praise not always to his liking, Barth was pursuing further readings that convinced him that he had not gone far enough in that book. Particularly, he felt that he had not sufficiently underscored the otherness of God. He had spoken of transcendence; but now he feared that he had not yet escaped from the liberal and romantic tendency to find God in the best of human nature. Also, he had not sufficiently stressed the contrast between the Kingdom of God and all human projects. He was now convinced that the Kingdom is an eschatological reality, one that comes from the Wholly Other, and not out of human construction. This led him to renounce the theology that had led him to join the Social Democrats. Although still a socialist, and still convinced that Christians ought to strive for justice and equality, he now insisted that none of these projects ought to be confused with the eschatological Kingdom of God.

Barth had just finished the second—and radically revised—edition of this *Commentary on Romans* when he left Safenwil in order to begin a teaching career in Göttingen—a career that he would later continue in Münster, Bonn, and finally in Basel. Kierkegaard's influence is clearly discernible in this second edition of Barth's *Commentary on Romans*—particularly in his insistence on the unsurmountable gap between time and eternity, between human achievement and divine action. It has also been said that this second edition was Barth's version of Kierkegaard's "attack on Christendom." By the time he began his teaching career, Barth was being credited with having begun a new theological school that some would call "dialectical theology," others "crisis theology," and still others "neo-orthodoxy." This was a theology of a God who is never ours, but always stands over against us; whose word is at the same time both "yes" and "no"; whose presence brings, not ease and inspiration in our efforts, but crisis. Around him gathered a number of theologians of stature: his fellow Reformed Emil Brunner, Lutheran pastor Friedrich Gogarten, and New Testament scholar Rudolf Bultmann. In 1922, Barth, Gogarten, Thurneysen, and others founded the theological journal *Zwischen den Zeiten—Between the Times*—to which Brunner and Bultmann also contributed. Soon, however, Bultmann and Gogarten drifted away from the group, which they considered too traditional in its approach to theology and not sufficiently engaged with the questions of modern doubt. Later, Brunner and Barth also parted company over the issue of the relationship between nature and grace—while Brunner felt that there must be in humans a "point of contact" for the action of grace, Barth insisted that this would lead to a reintroduction of natural theology, and that in any case it is grace that creates its own "point of contact."

Meanwhile, Barth had continued his theological pilgrimage. In 1927, he published the first volume of a projected *Christian Dogmatics,* wherein he declared that the object of theology is not the Christian faith, as Schleiermacher and others had made it appear, but the Word of God. The tone of his work had also changed, for in the *Commentary on Romans* he had been the prophet showing the error of past ways, and now he was the scholar trying to offer an alternative systematic theology. The theology of crisis had thus become a theology of the Word of God. But this entire project then became a false start. Through a study of Anselm, and then of nineteenth century Protestant theology, Barth became convinced that the *Christian Dogmatics* granted too much to philosophy. There, he had proposed that theology answers our deepest existential questions, and had used existentialist philosophy as the framework on which theology was built. Now he declared that the Word of God provides not only the answers, but also the questions. Sin, for instance, is not something we know by nature, and to which the gospel responds. It is the word of grace that convicts of sin. Without knowing that word, we know neither grace nor sin. This new perspective led Barth to begin his great systematic work once again, this time stressing the ecclesiastical grounding of theology by entitling it *Church Dogmatics.* The thirteen volumes of this work, which he never completed, were published between 1932 and 1967.

Church Dogmatics is unquestionably the great theological monument of the twentieth century. At a time when many felt that theological systems were a matter of the past, and that theology could at best consist in monographs, Barth wrote a work worthy of the best times of theological scholarship. On reading it, one immediately notices his profound acquaintance with earlier theological traditions, which he constantly brings to bear. But one is also aware of the inner coherence of the entire work, which from beginning to end—and over a period of almost four decades of writing—is true to itself. Shifting emphases there are in it; but no new starts. Most remarkable of all is Barth's own freedom and critical stance towards the entire task of theology, which he never confuses with the Word of God. Indeed, he insisted, theology, no matter how true or correct, always remains a human endeavor, and therefore must always be seen with a combination of freedom, joy, and even humor.

Renewed Conflicts

While Barth was preparing the first volume of his *Church Dogmatics,* ominous events were taking place in Germany: Hitler and the Nazi party were rising to power. In 1933, the Vatican and the Third Reich signed a concordat. Protestant liberals had no theological tools with which to respond critically to the new challenge. Indeed, many of them had declared that they believed in the perfectibility of the human race, and this was precisely what Hitler proclaimed. They had also tended to confuse the gospel with German culture, and the Nazi claim that Germany was called to civilize the world found echo in many Protestant pulpits and academic chairs. Hitler's own program included the unification of all Protestant churches in Germany, and their use in order to preach his message of German racial superiority, and of a divinely given mission. Thus arose the party of the "German Christians," joining traditional Christian beliefs, usually as they had been reinterpreted by liberalism, with notions of racial superiority and German nationalism. Part of their program was to reinterpret Christianity in terms of opposition to Judaism, thus contributing to the anti-Semitic policies of the Reich. In 1933, following the directions of the government, a united German Evangelical Church was formed. When its presiding bishop showed himself unwilling to obey the Reich in all matters, he was deposed, and another named in his place. In 1934, several professors of theology, including Barth and Bultmann, signed a protest against the directions the united church was taking. Then, a few days later, Christian leaders from all over Germany, both Lutheran and Reformed, gathered at Barmen for what they called a "witnessing synod," and issued the "Barmen Declaration," which became the foundational document for the "Confessing Church," a body that opposed Hitler's policies in the name of the gospel. The Barmen Declaration rejected "the false doctrine, that the church ought to accept as the basis for its message, besides and apart from the one Word of God, other events and powers, figures or truths, as if they were God's revelation." And it called all Christians in Germany to test its words by the Word of God, and to accept it only if they found it consistent with that Word.

The Reich's reaction was not slow in coming. Dr. Martin Niemöller, pastor in Berlin and an outspoken critic of the government, was arrested—he would remain in prison for eight years. Almost all pastors critical of the government were drafted into the army and sent to the battlefront. All professors in German Universities were required to sign a statement of unconditional support for the Reich (Barth refused to sign, and returned to Switzerland, where he taught at Basel until his retirement).

Most notable among those who suffered under Hitler's regime was young theologian Dietrich Bonhoeffer (1906–1945), who was a pastor in London when the Confessing Church invited him to return to Germany and head a clandestine seminary. His friends in England tried to dissuade him. But he felt that this was a call that he must accept, and returned to Germany knowing that he was endangering his life. In 1937, he published *The Cost of Discipleship,* in which he attempted to show the significance of the Sermon on the Mount for contemporary living. That same year his seminary was disbanded by direct order from the Reich. In spite of this order, Bonheoeffer again gathered two groups of students for continued theological instruction.

The experiences of these years of shared community in obedience and danger are reflected in his book on *Life Together,* published in 1939. By then, war was about to explode. Bonhoeffer was on a brief visit to London when friends from England and the United States (where he had been a student years earlier) insisted that he must not return to Germany. But return he did. Back in Germany, he decided to accept an invitation to spend a year in the United States. He had scarcely arrived, however, when he decided that he had made a mistake, for his fellow Germans would soon be forced to choose between patriotism and truth, and he declared: "I know which of those alternatives I must choose; but I cannot make that choice in security."

Bonhoeffer's life in Germany was increasingly difficult. In 1938, he was forbidden to live in Berlin. Two years later, his seminary was closed by order of the Gestapo, and he was forbidden from publishing anything or speaking in public. During the next three years, his involvement in the underground against Hitler increased. Until then, he had been a pacifist. But he came to the conviction that such pacifism, leaving others to make the difficult political and practical decisions, was a way of escaping from his own responsibility.

Dietrich Bonhoeffer, hanged by the Nazis shortly before their surrender, left behind some tantalizing suggestions regarding the need for a "religionless Christianity."

In a meeting with a friend in Sweden, Bonhoeffer told him that he was part of a conspiracy to assassinate Hitler. This was not something he liked to do, he said, but he felt that he had no other choice.

Bonhoeffer was arrested by the Gestapo in April 1943. While in prison, and later in concentration camp, Bonhoeffer won the respect of both guards and fellow prisoners, whom he served as chaplain. He also carried on correspondence with those outside, some of it censored by the authorities, and some smuggled with the help of sympathetic guards. In that correspondence, and in other papers he left behind, he showed that he was grappling with new ideas, some of which have tantalized later generations. For instance, he spoke of the world "coming of age," and of God's presence in such a world being much like that of a wise parent, who recedes into the background as a child grows. It was in this connection that he criticized Barth, whom he greatly admired, for having moved into what he called a "positivism of revelation," as if revelation let us know more than it actually does. But on other matters he took his cue from Barth, and tried to apply Barth's principles in daring fashion. For instance, Barth had declared that religion is a human effort by which we seek to hide from God, and on this basis Bonhoeffer spoke of a "religionless Christianity," while he groped for the future shape of such Christianity. Later generations would read these lines and feel compelled to follow Bonhoeffer's suggestions in a number of divergent ways.

As the American Army advanced, and defeat was unavoidable, the Third Reich moved to eliminate those it considered its worst enemies. Bonhoeffer was among them. After a hasty court-martial, he was condemned to death. The prison doctor later told of seeing him kneeling in his cell, praying in preparation for death. On April 9, 1945, two years and four days after his arrest, Dietrich Bonhoeffer was hanged. A few days later, the American Army captured the prison where he had been executed.

After the War

One result of the war was that vast areas of eastern and central Europe fell under Soviet domination. Most of these lands were predominantly Catholic, but in all of them there were significant Protestant minorities. The portion of Germany that fell under Soviet control was the cradle of Protestantism, where the population was overwhelmingly Protestant. This led both to difficulties between Protestants and Communist regimes, and to an increased dialogue between Marxists and Protestants. The nature of the relations between the state and the church varied from country to country, and from time to time. Although orthodox Marxist doctrine certainly saw Christianity as an enemy, some Communist leaders followed a policy of open opposition to the church, while others opted for benign neglect based on the conviction that religious faith was a matter of the past and would simply disappear. In Czechoslovakia and Hungary, the state continued the traditional policy of supporting the churches from public funds. In East Germany, on the other hand, Christians were placed under serious civil disabilities that kept them from pursuing an education or holding positions of significant responsibility.

In Czechoslovakia, the Marxist-Christian dialogue was associated with the name of Joseph Hromádka, dean of the Comenius Faculty of Theology in Prague. In order to understand his attitude, and that of other Protestants in Czechoslovakia, one must remember that this is the land of Huss, and also the land where the Thirty Years' War caused greatest devastation. Ever since, Protestants in that land have seen Catholics as their oppressors. Therefore, when the Communist regime declared that all churches would have equal standing before the government, Czech Protestants saw in this an act of liberation. The opposition of the Vatican to the new regime in Czechoslovakia they saw as an attempt to regain the privileges that Catholicism had lost, and therefore as a move to oppress them again. Also, from the times of the Hussite struggles against foreign invaders, they had been convinced that Christian faith must not be something private, but must also have an impact in society, leading it to greater justice. For these reasons, Hromádka and his followers have responded positively to the Marxist regime, while not abandoning their faith. Even before World War II, Hromádka had spoken of the possibility that Russian Communism might be the beginning of a new era in world history, one where issues of social justice would be paramount. As early as 1933, he had also warned of the dangers of Nazism. After the German invasion of his homeland, he fled to the United States, where he taught at Princeton Theological Seminary for eight years. At that time, he felt confirmed in his earlier belief that much of what passed for Christianity in the United States was little more than the justification of liberal democracy and capitalism. Furthermore, he was convinced that Christians should not be led astray by Marxist atheism, for the God whose existence the Marxists deny is no more than a fiction. The true God of Scripture and of Christian faith is not that God, but is One who is not touched by Marxism's futile atheism. There is indeed a radical difference between Marxism and Christianity. But the church must be careful not to confuse that difference with the polarization of the world due to the Cold War. Christians must be critical of the Marxist state; but they must not be so in such a fashion that they affirm the continuation of the injustices of the capitalist order—or of that which existed in Czechoslovakia before the war.

Elsewhere in Europe, a lively dialogue was taking place between Christians and Marxists. Often, the Marxist participants in this dialogue were not orthodox Marxist-Leninists, but rather revisionists who, while agreeing with the fundamental elements in Marx's analysis of history and society, wished to pursue those insights in their own way. A leader in this movement was Ernst Bloch, a Marxist philosopher who agreed with Marx that religion—and particularly Christianity in most of its history—has been used as an instrument of oppression. But, taking his cue from the young Marx himself, Bloch saw in early Christianity a movement of protest against oppression, and then went on to reinterpret Christian doctrines and biblical stories as having a positive value. For him, this value lies in the message of hope. The "principle of hope" was early Christianity's most significant contribution to human history. And this is of paramount importance, for from the perspective of hope humans are not determined by their past, but rather by their future. Such views, as well as those of other Marxist revisionists, paved the way for a dialogue that has continued into the last decades of the twentieth century. This dialogue—and particularly Bloch's work—has contributed to one of the main characteristics of Protestant theology in the twentieth century, namely, an emphasis on hope and on eschatology as a basic theme for Christian theology. A leader in this movement has been Jürgen Moltmann, whose books *Theology of Hope* and *The Crucified God* have been hailed as initiating a new era in theology. Moltmann argues that hope is the central category of biblical faith. God is not yet finished with the world. Our God, Moltmann argues, meets us and calls us from the future. Hope for the "last things" ought not to be the last chapter, but the first, of Christian theology. This is not a private, individualistic hope, but is rather the hope for a new order. Thus, a theology of hope must not lead the faithful to passive waiting for the future, but rather to join those struggles against poverty and oppression that signal the future of God.

Meanwhile, in those areas of western Europe that remained free of Soviet control, the process of secularization accelerated. Twenty years after the war, in traditionally Protestant areas such as Scandinavia, West Germany, and Great Britain, church attendance and participation had declined to the point that only a small minority—in some cases less than 10 percent—of the population had any significant contact with any form of organized Christianity. In those areas, the issue that most concerned Christian leaders and theologians was the relationship between Christianity and the modern, highly secular view of the world—an issue with which Bonhoeffer had been grappling in prison.

One of the most influential answers to this question was given by Rudolf Bultmann in an essay published during the war on *The New Testament and Mythology.* There, Bultmann argued that the message of the New Testament is couched in myth, and that for it to be heard today it must be "demythologized." This is important, not because without it faith would be impossible —people can force themselves to believe whatever they wish, no matter how irrational—but rather because without that demythologizing, faith is radically misunderstood. Faith is not an effort of the will to believe the unbelievable. The call of the New Testament to faith is not heard when one confuses it with the call to accept its myths. Myth is every attempt to express in images that which transcends this world. But in the New Testament, besides this basic myth, there is also a mythological worldview, one in which God and other supernatural forces intervene, and one in which the universe is seen as three tiers, with heaven above and hell below. The modern world can no longer accept the notion of a world open to supernatural interventions, nor does it view earth as hanging between hell and heaven. All this, as well as the basic attempt to speak of God in human terms, must be demythologized.

Bultmann's own suggestion as to how the New Testament is to be understood drew its inspiration from existentialist philosopher Martin Heidegger. This aspect of his program, however, has not been as widely accepted as his call for demythologization. Whatever the content of a new understanding of the New Testament may be, argue those who defend the program, it is clear that modern people no longer think in terms of a world open to supernatural intervention, and that therefore the stories of the New Testament, couched as they are in such terms, are an obstacle to faith. More than twenty years after the publication of Bultmann's essay, Anglican bishop John A. T. Robinson's *Honest to God,* which caused widespread debate and comment, was an attempt to popularize Bultmann's views—together with those of Bonhoeffer and Paul Tillich, to whom we shall return in our next chapter.

While growing secularism is a fact in Europe, this should not be interpre-

In order to make the faith believable, Rudolph Bultmann proposed the demythologization of the New Testament.

ted to mean that the churches have lost all vitality, or that theological discussions on the meaning of secularism are their main occupation. On the contrary, European Protestants, whose numbers have been reduced in many places in recent decades, continue to be an active leaven in their society, and have taken a place of leadership in the movement to stop the arms race, in issues of international justice, and in service to those disenfranchised or uprooted by industrial development and its consequences. In France, the Reformed Church of France was born in 1936 out of a union of two Reformed bodies with Methodists and Congregationalists. This church has shown great interest and success in evangelistic work in heavily industrialized areas. Likewise, in West Germany the Protestant churches employ a staff of 130,000 devoted to social assistance and relief, both in Germany itself and abroad. Behind that movement stand millions of committed Christians for whom the crucial question is not secularity, but obedience. In East Germany, after almost four decades in which the Communist regime had discouraged church attendance—particularly among children and youth—almost two-thirds of the population continued professing Christianity. In 1978, the government finally reached an agreement with the churches, promising to put an end to discrimination against Christian children and youth, allowing regional and national mass gatherings of believers, and authorizing the building of a number of churches. In 1983, the government and the churches—including Roman Catholics—joined in an uneasy alliance for the celebration of the fifth centennial of Luther's birth. While shaken by the momentous and even disastrous events of the twentieth century, and in some places reduced to a minority of the population, European Protestantism has not lost its vitality.

35/ Protestantism in the United States

We acknowledge our Christian responsibilities of citizenship. Therefore, we must challenge the misplaced trust of the nation in economic and military might. . . . We must resist the temptation to make the nation and its institutions objects of near-religious loyalty.

CHICAGO DECLARATION

From World War I to the Great Depression

Although the United States was involved in World War I, that conflict did not have the far-reaching consequences there that it had in Europe. The main reason was that the United States did not enter the war until its final stages, and even then its own lands were not the scene of battle. By and large, most Americans were spared the actual sight of destruction and bloodshed, and the sufferings of the civilian population did not compare with those of its counterpart in Europe. Although for a long time public opinion was in favor of keeping the nation out of what appeared to be a European conflict, once the United States declared war the entire affair was seen as a matter of glory and honor. The churches, which until 1916 had supported the peace movement, now joined in the rhetoric of war. Liberals and fundamentalists spoke of the need to "save civilization," and some among the more radical fundamentalists began interpreting the events of the time as the fulfillment of the prophecies of Daniel and Revelation. Except for the traditionally pacifist denominations—Mennonites and Quakers—war fever and national chauvinism were the order of the day, to the point that, from some pulpits, there was a call for the total extermination of the German people in the name of God. Naturally, this created enormous difficulties for those Americans of German descent who for whatever reasons felt the need for a more moderate stance —Walter Rauschenbusch among them.

The lack of critical reflection on the war and its causes had serious consequences in the years following. First of all, President Woodrow Wilson's hope for a treaty in which the vanquished were treated fairly, in order to avoid bitterness and renewed conflict, was shattered both by the ambition of the victorious allies and by lack of support at home. Second, his project of a League of Nations that would provide a forum for the resolution of international conflicts was so poorly received in a nation convinced by the rhetoric of war that the United States never joined the League of Nations. Although by that time many church leaders were trying to undo the prejudice they had fostered during the war, they found that their call for love and understanding was not as well received as their earlier message of hatred and prejudice.

Partly as a result of the war, the United States entered another period of isolationism, fear of everything foreign, and suppression of dissent. During the decade of the 1920s, the Ku Klux Klan enjoyed a revival and an unprecedented increase in its membership, in the North as well as in the South, by adding Catholics and Jews to blacks as the great enemies of American Christianity and democracy. Not a few religious leaders and churches contributed to this movement. This was the time of the "red scare," the first of a series of witch hunts for radicals, Communists, and subversives that has swept the United States during the twentieth century. Adding fuel to the fire and benefiting from it, many churches presented themselves and the Christian faith as the main line of defense against the red threat. Famous evangelist Billy Sunday declared that the deportation of "radicals" was too easy a punishment, and one that would be costly to the nation. Instead, he suggested, they should all be lined up and shot.

Some Christians, mostly in the mainline denominations, organized committees and campaigns to oppose these tendencies. Often such committees gained the approval of denominational headquarters. Thus appeared a phenomenon that would characterize many mainline denominations for decades: the split, in theology as well as in politics, between a national leadership of liberal tendencies, and a significant portion of the rank and file who felt misrepresented by their own denominational leaders.

The conflict between liberals and fundamentalists was exacerbated in the post-war period. Indeed, this was the time of the famous "Scopes trial," which symbolized the high point of the effort on the part of fundamentalists to ban the teaching of the theory of evolution in public schools. Almost all denominations were divided over the issue of fundamentalism—particularly the inerrancy of Scripture, which by then had become the hallmark of funda-

*Partly as a result of the war and of the fears
aroused by the new conditions, the Ku Klux
Klan enjoyed a period of unprecedented increase
in its membership.*

mentalist orthodoxy. In later years, these divisions would lead to open
schism. Thus, for instance, the work of the great defender of fundamentalism
among Northern Presbyterians, Princeton professor J. Gresham Machen, led
to the founding of a rival seminary and eventually of the Orthodox Presbyterian Church (1936).

During the 1920s, however, most Protestants were united in one great
cause: the prohibition of alcoholic beverages. Here was a cause that soon
enlisted the support both of liberals—for whom it was a practical application
of the Social Gospel—and conservatives—for whom it was an attempt to
return to the earlier times when the country had supposedly been purer.
Many joined drunkenness with all the evils they claimed had been brought
about by immigration of Jews and Catholics, thus appealing to the same
prejudices against foreigners, Jews, and Catholics that fueled the growth of
the Ku Klux Klan. The campaign first succeeded in a number of state legisla-

*The Scopes trial was the high point of a campaign, lasting for
several decades, against the theory of evolution.*

tures, and then tackled the federal Constitution. In 1919, by virtue of the
Eighteenth Amendment, prohibition became the law of the land, and it
remained so for more than a decade.

But it was easier to pass the law than to enforce it. Business interests,
gangsters, and the drinking public in various ways collaborated to break the
law. To the evils of drinking were then added those of corruption, encouraged by an illicit trade that had become inordinately profitable. By the time
the law was repealed, the notion that "one can't legislate morality" had
become commonplace in American folklore. This notion, popular at first
among those liberals who gave up the ideal of prohibition, would later be
used also by those conservatives who opposed legislation against racial segregation.

Through all those years of World War I and the following decade, the
basic American mood was one of high expectations. The war and its horrors
were dim memories from a distant land. In the United States, progress was
still the order of the day. In churches and pulpits, very little was heard of the
new theology that was developing in Europe, a theology that left behind the
optimism of earlier generations. What little was heard sounded alien, as

having do to with a world far removed from the cheerful expectations of the "land of the free and the home of the brave." Then came the crash.

Through Depression and World War

On October 24, 1929, panic gripped the New York Stock Exchange. With short periods of slight recovery, the market continued dropping until the middle of 1930. By then, most of the western world was in the middle of a great economic depression. One-fourth of the labor force in the United States was unemployed. Britain and other nations had social security systems and unemployment insurance. In the United States, fear of socialism had prevented such measures; therefore, the unemployed found themselves entirely on their own, or forced to seek charity from relatives, friends, or churches. Soup kitchens and breadlines became common sights in all major cities and many smaller towns. Runs on banks, bankruptcies, and foreclosures reached a record high.

At first, the nation faced the Great Depression with the optimism that had characterized earlier decades. President Hoover and his cabinet continued denying the existence of a depression for months after the market had crashed. When they finally admitted that there was a depression, they insisted that the American economy was sufficiently sound to rebound by itself, and that the free workings of the marketplace were the best way to ensure an economic recovery. Although the president himself was a compassionate man who suffered with the plight of the unemployed, there were around him those who rejoiced in the hope that the Depression would break the labor unions. When finally the government intervened to prevent further bankruptcies in industry and commerce, comedian Will Rogers quipped that money was being given to those at the top hoping that it would "trickle down to the needy."

All this put a halt to the optimism of the previous decade. Although historians have shown that the depression that had hit the United States late in the nineteenth century was much worse, the American public was much less psychologically prepared for the Great Depression of the 1930s. An entire generation that had never known want, and had been promised that things would inevitably improve, suddenly saw its dreams shattered. At a time when survival was at stake, facile promises of a rosy future seemed shallow.

It was then that less optimistic theologies began making an impact on the United States. Karl Barth's *The Word of God and the Word of Man,* published in English just before the crash, began to make sense to Americans in whom the Great Depression had an effect similar to that of World War I on Barth and his generation. The theology of the two Niebuhr brothers,

Reinhold (1892–1970) and H. Richard (1894–1962), came to the foreground. In 1929, H. Richard Niebuhr published *The Social Sources of Denominationalism,* in which he argued that denominationalism in the United States
was an adaptation of the gospel to the various racial and socioeconomic strata
of society, thus showing "the domination of class and self-preservative church
ethics over the ethics of the gospel."* His conclusion, made all the more
poignant because the world was approaching the worst war it had ever
known, was that "a Christianity which surrenders its leadership to the social
forces of national and economic life, offers no hope to the divided world."**
In 1937, his book on *The Kingdom of God in America* further indicted this sort
of religion by declaring that in it "A God without wrath brought men
without sin into a kingdom without judgment through the ministrations of
a Christ without a cross."***

Meanwhile, his brother Reinhold, who had been a parish minister in
Detroit until 1928, came to the conclusion that unbridled capitalism was
destructive, and in 1930 he and others joined in the Fellowship of Socialist
Christians. He was convinced that, left to its own devices, any society is
morally worse and more self-seeking than the sum of its members—a view
that he forcefully expounded in a book entitled *Moral Man and Immoral
Society.* In reaction against theological liberalism, he shared the doubts of the
neo-orthodox concerning human capabilities, and soon commented that a
more correct title for his book would have been "immoral man and even
more immoral society." He meant that it was time Christians recovered a
balanced view of human nature, including both a deeper understanding of
sin and its ramifications, and a radical view of grace. This he attempted to
do in 1941 and 1943, in two volumes on *The Nature and Destiny of Man.*

In 1934, thanks to the interest and support of Reinhold Niebuhr, German theologian Paul Tillich joined him in the faculty of Union Theological
Seminary. It was the time of the rise of Hitler in Germany, and Tillich, a
moderate socialist, was one of the first forced to leave the country. He was
not a neo-orthodox, but rather a theologian of culture who made use of
existentialist philosophy in order to interpret the gospel and its relationship
to the modern world. In contrast to Barth's emphasis on the Word of God
as the starting point of theology, Tillich proposed what he called the
"method of correlation," which consisted in examining the most profound
existential questions of modern people—particularly what he called their
"ultimate concern"—and then showing how the gospel responds to them.
His *Systematic Theology* was an attempt to deal with the central themes of
Christian theology on the basis of this method. He was also a socialist, who
did apply a revised form of Marxist analysis to try to understand the short-

---

*1959 reprint (New York: Meridian), p. 21.
**Niebuhr, *The Social Sources,* p. 275.
***(New York: Harper & Brothers, 1937), p. 193.

*Reinhold Niebuhr was one of the leading
figures in a new theology—a theology that was
not ready to accept the facile optimism of
liberalism or to confuse American culture and
traditions with the Christian faith.*

comings of western civilization. But after his move to the United States, this particular element of his thought was overshadowed by his interest in existentialism and in modern psychology.

It was not only in theological faculties that the Depression produced a critique of the economics of laissez faire. In 1932, both the Methodist Church and the Federal Council of Churches (founded in 1908 by thirty-three denominations) went on record as supporting government participation in economic planning and in providing means to safeguard the wellbeing of the poor. This was considered radical socialism, and a reaction was soon forthcoming.

That reaction combined elements of traditional fundamentalism with anti-socialist—and sometimes Fascist—political views. As the leadership of various mainstream denominations moved towards the conviction that a system of social security, unemployment insurance, and antitrust laws was necessary, many in the rank and file moved in the opposite direction, accusing that leadership of having been infiltrated by Communism. As the war approached, a significant sector of this movement allied itself with Fascism, and some of its leaders even declared that Christians ought to be thankful for Adolf Hitler, because he was halting the advance of socialism in Europe. Seldom was any distinction made between Russian Communism and other forms of socialism, and even then all were declared to be equally ungodly.

The advent of Roosevelt and the New Deal implemented many of the policies that the "socialists" in the leadership of the churches had been advocating. Some historians have credited the very moderate steps taken at that time for the relief of the poor, and for the security of the labor force, with having saved the capitalist system in the United States. In any case, although the New Deal did improve conditions for the poor, the economy recovered slowly, and the last vestiges of the Depression disappeared only in 1939, as the nation was once again preparing for the eventuality of war. In a way, it was the war, and not the New Deal, that put an end to the Great Depression.

The nation was deeply divided over the possibility of entering the war that was already raging in Europe and the Far East. Those who opposed the war did so for a variety of reasons: some were Christians who still felt remorse for the unrestrained militarism and nationalism exhibited during the previous war; others were Fascists, or at least people whose fear of Communism overrode every other consideration; among Americans of German and Italian extraction some felt sympathy for the lands of their ancestors; isolationists simply believed that the nation should leave the rest of the world to its own devices; and those who harbored racist and anti-Semitic attitudes felt that the United States should do nothing to hinder Hitler's program.

In the end, however, the nation was not given the chance to decide whether to enter the war. That decision was made by the attack on Pearl Harbor, on December 7, 1941. After that, the national loyalty of any who opposed the war effort was questioned. Japanese-Americans—including many whose ancestors had been in the United States for generations—were interned as potential spies. Sadly, the churches had little to say about this, while smooth operators took over the property and businesses of those interned. In general, perhaps chastized by their wholesale support of the previous war, the churches spoke with moderation during the conflict. They did support the war effort, provided chaplains for the armed forces, and declared their abhorrence for the crimes of Nazism. But most leaders took care not to confuse Christianity with national pride. It is significant that at the same time there were in Germany those who insisted on a similar distinction, even at much higher cost. While the world was torn apart by war, Christians living on both sides of the conflict were seeking to build bridges. After the end of the conflict, such bridges would bear fruit in the ecumenical movement (see chapter 36).

The Postwar Decades

The war ended with the horrors of Hiroshima and the dawn of the nuclear age. While at first there was much talk of the great promises of nuclear power, its destructive effect was also evident. For the first time in history, a generation grew up under the specter of nuclear holocaust. It was also the largest generation in American history—the "baby boom" generation. In spite of the horrors of Hiroshima, the postwar years were a period of unprecedented prosperity both for the economy of the nation and for its churches. After long decades in which depression and war had limited the availability of material goods, there came a period of abundance. The industrial production of the nation had been accelerated during the war, in order to provide the materials necessary for the conflict. Now that production continued, thus producing the most affluent consumer society the world had ever seen. There were opportunities for financial and social advancement for any who were willing to take them. Millions flocked to new areas in search of those opportunities and, having found them, settled in suburbia. The inner cities were progressively abandoned by the affluent, and remained as the abode of the lower classes—particularly poor blacks and other minorities. In the mobile society of suburbia, the churches came to play an important function as a source of both stability and social recognition.

It was also the time of the Cold War. Hardly had the Axis been defeated, when a new and more dangerous enemy appeared: Soviet Russia. This enemy seemed all the more insidiuous inasmuch as it had sympathizers in the western world. In the United States, there was a renewed witch hunt for Communists and socialists of every stripe. During the heyday of the "McCarthy era," lack of church membership was viewed as a possible indication of anti-American inclinations.

For all these reasons, churches in suburbia grew rapidly. The 1950s and early 1960s were the great age of church architecture, with local and affluent congregations financing the building of vast and beautiful sanctuaries, educational buildings, and other facilities. In 1950, the Billy Graham Evangelistic Association was incorporated. This was more than simply a continuation of the old American tradition of revivals, for it enjoyed abundant financial resources with which it made use of the most advanced tools and techniques of communication. Although basically conservative in its outlook, the Billy Graham Association usually followed a policy of avoiding conflict with Christians of other persuasions. It soon spread throughout the world, thus leaving the mark of the American revivalist tradition on every continent.

All, however, was not well. By and large, the mainline churches had abandoned the inner cities, now populated by the poor and by racial minorities. In spite of valiant efforts on the part of some, mainline Christianity had become so acculturated to the ethos of the newly affluent suburban areas, that it lost contact with the masses in the cities and with its rural roots and constituency. In rural areas, those who remained members of their traditional denominations were increasingly suspicious of the new leadership. In the cities, the Holiness churches sought to fill the gap; but vast numbers lost all contact with any form of organized Christianity. Twenty years after the great

*The Billy Graham Evangelistic Association was both a
continuation of the American tradition of revivals, and its
adaptation to social conditions in the mid–twentieth century.*

religious revival of the 1950s, the call was repeatedly heard for a renewed mission to the cities; but few had a clear idea how to accomplish that mission. It was not until the 1980s that there were signs of renewed religious vitality in the inner cities—and even then, such signs were closely connected with the return of the moderately affluent to the city.

Another feature of the post-war revival was an understanding of the Christian faith as a means to inner peace and happiness. One of the most popular religious authors of the time was Norman Vincent Peale, who promoted faith and "positive thinking" as leading to mental health and happiness. Historian Sydney E. Ahlstrom correctly speaks of the religiosity of the times as "faith in faith," which promised "peace of mind and confident living."* This form of religiosity was well suited for the times, for it provided peace in the midst of a confusing world, it said little about social responsibilities, and it did not risk conflict with those whose cold war mentality had made them Grand Inquisitors of American political opinion. Ahlstrom's conclusion is a serious indictment:

The churches by and large seem to have done little more than provide a means of social identification to a mobile people who were being rapidly cut loose from the comfort of old contexts.**

*A Religious History of the American People, vol. 2 (New York: Doubleday, 1975), p. 451.
**Ibid, p. 460.

There were, however, other factors at work within American society. Although during the post-war years these new elements were not sufficient to undo the prevailing optimistic mood of the nation, the next decade would bring them to the foreground, and bring about radical changes in the nation's outlook.

One of these factors was the black movement, which had been brewing for decades. The National Association for the Advancement of Colored People (NAACP), founded in 1909, had won a number of court battles long before the movement came to the foreground. Some in the black community persisted in finding refuge in an understanding of religion that promised otherworldly rewards, or gave them a sense of belonging to the small body of the faithful, without challenging the existing order. In some cases, this led to new religions with leaders who declared themselves to be incarnations of the divine. Most successful of these were "Father Divine" (who died in 1965) and "Sweet Daddy Grace" (who died in 1960). Black soldiers and sailors returning from the war—where they had fought in separate military units from whites—found that the freedom for which they had fought abroad was wanting at home. Government responded by desegregating the armed forces in 1949 and by the historic Supreme Court decision of 1952 that ordered the integration of public schools. A number of whites also supported the movement for integration, and in the early years their support and encouragement was valuable. The National Council of Churches (formerly the Federal Council of Churches), as well as most major denominations, also took a stance against segregation. But what made the movement irresistible was the participation and leadership of blacks themselves. Most of that leadership, until well into the 1960s, was drawn from black clergy—most notable among them Adam Clayton Powell, Jr., during the war and post-war years, and Martin Luther King, Jr., in the late 1950s and early 1960s. In an unprecedented manifestation of faith, courage, and perseverance, blacks by the thousands showed their determination to defy and unmask the oppressive laws and practices under which they lived. Through sit-ins, arrests, beatings, and even death, and in places such as Montgomery and Selma, Alabama, they showed the world that they were at least the moral equals of those who had repeatedly accused them of being inferior. "We shall overcome" became both a cry of defiance and a confession of faith.

The Southern Christian Leadership Conference (SCLC), which Dr. King founded, and a number of other Christian nonviolent organizations, did not suffice to channel all the frustration and anger that had accumulated in the black community. For several decades, more militant blacks had seen in Islam a religion not dominated by whites, and thus were the Black Muslims and several similar movements born. Others, particularly in the crowded ghettoes of cities such as New York and Los Angeles, vented their anger through riots —of which the most famous was the 1965 riot in the Watts area of Los

*Most of the early leadership of the black civil
rights movement was drawn from the clergy.*

Angeles. By the middle of the decade, blacks had come to the conclusion that they would not attain full rights until they had their just measure of power. Thus, the cry of "black power" arose—a cry often misinterpreted to mean that blacks intended to become masters over whites.

At the same time, due partly to its Christian inspiration, Dr. King's movement was branching out into other concerns that were not strictly racial. He and several other members of the SCLC became convinced that their struggle was against injustice of every sort. It was the time of the war in Southeast Asia, and Dr. King began criticizing the government's policies in the region, both because it was clear that the Selective Service System discriminated against blacks and other minorities, and because he was convinced that the United States was perpetrating in Southeast Asia an injustice similar to what had been perpetrated against blacks at home. In the United States itself, Dr. King now felt that the struggle must involve all poor people of whatever race. He was leading a "poor people's march" when he was assassinated in 1968.

The entire movement found much of its inspiration in the Christian faith of the black community. The old "spirituals" gained new meaning—or rather, they were given once again the defiant meaning they had when first sung in the old plantations. Churches became gathering and training places for protesters. Preachers articulated the connection between the gospel and the movement. Finally, a "black theology" emerged. This was a theology that was both essentially orthodox and an affirmation of the black reality, hope, and struggle. Its main figure was Union Theological Seminary professor James Cone, who declared:

There can be no Christian theology which is not identified unreservedly with those who are humiliated and abused. In fact, theology ceases to be a theology of the gospel when it fails to arise out of the community of the oppressed. For it is impossible to speak of the God of Israelite history, who is the God who revealed himself in Jesus Christ, without recognizing that he is the God *of* and *for* those who labor and are heavy laden.*

At the same time, another movement, at first less publicized, was gaining momentum. This was the feminist movement. For over a century, women in the United States had been claiming their rights. They had showed and strengthened their political muscle in the antislavery campaign, the Women's Christian Temperance Union, and their struggle for the right to vote—which they finally won in 1920. A few churches did ordain women during the nineteenth century. But, by the middle of the twentieth century, most denominations still did not allow the ordination of women, and all were under the control of men. During the 1950s, both in the church and in society at large, and as the result of vast changes in the fiber of society, the women's movement gained in strength, experience, and solidarity. In the churches, the battle was fought mainly on two fronts: women's right to have their call to ministry validated by ordination, and the critique of a theology that had traditionally been done and dominated by males. By the mid-1980s, most major Protestant denominations did ordain women; and in the Roman Catholic Church, which refused to do so, there were strong and vocal organizations campaigning against the ban on the ordination of women. In the field of theology, a number of women—notably Presbyterian Letty M. Russell and Roman Catholic Rosemary R. Reuther—proposed what were essentially orthodox corrections to traditional male theology. More radical were the views of Mary Daly, who declared herself a "graduate" from the male-dominated church and called on her sisters to await a "female incarnation of God."

While these movements were involving significant numbers of blacks and women, other international and national events were also shaping the mind of the nation. Foremost among these was the war in Southeast Asia. What started as a relatively small military involvement, in 1965 began escalating into the longest war the United States ever fought. It was a war in which, with the hope of halting Communist advance, the United States found itself supporting corrupt governments, and unsuccessfully using its enormous firepower against a nation much smaller than itself. The media brought the atrocities of the war into every living room. Then it was discovered that the public—and Congress—had been purposefully misinformed on the "Tonkin Gulf incident," which had precipitated the escalation of the war. Protests, bitterness, and patriotic disappointment swept the nation's campuses. Eventually, armed force was used against protesting students, resulting in fatalities

---

*James Cone, *A Black Theology of Liberation* (Philadelphia: J. B. Lippincott, 1970), pp. 17–18.

at Kent State University and Jackson State College. In the end, the United States, for the first time in its history, lost a war. But more than that, it lost its innocence. The notion of "the land of the free and the home of the brave" —exemplifying freedom and justice at home, and defending it abroad—was brought into question. The very prosperity that resulted from the war— followed as it was by a significant recession—led some to wonder if the economic system on which the nation was founded did not require the artificial stimulus of war. To this were added all the questions and doubts kindled by the Watergate scandal, which finally led to the resignation of President Nixon.

While all these events were taking place in society at large, the churches were also undergoing stress. The Protestant theological enterprise became fragmented, with theologians pursuing radically different avenues. Attempts to express the Christian message in secular terms led to the much-publicized "theology of the death of God." Taking a different tack, Harvey Cox's *The Secular City* sought to reinterpret the Christian message in the light of an urban society, and to see the opportunities and challenges that such a society offers. John Cobb and others set about the task of developing an understanding of the Christian faith on the basis of process philosophy. Moltmann's theology of hope found its counterparts on American soil. And many white male theologians began studying black, feminist, and Third World theologies as clues for a renewed understanding of the biblical message. In this vast array of different and even divergent theologies, there are three common themes: an orientation towards the future, an interest in sociopolitical realities, and an attempt to bring these two together. In other words, the dominant feature of these theologies taken as a whole is the recovery of eschatology as a future hope that is, however, active in present-day social involvement. This has been joined to a liturgical renewal emphasizing the eschatological dimension of worship and its social relevance.

This interest in social issues was further awakened by the international contacts of the churches. Questions of hunger, political freedom, and international justice became much more significant for those who were in almost constant contact with Christians in other nations suffering under those circumstances. Therefore, the National Council of Churches, the World Council of Churches, and the boards of missions of practically every major denomination were under attack by political conservatives who accused them of being infiltrated by Communists, or at least of being dupes for Communism.

Meanwhile, the charismatic movement that began early in the century in Azusa Street had taken a new shape. During the first half of the century, it had made an impact mostly among the lower classes and the Holiness churches. Beginning in the late 1950s, it spread in suburbia and within mainline denominations—including the Catholic Church. Most of those involved in this new charismatic wave remained loyal members of their churches; but at the same time there was a feeling of kinship among charismatics of various denominations, thus giving rise to an ecumenical movement that had little or no connection with organized ecumenism. Although sometimes seen by critics as the religious counterpart of the escape to suburbia, in truth the charismatic movement was quite varied, including within its ranks both some who felt that their experience with the Spirit should lead them away from the world, and those who felt that it should lead them to daring social action.

Evangelicalism was similarly divided. In the late 1970s and early 1980s, its radio and television work grew enormously. Some television preachers are presently creating and heading vast corporations for the furtherance of their work—a widespread phenomenon dubbed by critics "the electronic church." A common theme of many of these evangelists is the loss of traditional values and the breakdown of society that will result from it—a theme that has been heard since the time of Prohibition and its repeal. Taking their cue from the earlier struggle against alcohol, some evangelical leaders organized the "Moral Majority" to defend moral values and to support conservative economic and social policies.

On the other hand, growing numbers of evangelicals began to feel that their faith led them to a commitment to critique the existing economic and social order, both at home and abroad. Christians, they believed, must strive against all forms of injustice, suffering, hunger, and oppression. In 1973, a group of leaders of similar convictions joined in the "Chicago Declaration," which articulated what seemed to be the growing conviction of committed Christians in the United States:

As evangelical Christians committed to the Lord Jesus Christ and the full authority of the Word of God, we affirm that God lays total claim upon the lives of his people. We cannot, therefore, separate our lives in Christ from the situation in which God has placed us in the United States and the world.

We confess that we have not acknowledged the complete claims of God on our lives.

We acknowledge that God requires love. But we have not demonstrated the love of God to those suffering social abuses.

We acknowledge that God requires justice. But we have not proclaimed or demonstrated his justice to an unjust American society. Although the Lord calls us to defend the social and economic rights of the poor and the oppressed, we have mostly remained silent. We deplore the historic involvement of the church in America with racism and the conspicuous responsibility of the evangelical community for perpetuating the personal attitudes and institutional structures that have divided the body of Christ along color lines. Further, we have failed to condemn the exploitation of racism at home and abroad by our economic system. . . .

We must attack the materialism of our culture and the maldistribution of the nation's wealth and services. We recognize that as a nation we play a crucial role in the imbalance and injustice of international trade and development. Before God and a billion hungry neighbors, we must rethink our values . . .

We acknowledge our Christian responsibilities of citizenship. Therefore we must challenge the misplaced trust of the nation in economic and military might. . . . We must resist the temptation to make the nation and its institutions objects of near-religious loyalty. . . .

We proclaim no new gospel, but the gospel of our Lord Jesus Christ, who, through the power of the Holy Spirit, frees people from sin so that they might praise God through works of righteousness.

By this declaration, we endorse no political ideology or party, but call our nation's leaders and people to that righteousness which exalts a nation.

We make this declaration in the biblical hope that Christ is coming to consummate the Kingdom and we accept his claim on our total discipleship till he comes.*

It is significant that this declaration was very similar to others being made by Christians in varied situations throughout the world, often coming out of an entirely different theological background, but reaching parallel conclusions. From a worldwide perspective, it seemed that the church in the United States was finally coming to grips with the challenges of a post-Constantinian and an ecumenical age. It was also a church responding to the new vision of the "space age"—an age when for the first time we have seen the earth from space, and seen it as a fragile "spaceship" in which we must either learn to live together or perish together.

---

*Ronald J. Sider, ed. *The Chicago Declaration* (Carol Stream, Illinois: Creation House, 1974), cover and pp. 1–2.

36/ From the Ends of the Earth

*We bless God our Father, and our Lord
Jesus Christ, Who gathers together in one
the children of God that are scattered
abroad. . . . We are divided from one
another not only in matters of faith, order,
and tradition, but also by pride of nation,
class, and race. But Christ has made us
one, and He is not divided. In seeking Him
we find one another.*

FIRST ASSEMBLY OF THE WORLD COUNCIL OF
CHURCHES

The nineteenth century had brought about the existence of a truly
worldwide church. By the latter half of that century, there were
movements seeking further collaboration among the various
churches in each region. In 1910, the World Missionary Conference in Edinburgh gave further impulse to a movement that, although interrupted by two world wars, would eventually lead to the founding of the
World Council of Churches and to other visible manifestations of Christian
unity. Soon, however, it was discovered that such unity did not mean that
Christians from other parts of the world would become one in an essentially
western church; rather, it meant that all Christians, whatever their race or
nationality, would engage in a common search for the meaning of obedience
to Christ in the modern world. Thus, the ecumenical movement had two
facets. The first and most obvious was the quest for greater and more visible
unity. The second, with perhaps even more drastic consequences, was the

birth of a worldwide church to whose mission and self-understanding all would contribute. We shall take these two in order.

The Quest for Unity

The World Missionary Conference of 1910 appointed a Continuation Committee, which in turn led to the founding of the International Missionary Council in 1921. By that time, other regional and national organizations for missionary cooperation had appeared in Europe, the United States, Canada, and Australia, partly as a result of the work done at Edinburgh. These organizations provided the nucleus for the new body; but it was also decided that the "younger churches" that had resulted from missionary work would be directly represented. Again, the International Missionary Council did not intend to set guidelines or rules for missionary work, but rather to serve as a meeting place where strategies, experiences, and various resources could be shared. At the First Assembly of the International Missionary Council (which was, appropriately, held in Jerusalem in 1928), almost a fourth of the delegates belonged to the younger churches—a great advance from the seventeen who had been present at Edinburgh. Both in Jerusalem and in the Second Assembly, held in Madras, India, in 1938, the question of the nature of the church and the content of the Christian message came to the foreground, thus indicating that it was impossible to exclude theological discussion from a truly open encounter on the world mission of the church. Then the work of the Council was interrupted by World War II, and the Third Assembly, held in Whitby, Canada, in 1947, devoted most of its attention to reestablishing the links broken by the war, and to planning for the reconstruction of missionary work ravaged by the conflict. By then, however, there was a growing consciousness of the indissoluble union between church and mission, so that it seemed unwise to discuss missionary matters without also entering a dialogue on the nature of the church and other theological matters. This theme was increasingly heard in the next two assemblies of the International Missionary Council, held, respectively, in Willingen, Germany, in 1952, and in Ghana, from 1957 to 1958. By then, it was decided that the International Missionary Council should join the World Council of Churches, which it did at the New Delhi assembly of the World Council, in 1961. At the time of this merger, steps were taken so that bodies that would not or could not join the World Council of Churches itself could still be fully represented in the division that fell heir to the work of the International Missionary Council.

Another major movement leading to the founding of the World Council of Churches was "Faith and Order." To allay suspicions, the convocation of the World Missionary Conference of 1910 had explicitly excluded matters of faith and order—meaning any discussion of the beliefs of churches, or of their understanding and practice of ordination, sacraments, and so forth. Although this was a necessary exclusion in order to make the conference as inclusive as possible, many were convinced that the time had come to open a forum for the discussion of those very issues. Foremost among these was a bishop of the Episcopal Church, Charles H. Brent. At his prodding, the Anglican communion took the first steps in calling for a meeting on faith and order. Others soon joined, and after the interruption of World War I, and prolonged negotiations thereafter, the First World Conference on Faith and Order gathered in 1927 at Lausanne, Switzerland. Its four hundred delegates represented 108 churches—Protestant, Orthodox, and Old Catholic (those who had left Roman Catholicism at the time of the promulgation of papal infallibility). Many of them had gained experience in international and ecumenical gatherings through their participation in the Student Christian Movement—which for decades provided most of the leadership for several branches of the ecumenical movement. At the conference, it was decided not to seek unanimity by either very broad and therefore meaningless statements, or by doctrinal definitions that would necessarily exclude some. On the contrary, the method followed was frank and open discussion of issues, with the drafting of a document that began by stressing those points on which agreement had been reached, and then clearly stating those other points on which differences still remained. Thus, the documents were characterized by phrases such as "we agree," or "we believe," followed by points of clarification introduced by phrases such as "there are among us divergent views," or "it is held by many churches represented in the Conference." By the end of the meeting, it was clear to all present that their agreements were much more significant than their disagreements, and that a number of the latter could probably be overcome by further dialogue and clarification. Before adjourning the conference, a Continuation Committee was appointed, under the leadership of William Temple, archbishop of York (and later of Canterbury). After Temple's death, Brent succeeded him, and the Second World Conference on Faith and Order finally gathered at Edinburgh in 1937. It followed the same method of Lausanne, again with valuable results. But its most significant decision was to agree with the call of the Second Conference on Life and Work, gathered at Oxford the previous month, for the founding of a "World Council of Churches."

The Life and Work movement was also the result of the missionary experiences of earlier generations, as well as of the conviction that the various churches must join in every practical endeavor in which such collaboration was possible. Its foremost leader was Nathan Söderblom, Lutheran archbishop of Uppsala in Sweden. World War I, while interrupting the plans for an international gathering, did give Söderblom and others the opportunity to work together in finding solutions to the enormous problems caused by the conflict. Finally, the first conference on "Practical Christianity"—the early name of the movement—gathered in Stockholm in 1925. Its agenda consisted in seeking common responses to contemporary problems on the basis of the gospel. Its delegates were divided into five sections, each discussing one of five main themes and its ramifications: economic and industrial matters, moral and social issues, international affairs, Christian education, and means by which churches could join in further collaboration. From the beginning, this movement took a firm stance against every form of exploitation or imperialism. Thus, at a time when mechanization was causing unemployment, weakening unions, and lowering wages, the Conference echoed "the aspirations of the working people towards an equitable and fraternal order, the only one compatible with the divine plan of redemption." Also, with a prophetic voice whose truthfulness would be confirmed decades later, it noted a "general resentment against white imperialism" that threatened to break into open conflict. This conference also appointed a Continuation Committee that organized the Second Conference on Life and Work. This gathered at Oxford in 1937, and its final documents included a strong word against every form of totalitarianism, and a condemnation of war as a method

Those who presided over the World Council of Churches in its early years were people who had long experience in various other ecumenical endeavors. American Methodist John R. Mott is second from the top.

to solve international conflict. Also, as has been noted, it called for the joining of Life and Work with Faith and Order in a single World Council of Churches.

With that decision, and the concurrence of Faith and Order, the stage was set for the founding of such a council. The two movements appointed a joint committee, and work began towards the convocation of the council's first assembly. World War II, however, interrupted such plans. During the conflict, contacts made through the nascent ecumenical movement were instrumental in establishing networks of Christians on both sides of the battlefront, giving support to the Confessing Church in Germany, and saving Jews in various lands under Nazi rule. Finally, on August 22, 1948, the First Assembly of the World Council of Churches was called to order in Amsterdam. One hundred and seven churches from forty-four nations were part of it. The opening sermon was delivered by D. T. Niles, a Methodist from Ceylon, who had ample experience as a leader of the Student Christian Movement. Other speakers were Karl Barth, Joseph Hromádka, Martin Niemöller, Reinhold Niebuhr, and John Foster Dulles. The Council was organized so as to include the concerns previously related to Life and Work as well as those of Faith and Order—under its Division of Studies, there was a Commission on Faith and Order that continued meeting and organizing world conferences, while the more practical concerns of Life and Work were generally included under the Division of Ecumenical Action.

While rejoicing in the unity that the very existence of the Council manifested, the delegates also looked at the world around them, and sought to deal with the issues confronting that world. Significantly, at a time when the Cold War was beginning, the Council called on all churches to reject both Communism and liberal capitalism, and to oppose the mistaken notion that these two systems exhaust all possible alternatives. As could be expected, this declaration, and similar later ones, were not always well received.

After 1948, the membership of the World Council of Churches continued growing. Most significant was the increased participation of the Orthodox, who had jointly decided not to attend the Amsterdam assembly. When it was clarified that the World Council was not and did not claim to be an "ecumenical council" after the fashion of Nicea, and that it had no intention of becoming a church, the Orthodox did join the Council. Since several Orthodox churches existed under Communist regimes, and their delegates could only attend World Council meetings with government approval, this increased the suspicion on the part of many that the World Council was becoming the instrument of an international Communist conspiracy. In any case, by the time of the Second Assembly, gathered in Evanston, Illinois, in 1954, 163 churches were present. The Council began to turn its attention to the church in its local concreteness, trying to avoid the dangers of forgetting that those who gathered in its assemblies were, after all, the representatives of millions living and worshiping in every corner of the globe. When the Third Assembly gathered in New Delhi, in 1961, the member churches numbered 197. The merging at New Delhi of the International Missionary Council with the World Council of Churches also gave the latter more direct contacts with the Third World and the younger churches. Such contacts were increased by the membership in the Council of two Pentecostal churches from Chile—the first such bodies to join. This assembly also continued the earlier emphasis on the church at the parish level by speaking of the unity of "all in each place." Later assemblies in Uppsala (1968), Nairobi (1975), and Vancouver (1983) continued these trends. At Vancouver, the delegates insisted on relating issues of peace and justice, speaking of the "dark shadow" of the most perilous arms race and the most destructive "systems of injustice" the world has ever known. By then, in response to the new openness of the Catholic Church connected with the work of John XXIII and the Second Vatican Council, the World Council had also established fruitful conversations with the Catholic Church, often leading to collaboration in various projects and studies.

While these events were taking place at the global level, at the regional and national levels there was a similar movement towards Christian unity. This was manifested in regional, national, and local councils of churches, and in the organic unions that many churches sought. Most of these unions, particularly in Europe and the United States, comprised churches of very similar backgrounds and theology; but other areas took the leadership in more daring church unions. In 1925, the United Church of Canada was formed. Through a long series of unions—nineteen in all—that church comprised what had originally been forty different denominations. In 1922, the National Christian Council in China called on the missionaries and sending churches to "remove all obstacles" in the way of organic union. In 1927, the first synod of the Church of Christ in China was called to order. It included Christians of the Reformed tradition, Methodists, Baptists, Congregationalists, and others. During World War II, under pressure from the government, the Church of Christ in Japan—or Kyodan—was founded, with the participation of forty-two denominations. After the war, some of these groups withdrew; but most remained, convinced that obedience to the gospel demanded of them a common witness. In 1947, the Church of South India was founded. This merger was particularly significant, for this was the first time that such a union included Christians who insisted on bishops with apostolic succession —the Anglicans—and others who did not even have bishops. Since that time, there have been hundreds of union conversations throughout the world, and the mergers that have taken place are too numerous to mention. In the United States, the Consultation of Church Union (COCU) proposed to its participating denominations a plan for a "Church of Christ Uniting."

Mission from the Ends of the Earth

The missionary enterprise has always declared that its purpose is to found indigenous and mature churches in various parts of the world. In Roman Catholic circles, this has traditionally meant the planting of a church with its own hierarchy—and eventually a native one. Among Protestants, the goal has often been expressed in terms of the "three selves": self-government, self-support, and self-propagation. In most of these early formulations, however, it was taken for granted—both by Catholics and Protestants—that Christian theology in general would have little to learn from the younger churches. At most, it was hoped that these various churches would express western theology in terms of their own cultural setting. But the ecumenical movement, the end of colonialism, and a growing self-assurance on the part of the younger churches have produced unexpected results, for some of those churches are posing questions and offering answers that offer, not a mere adaptation, but a challenge to much of traditional theology.

Among Protestants, a number of books in recent decades have performed this function. In Asia, former Japanese missionary to Thailand Kosuke Koyama wrote *Waterbuffalo Theology*. A few years later, Chinese Choan-Seng Song published *Third-Eye Theology: Theology in Formation in Asian Settings* and *The Compassionate God*. In Africa, in the midst of the struggle against South African apartheid, Allan A. Boesak wrote *Farewell to Innocence*. In Latin America, Argentinian Methodist José Míguez Bonino wrote *Doing Theology in a Revolutionary Situation* and *Christians and Marxists*. While widely different from each other, these various books—and dozens of others—had one characteristic in common: they sought to look at the whole of Christian theology from an entirely different perspective than the traditional one. Most commonly, what made this perspective different was not only its cultural setting, but also that it took into account the social and economic struggles of the oppressed.

Among Catholics, the most surprising and far-reaching developments were taking place in Latin America. There, several factors coalesced to give birth to a new theology. First (as was pointed out in Volume 1 of this work) from its very beginnings Latin American Roman Catholicism had been divided between a church serving the interests of the powerful, and a mission-oriented church led by friars with vows of poverty who lived among the poor and participated in their struggle. Second, the existence of a regional organization including all Latin American bishops (CELAM), and the tendency towards greater freedom of action on the part of bishops, provided the vehicle for posing continent-wide questions as to the mission of the church. Finally, the Second Vatican Council, with its opening to the modern world, provided the impulse necessary for a daring look at the church's mission in

Latin America. After some preliminary work, that daring reexamination took place at Medellín, Colombia, in 1968. There, the bishops of Latin America rejected both capitalism and communism. Speaking of an "injustice that cries to heaven," the bishops committed themselves to the cause of justice, and called on Christians to take the side of peasants and Indians in their struggle for dignity and better living conditions. "The Christian quest for justice," they declared, "is a demand of biblical teaching."

Behind such assertions stood the work of a number of pastors and theologians who had come to the conclusion that the gospel required that the church side with the poor in their struggle for liberation. Leaders among these "liberation theologians" were Gustavo Gutiérrez and Juan Luis Segundo. What they proposed was not simply a theology that dealt with the issue of liberation, but rather one that looked at the entirety of Christian doctrine and life from the perspective of the poor who are being empowered by God—as they said, "from below." From such a perspective, they claimed, they could affirm orthodox Christian belief while interpreting it in a radically new fashion. Particularly, they discovered in Scripture elements they felt most traditional theology had ignored or obscured. Thus, their work became a challenge, not only to the powerful in Latin America, but to the entire Christian community throughout the world, which had to respond to their radical interpretation of the gospel.

That response was not slow in coming. Rome applied pressure on the bishops of Latin America, and when their next conference approached there were indications that it would back away from the declarations of Medellín. But at that next conference, held at Puebla, Mexico, in 1978, the bishops reaffirmed their earlier stance. In the western press, liberation theology was often interpreted in terms of the East-West conflict, and oversimplified as "Marxist theology." In Latin America itself, there were those who reacted violently against it. As confrontations became more violent, opposing parties solidified. In El Salvador, Archbishop Oscar A. Romero was slain by those who considered him a threat to the established order. In Brazil, Helder Camara and Paulo Evaristo Arns led the bishops who called for a new order. In Nicaragua, there was a growing confrontation between the Sandinista regime and the episcopacy. In Guatemala and other countries, Catholic lay catechists by the hundreds were killed by those who considered them subversive. In the United States and Europe, some declared that the new theology was anathema, while many theologians and Christian leaders declared that its call for a new look at the radical implications of the gospel was justified.

Where such debates and confrontations will lead, nobody knows. But one thing is clear: the last decades of the twentieth century will be marked by increased tensions between the North and the South. From the perspective of the North, the great issue is the confrontation between East and West. For many Christians in the United States and Europe, this means the confron-

*Immediately after his death, Archbishop Oscar
A. Romero became a symbol of Christian
commitment and pastoral concern for the poor.*

tation between capitalism and democracy on the one hand, and Communism and totalitarianism on the other. From the perspective of the South, the main issues are very different: the search for an economic order that will not continue impoverishing the Third World, distribution of wealth within the nations themselves, and fear of being the battlefront for wars by proxy between the great powers of the North.

While all this is taking place, it is also evident that the North is becoming increasingly de-Christianized, while the greatest numeric gains of the church are taking place in the South. Likewise, churches in the South that have long been considered dormant—including the Catholic Church in Latin America—are registering an unexpected vitality. While, in 1900, 49.9 percent of all Christians lived in Europe, by 1985 that number is estimated to be 27.2 percent. And, while in 1900 81.1 percent of all Christians were white,

Pope John Paul II's visit to Latin America symbolized the growing importance of that continent, and of other poor areas of the world, to the future of Christianity.

projections are that by the year 2000 that number will be reduced to 39.8 percent.* Therefore, no matter how one reacts to the various emerging theologies of the Third World, it seems likely that the twenty-first century will be marked by a vast missionary enterprise from the South to the North. Thus, the lands that a century before were considered the "ends of the earth" will have an opportunity to witness to the descendents of those who had earlier witnessed to them.

---

*David K. Barrett, ed., *World Christian Encyclopedia* (Nairobi: Oxford University Press, 1982), global tables 18 and 29.

Suggested Readings

Sydney E. Ahlstrom. *A Religious History of the American People,* vol. 2. Garden City, New York: Doubleday & Company, 1975.

Roger Aubert, et al. *The Church in a Secularized Society.* New York: Paulist Press, 1978.

Robert McAfee Brown. *The Ecumenical Revolution.* Garden City, New York: Doubleday & Company, 1967.

Alasdair I. C. Heron. *A Century of Protestant Theology.* Philadelphia: Westminster, 1980.

Kenneth Scott Latourette. *Christianity in a Revolutionary Age,* vols. 4–5. New York: Harper & Row, 1961–1962.

Stephen Neill, ed. *Twentieth Century Christianity.* London: Collins, 1961.

Ruth Rouse and Stephen Neill, eds. *A History of the Ecumenical Movement, 1517–1948.* Philadelphia: Westminster, 1968.

S. Paul Schilling. *Contemporary Continental Theologians.* Nashville: Abingdon, 1966.

L. S. Stavrianos. *Global Rift: The Third World Comes of Age.* New York: William Morrow and Company, 1981.

Index

Credits